Friedrich K. Feldbausch
Johannes Feldbausch

BANK-WÖRTERBUCH

Banking Dictionary

Deutsch-Englisch
Englisch-Deutsch

Friedrich K. Feldbausch
Johannes Feldbausch

BANK-WÖRTERBUCH

Banking Dictionary

Deutsch-Englisch
Englisch-Deutsch

4. aktualisierte und erweiterte
Auflage 1997

VERLAG WIRTSCHAFT UND FINANZEN
EIN UNTERNEHMEN DER
VERLAGSGRUPPE HANDELSBLATT GMBH, DÜSSELDORF

1. Auflage 1972
4. Auflage 1997

Copyright für diese Ausgabe:
© Verlag Wirtschaft und Finanzen, Verlagsgruppe Handelsblatt GmbH,
Düsseldorf.

© Ursula Kommorowski, EDV-Software und Verlag, Bochum.

Alle Rechte der Verbreitung vorbehalten. Das vorliegende Werk ist in allen
seinen Teilen urheberrechtlich geschützt. Jede Verwertung außerhalb der
engen Grenzen des Urheberrechtsgesetzes ist ohne Zustimmung des
Verlages unzulässig und strafbar. Das gilt insbesondere für Vervielfältigungen
und die Einspeicherung und Verarbeitung in elektronischen Systemen.

Ausstattung: Thomas Brink, Viersen
Gesamtherstellung: Parzeller & Co., Fulda

ISO 9706

ISBN 3-87881-110-1

Vorwort zur 4. Auflage

Die positiven Reaktionen der Leser der 3. Auflage dieses Bank-Wörterbuchs haben die Verfasser veranlaßt, eine vierte, wesentlich erweiterte Fassung zu schreiben.

Das vorliegende Bank-Wörterbuch ist um rd. 3.000 neuentstandene Bankwörter und Begriffe ergänzt worden. Sie umfassen die Bereiche: Eurobank-Produkte und Organisationen, Wertpapier- und Devisenhandel, derivative Finanzinstrumente sowie Finanz- und andere Bankdienstleistungen. Das Wörterbuch wurde auch im Hinblick auf die europäische Einigung überarbeitet. Die Europäische Union umfaßt heute, 1997, rd. 370 Millionen Menschen. Deutsch und Englisch sind die wichtigsten Sprachen in diesem neuen Europa. Mit der europäischen Integration, d. h. dem freien Verkehr von Gütern und Dienstleistungen sowie der Wirtschafts- und Währungsunion, entsteht ein gigantischer Markt für Bankgeschäfte.

Zielgruppe für dieses Bank-Wörterbuch ist daher der europäische Benutzer: Banker, Geschäftsleute, Mitarbeiter von Behörden und multinationalen Unternehmen, Studenten und alle diejenigen, die sich häufig mit wirtschaftlichen Fragen im Bank- und Finanzbereich in den beiden Sprachen auseinandersetzen.

Jede Fachsprache ist dynamisch. Ihr Wortschatz ändert sich und wächst jährlich. Aus diesem Grund bitten die Autoren alle fachkundigen Benutzer dieses Bank-Wörterbuchs um Anregungen und Verbesserungsvorschläge für spätere Auflagen.

Zum Abschluß danken die Autoren Frau Uta Feldbausch-Ladusch, die an der Durchsicht und Korrektur mitgearbeitet hat.

Saarbrücken, im März 1997

Dr. Friedrich K. Feldbausch
Dipl. Btw. Johannes Feldbausch

Vorwort zur 3. Auflage

Die vorliegende 3. Auflage wurde umfassend überarbeitet. Dabei wurden die seit dem Erscheinen des Bank-Wörterbuches in 1972 notwendigen Ergänzungen und Änderungen vorgenommen. Soweit dieses bei einem Wörterbuch überhaupt möglich ist, wurde das Buch dadurch auf den neuesten Stand gebracht.

Saarbrücken, im August 1984　　　　　　　　　　　　　　　　　　Dr. Friedrich K. Feldbausch

Aus dem Vorwort zur 1. und 2. Auflage

Das vorliegende Bank-Wörterbuch ist das Ergebnis langjähriger Studien über das Bankvokabular im englisch- (USA und England) und deutschsprachigen Raum (Deutschland, Österreich, Schweiz). Seine Zielsetzung war es, alle wichtigen Fachausdrücke des Bankwesens zu erfassen. Dabei wurde auch der Bereich Bankautomation (Datenverarbeitung) – soweit bekannt, erstmalig in einem Bank-Wörterbuch – mit berücksichtigt. Entsprechende Unterlagen verdankt der Verfasser der Siemens AG.

Nachdem der Verfasser den englisch-deutschen Teil des Wörterbuchs fertiggestellt hatte, wurde die weitere Verarbeitung dem Siemens-Programmsystem TEAM überlassen. Für diese Hilfe spricht der Verfasser dem Hause Siemens seinen herzlichen Dank aus.

Daneben gilt der aufrichtige Dank des Verfassers folgenden Damen und Herren, die ihn sowohl in sprachlicher als auch in technischer Hinsicht beraten und unterstützt haben:

Frau Herta Gebhardt, München; Mr. Erving Adler, New York; Herrn Karl-Heinz Brinkmann, München; Mrs. Ursula Dayton, Frankfurt a. M.; Mr. Sigfrid W. Kessler, Los Angeles; Frau Erika Müller, Saarbrücken; Mr. Peter Muller, London; Herrn Dr. Reinhard Niederhoff, München; Herrn Eberhard Tanke, München.

Last but not least gilt der Dank des Autors einerseits Frau Dipl.-Volksw. Tatjana Strunkmann-Meister, die das vom Verfasser mehr als Liebhaberei entwickelte Manuskript entdeckte und die Zusammenarbeit zwischen den verschiedenen Stellen koordinierte, und andererseits Fräulein Renate Heuer und Frau Ingrid Mildenberger, die das teilweise schwer lesbare Manuskript auf Grund ihrer guten Bank- und Sprachkenntnisse in die richtige Form brachten.

Zum Abschluß noch eine Bitte an die Benutzer und Kritiker dieses Bank-Wörterbuchs:

Sprachen sind nicht statisch, sondern dynamisch, ihr Wortschatz ändert sich und wächst, so daß jedes Wörterbuch von Zeit zu Zeit der Ergänzung bedarf. Aus diesem Grunde bittet der Verfasser, ihm mitzuteilen, welche Begriffe Sie vermissen oder für welche Begriffe Sie andere oder zusätzliche Termini zu finden wünschen. Nur so wird es möglich sein, dieses Bank-Wörterbuch auf die Dauer lebendig und aktuell zu halten, damit es seinen Zweck erfüllen kann: einen Beitrag zum besseren Verständnis im internationalen Geschäftsverkehr der Banken zu leisten.

　　　　　　　　　　　　　　　　　　　　　　　　　　　　　　　　Dr. Friedrich K. Feldbausch

Hinweise für die Benutzung des Wörterbuches

Die Stichwörter sind in alphabetischer Reihenfolge angeordnet, wobei die Umlaute im Deutschen wie die entsprechenden Grundbuchstaben und das »ß« wie »ss« behandelt werden.

Als Stichwörter gelten hier generell das erste (evtl. einzige) Wort einer Benennung. Darüber hinaus können auch, je nach Wichtigkeit, einzelne folgende Wörter einer Mehrwortbenennung als Stichwort behandelt werden, so daß diese Benennung (in umgestellter Form) auch an der entsprechenden alphabetischen Stelle im Wörterbuch erscheint. (So ist z. B. »abgenutzte Münze« sowohl dort als auch unter »Münze« zu finden.)

Die vorrangige Sortierung nach den Stichwörtern hat zur Folge, daß z. B. »informational aesthetics« hinter »information unit« zu finden ist. Hinter dem Stichwort wird die Sortierung in der gewohnten und angegebenen Reihenfolge fortgesetzt.

Benennungen, die dasselbe Stichwort enthalten, werden zu Gruppen zusammengefaßt. Innerhalb dieser Gruppen wird das Stichwort durch eine Tilde ersetzt. Es handelt sich dabei immer um ganze Wörter, nie um Teile eines Wortes. Die Sortierung wird so durchgeführt, daß hierbei zuerst die Benennungen, in denen das Stichwort (und damit die Tilde) am Anfang steht, angeführt werden, danach diejenigen Benennungen, in denen es in der Mitte oder am Ende erscheint.

Preface to the fourth edition

Positive readers' reactions encouraged the authors to prepare this fourth edition. It now includes another 3.000 new banking terms and phrases ranging from Euro-products and -organizations, stock trading and foreign-exchange dealing, derivative financial products, to financial and banking services.

This »Banking Dictionary« has been reviewed with regard to the common European market. Today, in 1997, the European Community consists of about 370 million people. German and English are the major languages within this new Europe. The continuing European integration, including the free flow of goods and services, creates with its economic and monetary union a tremendous domestic market for banking.

Thus, target group of this fourth Banking Dictionary edition is the European user: bankers, business men, employees of public authorities or multi-national companies, students and all those constantly dealing with banking business or finance in these two languages.

Every specialist language is dynamic. Since its vocabulary changes and grows every year, the authors request all users of this edition for additional expressions to prepare subsequent editions.

Finally, the authors are very much obliged to Mrs. Uta Feldbausch-Ladusch who helped correcting the manuscript.

Saarbrücken, March 1997   Dr. Friedrich K. Feldbausch
                                                                                         Dipl. Btw. Johannes Feldbausch

Preface to the third edition

This present third edition was completely revised. With regard to the fact that the first edition of this »Banking Dictionary« was published in 1972, the necessary completions and alterations were made. As far as it is possible, the dictionary is now up to date.

Saarbrücken, August 1984   Dr. Friedrich K. Feldbausch

From the Preface to the first and second edition

The Banking Dictionary is the product of a study, extending over many years, of the vocabulary of banking employed in the U.S., England, Germany, Austria and German-speaking Switzerland. In it, an attempt has been made to compile all important banking terms and usages, including – as far as can be determined, for the first time in a dictionary of banking terminology – terms current in the sector of banking automation (data processing). The author is indebted to Siemens AG for providing information pertinent to this field.

After the English-German section of the dictionary had been completed by the author, the task of evolving the complementary German-English portion was assumed by the Siemens TEAM program system. For this invaluable assistance, the author extends sincere thanks to the Siemens organization.

The author's heartfelt thanks for support and advice in questions of language, as well as in technical matters, are also due to Mrs. Herta Gebhardt, Munich; Mr. Erving Adler, New York; Mr. Karl-Heinz Brinkmann, Munich; Mrs. Ursula Dayton, Frankfurt a. M.; Mr. Sigfrid W. Kessler, Los Angeles; Mrs. Erika Müller, Saarbrücken; Mr. Peter Muller, London; Dr. Rheinhard Niederhoff, Munich; and Mr. Eberhardt Tanke, Munich.

Last but not least, I should like to express my gratitude to Mrs. Tatjana Strunkmann-Meister – who discovered the manuscript developed more or less as a hobby by the author – for her service in coordinating and expediting collaboration among the various contributors, and to Miss Renate Heuer and Mrs. Ingrid Mildenberger who by dint of her knowledge of banking and language, imposed proper form on an often barely legible manuscript.

In conclusion, I wish to make a request to the users and critics of this book. Language is not static, but dynamic; its vocabulary changes and grows. Consequently, every dictionary requires revision and expansion from time to time. For this reason, I should like to know which concepts you have looked for and not found, or for which concepts you would like to see other or additional terms. Only in this manner the Banking Dictionary can be kept viable and up-to-date, so that it may continue to serve its purpose of advancing understanding and effective communication in the sector of international banking.

Dr. Friedrich K. Feldbausch

Explanatory notes for the use of the dictionary

The key-words are arranged in strictly alphabetical order, the »umlauts« and the »ß« in German words being treated like the appropriate basic letters and »ss«, respectively.

A key-word is always the first (and sometimes only) word of a term. In addition, individual subsequent words of a term of several words may be listed as key-words, depending on their importance, so that such a term (in rearranged form) may appear several times in the dictionary. (Thus, for example »abgenutzte Münze« may be found under »abgenutzt« and also under »Münze«.)

The scheme adopted – namely that of giving priority to the keywords – means, for example, that »informational aesthetics« appears after »information unit«. The words following the key-word are listed in the same alphabetical order as the key-words. Terms containing the same key-word are grouped together. Within these groups the key-words are replaced by a swung dash. Complete words are always concerned here, never parts of a word. The items are so ordered that the terms in which the key-word (and thus the swung dash) appears at the beginning are listed first, thereafter the terms in which the key-word appears in the middle or at the end.

Abkürzungen – Abbreviations

m.	Maskulinum	Masculine Noun
f.	Femininum	Feminine Noun
n.	Deutsch: Neutrum Englisch: Substantiv	German: Neuter Noun English: Noun
pl.	Plural	Plural
plt.	Pluraletantum	Pluraletantum
v.	Verb	Verb
adj.	Adjektiv	Adjective
adv.	Adverb	Adverb
A.	Abkürzung	Abbreviation
GB	in Großbritannien gebräuchlich	British usage
US	in den USA gebräuchlich	U.S. usage
i.Zus.	in Zusammensetzungen	in compound expressions

Deutsch–Englisch

A

Abänderung f alteration n, modification n, change n
Abandonklausel f abandonment clause
Abbau m reduction n (e.g. of trade barriers)
abbestellen v counterorder v, cancel v; *einen Auftrag* ~ annual an order
abbröckeln v (Kurse) ease v
abbuchen v write-off, debit directly
Abbuchung f write-off n
Abbuchungsverfahren n direct debiting
abdecken; *Schulden* ~ cover debts
Abdeckung f repayment n (of credits)
abdisponieren v pay out, withdraw, transfer
Abdisposition f outpayment, withdrawal, transfer
Abendkassenbestände m pl overnight cash holdings
Aberdepot n bonds account
Abfindung f compensation n
Abfindungsangebot n offer of compensation payment, compensation offer
Abfindungssumme f amount of compensation
Abfindungsvertrag m deed of settlement
Abfindungszahlung f compensation payment
abflauen drop, sag, slow down
Abfluß m (von Geldern in das Ausland) drain n
Abfragemöglichkeit f interrogation facilities, inquiry facilities
Abfragestation f inquiry terminal
abführen v pay off, transfer, discharge v
Abgabe f charge n, contribution n, impost n
Abgabedruck; *massiver* ~ (Börse) heavy selling pressure
Abgabepflichtige f u. m taxpayer n
Abgabesatz m selling-rate
abgefundener Gläubiger paid off creditor
abgekürzt adj shortened adj, abbreviated adj
abgelegt adj filed for record
abgelöste Hypothek paid off mortgage
Abgeltung f settlement n, compensation n
abgenutzte Münze defaced coin
abgerechnet adj settled adj

abgeschlossen adj settled adj
abgeschwächter Markt sagging market
abgesichert; *vertraglich* ~ covered by contract
abgesicherter Kredit secured credit, secured loan
abgestempelt adj stamped adj
abgetrennte Kupons detached coupons
abgetretenes Konto assigned account (US)
abhaken v (von Posten) tick off (items)
abhängige Person dependent n
abheben v withdraw v; *Geld von der Bank* ~ draw out money from the bank
Abhebung f withdrawal n
Abhebungen f pl drawings n pl
abkaufen v buy, purchase
Abkommen n agreement n; ~ (Konvention) convention n; *unwiderrufliches* ~ binding agreement
abkürzen v abridge v
Abladehafen m port of shipment
Abladekonnossement n shipped bill of lading
abladen v unload, ship
Abladen n unloading, shipment
Ablader m shipper n
Ablagefach n stacker n, reception pocket, storage bin, receiving magazine, card stacker, card receiver
Ablauf m expiration n, expiry n
ablaufen v expire v
ablaufend adj expiring adj
ablegen v file v
ablehnen v refuse v, reject, turn down
Ablehnung f refusal n
Ablichtung f photocopy
abliefern v deliver v
Ablieferung f delivery n
ablösbar adj redeemable adj
Ablösbarkeit f redeemableness n
Ablösung f repayment, redemption n; ~ f (Abfindung) settlement n
Ablösungsbetrag m redemption capital
Ablösungsfonds m sinking fund
Ablösungshypothek f refunding mortgage

Ablösungssumme f amount of redemption
Ablösungsschuldverschreibungen f pl refunding bonds, unified bonds
Abmachung f agreement n; ~ f (förmlich) covenant n; *allgemeine* ~ general covenant
Abnahme f (Rückgang) reduction, decrease n
Abnahmegarantie f underwriting guarantee
Abnahmerecht n (beim Prämiengeschäft) right of calling
abnehmen v decrease v
abnehmend adj decreasing adj
Abnehmer m consumer n; ~ m (Börse) taker n
abnutzbare Wirtschaftsgüter wasting assets
abrechenbar adj invoiceable
abrechnen v clear, settle, balance
Abrechnung f settlement n; ~ *des Börsenmaklers* contract sheet; *börsentägliche* ~ market-to-market settlement
Abrechnungsposten m clearance item
Abrechnungsstelle f clearing house, clearing-office
Abrechnungssystem n clearing system
Abrechnungstag m settlement (settling) date; ~ m (Devisen) value date
Abruf m call, calling
abrufbar adj callable adj
Abrufbetrieb m (EDV) polling mode
Abrufkredit m call facility
abrunden v round off
Absage f refusal n
absagen v call of, refuse, counterorder v, countermand v
Absatz m sale n
absatzfähig adj marketable adj, sal(e)able adj
Absatzfinanzierung f sales financing
Absatzfinanzierungsgesellschaft f sales financing company
Absatzförderung f marketing n
Absatzgebiet n market n
Absatzkredit m sales credit
Absatzmarkt m outlet n (market)
Absatzmethode f marketing n
abschaffen v abolish v
Abschaffung f abolition n

abschätzbar adj appraisable adj
abschätzen v appraise v
abschicken v send v, dispatch v
Abschlag m discount n; ~ m (Preise) drop n, fall n; *einen* ~ *gewähren* make an allowance
abschlagen v refuse v, turn down
Abschlagsdividende f dividend on account, interim dividend; ~ f (erste) initial dividend (GB)
Abschlagszahlung f instalment n, payment on account
abschließen v (Konten) balance v; ~ v (Geschäfte) conclude v; *einen Vertrag* ~ enter into a contract; *in notarieller Form* ~ notarize v
Abschluß m (Börse) close n; ~ m (Vertrag, Geschäft) conclusion n; ~ m sale n; ~ *von Deckungsgeschäften* hedging n; *zum* ~ *bringen* terminate v
Abschlußabteilung f closing department
Abschlußagent m closing agent
Abschlußbericht m closing statement
Abschlußbuchung f closing entry
Abschlußgebühr f completion fee
Abschlußkonto n final account
Abschlußkurs m contract price, trading price
Abschlußposten m end-of-year item
Abschlußprüfer m auditor
Abschlußprüfung f audit of annual account
Abschlußrechnung f account of settlement
Abschlußtermin m closing date
Abschlußvergütung f end-of-year bonus
Abschlußvollmacht f power to contract
Abschlußzahlung f final payment
Abschnitt m (A. einer Anleihe) tranche, denomination unit
abschreiben v copy v; ~ v (Wert) depreciate v; ~ v (Schuld oder Forderung) wipe off, charge off v, write off v
Abschreibung f (Wert) depreciation n; ~ f (Schuld oder Forderung) write-off n, charge-off n; ~ *auf Betriebsanlagen* depreciation of plant; *lineare* ~ straight-line depreciation; *übermäßige* ~ overdepreciation n
Abschreibungen auf Inventar inventory write-downs; *verdiente* ~ amount of depreciation earned

Abschreibungsbetrag m depreciable amount
abschreibungsfähig adj depreciable adj
Abschreibungsfonds m depreciation fund, depreciation reserve, accrued depreciation, reserve for depreciation, allowance for depreciation
Abschreibungsgesellschaft f tax-loss company
Abschreibungskonto n depreciation account
Abschreibungslasten f pl amortization charges
Abschreibungsreserve f depreciation fund, depreciation reserve, accrued depreciation, reserve for depreciation, allowance for depreciation
Abschreibungsrücklage f depreciation fund, depreciation reserve, accrued depreciation, reserve for depreciation, allowance for depreciation
Abschreibungssatz m depreciation rate, rate of depreciation
Abschrift f copy n
abschwächen v (Kurse) ease off
Abschwächung f sag n, easing-off n; ~ **der Geldsätze** easing in money rates
Abschwächungstendenz f downward trend
Abschwung m down swing, decline, slow down
absenden v send v, dispatch v
Absender m sender, address, consignor n
absetzen v deduct v
Absetzung für Abnutzung allowance for wear and tear
absichern v cover, hedge, guard against
Absicherung f hedge, hedging, cover, covering
Absicherungsmöglichkeiten f pl hedging options (opportunities)
Absicht f intent n, intention n
Absichtserklärung f letter of intent
absondern v segregate v, separate v
Absonderungsanspruch m creditor's preferential claim, claim made by a secured creditor
abstammen v descend v
Abstammung f descent n
Abstand nehmen von desist from

absteigende Reihenfolge descending order, descending sequence
Abstempelung f stamping n
abstimmen v (Konten) reconcile v, balance v; ~ v (Wahl) vote v
Abstimmung f (von Konten) reconciliation n (of accounts), balancing n (of accounts); ~ f (Wahl) vote n
abstrakte Garantie naked guarantee
abstreiten v dispute v, challenge v, contest v
Abteilung f department n; ~ f division n; ~ **für festverzinsliche Wertpapiere** bond department (US)
Abteilungsleiter m head of department, department manager
abtrennen v separate, detach v
abtretbar adj assignable adj
Abtretbarkeit f assignability n
abtreten v assign v, convey v
Abtretende f u. m assignor n, cedent n, transferor n
Abtretung f assignment n, assignation n, cession n
Abtretungserklärung f declaration of assignment, act of transfer
Abtretungsurkunde f deed of assignment, deed of conveyance, deed of release, deed of transfer
Abwärtsbewegung f downward movement
abweichen v differ v
Abweichung f discrepancy n, difference
Abweisung f refusal n
abwerben; Kunden ~ draw away customers, alienate customers
abwerfen; einen Gewinn ~ leave a margin, leave a profit; **einen Nutzen ~** show a profit
abwerten v devalorize v, devalue v, devaluate v
Abwertung f devalorization n, devaluation n; ~ **aus Wettbewerbsgründen** (Währung) competitive devaluation (of a currency)
Abwesenheitspfleger m curator in absentia
abwickeln v settle, liquidate v, wind up
Abwickler m liquidator
Abwicklung f settlement, handling, processing, liquidation

Abwicklungsbank

Abwicklungsbank f liquidation bank, settlement bank
Abwicklungskonto n liquidation account
Abwicklungsprovision f handling commission
Abzahlung f instalment n, payment on account
Abzahlungsfinanzierungsgesellschaft f personal loan company (US)
Abzahlungsgeschäft n instalment business, instalment transaction, instalment lending business, instalment buying
Abzahlungskredit m instalment credit
Abzahlungsvertrag m credit sales arrangement
Abzahlungswechsel m instalment bill
abziehbar adj deductible adj
abziehen v deduct v; ~ v (Math.) subtract v
abzinsen v discount
Abzinsung f discount, deduction
Abzinsungsanleihe f discount bond, zero coupon bond
Abzinsungsbetrag m discount, amount discounted
Abzinsungssatz m discount rate
Abzug m allowance n; ~ m deduction n; *im voraus gemachter* ~ unearned discount
abzüglich minus, less
abzugsfähig adj deductible adj
addieren v add v
Addiermaschine f adding machine
Addition f addition n
Adrema f addressograph n
Adressant m sender n, adresser n
Adressat m addressee n
Adreßdatei f address file, address tape
Adresse f address n; *bonitätsmäßig erste* ~ first-class name; *bonitätsmäßig zweite* ~ second-class name
Adressenausfallrisiken n pl counterparty risk
adressieren v address v
Adressiermaschine f addressograph n
Adressierung f addressing n
Adressierungsverfahren n addressing method, addressing technique
Affidavit n statutory declaration, affidavit n, sworn declaration
Agent m agent n

Agentur f agency n
Agio n agio n, premium n
Agrarkredit m farm loan, farm credit, agricultural loan
akademische Ausbildung academic training
akkreditieren v accredit v
Akkreditiv n letter of credit, documentary credit; ~ *mit aufgeschobener Zahlung* deferred payment documentary credit; ~ *ohne Dokumente* clean letter of credit; *automatisch sich erneuerndes* ~ revolving letter of credit; *bestätigtes unwiderrufliches* ~ irrevocable confirmed letter of credit, straight letter of credit; *ein* ~ *stellen* open a letter of credit; *nicht bestätigtes* ~ unconfirmed letter of credit; *revolvierendes* ~ revolving documentary credit; *übertragbares* ~ transferable letter of credit; *widerrufliches* ~ revocable letter of credit
Akkreditivauftrag m order to open a letter of credit
Akkreditivbedingungen f pl terms and conditions of the letter of credit, conditions of the documentary credit
Akkreditivbegünstigte f u. m beneficiary of a letter of credit
Akkreditivbestätigung f confirmation of letter of credit
Akkreditivbetrag m amount of the documentary credit
Akkreditiveröffnung f opening of a letter of credit
Akkreditivgeschäfte n pl documentary credit transactions
Akkreditivinhaber m accreditee n
Akkreditivkonto n letter of credit account
akkumulierte Habenumsätze accumulated credit activity; ~ *Nachtragsliste* accumulated adjustment register; ~ *Sollumsätze* accumulated debit activity
Akkumulierung f accumulation n
Akquisition f acquisition, business getting
Akquisitionsabteilung f business department
Akte f file n

Aktenstück *n* file *n*, record *n*

Aktie *f* share *n*, stock *n*; **- aus dem Umweltbereich** environmental share; **- einer Bergwerksgesellschaft** share of a mining company; **- ohne Nennwert** no-par stock, no-par share, share of no-par value; **amtlich eingeführte -** listed stock (US); **börsengängige -** share listed on the stock exchange; **gängige -** active stock; **international gehandelte -** euro equity; **junge -** new share; **mit Fremdkapital finanzierte -** leveraged stock; **nennwertlose -** no-par stock, no-par share, share of no-par value; **stimmberechtigte -** voting share; **unfreie -** non-free share; **voll eingezahlte -** fully paid share, fully paid-up share

Aktien *f pl* shares, stocks *n pl*; **- an der Börse einführen** issue stocks at the stock exchange; **- auflegen** announce shares; **- beziehen** take up shares; **- der Schwerindustrie** heavy industrials; **- mit garantierter Dividendenzahlung** guaranteed stocks; **- mit geringem Kurswert** low-prices shares; **- mit geringer Marktkapitalisierung** small caps; **- mit Gewinnbeteiligung** participating stock; **- oder Obligationen von privaten Versorgungsbetrieben** public utilities; **- und andere nicht festverzinsliche Wertpapiere** shares and other non-fixed-income shares; **- veräußern** realize shares; **- voll zuteilen** allocate shares to all applicants; **- zeichnen** take up shares; **an der Börse nicht eingeführte -** unlisted shares; **effektiv im Besitz befindliche -** long stock (US); **eigene -** treasury stock; **kumulative -** cumulative stocks (US); **lombardierte -** pawned stocks; **nicht ausgegebene -** potential stock, unissued stock, unissued capital, unissued shares; **nicht bevorrechtigte -** (in bezug auf Dividendenzahlungen) deferred shares (US); **nicht gezeichnete -** unsubscribed stock; **nicht nachschußpflichtige -** nonassessable stocks; **nicht notierte -** displaced shares; **nicht zugeteilte -** unallotted shares; **verpfändete -** pawned stock (GB); **Wertminderung von -** dilution of shares

Aktienanteilsschein *m* certificate of stock (US), stock transfer warrant (GB), share certificate, stock certificate, share warrant, stock warrant, stock trust certificate

Aktienausgabe *f* issue of stock (US), share issue

Aktienauswahl *f* (unter Renditeaspekt) stock picking

Aktienbank *f* joint stock bank (GB)

Aktienbesitz *m* shareholdings *n pl*, stockholdings *n pl*

Aktienbesitzer *m* stockowner *n*

Aktienbestand *m* shareholdings *n pl*, stockholdings *n pl*

Aktienbezugsrecht *n* stock warrant

Aktienbezugsschein *m* stock warrant

Aktienbörse *f* stock exchange

Aktienbuch *n* register of shares, share ledger (GB)

Aktiendepot *n* share (stock) portfolio

Aktiendividende *f* share dividend

Aktienemission *f* stock (share) issue

Aktienfonds *m* investment fund for shares

Aktiengeschäft *n* stock trade

Aktiengesellschaft *f* stock corporation (US), joint-stock company (GB); **börsennotierte -** listed company; **eingetragene -** registered company

Aktiengesetz *n* law governing the operation of stock corporations, stock corporations law

Aktienhandel *m* stockbrokerage *n*, stockbroking *n*, dealings in stocks (US)

Aktienindex *m* share index; **- der Financial Times** All-Share Index; **- Future** stock index future

Aktieninhaber *m* shareholder *n*, stockholder *n*

Aktienkapital *n* share capital, stock capital; **effektiv ausgegebenes -** issued stock (US), issued capital (GB); **für eine Kapitalerhöhung genehmigtes -** authorized capital; **verwässertes -** watered (diluted) capital, watered stock (US)

Aktienkauf

Aktienkauf m stock purchase, purchase of shares
Aktienkaufoption f stock call option
Aktienkorb m stock basket
Aktienkurs m rate of shares, share price, share quotation
Aktienkursliste f share list, stock list (US)
Aktienkurszettel m share list, stock list (US)
Aktienmakler m stockbroker n, securities dealer (US)
Aktienmantel m bare shell, share certificate, stock certificate
Aktienmarkt m share (stock) market
Aktienmehrheit f majority of shares, majority of stocks
Aktiennotierung f rate of shares, share price, stock price, share quotation
Aktienoption f stock option
Aktienoptionsschein m stock (share, equity) warrant
Aktienpaket n block of shares, parcel of shares; *heimlicher Kauf eines größeren -s* sneak attack (US)
Aktienplazierung; *internationale -* international placement of shares
Aktienpreis m rate of shares, share (stock) price, share quotation
Aktienrecht n company law, corporation law
Aktienrechtsreform f amendment of stock laws
Aktienregister n share register
Aktienrendite f yield on shares
Aktienrückkauf m buyback of shares
Aktienschein m certificate of stock (US), stock transfer warrant (GB), share certificate, stock certificate, share warrant, stock warrant, stock trust certificate
Aktienspekulant m speculator n
Aktienspekulation f speculation in stocks
Aktiensplit m split (of shares)
Aktiensymbol n ticker symbol
Aktientausch m exchange of shares
Aktienteilung f split n, splitting n
Aktienterminhandel m stock futures and options trading
Aktienübernahmekonsortium n share (stock) underwriting group
Aktienübertragung f assignation of shares, assignment of stock, stock transfer, transfer of shares (GB), transfer of stock (US)
Aktienumschreibung f assignation of shares, assignment of stock, stock transfer, transfer of shares (GB), transfer of stock (US)
Aktienumtauschangebot n capital stock exchange offer
Aktienverkäufe m pl share sales
Aktienverkäufer; *betrügerischer -* share pusher
Aktienverwahrung f safekeeping of securities
Aktienwert m share value
Aktienzeichnungsbuch n subscription ledger
Aktienzeichnungsliste f allotment sheet
Aktienzertifikat n certificate of stock (US), stock transfer warrant (GB), share certificate, stock certificate, share warrant, stock warrant, stock trust certificate
Aktienzusammenlegung f reverse split
Aktienzuteilung f allocation of shares
Aktionär m shareholder n, stockholder n; *Minderheitenrechte des -s* minority shareholder rights
Aktionärsbuch n shareholders' ledger, stockholders' ledger
Aktionärsversammlung f meeting of shareholders (GB), meeting of stockholders (US), annual meeting, shareholders' meeting, stockholders' meeting
Aktionärsverzeichnis n dividend book, list of shareholders, shareholders' register (GB), list of stockholders (US)
aktiv adj active adj; *- adj* (Zahlungsbilanz) favo(u)rable adj
Aktiva plt assets n pl; *- einer Bank* bank resources; *- und Passiva* assets and liabilities; *flüssige -* floating assets, current assets, circulating assets, current funds, current receivables, fluid assets; (US), liquid assets, revolving assets; *gezielter Verkauf der -* asset stripping; *immaterielle -* intangible assets; *jederzeit greifbare -* available assets; *leicht realisierbare*

~ (z. B. Kasse, Bank, Postscheckguthaben, börsengängige Wertpapiere, Außenstände) quick assets; **leicht verwertbare** ~ easily marketable asset; **nicht greifbare** ~ intangible assets; **schwer verwertbare** ~ sticky assets; **transitorische** ~ prepaid expenses

aktive Handelsbilanz active trade balance

Aktiven *plt* assets

Aktivgeschäft *n* (einer Bank) assets-side business, loan business

aktivieren *v* activate

Aktivierung *f* activation

Aktivmasse *f* assets *n pl*

Aktivposten *m* asset *n*

Aktivsaldo *m* (Handelsbilanz) active balance; ~ *m* credit balance

Aktivseite *f* assets, active side, assets side

Aktivüberschuß *m* credit surplus

Aktivum *n* asset *n*

Aktivwert *m* assets value

Aktivzins *m* loan interest rate, interest receivable, interest earned

Akzept *n* acceptance *n*, bill of acceptance; **bedingtes** ~ qualified acceptance, conditional acceptance; **bedingungsloses** ~ clean acceptance; **Dokumente gegen** ~ documents against acceptance; **mit einem** ~ **versehen** accepted *adj*; **reines** ~ clean acceptance; **vor Fälligkeit bezahltes** ~ acceptance under rebate (GB), rebated acceptance (US), anticipated acceptance; **vorbehaltloses** ~ clean acceptance; **Wechsel mit einem** ~ **versehen** provide a bill with acceptance

Akzeptant *m* acceptor *n*; **bankrotter** ~ bankrupt acceptor

Akzeptbank *f* acceptance bank, acceptance house, accepting house

Akzeptbesorgung *f* presentment for acceptance

Akzeptbuch *n* acceptance ledger

Akzeptgebühr *f* acceptance charge

Akzeptgläubiger *m* acceptance creditor

akzeptieren; **blanko** ~ accept in blank; **einen Wechsel** ~ accept a bill

akzeptiert *adj* accepted *adj*

akzeptierter Wechsel acceptance *n*, bill of acceptance

Akzeptkonto *n* acceptance account

Akzeptkredit *m* acceptance credit, banker's acceptance credit; **dokumentärer** ~ documentary acceptance credit

Akzeptkreditlinie *f* line of acceptance, acceptance line

Akzeptkreditrahmen *m* line of acceptance, acceptance line

Akzeptlimit *n* line of acceptance, acceptance line (limit)

Akzeptprovision *f* accepting commission, commission for acceptance

Akzeptschuldner *m* acceptance debtor

Akzeptumlauf *m* acceptance commitments

Akzeptverbindlichkeit *f* acceptance liability

Akzeptverweigerung *f* non-acceptance *n*

Akzeptvorlage *f* presentation for acceptance

Alleingesellschafter *m* sole proprietor

Alleinverkaufsrecht *n* franchise *n*

Alleinvertrieb *m* exclusive sale, monopoly *n*

Alleinzeichnungsberechtigte *f u. m* sole authorized signatory

Allfinanz *f* universal financing; **Anbieter von** ~ **für Firmenkunden** financial boutique

Allfinanz-Dienstleistungen *f pl* multi function financial services, one-stop financial services

allgemeine Abmachung general covenant

Allgemeine *Geschäftsbedingungen* General Business Conditions, boilerplate (informal) (US); ~ **Kreditvereinbarungen** General Agreement to Borrow (GAB)

allgemeine Kosten overhead charges, overhead expenses, general expenses

Allgemeine Zoll- und Handelsabkommen *n* General Agreement on Tariffs and Trade (GATT)

Allonge *f* allonge, fly leaf

alte Rechnung completed period

älter *adj* senior *adj*

Alternativbegünstigte *f u. m* alternative payee

Alternativbezogene *f u. m* alternative drawee

Alternativverpflichtung

Alternativverpflichtung f alternative obligation
Altersrente f old age pension
Altersversorgung f pension
Altersversorgungsplan m pension plan, retirement plan
amerikanische *Buchführungsmethode* tabular bookkeeping; **~ *Eisenbahnwerte*** (Börse) American rails
Amerikanische Option f American option
Amortisation f amortization n, redemtion, paying off
Amortisationsanleihe f redemption bond
Amortisationsfonds m sinking fund
Amortisationshypothek f sinking fund mortgage loan, amortising mortgage
Amortisationsquote f amortization instalment
Amortisationszahlung f amortization payment, redemption payment
amortisierbar adj amortizable adj, redeemable adj
Amortisierbarkeit f redeemableness n
amortisieren v amortize v, repay, redeem
amortisiert adj redeemed adj
Amt n office n
amtlich adj official adj; **~ *beglaubigen*** legalize v; **~ *eingeführte Aktie*** listed stock (US); **~ *eingetragen*** incorporate adj
amtliche *Beglaubigung* legalization n; **~ *Eintragung einer Gesellschaft*** incorporation n
amtlicher *Einheitskurs* official cash market quotation; **~ *Kurs*** official price (rate); **~ *Makler*** official broker
Amtsdauer f term of office
Amtsgewalt f authority n
Analogrechner m analog computer
Analyse; *technische* ~ technical analysis
Analysenabteilung f analysis department
analysieren v analyse v
anbieten v offer v
Anbieter m seller, supplier n
anbinden tie (to peg); ***an die Europäische Währungseinheit*** ~ tie to the European Currency Unit
Anderdepot n third-party security deposit
Anderkonto n trust account
ändern v change v

Änderung f alteration n, modification n, change n
Änderungsdienst m revision service, modification service, updating service, file maintenance (service)
Änderungsmitteilung f modification notice, file maintenance notice
Änderungsschlüssel m modification code, file maintenance code
andienen v tender v (e.g. payment), offer v (e.g. a document)
aneignen (sich) v appropriate v
Aneignung f appropriation n
Anerbieten n offer n
anerkannt adj approved adj
anerkennen v (Recht, Urteil) abide by; **~** v acknowledge v; ***nicht*** ~ disclaim v
Anerkenntnis n acknowledgement n
Anerkenntnisurteil n decree of registration
Anfangskapital n initial capital, opening capital
Anfangskurs m opening price, starting price
Anfangsparität f (IMF) initial parity
Anfechtbarkeit f defeasibility n
anfordern v call for
Anforderung f requirement n
Anfrage f inquiry n, investigation n; **~ *wegen einer Kreditauskunft*** status inquiry
anfragende Bank calling bank
Anfuhrgebühren f pl cartage n
angeben v state v, (Wert) declare
Angebot n offer, bid n; **~** n (Börse) securities on offer, offerings n pl (US); **~ *und Nachfrage*** supply and demand; ***das tägliche*** ~ the floating supply
angeboten adj (Börse) asked adj
Angebotsdruck m selling pressure
Angebotssatz m offered price (rate)
Angehörige f u. m dependent n
angelegtes Geld invested money
angenommen adj accepted adj
angepaßt adj adapted adj
angeschlossen adj attached adj; ***direkt*** ~ on-line
angespannt adj (Börse) tight adj
angestellt adj employed adj
Angestelltenpensionskasse f staff pension fund

Angestellte f u. m employee n, employe n (US); *leitende* - executive n
angleichen v adjust v
Angleichung f adjustment n
Angstkäufe m pl scare buying
Angstverkauf m panic selling
anhaken v tick off (items)
Anhang m allonge, addendum, annex n, appendix n
anhängend adj annexed adj
anhängig; noch - pending adj, unsettled adj
anhäufen v accumulate v
Anhäufung f accumulation n
anheften v attach v
Anhörung f hearing n
Ankauf m buy n, purchase n, purchasing n
Ankaufsermächtigung f authority to purchase
Ankaufskurs m buying rate, purchase price
ankündigen v announce v, declare v
Ankündigung f announcement n, notice n
ankurbeln v stimulate v
Anlage f enclosure n, annex n, supplement n; - f (Investition) investment n, employment of funds; *besonders sichere* - eligible investment (US); *langfristige* - long position; *sichere* - safe investment; *vorübergehende* - current investment
Anlageabgänge m pl asset sales, loss in assets
Anlageberater m investment adviser, investment consultant
Anlageberatung f investment advisory service
Anlagebewertung f assets valuation, investment rating (US)
Anlageempfehlungen f pl investment recommendations
Anlageerneuerung f asset, replacement n
Anlagefinanzierung f fixed investment financing
Anlagefonds m investment fund; - *mit spekulativer Anlagepolitik* go-go fund; *gemischte* - mixed investment trust
Anlagefondsanteilsscheine m pl investment trust securities
Anlagegeschäft n investment business

Anlagegesellschaft f investment company
Anlagegrundsätze m pl investment standards
Anlagekapital n fixed capital, invested capital
Anlagekäufe m pl assets purchases
Anlageklima n climate for investment
Anlagekonto n property account
Anlagekundschaft f investing customers
Anlagemittel n pl funds available for investment
Anlagen; feste - gross plant, gross property, property assets; *unproduktive* - dead assets
Anlagenbau m plant construction
Anlagenkonfiguration f system configuration
Anlagenverwaltung f asset (investment) management
Anlageobjekt n object of investment
Anlagepapiere n pl investment securities, investment stocks; *mündelsichere* - legal investments (US), gilt-edged securities, gilt-edged investment, savings securities, widow and orphan stock (US)
Anlageplan m investment plan
Anlagepolitik f investment policy
Anlagepublikum n investors n pl, investing public
Anlagestatus m assets status
Anlagevermögen n fixed assets, property investments
Anlagevorhaben; langfristige - capital projects
Anlagewert eines Wertpapiers (auf Grund der Rendite) investment value
Anlaufdividende f start-up dividend
Anlaufkosten plt initial costs, launching cost
anlegen v invest in v
Anleger m investor n
Anleihe f bond n, loan n; - *ausländischer Schuldner* foreign bond issue; - *bei der Mantel und Zinsscheine getrennt sind* stripped bond; - *eines Emittenten erster Bonität* investment-grade bond (e.g. rated AAA); - *mit hohem Disagio und niedrigem Zins* debt-discounted bond; - *mit hohem Risiko* junk bond; - *mit Kündigungsschutzrecht*

Anleiheagio

des Gläubigers put bond; *- mit möglicher Laufzeitverkürzung* retractible bond; *- mit niedrigem Nominalwert* baby bond; *- mit Optionsschein auf Aktien* equity-linked issue; *- mit Optionsscheinen* bond cum warrants; *- mit überdurchschnittlicher Rendite* cushion bond; *- mit variablem Zinssatz* floating rate bond (FRB), floater; *- mit variabler, dem Marktzins entgegengesetzter Verzinsung* reverse floater; *- mit Verlängerungsrecht* extendable bond; *- mit Wahlrecht zwischen Barzahlung und zusätzlichen Stücken* multiplier bond; *- mit Währungsoption* bond issue with monetary option; *- mit zunehmender Verzinsung* step-up bond; *- ohne Optionsscheine* bond ex warrants; *- ohne Verfallfrist* dead loan (GB); *- ohne Wandel- oder Optionsklausel* straight note; *eine - auflegen* float a bond issue, float a loan issue, launch a loan; *eine - begeben* float a bond issue, float a loan issue, launch a loan; *eine - überzeichnen* oversubscribe a loan; *festverzinsliche - mit indexgekoppeltem Rückzahlungsbetrag* condor fund; *konsolidierte -* unified stock, consolidated loan; *nicht am Markt plazierte -* private placement; *nicht handelbare -* straight loan; *nicht in voller Höhe gezeichnete -* undersubscribed loan; *notleidende -* bond issue in default, assented bond (US); *öffentliche -* civil loan (US), public loan, public credit; *steuerbegünstigte -* taxfavo(u)red loan; *steuerfreie -* tax-free loan; *unbesicherte -* unsecured loan; *ungedeckte -* fiduciary loan; *unkündbare -* bullet bond; *unveränderliche -* closed issue; *zinslose -* interest-free bond, zero coupon bond

Anleiheagio n loan (bond) premium
Anleihebedarf m bond demand
Anleihebedingungen f pl bond terms
Anleihebetrag m bond amount
Anleihedienst m bond service
Anleiheerlös m proceeds from bond business
Anleihefinanzierung f loan (bond) financing
Anleihegarant m underwriter n
Anleihegeber m lender n, credit grantor
Anleihegeschäft n bond issue business
Anleihegläubiger m bond holder
Anleihekapital n bond capital, loan capital
Anleihekonsortium n bond (underwriting) syndicate
Anleihekonto n bond account
Anleihekonversion f bond conversion, loan conversion
Anleihekurs m bond price
Anleihelaufzeit f life of a bond
Anleihemarkt m bond market
Anleihen- und Schuldverschreibungen bonds and notes
Anleiheoptionsschein m bond warrant
Anleihepapier n bond n, debenture n, obligation n
Anleiheschein m bond certificate
Anleiheschuld f bond debt, bonded debt
Anleiheschuldenlast f bonded indebtedness
Anleiheschuldner m borrower n, bond debtor
Anleihestücke zurückkaufen retire a loan
Anleihetilgung f amortization of a bond
Anleiheumlauf m bond circulation
Anleihevertrag m bond contract, loan agreement
Anleiheverzinsung f bond service
Anleihezinsen m pl bond interest
Anlernling m learner n
anliegend adj annexed adj
anmelden; *einen Anspruch -* file a claim
Annäherung f approximation n
Annäherungswert m approximate value
Annahme f (eines Wechsels) acceptance n; *~ f (Rechte, Pflichten)* assumption n; *- verweigern* refuse acceptance; *- verweigert* acceptance refused; *bedingte -* qualified acceptance, conditional acceptance; *gegen -* against acceptance
Annahmestelle f register office
Annahmeurkunde f instrument of acceptance
Annahmeverpflichtung f purchase commitment

Annahmeverweigerung f non-acceptance n, refusal to accept
annehmbarer Preis reasonable price
annehmen v accept v
Annonce f advertisement n, ad n
annoncieren v advertise v
Annuität f annuity n; *hinausgeschobene* ~ deferred annuity
Annuitätenanleihe f annuity bond
annullierbar adj annullable adj, defeasible adj, rescindable adj
annullieren v annul v, nullify v
annulliert adj cancelled adj
Annullierung f annulment n
anordnen v (ordnen) arrange v, order, instruct
Anordnung f (Ordnung) arrangement n; ~ f instruction n
Anordnungen f pl dispositions n pl
anrechenbar adj chargeable adj
anrechnen v count towards, take into account; ~ *auf* charge up against
Anrecht n right n
Anrede f address n
Anreiz m incentive n
ansammeln v accumulate v
Ansammlung f accumulation n
anschaffen v provide v (e.g. funds), remit v (e.g. a sum to a bank)
Anschaffung f acquisition n
Anschaffungsdarlehen n consumer loan, personal loan
Anschaffungskapital n initial capital
Anschaffungspreis m initial cost
Anschaffungswert m cost value, acquisition value
Anschluß m connection n
Anschlußadresse f (bei Großspeicherdateien) chain address, linking address, chaining address, link address
Anschlußfinanzierung f follow-up financing
Anschlußpfändung f second distress
Anschreibekredit m credit in account
anschreiben v mark up
Anschrift f address n
Ansehen n standing n, reputation n; *geschäftliches* ~ business reputation
ansparen v save up
Ansparung f funds saved

Ansprache f address n, speech n
Anspruch m claim n; *einen ~ anmelden* file a claim; *einen ~ befriedigen* satisfy a claim; *einen ~ erheben* advance a claim, raise a claim, lodge a claim; *einen ~ geltend machen* advance a claim, raise a claim, lodge a claim; *einklagbarer ~* right of action; *zweifelhafter ~* doubtful claim
Anstalt f corporation, institution n
ansteigen; *rapide ~* (Preise, Kurse) boom v
Anstellung f employment n
Anstrengung f endeavor n (US), endeavour n (GB)
Anteil m share; ~ m (Teil) portion n; ~ m (Verhältnis) proportion n; ~ *an einem verbundenen Unternehmen* share of an affiliated company; ~*e an verbundenen Unternehmen* investments in affiliated enterprises
anteilmäßig adj pro rata, proportionate adj; ~ *berechnen* pro-rate v
Anteilseigner m shareholder n, stockholder n
Anteilsschein m participation certificate (US); ~ m (eines Investmentfonds) share certificate (of an investment company); ~ *einer Aktie* share, share certificate, scrip certificate (US)
Anteilsübertragung f assignment of interest
Antikapitalismus m anti-capitalism n
antikapitalistisch adj anticapitalistic adj
antizipative Posten (auf der Passivseite) accrued expenses, (auf der Aktivseite) accrued income
Antrag m application n; ~ *stellen* file an application
Antragsformular n application blank, application form, form of application
Antragsteller m applicant
Antwort f answer n
antworten v answer v
Antwortzeit f response time
anvertrauen v entrust v
anwachsen v increase v, accumulate v, accrue v
Anwalt m counsel n, counsellor n; ~ m lawyer n, attorney n, solicitor n (GB)

Anwaltsgebühren f pl counsel's fee, lawyer's fee, attorney's fee
Anwaltsgebührenrechnung f bill of costs
Anwärter m applicant n
anwartschaftlich adj reversionary adj
Anwartschaftsberechtigter m reversioner n
Anwartschaftsgut n remainder estate
Anwartschaftsrecht n contingent right, reversionary interest
anweisen v instruct v, direct v
Anweisung f order, instruction n; **wechselähnliche -** bill-like payment order
Anwender m user n
Anwendung f application n
Anwendungsbereich m range of application
Anzahlung f down payment, payment on account
Anzahlungen verrechnen allow for sums paid in advance
Anzahlungsbürgschaft f downpayment guarantee
Anzeige f (Werbung) advertisement n, ad n; ~ f advice n, notification n; ~ f announcement n, notice n
Anzeigegerät n display unit
anzeigen v announce v, declare v
Anzeigentarif m advertising rates
anziehen v rise, increase
Anziehen der Preise stiffening of prices; **leichtes ~ der Effektenkurse** slight improvement of share prices
Anziehungskraft f appeal n
Arbeit f work n
arbeitendes Kapital active capital
Arbeiterbank f workers bank
Arbeitgeber m employer n
Arbeitgeber-Arbeitnehmer-Verhältnis n industrial relations, labor relations (US), labour relations (GB)
Arbeitnehmer m employee n
Arbeitsablauf m processing sequence
Arbeitsbeschaffungskredit m jobcreating loan
Arbeitsentgelt n wage n, wages n pl
Arbeitsgang m (Stufe, Abschnitt) work segment, pass n
Arbeitskämpfe m pl labour disputes

Arbeitskräfte f pl manpower, labour force
Arbeitslohn m wages, pay
Arbeitslose f u. m unemployed, jobless
Arbeitsphase f work phase, processing phase
Arbeitsplatzteilung f (mit Teilzeitkräften) job sharing
Arbeitsteilung f division of labo(u)r
Arbeitsverhältnis n employment n
Arbeitsvertrag m contract of employment
Arbeitszeit f working hours
Arbitrage f arbitration n, arbitrage n
Arbitrageur m arbitrager n, arbitragist n
Archiv n archives n pl, records n pl
Arrangement n arrangement n
arrangieren v arrange v
Arrest m arrest n, distraint
Arrondierungskäufe m pl rounding-off buying
Artikel m article n, item n, commodity n
Asiatische Währungseinheit f Asian Currency Unit (ACU)
Asien-Dollar m Asian dollar
Assekuranz f assurance n (GB), insurance n
Attentismus m (am Kapitalmarkt) wait-and-see attitude (in the capital market)
auf Abruf at call
Aufbaukredit m build-up loan
Aufbewahrung f custody n, safe keeping
aufbrauchen v consume v, use up
Aufdecken n (von Schiebungen) racket busting (US)
Aufenthaltsbewilligung f residence permit
auferlegen v impose v
Auffanggesellschaft f lifeboat
auffordern; zur Abgabe von Zeichnungsangeboten ~ invite tenders
Aufforderung zur Rückzahlung recall for redemption
auffüllen v replenish v
Auffüllkredit m replenishment loan
Aufgabe f abandonment n; **~ des Goldstandards** abandonment of the gold standard
Aufgabenstellung f problem definition
aufgeben v relinquish v give up
aufgehoben adj cancelled adj
aufgelaufen adj accrued adj

aufgelaufene Kosten accrued charges; **~ Zinsen** interest accrued
Aufgeld n agio n, premium n
Aufgeldkonto n agio account
aufgenommener Kredit borrowed money
aufgeschobener Kredit deferred credit
aufgliedern v break down, split up
Aufgliederung f breakdown n, analysis n
aufhebbar adj annullable adj, defeasible adj, rescindable adj
Aufhebbarkeit f defeasibility n
aufheben v annul, cancel, rescind v
Aufhebung f abrogation n (of a law); **~ f** rescission n, cancellation n; **einstweilige ~** suspension n
Aufkauf m buying up
aufkaufen v buy up
Aufkäufer m buyer, raider
aufkündigen v cancel v, terminate v (e.g. a contract)
Auflage f condition n
Auflassung f (Grundstück) conveyance of property
Auflassungsvormerkung f entry of conveyance
auflaufen v accrue v
auflegen; eine Anleihe ~ float a bond issue, float a loan issue, launch a loan; **neu ~** reissue v
Auflegungsdatum n launch date
aufliegen v be exposed (for sale), be offered (for subscription)
auflösen v dissolve v; **~** v liquidate v, wind up; **ein Konto ~** eliminate an account
Auflösung f dissolution n, cancellation
Aufnahme f admission n
aufnahmefähiger Markt broad market, ready market
aufnehmen; einen Kredit ~ borrow money
aufnehmende Gesellschaft absorbing company
aufrechnen v set-off, offset, add up
Aufrechnung f set-off, offset n
Aufrechnungsanspruch m right of set-off
Aufruf m call n
aufrufen v call v
Aufruhrversicherung f civil commotion insurance
aufrunden v round off

aufschiebbar adj delayable adj, adjournable adj, deferrable adj
aufschieben v postpone v
aufschlagen v increase, charge an extra
Aufschub m (auch: Zurückstellung vom Militärdienst) deferment n; **~ m** respite n
Aufschwung nehmend booming adj (US)
Aufseher m controller n
Aufsichtsamt n supervisory office
Aufsichtsrat m supervisory board
Aufsichtsratsmitglied n member of the supervisory board, board member
Aufsichtsratsposten m directorship n
Aufsichtsratssitzung f meeting of the supervisory board, board meeting
Aufsichtsratsvergütung f remuneration of the supervisory board, directors fees
Aufsichtsratsvorsitzende f u. m chairman of the supervisory board, board chairman (US)
Aufsichtsratswahl f election of the supervisory board
aufsteigende Reihenfolge ascending order, ascending sequence
Aufstellung f list n, statement n
aufstocken v raise, increase, stock up
Aufstockung des Kapitals capital increase
Aufstockungsaktien f pl bonus shares
aufteilbar adj apportionable adj, allocable adj
aufteilen v distribute v, divide v, split v
Aufteilung f (Teilung) partition n; **verhältnismäßige ~** apportionment n
Auftrag m (Beauftragung) commission n; **~ m** order n; **~ Aktien billigst zu kaufen** stop order; **bedingter ~** conditional order; **einen ~ erteilen** give an order; **im ~ und für Rechnung** on behalf and for account of, by order and for account of
Auftraggeber m employer n; **~ m** principal n, mandator n
Auftragnehmer m supplier n, manufacturer n
Auftragsbestand m backlog n (of orders), unfilled orders
Auftragsbestätigung f confirmation of order
Auftragserteilung f order placing
Auftragsstimmrecht n (Depotstimmrecht) proxy voting right

Aufwand

Aufwand m expenditure, amount provided; *sonstiger* - other charges
Aufwandseite f expenses side
Aufwand-und-Ertrags-Konten n pl profit and loss accounts
Aufwärts-Abwärts-Index m advance-decline-index n
aufweisen; *einen Gewinn* - show a profit; *einen Saldo von ...* - show a balance of ...
aufwenden v spend v, use
Aufwendungen f pl expenses n pl, expenditure(s); *außerordentliche* - extraordinary expenses; *betriebliche* - operating expenses
aufwerten v revalue v
Aufwertung f (einer Währung) upvaluation n (of a currency), revaluation n; - f (eines Marktpreises) valorization n
Aufwertungsanleihe f stabilization bond
aufzählen v list v, enumerate v
aufzeichnen v register v, record v
Aufzeichnung f record n, note n
aufzinsen v add on interest
Aufzinsung f accrued interest
Aufzinsungsanleihe f premium bond
Auktion f auction n; *auf einer - kaufen* buy by auction
Auktionator m auctioneer n
ausarbeiten v elaborate v, work out, plan v
ausbauen v extend v
Ausbeutung eines Unternehmens milking n (US)
ausbezahlt adj paid off
Ausbildung f training n; *akademische* - academic training
Ausbildungskredit m education (student) loan
Ausbildungskurs m course of training
ausbuchen v write-off, take off the books
Ausbuchung f writing off, write-off
ausdehnen v expand v
Ausdehnung f expansion n
Ausfall m loss n
Ausfallbürgschaft f letter of indemnity (GB), bond of indemnity (US)
ausfallgefährdete Ausleihungen problem lendings
Ausfallquote f loss rate
Ausfallrisiko n risk of non-payment

ausfertigen v make out v, issue v
Ausfertigung f copy n; *in dreifacher* - in triplicate
Ausfuhr f export n, exportation n
Ausfuhrabgabe f export duty
ausführbar adj exportable adj; - adj realizable adj
Ausfuhrbescheinigung f export certificate
Ausfuhrbeschränkungen f pl restriction of exports
Ausfuhrbestimmungen f pl export regulations
Ausfuhrbewilligung f export licence, export permit
ausführen v execute, implement, carry out, effect; - v export; *einen Auftrag* - execute an order
Ausfuhrerlöse m pl export earnings
ausfuhrfähig adj exportable adj
Ausfuhrfinanzierung f export financing
Ausfuhrförderungskredit m export promotion credit
Ausfuhrgenehmigung f export licence, export permit
Ausfuhrhandel m export trade
Ausfuhrkredit m export credit
Ausfuhrkreditversicherung f export credit insurance
Ausführlichkeit f particularity n
Ausfuhrschein m export document
Ausfuhrüberschuß m export surplus, surplus of exports
Ausführung f execution n
Ausführungsbestimmung f regulation n
Ausführungsprovision f execution commission
Ausfuhrzoll m export duty
Ausfuhrzolltarif m export tariff
Ausgabe f disbursement n, outlay n; - f edition n; - f (von Wertpapieren) issue n (of securities), issuing n (of securities), emission n; - *geringeren Ranges* junior issue; - *neuer oder junger Aktien* (gegen Barzahlung) new issue of shares (for cash); - *von Gratisaktien* issue of bonus shares
Ausgabeaufschlag m front-end load
Ausgabekurs m offering price, issue part (GB), issue price, rate of issue; - *des Optionsscheins* warrant offering price

Ausgaben f pl expenses n pl, expenditure(s); *unbezahlte* - outstanding expenses
Ausgabenschätzung f estimate of expenditure
Ausgabetag m date of issue, day of issue
Ausgabewert m issue price; *- m* value
Ausgangssortierung f (beim Beleglesen) final sort pass
ausgeben v (verauslagen) disburse v; *- v* (Wertpapiere) emit v, issue v; *- v* spend v
Ausgeber m issuer n, emitter n
ausgebildetes Personal skilled personnel
ausgefülltes Giro special endorsement, special indorsement, direct indorsement (US)
ausgeglichen adj settled adj
ausgeloste Obligation drawn bond
ausgemacht adj stipulated adj, fixed adj
ausgeschüttete Dividende in Prozenten des Kapitalertrags payout-ratio n
ausgeschütteter Gewinn distributed profits
ausgewählt adj assorted adj
ausgezahlt adj paid off
Ausgleich m set-off, offset n; *zum - unserer Rechnung* in payment of our account
ausgleichen v balance, adjust v
Ausgleichsbetrag m adjusting amount
Ausgleichsbuchung f balance entry
Ausgleichsdividende f equalizing dividend
Ausgleichsfehler m counter error
Ausgleichsfonds m equalization fund
Ausgleichsforderungen f pl recovery claims
Ausgleichskonto n balance account
Ausgleichskredit m stopgap loan
Ausgleichsposten m adjusting item; *- für Anteile im Fremdbesitz* minority shareholders interest
Ausgleichsstelle f clearing house
Ausgleichswechsel m bill in full settlement
Ausgleichszahlung f compensatory payment
Aushandeln n bargaining
Aushändigung f surrender n, delivery n
Auskunft f information n
Auskunftei f commercial agency (US)
Auskunftersuchen n letter of inquiry
Auskunftsbuch über Kunden opinion book (GB)
Auskunftsbüro n information bureau
ausladen v discharge v
Ausladen n discharge n
Auslage f disbursement n, outlay n
Auslagen f pl expenses n pl, outlay n
Auslagenrechnung f note of disbursements
Ausland n foreign countries
Ausländer m non-resident n, foreigner n
Ausländerdepot n non-resident securities account
Ausländervermögen n foreign-owned property
ausländisch adj foreign
ausländische *Banknoten und Münzen* foreign notes and coin; *- Gesellschaft* alien corporation (US); *- Obligationen* foreign bonds; *- Währung* foreign currency, foreign exchange (US), foreign exchanges (GB)
Auslandsabteilung f foreign department
Auslandsakkreditiv n credit opened in a foreign country
Auslandsaktiva plt foreign assets
Auslandsakzept n foreign acceptance
Auslandsanlage f investment abroad, foreign investment
Auslandsanleihe f external loan, external bond, foreign bond issue; *- in Großbritannien* (in Pfund Sterling) bulldog bond; *- in Japan* (in Yen) samurai bond; *- in Japan* (nicht in Yen) shogun bond; *- in neuseeländischer Währung* kiwi-bond
Auslandsauftrag m order from abroad
Auslandsbank f foreign bank
Auslandsbeteiligungen f pl foreign shareholdings
Auslandsdirektion f international division
Auslandsgeschäft n foreign business, international banking, international business, international operations, foreign transaction
Auslandsguthaben n foreign balances
Auslandskassenverein m foreign security clearing association
Auslandskonto n external account

Auslandskredit *m* foreign credit; foreign borrowing
Auslandspassiva *plt* foreign liabilities
Auslandspostanweisung *f* foreign postal money order
Auslandsscheck *m* foreign check (US), cheque (GB)
Auslandsvermögen *n* foreign assets
Auslandsverschuldung *f* external debt
Auslandswechsel *m* bill in foreign currency, foreign bill
Auslandswerte *m pl* foreign securities, foreign stock
Auslandswertpapiere *n pl* foreign securities, foreign stock
Auslandszahlungsverkehr *m* foreign payments
Auslastung *f* (eines Systems) system utilization, system loading, utilization *n*
auslegen *v* interpret *v*
ausleihen *v* lend *v*; *Geld* - put out money, accommodate with money
Ausleiher *m* lender *n*, credit grantor
Ausleihungssatz *m* loan rate, borrowing rate
ausliefern *v* deliver
Auslieferung *f* delivery
Auslieferungsauftrag *m* delivery order
Auslieferungslager *n* depot
Auslieferungstermin *m* delivery date
auslösbar *adj* redeemable *adj*
auslosen *v* distribute by lots, draw by lot
Auslosung *f* (von Wertpapieren) drawing
Ausmünzung *f* mintage *n*
ausprägen *v* coin, monetize *v*
Ausprägung *f* coinage, mintage *n*
Ausrechnung *f* calculation *n*
Ausrüstung *f* equipment *n*
ausschalten *v* eliminate *v*
ausscheiden *v* leave office, eliminate *v*
ausschließen *v* exclude *v*
Ausschließlichkeitsklausel *f* exclusiveness agreement
ausschreiben *v* tender, invite tenders for, announce
Ausschreibung *f* tender
Ausschreibungsverfahren *n* tender procedure
Ausschuß *m* board *n*, committee *n*

ausschütten; *eine Dividende* - distribute a dividend, strike a dividend
Ausschüttung *f* distribution *n*, pay out
Ausschüttungsbedarf *m* dividend requirements
Ausschüttungsfonds *m* distribution fund
Ausschüttungsquote *f* pay-out ratio
Außenfinanzierung *f* external financing
Außenhandel *m* foreign trade
Außenhandelsbank *f* export bank, foreign trade bank
Außenhandelsdefizit *n* trade deficit, trade gap
Außenhandelsfinanzierung *f* foreign trade financing
Außenhandelsüberschuß *n* trade surplus
Außenstände *m pl* active debts, receivables *n pl* (US), accounts receivable
Außenwert *m* (einer Währung) external value (of a currency)
außerbörslich *adj* (Handel mit nicht notierten Wertpapieren) over-the counter
außerbörslicher *Effektenhandel* over-the-counter business; - *Kurs* curb market price
außergerichtliche Liquidation liquidation by arrangement
außergerichtliches Vergleichsverfahren settlement out of court
außer Kraft setzen *v* repeal *v*, abrogate *v*
Außerkurssetzung *f* demonetization *n*
außerordentlich *adj* special *adj*, extraordinary
außerordentliche *Aufwendungen* extraordinary expenses; - *Dividende* bonus *n*, surplus dividend, superdividend *n*, special dividend; - *Reserve* provident reserve fund
außerordentlicher Reservefonds contingency fund
aussetzen *v* (Rente) settle *v*; - *v* suspend *v*, defer *v*, postpone *v*
Aussicht *f* prospect *n*, outlook
aussondern *v* pick out, sort out; set apart, separate *v*; - *v* (Qualitätskontrolle) reject *v*
Aussonderungsanspruch *m* claim of exemption (US)
aussonderungsfähig *adj* recoverable *adj*

Aussonderungsverfahren n reclamation proceedings (US)
ausstatten v endow v; *jemanden mit Generalvollmacht* - furnish a person with full power
Ausstattung f equipment n; - f (einer Anleihe) terms n pl (of a bond)
ausstehen v be outstanding, be overdue
ausstehende *Einlagen auf das Grundkapital* subscribed capital stock; - *Forderungen* active debts, receivables n pl (US), accounts receivable
ausstehender Kupon outstanding coupon
ausstellen v make out v, issue v
Aussteller m issuer n, emitter n; - m (Wechsel) maker n, drafter n, drawer n
Ausstellung f (eines Schecks) issue, writing
Aussteuer f dot n, dotal property, dowry n
Aussteuerversicherungspolice f endowment insurance policy
ausstreichen v cancel v, cross out, delete v
Austausch m exchange, swap
Austauschbarkeit f convertibility
austauschen v exchange v, change v; - v (gegenseitig) interchange v
austeilen v deal out
Australische Anleihen f pl Aussie-bonds
Austritt m retirement n
ausüben v practice v, exercise v
Ausübung des Prämienrechts exercise of option
Ausverkauf m (Verkauf zu herabgesetzten Preisen) bargain sale; - m (Räumungsverkauf) clearing sale, clearance sale
Ausverkaufspreis m bargain price
Auswahl f choice n, selection
auswechselbar adj interchangeable adj
auswechseln v interchange v
Ausweis m statement n, return n (GB)
ausweisen; *einen Saldo von ...* - leave a balance of ...
Ausweiskarte f identification card, identification papers, identity card
Ausweispflicht f reporting requirement
Auswertung; *statistische* - statistical evaluation
Auswirkung f reaction n, consequence

auszahlen v pay out, pay off
Auszahlung f payment n; *telegrafische* - (Kurs) cable transfer rate, telegraphic transfer rate
Auszahlungsanweisung f cash note (GB)
Auszahlungsbeleg m voucher n
Auszahlungsbetrag m amount paid out
Auszahlungsgarantie f advance payment guarantee
Auszahlungskasse f paying department
Auszahlungskassenschalter m paying teller's window (US)
Auszahlungskonto n disbursing account
Auszahlungskurs m outpayment rate
Auszahlungsschalter m teller's window
Auszahlungsverkehr m outpayments, outpayment business
auszeichnen (sich) v exceed in
Auszug m abstract n; - m (kurze Übersicht) summary n
authentisch adj genuine adj, true adj
Autobahngebühr f motorway toll
Autobank f drive-in window
Autokredit m car-purchase loan
Automation f automation n, automatization n
automatisieren v automate v, automatize v
Automatisierung f automation n, automatization n
Automobilaktien f pl motors n pl
Autorisation f authorization n
autorisieren v authorize v
autorisiert adj authorized adj, empowered adj
Autorität f expert, authority n
Autoschalter m drive-in-window; *Bank mit* - drive in bank
Aval n guarantee, guarantee of a bill of exchange, aval n
avalierter Wechsel backed bill
Avalkonsortium n guarantee syndicate
Avalkredit m guarantee credit, surety credit
Avallinie f guarantee line
Avalprovision f guarantee commission
Avalrechnung f aval account
avisieren v advise v, notify

B

Back-up-Fazilitäten f pl back-up facilities
Bagatellgrenze f minimum limit
Bagatellkonto n ultra-small account
bahnamtlicher Spediteur railway express agency
Bahnanleihe f railway bond
Bahnfrachtbrief m railway bill
Bahnfrachtkosten plt rail freight charges
Bahnspediteur m railway carrier
Bahnspedition f railway express agency
Bahntarif m railway tariff
Baisse f sharp drop, bear market; *auf - ausgerichtet* bearish adj; *auf - spekulieren* bear v, sell a bear, speculate on a fall; *eine - herbeiführen* bear the market, bear the stocks
Baisse-Angriff m bearish operation, drive n (US)
Baisse-Engagement n (B.-Position) short position
Baisse-Gerüchte n pl bear rumours
Baisse-Haltung f bearish attitude
Baisse-Markt m bear market, bearish market
Baisse-Partei f short side
Baisse-Position f bear account
Baisse-Spekulant m short n (US), bear seller, bear n
Baisse-Spekulation f bear speculation, bearish operation, bear operation
Baisse-Tendenz f bearish tendency
Baissier m short n (US), bear seller, bear n; *geschlagener -* stale bear
BAK n (in Deutschland) = *Bundesaufsichtsamt für das Kreditwesen* Federal Banking Supervisory Authority
Ballen m (Ware) bale n
Bandbreite f spread, band n, fluctuation margin, band of permitted fluctuation
Bandbreitenoptionsschein m range warrant
Bandorganisation f tape organization
Bank f bank n; *- außerhalb des Clearingsystems* non-member bank, non-par bank; *- für Internationalen Zahlungsausgleich* f = **BfZ** Bank for International Settlements; *- von England* f Bank of England (GB); *bezogene -* drawee bank; *dem Clearingsystem angehörende -* member bank (US); *einziehende -* collecting bank; *ermächtigte -* authorized bank; *führende - eines Konsortiums* syndicate manager; *konzessionierte -* chartered bank (GB); *multinationale -* multinational bank; *negozierende -* negoting bank; *Pfandrecht der -* bank lien, banker's lien; *privilegierte -* chartered bank (GB); *von einem Einzelstaat zugelassene -* state bank (US); *weltweit tätige -* internationally operating bank; *Zurückbehaltungsrecht der -* bank lien, banker's lien
Bankabhebung f bank withdrawal
Bankabrechnungsstelle f banker's clearing house (GB)
Bankabteilung f banking department
bankähnlich adj quasi-banking
bankähnliche Unternehmen near banks
Bankaktie f bank share, bank stock
Bankaktien f pl banks
Bankaktionär m bank shareholder
Bankakzept n bank acceptance, banker's acceptance
Bank-an-Bank-Kredit m interbank lending
Bankangelegenheiten f pl banking matters, banking affairs
Bankangestellte f u. m bank clerk, bank assistant, bank employee, bank official
Bankanteil m banking interest
Bankanweisung f bank money order
Bank-auf-Bank-Ziehung f bank on bank-drawing
Bankaufsicht; staatliche - state banking department (US)
Bankaufsichtsratsmitglied n bank supervisory board member, bank director (US)
Bankauftrag m banker's order (GB)
Bankauskunft f banker's reference, bank inquiry, bank reference

bankgeschäftlich

Bankausweis *m* balance of the bank, bank report
Bankauszug *m* bank statement
Bankautomat *m* automatic teller machine (ATM)
Bankautomation *f* bank automation
Bankbehörde *f* banking authority
Bank-bei-Bank-Einlage *f* interbank deposit
Bankbelege *m pl* bank records
bankbestätigter Scheck certified check (US), certified cheque (GB)
Bankbestätigung *f* bank confirmation
Bankbeteiligungen *f pl* bank holdings, banking investments
Bankbetrieb *m* banking, banking operations
Bankbevollmächtigter im Clearinghouse in-clearer *n* (GB)
Bankbilanz *f* bank balance sheet
Bankbote *m* bank messenger
Bankbuch *n* pass-book *n* (US), bank book, deposit book
Bankbuchhalter *m* bank accountant
Bankbuchhaltung *f* bank accounting
Bankbürgschaft *f* bank guarantee
Bankdarlehen *n* bank loan, bank credit
Bankdebitoren auf Sicht due from banks on demand; *- auf Zeit* due from banks on time
Bankdirektor *m* bank director, bank manager, manager of a bank
Bankdiskont *m* bank discount, banker's discount
bankdomiziliert *adj* bank-domiciled
bankeigenes Haus house owned by the bank
Bankeinbruchversicherung *f* bank burglary insurance
Bankeinlage *f* bank deposit, banker's deposit
Bankeinzahlungsschein *m* bank payment slip
Banken; *vom Bundesstaat zugelassene* *-* national banking system (US)
Bankenbonifikation *f* bank's commission
Bankenclearing *n* bank clearing
Bankendebitoren *m pl* accounts receivable from banks, balances with other banks
Bankenfusion *f* bank merger, consolidation of banks

Bankengelder *n pl* money from banks
Bankengeldmarkt *m* interbank money market
Bankengesetz *n* Banking Law
Bankenkommissar; *staatlicher* - state bank examiner (US)
Bankenkommission *f* bank commission
Bankenkonsortium *n* banking syndicate, consortium of banks; *- für den Verkauf von Obligationen* selling group
Bankenkreditoren *m pl* accounts payable to banks, balances of other banks
Bankenkrise *f* banking crisis
Bankenmarkt *m* interbank market
Bankenstimmrecht *n* banks' voting right
Bankenstützungsaktion *f* banking support
Bankenvereinigung *f* banking association, banker's association
Bankenwerbung *f* bank advertising, bank publicity
Bankfach *n* safe deposit box, safe box
bankfähig *adj* discountable *adj*, bankable *adj*, eligible *adj* (US)
bankfähiger Wechsel discountable bill
bankfähiges Papier bank paper
Bankfazilitäten *f pl* bank facilities, banking facilities
Bankfeiertag *m* bank holiday
Bankfiliale *f* bank branch
Bankgarantie *f* bank guarantee (US), banker's guarantee
Bankgebäude *n* bank building, bank premises
Bankgebühren *f pl* bank charges
Bankgeheimnis *n* bank secrecy, banker's discretion, banking secrecy
Bankgeld *n* bank money, deposit money, deposits *n pl*
Bankgeschäft *n* banking trade, banking business; *neutrales* - off-balance-sheet business, non-credit business of bank
Bankgeschäfte *n pl* banking operations, banking transactions; *- außerhalb nationaler Grenzen* off-shore banking; *- im Warenhaus* shop-in-shop banking; *- innerhalb nationaler Grenzen* on-shore banking; *elektronische Abwicklung der* - telebanking
bankgeschäftlich *adj* relating to banking business

Bankgeschäftsstelle f banking office
Bankgesetz n bank law
Bankgewerbe n banking trade, banking business
bankgiriert adj bank-endorsed
Bankgiro n bank giro
Bankguthaben n balance at the bank, bank balance, cash in bank, cash at bankers, credit at the bank; *- bei der Zentralbank* Federal funds; *gegenseitige -* interbank deposits
Bankhauptbuch n bank ledger
Bankhaus n banking house
Bankherr m proprietor of a bank
Bankier m banker n
Bankierbonifikation f underwriting commission
Bankiersvereinigung f Institute of Bankers (GB)
Bankinhaber m proprietor of a bank
Bankinspektor m superintendent of banks
Bankinstitut n banking institution
Bankjustitiar m legal adviser of a bank
Bankkapital n bank funds
Bankkassierer m bank cashier, bank receiver, bank teller
Bankkaufmann m banker, bank clerk, bank officer
Bankkommissar m superintendent of banks
Bankkonditionen f pl interest rates and fees charged by bank
Bankkonkurs m bank failure, banking failure, bank crash
Bankkonto n bank account, banking account, account in bank
Bankkontoauszug m bank statement, account statement
Bankkonzern m banking group
Bankkrach m bank failure, banking failure, bank crash
Bankkredit m bank loan, bank credit
Bankkreditoren *auf Sicht* due to banks on demand; *- auf Zeit* due to banks on time
Bankkreise m pl banking circles
Bankkunde m bank customer
Bankkundschaft f customers of a bank
banklagernd retained correspondence

Banklehre f bank training, apprenticeship in banking
Banklehrling m bank trainee
Bankleitung f bank management
Bankleitzahl f bank code, routing symbol, bank identification number
Bankliquidität f bank liquidity
bankmäßig adj banking adj
bankmäßige Sicherung normal banking security
Banknote f bank note; *durch Werterhöhung gefälschte -* raised bill (US); *falsche -* stumer n (GB)
Banknoten f pl paper currency, paper money; *- in Umlauf setzen* issue bank notes; *ausländische -* foreign bank notes; *ausländische - und Münzen* foreign notes and coins; *wieder ausgebbare -* reissuable notes
Banknotenbündel n bundle of notes, bank roll (US)
Banknotendruck m bank note printing
Banknotenfälscher m counterfeiter of bank notes
Banknotenfälschung f counterfeiting n
Banknotenprivileg n right to issue bank notes
Banknotenumlauf m active circulation (GB), bank note circulation, circulation of bank notes, circulating bank notes, notes in circulation
Bankobligation f bank bond
Bankomat m cash dispenser, automatic teller machine (ATM)
Bankorganisation; *schlanke -* lean banking
Bankplatz m banking center, banking place
Bankpolitik f bank policy
Bankpraxis f banking practice, banking usage
Bankprokurist m assistant manager, authorized signatory of a bank
Bankprovision f bank agio, banker's commission
Bankquittung f bank receipt
Bankrate f discount rate
Bankrecht n banking law
Bankregel f banking rule; *goldene -* golden rule of banking (e.g. long-term assets need long-term liabilities)

Bankrembours *m* bank documentary credit
Bankreserve *f* bank reserve, banking reserve
Bankrevision *f* bank examination (US)
Bankrevisor *m* bank auditor, bank examiner (US), bank inspector
bankrott *adj* bankrupt *adj*, insolvent *adj*
Bankrott *m* bankruptcy *n*, failure *n*, insolvency *n*; *- machen* go bankrupt, fail *v*; *betrügerischer -* fraudulent bankruptcy
Bankrotterklärung *f* bankruptcy notice, declaration of bankruptcy
Bankrotteur *m* bankrupt person, bankrupt *n*
Banksatz *m* bank rate
Bankschalter; *über den -* over the counter
Bankscheck *m* bank cheque, bank check, banker's check, cashier's check (US)
Bankschulden *f pl* bank debts
Bankschuldner *m* debtor of a bank
Bankschuldverschreibung *f* bank bond
Banksicherheit *f* bank security, bank collateral
Banksparen *n* saving at banks
Bankspesen *plt* bank charges
Bankstatistik *f* banking statistics
Bankstelle *f* bank office, branch
Bankstellennetz *n* bank office network
Banksystem *n* banking system
Banktätigkeit *f* banking activity; *eine - ausüben* bank *v*
Banktratte *f* bank draft
Banktresor *m* bank vault
Banküberweisung *f* bank transfer
banküblich *adj* normal in banking
Bankusancen *f pl* banking practice, banking usage
Bankvaloren *plt* bank stocks (US), bank shares
Bankverbindung *f* banking connection
Bankverein *m* banking association, bankers association
Bankvereinigung *f* association of banks
Bankverkehr *m* interbank dealings
Bankvermögen *n* assets of a bank
Bankverpflichtungen; *gegenseitige -* interbank balances
Bankvertreter *m* bank agent

Bankvorstand *m* bank management, board, board of management
Bankwechsel *m* banker's bill, banker's draft (US)
Bankwelt *f* banking world
Bankwerte *m pl* bank stocks (US), bank shares
Bankwesen *n* banking trade, banking business; *genossenschaftliches -* cooperative banking
Bankzahlung *f* banker's payment
Bankzahlungsmittel *n* bank payment media
Bankzentrum *n* financial centre
Bankziehung *f* bill drawn by a bank
Bankzinsen *m pl* interest charged by banks
Bank-zu-Bank-Ausleihung *f* interbank lending
Bankzusammenbruch *m* bank crash
bar in cash; *- abzüglich Diskont* cash less discount; *- bezahlen* pay in cash; *- gekauft* bought for cash
Barabhebung *f* cash withdrawal
Barakkreditiv *n* cash letter of credit
Barangebot *n* cash offer
Baranschaffung *f* cash payment
Barausgleich *m* cash settlement
Barausschüttung *f* cash distribution
Barbetrag aus einem Grundbesitz proprietary equity
Barbonus *m* cash bonus
Bardepot *n* cash deposit
Bardividende *f* cash dividend
Bareinlage *f* cash deposit
Bareinnahmen *f pl* cash earnings, cash receipts
Bareinzahlung *f* cash inpayment, cash deposit
Barerlös *m* cash proceeds
bares Geld ready money
Bargeld *n* cash *n*
Bargeldauszahlungsautomat *m* cash dispensing machine, cash dispenser
bargeldlos *adj* cashless *adj*, without using cash
bargeldlose *Gesellschaft* cashless society; *- Zahlungsmittel* deposit currency (US), money in account, deposit money, bank money, check book money (US)

bargeldloser Zahlungsverkehr

bargeldloser Zahlungsverkehr *m* cashless transactions
Bargeldumlauf *m* notes and coins in circulation
Bargeschäft *n* cash transaction, cash operation
Barguthaben *n* cash balance, cash in hand
Barhinterlegung *f* cash deposit
Barkapital *n* cash capital
Barkasse *f* cash department
Barkauf *m* cash purchase
Barkredit *m* cash credit
Barkreditgeschäft *n* cash credit business
Barliquidität *f* cash liquidity
Barmittel *n pl* cash, cash funds, cash assets
Barposition *f* cash position
Barrabatt *m* cash discount
Barren *m* bar, bullion
Barreserve *f* cash funds, cash reserve
Barscheck *m* open check, uncrossed check, check to cash
Barsendung *f* remittance in cash
Barüberschuß *m* cash surplus
Barüberweisung *f* cash remittance
Barvergütung *f* cash refund
Barverkauf *m* cash sale
Barvermögen *n* cash in hand
Barvorschuß *m* cash advance
Barwert *m* cash value, present value
Barzahlung *f* cash payment, cashdown payment; *gegen* - cash down
Barzahlungsauftrag *m* cash order
Barzahlungssystem *n* cash system
Basis *f* bais *n*, foundation *n*
Basisaktie *f* underlying stock
Basispreis *m* striking price, exercise price
Basispunkt *m* basis point (0.01 percent), tick
Basissatz *m* basis rate, strike rate
Basiswert *m* underlying stock
Bau *m* construction *n*
Bauaktien *f pl* building stocks (US)
Baudarlehen *n* building loan; - *der Bausparkassen* building society loans
Bauernbank *f* farmers bank
Baufinanzierung *f* building finance, finance of building
Baugrundstück *n* building estate
Bauhypothek *f* construction mortgage

Baukapital *n* building capital
Baukosten *plt* cost of construction
Baukredit *m* building loan
Baumarkt *m* building market
Baumwollbörse *f* cotton exchange
Baupachtrecht *n* building lease
Bauplatz *m* building ground
baureifes Grundstück building estate
Bauspardarlehen *n* loan extended by a building society
Bausparen *n* saving through a building society
Bausparfinanzierung *f* financing with building society funds
Bauspargeld *n* savings at building societies
Bauspargeschäft *n* building society business
Bausparkasse *f* savings and loan association (US), building and loan association, building society (GB)
Bausparkredit *m* building society loan
Bausparvertrag *m* building loan contract, building society savings agreement
Bauwechsel *m* building bill
Bauwert *m* adjusted building costs
Bauzwischenkredit *m* intermediate building credit
Beamte *m* officer *n*, official *n*; *zuständige* - officer in charge
Beamtenbank *f* officials bank
beanspruchen *v* claim *v*, demand
Beanstandung *f* complaint *n*, objection *n*
beantragen *v* apply for, request *v*
beantworten *v* answer *v*
Bearbeitung *f* processing *n*
Bearbeitungsgebühr *f* service charge
Bearbeitungsprovision *f* handling commission
beaufsichtigen *v* control *v*, supervise *v*
Beaufsichtigung *f* control *n*, supervision *n*
beauftragt *adj* commissioned *adj*
Beauftragte *f u. m* agent *n*, mandatory *n*
bebautes Gebiet built-up area
Bedarf *m* demand *n*
Bedarfsfall; im - in case of need
Bedeutung *f* weight *n*, importance *n*
bedienen *v* (Gerät) operate *v*; - *v* serve *v*, attend *v*, be of service
Bedienungsanleitung *f* (Operatoranweisung) operator instructions

Bedienungsfehler m operator error
Bedienungsfeld n keyboard n
Bedienungskraft f operator n
bedingt adj conditional adj
bedingte Annahme qualified acceptance, conditional acceptance; *- Einlage* deposit in escrow
bedingter Auftrag conditional order
bedingtes Akzept qualified acceptance, conditional acceptance; *- Indossament* qualified endorsement
Bedingung f clause n; *-* f (Kondition) condition n; *-* f (Vorbehalt) proviso n
Bedingungen f pl terms n pl
bedingungsloses Akzept clean acceptance
Bedürfnis n requirement n, need
bedürftig adj indigent adj, needy adj, poor adj
Beeinflussung f manipulation n
Beeinträchtigung f impairment, interference
beendigen v terminate v
befähigen v enable v
Befähigung f competence n, qualification
befördern v convey v; *-* v promote v
Beförderung f transport n, transportation n, carriage n
beförderungsfähig adj conveyable adj, transportable adj
Beförderungsmittel n means of transport
Beförderungsschein m waybill n
befrachtbar adj charterable adj
befrachten v freight v (e.g. ship, plane), load v (e.g. vehicle)
Befrachter m charterer n
befrachtet adj loaded adj
Befrachtung f affreightment n
befreien v dispense v
befreit adj free adj
befriedigen; *einen Anspruch -* settle a claim; *Zahlungsansprüche -* meet demands for payment
befristete Einlage time deposit, fixed deposit
befristetes Darlehen term loan, time loan
Befugnis f authority n
befugt adj authorized adj, empowered adj
begebbar adj negotiable adj

begebbare Wertpapiere negotiable papers, negotiable securities
begeben v negotiate v; *eine Anleihe -* float a bond issue, float a loan issue, launch a loan; *wieder -* reissue v
Begebende f u. m endorser n, indorser n
Begebung f issue n (of securities), issuing n (of securities), emission n
beglaubigen v attest v; *ein Dokument - lassen* have a document legalized; *notariell -* acknowledge v; *öffentlich -* authenticate by a notary public or court
Beglaubiger m attestor n
beglaubigt adj attested adj
beglaubigtes Konnossement certified bill of lading
Beglaubigung f certification n, attestation n, official certification; *-* f (Echtheit, Gültigkeit) authentication n; *notarielle -* acknowledgement n
Begleichung f settlement n
Begleitbrief m cover letter, covering letter
Begleitschein m delivery note, bill of delivery, delivery order
Begleitschreiben n cover letter, covering letter
begrenzt adj limited adj, restricted adj
begrenzter Kauf- oder Verkaufsauftrag limited order
Begrenzung f limitation n, restriction n
begünstigen v benefit v, favo(u)r v
Begünstigte f u. m beneficiary n
Behälter m container n
behandeln v handle v; *-* v treat v
behauptet unchanged
beherrschtes Unternehmen controlled company
Beherrschungsvertrag m control contract
Behörde f public authority
Beiakten f pl ancillary papers
beibringen v procure v
beiderseitig adj reciprocal adj
beifügen v enclose v
beigefügt adj attached adj
beiladen v add to the cargo
Beiladung f cargo added
Beilage f enclosure n, annex n, supplement n
beilegen v enclose v

Beirat

Beirat *m* advisory board, prudential committee (US)
Beisatz *m* (EDV) trailer *n* (EDP)
beiseite bringen remove *v*
Beispiel *n* example *n*
Beistandskredit *m* stand-by credit
beisteuern *v* contribute *v*
Beitrag *m* contribution *n*
beitragen *v* contribute *v*
Beitragszahler *m* contributor
Beitragszahlung *f* premium payment
beitreibbar *adj* recoverable *adj*
Beitreibung *f* enforced collection, exaction *n*
bekannt *adj* renowned *adj*, wellknown *adj*, prominent *adj*
bekanntmachen *v* announce *v*, declare *v*
Bekanntmachung *f* announcement *n*, notice *n*; *~ f* (förmlich) notification *n*, notice *n*, advice *n*
Beklagte *f u. m* defendant *n*
belastbar *adj* debitable *adj*, chargeable
belasten *v* (Konto) charge *v*, debit *v*; **dinglich ~** hypothecate *v*, mortgage *v*, encumber *v*; **hypothekarisch ~** encumber *v*; **mit einer Hypothek ~** hypothecate *v*, mortgage *v*, encumber *v*; **zuviel ~** overcharge *v*, overdebit *v*
belastet; dinglich ~ encumbered *adj*, mortgaged *adj*; **hypothekarisch ~** encumbered *adj*, mortgaged *adj*
belastetes Grundstück burdened estate
Belastung *f* burden *n*, charge *n*, load *n*; *~ f* (Buchung) debit entry, debit item
Belastungsanweisung *f* debit ticket, charge ticket (US)
Belastungsanzeige *f* debit advice, debit note
belaufen auf (sich) amount to, come to, run to
Beleg *m* voucher *n*
Belegablage *f* voucher storage
Belegaufbereitung *f* document preparation
Belegfuß *m* document flow
belegloser Zahlungsverkehr paperless payments
Belegschacht *m* (bei Buchungsstationen) document bin, document chute
Belegschaft *f* staff *n*
Belegschaftsaktie *f* employees' share

Belegschaftsaktienausgabe *f* employee stock ownership plan (US)
Belegsortiermaschine *f* document sorter
Belegtransport *m* document transport
beleihbar *adj* acceptable as collateral, eligible as collateral
Beleihbarkeit *f* hypothecary value
Beleihung *f* hypothecation *n*
beleihungsfähig *adj* acceptable as collateral for a loan
Beleihungsgrenze *f* limit of credit, lending limit
Beleihungsobjekt *n* collateral
Beleihungswert *m* collateral value, loan value
belohnen *v* reward *v*
Belohnung *f* reward *n*
Bemessung *f* rating *n*, appraisal *n*, assessment *n*
Bemühung *f* endeavor *n* (US), endeavour *n* (GB)
benachrichtigen *v* inform *v*, notify *v*, advise *v*, communicate *v*
Benachrichtigung *f* notification *n*, notice *n*, advice *n*
benachteiligen *v* discriminate against
benachteiligte Partei injured party
Benachteiligung *f* discrimination *n*
Benennung *f* denomination *n*
Benutzer *m* user *n*
Benzingutschein *m* cheap petrol voucher for tourists
beraten *v* advise *v*; **schlecht ~** ill advised
beratend *adj* consultative *adj*
Berater *m* adviser *n*, consultant *n*, counselor *n*
Beratung *f* consultation *n*; **~ von Organisationen** advisory business
Beratungsauftrag *m* consultancy contract
Beratungsgeschäft *n* advisory business
berechenbar *adj* calculable *adj*
Berechenbarkeit *f* calculability *n*
berechnen *v* calculate *v*, compute *v*; **nach Verhältnis ~** pro-rate *v*
berechnet *adj* billed *adj*
Berechnung *f* computation *n*, charge
Berechnungsgrundlage *f* basis of calculation
berechtigen *v* entitle *v*
berechtigt *adj* entitled *adj*

38

berechtigte Unterschrift authorized signature
Bereich m (Gebiet) area n; ~ m range n, scope n; ~ m (Wirkungskreis) sphere n
bereichern (sich) v enrich v
Bereicherung f enrichment n
Bereichsabkommen n area agreement
bereinigen; *eine Bilanz* ~ clean up a balance sheet
Bereitschaftskredit m stand-by credit
bereitstellen v make available
Bereitstellung von Geldern (für einen bestimmten Zweck) earmarking of funds
Bereitstellungsfonds m appropriation account
Bereitstellungsprovision f commitment fee
Bereitstellungszins m commitment interest
Bergbauaktie f mining share, share of a mining company; *südafrikanische* ~ Kaffir
Bergregalabgabe f dead rent (GB)
Bericht m report n
berichtigen v correct v, rectify v
berichtigter Wert absorption value
Berichtigung f (Werte, Preise) adjustment n; ~ f correction n
Berichtigungsaktie f bonus share
Berichtigungsbuchung f adjusting journal entry, correcting entry, rectifying entry
Berichtigungseintragung f adjustment entry
Berichtigungskonto n adjustment account
Berichtsjahr n year under review
Berliner Testament n mutual testament, mutual will, double will
Beruf m (freier oder akademischer) profession n; ~ m (praktischer) trade n
berufen v (Amt) appoint v
Berufsgruppenschlüssel m occupation code
Berufshandel m professional traders
Berufung f appeal n; ~ f nomination n, appointment n
beschädigen v damage v
beschädigt adj (Wertpapiere) mutilated adj
Beschädigung f damage n
beschaffen v procure v

beschäftigt adj employed adj; ~ adj engaged adj, occupied adj
Beschäftigte f u. m employed person
Beschäftigung f employment
bescheinigen v (durch Zeugnis) certificate v; ~ v certify v
bescheinigt adj certified adj
Bescheinigung f certificate n; ~ *über das Eigentum* (an einem bestimmten Wertpapier) ownership certificate
Beschlag; *in* ~ *nehmen* embargo v; *mit* ~ *belegen* seize v
Beschlagnahme f attachment n, arrestment n, distraint n; ~ f (Privateigentum) confiscation n; ~ f seizure n
beschlagnahmefähig adj seizable adj, attachable adj
beschlagnahmen v attach v; ~ v (Privateigentum) confiscate v; ~ v seize v
beschlagnahmtes Konto sequestered account
beschließen v decide, vote, approve
Beschluß m decision, vote, resolution
Beschlußfähigkeit f quorum n
Beschlußfassung f resolution n
beschränken v restrict v, limit v
beschränkt adj limited adj, restricted adj; ~ *haftender Gesellschafter* special partner, limited partner; ~ *haftender Teilhaber* special partner, limited partner
beschränkte Konvertierbarkeit limited convertibility
beschränktes Giro conditional endorsement, restrictive endorsement
Beschränkung f restriction n
Beschwerde f complaint n, objection n
beschweren (sich) v complain v
besichern v secure
Besicherung f securing
besichtigen v inspect v
Besitz m (Wertpapiere, Land) holdings n pl; ~ m possession n, ownership n; ~ *an beweglichem Vermögen* personal estate; ~ *ergreifen* appropriate v; *in* ~ *nehmen* take possession of
besitzen v hold v; ~ v (als Eigentümer) own v; *voll und ganz* ~ own outright
Besitzer m proprietor n, possessor n, owner; *gutgläubiger* ~ bona fide holder, holder in due course

Besitzstand *m* proprietary *n*
Besitztitel *m* possessory title
Besitzurkunde *f* (Grundbesitz) root of title; *- f* title deed, deed of ownership
Besitzwechsel *m* change of ownership, change of title
besondere Kreuzung (eines Schecks) special crossing (of a check)
Besonderheit *f* particularity *n*
besonders *adj* particular *adj*; *- adv* in particular, especially *adv*, separately *adv*
besorgen *v* procure *v*, obtain
Besprechung *f* conference *n*; *geschäftliche -* business conference
bessern (sich) *v* improve *v*
Besserungsschein *m* debtor warrant
Bestand *m* inventory *n*; *- m* stock in hand; *eiserner -* reserve fund
Beständigkeit *f* stability *n*
Bestandsaufnahme *f* stocktaking *n*, inventory *n*
Bestandsband *n* (EDV) master tape (EDP)
Bestandsglattstellung *f* (Börse) closing out a position, positionsquaring
Bestandskonto *n* assets account
Bestandssatz *m* (EDV) master record (EDP)
Bestandsverzeichnis *n* inventory *n*
Bestandteil *m* component *n*
bestätigen *v* (Empfang) acknowledge *v*; *- v* confirm *v*; *einen Scheck -* certify a check
bestätigter Kredit confirmed credit; *- Scheck* marked cheque (GB)
bestätigtes unwiderrufliches Akkreditiv irrevocable confirmed letter of credit, straight letter of credit
Bestätigung *f* (Empfang) acknowledgement *n*; *- f* confirmation *n*; *- des Kontoauszugs* bank confirmation; *- vom Buchprüfer* certificate of account (US)
Bestätigungsbank *f* confirming bank
Bestätigungsschreiben *n* confirmation note
Bestätigungsvermerk *m* (einer Prüfungsgesellschaft) auditors' report
Bestechung *f* bribe *n*, graft *n* (US); *- f* bribery *n*, corruption *n*
bestellen *v* (Amt) appoint *v*; *- v* order *v*
Bestellung *f* order *n*; *- f* purchase order

bestens at best; *-* (Börsenauftrag ohne Preislimit) at the market
Bestens-Auftrag *m* market order (US)
besteuerbar *adj* taxable *adj*
Besteuerbarkeit *f* taxableness *n*
besteuern *v* tax *v*
besteuert *adj* taxed *adj*
Besteuerte *f u. m* assessed *n*
Besteuerung *f* taxation *n*; *direkte -* direct taxation
bestimmen *v* designate *v*, order
Bestimmung *f* designation *n*; *- f* (Vertrag) provision *n*; *gesetzliche -* enactment *n*
Bestimmungen *f pl* terms *n pl*, conditions, provisions
Bestimmungsland *n* country of destination
Bestimmungsort *m* destination *n*
bestmöglich (Börse) at best
bestrafen *v* fine *v*
bestreiten *v* disclaim *v*; *- v* dispute *v*, challenge *v*, contest *v*
beteiligen (sich) *v* participate, take an interest in
beteiligt *adj* concerned *adj*, interested *adj*; *- adj* (an) interested *adj* (in); *- sein* participate *v*
Beteiligte *f u. m* partner *n*
Beteiligung *f* (Kapital) investment *n*; *- f* participation *n*; *dauernde -* permanent holding
Beteiligungen *f pl* investments *n pl*, shareholdings *n pl*; *- an assoziierten Unternehmen* holdings of affiliated companies; *- an Gesellschaften* investments in companies; *- erwerben* secure interests
Beteiligungsfinanzierung *f* equity financing
Beteiligungsfonds *m* equity fund
Beteiligungsgeschäft der Bank equity banking, mergers and acquisitions activities
Beteiligungsgesellschaft *f* associated company, company in which an interest is held
Beteiligungskapital *n* equity capital; *Expansionsfinanzierung mit -* expansion stage financing, later stage financing; *Gründungsfinanzierung mit - * early stage financing

Beteiligungskonto n investment account
Beteiligungsquote f interest share
Beteiligungsvermittlung (M&A) f M&A, mergers and acquisitions
Beteiligungsvertrag m partnership contract, joint venture agreement
beträchtlicher Rückgang material recession
Betrag m amount n, sum n; ~ m (Gesamtbetrag) total n; **bis zum ~ von** to the extent of
betragen (sich) v amount to, come to, run to
betrauen v entrust v
betreffend adj concerning adj
betreiben v operate v
Betrieb m firm n, enterprise n, company n, concern n; ~ m plant n, operation n, business n
betriebliche Aufwendungen operating expenses; ~ **Einsparungen** business savings; ~ **Investition** business investment; ~ **Unternehmensforschung** operations research
Betriebsabteilung f operating department
Betriebsausrüstung f industrial equipment
Betriebsergebnis n operating result
Betriebsertrag m business proceeds
Betriebserweiterung f factory extension
Betriebsfinanzen plt business finance
Betriebsführung f business management, industrial management
Betriebsgeheimnis n business secret
Betriebsgemeinkosten plt overheads n pl
Betriebsgewinn m earned surplus
Betriebsgrundstück n business property
Betriebsinventar n business inventory; ~ n (Bilanz) plant n
Betriebsjahr n financial year (GB), fiscal year, fiscal accounting year
Betriebskalkulation f cost accounting
Betriebskapital n floating capital, circulating capital, current capital, rolling capital, trading capital, working capital
Betriebskonto n trading account
Betriebskosten plt cost of operation, working expenses
Betriebskredit m working credit
Betriebsleiter m manager n

Betriebsmittel n pl floating capital, circulating capital, current capital, rolling capital, trading capital, working capital
Betriebsmittelkredit m working capital loan
Betriebsschulden f pl business liabilities, business debts
Betriebssparen n industrial savings
Betriebsüberschuß m net operating income (profit)
Betriebsunfall m industrial accident
Betriebsunkosten plt operating expenses (US)
Betriebsunterbrechungsversicherung f loss-of-profit insurance, business interruption insurance
Betriebsverlust m operating deficit, trading loss
Betriebsvermögen n assets n pl; ~ n operating assets
Betriebswirtschaft f business administration, business economics
Betriebswirtschaftslehre f business administration, business economics
Betrug m defraudation n; ~ m fraud n
betrügen v defraud v
betrügerisch adj fraudulent adj
betrügerischer Aktienverkäufer share pusher; ~ **Bankrott** fraudulent bankruptcy
beurkunden v authenticate v
Beurkundung f authentication n
beurteilen v judge v
bevollmächtigen v authorize v
bevollmächtigt adj authorized adj, empowered adj
Bevollmächtigte f u. m proxy n, authorized person
Bevollmächtigung f authorization n
bevorrechtigt adj privileged adj; ~ adj (Konkursrecht) secured adj
bevorrechtigte Forderung preferential debt, preferred debt, privileged debt, secured debt; ~ **Schuld** preferential debt, preferred debt, privileged debt, secured debt; ~ **Wertpapiere** senior securities
bevorrechtigter Gläubiger preferential creditor (GB), preferred creditor (US)
bevorrechtigtes Pfandrecht prior lien; ~ **Zurückbehaltungsrecht** prior lien

bewährt

bewährt *adj* approved *adj*
bewegliches Eigentum chattels *n pl*, personal property, movables *n pl*; **- und unbewegliches Vermögen** movables and immovables; **- Vermögen** movable estate, movable goods, movables *n pl*, goods movable
bewegte Börse disturbed market; **- Konten** active accounts
beweisen *v* prove *v*
Beweismaterial *n* evidence *n*
bewerben (sich) *v* apply for, bid for
Bewerber *m* applicant *n*
Bewerbung *f* application *n*
bewerten *v* appraise *v*; **-** *v* assess *v*; **-** *v* value *v*; **zu niedrig -** undervalue *v*, underestimate *v*
Bewertung *f* rating *n*, appraisal *n*, assessment *n*
bewilligen *v* concede *v*, approve, permit
Bewilligung *f* approval *n*, permission *n*
Bewirtschaftungssystem *n* allocation system
bewohnbar *adj* habitable
bezahlen *v* pay *v*; **-** *v* (Rechnung) settle *v*; **eine Schuld -** retire a debt; **im voraus -** pay in advance, make a payment beforehand; **voll -** pay up
bezahlt *adj* paid *adj*; **-** *adj* (Rechnung) settled *adj*; **- machen** (sich) pay well
bezahlte Rechnung account settled
Bezahlkurs *m* price paid
Bezahlung *f* pay *n*, payment *n*
bezeichnen *v* designate, describe *v*
Bezeichnung *f* designation, description *n*
bezeugen *v* vouch *v*; **-** *v* witness *v*
Beziehungen aufnehmen mit enter into relations with, open up a business connection with
Bezirk *m* district *n*
Bezirksagentur *f* district office
bezogene Bank drawee bank
Bezogene *f u. m* drawee *n*; **bankrotte(r) -(r)** bankrupt drawee
Bezüge *plt* income, earnings *n pl*
Bezugsberechtigte *f u. m* beneficiary; **-(r) einer Versorgungsstiftung** beneficiary of provident fund
Bezugskurs *m* subscription price

Bezugsrecht *n* subscription right, right to subscribe, pre-emptive right; **mit -** cum rights; **mit - auf neue Aktien** cum new; **nicht zur Zeichnung einer neuen Aktie ausreichendes -** fractional right; **ohne -** ex new, ex rights
Bezugsrechtbewertung *f* subscription right valuation
Bezugsrechtzuteilung *f* allotment certificate (US), allotment letter (GB), letter of allotment (GB)
Bezugsschein *m* subscription certificate
bieten *v* bid *v*, offer *v*
Bieten *n* bidding *n*
Bietende *f u. m* bidder *n*
Bieter *m* bidder *n*
Bietungsgarantie *f* bid bond
Bilanz *f* balance of accounts; **-** *f* balance sheet, statement of assets and liabilities (US); **eine - aufstellen** draw up a balance; **eine - bereinigen** clean up a balance sheet; **Genehmigung der -** approval of the balance sheet; **geprüfte -** audited balance sheet; **konsolidierte -** consolidated balance sheet, consolidated financial statement; **letzte -** ultimate balance; **provisorische -** trial balance; **verkürzte -** condensed balance sheet, summary of assets and liabilities
Bilanzabschluß *m* balancing of the books
Bilanzabteilung *f* accounting department
Bilanzanalyse *f* ratio analysis, statement analysis
Bilanzaufgliederungsbogen *m* analysis sheet; **monatlicher -** monthly balance sheet
Bilanzaufstellung *f* balance sheet, statement of assets and liabilities (US)
Bilanzauszug *m* condensed balance sheet, summary of assets and liabilities
Bilanzbildverbesserung *f* window-dressing
Bilanzbogen *m* balance sheet, statement of assets and liabilities (US)
Bilanzbuch *n* balance sheet book
Bilanzbuchhalter *m* balance sheet clerk
Bilanzergebnis *n* balance sheet result
Bilanzexperte *m* accounting practitioner, accounting expert

42

Bilanzfrisur f tampering with a balance sheet, window-dressing
Bilanzgewinn m net profit, net income, annual profit
bilanzieren v balance v
Bilanzierung f balancing of accounts
Bilanzierungsgrundsätze m pl accounting axioms, accounting principles
Bilanzierungsperiode f accounting period
Bilanzierungsrichtlinien f pl accounting axioms, accounting principles
Bilanzkonto n balance sheet account
Bilanzkosmetik f creative accounting
bilanzneutrale Bankgeschäfte off-balance-sheet business, non-credit business of banks
Bilanzpolitik f accounting policy
Bilanzposten m balance sheet item
Bilanzprüfer m certified accountant, comptroller n (US)
Bilanzprüfung f balance sheet audit
Bilanzrichtlinien f pl Statements of Standard Accounting Practice (SSAP) (US)
Bilanzschema n statement heading
Bilanzstichtag m balance date
Bilanzsumme f (Bilanzvolumen) total assets, balance sheet total
bilanztechnischer Ausdruck balance sheet term
Bilanzvolumen n total assets
Bilanzwert m balance value, book value
Bilanzziehung f balancing n
Bilanzziffern f pl balance sheet figures
Bild n (eines Unternehmens in der Öffentlichkeit) image n
billige Geldsätze cheap money, easy money
billigen v approve v
billiges Geld cheap money, easy money
Billigkeit f equity n, low price
Billigkeitspfand n equitable mortgage
Billigkeitsrecht n law of equity n
billigst adj (Börse) at best
Billigung f approval n
Billion f (1.000.000.000.000) billion n (GB), trillion n (US)
bindend adj binding adj
bindende Wirkung binding effect
Binnen- (in Zus.) domestic adj, internal adj

Binnenhandel m domestic trade, internal commerce (US)
Binnenkonnossement n inland bill of lading
Binnenland n inland n
Binnenmarkt m internal market
Binnenschiffahrtsweg m inland waterway
Binnenwert m internal value of a currency
Binnenzoll m internal duty
BIZ f = *Bank für Internationalen Zahlungsausgleich* Bank for International Settlements (BIS)
Blankett n blank form
blanko adj blank adj, unsecured adj; **- akzeptieren** accept in blank; **- giriert** endorsed in blank, indorsed in blank
Blanko- (in Zus.) blank adj
Blankoakzept n blank acceptance
Blankoannahme f blank acceptance
Blankoauftrag m blanket order
Blankoformular n blank form, blank n
Blankogeschäft n blank transaction
Blankogiro n assignment in blank, blank endorsement, endorsement in blank, indorsement in blank
Blankoindossament n assignment in blank, blank endorsement, endorsement in blank, indorsement in blank
Blankokredit m blank advance, unsecured credit, blank credit, unsecured loan
Blankopapier n blank certificate, blank paper
Blankoscheck m blank check, blank cheque (GB)
Blankounterschrift f blank signature
Blankovollmacht f blank power of attorney
Blankovorschuß m blank advance, unsecured credit, blank credit, unsecured loan
Blankowechsel m blank bill
Blankozahlung f clean payment
Blankozession f assignment in blank
Block m block n
Blockhandel m lot trading
blockieren v block v, embargo v
blockierte Devisen blocked foreign exchange
blockiertes Konto frozen account, blocked account
Blocklänge f (EDV) block length

Blocklücke

Blocklücke f (EDV) interblock space, interblock gap, block gap
Blockungsfaktor m (EDV) blocking factor, block factor
Bodenkreditbank f land mortgage bank, land bank
Bodmerei f bottomry n
Bodmereibrief m bill of bottomry, bottomry bond; *- auf Schiff und Ladung* respondentia bond
Bodmereigläubiger m bottomry bondholder
Bodmereischuld f bottomry debt
Bogen m (Wertpapier) coupon sheet
Bogenerneuerung f coupon sheet renewal
bogenlos adj couponless
Bonifikation f compensation n, allowance n
Bonität f credit worthiness, soundness n, standing n, reliability n
Bonitätsprüfung f credit check; *- von Anleihen* bond rating
Bonitätsvermerk m credit rating
Bonus m bonus n, surplus dividend, superdividend n, special dividend
Bonusaktie f bonus share
Bord; *an - gehen* embark v
Bordkonnossement n on-board bill of lading
borgen v borrow v
Borgen n borrowing n
Börse f stock exchange, securities exchange, stock market; *Aktien an der - einführen* introduce shares on the market; *bewegte -* disturbed market; *empfindlich reagierende -* sensitive market; *flaue -* dull market, stale market; *leicht reagierende -* sensitive market; *lustlose -* dead market; *umsatzschwache -* dead market
Börsenabkürzungen f pl ticker abbreviations (US)
Börsenabrechnung f broker's ticket, stock exchange settlement
Börsenabteilung f securities trading department, stocks and bonds department
Börsenagent m stockbroker
Börsenaufsicht f exchange supervision; *- f* Securities and Exchange Commission (SEC) (US)

Börsenauftrag m stock exchange order; *- zum bestmöglichen Kurs* composite trading (US); *unlimitierter -* market order; *widerrufbarer -* revocable stock order
Börsenauftragsbuch n stock market order book
Börsenbericht m stock market report
Börsenbesucher m stock exchange member, operator n (US)
Börsenblatt n financial paper
Börsenbrauch m stock exchange customs
Börsencoup m deal on the stock exchange
Börsendiener m waiter n (GB)
Börsendilettant m dabbler n
Börseneinführung f stock exchange introduction, stock exchange listing; *Anmeldung zur -* registration
Börseneinführungsprovision f listing commission
Börsenentwicklung f tendencies of the market
börsenfähig adj marketable adj, sal(e)able adj
Börsenfähigkeit f marketability n
Börsenfernschreibdienst m ticker service (US)
Börsenfernschreiber m quotation ticker (US), tape machine, ticker n (US)
Börsenflaute f dullness n
Börsengang m going public
börsengängig adj current on exchange
börsengängige Aktie share listed on the stock exchange; *- Wertpapiere* stock exchange securities, marketable securities
Börsengeschäft; *ein kurzfristiges - machen* be in and out of the market
Börsengeschäfte n pl stock exchange dealings, stock exchange transactions, stock broking, stock market transactions; *kleiner als übliche -* odd lots (US), fractions; *mit Kredit finanzierte -* on margin, leveraged stock broking
Börsengeschehen n stock exchange business
Börsengesetz n stock exchange law
Börsengewinn m exchange profit; *ein leicht erzielter -* velvet n (US)

börsengültig für einen Tag valid for one day
Börsenhandel m stock exchange trading, stockbrokerage n, stockbroking n, dealings in stocks (US)
Börsenhändler m securities dealer, security dealer, dealer in stocks (US)
Börsenindex m stock exchange index, stock price average
Börsenkapitalisierung f market capitalization
Börsenklima n tone of the market
Börsenkommissionsfirma f commission broker
Börsenkommissionsgeschäft n broker's business, stockbroking transaction
Börsenkompensationsgeschäft n cross trade
Börsenkrach m crash, market crash
Börsenkredit m stock exchange loan
Börsenkurs m market price, exchange price, market rate, quoted value
Börsenkursblatt n list of quotations
Börsenkursgrafik f chart
Börsenkurszettel m stock exchange list
Börsenmakler m exchange broker; *unreeller* - bucketeer n (US)
Börsenmanöver n rig n, sharepushing n, stock exchange manoeuvre; *ein - durchführen* rig the market
börsenmäßig adj in accordance with stock exchange procedures
Börsenmitglied; das für eigene Rechnung spekulierende - floor trader (US)
Börsenname m (von Effekten) nickname n
börsennotierte Aktie (Anleihe) listed share (bond)
Börsennotiz f stock exchange quotation; *eine - aufheben* v delist v
Börsenorder f stock exchange order
Börsenordnung f rules of the stock exchange, stock exchange regulations
Börsenpreis m stock market price
Börsenreform f reorganization of the stock exchange
Börsensaal m floor n, trading floor
Börsenscheingeschäft n wash sale (GB), washing n (US)
Börsenscheinverkauf m wash sale (GB), washing n (US)

Börsenschluß m close of exchange
Börsensitz m seat n (on the stock exchange)
Börsenspekulant m bargain hunter
Börsenstimmung f market sentiment
Börsentag m trading day
börsentägliche Abrechnung market-to-market settlement (e.g. of profits or losses of future contracts)
Börsentelegraf m quotation ticker (US), tape machine, ticker n (US)
Börsentermingeschäft n dealing for future settlement, time bargain
Börsentheorien f pl market theories
Börsentip m tip n, hint n
Börsenumsätze m pl stock exchange turnover
Börsenumsatzsteuer f stock exchange turnover tax
Börsenusancen f pl stock exchange customs
Börsenvertreter m exchange agent
Börsenvorstand m committee of the stock exchange
Börsenwert m stock market value
Börsenwerte m pl listed companies, stock exchange securities, marketable securities
Börsenzettel m stock exchange list
Börsenzulassung; Antrag auf - application for listing (US); *Vorschriften zur -* listing requirements
Börsenzusammenbruch m collapse of the market, crash
Börsianer m stock exchange operator
Bote m messenger n
Botendienst m messenger service
brachliegendes Kapital dead capital, dead money, barren money, dormant capital, dormant money, idle capital
Branchenfonds m fund investing in an individual industry
Branchengliederung f branch-of-business classification
Branchenrendite f branch-of-business profitability
Branchenrisiko n industrial risk
Branchenstatistik f branch-of-business statistics
Brauereiaktien f pl breweries n pl (US)

Brief *m* (Börse) asked; *- und Geld* bills and money
Briefhypothek *f* certified mortgage
Briefkastenfirma *f* tax heaven corporation
Briefkopf *m* letterhead *n*
Briefkurs *m* asked quotation, offer price, selling rate, asked price; *- m* (Devisen) drawing rate
Briefmarke *f* stamp *n*
Briefumschlag *m* (Kuvert) envelope *n*, cover *n*
Britannia *f* Britannia = 100 Pound (Sterling) British gold coin
broschiert *adj* stitched *adj*
Bruchzins *m* broken-period interest
Bruttobetrag *m* gross amount
Bruttoertrag *m* gross proceeds
Bruttogewinn *m* gross profit
Bruttorendite *f* gross yield
Bruttosozialprodukt *n* Gross National Product (G.N.P.)
Bruttospanne *f* gross spread, gross margin
Bruttoumsatz *m* gross sales
Bruttoverzinsung *f* gross interest return
Buchabschluß *m* balancing of the books
buchen *v* book *v*, enter *v*; *gleichlautend -* enter in conformity, book in conformity; *tagfertig -* post up
Bücher abschließen close books, balance books; *- abstimmen* agree the books; *- revidieren* check the books; *- überprüfen* audit the accounts
Bücherabschluß *m* closing of books
Bücherfälschung *f* cooking of accounts
Bücherrevision *f* audit *n*, auditing of accounts, checking of accounts
Bücherrevisor *m* auditor *n*, chartered accountant, public accountant
Buchforderung *f* book claim
Buchforderungen *f pl* active debts, receivables *n pl* (US), accounts receivable
Buchführer *m* bookkeeper *n*, accountant *n*
Buchführung *f* accountancy *n*, accounting *n*, bookkeeping *n*; *doppelte -* bookkeeping by double entry, double entry bookkeeping, dual system; *einfache -* bookkeeping by single entry; *kaufmännische -* commercial bookkeeping
Buchführungsarbeit *f* bookkeeping work

Buchführungsbelege *m pl* accounting records
Buchführungsmethode *f* accounting method; *amerikanische -* tabular bookkeeping
Buchführungspflicht *f* record-keeping duty
Buchführungsunterlagen *f pl* accounting records
Buchführungsvorgang *m* accounting process
Buchgeld *n* deposit currency (US), money in account, deposit money, bank money, check book money (US)
Buchgewinn *m* book profit
Buchgläubiger *m* book creditor
Buchgrundschuld *f* registered land charge
Buchguthaben *n* credit balance in account
Buchhalter *m* bookkeeper *n*, accountant *n*
Buchhaltung *f* accountancy *n*, accounting *n*, bookkeeping *n*
Buchhaltungsabteilung *f* accounting department, bookkeeping department
Buchhaltungsbeleg *m* booking voucher, accounting voucher, entry ticket
Buchhaltungsbuch *n* ledger *n*
Buchhaltungschef *m* accounting supervisor
Buchhaltungskosten *plt* bookkeeping expense
Buchhaltungsmaschine *f* ledger machine
Buchhaltungssystem *n* accounting system
Buchhaltungsvorgang *m* accounting transaction
Buchhypothek *f* registered mortgage
Buchkredit *m* book credit, credit in current account
buchmäßiger Überschuß book surplus
Buchprüfer *m* auditor *n*, chartered accountant, public accountant
Buchprüfung *f* audit *n*, auditing of accounts, checking of accounts
Buchprüfungsbericht *m* auditor's report, audit report
Buchsachverständige *f u. m* auditing expert
Buchsaldo *m* (im Sparbuch eingetragener Saldo) passbook balance
Buchschuld *f* book debt

Buchschulden f pl ordinary debts
Buchschuldner m book debtor
Buchung f (Tätigkeit) booking n; ~ f entry n
Buchungen f pl postings n pl
Buchungsaufgabe f entry advice, statement of accounting entry
Buchungsbeleg m booking voucher, accounting voucher, entry ticket
Buchungsdatum n date of entry
Buchungsformular n bookkeeping form
Buchungsgebühr f entry fee
Buchungsmaschine f accounting machine, bookkeeping machine
Buchungsplatz m booking terminal
Buchungsposten m booking item, bookkeeping entry; *einen ~ abstreichen* check an entry
Buchungspostenzahl f number of transactions
Buchungsschnitt m accounts closing day
Buchungsstelle f accountancy office
Buchungstext m entry legend
Buchungsunterlagen f pl bookkeeping records, accounting records
Buchungsverfahren n bookkeeping method
Buchverlust m bookkeeping loss
Buchwert m accounting value, book cost, book value
Buchwerte m pl book figures
Budget n budget n
budgetmäßig adj budgetary adj
Bündelung f (von Bankdienstleistungen) bundling
Bullenfalle f (Börse) bull trap
Bundesanleihe f Federal government bond
Bundesanleihekonsortium n Federal board syndicate
Bundesaufsichtsamt für das Kreditwesen n (in Deutschland) = *BAK* Federal Banking Supervisory Authority
Bundesbahnanleihe f Federal Railway bond
Bundesbank f Federal Bank
bundesbankfähiger Wechsel m rediscountable (eligible) bill of exchange at the Bundesbank
Bundesbankgesetz n Bundesbank Act
Bundesobligation f Federal medium-term note

Bundespostanleihe f Federal Post Office bond
Bundesschatzanweisung f Federal treasury note
Bundesschatzbrief m Federal savings bond
Bundesschatzwechsel m Federal treasury bill
Bundeswertpapiere n pl Federal government securities
Bund Futures m pl Federal government futures
Bürge m guarantor n, surety n; ~ m (für Einwanderer) sponsor n
bürgen v guarantee, stand surety
bürgerliches Recht civil law
Bürgschaft f bail n; ~ f guarantee n (GB), guarant n (US); ~ f surety n, suretyship n; *eine ~ leisten* stand surety; *einfache ~* ordinary guarantee; *gesamtschuldnerische ~* joint and several guarantee; *nicht durch dingliches Vermögen abgesicherte ~* personal security; *persönliche ~* personal security; *selbstschuldnerische ~* guarantee with direct liability as co-debtor, joint and several guarantee
Bürgschaftsbank f guarantee bank
Bürgschaftsdarlehen n loan secured by a personal guarantee
Bürgschaftserklärung f declaration of guarantee
bürgschaftsfähig adj bailable adj
Bürgschaftskredit m guaranteed loan
Bürgschaftsleistung f bailment n
Bürgschaftsnehmer m guarantee
Bürgschaftsschein m guarantee deed, deed of suretyship, security bond, bail bond
Bürgschaftsurkunde f guarantee deed, deed of suretyship, security bond, bail bond
Bürgschaftsvertrag m contract of guarantee, contract of suretyship, guarantee agreement
Büro n office n; ~ *eines Freiverkehrsmaklers* bucketshop n (GB)
Business-Plan m siehe *Geschäftsplan*
Buße f fine n, penalty n

C

chancenreich *adj* promising *adj*
Charter *m* charterer *n*
chartern *v* affreight *v*, charter *v*
Charterverkehr *m* charter traffic
Chartervertrag *m* charter-party *n*, charter contract
Chefhändler *m* chief dealer
Chefprokurist *m* Assistant Manager (GB), Second Vice President (US)
Chefsyndikus *m* chief legal adviser
Chemiewerte *m pl* (Börse) chemicals, chemical stocks
chiffrieren *v* code *v*
Circa-Auftrag *m* near-limit order
Circa-Kurs *m* approximate price
Clearing *n* clearing *n*
Clearingabkommen *n* clearing agreement
Clearingbank *f* clearing bank
Clearinghaus *n* clearing house, clearing center
Clearingstelle *f* clearing house, clearing center
Clearingsystem für Euroanleihen *n* Euroclear (CEDEL)
Coderahmen *m* code structure
Codiergerät *n* coder *n*, code selector, encoding machine, encoder *n*
Codierzeile *f* coding line, coded line
Commonwealth *n* Commonwealth *n*
Computer *n* computer; *umstellen auf* ~ *v* computerize
Computerchip *m* chip (computer chip)
Computerfehler *m* computer error
computergestützt computer-assisted (aided)
Computerhandelssystem *n* computer trading system
computerlesbar computer readable
Computerprogramm *n* computer programme
Conto pro Diversa *n* = *CpD* suspense account, sundries account
Coupon *m* (Kupon) coupon *n*
Couponbogen *m* (Kuponbogen) coupon sheet
Courtage *f* brokerage *n*, broker's fee, broker's commission
Courtagetarif *m* scale of commission (GB); ~ *m* schedule of commission charges
CpD *n* = *Conto pro Diversa* suspense account, sundries account
Cross-Rate *f* cross rate
Cum-Anrechte *n pl* cum rights
Cum-Dividende *f* cum dividend

D

Dachfonds m holding fund, fund of funds
Dachgesellschaft f parent company
Damnum n discount
Dänenkrone f Danish Krone
Darlehen n loan n; *- der Landeszentralbank* reserve bank credit; *befristetes -* term loan, time loan; *ein - gewähren* lend v; *gedecktes -* secured advance; *kurzfristiges -* short-term loan; *landwirtschaftliches -* farm loan, farm credit, agricultural loan; *langfristiges -* long-term loan; *mittelfristiges -* medium-term loan; *nachrangiges -* junior mezzanine debt; *unbesichertes -* unsecured loan; *unsicheres -* precarious loan; *zinsloses -* interest-free loan; *zweckgebundenes -* tied loan
Darlehensbetrag m loan amount
Darlehensfinanzierung f financing on loans
Darlehensgeber m lender n
Darlehensgeschäft n loan business
Darlehenshypothek f loan mortgage
Darlehenskasse f loan bank, credit bank
Darlehenskonto n loan account
Darlehenskosten plt loan charges
Darlehensnehmer m borrower n
Darlehensschein m loan certificate
Darlehensschuld f loan debt
Darlehenssumme f loan amount
Darlehensvaluta f loan proceeds
Darlehensvermittler m loan broker
Darlehensvertrag m loan contract, loan agreement
Darlehenszinsen m pl loan interest
Darlehenszinssatz m loan rate, borrowing rate
Darlehenszusage f approval of a loan, promise of a loan
darniederliegen v stagnate v
Dateiaufbau m file format
Dateiorganisation f file organization
Daten plt data, information
Datenaustausch m data communication; *elektronischer -* Electronic Data Interchange (EDI)

Datenbank f data bank, data base
Datenendgerät n data-processing terminal
Datenendplatz m data-processing terminal
Datenerfassung f data collection, data acquisition
Datenfernübertragung f long-distance data transmission
Datenfernverarbeitung f teleprocessing n, remote data processing
Datenkomprimierung f data compression
Datensammelsystem n data gathering system, data acquisition system
Datensichtgerät n CRT terminal (Cathode Ray Tube), video data terminal, video display
Datenträgeraustausch m exchange of data media, exchange of data carriers
Datentransport m data transfer
Datenübertragung f data transmission
Datenübertragungsleitung f data transmission line
Datenverarbeitungsanlage f computer centre, data processing machine
Datenverarbeitungssytem n data processing system; *voll integriertes -* fully integrated processing system
Datenverkehr m data traffic (as opposed to voice traffic)
Datenverschlüsselung f data codification
Datenzwischenträger m interim data files, intermediate data medium, data medium for temporary storage
datieren v date v; *im voraus -* date in advance
Datierung f dating n
Datowechsel m after-date bill, bill after date
Datum n date n
Datumsstempel m date stamp
Dauer f duration n; *- einer Anleihe* life of a loan, term of a loan
Daueranlage f long-term investment, permanent investment
Daueranleger m long-term investor
Dauerauftrag m standing order

Dauergarantie

Dauergarantie f continuing guarantee (US), continuing security
dauerhaft adj permanent adj
Dauerkredit m long-term loan
Dauerkunde m regular customer
dauernde Beteiligungen permanent holdings
Dauerschuld f long-term debt
Dauerschuldverschreibung f perpetual debenture
Dauerzahlungsauftrag m standing payment order
DAX m = *Deutscher Aktienindex* German stock market index
Dax-Future-Option f Dax-future option
Debet n debit n
Debetbuchung f debit entry, debit item
Debetkonto n debtor account
Debetsaldo m debit balance, debit balance
Debetseite f debit side
Debetzinsen m pl debit interest, interest on debit balances
Debitor m debtor n
Debitoren m pl active debts, receivables n pl (US), accounts receivable; *- aus Schuldscheinen, Wechseln und Akzepten* notes receivable (US); *Finanzierung durch Abtretung der -* accounts receivable financing
Debitorenaufstellung f accounts receivable statement; *- nach Fälligkeit* aging schedule
Debitorengeschäft n lending business
Debitorenkonto n debit account
Debitorenkredit m accounts receivable loan
Debitorenreserve f reserve for bad debts
Debitorensätze m pl lending rates
Debitorenverkauf m factoring n
Debitorenverluste m pl losses on receivables
Debitorenziehung f bill drawn on a debtor
debitorisch adj as a debtor, on the debit side
decken v cover v; *ein Defizit -* cover a deficit, make up a deficit
Deckung f cover n; *Verkauf ohne -* short sale
Deckungsauftrag m covering order
Deckungsbestand m cover funds

deckungsfähig adj eligible as cover
Deckungsgeschäft n covering (hedging) transaction
Deckungskapital n coverage capital
Deckungskauf m bear covering, covering purchase
Deckungskonto n cover account
Deckungsmittel n covering funds
Deckungsschuldverschreibung f collateral bond
Deckungsstock m cover funds
Deckungsverhältnis n cover ratio
Deckungszusage f (Versicherung) binder n; *-* f binding receipt; *vorläufige -* cover note (GB), covering note
Defizit n deficit n
defizitär adj indeficit
Deflation f deflation n
deflationär adj deflationary
Deflationspolitik f deflationary policy
Degression f degression n
degressiv adj degressive, declining
dehnbares Limit elastic limit, flexible limit
Deklaration f declaration n
deklarieren v declare v
deklariert adj declared adj
Delegation f delegation n
delegieren v delegate v
Delkredere n delcredere
Delkredere-Konto n delcredere account
Delkredere-Risiko n delcredere risk, credit risk
Delkredere-Rückstellung f contingency reserve, contingent reserve, contingent fund (US)
Delkredere-Versicherung f credit insurance
Depesche f cable n
depeschieren v cable v
Deponent m depositor n, bank depositor
deponieren v deposit v
Deponierung f consignment n (Scotch Law); *-* f deposit n
Deport m backwardation n (GB)
Deportgeschäft n backwardation business (GB)
Deportkurs m backwardation rate
Depositen plt (Einlagen) deposits n pl
Depositenabteilung f deposit banking division, deposit department

Depositenbank f deposit bank, bank of deposit
Depositenbuch n pass-book n (US), bank book, deposit book
Depositeneinlagen f pl deposited funds, deposits n pl
Depositengelder n pl deposited funds, deposits n pl
Depositengeschäft n deposit banking
Depositeninhaber m depositor n, bank depositor
Depositenkasse f sub-office n, subbranch n, branch n, branch office
Depositenkonto n deposit account (US); ~ n deposit ledger (GB), depositors ledger
Depositenregister n deposit ledger (GB), depositors ledger
Depositenschein m certificate of deposit
Depositenversicherung f bank deposit insurance, deposit insurance
Depositenzertifikat n certificate of deposit (CD)
Depot n (bei einer Bank) securities account, securities portfolio, custodianship account, custodian account (US), safe custody account (GB); ~ n (Lagerplatz) depot n; **geschlossenes** ~ sealed safekeeping account; **offenes** ~ ordinary safekeeping account
Depotabsicherung f portfolio insurance
Depotabteilung f customer's security department, safe custody department (GB)
Depotanalyse f safekeeping account analysis
Depotaufstellung f statement of securities deposited
Depotauszug m statement of securities
Depotbank f depositary bank
Depotbesitz m securities portfolio
Depotbestand m portfolio value
Depotbewertung f portfolio evaluation
Depotbuchhaltung f securities accounts department
Depotgebühr f safe custody fee, safekeeping fee, custody charge
Depotgebühren f pl security safekeeping account charges

Depotgeschäft n custody business, custodianships n pl (US), safe custodies (GB)
Depotgutschrift f credit-entry in a safe-custody account
Depotjahresauszug m yearly statement of deposited securities
Depotkonto n custodianship account, custodian account (US), safe custody account (GB)
Depotkosten plt custody costs
Depotkredit m loan against securities in custodian account
Depotkunde m customer having a safe-custody account
Depotquittung f custody receipt, deposit receipt, deposit slip
Depotschein m custody receipt, deposit receipt, deposit slip
Depotstelle f depository
Depotstimmrecht n deposited shares voting right, proxy voting right
Depotübersicht f list of deposited securities
Depotumbuchung f transmission of shares
Depotversicherung f safe deposit box insurance
Depotverwahrung f securities custody
Depotverwahrungsart f type of securities deposit
Depotwechsel m bill deposited as security, bill in pension, bill on deposit
Depotwertvergleich m comparative valuation of deposited securities
Depression f depression n
Deputat n allowance n
Deregulierung f deregulation
derivative Instrumente derivative instruments
designieren v elect v
desinvestieren v disinvest
Detailgeschäft n retail n, retail trade
detaillieren v detail v
Detaillist m retailer n
Detailpreis m retail price
Deutsche Aktienindex m = **DAX** German stock market index; ~ **Bundesbank** f German Federal Bank; ~ **Kreditwesengesetz** n (KWG) German Banking Act;

Devisen

- **Mark** f German mark; **- Rentenindex** m **= REX** German bond market index; **- Terminbörse** f **= DTB** German Options and Financial Futures Exchange Ltd. (GOFFEX)

Devisen f pl foreign currency, foreign exchange (US), foreign exchanges (GB); *blockierte* - blocked foreign exchange; *eingefrorene* - blocked foreign exchange; *Kurssicherung von* - rate-hedging; *nicht frei konvertierbare* - blocked currency

Devisenabrechnung f foreign exchange settlement

Devisenabteilung f foreign exchange department

Devisenarbitrage f exchange arbitration; *- in drei verschiedenen Währungen* triangular exchange

Devisenausländer m non-resident n

Devisenbank f exchange bank

Devisenbeschränkungen f pl exchange restrictions, currency restrictions, foreign exchange restrictions

Devisenbestand m foreign currency holdings, foreign currency reserve

Devisenbestimmungen f pl exchange regulations, currency regulations, exchange control regulations

Devisenbewirtschaftung f exchange control, currency control

Devisenbörse f foreign exchange market

Devisendeckung f exchange cover

Devisenengagement; *Aufstellung der* - s position sheet, foreign exchange position

Devisenerklärung f currency declaration

Devisenfreigrenze f foreign exchange allowance

Devisengenehmigung f exchange permit

Devisengeschäft n foreign exchange business, dealings in foreign exchange

Devisengeschäfte; *einfache* - outright operations

Devisengesetz n foreign exchange law

Devisenhandel m foreign exchange business, dealings in foreign exchange

Devisenhändler m exchange dealer, currency dealer, foreign exchange dealer

Deviseninländer m resident n

Devisenkassahandel m spot exchange dealings, spot business in foreign exchange

Devisenkauf m spot purchase of a currency

Devisenkaufoption f currency call option

Devisenkonto n foreign currency account

Devisenkontrolle f foreign exchange (forex) control, currency control

Devisenkredit m foreign currency loan

Devisenkurs m rate of exchange, exchange rate, commercial rate of exchange (US), foreign exchange rate; *künstlich gehaltener* - pegged exchange

Devisenkursberechnung f calculation of exchange

Devisenkursblatt n list of foreign exchanges (GB)

Devisenkurse; *in Pennies notierte* - pence rates (GB); *in Pfund Sterling notierte* - currency rates (GB)

Devisenkursliste f exchange list, bill of course of exchange

Devisenkurssicherung f currency hedging, foreign exchange covering

Devisenlage f foreign exchange position

Devisenmakler m foreign exchange broker

Devisenmarkt m foreign exchange market

Devisenoption f foreign exchange (forex) option

Devisenposition f foreign exchange position; *- f* position sheet

Devisenreserven f pl foreign currency reserves

Devisenschiebung f currency racket

Devisensperre f exchange embargo

Devisentermingeschäft n forward exchange deal

Devisenterminhandel m forward exchange transactions

Devisenterminkontrakt m currency futures (contract)

Devisenvergehen n currency offense

Devisenverkauf m selling foreign currency

Devisenverkaufsoption f currency put option

Devisenverluste m pl losses on foreign exchange

Devisenwährung f currency exchange standard

Devisenwechsel m currency bill

Devisenzufluß m inflow of foreign currency
Devisenzuteilung f allocation of currency, foreign currency allocation
Devisenzwangswirtschaft f exchange control
dezimal adj decimal adj
Dezimalstelle f decimal place
Diebstahlversicherung f theft insurance
dienen v serve v, attend v, to be of service
Dienstleistung f service n
Dienstleistungsgebühr f service charge
Dienstprogramm n utility programme
Dienstvertrag m employment contract
Differenz f difference n; - f (zwischen Preisen, Kursen) spread n
Differenzgeschäfte machen speculate for differences
Differenzkonto n difference account (US)
differieren v differ, vary
dilatorisch adj dilatory adj
dinglich; - **belasten** hypothecate v, mortgage v, encumber v; - **belastet** encumbered adj, mortgaged adj
dingliche Sicherheit real security
direkt adj direct
Direktabbuchung f direct charge-off
Direktanlagebank f discount broker (US)
Direktbuchung f on-line posting
Direktbuchungsprogramm n on-line posting programme
Direktbuchungssystem n on-line accounting system
Direktdiskont m direct discounting
direkte Besteuerung direct taxation
direkter Zugriff direct access, random access
Direktion f management n
Direktkredite m pl direct borrowings
Direktor m manager, director, Senior Vice President; **geschäftsführender** - president n (US); **stellvertretender** - assistant manager, deputy manager, First Vice President
Direktorium n supervisory board, Board of Directors (the Board)
Direktwerbung f direct advertising
Disagio n disagio n
Diskont â forfait m discount without recourse

Diskont m discount, rediscount (US); - **einräumen** allow a discount; **bar abzüglich** - cash less discount
Diskontbank f bank of discount, discount bank, discount company, discount house
Diskontbedingungen f pl discount terms
Diskontbroker m discount broker
Diskonten plt discounts plt, discounted bills
Diskonterhöhung f increase in the discount rate, increase in the bank rate
Diskonterlös m proceeds n pl
Diskontermäßigung f reduction in the discount rate
diskontfähig adj discountable adj, bankable adj, eligible adj (US)
Diskontgeschäft n discounting business
diskontierbar adj discountable adj, bankable adj, eligible adj (US)
Diskontierbarkeit f discountability n
diskontieren v discount v
Diskontierer m discounter n
diskontiert adj discounted adj
Diskontierung f discounting n; - **von Wechseln** discounting of bills
Diskontierungstag m date of discount
Diskontkredit m discount credit, rediscount credit (US)
Diskontmarkt m discount market, bill market
Diskontmaterial n bills eligible for discount
Diskontnote f bill of discount
Diskontpolitik f bank rate policy, discount policy
Diskontsatz m discount rate, rate of discount, rediscount rate (US); - **der Federal Reserve Bank** Federal Reserve Rediscount Rate (US); - **der Notenbank** bank rate (of discount); **offizieller** - official discount rate
Diskontwechsel m pl discounts n pl, discounted bills
Diskontwechselbuch n discount ledger
Diskontwechselhändler m note broker (US)
Diskontwert m discounted value
Diskontzinsen m pl discount interest
diskreditieren v discredit v
Diskrepanz f discrepancy n
diskriminieren v discriminate v
Diskriminierung f discrimination n

Dispacheur

Dispacheur *m* average adjuster, average stator, average agent
Disparität *f* disparity *n*
disponibel *adj* disposable *adj*
disponieren *v* make arrangements, place orders
Disposition *f* disposal *n*; *zur ~ stellen* make available
Dispositionen treffen make arrangements, place orders
Distanzgeschäft *n* non-local transaction
Distanzscheck *m* out-of-town check
Distanzwechsel *m* out-of-town bill
diverse Kreditoren (Kontobezeichnung) sundry creditors account (GB)
Diverse *n* sundries *n pl*
Diversifikation *f* diversification
Dividende *f* dividend *n*; *außerordentliche ~* bonus *n*, surplus dividend, superdividend *n*, special dividend, melon *n* (US); *eine ~ ausfallen lassen* omit a dividend; *einschließlich ~* dividend on (US); *festgesetzte ~* declared dividend; *fiktive ~* sham dividend; *kumulative ~* cumulative dividend; *mit ~* cum dividend; *nicht kumulative ~* noncumulative dividend; *ohne ~* ex dividend
Dividendenabschlag *m* ex-dividend markdown
Dividendenanfall *m* accrual of dividends
Dividendenausfall *m* dividend omission
Dividendenausschreibung *f* declaration of dividends
Dividendenausschüttungen *f pl* dividend disbursement
dividendenberechtigt *adj* eligible for dividend payment
Dividendenbogen *m* dividend coupon sheet
Dividendeneinnahme *f* dividend income
Dividendenerhöhung *f* dividend increase
Dividendenerklärung *f* declaration of dividends
Dividendenertrag *m* dividend yield
Dividendenfonds *m* bonus fund, dividend fund
Dividendengarantie *f* dividend guarantee
Dividendenkonto *n* dividend account
Dividendenkupon *m* dividend coupon

Dividendenkürzung *f* dividend cut, reduction of dividends
dividendenlos *adj* dividendless
Dividendenpapiere *n pl* equity securities, equities *n pl*, dividendpaying stock
Dividendenrechte *n pl* dividend rights
Dividendenrendite *f* dividend yield
Dividendenreserve *f* bonus reserve
Dividendenrücklage *f* dividend reserve fund
Dividendensatz *m* dividend rate
Dividendenscheck *m* dividend check
Dividendenschein *m* dividend warrant, dividend coupon
Dividendenstock *m* dividend fund
Dividendenstopp *m* dividend freeze
Dividendenvoraussage *f* dividend forecast
Dividendenvorschlag *m* dividend recommendation
Dividendenwerte *m pl* dividend-bearing securities
Dividendenzahlung *f* dividend payment
dividieren *v* divide *v*
DM-Anleihe-Emittent *m* DM-bond issuer
DM-Auslandsanleihe *f* foreign DM-bond
Dock *n* wharf *n*, quay *n*
Dockgebühren *f pl* dock charges, dockage *n*, dock dues, wharfage *n*, quayage *n*
Docklagerschein *m* dock warrant
Dokument *n* document *n*, instrument *n*; *zu getreuen Händen hinterlegtes ~* escrow *n*
dokumentärer Akzeptkredit documentary acceptance credit
Dokumente *n pl* documents *n pl*; *~ gegen Akzept* documents against acceptance; *~ gegen Zahlung* documents against payment, cash against documents; *Akkreditiv ohne ~* clean letter of credit; *Kasse gegen ~* documents against payment, cash against documents; *Tratte ohne ~* clean draft
Dokumentenakkreditiv *n* documentary credit, documentary letter of credit; *widerrufliches ~* revocable documentary credit
dokumentengebunden *adj* linked to a document
Dokumenteninkasso *n* collection of documents, documentary collection

Dokumentenkredit *m* documentary credit, documentary letter of credit
Dokumententratte *f* commodity paper (US), documentary draft
Dokumentenvorschuß *m* advance against documents
Dokumentenwechsel *m* acceptance bill, documentary bill
Dollar *m* dollar *n*, (informal) greenback
Dollaranleihe *f* dollar bond
Dollarblock *m* dollar area
Dollarlücke *f* dollar gap
Dollarraum *m* dollar area
Dollarschwund *m* dollar drain
dolmetschen *v* interpret *v*
Dolmetscher *m* interpreter *n*
Domizil *n* domicile *n*, residence *n*
Domizilgesellschaft *f* domiciled company
domizilieren *v* domicile *v*, domiciliate *v*
Domizilierung *f* domiciliation *n*
Domizilprovision *f* commission for domiciling
Domizilwechsel *m* addressed bill, domiciled bill
Doppel *n* double *n*
Doppelbelegung *f* (bei einer Großspeicherorganisation) overlay *n*
Doppelbesteuerung *f* double taxation
Doppelbesteuerungsabkommen *n* double-tax agreement
Doppelquittung *f* double receipt
doppelte Buchführung bookkeeping by double entry, double entry bookkeeping, dual system
Doppelwährung *f* dual currency standard, double standard, parallel standard
Doppelwährungsanleihe *f* dual currency bond, heaven and hell bond (informal); *- mit variablem Wechselkurs für die Rückzahlung* reverse dual currency bond
Doppelzentner *m* quintal *n*
Dossier *n* dossier *n*
Dotation *f* endowment *n*
Dotationskapital *n* endowment capital
dotieren *v* endow *v*
Dotierung *f* dotation *n*; *- eines Kontos* alimentation of an account
Drahtakzept *n* telegraphic acceptance
Drahtanschrift *f* telegraphic address

Drahtwort *n* telegraphic address
Draufgeld *n* bargain money, bargain penny
dreifach *adj* triple *adj*, threefold *adj*
Dreimonatsgeld *n* ninety days loan
Dreimonatsgelder *n pl* ninety-day deposits
Dreimonatswechsel *m* three months bill, three months draft
dringende Notlage emergency *n*
Dringlichkeit *f* priority *n*
Dringlichkeitsstufe *f* priority *n*
Drittland *n* third country
Drittschuldner *m* third-party debtor, garnishee
Druckband *n* print tape
Druckbild *n* printing format
Druckdatei *f* print file
drücken *v* (Preise) beat down
Druckgeschwindigkeit *f* printing rate
druckintensiv *adj* said of a programme that requires a large volume of printer output
Druckplatte *f* (Plattenspeicher, der Druckdaten enthält) print file on disc
Druckpuffer *m* print buffer
Druckzeile *f* print line
DTA *m* = *Datenträgeraustausch* exchange of data carriers
DTB *f* = *Deutsche Terminbörse* German futures and options exchange
Dubiosa; *Rückstellung für -* doubtful debts provision
dubiose Forderungen doubtful debts, notes and accounts (US)
Dubiosenrückstellung *f* allowance for bad debts
Dumping *n* dumping *n*; *- betreiben* dump *v*
Duplikat *n* duplicate *n*
durch Wechsel garantierte Schuldverschreibung endorsed bond, indorsed bond
Durchfinanzierung *f* financing to completion
Durchfuhr *f* transit *n*
Durchführbarkeitsstudie *f* feasibility study
durchführen *v* carry through, carry out
Durchfuhrschein *m* transit bill
Durchführung *f* execution *n*
Durchführungsbestimmung *f* regulation *n*
Durchfuhrzoll *m* transit duty
Durchgangsposten *m* item in transit
Durchgangsverkehr *m* transit *n*

Durchkonnossement

Durchkonnossement *n* through bill of lading
durchlaufende Gelder cash in transit
Durchlaufkonto *n* suspense account
durchleiten *v* transmit, pass on
Durchleitungsbank *f* pass-through bank
Durchleitungskredit *m* pass-through loans
durchleuchten *v* check, examine, investigate
Durchschlag *m* copy *n*
Durchschnitt *m* average *n*
durchschnittlicher Saldo eines Einlagenkontos line of deposit (US)
durchschnittlicher Zahlungstermin equation of payments
Durchschnittskurs *m* average price (rate), market average, middle price
Durchschnittslaufzeit *f* duration, average life
Durchschnittssaldo *m* average balance
Durchsicht *f* review *n*
durchzählen *v* recount *v*, count over, count again
Dynamik *f* dynamics
dynamischer Markt fast-growing market
Dynamisierung *f* index-linking, indexation

E

ec m = **Euroscheck** eurocheque
ec-Karte f ec-card
echt adj genuine adj, authentic adj, real
echte Unterschrift genuine signature
echter Gewinn actual profit; **~ Wechsel** real bill (US)
echtes Gold sterling gold
Echtzeit f real-time
Eckdaten plt key figures
Eckzins m base rate, basic rate of interest
Edelmetall; ungemünztes ~ bullion n
Edelmetalle n pl precious metals
EDV f = **Elektronische Datenverarbeitung** electronic data processing
Effekten plt (Bilanz) investments n pl (balance sheet); **~ plt** securities n pl; **~ beleihen** advance money on securities, lend money on securities; **~ eines Investmenttrusts** investment trust securities; **~ hinterlegen** lodge securities; **international gehandelte ~** international securities, international stocks (US), internationals n pl; **lombardierte ~** pledged securities; **nicht abgestempelte ~** unassented securities (US); **Zulassung von ~ zum Börsenhandel** admission of securities
Effektenabrechnung f contract note, securities trading statement
Effektenabteilung f securities department
Effektenanlage f investment in securities
Effektenbeleihung f advances against securities, advances on securities, stock loan, share loan, margin loan (US)
Effektenbesitzer m stockowner n
Effektenbestand m investment portfolio, portfolio n
Effektenbewertung f ratings n pl (US)
Effektenbörse f stock exchange, securities exchange, stock market
Effektendepot n security account (US), register of securities
Effektendifferenzgeschäft n margin business (US)

Effektenemission f securities issue (offering)
Effektengarantie f underwriting n
Effektengattung f description of securities, category of securities
Effektengeschäft n securities transaction (deal), business in securities; **~ mit Einschuß** margin call (US)
Effektengirobank f securities clearing bank
Effektengiroverkehr m transfer of securities through a clearing system, clearing system for settling security transactions
Effektenhandel m security trading, stockbrokerage n, stockbroking n, dealings in stocks (US); **außerbörslicher ~** over-the-counter business
Effektenhändler m jobber n, stockjobber n; **~ m** securities dealer, security dealer, dealer in stocks (US)
Effektenindex m index of number of securities
Effektenkauf mit Einschuß buying on margin
Effektenkonto n securities account, safe custody deposit
Effektenkredit m loan on securities, margin loan (US)
Effektenkurse m pl securities prices, security prices
Effektenleihe f securities lending
Effektenlombard m advances against securities, advances on securities, stock loan, share loan, margin loan (US)
Effektenlombardkredit m advances against securities, advances on securities, stock loan, share loan, margin loan (US)
Effektenmakler m securities broker, stockbroker n
Effektenmarkt m securities market, security market, stock market
Effektenportefeuille n securities portfolio, portfolio n
Effektenprovision f stock exchange commission

Effektenschalter *m* bargain counter
Effektensparen *n* saving through investment in securities
Effektenspekulation *f* bargain hunting, stock adventure (GB)
Effektenstempelsteuer *f* stamp duty on securities
Effektenstrazze *f* securities blotter (US)
Effektenverkaufsvollmacht *f* stock power (US)
Effektenverwaltung *f* security management, custodianship (US)
effektiv *adj* actual *adj*; *~ ausgegebenes Aktienkapital* issued stock (US), issued capital (GB); *~ ausgegebenes Kapital* issued stock (US), issued capital (GB)
Effektivbestand *m* actual amount
effektiver Saldo actual balance; *~ Wert* actual value
Effektivverzinsung *f* effective yield
ehelich *adj* marital *adj*, matrimonial *adj*, legitimate *adj*
Ehevertrag *m* marriage settlement
Ehrenakzeptant *m* acceptor for honour
Ehreneintritt *m* act of honour
eidesstattliche Erklärung statutory declaration, affidavit *n*, sworn declaration
Eigenakzept *n* promissory note
Eigenanteile *m pl* proprietary interests
Eigenbesitz *m* own holdings, proprietary possession
eigene Aktien treasury stock; *~ Mittel* capital (equity) resources
Eigenfinanzierung *f* self-financing *n*, own financing
Eigenfinanzierungsgrad *m* equity ratio
Eigengeschäft *n* business for own account
Eigenhändler *m* dealer (trader) for own account, floor trader (US)
Eigenheim *n* homestead *n* (US), private home
Eigenheimbesitzer *m* homeowner *n* (US)
Eigenheit *f* particularity *n*
Eigenkapital *n* equity capital, capital, equity, net worth, proprietary capital, owners' capital; *~ n* (Bilanz), shareholders' equity, stockholders' equity (US); *~ im Vergleich zur Bilanzsumme* free capital ratio; *~ verwässern* *v* dilute equity; *gezeichnetes ~* subscribed equity; *haftendes ~* liable capital
Eigenkapitalausstattung *f* own capital resources
Eigenkapitalbedarf *m* equity requirements
Eigenkapitalbestimmungen *f pl* capital resources rules
Eigenkapitalrendite *f* return on equity, earnings-equity ratio
eigentlich *adj* actual, real *adj*
Eigentum *n* property *n*, ownership, possession; *~ beanspruchen* claim a title; *~ übernehmen* assume ownership; *bewegliches ~* chattels *n pl*, personal property, movables *n pl*; *wirtschaftliches ~* business ownership
Eigentümer *m* owner *n*, proprietor; *~ sein* own *v*; *materieller ~* beneficial owner, beneficiary owner; *rechtmäßiger ~* rightful owner; *unbeschränkter ~* absolute owner; *uneingeschränkter ~* freeholder *n*
Eigentümereigenschaft *f* ownership *n*
Eigentümerhypothek *f* owner's mortgage
eigentumsberechtigt *adj* beneficially entitled
Eigentumserwerb *m* acquisition of property
Eigentumsrecht *n* proprietary right; *unbeschränktes ~* absolute ownership
Eigentumsübertragung *f* transfer of ownership, transfer of property
Eigentumsurkunde *f* (Grundbesitz) root of title; *~ f* title deed, deed of ownership
Eigentumsverhältnis *n* ownership *n*
Eigentumsvorbehaltsklausel des Lieferanten Romalpa clause
Eigentumswechsel *m* change of ownership, change of title
Eigentumswohnung *f* owner-occupied flat, freehold flat
Eigentumszeichen *n* earmark *n*
Eigenvermögen *n* net worth, proprietary capital, owners' capital
Eigenverwahrung *f* owner custody
Eigenwechsel *m* promissory note, single bill, sola bill
Eilsendung *f* special delivery
Eilüberweisung *f* urgent transfer

Einnahmequellen f pl revenue sources
einbehalten v retain v, keep back, withhold v
einbehaltene Garantiesumme retention money
einberufen v call v; *eine Hauptversammlung* - call a meeting of shareholders, call a meeting of stockholders
einbringen v invest v; *Kapital* - contribute capital
Einbruchversicherung f burglary insurance
einbüßen v lose v
eindecken v cover, buy ahead
Eindeckung f covering, buying ahead
Eindeckungspflicht f coverage requirement
einfache *Buchführung* bookkeeping by single entry; *- Bürgschaft* simple guarantee
einforderbar adj claimable adj
Einfuhr f import n, importation n
Einfuhrabgabe f import deposit (GB); *- f* import duty, import tariff
Einfuhrbescheinigung f import certificate
Einfuhrbeschränkungen f pl import restrictions, import cuts
einführen v import v, introduce v
Einfuhrerklärung f declaration of imports
Einfuhrerlaubnis f import licence, import permit
Einfuhrfinanzierung f financing of imports
Einfuhrfreigabe f release for import, import release
Einfuhrgenehmigung f import permit
Einfuhrgeschäft n import trade
Einfuhrhandel m import trade
Einfuhrkredit m import credit
Einfuhrkreditbrief m import letter of credit
Einfuhrliberalisierung f decontrol of imports, liberalization of imports
Einfuhrlizenz f import licence, import permit
Einfuhrschein m import certificate
Einfuhrsteuer f import excise tax (US), import tax
Einfuhrüberschuß m import surplus
Einführungsschreiben n letter of introduction, recommendary letter
Einfuhrverbot n import ban, embargo on imports

Einfuhrwaren f pl imports n pl
Einfuhrzoll m import duty, import tariff
Eingabefehler m (EDV) input error
Eingang m receipt n; *- vorbehalten* due payment provided, subject to collection; *nach* - upon entry
Eingangsdatum n date of receipt
Eingangssortieren n (beim Beleglesen) entry pass
eingebrachtes *Gut* separate estate; *- Kapital* capital brought in
eingefroren adj frozen adj
eingefrorene Devisen blocked foreign exchange
eingefrorener Kredit frozen credit, frozen loan
eingefrorenes Konto frozen account, blocked account
eingehen; *Verbindlichkeiten* - assume obligations; *Verpflichtungen* - contract liabilities
eingehend prüfen examine closely
eingelöste Hypothek closed mortgage
eingelöster Wechsel discharged bill
eingeräumter Kredit credit line, line of credit, credit limit
eingetragen adj inscribed adj, registered adj
eingetragene *Genossenschaft* registered cooperative; *- Handelsgesellschaft* registered company
eingetragener Verein registered society
eingetragenes Kapital registered capital (GB)
eingeweihte Kreise insiders n pl
eingezahltes Kapital paid-in capital, paid-up capital
einhalten v comply with, conform with
Einheit f unit n
Einheitliche Europäische Akte f The Single European Act
Einheitliche Richtlinien und Gebräuche für Dokumentenakkreditive Uniform Customs and Practice for Documentary Credits (UCP)
Einheitsbilanz f unified balance sheet
Einheitsgebühr f standard rate
Einheitshypothek f unified mortgage
Einheitskurs m uniform price
Einheitswährung f standard currency

Einheitswert

Einheitswert *m* (eines Grundstücks) basic value, tax value
einkassierbar *adj* collectible *adj*, collectable *adj*, cashable *adj*, redeemable *adj*
einkassieren *v* cash *v*, encash *v* (GB)
Einkassierung *f* collection *n*, encashment *n*
Einkauf *m* buy *n*, buying *n*, purchase *n*, purchasing *n*
einkaufen *v* buy *v*, purchase *v*
Einkaufsgenossenschaft *f* cooperative buying association
einklagbarer Anspruch right of action
Einkommen *n* income *n*, revenue *n*, earnings *n pl*; *- aus Grundbesitz* property income; *festes -* fixed income, settled income; *steuerpflichtiges -* taxable income; *zurückbehaltenes -* retained income
Einkommensbetrag *m* amount of income
Einkommensstufe *f* income bracket
Einkommensteilung *f* split *n*, splitting *n*
Einkommensteuer *f* individual income tax, income tax
Einkommensteuererklärung *f* income tax return *n*, income tax statement (US)
Einkünfte *f pl* income *n*, revenue *n*, earnings *n pl*; *- aus Kapitalvermögen* investment income, returns *n pl*
Einlage *f* deposit *n*; *bedingte -* deposit in escrow; *befristete -* time deposit, fixed deposit
Einlageheft *n* pass-book *n* (US), bank book, deposit book
Einlagen *f pl* deposited funds, deposits *n pl*; *- der öffentlichen Hand* government deposits (US); *- der Regierung* government deposits (US)
Einlagenabteilung *f* deposit banking division, deposit department
Einlagenbestand *m* total deposits
Einlagenbuch *n* pass-book *n* (US), bank book, deposit book
Einlagengeschäft *n* deposit business
Einlagenkonto *n* deposit ledger (GB), depositors ledger
Einlagenschein *m* certificate a deposit
Einlagensicherungsfonds *m* deposit insurance fund
Einlagenversicherung *f* bank deposit insurance, deposit insurance

Einlagenzertifikat *n* certificate of deposit (CD)
Einlagenzinssatz *m* banker's deposit rate
Einlagerungskredit *m* storage loan, stockpiling credit
Einlagerungswechsel *m* storage bill
einlegen *v* deposit *v*
Einleger *m* depositor *n*, bank depositor
Einlegerkonto *n* deposit account (US)
Einlegerschutz *m* depositor protection
einlösbar *adj* collectible *adj*, collectable *adj*, cashable *adj*, redeemable *adj*; *nicht -* inconvertible *adj*
einlösen *v* (z. B. einen Scheck oder einen Wechsel) honour *v* (GB), honor *v* (US); *- v* redeem *v*; *eine Schuld -* retire a debt; *einen Wechsel -* cash a bill, clear a bill, discharge a bill, draw in a bill, retire a bill, take up a bill, honor a bill, answer a bill of exchange; *in bar -* cash *v*, encash *v* (GB)
Einlösungskurs *m* rate of redemption
Einlösungsstelle *f* paying agent, paying office
einmalig *adj* single *adj*, nonrecurring *adj*, unique *adj*
einmalige Summe lump sum
Einnahmen *f pl* earnings, revenue, receipts *n pl*
Einnahmen-und-Ausgaben-Buch *n* book of receipts and expenditures
Einnahmen-und-Ausgaben-Rechnung *f* bill of receipts and expenditures
Einnahmequelle *f* revenue source
einnehmen *v* receive *v*, earn
einräumen *v* concede *v*, grant (loan)
Einrede *f* plea, demurrer *n*, objection *n*
einreichen *v* lodge *v*; *- v* submit *v*, present *v*
Einreicher *m* presenter *n*, depositor
Einreicherobligo *n* discounter's liability
Einreiseerlaubnis *f* entry permit
einrichten *v* organize *v*; *einen Kredit -* establish a credit
Einrichtung *f* (Gerät) equipment *n*; *- f* institution *n*
Einrichtungskredit *m* installation loan
einschätzen *v* rate *v*; *unter dem Wert -* undervalue *v*, underestimate *v*
Einschätzung *f* rating *n*, appraisal *n*, assessment *n*

60

einschiffen (sich) v embark v
Einschiffung f embarkation n
einschränken v limit, restrict, restrain
Einschränkung f limitation, restriction, reduction n
Einschreibesendung f registered mail
Einschußkonto n margin account (US)
Einschußmarge f initial margin
Einschußzahlung auf Terminkontrakt maintenance margin
einseitige Rechtserklärung deed poll
einsetzen v set up, use, institute v
einsparen v save, economize
Einsparung von Kosten saving costs, cutting down costs
Einsparungen f pl economies n pl; *betriebliche* - business savings; *geschäftliche* - business savings
Einspruch m appeal n; - *erheben* protest v
Einstandspreis m cost n, initial cost, cost price
Einstandswert m cost n, initial cost
einstellen v discontinue v, suspend v
Einstellung f (Beendigung) stoppage n, cessation n; *vorübergehende* - suspension n
Einstufung f (eines Debitors) rating, classification (of a debtor)
Eintastfehler m keying error
Eintastgeschwindigkeit f keying speed
Eintrag m record n; - *in das Hauptbuch* post into the ledger; - *in die Bücher* enter in the books
eintragen v enter, register, record, inscribe
einträglich adj lucrative adj, remunerative adj, profitable adj
Eintragung f entry, registration, recording; - *eines Eigentumsrechts in das Grundbuch* registration of a title to property; - *im Aktionärsregister* registration of stock; - *von Belastungen* registration of charges; - *von Urkunden* registration of deeds
eintragungsfähig adj registrable adj
eintragungspflichtig adj subject to registration
eintreibbar adj collectible adj, collectable adj, cashable adj, redeemable adj, *nicht* - noncollectable adj

eintreiben; *eine Zahlung* - enforce payment
Eintreibung f collection n, encashment n; - *von Schulden* recovery of debts
eintreten; *für jemanden* - intercede for somebody
Einvernehmen n agreement, approval
einvernehmlich adj by agreement
Einverständnis n agreement, approval, consent
Einverständniserklärung f letter of consent
Einwand m demurrer n, objection n; *formaler* - technical objection
einwandern v immigrate v
Einwanderung f immigration n
einwandfrei adj clean adj, flawless adj, correct adj
Einwendungen erheben demur v
einwilligen v agree v
Einwilligung f agreement n
einzahlen v pay in; *voll* - pay up
Einzahler m depositor n, bank depositor
Einzahlung f payment n, inpayment n
Einzahlungsaufforderung f call letter, call to pay up
Einzahlungsbeleg m paying-in slip
Einzahlungsbuch n paying-in book (GB)
Einzahlungskasse f cash inpayment section
Einzahlungsschein m payment slip
Einzahlungsverpflichtung des Aktionärs stockholder's liability
Einzelfirma f sole proprietorship (US), one-man business (GB)
Einzelformular n single-copy form
Einzelhandel m retail n, retail trade
Einzelhandelsfirma f retail firm, retail company
Einzelhandelspreisindex m retail price index
Einzelhändler m retailer n
Einzelheit f detail n
Einzelheiten; *alle* - *einer Sache* ins and outs of a matter
Einzelkaufmann m one-man firm, sole trader
Einzelkredit m individual loan
einzeln adj single adj; - *aufführen* itemize v, specify v

Einzelverkauf m retailing n
Einzelverwahrung f separate custody of securities
Einzelwährung f monometallism n
Einzelwertberichtigung f provision against specific debts
einziehbar adj collectible adj, collectable adj, cashable adj, redeemable adj
einziehen v call in v; ~ v collect v; ~ v (Münzen) demonetize v
Einziehen n collection, cashing n
einziehende Bank collecting bank
Einziehung f collection n, encashment n
Einziehungsauftrag m collection order
Einziehungskosten plt recovery charges
Einziehungsschalter m collection window
Einziehungsspesen plt recovery charges
Einzug m collection n, encashment n; **Wert zum** ~ value for collection
Einzugsermächtigungsverfahren n direct debiting
Einzugsgebühr f collection charge
Einzugsprovision f commission for collecting
Einzugsspesen plt collecting charges, collection charges, collecting commission, collection fee
Einzugswechsel m bill for collection
Einzugsweg m collection procedure
einzulösender Wechsel bill receivable
Eisenbahnanleihe f railway loan
Eisenbahnfrachtbrief m railroad bill of lading
Eisenbahnobligation f railway debenture
Eisenbahnschuldverschreibung f railway bond
Eisenbahntransport m carriage by rail
Eisenbahnwerte m pl (Börse) railroad stocks; **amerikanische** ~ American rails
eiserner Bestand reserve fund
elektronische Bank electronic banking; ~ **Börse** electronic stock exchange; ~ **Datenverarbeitung** (EDV) electronic data processing (EDP); ~ **Kasse** electronic cash terminal; ~ **Rechenanlage** computer; ~ **Zahlkarte** (Geldkarte) electronic purse (prepaid card)

elektronischer Schalter electronic counter; ~ **Zahlungsverkehr** electronic fund transfer (EFT)
elektronisches Geld electronic money; ~ **Übertragungssystem** electronic delivery system
Elektrowerte m pl (Börse) electrical engineering stocks
Embargo n embargo n; **einem** ~ **unterwerfen** embargo v
Emission f issue, offering, going public; ~ **bei Aktienumtausch** wallpaper; ~ **für bestimmte Anleger(gruppen)** targeted issue; ~ **mit existierendem Sekundärmarkt** seasoned issue; ~ **ohne existierenden Sekundärmarkt** unseasoned issue; **eine** ~ **zeichnen** v underwrite an issue; **internationale** ~ going international; **zweigeteilte** ~ two-tranche issue
Emissionsabteilung f issue department
Emissionsanzeige f (informal) tombstone
Emissionsbank f issuing house, investment bank (US)
Emissionsbeteiligung mit Namensnennung im Prospekt »en nom« participation
emissionsfähig adj eligible for issuance
Emissionsgebühren f pl issuance fees
Emissionsgeschäft n issuing business, underwriting business, investment banking (US); **festes Bankangebot an den Emittenten im** ~ bought deal
Emissionshaus n investment bank, issuing house (GB), issuing company
Emissionskonsortium n underwriting syndicate
Emissionskontingentierung f fixing a maximum for new issues
Emissionskredit m credit obtained trough placing a new issue
Emissionskurs m issuing price, issue price, rate of issue
Emissionsmarkt m (security) issue market
Emissionspreis m issue price
Emissionsprospekt m issue prospectus; **vorläufiger** ~ pathfinder prospectus
Emissionssyndikat n underwriting syndicate
Emissionstag m date of issue, day of issue

Emissionsübernahme n underwriting of an issue; *- mit Plazierungsrisikoübernahme* standby agreement; *- ohne Plazierungsrisikoübernahme* best-efforts underwriting
Emissionsvergütung f underwriting commission
Emittent m issuer n, emitter n
emittieren v emit v, issue v
Empfang; den - bestätigen acknowledge receipt
empfangen v receive v
Empfänger m (von Überweisungsgutschriften) payee n; *-* receiver n; *- m* (Bedachter) recipient n
Empfängerbank f payee's bank, recipient bank
Empfängerinstitut n payee's bank
Empfangsbescheinigung f receipt n, acknowledgement of receipt
Empfangsbestätigung f acknowledgement of receipt
Empfangskonnossement n receipt for shipment bill of lading, received bill of lading
Empfehlung; geschäftliche - business reference
empfindlich reagierende Börse sensitive market
Endfälligkeitstilgung f balloon payment
Endkreditnehmer m ultimate borrower
Endlospapierstreifen m continuous paper tape
Endsumme f grand total
Energiewerte m pl energy stocks
Engagement n (Börse) commitment n; *- n* engagement n; **ungedecktes -** open position
engagieren v engage v, invest, commit
engagiertes Kapital locked-up capital
enger Markt narrow market
Enkelgesellschaft f sub-subsidiary
entbinden v dispense v, release, discharge
enteignen v disappropriate v, dispossess v, expropriate v
Enteignung f disappropriation n, dispossession n, expropriation n
enterben v disinherit v
entfernen v remove v

entflechten v deconcentrate v, decartelize v
Entflechtung f deconcentration n
entgegengesetzt adj opposite adj, contrary adj
entgegenkommend adj compliant adj, obliging adj
entgegennehmen v receive v
Entgelt n remuneration n, payment n, compensation n, consideration n
entgeltlich adj for a consideration, against payment
Entkartellisierung f decartelization n
entladen v discharge v
Entladen n discharge n
entlassen v dismiss v
Entlassung f dismissal n
entlasten v relieve, unburden
Entlastung f relieving, reducing the burden
entleihen v borrow v
Entmündigung f incapacitation n
Entnahme f withdrawal n
entnehmen v withdraw v
entschädigen v indemnify v, compensate v, reimburse v
Entschädigende f u. m indemnitor n
Entschädigung f compensation n; *- f* indemnification n, indemnity n
Entschädigungsempfänger m indemnitee n
Entschädigungsgewinn m indemnity benefits
Entschädigungsnehmer m indemnitee n
Entschädigungssumme f damages n pl (compensation); *- bestimmen* assess damages
Entschädigungsvertrag m indemnity contract
Entschädigungsvorteil m indemnity benefits
Entscheidung am grünen Tisch armchair decision
Entscheidungtabelle f decision table
entschulden v clear the debt, (Grundstück) disencumber v (an estate)
Entschuldung f debt clearance, disencumbrance n
entsperren v (Guthaben) deblock v
entsprechen v conform v
entstehen v develop, arise, accrue v

entwerten v depreciate v, cancel
entwerteter Scheck cancelled check
entwertetes Geld depreciated currency; *- Papiergeld* rag money (US)
Entwertung f depreciation n, cancellation
Entwertungsstempel m defacer n
entwickeln v develop v, evolve
Entwicklung f development n
Entwicklungsbank f development bank
Entwicklungshilfebank f development aid bank
Entwicklungsland n developing country, undeveloped country
Entwurf m design n, draft n, outline n
entziehen v withdraw v
erarbeiteter Gewinn earnings n pl
Erbbaurecht n leasehold
Erbberechtigung f right of inheritance, right to succeed, claim to inheritance
Erbe m heir n, inheritor n, successor
erben v inherit v
Erbengemeinschaft f joint heirs, community of heirs
erbfähig adj heritable adj
Erbfähigkeit f ability to inherit
Erbfolge f succession n
Erbfolgerecht n right of succession (GB)
Erbin f female heir, inheritress n
Erblasser m testator n, legator n
Erblasserin f testatrix n
erblich adj hereditary adj, inheritable adj
Erbmasse f estate, assets
Erbnachweis m proof of inheritance
Erbpachtgut n customary freehold
Erbpachtvertrag m building lease
Erbrecht n law of inheritance
Erbschaft f inheritance n, heritage n; *eine - ausschlagen* disclaim an estate; *gemeinsame -* coheritage n
Erbschaftsanspruch m right of inheritance, right to succeed, claim to inheritance
Erbschaftssteuer f inheritance tax (US), death duty (GB), estate duty (GB)
Erbschein m certificate of inheritance
Erbschleicherei f legacy hunting
Erbteilung f estate distribution
Erbzins m rent charge
Erdgaswerte m pl natural gas shares
Erdölaktien f pl oil stocks, oils
Ereignis; *ungewisses -* contingency n

ererbt adj inherited adj
erfahren adj experienced adj
Erfahrung f experience n
Erfassen des richtigen Zeitpunkts timing n
Erfassung f (von Daten) collection n (of data), acquisition n (of data)
Erfolg m success, profit, performance
Erfolgsbilanz f surplus statement
Erfolgshonorar n result fee
Erfolgsrechnung f income statement (US), profit and loss account, earnings statement
erfüllen v fulfill; *Verpflichtungen -* meet commitments
Erfüllung f fulfillment n, performance n
Erfüllungsgarantie f performance bond
Erfüllungsort m place of performance
Erfüllungsrisiko n settlement risk
ergänzen v complement v, supplement
Ergänzung f supplement n, complementing
Ergänzungsabgabe f income tax surcharge
Ergänzungssteuer f supplementary tax
ergeben (sich) (aus) ensue v (from)
Ergebnis n result, profit, income (loss), return, performance
Ergebnis vor Steuern und Zinsen earnings before interests and taxes (EBIT)
Ergebnisabführungsvertrag m profit and loss transfer agreement
Ergebnisübernahmevertrag m profit and loss assumption agreement
erhalten; *als Lohn -* earn v
erhaltene Zahlung payment received
erhältlich adj available adj
Erhebung f (Umfrage) inquiry n, investigation n; *- f* levy n
Erhebungen anstellen make investigations
erhöhen v raise v; *das Grundkapital um ... -* increase the original capital by ...; *im Preis -* mark up
Erhöhung f increase, rise, advance
Erholung f (Börse) rally n (stock exchange); *- f* recovery n
Erinnerungswert m pro-memoria item
erkennen mit credit with
erklären v declare v, explain, state, express
Erklärung f statement n; *eidesstattliche - statutory declaration, affidavit n, sworn

declaration; **garantieähnliche -** patronage letter
Erklärungstag m date of declaration
erkundigen (sich) v inquire v, ask, investigate
Erkundigung f inquiry n, investigation n
erlangen v obtain, read
Erlaß m (Schuld, Strafe) remission n; **- einer geringfügigen Schuld** acceptilation n; **- eines Gesetzes** enactment n
erlauben v permit v, grant v
Erlaubnis f permission n
erledigen v handle v, settle
erledigt adj settled adj
Erledigung f settlement n
erleichtern v ease v
Erleichterung am Geldmarkt easing in money rates
Erlös m proceeds n pl
Erlös-Kosten-Verhältnis n earnings/cost-ratio
erloschen adj expired, statute-barred adj (GB)
erlöschen v run out, lapse, expire v
erloschener Frachtbrief spent bill of lading
ermächtigen v authorize v, empower v
ermächtigt adj authorized adj, empowered adj
ermächtigte Bank authorized bank
Ermächtigung f authorization n
ermäßigen v abate v, lower v
Ermäßigung f abatement n, reduction n; **-** f (Steuer) relief n
Ermessen n discretion n, assessment
Ernannte f u. m appointee n
ernennen v appoint v
Ernennung f appointment n
erneuern v renew v, prolong v
Erneuerung f renewal n
erneuerungsfähig adj renewable adj
Erneuerungsrücklage f reserve for renewals and replacement
Erneuerungsschein m talon n, counterstock n, countertally n, apron n, renewal coupon, counterfoil n
Erntestützungskredit m crop support loan
eröffnen; einen Kredit - establish a credit
Eröffnung f opening n

Eröffnungsbilanz f opening balance, opening balance sheet
Eröffnungskurs m opening price, starting price
ERP-Kredite m pl European Recovery Programme (ERP-loans)
ERP-Sondervermögen n European Recovery Programme
Erpressung f extortion n, blackmail n
Ersatz m replacement n; **- leisten** reimburse v, refund v
Ersatzbeleg m substitute document
erscheinen v appear v
Erscheinungsbild n (eines Unternehmens) corporate identity
erschöpfen v exhaust v
Erschöpfung f exhaustion, depletion n
ersetzen v reimburse v, refund v; **-** v replace, substitute v
ersparen v save v
Ersparnis f saving n
Ersparnisse f pl savings n pl; **- machen** save v
erspartes Geld savings n pl
erstatten v reimburse v
Erstattung f reimbursement n
Erstattungsanspruch m claim to reimbursement
Erstausgabepreis m initial offering price
erste Hypothek first mortgage; **- Kursnotierung** first board
erstehen v buy v, purchase v
ersteigern v purchase at auction
erstellen v prepare v, set up
Ersterwerber m first taker
erstklassig adj (Wertpapiere, Kapitalanlagen) first-class, top quality
erstklassige Inhaberpapiere floaters n pl (GB); **- Kapitalanlagen** high-grade investments; **- Wertpapiere** first-class securities
erstklassiger Wechsel prime bill, first-class paper
erstrangig adj first-class adj, first-rank
erstrangiges Pfandrecht first lien; **- Zurückbehaltungsrecht** first right of retention
erststellige Hypothek first mortgage
erststelliges Hypothekendarlehen first mortgage loan

Ersuchen n request n
Ertrag m income n, revenue n, earnings n pl; **~ m proceeds** n pl; **~ m return** n; **~ abwerfen** yield v; **~ je Aktie** fully diluted earnings per share; **laufender ~** current yield; **monatlicher ~** monthly earning; **risikofreier ~** risk-free return
ertragbringend adj profitable adj
Erträge aus Beteiligungen earnings from investments; **sonstige ~** other income
ertraglos adj profitless adj
ertragloses Kapital dead assets
Erträgnisaufstellung f income statement (US), profit and loss account, earning statement
Ertragsbericht m earnings report
Ertragsbesteuerung f taxation of earnings
Ertragschance f change of making a profit, yield prospect
Ertragsfähigkeit f earning power, earning capacity
Ertragskonto n income account
Ertragskraft f earning power, earning capacity
Ertragslage f earnings situation
Ertragsminderung f decline in earnings
Ertragsrechnung f income statement (US), profit and loss account, earnings statement
Ertragsschätzung f estimate of profits
Ertragsschein m coupon
Ertragsteuer f tax on earnings
Ertragsüberschuß; nicht vorkalkulierter ~ unappropriated income
Ertragswert m capitalized income, earnings value, property value
Ertragszinsen m pl interest received
erübrigen v spare v, save v
erübrigtes Geld spare money
erwählen v elect v
Erwartung f expectation, anticipation n
erweitern v expand v
Erweiterung f expansion n
Erwerb m acquisition n; **auf ~ gerichtet** acquisitive adj; **gutgläubiger ~** bona fide transaction
erwerben v purchase v, buy v; **Beteiligungen ~** secure interests

Erwerber m purchaser, buyer; **gutgläubiger ~** good faith taker, purchaser in good faith
Erwerbsfähigkeit f earning power, earning capacity
Erwerbsgenossenschaft f cooperative association
Erwerbsgesellschaft f trading company, trading corporation
erwerbstüchtig adj acquisitive adj
Erwerbsurkunde f title deed, deed of ownership
Erwerbswert m cost value, acquisition value
Erwerbung f acquisition n, purchase
Erzeuger m manufacturer n, producer n
Erzeugnis n product n
Erziehung f education n, upbringing n, training
erzielen; Gewinne ~ secure profits
erzwingbar adj enforceable adj
eskomptieren v (abzinsen) to discount in advance
Etagenwohnung f apartment n (US)
Etat m budget n
etatmäßig adj budgetary adj
Etatplanung f budgeting n
Euroaktien f pl Euro-equities
Euroanlagen f pl investments on the euro market
Euroanleihe f euro loan, eurobond
Euroanleihen f pl euro loans, eurobonds; **~ in ECU-Währung** ECU-bonds; **~ japanischer Emittenten** (nicht in Yen) sushi bonds; **~ mit einer Zinswiederanlageoption** bunny bonds; **~ mit Währungsoption** indexed currency option note (ICON); **Clearingsystem für ~** Euroclear (CEDEL)
Euroanleihenmarkt m euro bond market
Eurocard f Eurocard
Eurocheque m eurocheque
Euroeinlage f eurodeposit
Eurodevisen f pl euro currencies
Eurodollars m pl eurodollars
Eurogelder n pl euro funds
Eurogeldmarkt m euro money market
Eurokapitalmarkt m euro capital market
Eurokredit m eurocredit (euro credit)

Eurokreditmarkt m eurocredit market
Euromarkt m euromarket (euro market); **kurzfristige Schuldverschreibung am** - Eurocommercial
Eurooption f euro-option
Europäische Bank für Wiederaufbau und Entwicklung f European Bank for Reconstruction and Development (EBRD); **- Fonds für Währungspolitische Entwicklung** m European Regional Development Fund (ERDF); **- Fonds für Währungspolitische Zusammenarbeit** m European Fund for Monetary Co-operation; **- Freihandelsgemeinschaft** f European Free Trade Association (EFTA); **- Gemeinschaft** f (EG) European Community (EC); **- Investitionsbank** f European Investment Bank (EIB)
europäische Option European option (exercise on final exercise date only); **- Rechnungseinheit** European unit of account
Europäische Union f (EU) European Union (EU); **- Währungseinheit** f (EWE) European Currency Unit (ECU)
europäische Währungspolitik European monetary policy
Europäische Währungsschlange f European Currency Snake; **- Währungssystem** n (EWS) European Monetary System (EMS); **- Wirtschaftsgemeinschaft** f (EWG) European Economic Community (EEC), Community of the Six
europäischer Währungskredit European currency loan
Euroscheck m = ec eurocheque
Euroschuldtitel mit kurzer Laufzeit eurocommercial paper (ECP)
Eurowährung f euro currency
Eurowährungseinlagen f pl eurocurrency deposits
Eurowährungsinhaberschuldschein m; **kurzfristiger -** euronote
Eurowährungskredit m eurocurrency loan
Euro-Yen m euroyen
Eurozins m euro market interest rate
Eventualforderung f contingent claim
Eventualverbindlichkeit f contingent liability
Eventualverpflichtung f contingent liability
ewige Rente bond issue without fixed maturity
ex-Anrecht ex-right
ex-Dividende (Aktie) ex-dividend (stock)
ex-Tag ex-date
Exekutive f executive n
Existenzaufbaudarlehen n business set-up loan
Existenzgründer m new start-ups
Exotenfonds m offshore fund
Expansionsfinanzierung f later stage financing, expansion stage financing
expedieren v forward v, dispatch v
Expedition f forwarding, dispatch n
Expertenrat m brain trust
Export m export n, exportation n
Exportabteilung f export department
Exportakkreditiv n export letter of credit
Exportauftrag m export order
Exportbescheinigung f export certificate
Exportbewilligung f export licence, export permit
Exportdevisen f pl export exchange
Exporte m pl exports n pl
Exporteur m exporter n
Exportfeldzug m export drive
Exportfinanzierung f export financing; **revolvierende - auf Basis eines Kaufvertrages** asset-backed trade finance
Exportfinanzierungskredit m export financing credit
Exportfirma f export firm
Exportförderungskredit m export promotion credit
Exporthandel m export trade
Exporthaus n export firm
exportieren v export v
Exportindustrie f export industry
Exportkontingent n export quota
Exportkredit m export credit
Exportkreditversicherung f export credit insurance
Exportquote f export ratio
Exportrisikogarantie f export risk guarantee
Exportsteuer f export tax, tax on exports
Exportüberschuß m export surplus

Export-und-Import-Finanzierung f foreign trade financing
Exportwaren f pl exports n pl
Expreßbrief m special delivery
extra adj extra adj
Extra- (in Zus.) extra adj
Extradividende f bonus n, surplus dividend, superdividend n, special dividend
Extrakt m extract n, excerpt n
Extraprämie f overagio n (GB)
Extraspesen plt extra charges
extreme Kursschwankungen sharp price swings
Exzedentenversicherung f excess insurance
Exzerpt n extract n
exzessive Verschuldung excessive indebtness

F

Fabrik f factory n
Fabrikanlage f plant n
Fabrikant m manufacturer n, producer n
Fabrikarbeiter m industrial worker
Fabrikat n product n, manufacture n, brand n, make n
Fabrikation f fabrication n, manufacture n
Fabrikbesitzer m manufacturer n, producer n
fabrikmäßig hergestellt manufactured adj
Fabrikunfall m industrial accident
Fabrikzeichen n trademark n
fabrizieren v manufacture v, produce v
Fachmann m expert n
Fachschlüssel m (beim Beleglesen) pocket key
Façonwert m good will
Factoring n factoring n, purchase of book debts against a discount; *echtes -* non-recourse factoring; *unechtes -* recourse factoring
fähig adj capable adj, efficient adj, able adj; *- adj* competent adj
Fähigkeit f competence n
fahrbare Zweigstelle mobile subbranch
Fahrgeld n fare n
fahrlässig adj negligent adj, reckless adj
Fahrlässigkeit f negligence n, recklessness n
Faksimile n facsimile n
Faktura f invoice n, commercial invoice
Fakturawert m invoice value
Fakturierabteilung f billing department
fakturieren v invoice v, bill v
Fakturiermaschine f billing machine
Fakturierung f billing n, invoicing
Fakultativklausel f option clause
Fall m case n
fallen v drop v, fall, decline; *im Wert -* depreciate v
Fallen n fall, (Rückgang) fall, drop, decline
fällig adj due adj; *- werden* mature v, fall due, become due
fällige Schuld debt owing; *- Wechsel* notes payable (US), bills payable; *- Zinsen* interest due

Fälligkeit f maturity n; *- eines Wechsels* date of a bill; *vor -* prior to maturity
Fälligkeitsklausel f acceleration clause
Fälligkeitsschlüssel m maturity code
Fälligkeitstag m due date, due day, date of expiration, date of maturity, maturity date, accrual date
Fälligkeitstermin m due date, due day, date of expiration, date of maturity, maturity date, accrual date
falsch adj false adj, wrong; *- verwenden* misapply v
falsche *Banknote* stumer n (GB); *- Münze* base coin (GB)
fälschen v (Geld, Wechsel) counterfeit v, falsify v, forge v; *eine Bilanz -* fake a balance sheet
Fälscher m forger n, counterfeiter n, faker n, falsificator n
Falschgeld n bad money, counterfeit money
Falschmünzen f pl counterfeit coins
Falschmünzer m counterfeiter n, falsifier n
Falschmünzerei f counterfeiting n
Fälschung f counterfeit n, fake n, falsification n, forgery n
Falsifikat n counterfeit n, fake n, falsification an, forgery n
Familienkonsortium n consortium of families
Familienstiftung f private trust
Familienunternehmen n family company
fauler Wechsel query bill
Faustpfand n pawn n, pledge n
Faustpfandkredit m loan against pledge
Favoriten m pl seasoned securities
FAZ- (Frankfurter Allgemeine Zeitung-) Aktienindex m FAZ-stock-index
Fazilität f facility n
federführend adj leading adj, responsible for centralized control
Federführer m syndicate leader, lead manager
Federführung f lead management
Fehlbetrag m deficit n
Fehldisposition f wrong planning, bad arrangement

fehlen

fehlen v be missing, be absent
Fehler m fault n, mistake n, error n
fehlerfrei adj clean adj, flawless adj, correct adj
fehlerhaft adj false adj, faulty adj
fehlerhaftes Konnossement unclean bill of lading
Fehlerhäufigkeit f error frequency
Fehlerkorrektur f error correction
Fehlerquelle f source of error
Fehlersuchprogramm n diagnostic programme
Fehlerwahrscheinlichkeit f error probability
Fehlinvestition f misdirected investment, unprofitable investment
Fehlschlag m failure n
Fehlspekulation f wrong speculation
feilschen v bargain v
Feilscher m bargainer n, haggler n
Feingehalt m fineness n
Feingold n pure gold, standard gold
Feinsortierung f (beim Beleglesen) fine sort
Feriensparkonto n (ein Sparkonto, das angelegt wird, um die Kosten für einen Urlaub aufzubringen) vacation club account
Fernbuchung f remote entry
Fernscheck m out-of-town check
Fernschreiben n telex n
Fernschreiber m teleprinter n, teletypewriter n
fernschriftlich by teleprinter, by telex
Fernverarbeitung f remote processing, teleprocessing n
Fertigstellungsgarantie f completion guarantee, completion guaranty (US)
Fertigung f fabrication n, manufacture n, production n
Fertigungsprogramm n range of products
fest adj firm adj; *- angestellt* salaried adj
Festangebot n binding offer, firm offer
feste Anlage abzüglich vorgenommener Abschreibungen net plant, net property; *- Anlagen* gross plant, gross property, property assets; *- Ausgaben* fixed charges; *- Börse* firm market, strong market; *- Schuld* fixed debt

fester Termin fixed term; *- Umrechnungskurs* direct exchange; *- Verkauf* firm sale; *- Vorschuß* fixed advance; *- Wechselkurs* fixed exchange rate; *- werden* stiffen v, harden v
festes Einkommen fixed income, settled income; *- Gehalt beziehend* salaried adj; *- Verkaufsangebot* firm offer
Festgeld n time deposit
Festgeldkonto n deposit account (US)
Festgeldverlängerung f deposit roll-over
festgesetzt adj stipulated adj, fixed adj
festgesetzte Dividende declared dividend
festgesetztes Kapital declared capital
festgestellte Schuld liquidated debt
Festhypothek f fixed-date mortgage
festigen (sich) (Börse) strengthen v
Festigung f stabilization n; *- der Börse* recovery n
Festlandbörse f continental bourse
festlegen; Kapital ~ lock up capital
Festlegung f locking up (e.g. of capital); *- amtlicher Kurse* (feststellen) fixing
Festpreis m fixed price
festsetzen v (vereinbaren) stipulate v, fix, establish
Festsetzung f stipulation n, fixing, determination
feststellen v ascertain v
Feststellungsurteil n decree of constitution
Festübernahme f firm underwriting, direct underwriting; *- von Wertpapieren* firm commitment (underwriting)
festverzinslich adj fixed interest bearing
festverzinsliche Anleihe mit indexgekoppeltem Rückzahlungsbetrag condor fund; *- Obligationen* active bonds (GB); *- USD-Anleihe* dollar straights; *- Wertpapiere* fixed interest bearing securities, fixed income securities, fixed interest issues
festverzinsliches Wertpapier fixed-interest security
Festzinshypothek f mortgage with fixed interest
Festzinssatzemission f fixed rate deal
Feuerversicherung f fire insurance
Feuerversicherungsgesellschaft f fire underwriters

Feuerwehrfonds *m* (informal) deposit insurance fund
FIBOR *m* = **Frankfurter Interbanken-Angebotszinssatz** Frankfurt Interbank Offered Rate
Fiduziar *m* trustee *n*
fiduziarisch *adj* fiduciary *adj*
fiduziarisches Rechtsgeschäft trust transaction
fiktiv *adj* fictitious *adj*
fiktive Dividende sham dividend; **- Gebote** rigged bids
Filialbank *f* branch bank
Filialbanksystem *n* branch banking, chain banking system
Filialbankwesen *n* chain banking, group banking, branch banking activities
Filiale *f* branch *n*, branch office
Filialkonto *n* agency account, branch account
Filialleiter *m* branch manager
filiallos *adj* branchless
Filialnetz *n* network of branch offices, branch network
Finanzier *m* financier *n*
Finanzabteilung *f* finance department, finance division
Finanzamt *n* inland revenue office (GB), tax office (US)
Finanzanalyse *f* financial analysis
Finanzanlagen *f pl* financial investments
Finanzanlagevermögen *n* financial assets
Finanzausschuß *m* financial committee
Finanzbuchhaltung *f* financial accounting (department)
Finanzdienste *m pl* financial services; **- von banknahen Unternehmen** near-bank banking; **- von Nichtbanken** / non-bank banking
Finanzdisponent *m* treasurer *n*
Finanzen *plt* finances *n*
Finanzerträge *m pl* financial income
Finanzgeschäfte *n pl* financial operations
Finanzgesellschaft *f* finance company; **bankähnliche -** near-bank (US); **bankfremde -** non-bank
Finanzhaushalt; gesellschaftlicher - corporate housekeeping activities
finanziell *adj* financial *adj*

finanzielle Haftung financial responsibility; **- Lage** financial condition, financial situation; **- Schwierigkeiten** financial difficulties, involvement *n*; **- Unterlagen** financial records; **- Unterstützung** financial backing
finanzieller Stand financial rating; **- Zusammenbruch** financial failure
finanzieren *v* finance *v*
Finanzierung *f* financing *n*; **- durch Abtretung der Debitoren** accounts receivable financing; **- mit eingeschränktem Rückgriff** limited recourse financing
Finanzierungsbedarf *m* financing needs
finanzierungsfähig capable of being financed
Finanzierungsform *f* form of financing
Finanzierungsgeschäft *n* financing business
Finanzierungsgesellschaft *f* commercial finance company, financing company; **- für Industriebedarf** industrial trust (US)
Finanzierungsinstitut *n* financial house, financial institution
Finanzierungskosten *plt* cost of finance, cost of financing, finance charge
Finanzierungslast *f* burden of financing
Finanzierungsmethoden *f pl* financing methods
Finanzierungsmittel *n pl* finance, financing instruments
Finanzierungsplan *m* financial plan, financial arrangement
Finanzierungsschätze *m pl* finance notes
Finanzierungstechnik *f* financial engineering
Finanzierungsunterlagen *f pl* financing documents
Finanzierungswechsel *m* finance bill
Finanzinnovationen *f pl* financial innovations derivative, financial products
Finanzjahr *n* financial year (GB), fiscal year, fiscal accounting year
Finanzkontrolle *f* financial control
Finanzkredit *m* financial loan
Finanzkreise *m pl* financial quarters
Finanzlage *f* financial condition, financial situation, financial position

Finanzleistungen

Finanzleistungen f pl financial services
Finanzmakler m finance broker
Finanzmann m financier n
Finanzmarkt m capital market
Finanzmärkte m pl financial markets
Finanzministerium n Board of the Exchequer (GB), Treasury Board (GB), Treasury Department (US)
Finanzplanung f budgetary accounting
Finanzprodukte n pl financial products; ***derivative*** - derivative financial products
Finanzraum m financial area; ***integrierter*** - integrated financial area
finanzschwach adj financially weak
finanzstark adj financially strong
Finanzstudie f financial study
Finanzstudienabteilung f analysis department
Finanzsupermarkt m financial supermarket
Finanzswap m financial swap
finanztechnisch adj financial adj
Finanzterminkontrakte m pl financial futures
Finanzvolumen n financing limit
Finanzwechsel m finance bill
Finanzwelt f financial world; ***Senkrechtstarter in der*** - whizz kid
Finanzwesen n finance n; ***öffentliches*** - public finance; ***staatliches*** - public finance
Finanzwirtschaft f finance n
Finanzzentrum n financial centre
fingieren v simulate v, feign v
fingiert adj fictitious adj
Finnmark f Finnish Markka
Firma f firm n, enterprise n, company n, concern n, business
Firmenbezeichnung f trade name, firm name
Firmenbilanz f corporate statement, company statement
Firmenforderung f debt owed to the firm
Firmengeschäft n (der Banken) corporate banking
Firmengründung f company foundation
Firmenhaftung f corporate liability
Firmeninventar n business inventory

Firmenkauf; *fremdfinanzierter* - leveraged corporate acquisition
Firmenkredit m business loan
Firmenkunde m business customer, corporate customer
Firmenkundengeschäft n corporate banking, business with corporate customers
Firmenname m trade name, firm name
Firmenschuld f debt owed by the firm
Firmenwert m goodwill n
Firmierung f business style
Fiskus m financial authorities
Fixauftrag m firm order
fixe Kosten fixed costs, overhead expenses
fixen v sell short, short seller, bear v, sell a bear, speculate on a fall
Fixer m short n (US), bear seller, bear n
fixer Teil (bei Bestandssätzen) fixed portion
flau adj dull n, slack adj, stagnant adj, flat adj; - ***sein*** stagnate v
flaue Börse dull market, stale market
flauer Markt dull market, stale market
Flaute f dullness n
flexible Wechselkurse floating exchange rates, freely fluctuating exchange rates
floaten v to float (the exchange rate)
Floaten n floating n; ***sauberes*** - clean floating
Floater m floater, floating rate note (FRN); - ***mit Zinsuntergrenze*** drop lock bond; ***umgekehrter*** - reverse floater
Floatgewinn m float profit
Floating n floating n
Fluchtgelder n pl hot money
Flughafen m airport n
Fluglinie f airline n
Flugpost f airmail n
Flugzeug n aircraft n
Flugzeughypothek f aircraft mortgage
Flugzeugwerte m pl (Börse) aircrafts n pl (stock exchange)
flüssig adj fluid adj, liquid adj; - ***machen*** realize v, convert into cash; ***nicht*** - illiquid; - ***sein*** hold liquid funds
flüssige Aktiva floating assets, current assets, circulating assets, current funds, current receivables, fluid assets (US), liquid assets, revolving assets; - ***Mittel*** liquid

72

reserves, liquid resources; *- Reserven* liquid reserves, liquid resources
flüssiges Kapital active capital
Flüssigmachung f realization n
Folgearbeit f (z. B. im Anschluß an Verbuchungsprogramme) subsequent processing
folgend adj subsequent adj, following adj
folgern v conclude v
Fonds m fund n; *- für allgemeine Bankrisiken* fund for general banking risks; *Auflegungsdatum eines -* launch date; *Ausgabeaufschlag eines -* front-end load of a fund; *geschlossener -* closed fund; *offener -* open-end fund, mutual fund (US); *thesaurierender -* cumulative fund
Fondsanteil m share, fund unit, investment fund share, mutual fund share (US)
Fondsgesellschaft f investment company
Fondshändler m jobber n, stockjobber n
Fondsmakler m bond broker (US)
Fondsvermögen n (Reinvermögen) net assets of a fund, net asset value
Förderer m promoter n; - m sponsor n
fordern v demand v, call for, ask, claim, request
fördern; *die Ausfuhr -* subsidize exports
Förderprogramm n support programme
Forderung f demand n, request n, claim, loan, debt, call; *bevorrechtigte -* preferential debt, preferred debt, privileged debt, secured debt; *eine - eintreiben* collect a claim; *getilgte -* debt paid
Forderungen; *- abkaufen* purchase debts; *- an Kreditinstitute* claims on banks; *- an Kunden* claims on customers; *ausstehende -* active debts, receivables, n pl (US), accounts receivable; *bedingte -* contingent receivables; *dubiose -* doubtful debts, notes and accounts (US); *täglich fällige -* callable receivables; *ungewisse -* contingent receivables
Forderungsabtretung f assignment of receivables, assignment of claim, assignment of debt
Forderungsberechtigte f u. m creditor n, debtee n, obligee n; - m rightful claimant, beneficiary n

Forderungseinziehung f collection of debts
Forderungsgläubige f u. m creditor n
Forderungsinhaber; gutgläubiger - bona fide creditor
Forderungspfändung f attachment of debts
Forderungsübernehmer m assignee n, cessionary n, transferee n
Forderungsverkauf m (Factoring) factoring
Forfaitierung f forfaiting, non-recourse financing
formal adj formal adj (e.g. difference)
formaler Einwand technical objection; *- Gegenwert* nominal consideration
Formalversprechen n convenant n
formell adj formal adj (e.g. person, validity)
formelles Recht law adjective
formlos adj informal adj
Formlosigkeit f informality n
Formular n form n, blank n
Formularbahn f form feeding track
Formulargestaltung f forms lay-out
Formularsatz m set of forms
Forschungsabteilung f research department
fortlaufend adj consecutive adj; *- notiert* bunched adj (US); *- numeriert* consecutively numbered
Fortschreibung f updating, current adjustment
Fortsetzung f continuation n
Fracht f freight n; *- berechnen* charge freight; *- gegen Nachnahme* freight forward; *- wird eingezogen* freight collect
Frachtberechnungsgrundlage f rate basis
Frachtbrief m (Bahn) bill of carriage; - m bill of consignment, bill of freight, consignment note, freight bill, letter of conveyance; - m bill of lading (US); *erloschener -* expired bill of lading
frachtfrei carriage paid (GB), freight paid
Frachtführer m carrier n
Frachtgut n cargo n
Frachtkonto n carriage account
Frachtkosten plt freightage n, carriage; *- per Nachnahme* carriage forward (GB)

Frachtpapiere

Frachtpapiere *n pl* forwarding documents
Frachtpolice *f* cargo policy
Frachtschiff *n* cargo ship
Frachttarif *m* freight rates
Frachtversicherung *f* cargo insurance
Frachtvertrag *m* charter-party *n*, contract of carriage
Franchise *f* franchise *n*
Franken *m* (Schweizer F.) Swiss Franc (Swiss currency unit)
Frankfurter Interbanken-Angebotszinssatz *m* = **FIBOR** Frankfurt Interbank Offered Rate; **- Wertpapierbörse** *f* Frankfurt Stock Exchange
franko *adv* carriage paid (GB), freight paid
Französische Franken *m* French Franc
frei *adj* free *adj*; **- an Bord** free on board (f.o.b.); **- bis zum Schiff** free alongside ship (f.a.s.)
Freibetrag *m* (tax) allowance, exemption *n*
Freibörse *f* curb *n*, curb exchange, curb market, kerb market, inofficial market, unofficial market (GB)
freie Aktiva assets at disposal; **- Ersparnisse** voluntary savings; **- Rücklage** voluntary reserve; **- Wechselkurse** floating exchange rates, freely fluctuating exchange rates
freier Grundbesitz freehold *n* (GB); **- Grundbesitzer** freeholder *n*; **- Kapitalverkehr** free flow of capital; **- Makler** non-member broker, outside broker; **- Markt** free market, open market
freies Grundeigentum freehold *n* (GB); **- Kapital** idle money
Freigabe *f* release *n*; **- des Wechselkurses** (einer Währung) floating *n* (of a currency)
freigeben; ein Guthaben - unfreeze funds, release funds
Freigrenze *f* exemption limit
Freihandelszone *f* free trade area
freihändig *adv* freely, in the open market, privately *adv*, by private contract
freistellen *v* release *v*, exempt
Freiverkehr *m* unofficial market, over-the-counter market (OTC); **im - gehandelte Wertpapiere** curb stocks (US)

Freiverkehrsbörse *f* curb *n*, curb exchange, curb market, kerb market, inofficial market, unofficial market (GB)
Freiverkehrshandel *m* dealings in the over-the-counter market
Freiverkehrsmakler *m* curb broker, curbstone broker, unofficial dealings broker
Freiverkehrsmarkt *m* curb *n*, curb exchange, curb market, kerb market, inofficial market, unofficial market (GB)
Freiverkehrswerte *m pl* unlisted securities
Freiwerden von Krediten release of credits
freiwillig *adj* voluntary *adj*
freiwillige Reserven voluntary reserves
Freizeichnungsklausel *f* non-liability clause
Fremdbesitz *m* third-party property
Fremde *f u. m* alien *n*, foreigner *n*
fremde Mittel deposits and borrowed funds
fremder Streubesitz widely distributed outside holdings
fremdes Geld outside money, borrowed money
fremdfinanzieren *v* finance from outside sources
Fremdfinanzierung *f* external financing, financing with outside capital
Fremdkapital *n* borrowed capital, outside capital, external funds
Fremdwährung *f* foreign currency, foreign exchange (US), foreign exchanges (GB)
Fremdwährungsanleihe *f* foreign currency bond (loan)
Fremdwährungskonto *n* foreign currency account
Fremdwährungsschuld *f* foreign currency debt
freundliche Stimmung (Börse) cheerful tone
Frisieren *n* (Bilanz) window-dressing
frisieren; eine Bilanz - cook a balance sheet
frisierte Bücher cooked accounts
Frist *f* limited period
Fristablauf *m* deadline *n*, expiry of a term
fristgemäße Rückzahlung repayment on due date
fristgerecht within the prescribed period
Fristtage *m pl* days of grace, days of respite

früher adj prior adj, former adj
Fuder n (Wein) tun n
führen v manage v, lead, keep
führend adj leading adj, prominent adj; ~ adj managerial adj
führende Bank leading bank; **~ Werte an der Börse** market leaders
Führer m manual n, guide book
Führungskräfte f pl executives n pl
Führungsprovision f lead management fee; **Anteil der Konsorten an der ~** participating fee
Fundamentalanalyse f basic analysis
fundieren v fund v, substantiate
fundiert adj funded adj
fundierte Schuld funded debt, bonded debt
fundiertes; gut ~ Unternehmen well-established enterprise
Fünfcentstück n nickel n (US)
fungibel adj fungible adj, interchangeable adj

fungieren v act v
Fürsorgefonds m provident fund
Fusion f merger; **Absicherungsmaßnahmen einer ~** lock up agreement (US); **anorganische ~** conglomerate merger; **horizontale ~** horizontal merger; **vertikale ~** vertical merger
fusionieren v merge v, fuse v
Fusionsabkommen n merger agreement, agreement of consolidation
Fusionsbilanz f consolidated balance sheet
Fusionsvertrag m agreement of consolidation, deed of merger, merger agreement
Futures plt (Termingeschäfte) futures; **~ auf US-Schatzanleihen** Treasury bonds-futures; **~ auf US-Schatzwechsel** Treasury bills-futures
Futures-Handel m futures trading
Futures-Kaufposition f long futures position
Futures-Verkaufsposition f short futures position

G

gangbar adj practicable adj, workable adj
gängige Aktie active stock; **~ Münze** common coin, current coin
Garant m warrantor n
Garantie f guarantee n (GB); guaranty n (US); **~ f** surety n, suretyship n; **~ auf Schadloshaltung** indemnity bond; **~ leisten** furnish a guarantee; **~ übernehmen** furnish a guarantee; **persönliche ~** personal bond
Garantiebrief m letter of guarantee
Garantiefonds m guarantee fund
Garantiefondszeichner m underwriter n
Garantiegeschäft n guarantee transactions
Garantiehinterlegung f guarantee deposit
Garantiekapital n guarantee funds, capital serving as a safeguard for depositors
Garantieklausel f clause of warranty
Garantiekonto n assigned account
Garantiemittel n pl guarantee funds
Garantienehmer m guarantee
garantieren v guarantee v, warrant v
garantierte Anleihe guaranteed bond
garantierter Kreditbrief guaranteed letter of credit
garantiertes Akkreditiv guaranteed letter of credit
Garantieschein m certificate of guarantee, guarantee coupon
Garantieschuldner m guarantor, drawer, indorser
Garantieträger m guarantor
Garantieübernahme f acceptance of a guarantee
Garantieverpflichtung f guarantee commitment
Garantieversicherung f commercial insurance
Garantievertrag m guarantee agreement, contract of guarantee
Gebäude abschätzen assess a building
Gebäudekonto n building account
Gebäudeversicherung f house insurance
Gebäudeverwaltung f building management

geben v (Geldhandel) sell, lend
Gebietsfremde f u. m non-resident
geborgt adj borrowed adj
Gebot n bid n; **ein ~ machen** bid v, offer v
gebotener Preis bid price
Gebrauch machen von avail oneself of, make use of
gebräuchlich adj customary adj
gebraucht adj second-hand adj, used adj
Gebühr f fee n, charge
Gebühren f pl charges n pl; **~ und Abgaben** rates and taxes
gebührende Sorgfalt due diligence, due attention
Gebührenerhöhung f increase in charges, fee increase
Gebührenermäßigung f abatement in fees, fee reduction
gebührenfrei free of charge, clear of charges
gebührenpflichtig adj taxable adj
Gebührenrechnung f note of charges
Gebührenverzeichnis n fee schedule
Gebührenvorschuß m retaining fee
Gebührenzuschlag m additional fee
gebundener Preis controlled price
gechartert adj chartered adj
gechartertes Schiff chartered ship
gedecktes Darlehen secured loan
gedrückt adj depressed adj, gloomy adj
gedrückter Markt heavy market
gefällig sein accommodate v, oblige v
Gefälligkeitsakzept n accommodation acceptance
Gefälligkeitsaussteller m accommodation maker
Gefälligkeitsindossament n accommodation endorsement
Gefälligkeitspapier n accommodation paper
Gefälligkeittratte f accommodation draft
Gefälligkeitswechsel m accommodation bill, accommodation note
gefälscht adj forged, counterfeit

gefälschte *Überweisung* forged transfer; *- Unterschrift* fiction n; *- Urkunde* fictitious instrument
gefälschter Scheck forged check, forged cheque (GB)
geforderter Preis (Börse) asked *adj*
gefragt *adj* in demand
Gegenakkreditiv n back-to-back credit (US), countervailing credit, dos-a-dos accreditif (US)
Gegenangebot n counter bid, counter offer
Gegenauftrag m counterorder n
Gegenbuchung f cross entry
Gegenbürgschaft f countersecurity n, backbond n, counterbond n
Gegendeckung f counterremittance n
Gegendienste erweisen (sich) reciprocate v
Gegenforderung f counterclaim n; *- f* (Aufrechnung) set-off, offset n
Gegengebot n counteroffer n
Gegengeschäft n countertransaction, countertrade
Gegengewicht n counterbalance n
Gegenkonto n contra account, counter account, control account
Gegenkredit m reciprocal credit
Gegenofferte f counteroffer n
Gegenorder f counterorder n
Gegenpartei f counterparty n
Gegenposten m contra item
Gegenrechnung f counterclaim n; **in** *- stellen* set-off, take as a set-off
Gegensaldo m counterbalance n
gegenseitig *adj* reciprocal *adj*
gegenseitige *Bankguthaben* interbank deposits; *- Bankverpflichtungen* interbank balances; *- Haftung* cross liability
gegenseitiger Vertrag reciprocal contract
gegenseitiges Testament mutual testament, mutual will, double will
Gegenseitigkeit; *Versicherungsverein auf* - benefit association, mutual insurance association, benefit society, beneficiary association, benefit club
Gegenseitigkeitsprinzip n reciprocity n
Gegenstand m article n, item n, commodity n; *- m* object n
Gegenübernahmeangebot n reverse bidding

Gegenverkauf m countersale n
Gegenwechsel m cross bill, counterbill n
Gegenwert m countervalue n, equivalent n
gegenzeichnen v countersign v
Gegenzeichner m countersigner n
Gegenzeichnung f countersignature n
Gehalt n salary, pay, earnings
Gehaltsempfänger m payroller n
Gehaltskonto n salary account
Gehaltskredit m personal loan
Gehaltsliste f payroll n
Gehaltspfändung f attachment of earnings
Gehaltsvorschuß m advance of salary
gehandelt (Börse) traded, listed
Geheimschrift f code n
Gehilfe m assistant n
geisteskrank *adj* insane *adj*, mentally deranged
Geisteskrankheit f insanity n
gekauft *adj* bought *adj*
gekreuzter Scheck check only for account, crossed check
gekündigt *adj* called *adj*
gekürzt *adj* condensed *adj*, shortened *adj*, abbreviated *adj*
Geländeerschließung f land development
Geld n (Börse) buyers n pl (stock exchange), money n; *- n* money n, (Bargeld) cash; *- auftreiben* raise money, scare up money; *- anzahlen* v pay money down; *- ausleihen* put out money, accommodate with money; *- schöpfen* create money; *- von der Bank abheben* draw out money from the bank; *- vorstrecken* advance money; *bares -* ready money; *billiges -* cheap money, easy money; *Brief und -* bills and money; *entwertetes -* depreciated currency; *erübrigtes -* spare money; *geliehenes -* borrowed money; *täglich fälliges -* call money, money at call, day-to-day money, demand money; *teures -* close money, dear money; *übriges -* spare cash; *zu - machen* cash v, encash v (GB)
Geld- (in Zus.) monetary *adj*
Geldabfluß m drain of money
Geldanlage f investment n
Geldanspannung f stress of money

Geldausgabeautomat *m* cash dispenser, bancomat, contomat, automatic teller machine (ATM)
Geldautomatenkarte *f* cash-card
Geldbestand; *gesamter* - monetary stock (US), money holdings
Geldbetrag *m* sum *n*, amount of money
Geldbewilligung *f* allocation of funds
Geldbrief *m* cash letter
Gelddisponent *m* money manager
Gelddisposition *f* monetary arrangements
Gelddispositionsabteilung *f* money dealings department
Geldeinheit *f* monetary unit
Geldempfänger *m* payee
Geldentwertung *f* inflation *n*
Gelder; *beim Treuhänder hinterlegte* - escrow funds; *durchlaufende* - cash in transit; *öffentliche* - public funds, public money; *vagabundierende* - erring funds; *verfügbare* - disposable funds
Geldfälscher *m* counterfeiter *n*
Geldflüssigkeit *f* liquidity *n*
Geldfülle *f* abundance of money
Geldgeber *m* financier *n*
Geldhandel *m* money dealings
Geldhändler *m* money jobber
Geldinstitut *n* financial house, financial institution
Geldkarte *f* prepaid card (electronic purse)
Geldkasse *f* till *n*, cash register
Geldkassette *f* cash box
Geldknappheit *f* lack of money, tightness of money; *zeitweilige* - *am Geldmarkt* money pinch
Geldkurs *m* buying rate, banker's buying rate
geldlich *adj* monetary *adj*
Geldmakler *m* money broker; - *für die Vermittlung von Personalkrediten* personal loan broker (US)
Geldmangel *m* lack of funds, impecuniosity *n*, destitution *n*
Geldmarkt *m* cash market, money market
Geldmarktanlage *f* investment on the money market
Geldmarktfonds *m* money-market fund
Geldmarktgeschäft *n* money market business

Geldmarktkonto; *verzinsliches - für öffentliche Stellen* super new account (US)
Geldmarktpapier *n* money market paper, certificate of deposit (CD)
Geldmarktpapiere *n pl* money market securities
Geldmarktsätze *m pl* market rates of interest (US)
Geldmenge *f* money supply
Geldmittel *n pl* means *n pl*; - *auftreiben* raise funds
Geldpolitik *f* monetary policy
Geldrolle *f* money parcel
Geldsatz *m* money rate
Geldschöpfung *f* creation of money
Geldschrank *m* safe *n*
Geldsender *m* remitter *n*
Geldsendung *f* cash remittance
Geldsorten *f pl* notes and coins
Geldstelle *f* cashiers department, money desk
Geldstrafe *f* fine *n*, mulct *n*; *eine* - *verhängen* fine *v*
Geldstück *n* coin *n*
Geldsumme *f* amount of money
Geldsystem *n* monetary system
Geldtheorie *f* monetary theory, theory of money
Geldüberweisung *f* money transfer; *telegrafische* - telegraphic money order, cable transfer
Geldumlauf *m* circulation of money, flux of money
Geld-und-Brief-Kurs *m* bid and asked quotations
Geldverkehr *m* circulation of money
Geldverlegenheit; *in* - *sein* be tight, be pressed for money
Geldverleiher *m* money lender
Geldvermögen *n* financial assets, monetary wealth
Geldversorgung *f* money supply
Geldvolumen; *rechnerisches* - statistical volume of money
Geldwäscherei *f* money-laundering
Geldwechselgeschäft *n* money exchange business
Geldwechsler *m* money dealer
Geldwert *m* monetary value

Geldwerttheorie f commodity theory of money
Geldwertverschlechterung f decline in money value, inflation
Geldwesen n money and finance n, monetary system
Geldzuweisung f appropriation of funds, allowance in money
Gelegenheitskauf m bargain n
gelerntes Personal skilled personnel
geliehen adj borrowed adj
geliehenes Geld borrowed money
Gemeinde f community n
Gemeindedarlehen n communal loan
Gemeindefinanzen plt local finances
Gemeindesteuer f local tax
gemeindlich adj communal adj
Gemeineigentum; Überführung in - socialization n, communization n
Gemeinkosten plt overhead n, overheads n pl; **verrechnete -** absorbed expenses
gemeinnützige Gesellschaft nonprofit corporation
gemeinsame Erbschaft coheritage n, coparcenary n, coparceny n
Gemeinsamer Markt m Common Market
gemeinsames Konto joint account
gemeinschaftliches Kontokorrentkonto joint current account
Gemeinschaftsdepot n joint deposit, joint custody
Gemeinschaftseigentum n collective ownership
Gemeinschaftsfinanzierung f joint financing
Gemeinschaftskonto n community account, joint account (GB)
Gemeinschaftsvertrag m joint contract
Gemeinschaftswerbung f joint advertisement
Gemeinschuldner m common debtor
gemeinwirtschaftliches Unternehmen public company (GB)
Gemeinwirtschaftsbanken f pl social economy banks
gemischte Anlagefonds m pl mixed investment trusts
genau adj exact adj, accurate
genehmigen v authorize, approve, permit
genehmigt adj approved adj, authorized adj

genehmigtes Kapital authorized capital (GB), authorized stock (US)
Genehmigung f approval n; - f concession n
General- (in Zus.) blanket adj, general adj
Generalbevollmächtigte f u. m (executive) manager, chief
Generaldirektor m general manager
Generalklausel f blanket clause
Generalkonsul m consul general
Generalkonsulat n consulate general
Generalpolice f blank policy, blanket policy
Generalunkosten plt overhead n, overheads n pl
Generalversammlung f general assembly, general meeting
Generalvollmacht f unlimited power of attorney; **jemanden mit - ausstatten** furnish a person with full power
Genosse m associate n
Genossenschaft f cooperative n
genossenschaftliches Bankwesen cooperative banking; **- Kreditinstitut** cooperative bank
Genossenschaftsanteile m pl shares in a cooperative society
Genossenschaftsbank f bank for cooperatives (US)
Genossenschaftskapital n cooperative stock
Genußrechtskapital n profit-participation certificate
Genußschein m profit-sharing certificate, dividend-right certificate, participation certificate
geparkte Gelder parked funds, funds temporarily invested
gepfändete Waren distrained goods
geprüfte Bilanz audited balance sheet
gerafft adj condensed adj, shortened adj, abbreviated adj
gerichtlich anerkannte Schuld judg(e)ment debt; **- anerkannter Gläubiger** judg(e)ment creditor, execution creditor
gerichtliche Testamentsbestätigung und Erbscheinerteilung probate n
Gerichtsbeschluß m court order
Gerichtsstand m place of jurisdiction, venue
Gerichtsverfahren n court procedure

Gerichtsverhandlung

Gerichtsverhandlung f trial
Gerichtsvollzieher m bailiff n (law)
geringfügiger Kursrückgang shading n
geringverzinslich adj low-interest
Gesamt- (in Zus.) blanket adj, general adj
Gesamtabrechnung f receipt in full
Gesamtbank f entire bank
Gesamtbetrag m total n, total amount
Gesamtbilanz f combined balance sheet
Gesamtbürgschaft f joint surety
Gesamtdauer f total life
Gesamteigentum n joint property
Gesamteinkommen n gross earnings
Gesamteinnahmen f pl total receipts
Gesamtengagement n total commitment
Gesamtergebnis n overall result
Gesamtgläubiger m general creditor
Gesamtgrundpfandrecht n multiple lien on property
Gesamthaftung f joint and several liability
Gesamthandeigentum n collectively owned property
Gesamthandgläubiger m collective creditor
Gesamthandschuldner m joint debtor
Gesamtheit f totality, entirety
Gesamthypothek f blanket mortgage, general mortgage, floating mortgage, consolidated mortgage (US); (mit Mobiliar) package mortgage
Gesamtkapital n total capital
Gesamtkosten plt all-in costs, total costs
Gesamtkredit m aggregate loan facility
Gesamtliquidität f overall liquidity
Gesamtpfandrecht n multiple lien on property
Gesamtpolice f joint policy
Gesamtquittung f receipt in full
Gesamtrendite f compound yield
Gesamtschuld f collective liability, community debt
gesamtschuldnerisch adj joint and several
gesamtschuldnerische Bürgschaft joint and several guarantee
Gesamtschuldnerschaft f joint and several liabilities
Gesamtsumme f total n, total amount
Gesamtwert m total value; **~ einer öffentlichen Anleihe** omnium n (GB)

Geschäft n business, trade, deal, bargain; **ein ~ aufgeben** close down business, retire from business; **ein ~ wiederaufnehmen** reopen business; **ein ~ wiedereröffnen** reopen business; **tägliches ~** daily business
Geschäfte in verschiedenen Effekten spreading operations (GB); **gewagte ~ machen** speculate v, gamble v, job v; **laufende ~** current business
Geschäftemacherei f racket n (US), racketeering n
geschäftliche Besprechung business conference; **~ Einsparungen** business savings; **~ Empfehlungen** business reference; **~ Referenz** business reference; **~ Verabredung** business appointment; **~ Verpflichtungen** business commitments
geschäftliches Ansehen business reputation; **~ Unternehmen** business enterprise
Geschäftsabschluß m deal, trade, transaction, business transaction, conclusion of a bargain
Geschäftsabwicklung f handling of business
Geschäftsanteil m business interest, share n (in a business)
Geschäftsaussichten f pl business prospects, business outlook
Geschäftsbank f commercial bank
Geschäftsbedingungen; Allgemeine ~ (AGB) General Business Conditions
Geschäftsbeginn m commencement of business
Geschäftsbelebung f business revival
Geschäftsbereich m sphere of business, scope of business; **~ mit Ertragsverantwortung** profit center
Geschäftsbericht m business report; **~ m** (Finanzbericht) fiscal report; **jährlicher ~** annual report, annual return (GB)
Geschäftsbeteiligung f business participation, business interest, share in a business
Geschäftsbewertung f survey n
Geschäftsbeziehungen f pl business relations, business connections
Geschäftsbrief m business letter

Geschäftsbücher *n pl* business records
Geschäftsdomizil *n* residence *n*
Geschäftseinkommen *n* business income
Geschäftseröffnung; Antrag auf - business application
Geschäftsertrag *m* business proceeds
geschäftsfähiges Alter responsible age
Geschäftsfreund *m* business friend
geschäftsführend *adj* managing *adj*
geschäftsführender *Gesellschafter* managing partner, acting partner; *- Teilhaber* managing partner, acting partner
Geschäftsführer *m* manager *n*; *- ohne Auftrag* agent of necessity
Geschäftsführertätigkeit *f* managership *n*
Geschäftsführung *f* management *n*
Geschäftsgang *m* course of affairs, trend of affairs
Geschäftsgebrauch *m* business custom
Geschäftsgeheimnis *n* business secret
Geschäftsgewinn *m* business profit, commercial profit
Geschäftsgrundlage *f* business basis
Geschäftsgrundstück *n* business property
Geschäftsgründung *f* foundation of a business
Geschäftshaus *n* business house, office building
Geschäftsinventar *n* business inventory
Geschäftsjahr *n* business year, financial year (GB), fiscal year (US)
Geschäftskapital *n* business capital
Geschäftskarte *f* business card
Geschäftskonjunkturauftrieb *m* business prosperity
Geschäftskonjunkturrückgang *m* business recession
Geschäftskonto *n* business account, commercial account
Geschäftskredit *m* business loan
Geschäftsleitung *f* management *n*
Geschäftslokal *n* business premises, business office
Geschäftsmann *m* businessman *n*; *wichtiger -* tycoon
geschäftsmäßig *adj* businesslike *adj*
Geschäftspartner *m* business associate, partner *n*

Geschäftsplan bei einer Unternehmensgründung business plan
Geschäftsplanung *f* budgeting *n*
Geschäftspraxis *f* commercial practice
Geschäftsprognose *f* forecasting *n*
Geschäftsrahmen *m* sphere of business, scope of business
Geschäftsräume *m pl* business premises, business office
Geschäftsrückgang *m* business decline, decline in business, dip *n*
Geschäftsschulden *f pl* business liabilities, business debts
Geschäftsschwankungen *f pl* business fluctuations
Geschäftssinn *m* business acumen
Geschäftssitte *f* business custom
Geschäftssitz *m* place of business
Geschäftssitzung *f* business appointment
Geschäftssparte *f* business branch, business line, class of business
Geschäftsstelle *f* business unit
Geschäftsstellennetz *n* network of branch offices, branch network
Geschäftsübergabe *f* handling over a business
Geschäftsübernahme *f* taking over a business
Geschäftsumfang *m* business volume
geschäftsunfähig *adj* unable to contract, incompetent *adj*
Geschäftsunfähigkeit *f* contractual incapacity, legal incapacity
Geschäftsunkosten *plt* business expenses; *variable -* operating expenses (US)
Geschäftsunterlagen *f pl* books of corporation
Geschäftsunternehmen *n* business concern, business corporation (US)
Geschäftsusance *f* business custom
Geschäftsveräußerung *f* sale of a business
Geschäftsverbindung *f* business relations, business connections
Geschäftsverkehr *m* business activity
Geschäftsverlegung *f* removal of business
Geschäftsvermögen *n* business assets
Geschäftsvolumen *n* volume of business
Geschäftsvorfall *m* business transaction

Geschäftswert *m* goodwill *n*
Geschäftszeichen *n* file number, reference number
Geschäftszeit *f* business hours, hours of business
Geschäftszimmer *n* office *n*
Geschäftszweig *m* business branch, business line, class of business
Geschenk *n* gift *n*
Geschenksparbuch *n* gift savings book
geschlagener *Baissier* stale bear;
 ~ *Haussier* stale bull
geschlossenes Depot sealed safekeeping account
Gesellschaft *f* company *n*, partnership, corporation; ~ *des bürgerlichen Rechts* (GbR) partnership; ~ *des öffentlichen Rechts* statutory corporation; ~ *mit beschränkter Haftung* limited liability company; *aktive Geschäfte betreibende* ~ operating company; *aufnehmende* ~ absorbing company; *ausländische* ~ alien corporation (US); *bargeldlose* ~ cashless society; *gemeinnützige* ~ non-profit corporation; *im Ausland arbeitende* ~ foreign business corporation; *konzessionierte* ~ chartered company; *privilegierte* ~ chartered company; *stille* ~ dormant partnership
Gesellschafter *m* partner *n*; ~ *m* shareholder *n*, stockholder *n*, participator; *beschränkt haftender* ~ special partner, limited partner; *geschäftsführender* ~ managing partner, acting partner; *persönlich nicht haftender* ~ subpartner *n* (GB); *unbeschränkt haftender* ~ unlimited partner
Gesellschafterverhältnis *n* partnership *n*
Gesellschafterversammlung *f* company meeting, shareholders meeting
gesellschaftlicher Finanzhaushalt corporate housekeeping activities
Gesellschaftsanteil *m* share *n* (in company's capital)
Gesellschaftsbefugnisse *f pl* corporate powers
Gesellschaftsbericht *m* corporation report, corporate report
Gesellschaftsbilanz *f* corporate statement, company statement
Gesellschaftseigentum *n* corporate property
Gesellschaftsfinanzen *plt* company finances
Gesellschaftsform *f* corporate form
Gesellschaftsgewinn *m* company's surplus, corporate profit
Gesellschaftsgläubiger *m* partnership creditor
Gesellschaftsgründung *f* company foundation
Gesellschaftshaftung *f* corporate liability
Gesellschaftskapital *n* (einer OHG) partnership capital; ~ *n* (einer AG) share capital, stock capital
Gesellschaftsleitung *f* corporate management
Gesellschaftsrecht *n* company law
Gesellschaftsreingewinn *m* corporate net profit
Gesellschaftsschuld *f* partnership debt
Gesellschaftssitz *m* domicile *n*
Gesellschaftssteuer *f* capital investment tax
Gesellschaftsvermögen *n* (einer OHG) assets of a partnership, partnership assets; ~ *n* (einer AG) corporate assets
Gesellschaftsverpflichtungen *f pl* partnership liabilities, partnership obligations
Gesellschaftsvertrag *m* articles of incorporation and bylaws (US), memorandum and articles of association (GB), partnership agreement, statute *n*
Gesetz *n* act *n*; ~ *n* law *n*
Gesetzessammlung *f* statute book
Gesetzgebung *f* legislation *n*
gesetzlich *adj* legal *adj*, statutory *adj*;
 ~ *geschützt* patented *adj*; ~ *vorgeschriebene Bücher* statutory books; ~ *vorgeschriebene Quittung* statutory receipt; ~ *vorgeschriebene Reserve* legal reserve
gesetzliche Bestimmung enactment *n*;
 ~ *Hypothek* legal mortgage, statutory mortgage; ~ *Kündigungsfrist* statutory period of notice; ~ *Zahlungsmittel* lawful money (US), legal tender
gesetzlicher Zinssatz legal interest, legal rate of interest, statutory interest
gesetzwidrig *adj* illegal, unlawful

gesichert *adj* secured *adj*
gesicherter Gläubiger secured creditor; **~ Kredit** secured credit, secured loan
gespalten *adj* split, multiple
gespaltener Goldpreis split goldprice; **~ Wechselkurs** multiple exchange rate
gesperrtes Guthaben blocked balance; **~ Konto** frozen account, blocked account
gestalten *v* organize *v*, structure *v*, arrange *v*, design *v*
gestatten *v* allow *v*, grant *v*
Gestehungskosten *plt* prime cost, actual costs
gestrichener Kurs no price fixed, quotation cancelled
gestundete Ratenzahlung deferred payment
Gesuch *n* application, request, petition
gesucht *adj* in demand, asked
gesund *adj* sound *adj*
geteilt *adj* divided *adj*
getilgt *adj* redeemed *adj*
getilgte Forderung debt paid
Getränkesteuer *f* beverage tax
Getreidebörse *f* corn exchange
getrennter Markt für Mäntel und Kupons strips market
getreue Nachbildung facsimile *n*
gewagtes Geschäft speculation *n*, gamble *n*
Gewähr *f* guarantee, warranty; **~ leisten** guarantee *v*, warrant *v*
gewähren *v* grant, allow, concede, confer
Gewährleistung *f* guarantee, warranty
Gewährleistungsvertrag *m* warranty contract
Gewahrsam *m* custody *n*
Gewährsmann *m* guarantor *n*, surety *n*
Gewerbe *n* business *n*; **~ n** trade *n*
Gewerbebank *f* industrial bank
Gewerbebetrieb *m* trade, trading firm, business
Gewerbeimmobilie *f* commercial property, industrial property
Gewerbekapital *n* industrial capital
Gewerbekredit *m* business loan
Gewerbesteuer *f* municipal trade tax (on income and capital)
Gewerbetreibende *f u. m* traders *n pl*, craftsmen *n pl*, manufacturers *n pl*

gewerbliche Kreditgenossenschaft industrial loan company
gewerblicher Gewinn industrial profit
gewerbliches Einkommen industrial income
Gewerke *n* (Bergbau) mining company
Gewerkschaft *f* trade union
Gewicht *n* weight *n*, importance *n*
Gewichtsschein *m* bill of weight
Gewinn *m* (Zuwachs) gain *n*; **~ m** profit *n*; **~ abwerfen** render a profit; **~ des Börsenjobbers** jobber's turn (GB); **~ thesaurieren** accumulate profit; **~ vor Steuern** pre-tax profit; **anderen Gesellschaften zustehender ~** profit of minority interest's; **ausgeschütteter ~** distributed profits; **erarbeiteter ~** earnings *n pl*; **laufender ~** current yield; **nicht zweckgebundener ~** available surplus; **noch nicht realisierter ~** contingent profit; **verteilter ~** distributed profits
Gewinnabführungsvertrag *m* profit transfer agreement
Gewinnanalyse *f* surplus analysis
Gewinnansammlung *f* surplus accumulation
Gewinnanteilschein *m* coupon *n*
Gewinnausschüttung *f* distribution of profits, dividend payment
Gewinnausschüttungsquote *f* pay-out ratio
Gewinnberechnung *f* calculation of profits
gewinnberechtigt *adj* participating *adj*
Gewinnbeteiligung *f* profit sharing; **Aktien mit ~** participating stock; **Obligationen mit ~** income debentures, participating bonds (US), profit-sharing bonds; **Rente mit ~** participating annuity; **Versicherung mit ~** participating insurance; **Vorzugsaktien mit zusätzlicher ~** participating preference shares (GB), participating preferred stocks (GB)
gewinnbringend *adj* lucrative *adj*, remunerative *adj*, profitable *adj*
Gewinne erzielen secure profits; **nicht ausgeschüttete ~** retained earnings, retained profits; **steuerpflichtige ~** taxable profits; **unrealisierte ~** paper

gewinnen

profits (US); ***zurückbehaltene*** - retained earnings, retained profits
gewinnen *v* gain *v*, win *v*
Gewinnentnahme *f* withdrawal of profits
Gewinnerwartung *f* profit expectation
Gewinnmitnahme *f* profit taking
Gewinnprämie *f* share bonus
Gewinnrealisierung *f* profit taking
Gewinnrendite *f* (d. h. Prozentsatz des Aktienkurswertes, der auf diese Aktie bei restloser Auszahlung entfallen würde) earnings yield
Gewinnrücklage *f* retained income
Gewinnrückstellung *f* surplus reserve (US)
Gewinnschätzung *f* estimate of profits
Gewinnschrumpfung *f* diminution of profits, profit shrinkage
Gewinnschuldverschreibung *f* (in Zusammenhang mit einer Reorganisation) reorganization bond (US)
Gewinnschuldverschreibungen *f pl* participating bonds; income bonds (US)
Gewinnspanne *f* profit margin, return on sales
Gewinnsteigerung *f* profit rise
Gewinnteilung *f* pooling of profits
Gewinnüberschuß *m* surplus earnings *n* (US), surplus profits (US)
Gewinnüberschußkonto *n* surplus account (US)
Gewinnübersicht *f* surplus statement
Gewinn-und-Verlust-Beteiligung *f* sharing of profit and losses
Gewinn-und-Verlust-Konto *n* revenue account
Gewinn-und-Verlust-Rechnung *f* income statement (US), profit and loss account, earnings statement; ***konsolidierte*** - consolidated profit and loss statement
Gewinnverteilung *f* distribution of profits
Gewinnvortrag *m* accumulated surplus, surplus brought forward (US)
Gewohnheit *f* custom, use, practice
Gewohnheitsrecht *n* customary right
gezeichnetes Kapital subscribed capital
Giralgeld *n* deposit currency (US), money in account, deposit money, bank money, check book money (US)
Girant *m* endorser *n*, indorser *n*
Giratar *m* endorsee *n*, indorsee *n*

girierbar *adj* endorsable *adj*, indorsable *adj*
girieren *v* endorse *v*, indorse *v*
giriert *adj* endorsed *adj*, indorsed *adj*; ***blanko*** - endorsed in blank, indorsed in blank
Giro *n* endorsement *n*, credit transfer, giro; ***ausgefülltes*** - special endorsement; ***beschränktes*** - conditional endorsement, restrictive endorsement; ***mit - versehen*** endorse *v*, indorse *v*, endorsed *adj*, indorsed *adj*; ***ohne*** - unindorsed *adj*, unendorsed *adj*; ***Übertragung durch*** - transfer by means of indorsement
Giroabteilung *f* giro department
Girobank *f* giro transfer bank, transfer bank
Giroeinlage *f* giro account deposit
Girogeschäft *n* giro business, giro operations
Girokonto *n* giro account
Girosammeldepot *n* collective securities account
Girosammelverwahrung *f* collective custody
Giroverkehr *m* clearing operations
Girowesen *n* giro transfer system
Girozentrale *f* Central Savings Bank
glattstellen *v* settle *v* (e.g. account), liquidate *v* (e.g. debt); ***eine Position*** - close a position
Glattstellung *f* liquidation *n*; - ***von Verbindlichkeiten im Konzernverbund*** netting
Glauben; in gutem - bona fide, in good faith
Gläubiger *m* creditor; - ***aus Kontokorrentgeschäften*** trade creditor; ***abgefundener*** - paid off creditor; ***bevorrechtigter*** - preferential creditor (GB), preferred creditor (US); ***bevorzugter*** - preferential creditor (GB), preferred creditor (US); ***gerichtlich anerkannter*** - judg(e)ment creditor, execution creditor; ***gesicherter*** - secured creditor; ***öffentlicher*** - public creditor; ***ungesicherter*** - unsecured creditor; ***zweifacher*** - double creditor
Gläubigerausgleich *m* arrangement with creditors
Gläubigerausschuß *m* board of creditors, creditors committee

Gläubigerkonten *n pl* accounts with creditors
Gläubigerschutz *m* protection of creditors
Gläubigervergleich *m* settlement with creditors
Gläubigerversammlung *f* creditors meeting, meeting of creditors
gleich *adj* equal, same, uniform
gleichberechtigt *adj* pari passu
gleichlautend buchen enter in conformity, book in conformity
gleichmäßig *adj* equal, even
gleichmäßige Produktion settled production
gleichordnen *v* coordinate *v*
Gleichordnung *f* coordination *n*
gleitende Neuwertversicherung floating policy
Gleitklausel *f* escalator clause, index clause
gliedern; nach Posten - itemize *v*, specify *v*
global *adj* world-wide *adj*, overall *adj*
Globalbetrag *m* bloc amount, round sum
Globalfinanzierung *f* bloc financing
Globalisierung *f* (Internationalisierung) globalisation
Globalzession *f* blanket assignment
Going-Public-Optionsanleihe *f* going public warrant issue
Gold von geringem Feingehalt base gold; **echtes -** sterling gold
Goldabfluß *m* drain of bullion (GB), drain of gold
Goldbarren *m* gold bar
Goldbestand *m* gold holdings
Golddeckung *f* gold cover
Golddeckungsvorschriften *f pl* gold backing requirements, gold cover requirements
Golddevise *f* gold currency
Golddevisenwährung *f* gold exchange standard
goldene Bankregel golden rule of banking
goldene Bilanzregel golden rule for balance sheet
goldgesichert *adj* secured by gold
Goldgräber *m* prospector *n*
Goldkernwährung *f* gold bullion standard
Goldklausel *f* gold clause
Goldkredit *m* gold credit

Goldmünze *f* gold coin; **- mit geringem Agio** bullion coin
Goldobligationen *f pl* gold bonds (US)
Goldoption *f* gold option
Goldpool *m* Gold Pool
Goldpreis *m* gold price; **gespaltener -** two-tier gold system
Goldpunkt *m* gold point, bullion point, specie point; **oberer -** gold export point; **unterer -** gold import point
Goldreserven *f pl* gold reserves
Goldstandard *m* gold standard; **Aufgabe des -s** abandonment of the gold standard
Goldstück *n* gold piece, gold coin
Goldtranche *f* (IMF) gold tranche
Gold-und-Silber-Bestand *m* bullion reserve
Goldwährung *f* gold standard
Goldwertklausel *f* gold value clause
Goodwill *m* goodwill *n*
Gradmesser *m* standard
Gratifikation *f* bonus *n*; **- f** gratuity *n*
Gratisaktie *f* bonus share (GB), bonus stock (US)
Gratisaktien; Ausgabe von - issue of bonus shares
Gratisrecht *n* bonus right
grauer Markt grey market
greifbare Mittel liquid funds
Grenz- (in Zus.) marginal *adj*
Grenzbetrieb *m* marginal producer
Grenze *f* limit *n*; **dehnbare -** elastic limit, flexible limit
Grenznutzen *m* marginal utility
Griechische Drachme *f* Greek Drachme
Grobsortierung *f* (beim Beleglesen) rough sort, pre-sort *n*
Großaktionär *m* major shareholder
Großbank *f* big bank, large bank, major bank
Großemission *f* jumbo issue (deal)
Größenklassengliederung *f* breakdown by size, classification by size
Größenordnung *f* order of magnitude
Großhandel *m* wholesale trade *n*
Großhandelsrabatt *m* trade allowance
Großhandelsverkauf *m* wholesale trade *n*
Großhändler *m* wholesaler *n*, wholesale dealer
Großkundengeschäft *n* wholesale banking

Grossist m wholesaler n, wholesale dealer
Großkredit m large loan
Großkunde m large corporate customer, key account
Grund und Boden realty n, real property, landed property, real estate, real assets
Grundausbildung f basic training
Grundbesitz m realty n, real property, landed property, real estate, real assets; *Barbetrag aus einem -* proprietary equity; *freier -* freehold n (GB)
Grundbesitzanlage f real estate investment
Grundbesitzer; *freier -* freeholder n
Grundbuch n land register, real estate register (US), cadastre n
Grundbuch- (in Zus.) cadastral adj
Grundbuchamt n land registration office
Grundbuchbeamte m registrar of deeds (US), registrar of mortgages
Grundbucheintragung f real estate recording (US)
Grunddienstbarkeit f real servitude, rent charge
Grundeigentum n realty n, real property, landed property, real estate, real assets; *freies -* freehold n (GB)
Grundeigentümer m land owner, registered proprietor
gründen; *eine Gesellschaft -* form a company
Gründer m founder n
Gründeraktien f pl founders shares
Gründerrechte n pl founders preference rights
Grunderwerbsbescheinigung f certificate of purchase
Grunderwerbsteuer f realty transfer tax
Grundgebühr f basic fee
Grundgeschäft n underlying transaction
Grundkapital n capital stock (US), share capital, capital fund, original capital
Grundlage f basis n, foundation n
Grundpacht f land rent
Grundpfand n real security
Grundpfandbriefe m pl real estate bonds (US)
Grundpfandrecht n lien upon real estate
Grundpfandrechte; *durch - gesicherter Kredit* real estate-backed loan

Grundpreis m basic price
Grundsatz m axiom n, principle n, rule n
Grundschuld f land charge, registered charge
Grundschuldbrief m land charge deed
Grundschuldforderung f land charge claim
Grundsteuer f real property tax, real estate tax
Grundstoffindustrie f basic industry
Grundstück n land, piece of land; *belastetes -* burdened estate; *unbelastetes -* clear estate
Grundstücke mit allen Nebengebäuden premises n pl
Grundstücksabschreibung f property depreciation
Grundstücksbelastung f property charge(s)
Grundstücksbewertung f real property valuation, survey
Grundstückseigentum n realty n, real property, landed property, real estate, real assets
Grundstückseigentümer m property owner
Grundstückserwerb m purchase of land, property purchase
Grundstücksgesellschaft f proprietary company
Grundstückskonto n (einer Bank) bank premises account
Grundstückskredit m mortgage loan, real estate loan
Grundstücksmakler m realtor n (US), real estate broker (US), real estate dealer
Grundstücksmarkt m property market, real estate market
Grundstücksobligationen f pl real estate bonds (US)
Grundstückspacht f ground lease
Grundstücksparzelle f lot n (US)
Grundstücksrecht n real property right
Grundstücksspekulation f land speculation
Grundstückssteuer f tax on real estate
Grundstücksübertragung f transfer of title to land, property conveyance
Grundstücksübertragungsurkunde f warranty deed (US)

Grundstücksumschreibung f transfer of title to land
Grundstücksvertrag m deed of real
Grundstückswert m real state value
Gründung f foundation, promotion
Gründungseinlage f original investment
Gründungsgesellschaft f company promotion business
Gründungskosten plt start-up expenditure, cost of promotion
Gründungsmitglied n founder member
Grundvermögen n real property, assets
Grundzahl f cardinal number
Gruppe f group, section
Gruppenumsatz m group sales
Gruppenversicherung f collective insurance
Guinee f (21 Schilling) guinea n (GB)
Gulden m florin n
gültig adj valid adj, effective, inforce; - *machen* validate v
Gültigkeit f validity n
Gültigkeitsdauer f validity n, period of validity
Gültigkeitserklärung f validation
Gummiaktien f pl rubbers n pl
günstig adj advantageous adj
gut *lieferbar* (Börse) good delivery (stock exchange); - *rentieren* (sich) pay well
Gut n (Vermögen) asset, property; *eingebrachtes* - separate estate
Gutachten n (eines Rechtssachverständigen) expert opinion n, counsel's opinion; - n survey n
Gutachter m expert, valuer, assessor
gutachtlich adj consultative adj

Gutdünken n discretion n
Güter n pl goods n pl, commodities n pl; *immaterielle* - intangibles
Gütertarif m railroad freight rate, railway rate
Gütertrennung f separation of property
Güterversicherung f cargo insurance
gutgläubig bona fide, in good faith
gutgläubiger *Besitzer* bona fide holder, holder in due course; - *Erwerb* bona fide transaction; - *Erwerber* good faith taker, purchaser in good faith; - *Forderungsinhaber* bona fide creditor; - *Inhaber* bona fide holder, holder in due course
Guthaben n credit, deposits, credit balance; - *bei Postgiroämtern* balances on postal giro accounts; - *bei Zentralnotenbanken* balances with central banks; *ein* - *freigeben* unfreeze funds, release funds; *gesperrtes* - blocked balance; *nicht zurückgefordertes* - dormant balance; *umsatzloses* - dormant balance
Guthabenkonto n creditor account
Guthabensaldo m credit balance, balance in one's favour
gütliche **Liquidation** liquidation by arrangement
gutschreiben v credit to an account
Gutschrift f credit advice, credit memorandum, credit note
Gutschriftsanzeige f credit advice, credit memorandum, credit note
Gutschriftsträger m credit voucher

Haben

H

Haben; ins - buchen credit v
Habenposten m credit item
Habensaldo m credit balance
Habenzinsen m pl credit interest, interest payable
Habenzinssatz m credit rate, deposit rate
Hafensperre f embargo n
haftbar adj responsible adj, liable adj
haften für guarantee v, be liable for, stand guarantee for
haftendes Eigenkapital liable capital
haftpflichtig adj liable adj
Haftpflichtversicherung f liability insurance; **~ f** third party liability insurance
Haftung f liability n; **~ f** responsibility n; **- für Schäden aus einem Mietgegenstand** impeachment of waste; **gegenseitige -** cross liability
Haftungsausschluß m exclusion of liability
Haftungsbeschränkung f limitation of liability
Haftungserklärung f warranty declaration
Haftungsfonds m guarantee fund
Haftungsgrenze f liability limit
Halbjahresabschluß m mid-year settlement
Halbjahresgeld n six-months money
Halbjahresrechnung f mid-year settlement
halbjährlich adj semi-annual adj, biannual adj
halbjährlicher Kontoauszug semiannual account
Halbmonatsabrechnung f settlement every fortnight
Hand; öffentliche - public authorities
Handbuch n manual n, handbook n
Handel m trade, dealings, trading;
 - bei Erscheinen when issued (WI);
 - und Gewerbe trade and commerce;
 - und Industrie trade and industry;
 einen - abschließen contract a bargain; **inoffizieller -** grey market;
 nebenbörslicher - pre-market dealings;
 permanenter - continuos trading;
 zwischenstaatlicher - (zwischen den einzelnen US-Bundesstaaten) interstate commerce (US)
handelbar adj negotiable adj; **schwer -** not easy marketable
handeln v (tätig sein) act, deal, trade, bargain; **- v** (Handel treiben) buy and sell, deal v, merchandise v, trade v
Handelsabkommen n trade agreement, commercial treaty
Handelsagent m agent n
Handelsakzept n trade acceptance
Handelsauskunftei f credit inquiry agency, mercantile agency (US)
Handelsbank f commercial bank
Handelsbeschränkung f restriction of trade
Handelsbetrieb m trading firm
Handelsbezeichnung f trade name
Handelsbilanz f balance of trade; **aktive -** active trade balance
Handelsbrauch m trade custom, commercial usage
Handelsbräuche m pl business usages
Handelsdokument n trade note, trade paper
Handelseinheit f trading unit
Handelsfinanzierung f trade financing
Handelsfirma f commercial firm, commercial concern
Handelsgericht n commercial court (GB)
Handelsgeschäft n commercial business, commercial transaction
Handelsgesellschaft f commercial company, commercial corporation, commercial partnership, company of merchants, trading company, trading corporation; **Offene -** f (OHG) general partnership
Handelsgesetzbuch n commercial code
Handelsgewinn m trading profit
Handelshaus n firm n, enterprise n, company n, concern n
Handelshochschule f commercial academy
Handelsinteressen n pl commercial interests

Handelskammer f Board of Trade (US), Chamber of Commerce (GB)
Handelskette f trading chain
Handelskorrespondenz f commercial correspondence
Handelskredit m commercial credit
Handelsniederlassung f factory n
Handelspapiere n pl commercial papers
Handelsrecht n commercial law, mercantile law
Handelsregister n commercial register, register of companies (GB); *Löschung im -* deregistration n
Handelsregisteramt n register office
Handelsregistereintragung einer Gesellschaft registration of a company (GB)
Handelssachen; *Kammer für -* court of trade
Handelsschule f business school
Handelsspanne f profit margin, trade margin
Handelsstand m traders n pl, merchants n pl, merchant class
Handelsunternehmen n trading company (enterprise)
Handelsusancen f pl trade customs
Handelsverbot n embargo n
Handelsverkehr m commerce n, trading n
Handelsvertrag m trade agreement, commercial treaty
Handelsvertreter m mercantile agent
Handelsware f merchandise n, commercial goods
Handelswechsel m commercial note, commercial bill, trade bill
Handelswelt f world of commerce
Handelswert m commercial value
Handelszeichen n trademark n
Handelszentrum n trade center, center of commerce, mart n
Handgeld n bargain money, bargain penny
Handhabung f handling, management
Händler m trader n, dealer n, tradesman n
Händlerobligo n dealer's engagement
Händlerposition f dealer position
Händlerprovision f dealer commission
Handlung f act, action

Handlungsbevollmächtigte f u. m assistant manager, authorized agent, assistant treasurer, officer
Handlungsgehilfe m commercial clerk
Handlungsreisende f u. m commercial travel(l)er, travel(l)ing salesman
Handlungsunfähigkeit f mental incapacity, inability to act
Handlungsvollmacht f limited power of representation, power of attorney
Handwerk n handicraft n, craft n, small trader
Handwerker m craftsman, small trader
Handzettel m hand bill
Härteklausel f hardship clause
Hartgeld n hard cash (US), hard money
Hartwährung f hard currency
Hauptaktionär m principal shareholder
Hauptanteil m bulk, main part (share)
Hauptbuch n general ledger
Hauptbuchhalter m chief accountant, general bookkeeper
Hauptbuchhaltung f general accounting department, general accounting
Hauptbuchsammelkonto n controlling account, control account
Hauptfiliale f main branch, regional head branch
Hauptgeschäftssitz m head office, headquarter
Hauptgläubiger m chief creditor
Haupthändler m main dealer
Hauptinhaber m senior partner
Hauptkasse f chief cash office
Hauptkassierer m cashier in charge of operations, chief cashier, head teller, cashier n (US)
Hauptkonto n general account
Hauptniederlassung f main office, head office, headquarter
Hauptsatz m (EDV) master record (EDP)
Hauptschuldner m principal debtor
Hauptsitz m head office, head quarter
Hauptversammlung f meeting of shareholders (GB), meeting of stockholders (US), general meeting, shareholders' meeting, stockholders meeting; *eine - der Aktionäre einberufen* call a meeting of shareholders, call a meeting of stockholders (US); *ordentliche - der Aktionäre*

annual meeting of stockholders (US), annual meeting of shareholders (GB), general meeting; **außerordentliche -** extraordinary general meeting

Hauptverwaltung f head office, central management

Hauptwechselschuldner m principal bill debtor

Hausbank f principal bank, borrower's bank

Hausbankverbindung f relationship banking

Hausbesitzbrief m house property certificate

haushalten v economize v

Haushaltsaufstellung f budgeting n

Haushaltskonto n budgetary account

haushaltsmäßig adj budgetary adj

Haushaltsplan; einen - aufstellen budget v

Haushaltsreform f budgetary reform

Hausse f boom n, bull market; **auf - spekulieren** buy for the rise, bull v, speculate for a rise; **im Hinblick auf eine - kaufen** buy for the rise, bull v, speculate for a rise; **in -** bullish adj

Hausse-Bedingungen f pl boom conditions

Hausse-Bewegung f bull movement

Hausse-Geschäft n bull transactions

Hausse-Gruppe f bull pool

Hausse-Kauf m bull buying, bull purchase (US)

Hausse-Kurs m boom price

Hausse-Markt m boom market, bull market, bullish market

Hausse-Nachricht f bullish report

Hausse-Partei f bull clique, long side, constructive side of the market (US)

Hausse-Position f bull account, bull position

Hausse-Spekulant m bull n, long n, speculator for a rise, bull operator

Hausse-Spekulation f bull operation, bull speculation

Hausse-Tendenz f bullish tendency, bullishness n

Haussier m bull n, bull operator n, speculator for a rise; **geschlagener -** stale bull

haussierend adj bullish adj

Hausverkauf m door-to-door market

Havarie f damage, average; **- nach Seebrauch** average accustomed

Havarieagent m average adjuster, average staker, average agent

Havarieerklärung f ship's protest

Havariegelder n pl average charges, average expenses, average money

Havarieklausel f average clause

Havarierechnung f average bill

Havarieschein m average bond

Hedgegeschäft n (Kurssicherung) hedging, immunization business

Heimatbörse f home stock exchange

Heimfall m escheat n

heißes Geld hot money

herabgesetztes Kapital reduced capital

Herabsetzen der Geldsätze cheapening of money

herabsetzen v (Preise) reduce v, lower v, cut back

herabsetzen; im Preis - mark down

Herabsetzung f lowering n, reduction n

Herbstultimo n last day of third quarter

Herkunftsbescheinigung f certificate of origin

Herkunftsland m country of origin

Hermes-Exportkreditgarantie f Hermes export credit guarantee

herrenlos adj unowned, vacant

Hersteller m manufacturer n, producer n

Herstellung f fabrication n, manufacture n, production

Herstellungsbetrieb m manufactory

Herstellungswert m cost value, cost of production

heruntergehen v decline, drop, fall

herunterhandeln v beat down

herunterkonvertieren v convert downwards

HIBOR m = Hongkonger Interbanken-Angebotszinssatz Hongkong Interbank Offered Rate

Hilfs- (in Zus.) assistant n

Hilfsmittel n pl resources n pl

Hilfsprogramm n auxiliary routine

hinauftreiben v force up, push up

hinausgeschobene Annuität deferred annuity

hinausschiebbar adj delayable adj, adjournable adj, deferrable adj

hinausschieben v delay v, defer v
hinkende Währung limping standard
Hinterlassenschaft f estate, property left
hinterlassungsfähig adj bequeathable adj
hinterlegen v deposit v
Hinterleger m depositor n, bank depositor
Hinterlegung f deposit, consignation n (Scotch Law); ~ f lodg(e)ment n; *unfreiwillige* ~ involuntary bailment
Hinterlegungsschein m certificate of deposit
Hinterlegungsstelle f depository n, custodian n
Hinterlegungsurkunde f letter of deposit, memorandum of deposit (GB)
hinterziehen v defraud v; *Steuern* ~ evade taxes
Hinterziehung f defraudation n
hinzurechnen v add v, include
hinzuzählen v add v
Hochfinanz f high finance (US)
Hochkonjunktur f business prosperity
Höchstbetrag m maximum amount, limit, ceiling n
Höchstbetragshypothek f floating charge (GB)
höchster Kurs top price
Höchstgebot n highest bid
Höchstgrenze f maximum, upper limit, ceiling n
Höchstkredit m credit line, line of credit, credit limit
Höchstkurs m high quotation (stocks), high rate (money), peak price
Höchstlaufzeit f maximum life (e.g. of loan)
Höchstpreis m peak price, ceiling price
Höchststand m highest level, top level
Höchstzinssatz m interest rate, cap
hochtreiben v force, send up, push up
höhere Gewalt act of God, force majeure
Holding f holding n
Holdingbilanz f holding company's balance sheet
Holdinggesellschaft f holding company
Holländische Gulden m Dutch Guilder
Home-Banking n (Bankgeschäfte mittels Telekommunikation) home banking
Hongkonger Interbanken-Angebotszinssatz m = HIBOR Hongkong Interbank Offered Rate

Honorar n fee n, honorarium n
honorieren v pay, honour v (GB), honor v (US); *einen Wechsel* ~ cash a bill, clear a bill, discharge a bill, draw in a bill, retire a bill, take up a bill, honor a bill, answer a bill of exchange
horten v hoard v, stockpile v
Hortungskauf m hoarding purchase
Hotelfinanzierung f hotel financing
Hundertstelstelle f percentile n
Hyperinflation f hyperinflation
Hypothek f mortgage n, real estate mortgage; *abgelöste* ~ paid off mortgage; *eine* ~ *aufnehmen* raise a mortgage; *eine* ~ *bestellen* register a mortgage; *eine* ~ *eintragen lassen* register a mortgage; *eine* ~ *tilgen* extinguish a mortgage; *eingelöste* ~ closed mortgage; *erste* ~ first mortgage; *für mehrere Gläubiger bestellte* ~ contributory mortgage; *gesetzliche* ~ legal mortgage, statutory mortgage; *landwirtschaftliche* ~ farm mortgage; *nachrangige* ~ junior mortgage, second mortgage; *rechtsgültige* ~ legal mortgage, statutory mortgage; *sicherungsweise abgetretene* ~ blanket bond; *stilliegende* ~ tacit mortgage; *zweitstellige* ~ junior mortgage, second mortgage
Hypothekardarlehen n mortgage loan
hypothekarisch adj hypothecary adj; ~ *belasten* hypothecate v, mortgage v, encumber v; ~ *belastet* encumbered adj, mortgaged adj; ~ *gesicherte Obligation* secured bond, mortgage debenture; ~ *gesicherte Schuldverschreibung* secured bond, mortgage debenture
hypothekarische Belastung mortgage n, real estate mortgage
Hypothekarkredit m mortgage loan, real estate mortgage
Hypothekarschuld f debt on mortgage
Hypotheken; mit ~ *belastet* burdened with mortgages
Hypothekenablösungsrecht n equity of redemption
Hypothekenabteilung f mortgage department

Hypothekenabtretung f assignment of mortgage, mortgage assignment
Hypothekenantrag m application for a mortgage
Hypothekenauszahlung f mortgage payment, amount paid out to borrower of a mortgage
Hypothekenbank f land bank, mortgage bank
Hypothekenbelastung f mortgage, encumbrance n, mortgage charge
Hypothekenbestellung f creation of a mortgage
Hypothekenbrief m mortgage bond, real estate mortgage note, mortgage deed
Hypothekendarlehen n mortgage loan
Hypothekeneintragung f registration of a mortgage
hypothekenfähig adj mortgageable adj
hypothekenfrei adj unmortgaged adj, unencumbered adj
Hypothekengeld n mortgage loan money
Hypothekengeschäft n mortgage business
Hypothekengläubiger m mortgage creditor, mortgagee n
Hypothekenklausel; negative - negative mortgage security clause
Hypothekenkredit m mortgage loan, real estate loan

Hypothekenlöschung f release of mortgage
Hypothekenpfandbrief m mortgage bond, real estate mortgage note, mortgage deed
Hypothekenregister n register of mortgages
Hypothekenschuldner m mortgage debtor, mortgager n, mortgagor n
Hypothekenschuldverschreibung f collateral mortgage bond, mortgage debenture
Hypothekenstock m mortgage loan portfolio
Hypothekentilgung f mortgage redemption
Hypothekenübernahme f assuming of a mortgage
Hypothekenurkunde f mortgage deed
Hypothekenvaluta f mortgage loan proceeds
Hypothekenvereinigung f tacking of mortgages
Hypothekenzinsen m pl mortgage interests
Hypothekenzusage f promise of a mortgage loan
Hypothekenzwangsvollstreckung f mortgage foreclosure

I

Identifikationsmethode f method of identification
Identität f identity n
illiquide adj illiquid, non liquid
immaterielle Aktiva intangible assets
immaterieller Firmenwert m goodwill, company's intangible asset
immaterieller Geschäftswert m goodwill
Immobilien plt immovables n pl, immovable property, real estate, real property
Immobilienanlage f real estate investment
Immobilienfinanzierung f real estate financing
Immobilienfonds m property fund, real estate fund
Immobiliengeschäft n real estate business
Immobiliengesellschaft f real estate firm
Immobilienhandel m dealings in real estate
Immobilienkauf n property purchase
Immobilienmakler m realtor n (US), real estate broker (US), real estate dealer
Immobilienmarkt m real estate market, property market
Immobilienzertifikat n property fund share, real estate fund certificate
Import m import n, importation n
Importakkreditiv n import letter of credit
Importartikel m pl imports n pl
Importbeschränkungen f pl import restrictions, import cuts
Importeur m importer n
Importgeschäft n import trade
importieren v import v
Importkredit m import credit
Importsteuer f tax on imports
Importware f articles of import
Inanspruchnahme f availment, use, amount drawn upon
Inbesitznahme f taking possession, appropriation n
Index m index n; *- der New Yorker Börse* (Durchschnittskurs einer Auswahl von US-Aktien) Dow-Jones-Index n, Standard and Poor's Composite Index (S & P)
Index-Anleihe f index-linked bond issue, indexed issue, index-linked loan
Index-Arbitrage f index arbitrage
Index-Fonds m index fund; *- der Tokioter Börse* Japanese stock price index (NIKKEI)
Index-Futures m pl index futures
indexgekoppelt adj index-linked
Index-Gewährung f index-linked currency
indexieren v link to an index
Index-Klausel f escalator clause, index clause, indossabel adj endorsable adj, indorsable adj
Indossament n endorsement n, endorsing n, indorsement n, indorsation n; *- fehlt* indorsement required; *- ohne Obligo* endorsement without recourse (GB); *- ohne Verbindlichkeit* indorsement without recourse; *bedingtes -* qualified endorsement; *durch - übertragen* endorse v, indorse v; *mit - versehen* endorsed adj, indorsed adj; *unbeschränktes -* absolute endorsement; *vollständiges -* full endorsement, full indorsement
Indossamentsverbindlichkeiten f pl contingent liabilities in respect of endorsements
Indossant m endorser n, indorser n
Indossat m endorsee n, indorsee n
Indossatar m endorsee n, indorsee n
indossierbar adj endorsable adj, indorsable adj
indossieren v endorse v, indorse v
indossierter Wechsel made bill (GB)
Indossierung f endorsement n, endorsing n, indorsement n, indorsation n
industrialisieren v industrialize v
Industrialisierung f industrialization n
Industrie f industry n
Industrieaktien f pl industrial shares
Industrieakzept n industrial bill
Industrieanleihe f corporate bond
Industriebank f industrial bank
Industriebörse f commodity exchange
Industrieemissionen f pl industrial issues
Industrieentwicklung f industrial development

Industriekapazität f industrial capacity
Industriekapital n industrial capital
Industriekonzern m industrial combination
Industriekredit m industrial loan, loan to industry
Industrielle f u. m industrial producer, industrialist n
Industriemagnat m Tycoon
Industrieobligationen f pl industrial bonds
Industriepapiere n pl industrials n pl, industrial securities, industrial shares, industrial stocks
Industrieproduktion f industrial output, industrial production
Industriestaat m industrial country, industrial state
Industrie- und Handelskammer (IHK) f chamber of industry and commerce
Industrieunternehmen n industrial concern, industrial enterprise, industrial company, industrial undertaking
Industrieverband m industrial federation, industrial association
Industrieverlagerung f relocation of industry
Industrievermögen n industrial property, industrial wealth
Industriewerte m pl industrials n pl, industrial securities, industrial shares, industrial stocks
Industriezentrum n industrial centre
Industriezweig m industry n
Inflation f inflation n; *galoppierende* - runaway inflation
inflationieren v inflate
inflationistisch adj inflationary adj
inflationistische Konjunktur inflation boom
Inflationsbekämpfung f combatting inflation, disinflation
inflationsfeindlich adj anti-inflationary adj
inflationsfrei adj non-inflationary adj
Inflationsgefahr f inflation danger, inflation peril
Inflationsrate f rate of inflation
Inflationszeit f inflationary period
Informatiknetzwerk n informatic network
Information f information n; *vertrauliche* - confidential information
Informationsfluß m information flow

Informationsgehalt m information content
Informationsvolumen n information volume
informieren v inform v, notify v, advise v, communicate v
Infrastrukturkredit m infrastructure financing loan
Inhaber m owner, proprietor, holder n, bearer n; *- eines Zurückbehaltungsrechts* lienor n, lien creditor; *auf den - lautend* in bearer form; *gutgläubiger -* bona fide holder, holder in due course
Inhaberaktie f bearer share, bearer stock
Inhaberaktienzertifikat n share warrant to bearer
Inhaberanleihe f bearer bond
Inhabereffekten plt bearer securities
Inhabergrundschuldbrief m bearer land charge certificate
Inhaberobligation f bearer bond, bond to bearer, bearer debenture, coupon bond (US)
Inhaberoptionsanleihe f bearer warrant issue
Inhaberpapier n bearer instrument, instrument payable to bearer
Inhaberpapiere n pl bearer securities; *erstklassige -* floaters n pl (GB)
Inhaberscheck m bearer check
Inhaberschuldbrief m bearer mortgage note
Inhaberschuldverschreibung f bearer bond, bond to bearer, bearer debenture, coupon bond (US)
Inhaberwechsel m bill to bearer
Inhaberzertifikat n bearer certificate
Initiative f (z. B. vom Datenendplatz aus) request n, initiative n; *unternehmerische -* business initiative
Inkasso n collection n, encashment n; *- durch Boten* collection by hand (US); *- von Schecks* cheque collection (GB); *- zu Pari* par collection; *das - eines Wechsels besorgen* attend to the collection of a bill; *Wert zum -* value for collection
Inkassoabteilung f collection department
Inkassoabtretung f assignment of accounts receivable
Inkassoauftrag m collection order

Inkassobank f collecting bank
Inkassobeamte m collector n
Inkassobericht m clearing house report, tracer n
Inkassobestand m items on hand for collection
Inkassobüro n collecting agency
Inkassogebühren f pl collecting charges, collection charges, collecting commission, collection fee
Inkassogeschäft n collecting business
Inkassokonto n collecting account
Inkassoscheck m collection check
Inkassospesen plt collecting charges, collection charges, collecting commission, collection fee
Inkassotarif m collecting rates
Inkassotratte f agency draft
Inkassovollmacht f letter of delegation
Inkassowechsel m bill for collection, short bill
inklusive cum
Inland n home country, inland n
Inländer m resident n
Inländerkonvertierbarkeit f convertibility for residents
inländisch adj domestic adj, internal adj
Inlands- (in Zus.) domestic adj, internal adj
Inlandsabsatz m domestic sales
Inlandsanleihe f domestic bond
Inlandsbesitz m resident's holding
Inlandsbeteiligungen f pl domestic investments
Inlandseinlage f resident's deposit
Inlandsgeschäft n domestic business
Inlandskonto n internal account
Inlandsmarkt m domestic market, home market
Inlandsreisekreditbrief m domestic travellers letter of credit (US)
Inlandsschuldverschreibungen f pl domestic bonds
Inlandsspediteur m country shipper
Inlandswährung f domestic currency
Inlandswechsel m domestic bill, inland bill
Inlandszahlung f payment inside the country
innehaben v hold v
Innehabung f holding n

Innenfinanzierung f internal financing, self-financing
innerer Wert intrinsic value, net worth
innerlich adj intrinsic adj, real adj
Inserat n advertisement, ad n
Inserent m advertiser n
inserieren v advertise v
Insider m insider
Insidergeschäfte n pl insider transactions
Insiderhandel m insider trading
insolvent adj insolvent, bankrupt
Insolventenliste f black book, black list
Insolvenz f insolvency n
Inspektion f inspection n
Institut n institute, institution n
institutioneller Anleger institutional investor
Instruktion f instruction n, order
Instrumentarium n instruments, tools
integrierter Finanzraum integrated financial area
intensivieren v intensify v, stimulate v
Interbankendevisenmarkt m interbank forex market
Interbankengeschäft n interbank business
interbankmäßig adj interbank, between banks
Interbankverflechtung f interbank relations
Interbankzinssatz m interbank rate, Federal-funds rate (US)
Interesse n interest n, concern, attention; *ein ~ wahren* v safeguard interest
Interessenabstimmung f agreement of interests
Interessengegensatz m conflict of interests
Interessengemeinschaft f syndicate n
Interessenkäufe m pl buying by special interests
Interessenkonflikt m conflict of interests
Interessenten m pl interested parties
Interessentengruppe f pressure group
interessiert adj concerned adj, interested adj
Interimsdividende f dividend on account, interim dividend
Interimskonto n interim account, suspense account
Interimsschein m scrip n, certificate (GB)

Interimswechsel *m* bill at interim
international *adj* international *adj*; **- gehandelte Effekten** international securities, international stocks (US), internationals *n pl*; **- gehandelte Wertpapiere** international securities, international stocks (US), internationals *n pl*; **- operierendes Unternehmen** global player
internationale Aktienplazierung international placement of shares, going global; **- Zahlungsanweisung** international money order
Internationale Bank für Wiederaufbau und Entwicklung *f* International Bank for Reconstruction and Development; **- Entwicklungsbank** *f* International Development Association (IDA); **- Finanzgesellschaft** *f* International Finance Corporation (IFC); **- Handelsbestimmungen** *f pl* (Incoterms) International Commercial Terms (Incoterms); **- Handelskammer** *f* International Chamber of Commerce; **- Vereinigung der Wertpapierhändler** *f* International Securities-Dealer Market Association; **- Vereinigung für Swaps und derivative Instrumente** *f* = *ISDA* International Swap and Derivative Association Inc.; **- Währungsfonds** *m* = *IWF* International Monetary Fund (IMF)
internationales Bankwesen international banking
interpretieren *v* interpret *v*
intervalutarisch *adj* between different currencies
intervenieren *v* intervene *v*, mediate *v*
Intervention *f* intervention
Interventionskäufe *m pl* support buying
Interventionskurse *m pl* intervention rates
Interventionspunkte *m pl* intervention points
Invalidenversicherung *f* disability insurance
Invaliditätsfonds *m* disability fund
Invaliditätsrente *f* disability benefit
Invaliditätsunterstützung *f* disability benefit
Inventar *n* inventory, stock
Inventarkurs *m* inventory rate
Inventarverzeichnis *n* inventory sheet

Inventarwert *m* inventory value; *-* *m* (eines Investmentfonds) net asset value
Inventur *f* inventory, stock-taking; **eine - durchführen** take inventory; **permanente -** perpetual inventory
inverse Zinsstruktur inverse interest rate structure, reverse yield curve
investieren *v* invest *v*
investiertes Geld invested money
Investition *f* investment *n*, capital expenditure; **betriebliche -** business investment; **übermäßige -** overinvestment *n*
Investitionsanleihe *f* investment loan
Investitionsbedarf *m* capital investment requirements
Investitionsbeschränkungen *f pl* restriction of investment
Investitionsfinanzierung *f* investment financing, financing of capital projects
Investitionsgüter *n pl* capital goods
Investitionshilfe *f* investment aid, assistance
Investitionskapital *n* investment capital
Investitionskredit *m* investment loan, investment credit, capital investment loan
investitionsorientiert *adj* investment-oriented
Investitionsplan *m* investment plan
Investitionsplanung *f* investment planing
Investitionsquote *f* investment ratio
Investitionsrate *f* rate of investment
Investitionsrisikogarantie *f* investment risk guarantee
Investitionsvorhaben *n* capital project
Investitionszulage *f* investment allowance
Investitionszuschuß *m* investment grant (aid)
Investment *n* investment
Investmentanteil *m* investment fund share, mutual fund share (US)
Investmentbank *f* investment bank
Investmentfonds *m* investment fund; **- mit auswechselbarem Portefeuille** fund of funds; **- mit begrenzt auswechselbarem Portefeuille** semi-fixed fund; **- mit hoher Barausschüttung** income fund; **- mit Leihkapital** leverage fund; **auf hohen Wertzuwachs ausgerichteter -** perfomance fund

Investmentgeschäft *n* investment fund business
Investmentgesellschaft *f* investment company; *- die zum Kauf von Anlagen kein Fremdkapital einsetzt* non-leverage company
Investmentplan *m* investment programme
Investmenttrust *m* investment trust; *- in einem steuerbegünstigten Land* offshore fund
Investmentzertifikat *n* investment certificate, investment fund certificate
Investor *m* investor *n*
Irische Pfund *n* Irish Punt (Pound)
Irrtum *m* error *n*, mistake *n*

Irrtümer und Auslassungen vorbehalten errors and omissions excepted (E. and O.E.)
irrtümlich *adj* wrong, erroneous *adj*
ISDA *f* = *Internationale Vereinigung für Swaps und derivative Instrumente* International Swap and Derivative Association Inc.
Ist-Aufnahme *f* inventory *n*
Ist-Bestand *m* actual amount
Ist-Kosten *plt* actual cost
Ist-Leistung *f* actual performance
Ist-Zahlen *f pl* actuals
Italienische Lira *f* Italian Lira
IWF *m* = **Internationaler Währungsfonds** International Monetary Fund (IMF)

J

Jahrbuch n annual n, yearbook n
Jahresabschluß m annual accounts, annual financial statement
Jahresabschlußzahlung f end-of-year payment
Jahresausschüttung f year's dividend
Jahresausweis m annual statement
Jahresbericht m annual report, annual return (GB)
Jahresbilanz f annual financial statements, annual balance sheet
Jahreseinkommen n annual income
Jahresergebnis n year's result
Jahresertrag m year's earnings
Jahresfehlbetrag m annual deficit, year's net loss
Jahresgewinn m year's profit
Jahreshauptversammlung f annual general meeting
Jahreskonto n yearly account
Jahresproduktion f annual output, annual production
Jahresrate f annual rate, annual instalment
Jahresrechnung f annual account, annual statements of accounts, annual financial statement
Jahresrente f annuity n
Jahresüberschuß m net income for the year
Jahresultimo m year-end n
Jahresumsatz m annual turnover
Jahresvergleich m year-to-year comparison
Jahreswachstum n annual growth
Jahreszahlung f yearly payment, annuity n
Jahreszinsen m pl annual interests n; *effektive -* annual percentages
jährlich adj yearly, annual adj
jährlicher Geschäftsbericht annual report, annual return (GB)
Japanische Auslandsanleihe f shogun bond
Japanische Index der Tokioter Börse m Japanese stock price index (NIKKEI)
Japanische Yen m Japanese Yen
Journal n journal n, day-book n
Jubiläumsbonus m anniversary bonus
Jumboemission f jumbo, jumbo issue, jumbo deal
Jurist m lawyer n, attorney n, solicitor n (GB)
juristisch adj legal, juridical
juristische Person corporate body, juridical person, legal entity
juristischer Sachverständiger legal expert

K

Kabel *n* cable *n*
Kabelauftrag *m* cable order
Kabelauszahlung *f* (Kurs) cable transfer rate, telegraphic transfer rate
kabeln *v* cable *v*
Kabelsatz für Devisentermingeschäfte future cable rate (US)
Kabelüberweisung *f* telegraphic transfer, cable transfer
Kaduzierung von Aktien forfeiture of shares
Kaffeebörse *f* coffee exchange
Kai *m* wharf *n*, quay *n*
Kaiempfangsschein *m* dock receipt
Kaigeld *n* dock charges, dockage *n*, dock dues, wharfage *n*, quayage *n*
Kalender *m* calendar *n*
Kalenderquartal *n* calendar quarter
Kalendertag *m* calendar day
Kalkulation *f* costing, calculation *n*
Kalkulationsabteilung *f* cost department
Kalkulationsaufschlag *m* profit margin, trade margin
Kalkulationsfehler *m* miscalculation
Kalkulationsnorm *f* cost standard
Kalkulator *m* cost accountant
kalkulieren *v* calculate *v*, compute *v*
Kammer für Handelsaktivitäten court of trade
Kampagnekredit *m* crop financing loan, campaign credit
Kanalfracht *f* canal freight
Kandidat *m* candidate, nominee *n*
Kapazität *f* capacity *n*
Kapital *n* capital *n*, equity *n*; ~ *n* (im Gegensatz zu »Zinsen«) principal *n*; ~ **abziehen** alienate capital; ~ **beschaffen** finance *v*; ~ **einbringen** contribute capital; ~ **festlegen** lock up capital; ~ **flüssig machen** liberate capital; ~ **in ein Geschäft stecken** put capital into a business; ~ **und Eigentum eines Trust** corpus *n* (US); ~ **und Zinsen** principal and interest; **arbeitendes** ~ active capital; **brachliegendes** ~ dead capital, dead money, barren money, dormant capital, dormant money, idle capital; **effektiv ausgegebenes** ~ issued stock (US), issued capital (GB); **einbezahltes** ~ paid-up capital; **eingebrachtes** ~ capital brought in; **eingefordertes** ~ called up capital; **eingetragenes** ~ registered capital (GB); **eingezahltes** ~ paid-in capital, paid-up capital; **ertragloses** ~ dead assets; **festgesetztes** ~ declared capital; **flüssiges** ~ active capital; **freies** ~ idle money; **genehmigtes** ~ authorized stock capital; **in** ~ **umwandeln** capitalize *v*, convert into capital; **nicht angelegtes** ~ idle money; **nicht eingezahltes** ~ uncalled capital; **totes** ~ dead capital, dead money; **zu** ~ **machen** capitalize *v*
Kapital- oder Rentenzahlung nach Wahl (Versicherung) insurance option
Kapitalabfindung *f* financial indemnity, cash compensation
Kapitalabschreibung *f* capital depreciation, depreciation of capital
Kapitalabwanderung *f* capital drain, outflow of capital
Kapitalabzug *m* withdrawal of capital
Kapitalanlage *f* investment *n*; **langfristige** ~ capital investment
Kapitalanlageberater *m* investment advisor
Kapitalanlagegesellschaft *f* capital investment company, investment trust; ~ **mit Anlageverwaltung** management trust
Kapitalanlagen *f pl* investments, capital assets; **erstklassige** ~ high-grade investments
Kapitalanleger *m* investor *n*
Kapitalansammlung *f* capital accumulation
Kapitalanteil *m* equity share, amount of stock, capital share, stock share
Kapitalaufnahme *f* raising of capital
Kapitalaufstockung *f* capital increase, increase of capital
Kapitalaufwand *m* capital expenditure, capital cost, capital outlay
Kapitalausfuhr *f* capital export
Kapitalausschüttung *f* capital distribution

Kapitalausstattung

Kapitalausstattung f capital resources, capitalization n
Kapitalbasis f capital base
Kapitalbedarf m capital needs, capital demand, capital requirements, financial requirements
kapitalbedürftig adj needing capital
Kapitalbereitstellung f provision of capital, supply of capital
Kapitalberichtigung f adjustment of capital, capital adjustment, readjustment of capital stock
Kapitalberichtigungsaktie f bonus share (GB), bonus stock (US)
Kapitalbeschaffung f fund raising, raising of capital
Kapitalbesitz m capital holding
Kapitalbeteiligung f equity interest, capital interest
Kapitalbeteiligungsgesellschaft f equity investment company
Kapitalbetrag m amount of capital
Kapitalbewegungen zum Semesterultimo mid-year movements of funds
Kapitalbewertung f capital rating, capital valuation, movement of capital
Kapitalbildung f capital formation, capital accumulation
Kapitalbildungsplan m accumulation schedule
Kapitaldecke f capital base, capital cover
Kapitaldeckungsverfahren n adjustable-contribution procedure, formation of coverage capital
Kapitaldienst m principal repayments, service of capital
Kapitaleinfuhr f capital imports
Kapitaleinkommen n investment income, capital gain, profit derived from capital
Kapitaleinlage f contribution to capital, brought-in capital
Kapitaleinleger m contributor of capital
Kapitaleinsatz m capital invested
Kapitaleinzahlung f contribution to capital, brought-in capital
Kapitaleinziehung f retirement of stock
Kapitalentwertung f capital depreciation
Kapitalerhöhung f capital increase, increase of capital

Kapitalertrag m capital yield, yield on capital, investment income (US)
Kapitalertragsteuer f capital yield tax
Kapitalexport m capital export
Kapitalfestlegung f immobilization of capital
Kapitalflucht f exodus of capital, flight of capital
Kapitalfluß m capital flow
Kapitalforderungen f pl capital claims
Kapitalgeber m investor n
Kapitalgesellschaft f corporation n (US), joint stock company (GB)
Kapitalgewinn m capital gain, profit derived from capital
Kapitalgüter n pl capital goods
Kapitalherabsetzung f capital reduction, reduction of capital stock (US), reduction of share capital (GB)
Kapitalherkunft f source of funds
Kapitalhöhe f amount of capital
kapitalintensiv adj heavily capitalized
Kapitalinteresse; maßgebendes - controlling interest, majority interest
Kapitalinteressen n pl financial interests
Kapitalinvestition f capital investment
kapitalisierbar adj capitalisable, fundable adj
kapitalisieren v capitalize v, convert into capital; **nochmals -** recapitalize v
kapitalisiert adj capitalized
Kapitalisierung f capitalization n
Kapitalisierungsfaktor m capitalization factor
Kapitalismus m capitalism n
Kapitalist m capitalist n
kapitalistisch adj capitalistic adj
Kapitalknappheit f capital shortage
Kapitalkonto n capital account, proprietary account, share account, stock account
Kapitalkonzentration f concentration of capital
Kapitalkosten f capital cost
kapitalkräftig adj well-capitalized, financially strong
Kapitalmarkt m capital market; **Zugang zum -** access to the capital market
kapitalmarktfähig adj ready for the capital market

Kapitalmarktzins m capital market interest rate
Kapitalnehmer m borrower, capital raiser
Kapitalprämie f capital bonus
Kapitalrendite f return on investment
Kapitalrentabilität f return on capital employed (ROCE)
Kapitalreserve f revenue reserves (GB), capital reserve, investment reserve
Kapitalreserven f pl capital surplus
Kapitalrückflußdauer f payback period
Kapitalrücklage f capital reserve, capital surplus
Kapitalschnitt m capital write-down
Kapitalschutz m investors protection
Kapitaltransfer m transfer of capital, capital transfer
Kapitalüberschuß m capital surplus
Kapitalumsatz m capital turnover
Kapitalunterdeckung f capital deficiency, capital shortage
Kapitalverbindlichkeit f capital liability
Kapitalverflechtung f financial interrelation
Kapitalverhältnis n capital ratio
Kapitalverkehr m capital transactions, movement of capital
Kapitalverkehrssteuer f capital transaction tax
Kapitalverlust m capital loss
Kapitalvermögen n capital property, capital assets
Kapitalvermögenssteuer f capital tax
Kapitalverpflichtungen f pl capital commitments
Kapitalverwässerung f watering of stock
Kapitalverwendung f appropriation of capital (funds), employment of funds; *anderweitige ~* displacement of funds
Kapitalverzinsung f rate of return, investment return, investment revenue
Kapitalwert m capital value, principal value
Kapitalzinsen m pl interest on capital
Kapitalzufluß m inflow of capital
Kapitalzusammenlegung f capital consolidation, merger
Kapitalzuschuß m capital contribution
Kapitalzuwachs m capital growth
Karat n carat n
Karriere f career n

Kartell n pool n, combine n
Kartellamt n Federal Trade Commission
Kartellbestimmungen f pl cartel regulations
kartellfeindlich adj anti-trust adj
Kartellgesetzgebung f anti-trust legislation
kartellisieren v cartelize v
Kartellisierung f cartelization n
Kartellvertrag m cartel agreement, pooling agreement
Kartellwesen n cartelism n
Kartenkredit m card credit
Kassadevisen f pl spot exchange
Kassageschäft n cash transaction, cash operation, spot transaction; *~ per Termin* cash forward transaction
Kassakauf m cash buying, outright buying (US)
Kassakonto n cash account, cashier's account
Kassakurs m (Effektenbörse) spot price; *~* (Devisenmarkt) spot rate; *~ ist niedriger als Terminkurs* forwardation (contango)
Kassalieferung f spot delivery
Kassamarkt m cash market
Kassaskonto n cash discount
Kasse f cash n; *~* f (Abteilung) cash office, cash department, cashier's department, teller's department (US); *~ gegen Dokumente* documents against payment, cash against documents; *gegen ~ gekauft* bought for cash; *kleine ~* petty cash
Kassekonto n cash account, cashier's account
Kassenabschluß m teller's proof
Kassenabteilung f paying department
Kassenanweisung f cash note (GB)
Kassenausgänge m pl cash disbursements
Kassenausgangsbuch n cash payments book
Kassenauszahlung f cash disbursement
Kassenbeleg m cash record, cash voucher
Kassenbericht m cash report
Kassenbestand m cash in hand, cash assets, cash holding, cash in vault, money in cash, money in hand, amount in cash, balance in cash
Kassenbote m cash boy, collection clerk
Kassenbuch n cashier's book, till book

Kassendarlehen n cash loan, money loan
Kassendefizit n cash deficit, cash short, shortage of cash, short in cash
Kassendisposition f cash management
Kasseneingänge m pl cash receipts
Kassenfehlbetrag m cash deficit, cash short, shortage of cash, short in cash
Kassenkladde f cash diary, waste book
Kassenkonto n cash account, cashier's account
Kassenkredit m cash advance, cash credit
Kassenmarkt m spot market
kassenmäßig adj relating to cash
Kassenmittel n pl cash resources
Kassenobligation f medium-term bond
Kassenposten m cash item
Kassenprüfung f cash audit
Kassenquittung f cash receipt, cashier's receipt
Kassenraum m counter hall
Kassenreserve f cash reserve
Kassenrevision f cash audit
Kassensaldo m cash balance
Kassenschalter m cash desk, cashier's desk
Kassenscheck m counter check
Kassenschrank m money vault
Kassenstempel m teller stamp (US)
Kassenstrippe f cash register roll
Kassenstunden f pl business hours
Kassenüberschuß durch Irrtümer in der Kassenführung cash over, cash surplus
Kassenumsatz m cash turnover
Kassenverein m securities clearing bank
Kassenverwalter m treasurer n
Kassieren n cashing n
kassieren v cash v, encash v (GB)
Kassierer m cash clerk, cashier n, teller n (US); *- für Auszahlungen* paying teller (US); *- für Ein- und Auszahlungen* unit teller; *- für Einzahlungen* receiving teller; *- für postalisch eingehende Überweisungen* mail teller
Kataster m land register, real estate register (US), cadastre n
Kataster- (in Zus.) cadastral adj
Kauf m buy n, buying n, purchase n, purchasing n; *- auf Kredit* purchase on account; *- gegen Akzept* purchase for acceptance

Kauf-/Abnahmeverpflichtung f purchase commitment
Kaufangebot n offer to buy
Kaufauftrag m buy order, purchase order
Käufe und Verkäufe bids and offers
kaufen v buy v, purchase v; *auf Kredit -* buy on credit, buy on trust, buy on time; *auf Lieferung -* buy forward; *aus erster Hand -* buy at first hand; *gegen bar -* buy for cash, buy for ready money; *mit Verlust -* buy at a loss; *per Kasse gegen sofortige Lieferung -* buy outright (US); *über pari -* buy at a premium
Käufer m buyer n, purchaser n; *- m* (Börse) taker n
Käufermarkt m buyer's market
Käufermonopol n buyer's monopoly
Kaufhaus n department store
Kaufhauswerte m pl department store shares, stores
Kaufkraft f purchasing power; *- abschöpfen* absorb buying power
Kaufkraftindex m purchasing power index
Kaufkraftparität f purchasing power parity
Kaufkredit m purchase-financing loan
Kaufkurs m buying rate, banker's buying rate
käuflich adj buyable adj
Kaufmann m businessman, merchant
kaufmännisch adj commercial adj
kaufmännische Buchführung commercial bookkeeping
kaufmännischer Angestellter employee n; *- Lehrling* commercial trainee
Kaufoption f buyer's option, call option; *- auf einen Terminkontrakt* futures call option; *Kauf (Erwerb) einer -* buying a call; *Käufer (Erwerber) einer -* call buyer (holder); *Verkauf einer -* selling (writing) a call; *Verkäufer (Stillhalter) einer -* call writer, seller of a call; *verkaufte -* short call
Kaufoptionsschein m call warrant; *- mit sehr niedrigem Ausübungspreis* low exercise price option (LEPO); *- und Verkaufsoptionsschein mit dem gleichen Basispreis* call and put option with the same exercise price, straddle (US)

Kaufpreis m purchase price
Kaufpreisfinanzierung f purchase price financing
Kaufpreisminderung f abatement of purchase money
Kaufsumme f purchase money
Kaufvertrag m bill of emption, bill of sale, contract of purchase, contract of sale, deed of sale
Kaution f guarantee, security, bail
Kautionskredit m bank guarantee
Kautionsversicherung f surety insurance, guarantee insurance (GB)
Kautionsversicherungsgeschäft n surety insurance business
Kautionsversicherungsgesellschaft f bonding company, surety company (US)
Kautionswechsel m guarantee bill, collateral bill
keine Deckung (Bankvermerk auf Schecks) n.s.f. (abbreviation for »not sufficient funds«), N./F. (abbreviation for »no funds«)
Kellerwechsel m kite n, wind bill (GB), windmills n pl (GB)
Kenntnis; in ~ setzen inform v
Kennummer f code number; *persönliche* ~ personal identification number (PIN)
Kennwort n code word
Kennzeichen n earmark n
Kerngeschäft n core activity (business)
Kernspeicherabzug m core dump
Kette f chain n
KGV n = *Kurs-Gewinn-Verhältnis* price/earnings ratio (PER)
Kirchensteuer f church tax
KISS n = *Kurs-Informations-und-Service-System* price information system
Kladde f blotter n
klagbar adj actionable adj, suable adj
Klage f suit n; ~ *auf Rechnungslegung* action for accounting; ~ *auf Zahlung* action for payment; ~ *erheben* sue v
Klageerhebung f suit n
klagen v sue v
Kläger m plaintiff, suitor n
Klagerecht n right of action
klären v clear v
Klartext m clear text
klassifizieren v classify v, class v

klassifiziert adj classified adj
Klassifizierung f classification n
Klausel f clause n
Klauseln in Kreditverträgen covenants
Kleinaktien f pl low-prices shares, penny stocks
Kleinaktionär m small shareholder
Kleinbetrieb m small business; ~ *mit geringer Marktkapitalisierung* small cap
Kleindarlehen n small personal loan
Kleindarlehensgeschäft n small-loan business
kleine Kasse petty cash; ~ *Aufwendungen* petty expenses
Kleingeld n loose money, small change, small coins
Kleinhändler m retailer n
Kleinkredit m small personal loan; *persönlicher* ~ cash loan
Kleinkreditgeschäft n small-loan business
Kleinkreditkunde m small borrowing customer
Klient m client n
KMU = kleine und mittlere Unternehmen small and medium-sized enterprises (SME's)
knapp bei Kasse sein be tight, be pressed for money
Ko-Finanzierung f (Gemeinschaftsfinanzierung) co-financing
Kode m code n
Kodierzeile f line of code
kodifizieren v codify v
Kodifizierung f codification n
Kollege m colleague n
Kollektion f assortment n, collection n
Kollektivfrachtbrief m blanket waybill
Kombination f combination n; ~ *1 Kauf- und 2 Verkaufsoptionen* strip; ~ *2 Verkaufs- und 1 Kaufoption* strap; ~ *verschiedener Swaps* cocktail swap
Komitee n committee n
Kommanditgesellschaft f limited partnership; ~ *auf Aktien* company limited by shares with at least one general partner
Kommanditist m special partner, limited partner
Kommanditkapital n limited-liability capital

Kommanditvertrag *m* limited partnership agreement
kommerzialisieren *v* commercialize *v*
Kommerzialisierung *f* commercialization *n*
kommerziell *adj* commercial *adj*
Kommissar *m* commissioner *n*
Kommission *f* commission *n*
Kommissionär *m* commission merchant, commission agent, factor *n*
Kommissionsgeschäft *n* commission business, commission dealing
Kommissionshandel *m* commission business, commission dealing
Kommissionskonto *n* commission account
Kommissionsmakler *m* commission broker
Kommissionsmitglied *n* commissioner *n*
kommissionspflichtig *adj* subject to commission
Kommissionsverkauf *m* commission selling, sale on commission
Kommissionsvertrag *m* commission agreement
kommissionsweise Plazierung placing on commission
kommissionsweiser Verkauf sale on commission
kommunal *adj* communal, local, municipal
Kommunalanleihe *f* municipal bond (US), municipals *n pl*, municipal securities, corporation stocks (GB), corporation loan (GB), local authority loan (GB)
Kommunalbank *f* municipal bank
Kommunaldarlehen *n* public-sector loans (lendings)
Kommunalkredite *m pl* public lendings, public-sector loans, communal loans
Kommunalobligationen *f pl* public-sector debentures (loan), municipal bonds (US), municipals *n pl*, municipal securities
Kommunalschuldverschreibungen *f pl* municipal bonds (US), municipals *n pl*, municipal securities, corporation stocks (GB), corporation loan (GB), local authority loan (GB)
Kommunalsteuern *f pl* local taxes
Kommunalvermögen *n* county fund
Kommune *f* local government
Kompensation *f* compensation *n*

Kompensationsabkommen *n* compensation agreement
Kompensationsgeschäft *n* compensation business, compensation transaction
Kompensationskurs *m* rate of compensation
Kompensationsorder *f* cross order
kompensieren *v* counterbalance *v*, compensate *v*, offset *v*, sett off, indemnify
kompetent *adj* competent *adj*
Kompetenz *f* competence *n*
Komplementär *m* personally liable partner, general partner
komplett *adj* complete *adj*
Komplettkonto *n* comprehensive account
Kompromiß *m* compromise *n*; *einen - schließen* compromise *v*
Konditionen *f pl* conditions *n pl*, terms *n pl*
Konfektionsindustrie *f* clothing industry
Konferenz *f* conference *n*, meeting *n*
konfiszieren *v* confiscate *v*
Konfiszierung *f* confiscation *n*
Kongreß *m* congress *n*, conference
Konjunktur *f* business cycle, economic situation
Konjunkturablauf *m* trade cycle
Konjunkturanalyse *f* analysis of cyclical trends
Konjunkturbaisse *f* cyclical depression
konjunkturbedingt *adj* due to the economic situation
Konjunkturbelebung *f* business recovery, business revival
Konjunkturbeobachter *m* cyclical trend observer, forecaster *n*
Konjunkturberuhigung *f* easing in economic activity
Konjunkturbewegung am Markt market swing (US)
Konjunkturdämpfung *f* decline in economic activity
Konjunkturdiagnose *f* business forecasting
Konjunktureinfluß *m* cyclical influence
konjunkturell *adj* cyclical *adj*
Konjunkturforschung *f* business research
Konjunkturgewinn *m* boom profit
Konjunkturjahr *n* boom year
Konjunkturperiode *f* swing *n* (US)

Konjunkturpolitik f cyclical policy, economic policy
Konjunkturrückgang m depression n
Konjunkturschwankungen f pl economic fluctuations, business fluctuations
Konjunkturtendenz f cyclical trend
Konjunkturverlauf m business cycle
Konjunkturzyklus m business cycle
Konkurrent m competitor n, rival
Konkurrenz f competition n
Konkurrenzbeschränkung f restriction of trade
konkurrenzfähig adj competitive adj
konkurrenzfähiger Preis competitive price
Konkurrenzfähigkeit f competitive power
Konkurrenzkampf m business struggle
Konkurrenzpreis m competitive price
konkurrieren v compete v
konkurrierend adj competing adj
Konkurs m bankruptcy n, insolvency n; *- machen* go bankrupt, fail v; *- durch Gläubigerantrag herbeigeführter -* involuntary bankruptcy; *in - bankrupt* adj, insolvent adj; *in - gehen* become bankrupt, go bankrupt; *in - geraten* become bankrupt, go bankrupt; *unfreiwilliger -* involuntary bankruptcy; *zum - treiben* bankrupt v
Konkursanmeldung f bankruptcy notice, declaration of bankruptcy
Konkursantrag m bankruptcy petition
Konkursbestimmungen f pl bankruptcy rules
Konkurserklärung f bankruptcy notice, declaration of bankruptcy
Konkurseröffnung f adjudication in bankruptcy
Konkurseröffnungsantrag *eines Gläubigers* creditor's petition; *- eines Schuldners* debtor's petition
Konkurseröffnungsbeschluß m decree in bankruptcy
Konkursforderung anmelden prove a claim in bankruptcy
Konkursgericht n court of bankruptcy
Konkursgläubiger m creditor in bankruptcy
Konkursmasse f bankrupt's estate
Konkursordnung f bankruptcy act, bankruptcy statute

Konkursquote f dividend on winding up, dividend in bankruptcy
Konkursrecht n bankruptcy law
Konkursschuldner m bankrupt person, bankrupt n
Konkursverfahren n bankruptcy action, bankruptcy proceedings, bankruptcy examination
Konkursvergehen n act of bankruptcy
Konkursvergleich m composition in bankruptcy
Konkursverwalter m trustee in bankruptcy, liquidator in bankruptcy, bankruptcy commissioner (US)
Konkursverwaltung f receivership n (US)
Konnossement n bill of lading; *- ohne Einschränkung* clean bill of lading; *beglaubigtes -* certified bill of lading; *fehlerhaftes -* unclean bill of lading; *reines -* clean bill of lading; *vollständiger Satz für ein -* full set
Konnossementsdatum n date of bill of lading
Konsignant m consigner n, consignor n
Konsignation f consignment n
Konsignatar m consignee n
konsignieren v consign v
konsolidieren v consolidate v
konsolidierte Anleihe unified stock (GB), consolidated loan; *- Bilanz* consolidated balance sheet, consolidated financial statement; *- Gewinn-und-Verlust-Rechnung* f consolidated profit and loss statement; *- Papiere* consolidated stock (GB); *- Schuld* consolidated debt
Konsolidierung f consolidation n
Konsorte m syndicate member, underwriter, member (of a syndicate)
konsortial adj consortial adj
Konsortialabteilung f syndicate department
Konsortialangebot n syndicate offering
Konsortialbank f member bank of a syndicate
Konsortialbeteiligung f participation in a syndicate
Konsortialführer m lead manager, book runner, book keeper
Konsortialgeschäft n underwriting busi-

ness, syndicate business, syndicate operation
Konsortialkredit m syndicated loan, participating loan, syndicate credit, syndicate loan (US), participation loan
Konsortialmitglied n syndicate member, underwriter n
Konsortialprovision f underwriting commission
Konsortialvertrag m underwriting agreement, syndicate agreement
Konsortium n consortium n, syndicate n; *Mitführer eines -s* co-lead manager
Konstante f constant n
Konstruktion f construction n
Konsul m consul n
Konsulargebühren f pl consular fees
konsularisch adj consular adj
Konsularstatus m consular status
Konsulat n consulate n
Konsulatsdienst m consular service
Konsulatsfaktura f consular invoice
Konsultation f consultation n
konsultieren v consult v
Konsum m consumption n
Konsument m consumer n
Konsumentenkaufkraft f consumer purchasing power
Konsumentenkredit m customer's loan, retail book credit, retail credit (US), consumer credit, consumption credit
Konsumfinanzierung f consumer financing
Konsumfinanzierungswechsel m consumption-financing bill
Konsumgüter n pl consumer goods
konsumieren v consume v
Konsumkraft f consumptive power
Konsumkredit m consume credit
Konsumtrend m consumption trend
Konten n pl accounts n pl; *- abstimmen* agree accounts; *- bereinigen* adjust accounts; *nicht genügend gedeckte -* overextended accounts (US)
Kontenabschluß m balancing accounts, closing of accounts
Kontenabstimmung f (Bank) reconciliation of bank accounts
Kontenart f type of account
Kontenaufgliederung f account classification, breakdown of accounts

Kontenbewegung f account move, activity of accounts
Kontenführungsgebühr f accountkeeping charge
Kontengeschäft n accounts business
Kontenkalkulation f account costing
Kontenrahmen m systematic chart of accounts, systematic schedule of accounts
Kontensperre f blocking of account
Kontenübertrag m transfer in account
Kontenverzeichnis n accounts opened and closed book (US)
Kontenzahl f number of accounts
Kontingent n quote, share, contingent n
Konto n account n; *- für Diverses* sundries account; *- für Zinsen* reserved interest account (GB); *- in laufender Rechnung* current account, running account, open account; *- pro Diverse* sundries account; *- unter Zwangsverwaltung* sequestered account; *- »Verschiedenes«* sundries account; *blockiertes -* frozen account, blocked account; *eingefrorenes -* frozen account, blocked account; *ein - abschließen* balance an account; *ein - auflösen* close an account; *ein - ausgleichen* discharge an account, settle an account; *ein - belasten* charge an account; *ein - erkennen* credit an account; *ein - eröffnen* open an account; *ein - überziehen* overdraw an account; *ein - unterhalten* keep an account; *gemeinsames -* joint account; *gesperrtes -* frozen account, blocked account; *kreditorisches -* credit account; *offenes -* current account, running account, open account; *provisorisches -* suspense account; *totes -* dormant account, inoperative account (GB), broken account, dead account; *transitorisches -* suspended account, suspense account; *umsatzloses -* dormant account, inoperative account (GB), broken account, dead account; *umsatzreiches -* working account; *umsatzstarkes -* active account; *unbewegtes -* dormant account, inoperative account (GB), broken account, dead account; *vorläufiges*

~ suspended account, suspense account; ***zweckbestimmtes*** ~ earmarked account
Kontoabhebung; *Quittung über eine* ~ withdrawal receipt
Kontoabschluß *m* balancing accounts, closing statement
Kontoabtretung *f* assignment of account
Kontoanalyse *f* account analysis
Kontoänderung *f* change of account
Kontoanerkennung *f* approval of account
Kontoauszug *m* statement of account, abstract of account, extract of account, account statement; ***halbjährlicher*** ~ semi-annual account
Kontobearbeitungsgebühr *f* service charge
Kontobezeichnung *f* account title
Kontoblatt *n* account form, account ledger sheet
Kontobuch *n* account book, book of accounts
Kontoeröffnung *f* account opening
Kontofälschung *f* cooking of accounts
Kontofreigabe *f* release of a blocked account
kontoführende Bank accountholding bank
Kontoführer *m* account keeper, account(s) officer
Kontoführung *f* conduct of the account
Kontoführungsgebühr *f* accountkeeping charge
Kontoglattstellung *f* clearing of an account
Kontoguthaben *n pl* account balance, account deposits; ***ungenügende*** ~ n.s.f. (abbreviation for »not sufficient funds«), N/F. (abbreviation for »no funds«)
Kontoinhaber *m* account holder
Kontokarte *f* account card
Kontokorrentbuch *n* current account ledger, money lent and lodged book (GB)
Kontokorrentforderungen *f pl* debts founded on open account
Kontokorrentkonto *n* current account, running account, open account; ***gemeinschaftliches*** ~ joint current account
Kontokorrentkredit *m* advance on current account, current account credit, overdraft facility in current account, loan on overdraft, open credit
Kontokorrentverbindlichkeiten *f pl* deposit liabilities
Kontonummer *f* account number
Kontonummernsystem *n* account numbering system
Kontorist *m* clerk *n*
Kontoschließung *f* account close
Kontostand *m* account balance, state of an account
Kontoübertrag *m* transfer to another account, internal-transfer
Kontoüberziehung *f* overdraft *n*; ***kurzfristige*** ~ temporary overdraft; ***technische*** ~ technical overdraft
Kontoumsatz *m* account turnover
Kontounterlagen *f pl* account files
Kontountersuchung *f* account analysis
Kontoverbindung *f* accounting connection
Kontrahent *m* contractant *n*, contracting party, stipulator *n*
kontrahieren *v* contract *v*
Kontrakt *m* contract *n*
Kontrollabschnitt *m* counterfoil *n*, stub *n* (US)
Kontrollbuch über die ausgehenden Briefe letters dispatched book (GB)
Kontrolle *f* (Überprüfung) check *n*, checking *n*; ~ *f* (Einflußnahme) control *n*; ~ *f* (Überwachung) control *n*, supervision *n*; ~ ***durch das Heimatland*** home-country control; ***programmierte*** ~ programmed check
Kontrolleur *m* controller *n*
kontrollieren *v* control, check *v*
kontrollierende Gesellschaft controlling company
Kontrollinformation *f* checking information
Kontrollkonto *n* controlling account, control account
Kontrollnummer *f* test number, code number
Kontrolluhr *f* time clock
Kontrollvermerk *m* control note
Konventionalstrafe *f* contractual penalty
Konversionssatz *m* rate of conversion
Konversionsschuldverschreibung *f* conversion bond
Konvertibilität *f* convertibility *n*

konvertierbar *adj* convertible *adj*; **nicht -** inconvertible *adj*

konvertierbares Papiergeld convertible paper currency

Konvertierbarkeit *f* convertibility *n*; **beschränkte -** limited convertibility; **unbeschränkte -** full convertibility

konvertieren *v* convert *v*

Konvertierung *f* conversion *n*, exchange

Konvertierungsanleihe *f* conversion bond

Konzentration *f* concentration *n*

Konzentratornetz *n* concentrator network

Konzern *m* group of companies, trust *n*, combine *n*, group company, group

Konzernbilanz *f* consolidated balance sheet, consolidated financial statement, group balance sheet

Konzernentflechtung *f* demerger, spin-off

Konzernfirmen *f pl* group companies

Konzerngesellschaft *f* affiliated company (GB), affiliated corporation (US) group company

Konzerngewinne *m pl* group profits

Konzerngruppe *f* consolidated group

Konzernüberschuß *m* consolidated surplus (GB)

Konzernumsatz *m* group sales, turnover of a combine

Konzernverflechtung *f* interlocking combine

Konzertzeichner *m* stag *n* (GB)

Konzertzeichnung *f* stagging

Konzertzeichnungen; den Markt durch - beeinflussen stag the market

Konzession *f* franchise *n* (US), concession *n*

Konzessionär *m* concessionaire *n*, concessionary *n* (US)

konzessionierte Bank chartered bank (GB); **- Gesellschaft** chartered company

Konzessionsinhaber *m* concessionaire *n*, concessionary *n* (US)

koordinieren *v* coordinate *v*

Koordinierung *f* coordination *n*

Kopf; pro - per capita

Kopffiliale *f* main branch

Kopfsteuer *f* poll tax, capitation tax

Kopie *f* copy *n*

Kopierbuch *n* duplicating book

kopieren *v* copy *v*

Kopplungsgeschäft *n* package deal

Korbwährung *f* basket currency

Körper *m* body *n*

körperliche Wirtschaftsgüter tangible assets

Körperschaft *f* body, corporate body, corporation *n*; **- des öffentlichen Rechts** statutory company, statutory corporation; **öffentliche -** public corporation, corporation under public law

körperschaftlich *adj* corporate *adj*

Körperschaftssteuer *f* corporation tax

Körperschaftssteuervorauszahlung *f* advance corporation tax

korporativ *adj* corporate *adj*; - corporately, jointly and severally

Korrektur *f* correction *n*, adjustment *n*

Korrespondent *m* correspondent *n*

Korrespondenz *f* correspondence *n*

Korrespondenzbank *f* correspondent bank; **unverzinsliche Sichteinlagen bei einer -** compensation balance

Korrespondenzscheck *m* correspondence check

korrespondieren *v* correspond *v*

korrigieren *v* correct *v*, rectify *v*

kosten *v* cost *v*

Kosten *plt* cost, costs, expenses, expenditures, charges; **- nach Abschreibungen** amortized cost; **fixe -** fixed costs, overhead expenses; **laufende -** recurring costs; **nachträgliche -** after costs; **-, Versicherung, Fracht** cost, insurance and freight (c.i.f.)

Kostenanalyse *f* cost analysis

Kostenangaben *f pl* cost data

Kostenanschlag *m* tender *n*

Kostenaufteilung *f* cost breakdown

Kostenaufwand *m* expenses *n pl*, expenditure(s)

Kostenbeleg *m* cost record

Kostenberechnung *f* costing *n*, computation of costs

Kostenbeteiligung *f* cost sharing

Kostendegression *f* cost decrease, declining costs

Kosteneinheit *f* cost unit

Kostenerhöhung *f* cost increase

Kostenersparnis *f* cost saving

Kostenerstattung *f* refund of costs

kostenfrei *adj* cost-free *adj*
Kostengefüge *n* cost structure
Kosteninflation *f* cost push inflation
Kostenkalkulation *f* cost calculation, costing, computation of costs
Kostenkonto *n* cost account
Kostenkontrolle *f* cost control
kostenlos *adj* cost-free *adj*; **~** *adv* without charge, free of charge
Kosten-Nutzen-Analyse *f* cost-benefit analysis
Kostenpreis *m* cost price
Kostenrechner *m* cost accountant
Kostenrechnung *f* cost accounting, costing
Kostenrechnungsmethode *f* cost method
Kostensenkung *f* cost reduction, cost-cutting
Kostensteigerung *f* cost increase
Kostenstelle *f* cost center
Kostenüberprüfer *m* (Controller) comptroller *n* (US), controller
Kostenunterlagen *f pl* cost data
Kostenvoranschlag *m* cost estimate
Kostenvorschuß *m* advance on costs
kostenwirksam cost-effective
Kostenzuschlag *m* extra charges
kostspielig *adj* expensive *adj*; **~ sein** run into money
kotiert *adj* (Schweiz) quoted *adj*, listed *adj* (US)
Kraft; in ~ treten become effective
Kraftfahrzeugwerte *m pl* motors
kraftlos *adj* invalid, null and void
Kraftloserklärung *f* invalidation, annulment; **~ von Wertpapieren** cancellation of securities
Kredit *m* credit *n*; **~** *m* loan *n*; **~ gewähren** allow a credit; **abgesicherter ~** secured credit, secured loan; **aufgenommener ~** borrowed money; **aufgeschobener ~** deferred credit; **bei jemandem einen ~ eröffnen** lodge a credit with; **bestätigter ~** confirmed credit; **durchlaufender ~** transmitted loan; **einen ~ aufnehmen** contract a loan, borrow money; **einen ~ einräumen** allow a credit; **einen ~ einrichten** establish a credit; **einen ~ eröffnen** establish a credit; **einen ~ kündigen** draw in a loan; **eingefrorener ~** frozen credit, frozen loan; **endfälliger ~** bullet loan, balloon loan; **gesicherter ~** secured credit, secured loan; **in Anspruch genommener ~** credit in use; **landwirtschaftlicher ~** rural credit; **langfristiger ~** extended credit; **laufender ~** standing credit; **nicht in Anspruch genommener ~** unavailed credit; **normierter ~** standardized loan; **offener ~** advance on current account, current account credit, overdraft facility in current account, loan on overdraft, open credit; **öffentlicher ~** public loan, public credit; **ohne ~** uncredited *adj*; **revolvierender ~** revolving credit; **sich automatisch erneuernder ~** revolving credit; **syndizierter ~** syndicated loan; **täglich fälliger ~** day-to-day loan (GB), day loan, demand loan; **unbefristeter ~** evergreen credit (US); **vorläufiger ~** bridgeover *n*; **widerruflicher ~** revocable credit; **zinsloser ~** credit given flat; **zuviel ~ gewähren** overcredit *v*
Kreditabkommen *n* credit agreement
Kreditabteilung *f* credit department, loan department
Kreditakte *f* credit file, credit folder
Kreditangebot *n* loan offer, credit offer
Kreditanspannung *f* credit strain
Kreditanstalt *f* credit institution; **~ für Wiederaufbau** *f* **= KfW** Reconstruction Loan Corporation
Kreditantrag *m* loan application
Kreditantragsformular *n* credit form (US)
Kreditantragsteller *m* credit applicant
Kreditaufnahme *f* borrowing *n*
Kreditaufnahmemöglichkeiten *f pl* borrowing facilities
Kreditauftrag *m* credit order
Kreditausfall *m* loan loss, credit loss
Kreditauskunft *f* credit bureau report, credit information, credit report, status report; **Bitte um ~** credit enquiry; **gegenseitige ~** credit interchange
Kreditauskunftei *f* credit agency, credit bureau
Kreditauskunfteibericht *m* agency report (US)
Kreditauskunftsanfrage *f* credit enquiry

Kreditauskunftsorganisation f credit service organization
Kreditausschuß m loan committee
Kreditausweitung f credit expansion
Kreditbank f commercial bank, loan bank, credit bank
Kreditbasis f credit basis
Kreditbearbeiter m credit man
Kreditbedarf m borrowing requirements (needs)
Kreditbedingungen f pl credit conditions, credit terms
Kreditbedürfnis n credit requirement (US)
kreditbereit adj ready to lend
Kreditbereitschaft f readiness to lend
Kreditbereitstellung f loan arrangement, extension of a loan
Kreditbesicherung f security for a loan
Kreditbetrag m credit line, line of credit, credit limit
Kreditbetrug m credit robbery, obtaining money by false pretences
Kreditbewilligung f loan approval, lending, credit granting
Kreditbrief m letter of credit; *an eine bestimmte Bank gerichteter* ~ direct letter of credit (GB)
Kreditbriefinhaber m beneficiary of a letter of credit
Kreditbürgschaft f loan guarantee
Kreditbüro n credit department, loan department
Kreditdisagio n loan discount, debt discount
Krediteinschränkung f credit restriction
Kreditfachmann m credit expert
Kreditfähigkeit f creditability n, legal right to demand credit (e.g. through power of attorney)
Kreditfaktor m credit element
Kreditfazilitäten f pl credit facilities
Kreditformular n credit form (US)
Kreditgarantiegemeinschaft f credit guarantee association
Kreditgeber m lender n, lending bank
Kreditgenossenschaft f cooperative credit union, cooperative savings organization, credit cooperative
Kreditgeschäft n lendings, credit business
Kreditgeschäfte n pl credit operations

Kreditgesellschaft f credit society
Kreditgesuch n loan application
Kreditgewährung f lending n, granting of credit, credit accommodation
Kreditgewerbe n banks, banking industry, banking trade, banking business
Kreditgrenze f limit of credit, lending limit
Kreditgrundsätze m pl credit principles
Kredithai m (Wucherer) loan shark
Kredithilfe f financial aid
kreditieren v lend, credit v
Kreditinanspruchnahme f borrowing
Kreditinstitut n credit institution; *genossenschaftliches* ~ cooperative bank
Kreditinstrument n financial instrument
Kreditkapazität f lending capacity, credit capacity
Kreditkapital n borrowed capital
Kreditkarte f credit card; ~ *mit elektronischem System* memory card, smart card; *goldene* ~ gold card (for affluent private customers)
Kreditkauf m credit sale, purchase on credit, credit buying
Kreditknappheit f credit squeeze, credit stringency
Kreditkommission f credit commission
Kreditkonditionen f pl credit conditions, credit terms
Kreditkonto n loan account
Kreditkontrolle f (staatliche) credit control
Kreditkosten plt credit cost, cost of borrowing, charges on credits
Kreditkrise f credit crisis
Kreditkunde m borrowing customer
Kreditlimit n credit limit, lending limit; *revolvierendes* ~ revolving credit
Kreditlinie f credit line, line of credit, credit limit, swingline facility; ~ *für mehrere Währungen* multi-currency credit line; *nicht in Anspruch genommene* ~ undrawn overdraft facility
Kreditmanagement n credit management
Kreditmarge f credit margin
Kreditmaßstäbe m pl credit barometrics
Kreditmißbrauch m credit abuse
Kreditmittel n credit instrument; *staatliche* ~ state loans
Kreditmöglichkeiten f pl credit facility

Kreditnachfrage f demand for credit, credit demand
Kreditnehmer m borrower n
Kreditor m creditor n, debtee n, obligee n
Kreditoren m pl deposits; **~** m pl (aus Lieferantenschulden) accounts payable; **~** m pl payables n pl (US); **~ auf Sicht** demand deposits; **~ auf Zeit** time deposits; **~ in laufender Rechnung** account current creditors; **diverse ~** (Kontobezeichnung) sundry creditors account (GB)
Kreditorenabteilung f deposit banking division, deposit department
kreditorisch adj on the credit side, as a creditor
kreditorisches Konto creditor account
Kreditpapier n credit instrument
Kreditplafond m lending ceiling, borrowing limit, line of credit, credit limit (GB)
Kreditpolitik f credit policy, lending policy
kreditpolitisch adj relating to credit policy
kreditpolitische Situation credit situation
Kreditpotential n lending power
Kreditprogramm n lending programme
Kreditprolongation f renewal of credit
Kreditprovision f loan commission, credit commission
Kreditprüfung f loan review, credit checking
Kreditquellen f pl credit resources
Kreditrahmen m credit line, line of credit, credit limit
Kreditregister n credit ledger
Kreditrestriktion f credit restriction
Kreditrichtlinien f pl loan directives, credit rules, credit standards
Kreditrisiko n credit risk
Kreditsachbearbeiter m credit officer, loan officer
Kreditsaldo m loan balance
Kreditschöpfung f creation of credit
Kreditschrumpfung f credit contraction
Kreditsicherheit f loan collateral, credit collateral, security for credit; **Unterlegung durch eine ~** security backing
Kreditsicherstellung f safeguarding of credits
Kreditsituation f state of credit
Kreditsperre f stoppage of credit
Kreditsumme f loan amount

Kreditteilbeträge m pl transferable loan facility
Kredittranche f (IMF) credit tranche
Kreditüberschreitung (Kreditüberziehung) f overdraft n
Kreditunterbeteiligung f loan sub-participation
Kreditvaluta f proceeds of loan
Kreditverein m credit union
Kreditvereinbarung f credit arrangement
Kreditvereinbarungen; Allgemeine ~ General Agreement to Borrow (GAB)
Kreditvergabe mit beweglichem Kreditrahmen contingency lending; **unfreiwillige ~** involuntary lending
Kreditverkauf m credit sale, loan sale
Kreditverknappung f restriction of credit
Kreditvermittler m credit broker, loan broker
Kreditvermittlungsbüro n credit agency, credit bureau
Kreditversicherung f credit insurance, loan insurance
Kreditvertrag m loan contract, loan agreement; **~ mit gleichbleibenden Sicherheiten** continuing agreement (US)
Kreditvolumen n loan portfolio, credit volume
Kreditwechsel m credit bill
Kreditwesen n credit system
Kreditwesengesetz n Banking Law, German law concerning the credit system
Kreditwunsch m borrowing demand
kreditwürdig adj credit-worthy, creditable adj
Kreditwürdigkeit f creditability n, credit-worthiness n, borrowing power, credit standing
Kreditwürdigkeitsprüfung f credit scoring, credit rating (US), credit investigation
Kreditzinsen m pl loan interest
Kreditzinssatz m loan rate, borrowing rate
Kreditzusage f advance commitment, promise of a credit; **rechtsverbindliche ~** legally binding promise of a loan; **unwiderrufliche ~** irrevocable loan promise
Kreissparkasse f district savings bank

kreuzen v cross v; (gekreuzter Scheck) crossed cheque
Kriegsanleihe f war loan, victory loan (GB)
Krise f crisis n
Krone f crown n; ~ Krone (Danish and Norwegian currency unit)
Krügerrand m Krugerrand = South African gold coin (1 ounze gold)
Kulisse f unofficial market
kumulativ adj cumulative adj
kumulative Aktien cumulative stocks (US); **- Dividende** cumulative dividend; **- Vorzugsaktien** cumulative preference stocks
kündbar adj subject to notice, redeemable adj
kündbare Anleihe callable bond, puttable bond; **- Obligationen** optional bonds (US); **- Vorzugsaktien** redeemable preferred stock
kündbares Swapgeschäft puttable swap
Kunde m customer, client; **voraussichtlicher** - prospective customer; **zukünftiger** - prospect n
Kunden abwerben draw away customers, alienate customers
Kundenakzept n trade acceptance
Kundenauftrag m customer's order
Kundenbedürfnis n customer's needs
Kundenberater m customer adviser
Kundenberatungsdienst m advisory service for customers
Kundenbeschwerde f customer's complaint
Kundenbetreuung f customer service, client service
Kundendienst m service n
Kundendienstabteilung f service department
Kundenempfehlung f customer recommendation
Kundengelder n pl client money, customer deposits
Kundenkonten n pl accounts with customers
Kundenkonto n customer account, charge account
Kundenkredit m customer's loan, retail book credit, retail credit (US), consumer credit, consumption credit

Kundenkreis m customers, clientele n
Kundenliste f customers register
kundennah adj customer-oriented adj
Kundensichteinlagen f pl customers' sight deposits, customers' demand deposits
Kundenverkehr m customers' traffic
Kundenwartezeit f customer waiting time
Kundenwechsel m trade bill, bill on customers, customer's bill, customer's note; **~** m pl (Bilanz) trade notes receivable, bills receivable
Kundenwerbeabteilung f business department
Kundenwerbung f canvassing, winning new customers
Kundenwünsche m pl customer's wishes
kündigen v call in v, give notice
Kündigung f (einer Anleihe) call for redemption; **~** f notice n; **schriftliche ~** written notice; **wöchentliche ~** seven days' notice
Kündigungsfrist f term of notice, period of notice; **gesetzliche ~** statutory period of notice
Kündigungsgeld n money at notice
Kündigungsklausel f cancellation clause
Kündigungskonto n account subject to notice
Kündigungsrecht n right to give notice, right to call for redemption
Kündigungssperrfrist f notice of withdrawal period
Kündigungstermin m call date, last day for giving notice
Kundschaft f customers, clientele n
künstlich adj artificial adj; **- gehaltener Devisenkurs** pegged exchange
Kupfermünze f cooper coin
Kupfermünzen f pl coopers n pl
Kupon m coupon n; **abgetrennter ~** detached coupon; **ausstehender ~** outstanding coupon; **laufender ~** current coupon; **notleidender ~** overdue coupon; **unbezahlbarer ~** outstanding coupon
Kuponabteilung f coupon collection department
Kuponbogen m coupon sheet
Kuponeinlösung f collection of coupons, coupon service

Kuponinhaber m coupon holder
Kuponkasse f coupons paying department
Kuponkassierer m coupon collection teller (US), coupon teller
Kuponscheck m coupon check (US)
Kupontermin m coupon date
kurant marketable
Kurantgeld n current money
Kurantmünze f full legal tender coin
Kurator m administrator n
Kurs m price, rate, quotation; *~ m (Devisenbörse)* exchange rate; *~ für Termingeschäfte* futures rate (US); *außer ~ setzen* v *(Münzen)* demonetize v; *außerbörslicher ~* curb market price; *einen ~ heraufsetzen* advance the price, advance the rate; *höchster ~* top price; *nachbörslicher ~* curb market price; *nachträglicher ~* after price
Kursabschlag m discount, backwardation n (GB)
Kursänderung f change of rates
Kursanstieg m price increase, rise n
Kursanzeigetafel f exchange board
kursanziehend adj rising adj
Kursaussetzung f suspension of a quotation
Kursbeeinflussung f manipulation n
Kursbericht m *(Devisen)* exchange list, bill of course of exchange
Kursbewegung f price movement, price range
Kursbewegungen f pl share movements
Kursbildung f price movement, price range
Kursblatt n quotation list, stock exchange list
Kurs-Cash-flow-Verhältnis n prise/cash flow ratio
Kursdifferenz f price difference, exchange rate difference
Kurse drücken bear the market, bear the stocks; *~ in die Höhe treiben* rush v (US); *~ steigern* boom the market; *abgeschwächte ~* market off (US); *die ~ haben sich gebessert* prices have improved; *die ~ liegen schwächer* prices have decreased
Kurseinbruch m break in prices
Kursentwicklung f price movement, price range; *~ f (Devisen)* rate development

Kursfestsetzung f price making, rate fixing
Kursgarantie f exchange rate guarantee
Kursgewinne mitnehmen benefit by the exchange
Kurs-Gewinn-Verhältnis n (KGV) price/earnings ratio (PER)
Kursindex m price index
Kurslimit n price limit
Kursmakler m broker n
Kursmanipulierung f price rigging, price/rate manipulation n
Kursnotierung, *erste ~* first board; *verbindliche ~* firm quotation
Kursobergrenze f price cap
Kursparität f exchange parity
Kurspflege f price-regulating operations, price support
Kursrendite f yield on price, dividend yield
Kursrisiko n price risk, exchange risk
Kursrückgang *einer Aktie* decrease in stock price (US); *allgemeiner ~* retreat n; *geringfügiger ~* shading n
Kursschwankungen f pl price swings, price fluctuation
Kursschwankungsausmaß n volatility
Kurssicherung durch ein Devisentermingeschäft forward cover
Kurssicherung f hedge; *~ von Devisen* rate-hedging; *~ von Wertpapieren* hedge against price risks
Kurssicherungsgeschäft n rate-hedging transaction, rate fixing business
Kurssprünge m pl price jumps, spurts n pl
Kursstand m price level
Kurssteigerung f rise in stock prices; *plötzliche ~* sharp price advance n, spurt n
Kurssturz m break in prices; *plötzlicher ~* slump n
kursstützend adj price-supporting
Kursstützung f price support, peg n
Kursstützungsfaktoren m pl stabilizing factors of the market
Kursteilnehmer m trainee n
Kurstreiberei f market rigging
Kursunterschied m difference in rates
Kursus m course n
Kursverlust m loss on price, loss on exchange

Kursverlustversicherung *f* insurance against loss by redemption

Kurswert *m* market value, market price, exchange price, market rate, quoted value

Kurswertberechnung *f* rate calculation

Kurszettel *m* list of quotations; *-* *m* (Devisen) exchange list

kürzen *v* reduce v, cut down, cut v

kurzfristig *adj* short-term *adj*, short-dated *adj*; *- zurückzahlbare Schulden* quick liabilities

kurzfristige Anleihe short term bond, short-term credit, short-sighted loan; *- Finanzierung* short-term financing; *- Kontoüberziehung* temporary overdraft

kurzfristiger Kredit short-term loan, short-term credit, short-sighted loan; *- Wechsel* short-term bill

kurzfristiges Darlehen short-term loan, short-term credit, short-sighted loan

Kurzläufer *m* short (maturity) bond, short

kurzlebige Wirtschaftsgüter wasting assets

Kürzung *f* cut, curtailment, reduction

Kux *m* share of a mining company

KWG *n* = *Kreditwesengesetz* (Deutschland) German Banking Act

L

Ladebuch n cargo-book n
Ladefähigkeit f cargo capacity
Ladegebühr f loading charges
Ladegeschäft n loading business
Ladehafen m port of lading
laden v load
Laden m store n
Ladenbesitzer m shopkeeper n, store owner (US)
Ladenkasse f till n, cash register
Ladeschein m (Landtransport) carriage receipt; ~ m certificate of shipment
Ladung f load, shipment, cargo n
Ladungspapier n cargo document
Lage eines Grundstücks site n
Lager n warehouse n, store n, storehouse n
Lagerabbau m stock reduction
Lageraufüllung f stock replenishment
Lagerbestand m stock on hand, stock position, inventory
Lagerbestände m pl inventories n pl, stock in hand, supplies n pl
Lagerempfangsschein m warehouse receipt
Lagergeld n storage charges, warehouse fee
Lagerhalter m warehouseman n, stock clerk, store keeper
Lagerhalterpfandrecht n warehousemen's lien
Lagerhaltung f stock keeping
Lagerhaus n warehouse n, store n, storehouse n
Lagerkapazität f storage capacity
Lagerkosten pl t storage costs
Lagerplatz m place of storage, depot n, storing place
Lagerraum m warehouse space
Lagerschein m warehouse certificate (US), warehouse warrant; ~ **für sicherungsübereignete Waren** warehouse receipt
Lagerstelle f (im Depotgeschäft) safekeeping address
Lager- und Finanzierungskosten f pl carrying charges

Lagerverwalter m warehouseman n, stock clerk, store keeper
Landeplatz m landing place
Länderfonds m fund investing in a specific country
Länderrisiko n country risk
Länderstatistik f (international) statistics by countries; ~ f (Land, Provinz) statistics by states
Landesbank f Central Savings Bank, regional bank
Landeswährung f national currency
Landgut n estate n
landwirtschaftliche Hypothek farm mortgage
landwirtschaftlicher Kredit farm credit
landwirtschaftliches Darlehen farm loan, farm credit, agricultural loan
Landwirtschaftsbank f agricultural bank
Landwirtschaftskredit m farm loan, farm credit, agricultural loan
langfristig adj long-term adj, longdated adj
langfristige Anlagevorhaben capital projects; ~ **Kapitalanlage** capital investment; ~ **Schulden** long-term debt; ~ **Verbindlichkeit** capital liability; ~ **Verpflichtungen** long-term obligations
langfristiger Kredit long-term credit; ~ **Wechsel** long-term bill
langfristiges Darlehen long-sighted loan, long-term loan
Last f burden n, charge n, load n
Lasten; zu ~ von chargeable to
Lastenausgleichsbank f Equalization of Burdens Bank
Lastenumverteilung f (z. B. Umschuldung) burden sharing
Lastschrift f debit, direct debit, debit entry
Lastschriftbeleg m debit voucher
Lastschrifteinzug m debit transfer order collection
Lastschriftverfahren n debit charge procedure, direct debit system
Laufbahn f career n
laufen v (z. B. von Wechseln) run v

laufend *adj* current, consecutive, running, successive

laufende Kosten running costs, recurring costs; **~ Notierung** consecutive quotation; **~ Nummer** serial number; **~ Rendite** current yield; **~ Verbindlichkeiten** current liabilities; **~ Verzinsung** running yield (GB); **~ Zinsen** current interest

laufender Ertrag current yield; **~ Gewinn** current yield; **~ Kredit** standing credit; **~ Kupon** current coupon; **~ Zins** broken-period-interest

laufendes Konto current account, running account, open account

Laufzeit f maturity, duration; **~ f (eines Vertrages)** life n (of a contract); **~ f period** n; **~ einer Anleihe** life of a loan, term of a loan; **~ eines Kredits** credit period; **~ eines Wechsels** tenor of a bill; **mittlere ~** average term

Laufzeitbegrenzung f maturity cap

Laufzettel m tracer n

lautend auf issued to, made out to, payable to

Lead Manager m (Führer eines Konsortiums) lead manager, book keeper (runner)

Leasing n (Vermietung, Verpachtung) leasing n; **~ zwischen Konzernunternehmen in verschiedenen Ländern** inter-company leasing

Leasinggeber m lessor

Leasingnehmer m lessee

Leasingvertrag m lease agreement

Lebenshaltungskostenindex m cost of living index

Lebenshaltungskosten plt cost of living

lebenslange Rente life annuity, perpetual annuity; **~ Treuhandverwaltung** living trust (US)

Lebensrente f life annuity, perpetual annuity

Lebensversicherung f life assurance (GB), life insurance; **~ auf den Todesfall** whole-life insurance

Lebensversicherungsgesellschaft f life assurance company

lebenswichtige Güter essentials n pl, essential goods

lebhaft *adj* brisk *adj*, active *adj*

Leerkauf m fictitious purchase

Leerverkauf m short sale; **~ von Aktien** short stock sale

Leerverkäufe auf Baisse short selling

Leerverkaufsposition f short position

legalisieren v legalize v

Legalisierung f legalization n

Legat n legacy n, legate n, bequest n; **~ n taker** n (US)

legatsberechtigt *adj* beneficially entitled

Legierung f alloy n

Legitimation f proof of identity

legitimieren (sich) v prove one's identity, legitimate

Lehre f training n, apprenticeship n

Lehrgang m course n

Lehrling m trainee, apprentice n; **kaufmännischer ~** trainee

Lehrlingsausbildung f training

Lehrzeit f apprenticeship n

Leibrente f life annuity, perpetual annuity; **~ ohne Zahlung im Todesfall** non-apportionable annuity

Leibrentenvertrag m contract of annuity

leicht reagierende Börse sensitive market; **~ realisierbare Aktiva** (z.B. Kasse, Bank, Postscheckguthaben, börsengängige Wertpapiere, Außenstände) quick assets

leichtfertig *adj* negligent *adj*, reckless *adj*

Leichtfertigkeit f negligence n, recklessness n

leihen v lend v, loan v, borrow v

Leihen n lending n, loan n, borrowing n

Leihgeld n money lent

Leihkapital n borrowed capital

Leistung f (eines Investmentfonds) performance n (of a mutual fund); **geldliche ~** payment n

Leistungen; zusätzliche ~ fringe benefits

Leistungsbilanzüberschuß m current account surplus

Leistungsfähigkeit f efficiency n

Leistungsgarantie f performance guarantee

leistungsorientiert *adj* performance-minded

leistungsstark *adj* efficient

Leitbörse f leading stock exchange

leiten v direct v; - v manage v, supervise v, lead v
leitender Angestellter executive n
Leiter m manager n; **- des Rechnungswesens** controller n
Leitfaden m manual n, handbook n
Leitstelle f head office
Leitungsgeschwindigkeit f line speed
Leitungsnetz; sternförmiges - radial transmission network
Leitwährung f leading currency, key currency
Leitzinsen m pl basic interest rates
Leitzinssatz m prime rate
lenkbar adj manageable adj
lenken v control v, direct, regulate
Lenkung f control n, direction, regulation
letzte Bilanz ultimate balance
letzter Tag des Monats ultimo n; **- Wille** will n, testament n, last will
letztwillig adj testamentary adj
letztwillige Verfügung (über Grundbesitz) devise n, will n, testament n, last will
liberalisieren v decontrol v, liberalize v
Liberalisieren des Kapitalverkehrs liberalize of capital markets
LIBID m **= Geldmarktzinssatz am Londoner Interbanken-Geldmarkt** London Interbank Bid Rate
LIBOR m **= Londoner Interbanken-Angebotszinssatz** London Interbank Offered Rate; **- ohne Aufschlag** LIBOR flat
Liebhaberwert m sentimental value
Lieferant m supplier n
Lieferantenkredit m supplier credit
lieferbar adj deliverable adj
Lieferbedingungen f pl terms of delivery
Lieferkosten plt cost of delivery
liefern v deliver v; - v furnish v, supply v
Lieferort m delivery place, place of delivery
Lieferschein m delivery note, bill of delivery, delivery order
Liefertermin m delivery date
Lieferung f (Auslieferung) delivery n; - f supply n; **- gegen Kasse** comptant (c); **- ohne Spesen** freight prepaid; **- ohne Versandspesen** postage paid; **schlechte -** bad delivery, defective delivery; **zahlbar bei -** cash on delivery (C.O.D.)

Lieferungsanzeige f delivery ticket
Lieferungsbedingungen f pl terms of delivery
Lieferungstag m (Börse) account day (GB)
Liegenschaften f pl realty n, real property, landed property, real estate, real assets
Liegenschaftsfonds m real estate investment fund
LIFFE m London International Financial Futures Exchange
LIMEAN m = **mittlerer Geldmarktzinssatz zwischen LIBOR und LIBID** London Interbank Mean Rate
Limit n limit n; **dehnbares -** elastic limit, flexible limit
limitieren v limit
limitiert adj limited adj, restricted adj
limitierter Auftrag (Börsenorder) limited order
Limitkurs m limit price (rate)
lineare Abschreibung straight-line depreciation
Liquidation f liquidation n; **außergerichtliche -** liquidation by arrangement
Liquidationsanteil m liquidating dividend
Liquidationskonto n settlement account, realization and liquidation account
Liquidationsrate f liquidating dividend
Liquidationstag m (Abrechnungstag) settlement day, settling day
Liquidationswert m liquidating value
Liquidator m liquidator n, receiver n
liquide adj solvent adj; **- Anlagen** (Reserven) liquid investments; **- Mittel** available funds
liquidieren v liquidate v, wind up; - v (z. B. Investmentanteile) redeem v, liquidate v, realize v
Liquidierung f liquidation, winding-up, dissolution, realization n
Liquidität f liquidity n; **Planung, Steuerung und Kontrolle der -** cash management
Liquiditätsanspannung f strain on liquidity
Liquiditätsausweis m liquidity statement
Liquiditätsgrad m liquidity ratio, current ratio, »acid-test« ratio

Liquiditätsmangel

Liquiditätsmangel m squeeze n
Liquiditätsreserve f liquidity reserve
Liquiditätssteuerung (und Finanzplanung) treasury management
Liquiditätsumschichtung f change in liquidity
Liquiditätsverhältnis n liquidity ratio, current ratio, »acid-test« ratio
Lira f (italienische Lira) Italian Lira
Liste f list n
Listenbild n printer layout, list structure
Lizenz f licence n, license n
Lizenzgeber m licensor
Lizenzgebühr f royalty n, licence fee
Lizenznehmer m licensee
Lizenzvertrag m licence contract
Lohn m wage n, pay, wages n pl
Lohnabrechnung f payroll accounting
Lohnbuchhalter m timetaker n, timekeeper n
Lohnempfänger m wage earner
Lohnkonto n payroll account
Lohnliste f payroll n
Lohnpfändung f wage, garnishment (US)
Lohnscheck m pay check, wages check
Lohnsteuer f income tax, wage tax
Lohnstreitigkeiten f pl labor conflict
Lohnvorschuß m advance on wages
Lokalbank f local bank
Lokopreis m (Warenbörse) spot rate
Lombarddarlehen n lombard loan, securities collateral loan, credit on securities, loan upon collateral security (US), collateral credit, collateral loan
Lombarddepot n collateral security deposit
lombardfähig adj acceptable as collateral, eligible as collateral
Lombardforderungen f pl advances against security
Lombardgeschäft n lombard business, lending on securities, collateral loan business
lombardieren v pledge as collateral for a loan
lombardierte Aktien pawned stock (GB); **~ Effekten** pledged securities
Lombardierung f granting of a loan against securities, hypothecation n

Lombardkredit m lombard loan, securities collateral loan, credit on securities, loan upon collateral security (US), collateral credit, collateral loan
Lombardsatz m rate for collateral loans, lending rate (US)
Lombardschuld f collateral debt
Lombardvorschuß m collateral advance
Lombardwechsel m collateral bill
Lombardwert m hypothecary value
Lombardzins m bank rate for loans
Londoner ~ Börse für Finanzterminkontrakte f London Financial Futures Exchange (LIFFE); **~ Effektenbörse** f London Stock Exchange (LSE); **InterbankenAngebotszinssatz = LIBOR** London Interbank Offered Rate; **~ Parität** f London equivalent; **~ Schuldenabkommen** n London Debt Agreement; **Geldmarktzinssatz am ~ Interbanken-Geldmarkt** m = **LIBID** London Interbank Bid Rate
Loroeffekten plt loro securities
Lorokonto n loro account
Los n lot n (US)
löschen v annul, discharge, cancel v; **im Handelsregister ~** deregister v
Löschgeld n dock charges, dockage n, dock dues, wharfage n, quayage n
Löschung f cancellation n; **~ im Handelsregister** deregistration n
Löschungsgebühren f pl landing charges
Löschungsschein m landing certificate
Loseblattform f loose-leaf format
losen v draw lots
Loskurs m price drawn by lot
Loyalitätsbonus m loyalty bonus
Lücke f gap
Luftfahrt f aviation n
Luftfahrtwerte m pl (Börse) aircrafts
Luftfahrzeughypothek f aircraft mortgage loan
Luftfracht f air cargo, air carriage, air freight
Luftfrachtbrief m airway bill
Luftfrachtgeschäft n air cargo business
Luftfrachtgesellschaft f air cargo carrier
Luftpost f airmail n

Luftverkehrsgesellschaft f airline n
lukrativ adj lucrative adj, remunerative adj, profitable adj
lustlos adj dull n, slack adj, stagnant adj, flat adj; **- sein** stagnate v
lustlose Börse dead market

lustloser Markt dull equity market, sick market (US)
Lustlosigkeit f stagnancy n, stagnation n
Luxemburger Interbanken-Angebotszinssatz m = **LUXIBOR** Luxembourg Interbank Offered Rate

M

Machtbefugnis f authority n
Madrider Interbanken-Angebotszinssatz m = **MIBOR** Madrid Interbank Offered Rate
Magazin n warehouse n, store, storehouse n
Magnetband-Clearing-Verfahren m magnetic tape clearing procedure
Mahnbrief m reminder, letter requesting payment, dunning letter
Mahnung f reminder n, dunning n
Mahnwesen n delinquency procedure
Majorisierung f stagging
Makler m broker n; *- am Londoner Bankmarkt* inter dealer broker (GB); *- im Edelmetallhandel* bullion broker; *amtlich zugelassener -* certified broker, inside broker (GB); *auf eigene Rechnung arbeitender -* floor broker; *freier -* non-member broker, outside broker; *nicht zur offiziellen Börse zugelassener -* non-member broker, outside broker; *vereidigter -* sworn broker
Maklerdarlehen n broker's loan
Maklerfirma f brokerage concern, brokerage firm, brokerage house, brokerage office, commission house
Maklergebühr f brokerage n, broker's fee, broker's commission
Maklergeschäft n brokerage n, brokerage business, broking n
Maklergeschäfte; Betreiben unsauberer - bucketing n (US)
Maklerprovision f brokerage n, broker's fee, broker's commission
Maklerstand m broker's board
Maklersyndikat n board of brokers
Maklerusancen f pl brokerage practices
Maklerwesen n brokerage field
Management n management; *- Buyout* n management buyout (MBO); *schlankes -* lean management
Management-Informationssystem n Management Information System (MIS)
Managertum n managership n

Mandant m client n
Mandat n mandate n, directorship, board membership
Mandatar m proxy, mandatary n
Mangel m deficiency n, shortage, lack; *- im Recht* defect of title
mangelhafter Rechtstitel bad title
Mängelklage f impeachment of waste
mangels Zahlung for lack of payment
manipulierte Währung managed currency
Mantel m share or bond certificate without couponsheet and talon
Mantelabtretung f blanket assignment (of receivables)
Maple Leaf m Maple Leaf = kanadische Goldmünze, 50 $ Nennwert (1 Unze Feingold)
Marge f margin n
Marke f (Handelsmarke) brand n, trademark n; *- f (Markierung)* mark n
Markenartikel m branded goods
Markenbezeichnung f brand name, trademark
Marketing-Mix n marketing mix
Markt m market n; *- für amerikanische Werte* American market (GB); *- für international gehandelte Wertpapiere* international market; *- für Tagesgeld* call money market; *- für verschiedene Werte* miscellaneous market; *- im Telefonverkehr und am Schalter* over-the counter market; *- zweiter Ordnung* secondary market; *abgeschwächter -* market off (US); *flauer -* dull market, stale market; *freier -* free market, open market; *grauer -* grey market; *in engem Rahmen gehaltener -* pegged market (US); *lustloser -* sick market (US); *offener -* free market, open market; *schwacher -* thin market, weak market; *sehr gedrückter -* demoralized market; *Umschwung am -* turn in the market; *uneinheitlicher -* sick market (US); *zweigeteilter -* two-tier market
Marktanalyse f commercial survey, market analysis

120

Marktanteil *m* market share
Marktbericht *m* market report
Marktenge *f* narrowness of the market
Markterfordernis *n* market requirement
Markterholung *f* market recovery, market rally
marktfähig *adj* marketable *adj*, sal(e)able *adj*
Marktfähigkeit *f* marketability *n*
Marktforschung *f* market research
marktgerechte Anleihe bellweather bond
marktkonform *adj* in line with the market
Marktlage *f* market situation
Marktlücke *f* (Nische) gap in the market
Markt Maker *m* market maker, primary dealer (GB)
Marktnotierung *f* market quotation
Marktpapier *n* marketable paper
Marktpartner *m* market member
Marktpreis *m* actual price, market price, ruling price
Marktprognose *f* market forecast
Marktstützung *f* market support, price support, peg *n*
Marktverhältnis *n* market ratio (US)
Marktvolumen *n* market volume
Marktwert *m* actual market value, current value, market value
maschinelle *Anlagen* machinery *n*;
 - *Buchhaltung* machine posting;
 - *Weiterverarbeitung* subsequent machine processing
Maschinen *f pl* machinery *n*
Maschinenanlage *f* plant *n*
Maschinendurchlauf *m* run *n*, machine run
Masse *f* mass, bulk
Masseanspruch *m* claim against the estate
Massenerzeugung *f* mass production
Massenfabrikation *f* mass production
Massengeschäft *n* retail banking, mass business
Massenherstellung *f* mass production
Massenkaufkraft *f* mass purchasing power
Massenproduktion *f* mass production
Massenverkauf *m* wholesale trade
Massenzahlungsverkehr *m* bulk payment, largescale check payment system
Masseverwalter *m* liquidator *n*, receiver *n*
maßgebende Bank leading bank

maßgebendes Kapitalinteresse controlling interest, majority interest
maßgeblich *adj* considerable, substantial, sizeable
massiver Abgabedruck (Börse) heavy selling pressure
Material *n* (Börse) securities on offer, offerings *n pl* (US)
materielle Vermögenswerte physical assets
materieller Eigentümer beneficial owner, beneficiary owner
materielles Eigentum beneficial ownership
MATIF *m* = Marché à Terme International de France (französischer Terminmarkt) International Future Market of France
MATIS *n* = **Makler-Tele-Informations-System** price information system established by Germany's official brokers
Medaille *f* medal *n*
Medio *m* mid-month
mehr Angebot als Nachfrage sellers over (GB)
Mehraufwand *m* additional expenditure
Mehrbelastung *f* overcharge *n*
Mehreinnahmen *f pl* additional receipts
Mehrgewinn *m* surplus profit
Mehrgewinnsteuer *f* windfall profit tax
Mehrheit *f* majority; *beschlußfähige -* quorum *n*
mehrheitlich *adj* by a majority
Mehrheitsbeteiligung *f* controlling interest, majority interest
Mehrkosten *plt* additional charges
Mehrpunktverbindung *f* multi-point connection, multi-point drop
mehrseitig *adj* multilateral *adj*
Mehrstimmenrecht *n* plural vote
Mehrwährungsklausel *f* multi-currency clause
Mehrwertsteuer *f* value-added tax
Mehrwertsteuerbefreiung *f* zero-rating
mehrwertsteuerfrei zero-rated
Mehrzweckfeld *n* multi-purpose field
Meinungskäufe *m pl* speculative purchases
Meistbegünstigtenklausel *f* most favoured nation clause
Meistgebot *n* highest bid
Meldung *f* declaration, report, notification
Memorial *n* journal *n*, day-book *n*

Menge f quantity n
Mengen; in großen - bulk
Mengeneinkauf m bulk buying
Mengengeschäft n retail banking, mass business
Mengenrabatt m quantity discount
Mengentender m fixed-rate tender
merkantil adj mercantile adj
Merkmal n feature n, characteristic n; ~ n mark n
Messe f fair n, exhibition n
Metageschäft n deal on joint account, joint transaction
Metakredit m credit on joint account
Metall; unedles - base metal
Metallbörse f metal exchange
Metallgeld n specie n
Metallkonto n metal account
Metallwährung f metallic currency
Mezzanine f mezzanine finance
MIBOR m = **Madrider Interbanken Angebotssatz** Madrid Interbank Offered Rate
mietbar adj tenantable adj
Miete f (Mietverhältnis) lease n; ~ f (Wohnungsmiete) rent n; **überhöhte** ~ rackrent n
Mieteinkommen n rent income
Mieteinnahmen f pl rent receipts
Mieteinzieher m rent collector
Mieteinzug m rent collection
mieten v rent v, lease
Mieter m lessee n, renter n, rent payer, tenant n, leaseholder n
Mietertrag m rent return
Mietgeld n rent money
Mietinkasso n collection of rents
Mietkauf m lease purchase, hire purchase
Mietkonto n rent account
Mietobjekt n rented property
Mietrückstände m pl accrued rents
Mietsätze m pl rentals n pl
Mietshaus n apartment building, apartment house
Mietverhältnis n tenancy n
Mietvertrag m contract of lease, tenancy agreement, lease deed; **indexierter** ~ indexational lease deed
Mietzins m rent, rental n
Mikroprozessor m microprocessor

Milliarde f (1.000.000.000) billion n (US)
Million f million
Minderheitsbeteiligung f minority interest
minderjährig adj minor adj
Minderjährige f u. m infant n, minor n
Mindestbetrag m round lot
Mindesteinlage f minimum deposit
Mindesteinschuß m maintenance margin
Mindestertragsrate f hurdle rate (US)
Mindestreserve f statutory reserve, minimum reserve
Mindestreservevorschriften f pl reserve requirements
Mindestzinssatz m interest rate floor
Minenwerte m pl (Börse) mining shares (stocks)
Minimalpacht f dead rent (GB)
Minoritätsrechte der Aktionäre minority shareholder rights
Minuszins m negative interest
Mischfinanzierung f mixed financing
Mischkonzern m conglomerate
Mischkredit m mixed loan (credit)
Mischzinssatz m composite interest rate
mißgestimmt adj depressed adj (market), gloomy adj
Mißkredit m discredit n, disrepute n
Mißverhältnis n disproportion n
Mißwirtschaft f mismanagement
Mitarbeit f cooperation n, collaboration n
mitarbeiten v cooperate v
Mitarbeiter m collaborator, employee, assistant n; ~ m staff member;
~ **der die Wertpapiergeschäfte der Angestellten überwacht** compliance officer
Mitarbeiteraktien siehe **Belegschaftsaktien**
Mitbenutzer m co-user n
Mitbesitzer m joint proprietor, copartner n, partner n
Mitbestimmung f codetermination n
Mitbeteiligung f participation n
Mitbürge m joint surety, co-guarantor
Mitbürgschaft f joint guarantee, co-guarantee
Miteigentum n co-ownership n, part ownership, coproperty
Miteigentümer m joint owner; ~ m part owner, co-owner n, coproprietor

mündelsichere Anlagepapiere

Miterbe *m* coheir *n*, joint heir
Miterbschaft *f* coheritage *n*, coparcenary *n*
mitfinanzieren *v* co-finance
Mitführer eines Konsortiums co-lead (joint-lead) manager
Mitgift *f* dot *n*, dotal property, dowry *n*
Mitgläubiger *m* cocreditor *n*, fellow creditor, joint creditor
Mitgliedsbank *f* (d. Federal Reserve System) member bank (US)
mithaften *v* be jointly liable
Mithaftung *f* joint liability
Mitinhaber *m* joint proprietor, copartner *n*, partner *n*
Mitkonsorte *m* (einer Emission) co-manager
Mitnahme kleinster Spekulationsgewinne scalping *n* (US)
Mitschuldner *m* joint debtor, co-debtor *n*, fellow debtor
mitteilen *v* inform *v*, notify *v*, advise *v*, communicate *v*
Mitteilung *f* information, notification *n*, notice *n*, advice *n*
Mittel *n pl* funds *n pl*, means *n pl*;
 - vorschießen advance funds;
 flüssige - ready money; *liquide -* available funds, liquid funds; *nicht verteilte -* unappropriated funds; *geparkte -* parked funds
Mittelabfluß *m* money outflow
Mittelaufnahme *f* borrowing, raising funds
Mittelbedarf *m* borrowing requirements
Mittelbetrieb *m* medium-sized business
mittelfristig *adj* medium-term
Mittelkurs *m* middle rate; *-* *m* (Devisen) mean rate of exchange
mittellos *adj* destitute *adj*, impecunious *adj*, moneyless *adj*
Mittellosigkeit *f* lack of funds, impecuniosity *n*, destitution *n*
mittelständische Wirtschaft small and medium-sized enterprises (SME)
Mittelwert *m* mean value, average *n*
mittlere Laufzeit mid-range maturity, average term
mittlerer *Verfall* (Fälligkeit) average due time; *- Zahlungstermin* average due date
mitunterzeichnen *v* sign jointly, countersign *v*

Mitunterzeichnung *f* joint signature, countersignature *n*
Mitversicherung *f* coinsurance *n*
mitwirken *v* cooperate *v*
Mitwirkung *f* participation *n*
Möbelspediteur *m* mover *n* (US), removal contractor (GB)
Mobiliarhypothek *f* chattel mortgage
Mobiliarvermögen *n* movable property, movable goods, movables *n pl*, goods movable
Mobilien *plt* chattels *n pl*, personal property, chattels personal, movables *n pl*
Mobilienleasing *m* movable equipment leasing
mobilisierbar *adj* mobilisable
Mobilisierungswechsel *m* finance bill
Modul *n* module *n*
monatlich *adj* monthly *adj*
monatlicher *Bilanzaufgliederungsbogen* monthly balance sheet; *- Ertrag* monthly earning
Monatsausweis *m* monthly return (GB), monthly statement
Monatsbilanz *f* monthly balance
Monatsgeld *n* money for one month
Monatskonto *n* monthly account
Monatsultimo *m* month-end *n*
monetär *adj* monetary
monetäre Basis monetary basis
monetisieren *v* turn into money, monetize *v*
Monometallismus *m* monometallism *n*
Monopol *n* monopoly *n*
monopolähnlich *adj* semi-monopolistic *adj*
monopolisieren *v* monopolize *v*
Montanindustrie *f* coal and steel industry
Moratorium *n* stand still agreement, moratorium *n*, delay of payment
Moratoriumsurkunde *f* letter of protection, letter of respite
Motorenwerte *m pl* (Börse) motors *n pl*
multilateral *adj* multilateral *adj*
multinationale Bank multinational bank
multiple Wechselkurse multiple exchange rates
Mündel *n* ward *n*
Mündelgeld *n* trust money, ward money
mündelsichere *Anlagepapiere* legal investments (US), gilt-edged securities, gilt-edged investment, savings

123

Mündelsicherheit

securities, widow and orphan stock (US); **~ Kapitalanlage** trustee investments (GB); **~ Wertpapiere** legal investments (US), gilt-edged securities, gilt-edged investment, savings securities, widow and orphan stock (US)
Mündelsicherheit f trustee investment status, trustee security status
Mündige f u. m major n, adult n
Münz- (in Zus.) monetary adj
Münzamt n mint n
Münze f coin n; ~ f (Prägeanstalt) mint n; **abgenutzte ~** defaced coin; **falsche ~** base coin (GB); **gängige ~** common coin, current coin
Münzeinheit f monetary unit
münzen v coin v, strike coins
Münzen f pl coins n pl, coinage n; **ausländische Banknoten und ~** foreign notes and coins; **Sammeln von ~** numismatics
Münzer m coiner n

Münzfuß m monetary standard; **einen ~ festsetzen** monetize v
Münzgeld n coins n pl
Münzgerechtigkeit f moneyage n
Münzgewinn m seigniorage n, profit n
Münzhandel m dealing in coins
Münzhoheit f right of coinage
Münzkunde f (Numismatik) numismatics
Münzparität f mint par
Münzprägung f minting n, monetization n
Münzregal n coinage prerogative
Münzsorte f specie n
Münzstätte f mint n
Münzumlauf m coins in circulation
Münzverschlechterung f deficiency of coins
Muster n example, specimen, design, sample n
Muttergesellschaft f parent company
Mutterland n metropolitan country
Mutterumsatz m parent company's turnover

N

nachaddieren v check the addition of
nachbelasten v make an additional charge
Nachbezugsrecht n right to cumulative dividend
Nachbörse f after hours market, curb n, curb exchange, curb market, kerb market, inofficial market, unofficial market (GB)
nachbörslich adj after bourse hours, after market
nachbörslicher Kurs curb market price
Nachbürge m additional guarantor
Nachbürgschaft f additional guarantee
Nachcodierung f post-inscription n, post-qualification n (MICR)
nachdatieren v antedate v
nachdatierter Scheck antedated check
Nachdeckungspflicht f obligation to provide additional security
Nachemission f follow-up issue
Nacherbe m remainderman n
Nachfinanzierung f further financing
Nachfolge f succession n
Nachfolgebank f successor bank
Nachfolgegroßbanken f pl big three successors
Nachfolgeinstitut n successor institution
nachfolgend adj subsequent adj, following adj
nachfordern v call for more
Nachforderung f supplementary claim
Nachforschung f inquiry n, investigation n
Nachfrage f demand n; *äußerst lebhafte* - rush n; *große* - *nach Aktien* run on stocks; *spärliche* - slack demand
nachfragen v inquire v
Nachfrist f grace n (period)
Nachgangshypothek f subsequent mortgage
Nachgeben der Kurse decline in prices
Nachgebühr f postage due
nachgemacht adj (gefälscht) forged adj, counterfeit(ed) adj; - adj (imitiert) imitated adj, copied adj
Nachgeschäft n repeat option business
nachgiebig adj (Börse) declining, soft adj
nachkommen v (Anordnungen) comply with, conform with; - v (Verpflichtungen) meet v; *seinen Verbindlichkeiten* - meet one's liabilities
Nachlaß m (Erbrecht) estate, estate assets, deceased's estate, decedent's estate (US); - m (Steuer) relief n; - *gewähren* allow a discount; - *nach Zahlung aller Verbindlichkeiten* residuary estate; *zur Versilberung bestimmter* - blended fund (GB)
Nachlaßaufnahme f inventory n
nachlassen v ease v, slacken v
nachlässig adj careless adj
Nachlässigkeit f carelessness n
Nachlaßmasse f estate assets
Nachlaßpfleger m estate administrator
Nachlaßrest m residue n
Nachlaßschulden f pl debts of estate
Nachlaßsteuer f inheritance tax (US), death duty (GB), estate duty (GB)
Nachlaßverbindlichkeiten f pl liabilities of an estate
Nachlaßvermögen n deceased person's estate
Nachlaßverwalter f administration of an estate, estate administration, estate administrator; *als* - *tätig sein* administer v
Nachlaßverzeichnis n estate inventory
nachmachen v imitate v, copy v, forge v, counterfeit v
Nachmittagshandel m afternoon trade
Nachnahmepaket n cash parcel, C.O.D. parcel
Nachnahmesendung f cash-on delivery consignment
nachprüfen v check, control, verify v
Nachprüfung f check n, checking n
nachrangige Anleihe junior bond; - *Hypothek* junior mortgage, second mortgage
nachrangiger Gläubiger junior creditor
nachrangiges Pfandrecht second lien
Nachricht f news, information n
Nachrichtenaufbau n message format
Nachrichtennetz n communication system
Nachrichtensystem n communication system

nachrücken

nachrücken v move up
Nachrückungsrecht n right of a creditor to be brought forward
nachschießen v provide fresh funds, remargin v (US)
nachschüssig adj decursive adj
Nachschußmarge f variation margin, maintenance margin
Nachschußpflicht f obligation to provide extra funds, additional funding obligation, reserve liability
Nachschußzahlung f remargining n (US); *eine - fordern* call for additional cover
Nachsichtwechsel m after sight bill, fixed-dated bill
nachstehendes Pfandrecht junior lien
Nach-Steuer-Gewinn m after tax profit
Nachteil m detriment n; *-* m disadvantage n
nachteilig adj detrimental adj
Nachtrag m supplement n
nachtragen; *Posten -* book omitted items
nachträglich adj subsequent adj
nachträgliche Kosten after costs
nachträglicher Kurs after price
Nachtragsbuchung f subsequent entry, supplementary entry
Nachtsafe m night depository (US), night safe
Nachttresor m night depository (US), night safe
Nachvermächtnisnehmer m residuary legatee
Nachversicherung f additional insurance
Nachweis einer Forderung proof of debt
nachweisbare Schulden provable debts
nachweisen v prove v
nachzahlen v pay later, pay in addition
nachzählen v recount v, count over, count again
Nachzahlung f additional payment, supplementary payment
Nachzeichnung von Aktien subsequent subscription
Nachzugsaktien f pl (können erst nach Befriedigung der vorgehenden Aktien Dividende beanspruchen) deferred shares
Näherung f approximation n
nahestehende Gesellschaft associated company (GB)
Nahezubargeld n quasi-cash

Nahtstelle f (EDV) interface n
Namen; auf den *- lautend* inscribed adj, registered adj; *im - von* on behalf of
Namensaktie f registered share (GB), registered stock (US), inscribed stock (GB); *vinkulierte -* registered share with restricted transferability
Namenskonnossement n straight bill of lading (US)
Namenslagerschein m registered warehouse receipt
Namensobligation f registered debenture, registered bond
Namenspapier n registered certificate
Namenspapiere n pl registered securities; *- mit Zinsschein* registered coupon bonds
Namenspfandbriefe m pl registered mortgage bonds
Namensscheck m registered check
Namensschuldverschreibungen f pl registered bonds
Namensverzeichnis n index n
Namenszug m signature n
namhaft adj renowned adj, wellknown adj, prominent adj
Napoleon m Napoleon = 20 French francs gold coin
Nationalbank f national bank
Nationalbankwesen n national banking system (US)
Nationalökonom m economist n
Nationalökonomie f economics plt, national economy
Naturalgeld n commodity money
natürliche Person natural person, individual n
Nebenausgaben; *unvorhergesehene -* contingencies n pl
Nebenbürge m co-surety n
Nebengebühr f additional fee
Nebenkosten plt incidental expenses
Nebenmarkt m (Börse) sideline market
Nebenprodukt n by-product n
Nebensicherheit f collateral security
Nebenstelle f branch n, branch office
Nebenzweigstelle f sub-branch
negative Orderklausel »not to order« clause
Negativerklärung f negative declaration

126

Negativklausel f negative clause
Negativzins m negative interest
negoziieren (verhandeln, begeben, ankaufen) v negotiate v
Negoziierung f negotiation n
Nenn- (in Zus.) nominal adj
nennenswert adj appreciable adj, noticeable adj
Nennkapital n nominal capital
Nennwert m face value, nominal par, nominal value, par value; **unter dem** - below par; **zum** - at par
Nennwertaktie f par value stock (US)
nennwertlos adj of no par value
nennwertlose Aktie no-par stock, no-par share, share of no-par value
netto net, in net terms
Nettoaustauschverhältnis n net barter terms of trade (TOT)
Nettobetrag m net amount, clear amount
Nettobetriebskapital n net working capital
Nettoeinkommen n net income
Nettoerlös m net proceeds, net avails (US)
Nettoertrag m net earnings (income)
Nettogewinn m net profit, net proceeds, clear profit, clear gain, pure profit
Nettoguthaben n net credit balance
Nettoinvestition f net investment
Nettokonditionen f pl net terms
Nettokurs m net price
Nettomarge f net margin
Nettosatz m net interest rate
Nettoumsatz m net sales
Nettoverdienst m net earnings, take-home pay
Nettoverlust m net loss
Nettoverzinsung f net interest return
Nettowert m net value, clear value
Nettozinsen m pl pure interest, net interest
Netzaufbau m network lay-out, network configuration
neu aufgelegt reissued adj; **- auflegen** reissue v; **- schätzen** revalue v, reappraise v
Neuanlage f reinvestment n
Neubelegung f (von Lücken auf Großspeicherdateien) record insertion; ~ f (COBOL) redefinition n
neubewerten v revalue, reappraise v

nicht abgestempelte Effekten

Neubewertung f reappraisal n; ~ f (von Vermögen) revaluation n (of property)
neue Rechnung after account
Neuemission f new issue
neufinanzieren v recapitalize n
Neufinanzierung f recapitalization n
neufundierte Obligation redemption bond
Neukapitalisierung f recapitalization n
Neuschätzung f reappraisal n
Neuwertversicherung; gleitende ~ floating policy
New Yorker Effektenbörse f New York Stock Exchange (NYSE), Wall Street (informal)
New Yorker Interbanken-Angebotszinssatz m = **NIBOR** New York Interbank Offered Rate
nicht abgestempelte Effekten unassented securities (US); **- aktiver Teilhaber** nominal partner (GB); **- akzeptieren** dishonour v; **- anerkennen** disclaim v; **- angelegtes Kapital** idle money; **- ausgegebene Aktien** potential stock, unissued stock, unissued capital, unissued shares; **- bankfähig** unbankable adj; **- begebbar** unnegotiable adj; **- beglaubigt** uncertified adj; **- bestätigtes Akkreditiv** unconfirmed letter of credit; **- bezahlen** dishonour v; **- bezahlt** unpaid adj; **- diskontfähig** unbankable adj; **- eingeschränkt** unlimited adj; **- eingetragen** unincorporated adj; **- eingezahltes Kapital** uncalled capital; **- einkassierbar** uncollectable adj; **- einlösbar** inconvertible adj; **- einlösen** dishonour v; **- eintreibbar** noncollectable adj; **- einziehbar** uncollectable adj; **- einziehbare Werte** write-offs n pl (US); **- erfüllen** default v; **- flüssig** illiquid adj; **- freigemacht** unpaid adj; **- gedeckt** uncovered adj; **- geschäftsmäßig** unbusinesslike adj; **- gezeichnete Aktien** unsubscribed stock; **- giriert** unindorsed adj, unendorsed adj; **- greifbare Aktiva** intangible assets; **- gutgeschrieben** uncredited adj; **- in voller Höhe gezeichnete Anleihe** undersubscribed loan; **- indossiert** unin-

127

dorsed adj, unendorsed adj; **~ konvertierbar** inconvertible adj; **~ kumulative Dividende** non-cumulative dividend; **~ limitiert** unlimited adj; **~ notiert** unlisted adj (US), unquoted; **~ saldiert** unbalanced adj; **~ steuerpflichtig** non-taxable adj, tax-free adj; **~ stimmberechtigt** voiceless adj; **~ übertragbar** untransferable adj; **~ versicherungsfähig** uninsurable adj; **~ verteilte Mittel** unappropriated funds; **~ vorkalkulierter Ertragsüberschuß** unappropriated income; **~ zugeteilte Aktien** unallotted shares; **~ zurückgefordertes Guthaben** dormant balance; **~ zuteilbar** unassignable adj

Nichtakzeptierung f non-acceptance n
Nichtannahme f non-acceptance n; **~ f** refusal of acceptance
Nichtbanken f pl non-banks (ex: store chains)
Nichtbankenkundschaft f non-bank customers
Nichtbankenpublikum n non-bank public
Nichtbezahlung f non-payment n
Nichteinlösung f dishonour n
Nichterfüllung f default n
nichtig adj void adj; **für ~ erklären** annul v, nullify v; **für null und ~ erklären** consider as null and void, defeat v
Nichtigkeitserklärung f annulment
Nichtzahlung f non-payment n
Niederlage f defeat n
Niederlassung f branch n, branch office
Niederschrift f record n
Niederstwertprinzip n minimum value principle
niedrig adj low adj
niedrig notierte Aktie low-priced share
Niedrigpreis m rock bottom
niedrigster Stand bottom n
Niedrigstkurs m bottom price, low quotation (stock), low rate (money)
Nießbrauch m beneficial right, beneficial interest, right of usufruct, usufruct n; **~ an einem Vermögen** beneficial estate, beneficial property
Nießbrauchberechtigte f u. m beneficial occupant

Nießbraucher m usufructuary n, beneficial user
Nießbrauchsrecht n beneficial enjoyment
Nochgeschäft n (Börse) put of more, call of more
Nominal- (in Zus.) nominal adj
Nominalbetrag m nominal amount
Nominalkapital n nominal capital
Nominalwert m face value, nominal par, nominal value, par value
nominell adj nominal adj
nominieren v nominate v
Nonvaleurs m pl valueless securities
Norm f standard n
normaler Zinssatz standard interest
normalisieren v normalize v, rehabilitate v
Normalisierung f normalization n, rehabilitation n
Normalkondition f standard condition, normal condition
normierter Kredit standardized loan
Normierung f standardization n
Normvordruck m standard form
Norwegische Krone f Norway Krone
Nostroguthaben n credit balance with other banks, credit balance on a nostro account; **~ bei in- und ausländischen Banken** balance with home and foreign bankers
Nostrokonto n nostro account
Notadresse f address in case of need, notify address
Notar m notary public, notary n; **vor einem ~** notarial adj
Notariat n notary's office, notariate n
Notariatsakt m notarial act
Notariatsgebühren f pl notarial fees
notariell adj notarial adj; **~ beglaubigen** notarize v
Notenausgabe; **ungedeckte ~** fiduciary issue
Notenbank f Central Bank, bank of circulation, bank of issue, note-issuing bank, issue bank
Notenbankgeld n central bank money
Notenbankgeldmenge f central bank money
Notenbankinstrumentarium n powers of the central bank

Notenbankpolitik f central bank policy
Notenbankwesen n central banking
Notendeckung f note cover
Noteneinlösungspflicht f obligation to redeem bank notes
Notenmonopol n note-issuing privilege
Notennummer f serial number
Notenprivileg n right to issue bank notes
Notenumlauf m bank note circulation
Notgeld n emergency money
Notgroschen m nest-egg n; *~ m* spare money
notierbar adj quotable adj
notieren v note, quote, list
Notierung f quotation n, price n
Notifikation f notification n, notice n, advice n
Nötigung f duress n
Notiz f (Börse) quotation n, price n
Notklausel f escape clause
Notlage f distress n; ***dringende ~*** emergency n
notleidend adj in defaulted, dishonoured
notleidende *Obligationen* defaulted bonds; *~ **Währung*** depreciated currency
notleidender *Kupon* overdue coupon; *~ **Scheck*** dishonoured check; *~ **Wechsel*** bill in distress, dishonoured bill
Novation f substitution of debt
Nugget m Nugget = 100 Australian Dollar gold coin (1 ounce)

null und nichtig null and void, absolutely void
Nullkuponanleihe f zero bond, zero coupon bond; *~ **mit Wandelrecht in Aktien*** liquid yield option note (LYON)
Nullprobe f zero proof
Nullwachstum n zero growth
numeriert; fortlaufend *~* consecutively numbered
Numerierungsprinzip n numbering principle
Numismatik f (Münzkunde) numismatics
Nummerndepot m numbered securities account
Nummernkonto n numbered account
nur zur Verrechnung for deposit only
nutzbringend adj beneficial adj
Nutzen m profit, benefit n, privilege n;
 *~ **bringen*** benefit v, favo(u)r v;
 *~ **ziehen aus*** benefit by
Nutznießer m beneficial owner, beneficiary owner; *~ m* beneficiary n
Nutznießung f beneficial use, beneficial interest, right of usufruct, usufruct n; **lebenslängliche *~*** life interest
Nutznießungsrecht n beneficial enjoyment
Nutzung f use, utilisation
Nutzungsdauer f useful life
Nutzungsrecht n right of use, usufructuary right
Nutzwert m user value

Obergesellschaft

O

Obergesellschaft f ultimate holding company
Obergrenze f upper limit, cap
Objekt n object, property
Objektentwicklungsgesellschaft f property developer
oberer Goldpunkt gold export point
Objektkredit m investment property loan, loan against specific security
Obligation f bond n, debenture n, obligation n; ~ **mit variabler Verzinsung** floating rate issue; ~ **mit Vorzugsrecht** preference bond, preferred bond, senior bond; ~ **mit zusätzlichen Sicherheiten** collateral bonds (US); **ausgeloste** ~ drawn bond; **hypothekarisch gesicherte** ~ secured bond, mortgage debenture
Obligationen der amerikanischen Bundesstaaten state bonds (US); ~ **mit Gewinnbeteiligung** income debentures, participating bonds (US), profit-sharing bonds; ~ **mit kleiner Stückelung** small bonds, savings bonds, baby bonds; ~ **mit variabler Verzinsung** LIBOR bonds; ~ **ohne Konversions- oder Bezugsrechte** straight bonds; **aufgerufene und für ungültig erklärte** ~ obsolete securities (US); **auslösbare** ~ redeemable bonds; **durch Vorranghypothek gesicherte** ~ underlying bonds (US); **fest plazierte** ~ digested bonds (US); **festverzinsliche** ~ active bonds (GB); **kündbare** ~ optimal bonds (US); **neufundierte** ~ redemption bonds; **notleidende** ~ defaulted bonds; **pfandrechtlich gesicherte** ~ collateral trust notes; **prolongierte** ~ continued bonds (US); **serienweise rückzahlbare** ~ instalment bonds; **ungesicherte** ~ plain bonds; **ungültige** ~ disabled bonds (GB)
Obligationenbuch n bond register
Obligationenerlös m bond (loan) proceeds
Obligationenfonds m bond fund
Obligationenhandel m bond trading

Obligationenkupon m interest coupon
Obligationenkurs m bond price
Obligationenrecht n law of contracts
Obligationsagio n bond premium, bond discount
Obligationsinhaber m (Gläubiger) bond creditor, bond holder
Obligationsmarkt m bond market
Obligationsschuldner m bond debtor, obligor n, obligator n
Obligationstilgung f bond redemption
Obligationszinsen m pl bond interest
Obligo n liability n, commitment n; **ohne** ~ without recourse, without our liability
Obligobuch n acceptance register
Obligoführung f liability accounting
Obligoverzeichnis n acceptance ledger
Oderdepot n joint securities account
Oderkonto n joint account
offenbaren v disclose v
Offenbarungseid m debtor's oath
offene Handelsgesellschaft general partnership; ~ **Police** open policy; ~ **Reserven** official reserves, general reserves, declared (published) reserves; ~ **Rücklage** declared reserves; ~ **Schalterhalle** open banking hall
offener Kredit advance on current account, current account credit, overdraft facility in current account, loan on overdraft, open credit; ~ **Markt** free market, open market; ~ **Scheck** open check, uncrossed check
offenes Depot f standard custody account, ordinary safe keeping account; ~ **Konto** current account, running account, open account
Offenmarktpapier n open market paper
Offenmarktpolitik f open market policy
offenstehend adj outstanding adj
öffentlich adj public adj; ~ **beglaubigen** authenticate by a notary public or court
öffentliche Anleihe public sector bond, government bond; ~ **Arbeiten** public works; ~ **Finanzen** public

130

finance; **~ Gelder** public funds, public money; **~ Hand** public authorities; **~ Körperschaft** public corporation, corporation under public law; **~ Schuld** public debt; **~ Versteigerung** public sale

öffentlicher Gläubiger public creditor; **~ Kredit** civil loan (US), public loan, public credit; **~ Versteigerer** auctioneer n

Öffentlichkeit f (Allgemeinheit) public n

Öffentlichkeitsarbeit f public relations (P. R.)

öffentlich-rechtlich adj under public law

öffentlich-rechtliches Kreditinstitut public sector bank, credit institution under public law

Offerte f offer n

offiziell adj official adj

offizielle Zulassung zum Börsenhandel official listing (US)

offizieller Diskontsatz m official discount rate

Offshore-Bankgeschäfte n pl offshore banking

Offshore-Finanzplatz m offshore financial center

ohne Bezugsrecht ex rights; **~ Deckung** uncovered adj; **~ Dividende** ex dividend; **~ Giro** unindorsed adj, unendorsed adj; **~ Kosten** »no expense«; **~ Kredit** uncredited adj; **~ Obligo** without our liability; **~ Protest** without protest; **~ Testament** intestate adj; **~ Zinsen** ex interest

Ökofonds m fund investing in environment protecting industries

Ökonomie f economy n

ökonomisch adj economical adj, economic adj

Ölgelder n pl petro dollar

Ombudsmann m expert dealing with customers' complains

Oppositionsliste f stopping list

Option f (Börse) option n; **~ auf eine Zinsbegrenzungsvereinbarung** cap option, caption; **~ auf Tausch zinsvariabler in Festsatz-Obligationen** fixed debt option; **~ auf Terminkontrakte** futures option; **~ der Emissionsbank auf höhere Zuteilung** green shoe (option); **börsengehandelte ~** traded option; **nicht börsengehandelte ~** non traded option

Optionen ~ auf Devisen-Terminkontrakte options on currency futures; **~ verkaufen** write (sell) options

Optionsanleihe f warrant-linked bond, warrant issue, option loan, bond with warrants

Optionsberechtigte f u. m optionee n

Optionsbörse f options exchange; **~ von Frankreich** f Open-Market de France (OMF)

Optionsfonds m option fund

Optionsgeber m optioner n

Optionsgeschäfte n pl options trading

Optionskäufer m option buyer

Optionsnehmer m option taker

Optionspreis m option price

Optionsrecht n option, option right

Optionsrechte auf Aktien stock (share) purchase options, equity sweeteners (informal)

Optionsschein m warrant; **~ auf einen Aktienkorb** green warrants; **~ mit Zinsobergrenze** capped warrants

Optionsscheine auf USD-Anleihen dollar warrants

Optionsscheinpreis m warrant price

Optionsscheinmarkt m warrant market

Optionsverkäufer (Stillhalter) m option seller (writer)

Optionswährung f option currency

optische Zeichenerkennung optical character recognition (OCR)

Order f order n

Orderbuch n order book, blotter n

Orderklausel f order clause »to the order of«; **negative ~** »not to order« clause

Orderpapier n instrument payable to order, order instrument

Orderscheck m check to order, order check

Orderschuldverschreibung f order bond

Orderwechsel m bill to order

Ordnungsbegriff m classification key, classification criterion

ordnungsgemäß adv duly adv; **~ unterschrieben** duly signed

Organgesellschaft f subsidiary, controlled company
Organigramm n organization chart
Organisation f organization; **- Erdöl exportierender Länder** f Organization of Petroleum Exporting Countries (OPEC); **- für wirtschaftliche Zusammenarbeit** f Organization for Economic Cooperation and Development (OECD)
organisieren v organize v
Organkredite m pl loans extended by a corporation to its executives and their family members
Organschaftsvertrag m agreement between interlocking companies
Organträger m parent company (of an interlocking relationship)
Organverhältnis n group relationship
Organvertrag m agreement between interlocking companies
Orientierungsgröße f (Wertmaßstab) bench mark
Original n original n
originär adj original
Ortsschlüssel m geographic code
ortsüblich adj locally usual
Ortszeit f local time
Ortsgespräch n local call
Ortsnetzkennzahl f area code
Ostblock m Eastern bloc
Österreichische Schilling m Austrian Schilling
Outright-Geschäfte n pl outright operations
Over-the-counter-(Freiverkehr-)Geschäft n over-the-counter business (OTC business)

P

Pacht f lease n; ~ f (Pacht-, Mietbesitz) leasehold n; ~ f (Zahlung) rent n
pachtbar adj tenantable adj
Pachtbesitzer m leasehold
Pachtdauer f tenancy n
Pachteinkommen n rent income
Pachteinnahmen f pl rent receipts
pachten v rent, lease
Pächter m tenant n, leaseholder n
Pachtgeld n rent money
Pachtgrundstück n leasehold property
Pachtsätze m pl rentals n pl
Pachtverhältnis n tenancy n
Pachtvertrag m lease, contract of lease, tenancy agreement, lease deed
Pachtzins m rental rate
Pakethandel m block trading, large-lot dealing
Paketverkauf m large-lot sale
Paketzuschlag m share block premium, large-lot price supplement
Panda m (chinesische Goldmünze) Panda = 100 Yuan Chinese gold coin (1 ounce)
Panik f (Börse) scare n, panic n
Panzergewölbe n strong room, vault n
Papier n paper n, (Wertpapier) security
Papiere mit kurzen Laufzeiten shorts; *international gehandelte* ~ international securities, international stocks (US), internationals n pl; *konsolidierte* ~ consolidated stock (GB); *mündelsichere* ~ legal investments (US), gilt-edged securities, gilt-edged investment, savings securities, widow and orphan stock (US); *schwere* ~ high shares
Papiergeld n paper currency, paper money; *entwertetes* ~ rag money (US); *konvertierbares* ~ convertible paper currency
Papiergewinne m pl paper profits
Papierschneidemaschine f paper cutter
Papiertrennmaschine f paper burster, paper decollator
Papierwährung f paper currency
Papierwerte m pl (Börse) paper securities
Parallele f parallel

Parallelfinanzierung f parallel financing
Parallelkredit m parallel loan, back-to-back credit
Parallellauf m parallel run
Parallelmarkt m parallel market
pari par; *unter* ~ below par; *über* ~ above par
Pariemission f par issue, issue at par
Parikurs m par price
Pariser Interbanken-Angebotszinssatz m = **PIBOR** Paris Interbank Offered Rate
Parität f parity n
Paritätsklausel f parity clause
Pariwechsel m bill at par
Pariwert m face value, nominal par, nominal value, par value
Parkett n (Börse) floor n, trading floor
Partei f party n; *benachteiligte* ~ injured party
Partenreederei f shipowning partnership
Partizipationsschein m participation certificate
Partner m partner n, associate
Partnerbanken f pl partner banks
Partnerschaft f partnership, membership
passend adj appropriate adj
Passiva plt liabilities n pl; *transitorische* ~ suspense liabilities, accrued liabilities
Passivgelder n pl deposits
Passivgeschäft n deposit business
Passivseite f total liabilities and shareholders equity, liabilities side
Passivzins m interest payable
Passivzinsen m pl deposits interest rate, interest payable
Patent n patent n
patentfähig adj patentable adj
Patentfähigkeit f patentability n
patentierbar adj patentable adj
patentieren v patent v
patentiert adj patented adj
Patentinhaber m patent holder, patentee n
Patentrechte n pl patent rights
Patronatserklärung f patronage letter, letter of comfort
pauschal adj overall, lump sum, blanket-rate

Pauschalbetrag m lump sum
Pauschalsatz m flat rate
Pauschalsumme f lump sum
Pauschalversicherung f floating policy
Pauschalwertberichtigung f general loan loss reserves
Pauschalzahlung f lump sum payment
PC m = **Personalcomputer** personal computer (PC)
pekuniär adj pecuniary adj
Pension f pension n
pensionieren v retire, pension off
Pensionierung f retirement n
Pensionsfonds m pension fund, provident fund
Pensionsgeber m pledgee, borrower
Pensionsgeschäft n pledging against loan, buy-back agreement, repurchase agreement
Pensionskasse f pension fund
Pensionskonto n pension account
Pensionsnehmer m lender, recipient of bills or securities
Pensionsplan m pension plan, retirement plan
Pensionswechsel m bill in pension, bill on deposit
Pensionszuschüsse m pl pension payments, service apportionments
Pensionszuwendung f retirement pension, pension n, retirement benefit
per Erscheinen as if and when
Performancemaß n benchmark; *sich orientieren an einem - benchmarking*
permanente Zinsrechnung continuos interest calculation
permanenter Handel continuos trading
Person; *abhängige - dependent* n; *juristische - juridical person, legal entity, legal person, artificial person*
Personal n staff n, personnel; *ausgebildetes - skilled personnel; gelerntes - skilled personnel*
Personalabteilung f human resources department, personnel department, personnel division
Personalakte f personal file
Personalaufwand m staff expenses
Personalausweis m identification card, identification papers, identity card

Personalbarkredit m personal cash advance
Personalgesellschaft f (OHG oder KG) partnership n
Personalcomputer m = **PC** personal computer (PC)
Personalkredit m personal credit, personal loan (US); *ungedeckter - unsecured personal loan*
Personalkreditabteilung f personal loan department
Personenfirma f partnership, oneman firm
persönlich adj personal adj; *- haftender Gesellschafter* responsible partner
persönliche Bürgschaft personal security; *- Garantie* personal bond; *- Sicherheit* personal security
Persönliche Kenn-Nummer f = **PIN** personal identification number (PIN)
Petrodollars n pl petro dollars
Pfand n pawn n, pledge n; *als - unterhalten* hold in pledge; *ein - einlösen* redeem a pledge
Pfandanleihe f pledge loan
pfändbar adj seizable adj, attachable adj
Pfändbarkeit f attachability n
Pfandbestellung f pledging n, pawning n
Pfandbrief m mortgage bond, hypothecation bond
Pfandbriefabteilung f mortgage bond trading department
Pfandbriefagio n mortgage bond premium, bond discount
Pfandbriefanstalt f mortgage bank
Pfandbriefausgabe f mortgage bond issue
Pfandbriefbesitz m mortgage bond holdings
Pfandbriefe m pl land bonds (US); *durch erststellige Hypotheken gesicherte - first mortgage bonds; öffentliche - communal bonds*
Pfandbriefemission f mortgage bond issue
Pfandbrieffonds m mortgage bond fund
Pfandbriefgläubiger m mortgage bond creditor, mortgage bond holder
Pfandbriefhandel m mortgage bond trading
Pfandbriefinhaber m mortgage bond creditor, mortgage bond holder

Pfandbriefinstitut n mortgage bond house
Pfandbriefmarkt m mortgage bond market
Pfandbriefschuldner m mortgage bond debtor
Pfanddarlehen n loan against pledged securities
Pfanddepot n pledged securities deposit
pfänden v seize, attach, distrain v; *- v (Forderung beim Drittschuldner)* garnish v
Pfandgeber m pledger n (GB), pledgor n (US)
Pfandgegenstand m pledged property, pawn n, pledge n
Pfandgläubiger m pledgee, mortgagee, lienholder
Pfandinhaber m pledgee n, pawnee n
Pfandleiher m pawnbroker n
Pfandleihgeschäft n pawnbrokery n, pawnbroking n
Pfandnehmer m pledgee n, pawnee n
Pfandobjekt n pledged property
Pfandrecht n lien, charge; *- an einer beweglichen Sache* registered lien charge; *bevorrechtigtes -* prior lien; *erstrangiges -* first lien; *gesetzliches -* legal lien; *nachrangiges -* second lien; *nachstehendes -* junior lien
Pfandsache f pawn n, pledge n
Pfandschein m certificate of pledge
Pfandschuldner m pledgor
Pfändung f attachment n, arrestment n, distraint n
pfändungsfreier Betrag exemption n
Pfändungsgläubiger m attaching creditor
Pfändungsschuldner m judgement debtor, distrainee n
Pfandverkauf m sale of pledged property
Pfandvertrag m deed of pledge
Pfandverwahrung f custody of pledged property
Pfandverwertung f realization of pledged property
Pfleger m curator, guardian n
Pflegschaft f curatorship n, guardianship n; *- mit besonderen Pflichten* special trust n
Pflichtaktien f pl qualifying shares
Pflichteinlage f compulsory deposit
Pflichtreserve f required reserve
Pfundanleihe f sterling loan
Pfundblock m sterling area
Pfund Sterling n pound sterling
Pfund-Sterling-Staatsanleihe; *gestrippte britische -* f zero coupon eurosterling bearer or registered accruing security (ZEBRAS)
PIBOR m = **Pariser Interbanken-Angebotszinssatz** Paris Interbank Offered Rate
PIN f (persönliche Kennummer) personal identification number (PIN)
Plafond m ceiling n, limit n
Plan m scheme n, plan n
Plandividende f target dividend
planlos adj planless, unplanned
planmäßig adj according to plan
Planrechnung f budgeting n
Planung; *strategische -* (gemeinsame Problembewältigung) brainstorming
Planwirtschaft f planned economy, managed economy
Plastikgeld n plastic money
Platin n platinum
Plattenorganisation f (EDV) disc file organization (EDP)
Platz m place, centre n
Platzbank f local bank
Platzscheck m local cheque (GB)
Platzspesen plt local charges
Platzübertragung f local transfer
Platzusance f local custom
Platzwechsel m local bill, local draft, town bill (US)
Plausibilitätsprüfung f reasonableness check
Plazierung f placing n (GB), placement n (US); *kommissionsweise -* placement on commission
Plazierungsgeschäft n security placing business
Plazierungsrisiko n placing risk
Pleite f flop
Plombe f seal n
plombieren v seal v
plombiert adj sealed adj
Police f certificate of insurance, policy n; *offene -* open policy; *volleingezahlte -* paid-up policy

Policeninhaber m policy holder
Politik f policy n
Pool m pool n, cartel n, combine n
Poolbildung f (Zusammenlegung) pooling
Portefeuille n portfolio n, holdings;
- **eigener Aktien** reacquired capital stock
Portefeuille-Analyse f portfolio analysis
Porto n postage n
Portobuch n stamp book
Portogebühr f postage n
Portokasse f petty cash
Portokassenbuch n stamp book
Portospesen plt postage n
POS m = **Verkaufspunkt** point of sale (POS)
Position f position n, job, post
positionieren v position, place
Positionierung f positioning
Post; *mit der - senden* mail v (US)
Postabholung f collection of letters
Postanleihe f Federal Post Office bond
Postanschrift f mailing address
Postanweisung f money order (MO), postal money order; - f (für kleine Beträge) postal order (GB)
Postauftrag m mail order
Posteinlieferungsschein m certificate of posting
Postempfangsschein m postal receipt
Posten m article n, item n, commodity n; - *nachtragen* book omitted items; *vorläufige* - suspense items
Postengebühr f item charge
Postgiro n postal giro transfer
Postlauf m course of mail
Postlaufkredit m mail credit
Postlaufzeit f elapsed time between mailing and delivery at destination
Postleitzahl f zip code, postal code (GB)
Post-Marketing banking by mail
postnumerando payable in arrears
Postquittung f certificate of posting
Postscheck m postal check (US), postal cheque (GB)
Postscheckamt n postal check office
Postscheckguthaben n credit balance on a postal check account
Postscheckkonto n postal check account
Postscheckverkehr m postal giro service

Postsparbuch n postal savings book
Postsparguthaben n postal savings deposit
Postsparkasse f postal savings bank
Postsparkassenguthaben n postal savings deposit
Postsparkassenkonto n postal savings account
Postsparschein m savings certificate (GB)
Poststempel m date stamp
Postüberweisung f mail transfer
Postversandwerbung f direct mail advertising
Postwertzeichen n stamp n
Postzahlungsverkehr m postal payment system
Präferenz f preference
prägen v coin v
Prägung f (von Münzen) coinage n
Praktikant m trainee
Prämie f premium n; n (Optionsprämie) option premium; *durch - fördern* bonus v
Prämienanleihe f premium bond
Prämienaufgabe f abandonment of the option money
prämienbegünstigt adj premium-carrying
Prämienerklärung f declaration of options
Prämienerklärungstag m making up day
Prämiengeschäft n premium deal, option dealing, premium bargain, option put and call (US); *ein - eingehen* call an option
Prämiengewährung f bonus issue
Prämienhöhe f amount of premium
Prämienkauf m (Börse) purchase at option
Prämienkonto n bonus account
Prämienkurs m option price
Prämienmakler m privilege broker (US), put and call broker (GB)
Prämienobligation f premium bond
Prämienreserve f bonus reserve
Prämiensatz m rate of consideration
Prämienschein m premium bond
Prämiensparen n premium-account saving
Prämiensparer m premium saver
Prämiensystem n bonus plan
Prämienverdienst m bonus earnings
pränumerando payable in advance
Präsident m (eines Gremiums) chairman n; - m president n

Präsidentenstuhl m presidential chair
Präsidium n presidency n, chairmanship n
Preis m (Gewinn) prize n; ~ m quotation n, price n; **annehmbarer** ~ reasonable price; **gebotener** ~ bid price; **gebundener** ~ controlled price; **geforderter** ~ asking price; **im ~ herabsetzen** reduce v, cut the price of; **konkurrenzfähiger** ~ competitive price; **vernünftiger** ~ reasonable price
Preisabschlag m discount n
Preisangabe f quotation n, price n
Preisberechnung f costing n, computation of costs
Preise angeben quote v
Preisermittlung durch Zuruf oder Handzeichen open outcry (at the stock exchange)
Preisfestsetzung f price-fixing n
preisgebunden adj at fixed price
Preisgleitklausel f sliding-price clause
Preisgrenze f (für den An- und Verkauf von Wertpapieren) limit order
preisgünstig adj low price, cheap
Preislage f range of prices
Preisliste f price list
Preisrückgang m decline in price, drop in prices, price fall, price cut
Preisskala f range of prices
Preisnachlaß m discount, rebate
Preisspielraum m (innerhalb gewisser Grenzen) price range
Preissteigerung f price rise, increase in price
Preisstellung f quotation n, price n
Preisstop m price freeze
Preisstützung f price support, peg n
Preisunterschied m difference in price, price differential
Primadiskonten m pl prime acceptances
primadiskontfähig adj qualifying as prime acceptance
Primanote f journal n, day-book n
Primärmarkt m primary market
Primärprogramm n source programme
Primawechsel m first of exchange
Priorität f priority n
Prioritätsaktie f preference share (GB), preferred stock (US)
privat adj private adj

Privatbank f private bank
Privatbankier m private banker, individual banker (US)
Privatdiscount m prime bankers acceptance
Privatdiskontmarkt m prime acceptance market
Privatdiskontsatz m prime bank acceptance rate, prime rate, private discount rate
Privateigentum n private property
Privateinkommen n private income
privates Publikum general public
Privatkonto n personal account, private account
Privatkredit m personal loan
Privatkreditinstitut n personal loan institution
Privatkunde m individual customer
Privatkundschaft f private customers
Privatplazierung f private placement
Privatunternehmen n private enterprise
Privatvermögen n private property
Privatwirtschaft f private enterprise, private industry and commerce
Privileg n charter n; ~ n privilege n (priority)
privilegiert adj privileged adj
privilegierte Bank chartered bank (GB); ~ **Gesellschaft** chartered company
pro Kopf per capita, proportionate
Pro-Kopf-Einkommen n per-capita-income
Pro-rata-Zins m broken-period interest
Probe f sample, specimen n
Probebilanz f trial balance
Produkt n product n
Produktenmakler m (der für eigene Rechnung spekuliert) trader (US)
Produktion f production n, manufacturing, output; **gleichmäßige** ~ settled production
Produktionsgesellschaft f manufacturing company
Produktionskredit m production loan
Produktionsskala f range of products
produktiv adj productive adj
Produktivität f productivity n
Produzent m manufacturer n, producer n
produzieren v produce, manufacture
Profit-Center n profit center
Proformarechnung f proforma invoice

Prognose f forecast n
Programm n program(me) n
Programmaufteilung f programme subdivision
Programmfehler m programme error
Programmhandel m programme trading
programmierbar programmable
programmieren v programme v
Programmierer m programmer
programmierte Kontrolle programmed check; **~ Unterweisung** programmed instruction (PI)
Programmierung f programming
Programmpaket n programme package
Progression f progression n
progressive Zinsrechnung progressive interest calculation
Projekt n project, plan, scheme
Projektfinanzierung f project financing
Prokura f procuration n
Prokuraindossament n proxy endorsement
Prokurist m authorized signatory, Assistant Vice President
Prolongation f prolongation n, extension n, renewal n
Prolongationsabschnitt m prolongation bill
prolongationsfähig adj renewable adj
Prolongationsgebühr f renewal fee
Prolongationsgeschäft n carrying-over business (GB), speculating in contangos
Prolongationsrecht n right of renewal
Prolongationswechsel m renewal bill, continuation bill (GB)
prolongieren v renew v, prolong v
prolongierte Obligationen continued bonds (US)
proportional adj proportional adj
Prospekthaftung f liability for the prospectus, liability in respect of any untrue statement contained in the prospectus
Prospektmaterial n sales literature
Protektionismus m protectionism n
Protest m protest n; **~ erheben** raise a protest; **~ mangels Zahlung** protest for non-payment; **~ wegen Nichtannahme** protest for non-acceptance
Protestaufnahme f noting of a bill, protesting of a bill

Protestbenachrichtigung f notice of protest (US)
Protesterhebung f protesting, act of protest
protestieren v protest v; **einen Wechsel ~ lassen** enter protest of a draft
protestiert adj (Wechsel) noted for protest (bill of exchange)
protestierter Scheck protested check; **~ Wechsel** protested bill
Protestkosten plt protest charges
Protesturkunde f notarial protest certificate, note of protest, deed of protest, certificate of protest, bill of protest
Protokoll n (einer Sitzung) minutes n pl; **~ n** (Informationsverarbeitung) printout n, log n; **~ n** (Gerichts-) record n; **~ führen** keep the minutes
Protokollbuch n minute book
protokollieren v register v, record v
Provinz- (in Zus.) provincial adj, regional adj
Provinzbank f country bank (GB), interior bank (US)
Provinzbörse f out of town market
Provinzfiliale f country branch (GB)
provinziell adj provincial adj, regional adj
Provinzwechsel m country bill (GB)
Provision f commission n; **~ aus Konsortialbeteiligungen** underwriting commission; **eine ~ berechnen** charge commission; **eine ~ gewähren** accord a commission
Provisionsaufwand m commissions paid
Provisionsbelastung f (beim Kauf von Investmentanteilen) load n
Provisionsertrag m commissions surplus
provisionsfrei adj commission-free
Provisionskonto n commission account
provisionspflichtig adj commissionable adj
Provisionssatz m rate of commission
Provisionssätze m pl banking charges
Provisionsüberschuß m commission income
provisorische Bilanz trial balance
provisorisches Konto suspense account
Prozedur f (EDV) procedure n
Prozent n per cent, percent, percentage; **in ~ ausgedrückt** percentaged adj
Prozentpunkt m percentage point
Prozentsatz m percentage n

prozentual *adj* percental *adj*
Prozeß *m* process, case *n*, proceedings, litigation *n*, lawsuit *n*, action *n* (at law)
prozeßfähig *adj* actionable *adj*, suable *adj*
Prozeßkosten *plt* cost of the proceedings, legal charges
Prozeßpartei *f* party to a lawsuit
Prozeßvollmacht *f* power of attorney
prüfen *v* examine *v*; *eingehend* - examine closely
Prüfung *f* control, check, examination, audit (of company records)
Prüfungsauftrag *m* auditing mandate
Prüfungsbericht *m* audit report
Prüfungsbescheinigung *f* (für Waren) certificate of analysis
Prüfungsvermerk *m* accountant's certificate, audit certificate
Prüfungswesen *n* auditing *n*
Prüfziffer *f* (EDV) check digit
Prüfziffernrechnung *f* (EDV) check digit calculation
Prüfziffernverfahren *n* (EDV) check digit method
Pseudokonto *n* fictitious account
Publikum *n* the public
Publikumsbörse *f* general publics stock market
Publikumsgelder *n pl* customer deposits
Publikumsgesellschaft *f* public company
Publikumsöffnung *f* going public
Publikumswerte *m pl* (Börse) popular stocks
Publizität *f* publicity *n*
Pufferung *f* (EDV) buffer *n*, buffering *n*
Punkt *m* (bei der Notierung an der Börse) point *n*, base point (0,01 %), tick
pünktlich *adj* prompt *adj*, punctual *adj*
pünktliche Zahlung timely (prompt) payment

Q

Qualifikation f qualification n, standing n
Qualität f quality; **- des Schuldners** standing of the debtor
qualitativ adj qualitative
quantifizieren v quantify
Quantität f quantity n
quantitativ adj quantitative
Quantitätstheorie f quantity theory of money
Quantum n quantity n
Quartalsbetrag m quarterage n
Quartalsdividende f quarterly dividend
quasi begehbares Wertpapier quasi-negotiable instrument; **- übertragbares Wertpapier** quasi-negotiable instrument
Quasigeld n near liquid asset
Quellenbesteuerung f taxation at source, withholding of tax at source
Quellensteuer f withholding tax
quellensteuerfrei exempt from withholding tax

Querschreiben n crossing n (GB)
querschreiben v cross v
quittieren v acknowledge v; - v receipt v, make out a receipt
quittierter Wechsel receipted bill of exchange
Quittung f receipt n, acknowledgement of receipt; *eine - ausstellen* receipt v, make out a receipt; *- über Kontoabhebung* withdrawal receipt; *gesetzlich vorgeschriebene* - statutory receipt
Quittungsaustausch m exchange of acknowledgement signals
Quote f quota n, portion, share
Quotenaktien f pl shares without par value, shares of no-par value
quotenmäßig adj proportionate
quotieren v quote
Quotierung f quotation
Quotient m quotient

R

Rabatt m discount n; ~ m rebate n; **~ für Wiederverkäufer** trade allowance
Radio-und-Fernseh-Werbung f radio and TV advertising
Rahmen m frame, framework, limit
Rahmenfinanzierungsvertrag m block financing agreement
Rahmenkredit m credit line, block credit, blanket credit
Rahmenzusage f basic commitment
Raiffeisenbanken f pl Raiffeisen banks, agricultural credit cooperatives
Raiffeisenkasse f agricultural cooperative credit society (GB)
raketenartiges Steigen der Kurse skyrocketing n (US)
Rang m standing n, rank n
Rangfolge f order of priority
Rangordnung f order of priority
Rangrücktritt m subordination
rapide ansteigen v (Preise, Kurse) boom v
Rat m advice, recommendation, counsel n
Rate f instalment n, payment on account; ~ f (Satz) quota n
Ratenkredit m instalment loan
Ratensparvertrag m automatic savings plan
ratenweise adj by instalments
Ratenzahlung f payment by instal(l)ments, instalment payment; **gestundete ~** deferred payment
Ratenzahlungsgeschäft n instalment business, instalment transaction, instalment lending business, instalment buying
Ratenzahlungskredit m instalment loan
Ratgeber m adviser n, consultant n, counsellor n
Ratifizierung f ratification n
Rationalisierung f rationalization n
Ratschlag m advice n, counsel n
Raubüberfallversicherung f robbery insurance
Reaktion f reaction n; **technische ~** technical reaction
real adj real, actual, practical

realisierbar adj realizable adj
realisieren v realize v, convert into cash; **schnell mit kleinem Nutzen ~** scalp v (US)
Realisierung f realization n
Realkredit m loan against real property, credit on real estate
Realkreditinstitut n mortgage bank
Realwert m real value
Realzins m real interest
Rechenanlage; elektronische ~ computer n
Rechenaufwand m computational effort
Rechenfehler m miscalculation n
Rechenmaschine f calculating machine, calculator n
Rechenschaftsbericht m business report, financial statement
Rechenzentrum n computer centre
rechnen v calculate v, compute v
Rechnen n calculating n, reckoning n
Rechner m computer n
rechnerisches Geldvolumen statistical volume of money
Rechnung f (Bank) account n; ~ f bill n; ~ f (Berechnung) calculation n; ~ f (Warenrechnung) invoice n, commercial invoice; **eine ~ ablegen** account v; **eine ~ legen** render account; **eine ~ vorlegen** render account; **bezahlte ~** account settled; **für ~ von** on account of; **für Ihre ~ und Gefahr** for your account and at your risk; **in ~ gestellt** billed adj; **in ~ stellen** invoice v, bill v; **neue ~** new accounting period
Rechnungen bezahlen straighten accounts; **~ prüfen** audit v; **~ in Ordnung bringen** straighten accounts
Rechnungsabgrenzungsposten m pl = **RAP** deferred items, accounting-apportionment item; **aktive ~** prepaid expenses; **passive ~** prepaid income
Rechnungsabschluß m balance of accounts
Rechnungsaufstellung f accounting statement

Rechnungsauszug

Rechnungsauszug *m* statement of account, abstract of account, extract of account
Rechnungsbetrag *m* invoice amount
Rechnungseinheit *f* unit of account
Rechnungsjahr *n* financial year (GB), fiscal year, fiscal accounting year
Rechnungslegung *f* accounting
Rechnungsperiode; abgeschlossene - completed period
Rechnungsprüfer *m* auditor *n*, chartered accountant, public accountant
Rechnungsprüfung *f* audit *n*, auditing of accounts, checking of accounts
Rechnungswert *m* invoice value
Rechnungswesen *n* accountancy *n*, accounting *n*, bookkeeping *n*
Recht *n* (objektives Recht) law *n*; ~ *n* right *n*; *bürgerliches -* civil law; *formelles -* law adjective
Rechte; verbriefte - chartered rights; *wohlerworbene -* acquired rights, vested rights
rechtmäßig *adj* legitimate *adj*, lawful, rightful
rechtmäßiger Eigentümer rightful owner
Rechtsabteilung *f* legal department
Rechtsanspruch *m* legal claim, title *n*
Rechtsanwalt *m* lawyer *n*, attorney *n* (US), solicitor *m* (GB)
Rechtsbeistand *m* legal adviser
Rechtsberater *m* counsel *n*, counsellor *n*
Rechtseinwand *m* plea, legal objection *n*; *einen - vorbringen* interpose a demurrer, demur *v*
Rechtserklärung; einseitige - deed poll
Rechtsfähigkeit *f* legal capacity
Rechtsfall *m* case *n*
Rechtsform *f* legal form
Rechtsgang *m* course of law
Rechtsgeschäft *n* legal act, transaction
rechtsgültig *adj* effectual *adj*; *für - erklären* validate *v*
rechtsgültige Hypothek legal mortgage, statutory mortgage
rechtskräftiges Urteil final judg(e)ment
Rechtslage *f* legal position
Rechtsmangel *m* defect of title
Rechtsnachfolger *m* successor intitle, legal successor

Rechtspersönlichkeit *f* legal personality, legal status
Rechtssache *f* case *n*
Rechtsstreit *m* litigation *n*, lawsuit *n*, action (at law)
Rechtstitel *m* legal claim, title *n*; *mangelhafter -* bad title; *urkundlicher -* document of title
Rechtsübertragung *f* title transfer, assignment of a right, conveyance of title
rechtsungültig *adj* invalid
rechtsverbindlich *adj* legally binding *adj*
rechtsverbindliche Kreditzusage legally binding promise of a loan
Rechtsvorschriften *f pl* legal provisions
rechtswidrig *adj* unlawful, illegal
Rechtswirksamkeit *f* validity *n*
Rediskont *m* rediscount *n*
rediskontfähig *adj* rediscountable
rediskontieren *v* rediscount
Rediskontkredit *m* rediscount credit
Rediskontpapier *n* rediscountable paper
Rediskontrahmen *m* rediscount limit
Rediskontsatz *m* rediscount rate
Reeder *m* shipowner *n*
Referat *n* (Abteilung) unit, department *n*; ~ *n* (Bericht) report
Referenz; geschäftliche - business reference
refinanzieren *v* refinance *v*
Refinanzierung *f* refinancing *n*
refinanzierungsfähige Wechsel rediscountable bills
Refinanzierungshilfe *f* rediscount assistance
Refinanzierungsmöglichkeit *f* refinancing facility
Refinanzierungs-Swap *m* refinancing swap
Refinanzierungsvolumen *n* total recourse
Reflation *f* (Wirtschaftsbelebung) reflation
Regel *n* principle, rule *n*
regeln *v* settle *v*
Regelung *f* regulation, settlement *n*
regelwidriges Endorsement irregular endorsement
Regierungsanleihe *f* government bond
Regierungsbeamte *m* government official
regional *adj* provincial *adj*, regional *adj*
Regionalbank *f* regional bank

Register *n* register *n*; *- für Grundstücksbelastungen* register of charges
Registratur *f* register office
registrieren *v* register *v*, record *v*
Registrierkasse *f* cash register
registriert *adj* inscribed *adj*, registered *adj*
registrierungsfähig *adj* registrable *adj*
Regreß *m* recourse *n*; *- nehmen* have recourse to, recover *v*
Regreßanspruch *m* right of recourse
regreßpflichtig *adj* liable to recourse
regulieren *v* settle, pay; *leicht zu -* manageable *adj*
Regulierung *f* settlement, payment
rehabilitieren *v* rehabilitate *v*
rehabilitierter Konkursschuldner certificated bankrupt
Rehabilitierung *f* rehabilitation *n*
Reichtum *m* riches *n pl*, wealth *n*
Reihenfolge; *absteigende -* descending order, descending sequence; *aufsteigende -* ascending order, ascending sequence
rein *adj* net, clean
Reinbetrag *m* net amount, clear amount
Reinertrag *m* net income
reines Akzept clean acceptance
Reinfall *m* flop
Reingewinn *m* net profit, net proceeds, clear profit, clear gain, pure profit; *unverteilter -* unappropriated profits, undivided profits, unappropriated earned surplus (US); *Verwendung des -s* appropriation of net profit (GB)
Reinverlust *m* net loss
Reinvermögen *n* net assets, actual assets
Reisebestimmungen *f pl* passenger clause
Reisebüro *n* travel agent
Reisedevisen *plt* travel funds
Reisekosten *plt* travel expenses
Reisekreditbrief *m* traveller's letter of credit (US)
Reisescheck *m* traveler's check, traveller's cheque (GB)
Reisezahlungsmittel *n* payment instrument for travel
Reitwechsel *m* kite *n*, wind bill (GB), windmills *n pl* (GB)
Reklamation *f* complaint *n*, objection *n*
Reklame *f* advertising *n*

Reklamezettel *n* hand bill
reklamierbar *adj* claimable *adj*
reklamieren *v* complain *v*
Rektaindossament *n* conditional endorsement, restrictive endorsement
Rektaklausel *f* »not to order« clause
Rektapapiere *n pl* registered securities
Rektawechsel *m* non-negotiable bill
Rembours *m* reimbursement *n*
Remboursakkreditiv *n* reimbursement credit
Remboursauftrag *m* order to open a documentary credit
Remboursbank *f* accepting bank
Rembourskredit *m* reimbursement credit, banker's acceptance credit
Remittent *m* payee of a bill
Remittenten; für Rechnung des - (Kreuzung auf Schecks) account of payee
remittieren *v* remit *v*
Rendite *f* yield, return; *laufende -* current yield
Renditeaktie *f* high-yield stock
rentabel *adj* lucrative *adj*, remunerative *adj*, profitable *adj*; *gerade noch -* marginal *adj*
Rentabilität *f* earning power, earning capacity; *- f* profitability *n*
Rentabilitätsberechnung *f* calculation of earning power
Rentabilitätsgrenze *f* break-even point
rentabilitätsmäßig *adj* from the point of view of earning power
Rentabilitätsschwelle *f* break-even point
Rente *f* annuity *n*; *- f* pension *n*; *- mit Gewinnbeteiligung* participating annuity; *eine - abwerfend* yielding interest; *lebenslängliche -* life annuity, perpetual annuity; *sofort fällige -* immediate annuity; *steuerfreie -* clear annuity
Renten *f pl* fixed income bonds, annuities *n pl*
Rentenabteilung *f* annuity department
Rentenanleihe *f* perpetual bond, perpetual government loan
Rentenbarwert *m* annuity value
Rentenfonds *m* bond fund, investment fund
Rentengeschäft *n* fixed-interest security business

Rentenkurs m bond price
Rentenmarkt m bond market
Rentenpapier n fixed-interest security
Rentenrückkaufswert m annuity value
Rentenschein m annuity certificate, annuity coupon
Rentenschuldverschreibung f annuity bond
Rententitel m annuity bond
Rentenvertrag m contract of annuity
Rentenwahlrecht n annuity option
rentieren v yield
rentierlich adj yielding a return
Rentner m annuitant n, rentier n
Reorganisation f reorganization n; ~ f (zur Erschließung kundenorientierter Marktpotentiale) business reengineering
Reorganisationsablauf m (bei Großspeicherdateien) reorganization n, file reorganization
repartieren v scale down, apportion v; *Anleihen* ~ repatriate bonds
Repartierung f scaling down, apportionment n, subscribed allotment
Report m (Börse) carry-over transaction
Reportgeschäft n carry-over (contango) transaction, contango business
Reportierung f (Börse) carrying over (GB)
Reportprämie f contango rate (GB), continuation rate (GB)
Reportsatz m contango rate, continuation rate
Repräsentanz f representative n, agent n
Reserve f reserve n, reserve fund; ~ *zweiten Ranges* second reserve; *außerordentliche* ~ provident reserve fund; *gesetzlich vorgeschriebene* ~ legal reserve
reserveähnlich adj reserve-like
Reservebildung f accumulation of reserves, appropriation of surplus, creation of reserves
Reservefonds m pl reserve funds; ~ *für unvorhergesehene Verluste* contingent account (GB)
Reservekapital n revenue reserves (GB), capital reserve, investment reserve
Reservekonto n reserve account
Reserven; *aus Reingewinn gebildete* ~ earned surplus account; *flüssige* ~ liquid reserves, liquid resources; *nach der Satzung vorgeschriebene* ~ statutory reserves; *offene* ~ official reserves, published reserves, declared reserves; *stille* ~ hidden assets, hidden reserves, inner reserves, undisclosed reserves
Reservewährung f reserve currency
reservieren v reserve v
Respekttage m pl days of grace, days of respite
Ressort n department n
Rest m residue n
Restbestand m remainder n, remaining amount, pay-off amount (loans)
Restbetrag m remainder n, remaining amount, pay-off amount (loans)
Restbuchwert m residual costs, residual book value, written-down value
Restdividende f dividend balance
Restforderung f residual claim
Restitution f restitution n
Restkapital n remaining capital
Restkaufgeld n residual purchase money
Restkaufgeldhypothek f purchase money mortgage
Restnachlaß m residuary estate
Restrukturierung f restructuring, reorganisation
Restschulden f pl surviving debts
Restsumme f residual amount, arrearage n
Restvermächtnis n residuary legacy
Restzahlung f payment of the balance
Resultat n result n, outcome
Retourengutschrift f returns credit voucher
Retourenkonto n returns account
retourniert adj returned adj
Reuegeld n premium
revidieren v audit v; *Bücher* ~ check the books
Revision f audit n, auditing of accounts, checking of accounts; ~ *der Geschäfte einer Gesellschaft* investigation of a company's affairs
Revisionsabteilung f department audit (auditing)
Revisionsbericht m auditor's report, audit report
Revisionsbuch n audit book
Revisionsgesellschaft f auditing company

Revisionsrichtlinien *f pl* audit standards
Revisionsverband *m* joint auditing body
Revisonswesen *n* auditing *n*
Revisor *m* auditor *n*, chartered accountant, public accountant; *- m* comptroller *n* (US)
revolvierend *adj* revolving *adj*
revolvierender Kredit revolving credit
revolvierendes Akkreditiv revolving documentary credit; *- Konto* revolving account
Rezession *f* business recession
reziprok *adj* reciprocal *adj*
richterliche Verfügung juridical order
Richtgröße *f* benchmark
Richtigkeitsbestätigung *f* reconciliation statement
Richtigstellung *f* adjustment *n*; *- f* correction *n*
Rimesse *f* bill, draft, remittance *n*
Ring *m* pool *n*, cartel *n*, combine *n*
Risiko *n* risk *n*
Risiko-Arbitrage *f* risk arbitrage
risikoarm *adj* low-risk
risikobehaftet *adj* risky
Risikobetrag *m* amount of risk
Risikogeschäft *n* adventure *n*
Risikokapital *n* risk capital, venture capital
Risikomanagement *n* risk management
Risikoprämie *f* risk premium
Risiko-Rendite-Profil *n* risk/yield profile, risk/return profile
Risikoübernahme *f* risk taking
Risikoversicherung *f* risk assurance
Risikoverteilung *f* distribution of risk, pooling of risk, risk spreading
riskantes Unternehmen speculative venture
riskieren *v* risk *v*
Rohbilanz *f* rough balance
Rohertrag *m* gross proceeds
Rohgewinn *m* gross profit
Rohmaterial *n* raw material
Rohstoff *m* raw material
Rohstoff-Fonds *m* commodity fund
Rohstoff-Kreditgesellschaft *f* Commodity Credit Corporation (US)
Rohwarenbörse *f* commodity exchange
Rollgeld *n* freight charge, cartage *n*
Rollgut *n* carted goods

Roll-over-Kredit *m* roll-over credit, rollover loan facility (at the eurocredit market)
Royalty *n* (Lizenz-, Patentgebühr, Tantieme) royalty *n*
Rückbelastungsaufgabe *f* return debit voucher
Rückbuchung *f* retransfer, reversal *n*
Rückbürgschaft *f* back-to-back guarantee
Rückeinfuhr *f* reimportation *n*
rückerstatten *v* refund, reimburse *v*
Rückerstattung *f* refund *n*, reimbursement *n*
Rückfluß *m* flowback
Rückgabe *f* giving-back, return
Rückgang *m* decline *n*, decrease *n*, fall *n*, drop *n*; *- m* (Kurse) reaction *n*; *beträchtlicher* ~ material recession; *wesentlicher* ~ material recession
Rückgängigmachung *f* annulment, rescission *n*, cancellation *n*
rückgliedern *v* reincoporate
Rückgriff *m* recourse *n*
Rückgriffsrecht *n* right of recourse
Rückgriffsreserve *f* standby reserve
Rückhalt *m* financial support, stand-by
Rückkauf *m* repurchase (von Aktien), redemption by purchase; *- einer Schuld* (häufig mit Abschlag) cash buy back
rückkaufen *v* repurchase, buy back
Rückkaufswert *m* redemption value; *- m* (einer Versicherungspolice) surrender value, cash surrender value
Rückkaufverpflichtung der Emissionsschuldner purchase syndicate
Rückkoppelung *f* feedback
Rücklage *f* reserve *n*, reserve fund; *gesetzliche* ~ statutory reserve; *offene* ~ published reserve; *zweckgebundene* ~ surplus reserve (US)
rückläufig *adj* declining *adj*; *- adj* (Börse) downward tendency, retrograde *adj*
Rückläufigkeit *f* decline *n*
Rückmeldung *f* response *n*, answerback *n*
Rücknahme *f* taking back, repurchase
Rücknahmepreis *m* redemption price, repurchase price
Rückprämie *f* (Börsenprämiengeschäft) premium for put option

Rückrechnung f (Auslandswechsel) re-exchange n; ~ f return account
Rückscheck m returned check
Rückschlag m (Börse) reaction n; ~ m recession n, setback n
Rückseite f (eines Wechsels oder Schecks) back n
Rückspesen plt back charges
Rückstand m arrears, arrearage n; **im ~ behindhand** adj
rückständig adj unpaid adj
rückständige Zahlung overdue payment
Rückstellung f provision, reserve n, reserve fund; **~ für Amortisationen** amortization reserve; **~ für Anlageerneuerung** reserve for amortization; **~ für Schuldentilgung** reserve for debt redemption; **~ für zweifelhafte Forderungen** reserve for bad and doubtful debt provisions
Rückstellungen f pl (für noch nicht erkennbare Risiken) reserves for contingencies; **~ für Kreditverluste** loan loss provisions (reserves); **~ für Pensionen** pension provisions
Rückstellungskonto n appropriation account
Rückstellungsposten m reserve item
Rücktritt m (vom Amt) retirement n; ~ m (von einer Vereinbarung) withdrawal n
Rücktrittsprämie f premium
Rückübereignung f reconveyance n
Rückübertragung f retransfer, re-assignment n; ~ f (von Grundbesitz) reconveyance n
Rücküberweisung f retransfer, return remittance
Rückvaluta f backvalue n
rückvergüten v refund, reimbourse
Rückvergütung f refund n, reimbursement n
Rückversicherer m reinsurer n
rückversichern v reinsure v, reassure v

Rückversicherung f reinsurance n, reassurance n
Rückwechsel m re-exchange bill, return draft, returned bill
Rückwechselkonto n account of redraft
rückwirkend adj retroactive adj
Rückwirkung f retroactive effect, reaction n
rückzahlbar adj reimbursable adj, repayable adj
Rückzahlbuch n debenture book
rückzahlen v repay, reimburse v
Rückzahlung f repayment n, redemption n, amortization n; **zur ~ aufgerufen** called adj
Rückzahlungsagio n premium on redemption
Rückzahlungskurs m repayment price, rate of redemption
Rückzahlungstermin m date of redemption, date of repayment; ~ m (eines Kredits) repayment date, due date (of a loan)
Rückzahlungswert m redemption value
Rückzoll m drawback n, customs penny
Rückzug m withdrawal, retreat n
Ruf m call n, (Ansehen) reputation
rufen v call v
Ruhegeld n retirement pension, pension n, retirement benefits
Ruhestand m retirement n
rührig adj active adj
Ruin m ruin n
Rumpfgeschäftsjahr n abreviated financial year
Rumpfgesellschaft f rump company
runden v round off
Rundschreiben n circular, form letter
Rüstungsauftrag m armament order
Rüstungsindustrie f armament industry
Rüstungswerte m pl (Börse) armament securities, war securities
Rüstzeit f set-up time
rutschen slide, (Kurse) slip

S

Sachanlage *f* real investment
Sachanlagen *f pl* (Bilanzposten) tangible fixed assets
Sachanlagevermögen *n* tangible assets
Sachaufwendung *f* operating expenditure
sachdienlich *adj* appropriate *adj*
Sacheinlage *f* investment in kind
Sachgebiet *n* subject *n*, area of specialty, field of application, special field
Sachkonto *n* real account, impersonal account, nominal account
Sachkosten *plt* non-personnel cost, equipment and material cost
Sachregister *n* index *n*
Sachschaden *m* damage to property
Sachversicherung *f* property damage insurance
Sachverständigenrat *m* board of experts, brain trust
Sachwert *m* real value, intrinsic value
Sachwertdenken *n* thinking in terms of material value
Sachwertdividende property dividend (US)
Sachwertklausel *f* material value clause
Safe *m* safe *n*
Safemiete *f* safe deposit fee
saisonabhängig *adj* subject to seasonal influences
Saisonkredit *m* seasonal loan
Saisontendenz *f* seasonal tendency
Saldenanerkenntnis *f* confirmation of balance
Saldenliste *f* report of balances, list of balances
saldieren *v* balance *v*; ~ *v* (Konto) balance an account
Saldieren *n* balancing *n*
saldiert durch counterbalanced by
Saldierung *f* balancing, closing, netting
Saldo *m* balance *n*, account balance; *einen ~ ausgleichen* clear a balance; *einen ~ ziehen* balance *v*; *per ~ gutschreiben* credit by balance; *täglicher ~* daily balance; *umsatzloser ~* dormant balance
Saldomitteilung *f* balance notification
Saldovortrag *m* balance carried forward (B/F), balance brought forward (B/F), account carried forward
Sammelaktie *f* global share
Sammelauftrag *m* collective order
Sammelavis *m* summary advice
Sammeldepot *n* collective custody account
Sammelgutschrift *f* collection credit, credit for collected item(s)
Sammelkonnossement *n* collective bill of lading
Sammelkonto *n* collective account
sammeln *v* collect, gather
Sammeloptionsschein *m* global warrant
Sammelüberweisung *f* collective transfer
Sammelverwahrung *f* collective custody
Sammelzertifikat *n* global certificate
Samurai-Anleihe *f* samurai bond
sanieren *v* reconstruct, reorganize, recapitalize; *ein faules Konto ~* nursing an account (GB)
Sanierung *f* reorganization *n*, reconstruction *n*
Sanierungskonto *n* reorganization account
Satz *m* rate *n*; *~ für Kabelauszahlungen* rate for cable transfers; *~ für Tagesgeld* call rate; *voller ~ Dokumente* full set of documents
Satzlänge; *variable ~* (EDV) variable record length
Satzung *f* (einer Aktiengesellschaft) articles of incorporation and bylaws (US), memorandum and articles of association (GB), statute *n*; *~ f* statute *n*, rulebook
satzungsgemäß *adj* statutory *adj*
säumiger Zahler defaulter *n*
Säumnisgebühr *f* default fee
Schacherer *m* bargainer *n*, haggler *n*
Schachtelbeteiligung *f* intercompany participation
schaden *v* damage *v*
Schaden *m* damage, injury, claim; *~ m* (Einbuße) loss *n*; *~ feststellen* assess damages; *~ zufügen* damage *v*

Schadenersatz

Schadenersatz *m* damages compensation; ~ *m* (Entschädigung) indemnification *n*, indemnity *n*
Schadenersatzanspruch *m* damageclaim, claim for damages, claim for loss, right of recovery
Schadenersatzerklärung *f* letter of indemnity (GB), bond of indemnity (US)
Schadenersatzklage *f* action for damages
Schadenersatzsumme *f* damages *n pl* (compensation)
Schadenersatzversicherung *f* indemnity insurance
Schadenfestsetzung *f* adjustment of claims
Schadenfeststellung *f* ascertainment of loss
Schadenregulierer *m* claim adjuster, claim agent
Schadenregulierung *f* claim settlement
Schadenreserve *f* claim reserve
Schadensbericht *m* damage report
Schadenschätzer *m* claim adjuster, claim agent
Schadenversicherung *f* property damage insurance
Schadloserklärung *f* declaration of indemnity
schadlos halten (sich) indemnify *v*, compensate *v*, reimburse *v*
Schalter *m* counter *n*
Schalterangestellte *f u. m* counter-clerk *n*
Schalterautomat siehe *Bankautomat*
Schalterbeamte *m* counter-clerk *n*
Schalterbuchungsmaschine *f* tellerposting machine, teller machine
Schalterfach *n* post box
Schaltergeschäft *n* counter operations, over-the-counter business
Schalterhalle *f* banking hall; *offene* ~ open banking hall
Schalterquittungsmaschine *f* tellerreceipting machine
Schalterschluß *m* window closing time
Schalterstunden *f pl* banking hours
Schalterverkehr *m* window traffic, over-the-counter trading
Schatz *m* treasure *n*
Schatzamt *n* Exchequer *n* (GB); ~ *n* Treasury *n*

Schatzanleihe Treasury bond
Schatzanweisungen *f pl* Treasury notes; *unverzinsliche* ~ Treasury discount notes (US)
Schatzbrief *m* savings bond
schätzen *v* estimate *v*; ~ *v* value *v*; *eine Münze* ~ rate a coin; *neu* ~ revalue *v*, reappraise *v*
Schätzer *m* appraiser *n*, appriciator *n*, valuar *n* (GB), valuator *n* (US)
Schatzmeister *m* treasurer *n*
Schatzschein *m* treasury certificate
Schätzung *f* appraisal *n*; ~ *f* valuation *n*; *vorsichtige* ~ conservative estimate
Schätzungskosten *plt* cost of appraisal
Schatzwechsel *m* (kurzfristig) Exchequer bill (GB); ~ *m* Treasury bill, Treasury note
Schatzwechselkredite *m pl* borrowing on Treasury bills
Schätzwert *m* appraised value, estimated value
Scheck *m* check *n* (US), cheque *n* (GB); ~ *mit geprüfter Unterschrift* initialed check; ~ *ohne (volle) Deckung* rubbercheck (US); ~ *von begrenzter Höhe* limited cheque (GB); *bankbestätigter* ~ certified check; *bestätigter* ~ marked cheque (GB); *durch Werterhöhung gefälschter* ~ raised check (US); *einen* ~ *auf ein Konto ziehen* draw a check upon an account; *einen* ~ *bestätigen* certify a check; *einen* ~ *einkassieren* collect a check; *einen* ~ *einlösen* cash a check; *einen* ~ *einziehen* collect a check; *einen* ~ *kassieren* cash a check; *entwerteter* ~ cancelled check; *gekreuzter* ~ check only for account, crossed check; *nachdatierter* ~ antedated check; *nicht vollständig ausgefüllter* ~ inchoate check (US), inchoate cheque (GB); *notleidender* ~ dishonoured check; *offener* ~ open check, uncrossed check; *protestierter* ~ protested check; *über ein festgesetztes Kreditlimit hinausgezogener* ~ overcheque *n* (GB); *überfälliger* ~ overdue check; *ungedeckter* ~ check without provision, bad check, kite check, rubber check (US), uncovered

check; **ungekreuzter** - open check, uncrossed check; **verfallener** - overdue check; **verjährter** - stale check (US); **vordatierter** - postdated check
Scheckabteilung f check department
Scheckaussteller m writer (drawer) of a check
Scheckbegünstigte f u. m payee of a cheque
Scheckbestätigung f certification of a check
Scheckbestätigungsabteilung f certification department
Scheckbuch n check book
Scheckduplikat n duplicate check
Scheckeinzug m check collection
Scheckendnummer f check ending number
Scheckfälschung f alteration of checks
Scheckformular n check form (US), cheque form (GB)
Scheckheft n check book
Scheckinhaber m bearer of a check
Scheckinkasso n check collection
Scheckkarte f cheque card
Scheckkartenscheck m cheque card check
Scheckkontoinhaber m check account depositor
Scheckkontrolleur m receiving teller (US)
Scheckkurs m check rate
Scheckliste f check register
Schecknummer f check number
Schecks; im Einzug befindliche - float n (US); **Inkasso von** - cheque collection (GB)
Schecksperre f stop payment order
Scheckstempel m check stamp
Scheck-und-Wechsel-Verkehr m check and bill transactions (GB)
Scheckverrechnungsverkehr m check clearing system
Scheidemünze f divisional coin, subsidiary coin, base coin (US)
Schein m slip n
Scheindividende f sham dividend
Scheingeschäft n dummy transaction
Scheingewinne m pl paper profits (US)
Schema n scheme, diagram, form n
Schenkung f gift, donation

Schenkungsempfänger m donee n
Schenkungsurkunde f deed of donation, deed of gift
Schieber m racketeer n (US)
Schiebung f racket n (US), racketeering n
Schiedsgericht n arbitration court
schiedsgerichtlich adj arbitrational adj, arbitral adj
schiedsgerichtliche Entscheidung arbitration n, arbitrage n
schiedsgerichtsfähig adj arbitrable adj
Schiedsrichter m arbitrator n, arbiter n
Schiedsrichteramt n arbitratorship n
Schiedsspruch m arbitrator's award n; **durch - entscheiden** arbitrage v, mediate v, intervene v
Schiedsverfahren n arbitration n, arbitrage n
Schiff; gechartertes - chartered ship
Schiffahrtsaktien f pl shipping issues, shipping shares
Schiffbruch m wreck n
Schiffseigentümer m shipowner n
Schiffshypothek f ship mortgage
Schiffshypothekenbank f ship mortgage bank, bank granting loans on ship mortgages
Schiffsladung f cargo
Schiffsverpfändung f bottomry n
Schiffswerte m pl (Börse) shipping issues, shipping shares
Schilling m schilling (Austrian currency unit)
Schirmherr m sponsor n
schlanke Bankorganisation lean banking
schlankes Management lean management
schlecht beraten ill advised
schlechten Absatz finden run into heavy selling
schlechtes Geschäft bad bargain
Schleichhandel m illegal trade
Schleuderpreis m rock bottom
schlichten v arbitrage v, mediate v, intervene v
Schlichter m arbitrator n, arbiter n
Schlichtungsausschuß m board of arbitration
Schließfach n safe deposit box, safe box
Schließfachgebühr f safe deposit fee
Schluß m (Börse) close n

Schlußabrechnung

Schlußabrechnung f account of settlement
Schlußabrechnungstag m settling day
Schlußbestand m closing stock
Schlußdividende f final dividend, terminal bonus
Schlußeinheit f closing unit, round lot
Schlüssel m key; ~ m (Schlüsselnummer) code n
Schlußfolgerung f conclusion n
Schlußkurs m closing price
Schlußnote f sales note, broker's memorandum, broker's note, contract note, bought note
Schlußnotenregister n bargain book
Schlußschein m sales note, broker's memorandum, broker's note, contract note, bought note
Schlußscheinbuch n contract book
Schlußscheinstempel m contract stamp
Schlußtermin m closing date, latest date
schmälern v curtail v, cut down, cut v, impair v
Schmälerung f impairment, curtailment n, reduction n
Schmiergeld n bribe n, graft n (US)
Schmuggel m illegal trade
Schnellkurs m condensed course
Schnittstelle f (EDV) interface n
Schrankfach n safe deposit box, safe box
Schrankfachgebühr f safe deposit fee
Schreibbreite f (eines Schnelldruckers) line width, number of print positions
Schreibmaschine; auf der ~ schreiben typewrite v
Schreibtischtest m (von Programmen) desk check
Schriftführer m secretary n
schriftliche Garantieerklärung letter of indemnity (GB), bond of indemnity (US); **~ Kündigung** written notice; **~ Schuldanerkenntnis** cognitive note
Schriftwechsel m correspondence n
Schufa f = **Schutzgemeinschaft für allgemeine Kreditsicherung** creditors protection agency
Schuld f debt, indebtedness n, amount owed; **bevorrechtigte ~** preferential debt, preferred debt, privileged debt, secured debt; **eine ~ begleichen** discharge a debt; **fällige ~** debt owing; **festgestellte ~** liquidated debt; **für eine ~ einstehen** answer for a debt; **konsolidierte ~** consolidated debt; **öffentliche ~** public debt; **schwebende ~** floating debt, unfunded debt; **uneinbringliche ~** bad debt; **unfundierte ~** floating debt, unfunded debt; **unverzinsliche ~** passive debt; **verjährte ~** barred debt; **vertagte ~** deferred debt
Schuldablösung f repayment of a debt
Schuldanerkenntnis n acknowledgement of debt; **schriftliches ~** cognitive note
Schuldanerkennung f certificate of indebtedness, IOU (= I owe you), acknowledgement of indebtedness
Schuldauswechslung f substitution of debt
Schuldbrief m mortgage note
Schuldbuch n debt book, debt register
Schuldbuchforderung f debt register claim
schulden v owe v
Schulden f pl liabilities n pl; **~ abdecken** cover debts; **~ machen** contract debts; **~ übernehmen** assume debts; **Eintreibung von ~** recovery of debts; **kurzfristig zurückzahlbare ~** quick liabilities; **nachweisbare ~** provable debts
Schuldenabbau m debt reduction, debt retirement
Schuldendienst m debt service
Schuldenerlaß m release from debts, acquittance n, quittance n; **teilweiser ~** abatement of debts
schuldenfrei adj unencumbered adj, unmortgaged adj, unincumbered adj
Schuldenkonto n debtor account
Schuldensaldo m debt balance, debit balance
Schuldentilgung f amortization n; **~ f** debt redemption
Schuldentilgungsplan m redemption plan
schuldig sein owe v
Schuldner m debtor n; **flüchtiger ~** absconding debtor; **unbekannt verzogener ~** absconding debtor; **zahlungsunfähiger ~** bad debtor
Schuldnerland n debtor nation

Schuldrecht *n* law of contract
Schuldschein *m* promissory note, certificate of indebtedness, IOU (= I owe you), acknowledgement of indebtedness, borrower's note, note; **- mit Unterwerfungsklausel** judg(e)ment note; **einen - einlösen** discharge a bond; **hypothekarisch gesicherter -** mortgage note
Schuldscheinaussteller *m* recognizor *n*
Schuldscheindarlehen *n* loan against a promissory note
Schuldsumme *f* amount of the debt
Schuldtitel *m* debt, debt issue, debt security (note); **- des US-Schatzamtes** Treasuries (informal), Treasury bills and notes; **- öffentlicher Stellen** public sector securities; **- ohne Laufzeitbegrenzung** perpetuals, perpetual bonds; **- staatlicher Kreditnehmer** sovereign debt (GB); **kurzfristiger - auf revolvierender Basis** revolving underwriting facility (RUF); **nach oben begrenzter, zinsvariabler -** capped floating rate note; **ungesicherter, kurzfristiger -** commercial paper; **zinsvariabler -** countdown floater
Schuldübernahme *f* substitution of debt
Schuldurkunde *f* debt certificate, acknowledgement of debt
Schuldverschreibung *f* bond *n*, debenture *n*, obligation *n*, note; **- mit einjähriger Laufzeit** yearling bond; **- mit mittlerer Laufzeit** medium-term note; **- mit zusätzlicher Bürgschaft** bond with surety; **- über eine bevorrechtigte Forderung** trust debenture, trust bond; **durch Wechsel garantierte -** endorsed bond, indorsed bond; **hypothekarisch gesicherte -** secured bond, mortgage debenture; **ungesicherte -** debenture bond; **unverzinsliche -** passive bond, non-interestbearing bond, discount bond (US)
Schuldverschreibungen *f pl* (Bilanzposten) debt securities; **noch nicht ausgegebene -** unissued debentures; **sonstige -** other bonds; **tarifbesteuerte -** bonds subject to normal tax rates
Schuldverschreibungsurkunde *f* bond indenture
Schulung *f* training *n*
schützen *v* secure *v*, protect *v*, safeguard *v*, provide security for
Schutzbestimmungen *f pl* proactive covenants, safeguarding provisions
Schutzsystem *n* protectionism *n*
schwacher Markt thin market, weak market
Schwankungsbreite *f* swing *n* (US)
schwarze Börse black bourse; **- Liste** black book, black list; **auf die - Liste setzen** blacklist *v*
Schwarzmarkt *m* black market
Schwebe; in der - befindlich pending *adj*, unsettled *adj*
schwebend *adj* floating *adj*
schwebende Schuld floating debt, unfunded debt; **- Verbindlichkeiten** unadjusted liabilities
Schwebeposten *m pl* suspense items
Schwebezustand *m* abeyance *n*
Schweizer Franken *m* Swiss Franc
Schweizer Frankenanleihe ausländischer Schuldner *f* Swiss franc bond issues by foreign borrowers
Schweizerische Bankiervereinigung *f* Swiss Bankers Association
Schweizerische Nationalbank *f* Swiss National Bank
Schwellenpreis *m* threshold price
schwer verwertbare Aktiva sticky assets
schwere Papiere high shares
schwerfälliges Wertpapier lame duck (US)
Schwestergesellschaft *f* sister company
Schwierigkeit *f* difficulty, problem, dilemma
Schwindelfirma *f* wild cat company (US)
Sechsmonatslibor *m* six-month's Libor
sechsprozentige Papiere sixes *n pl*
Securitisierung *f* (Verbriefungstendenz) securitization
Seebrief *m* clearance certificate
Seefrachtbrief *m* bill of lading
Seelenmassage *f* (z.B. durch Bankesbank-Appelle) moral suasion

Seeschaden *m* damage by sea water, average
Seetransport *m* carriage by sea
Seetransportversicherung *f* marine insurance, sea insurance
Seeversicherung *f* marine insurance, sea insurance
Seeversicherungsgesellschaft *f* marine insurance underwriters
Seeversicherungspolice *f* marine insurance policy
sehr fest (Kurse) buoyant *adj*
Seitenleser *m* (EDV) page reader
Sekretär *m* secretary *n*
Sektor *m* sector *n*
Sektretariat *n* secretariat *n*
Sekundärmarkt *m* secondary market
Sekundawechsel *m* second of exchange
Selbstabholung *f* collection by the customer, collection by hand (US)
Selbstbedienungsbank *f* self-service bank
Selbstbedienungsterminal *n* customer-operated terminal
Selbstbehalt *m* retention *n*
Selbsteintritt *m* acting as principal, contracting for one's own account
selbstfinanzieren *v* self-finance *v*
Selbstfinanzierung *f* self-financing *n*, own financing
Selbstkosten *plt* prime cost, actual costs
Selbstkostenpreis *m* cost price
Selbstkostenrechnung *f* cost accounting, calculation of cost
selbstprüfende Kontonummer self-checking account number
selbstschuldnerische Bürgschaft directly unforceable guarantee, guarantee with direct liability as co-debotor
Selbstversicherer *m* self-insurer *n*
Selektion *f* selection *n*, choice between
senden *v* send, forward, remit *v*
Seniorchef *m* senior director
Senkrechtstarter im Finanzgeschäft whizz kid (informal)
Separatkonto *n* special account
Sequester *m* sequestrator *n*, receiver *n*
sequestrieren *v* sequestrate *v*, sequester *v*
Serie *f* series, tranche, issue
Serienanleihen *f pl* serial bonds

serienweise rückzahlbare Obligationen instalment bonds
Service *m* service *n*
SIBOR *m* = **Singapurer Interbanken-Angebotszinssatz** Singapur Interbank Offered Rate
sicher *adj* safe *adj*
sichere Anlage safe investment; **- Verwahrung** safekeeping *n*
sichergestellt *adj* secured *adj*
Sicherheit *f* safety *n*; **- f** security *n*; **dingliche -** real security; **genügende -** ample security; **persönliche -** personal security; **Verzicht auf -** abandonment of security; **wertlose -** dead security; **zusätzliche -** collateral security
Sicherheiten *f pl* collaterals, securities; **nachrangige -** junior securities; **verpfändete -** pledged collaterals; **verkehrsfähige -** marketable securities; **verwertbare -** fungible (interchangeable) securities
Sicherheitsempfänger *m* warrantee *n*
Sicherheitsgeber *m* warrantor *n*
Sicherheitsleistung *f* provision of security; **- für eine Anerkennung** recognizance *n*
Sicherheitsmarge *f* safety margin, collatered security margin; **- bei Eröffnung einer Terminposition** initial margin; **minimale -** marginal margin
Sicherheitsnehmer *m* warrantee *n*
Sicherheitspool *m* security pool
Sicherheitsrücklage *f* contingency reserve, contingent reserve, contingent fund (US)
Sicherheitsverwertung *f* realization (liquidation) of a security
Sicherheitswechsel *m* bill of security
sichern *v* secure *v*, protect *v*, safeguard *v*, provide security for
sicherstellen *v* secure *v*, protect *v*, safeguard *v*, provide security for
Sicherstellungsdepot *n* security deposit
Sicherung; - einer Kassaposition durch einen Terminkontrakt cross hedge; **bankmäßige -** normal banking security
Sicherungsabtretung *f* assignment of security

Sicherungsgegenstand *m* collateral *n*
Sicherungsgeschäft *n* hedge *n*
Sicherungshypothek *f* trust mortgage, covering mortgage
Sicherungsmaßnahmen *f pl* security measures, safety measures
Sicherungsrecht *n* (mit Besitz nicht verbunden) charging lien
Sicherungsschlüssel *m* (EDV) security code
Sicherungsübereignung *f* collateral assignment, assignment by way of security
Sicherungsübereignungsvertrag *m* deed of assignment, letter of lien
Sicherungsvorkehrungen *f pl* security precautions, safety precautions
Sicherungswechsel *m* collateral bill
sicherungsweise abgetretene Hypothek security mortgage
Sicht; *bei -* at sight
Sichteinlage *f* sight deposit, demand deposit (US)
Sichtkurs *m* (Devisenmarkt) demand rate; *- m* sight rate
Sichtpapier *n* demand instrument, demand note, demand paper
Sichttratte *f* demand draft, draft at sight, sight draft
Sichtwechsel *m* bill at sight, bill on demand, demand bill, sight bill, cash order (GB)
Sichtwechselkurs *m* sight exchange
Siedlungskredit *m* land settlement financing loan
Siegel *n* seal *n*
Silberbarren *m* silver bar
Silbermünze *f* silver coin
Silvester-Anleihe *f* New Year's bond
simulieren *v* simulate *v*, feign *v*
Simultanarbeit *f* parallel work, multi-programming *n* (EDP)
Singapurer Interbanken-Angebotszinssatz *m* = **SIBOR** Singapore Interbank Offered Rate
Sinken *n* sag *n*, easing-off *n*
sinnlos spekulieren plunge *v*
Sitz *m* domicile *n*, registered office
Sitzung *f* meeting *n*, session *n*; *eine - abhalten* sit *v*, meet *v*
Sitzungsbericht *m* minutes *n pl*
Sitzungsgeld *n* attendance fee

Sitzungssaal des Direktoriums board room
skontieren *v* discount *v*
Skonto *m* discount *n*
sofort fällige Rente immediate annuity; *- lieferbar* spot cash; *- zahlbar* spot cash
Sofortabbuchungssystem *n* on-line debit system
Sofortauskunftssystem *n* on-line information system
sofortige Zahlung cash payment, cash-down payment
Sofortzugriff *m* (EDV) immediate access
Solawechsel *m* note of hand, promissory note, single bill, sola bill, sole bill of exchange
Solidarbürge *m* joint guarantor
Solidarbürgschaft *f* joint and several guarantee
solidarisch (z. B. haften) corporately, jointly and severally
Solidarschuld *f* joint liability
Solidarschuldner *m* joint debtor, codebtor *n*, fellow debtor
solide *adj* sound *adj*
Soll *n* debit *n*; *- und Haben* credit and debit
Sollbeleg *m* debit voucher
Sollsaldo *m* debt balance, debit balance
Sollseite *f* debit side
Sollstellung *f* budget position, book position
Sollzinsen *m pl* debit interest, interest receivable
Sollzinssatz *m* debit rate
solvent *adj* solvent *adj*
Solvenz *f* solvency *n*
Solvenzkoeffizient *m* solvency factor
Sonder- (in Zus.) extra *adj*
Sonderabschreibung *f* special write-off, accelerated depreciation
Sonderbonus in bar cash bonus
Sonderdepot *n* specific deposit
Sondereinnahme *f* special revenue
Sondererträge *m pl* extraordinary income
Sonderkontingent *n* special quota
Sonderkonto *n* special account
Sonderkredit *m* special loan

Sonderkreditinstitut

Sonderkreditinstitut *n* special-purpose credit institution
Sonderposten mit Rücklageanteil (Bilanzposten) special items with partial reserve character
Sonderrecht *n* privilege *n* (priority)
Sonderrechte; mit -n ausgestattet privileged *adj*
Sonderrückstellung *f* special reserve
Sondersatz *m* special rate
Sondervermögen *n* separate estate, separate fund
Sonderwerte *m pl* (Börse) special stocks (US)
Sonderziehungsrechte *n pl* (IMF) special drawing rights (SDRs)
sonstige Erträge other income; **- Verpflichtungen** other liabilities
sonstiger Aufwand other charges
Sorgfalt *f* carefulness *n*; **gebührende -** due diligence, due attention
Sorte *f* type *n*, grade *n*, brand *n*
Sorten *f pl* foreign notes and coins
Sortengeschäft *n* business in foreign notes and coins
Sortenhandel *m* dealings in foreign notes and coins
Sortenkasse *f* foreign till - *f* (Abteilung) foreign money department
Sortenkonto *n* specie account
Sortenzettel *m* bordereau *n*
sortieren *v* sort *v*
Sortiergenerator *m* sort generator
Sortiergesichtspunkt *m* sort philosophy
Sortierkriterium *n* sort key, sort criterion
Sortierlauf *m* sort *n*, sort run
Sortiermodell *n* (beim Beleglesen) sort pattern
sortiert *adj* assorted *adj*
Sortierverfahren *n* sorting method, sort method
Sortiment *n* assortment *n*, collection *n*
Sovereign *m* (englische Goldmünze) Sovereign *n* (British gold coin);
 - debt Verschuldung durch den Staat;
 - risk Länderrisiko (politisches Risiko)
Sozialabgaben social security costs
Sozialaufwendungen *f pl* social expenditure
Sozialbilanz *f* social report

sozialisieren *v* socialize *v*, communize *v*
Sozialisierung *f* socialization *n*, communization *n*
Sozialleistung *f* social security expenditure
Sozialversicherung *f* social security, social insurance
Sozialversicherungsleistungen *f pl* social security benefits
Spaltung *f* split, splitting *n*
Spanne *f* margin *n*; **höchste - zwischen Geld- und Briefkurs** maximum spread
Sparabteilung *f* savings department, thrift department (US)
Sparbank *f* savings bank, savings association, savings and loan association
Sparbrief *m* savings bond
Sparbuch *n* savings book, savings passbook
Sparbüchse *f* money box, thrift box (US)
Spareckzins *m* basic savings rate
Spareinlage *f* savings deposit
Spareinlagen *f pl* savings *n pl*
Spareinlagenbildung *f* accumulation of savings
Spareinleger *m* savings depositor
sparen *v* save *v*
Sparen *n* saving *n*; **vermögenswirksames -** capital savings
Sparer *m* saver, depositor *n*
Sparer-und-Anleger-Schutz *m* protection of savers and depositors
Sparförderung *f* savings promotion; **staatliche -** save-as-you-earn (US)
Spargelder *n pl* savings *n pl*; **-** *n pl* thrift deposit (US)
Spargeschenkgutschein *m* savings gift credit voucher
Sparguthaben *n* savings account, special interest account (US), thrift account (US)
Sparkapital *n* savings capital
Sparkasse *f* savings bank, savings association, savings and loan association
Sparkassenabteilung *f* special interest department (US)
Sparkassenbrief *m* savings certificate
Sparkassenbuch *n* savings book, savings passbook
Sparkassenguthaben *n* credit with a savings bank

Sparkassenverband *m* savings bank association
Sparkassenwesen *n* savings banking
Sparkonto *n* savings account, special interest account (US), thrift account (US); **~ für Weihnachtseinkäufe** Christmas Club account (US), Xmas club (US)
spärliche Nachfrage slack demand
Sparpfennig *m* nest-egg *n*
Sparplan *m* savings plan
Sparprämie *f* savings premium
sparsam *adj* thrifty, economical *adj*, economic *adj*
Sparsamkeit *f* thriftiness
Sparschuldverschreibung *f* savings bond
Sparsumme *f* total saving
Spartätigkeit *f* savings activity
Sparte *f* line of business, branch *n*
Spartenaufgliederung *f* breakdown by branches
Sparverein *m* savings association (US)
Sparverkehr *m* savings activity, saving *n*
Sparvertrag *m* savings plan
Sparvorgang *m* saving *n*
Sparziel *n* saving target
Sparzugang *m* accrual of savings
Sparzulage *f* savings bonus
später *adj* later *adj*, subsequent *adj*
spätere Annahme after acceptation
Spediteur *m* forwarder *n*, forwarding agent, carrying agent; **bahnamtlicher ~** railway express agency
Spediteurempfangsschein *m* forwarder's receipt
Spedition *f* forwarding, forwarding agency
Speditionsgebühr *f* carriers charges
Speditionsrechnung *f* bill of conveyance
Speicherkapazität *f* (EDV) storage capacity, memory capacity, memory size
Spekulant *m* speculator *n*, adventurer *n*, gambler *n*, profiteer *n*; **großer ~** prospector *n*; **unerfahrener ~** lamb *n*; **wilder ~** wild catter
Spekulation *f* speculation *n*, gamble *n*
Spekulationsaktie *f* speculative stock
Spekulationsgeschäft *n* speculative transaction
Spekulationsgewinn *m* speculative gain
Spekulationsgewinne; Mitnahme kleinster ~ scalping *n* (US)
Spekulationskapital *n* risk capital, venture capital
Spekulationspapier *n* speculative security
Spekulationspapiere; unsichere ~ fancy stocks
Spekulationssteuer *f* short-term capital gains tax
spekulativ *adj* speculative *adj*
spekulativer Händler scalper *n* (US)
spekulatives Geld hot money
spekulieren *v* (Börse) speculate *v*, gamble *v*, job *v*; **auf schnellen Gewinn ~** scalp; **sinnlos ~** plunge *v*
Spende *f* donation *n*
spenden *v* donate *v*
Spender *m* donor *n*, donator *n*
Sperrdepot *n* blocked deposit, blocked security deposit
Sperre *f* (eines Kontos) blocking *n* (of an account); **~ *f*** (eines Schecks) stop payment order
sperren *v* block *v*, freeze *v*; **den Handelsverkehr ~** embargo *v*; **einen Scheck ~** earmark a check, stop payment of a check
Sperrfrist *f* blocking period
Sperrgeld *n* tolerance *n* (US)
Sperrgut *n* bulky goods
Sperrguthaben *n* blocked deposit
Sperrkonsortium *n* syndicate holdings veto power
Sperrkonto *n* frozen account, blocked account
Sperrliste *f* stopping list
Sperrminorität *f* blocking stock
Sperrstücke *n pl* blocked securities
Sperrvermerk *m* note of blocking
Sperrwort *n* password
Spesen *plt* charges, expenses
spesenfrei free of charge, clear of charges
spesenfreie Inkassi free items (US)
Spesenkonto *n* expense account, account of expenses, account of charges
Spesenrechnung *f* bill of costs
Spesenzettel *m* cost record
Spezialbank *f* specialized bank
Spezialfonds *m* special fund
Spezialkonto *n* special account
Spezialreserve *f* provident reserve fund

Spezialwerte

Spezialwerte m pl (Börse) special stocks (US)
spezifizieren v itemize v, specify v
Sphäre f sphere n
Spitzenbelastung f peak load
Spitzenbetrag m maximum amount
Spitzenergebnis n record n
Spitzengruppe f leading group
Spitzenpapier n first-rate security
Spitzenreiter m market leader
Spitzensatz m top rate
Spitzenwerte m pl (Börse) blue chips, blue chip stock
Split m split n, splitting n
splitten v split
Sponsoring n sponsoring
Spotpreise m pl bargain basement prices
spürbar adj appreciable adj, noticeable adj
Staat m state, government
staatlich adj public adj; - **gefördert** government sponsored; - **gelenkt** state controlled
staatliche *Bankenaufsicht* state banking department (US); - *Kreditmittel* state loans; - *Unterstützung* subvention n, subsidy n
staatlicher *Bankenkommissar* state bank examiner (US); - *Zuschuß* subvention n, subsidy n
staatliches Finanzwesen public finance
Staats- (in Zus.) public adj
Staatsanleihe f government bond (loan); *mündelsichere britische* - gilt (GB)
Staatsbank f governmentowned bank, national bank, state bank (US)
Staatsbetrieb m public business
Staatsgelder n pl state funds
Staatsgläubiger m state creditor
Staatshaushalt m state budget
Staatskasse f treasury n
Staatskonto n public account (GB)
Staatskredite m pl state loans
Staatspapiere n pl government bonds, government funds, government securities
Staatsschatz m national treasury, The Exchequer (GB)
Staatsschuld f national debt, state debt
Staatsschuldenaufnahme f state borrowing

Staatsschuldschein m state note
stabilisieren v (Preise) stabilize v (prices)
Stabilisierung f stabilization n
Stabilität f stability n
Stadtanleihe f municipal bonds (US), municipals n pl, municipal securities, corporation stocks (GB), corporation loan (GB), local authority loan (GB)
Stadtfiliale f city branch
städtisch adj municipal adj
Stadtsparkasse f municipal savings bank
Stadtzweigstelle f city sub-branch
Staffelmethode f daily balance interest calculation
Staffelzinsen m pl compound interest
Stagflation f stagflation
Stagnation f stagnancy n, stagnation n
stagnieren v stagnate v
stagnierend adj stagnant adj
Stahlaktien f pl steel shares, steels
Stahlfach n save deposit box, safe box
Stahlkammer f strong room, vault n
Stahlkassette f strong box
Stammaktie f ordinary share, ordinary stock, common stock (US), common share
Stammdaten n pl (für ein Konto) primary account data
Stammeinlage f (GmbH) original participation
Stammgesellschaft f parent company
Stammkapital n capital stock (US), share capital, capital fund, original capital
Stammkontonummer f primary account number
Stammkunde m regular customer
Stammpersonal n permanent staff
Stand m level n, position n, status n, state n; - m (Börse) post n
Standard m standard n
Standardisierung f standardization n
Standardwerte m pl (Börse) blue chips, blue chip stock
Standesamt n registration (registry) office
ständig adj permanent adj
Standverbindung f (EDV) point-to-point connection
Stapelplatz m entrepot n, depot n, storing place

Stapelprogramm n batchprocessing programme, batch programme
Starthilfekredit m business set-up loan
Startkapital n initial capital, seed money
Statistiken f pl statistics
statistische Auswertung statistical evaluation
statthaft adj allowed, permitted
Status m (Rang) state n; ~ m (Übersicht über die Vermögenslage) statement of affairs
Statut n articles of incorporation and by-laws (US), memorandum and articles of association (GB), statute n
statutengemäß adj statutory adj
steigen v rise, increase; **im Kurs ~** improve v
Steigen n rise n, rising n; **raketenartiges ~ der Kurse** skyrocketing n (US)
steigend adj rising adj
steigende Tendenz buoyancy n
steigern v increase, raise, push up, advance; **Kurse ~** boom the market
Steigerung f (Börse) rise n, increase n
Steigerungsrate f rate of increase
Stellagegeschäft n put and call premium business, straddle n (US), double option
Stellenbewerber m applicant n
Stellung f (Amt) office n; ~ f standing n, rank n
stellvertretend adj deputy, acting adj, vice
stellvertretender Direktor assistant manager, deputy manager; **~ Vorsitzender** deputy chairman
Stellvertreter m substitute n
Stellvertretung f (auf Grund einer Vollmacht) proxy n; ~ f substitution n
Stempelabgabe f stamp duty, stamp tax (US)
Stempelgebühr f stamp duty, stamp tax (US)
Stempelmarke f stamp n
stempeln v stamp v
Stempelpapier n stamped paper
Stempelsteuer f stamp duty, stamp tax (US)
Sterbegeld n death benefit
sterben (ohne Hinterlassung eines Testaments) die intestate; ~ (unter Hinterlassung eines Testamentes) die testate

Steuern betreffend

Sterlingblock m sterling area, sterling block
Sterlinggebiet n sterling area, sterling block
Sterlingobligationen f pl sterling bonds
sternförmiges Leitungsnetz radial transmission network
Steuer f tax n; **nach ~** after tax
steuerabgabepflichtig adj taxable
Steueramt n inland revenue office (GB), tax office (US), Internal Revenue Service (IRS)
steuerbar adj assessable adj
steuerbarer Wert taxable value, value for tax purposes
Steuerbarkeit f ratability n, rateability n
steuerbefreit adj tax-free, tax-exempt
Steuerbefreiung f tax exemption
steuerbegünstigt adj tax-privileged
steuerbegünstigte Anleihe taxfavo(u)red loan (bond)
Steuerbehörde f board of assessment, taxing authority, internal revenue office (US)
Steuerberatung f tax consultant's services
Steuerbescheid m tax bill (GB), tax assessment notice, tax assessment note, bill of taxes
Steuerbilanz f tax balance sheet
Steuereinkommen n tax revenue
Steuereinnehmer m collector n
Steuererhebung f taxation, levying a tax
Steuererklärung f tax return, tax sheet
Steuerflucht f tax dodging
steuerfrei adj non-taxable adj, tax-free adj
Steuerfreibetrag m exemption n
steuerfreie Anleihe tax-free loan; **~ Rente** clear annuity
Steuergeheimnis n fiscal secrecy
Steuergutschein m tax-anticipation note
Steuergutschrift f tax credit
Steuerhinterziehung f tax evasion
Steuerjahr n financial year (GB), fiscal year, fiscal accounting year
Steuerkarte f (Informationsverarbeitung) parameter card; ~ f tax card
Steuerkurswert m taxable market value
Steuerlast f burden of taxation
steuerlich veranlagen assess v
Steuern betreffend taxational adj; **mit ~ belegen** tax v

Steueroase f tax haven
steuerpflichtig adj subject to taxation, taxable adj, assessable adj
Steuerpflichtige f u. m taxpayer n
steuerpflichtige Gewinne taxable profits
steuerpflichtiger Wert taxable value, value for tax purposes
steuerpflichtiges Einkommen taxable income
Steuerquote f taxation ratio
Steuerrückerstattung f tax refund
Steuerrückstellungen f pl provision for taxes
Steuersatz m tax rate, rate of taxation
Steuerschätzer m assessor n
Steuerschulden f pl tax liabilities, accrued taxes
Steuertarif m tax rate
Steuertermin m tax maturity date
Steuerung f control n
Steuerveranlagung f taxation n
Steuervergünstigung f tax relief
Steuervorauszahlung f tax prepayment
Steuerwert m taxable value, value for tax purposes
Steuerwesen n taxation n
Steuerzahler m tax payer
Steuerzeichen n control character
Steuerzuschlag m surtax n
Stichprobe f sample test
Stichtag m deadline n, qualifying date, record date, declaration day
Stichzahl f test number, code number
Stifter m founder n
Stiftung f foundation n, donation n, endowment n, trust n; ~ f (Ausstattung mit Vermögensgütern) endowment n; ~ foundation n; **unwiderrufliche ~** irrevocable trust
Stiftungskapital n endowment capital
Stiftungsurkunde f deed of donation, deed of gift; ~ f foundation charter
Stiftungsvermögen n trust estate, trust fund, estate trust
stille Gesellschaft dormant partnership; **- Reserven** hidden assets, hidden reserves, inner reserves
stiller Teilhaber sleeping partner (GB), silent partner (US), dormant partner
Stillhalteabkommen n blocking

Stillhaltekredit m standstill credit arrangement
Stillhalter m seller of an option, writer (of an option)
Stillhaltergeschäft n sale of an option
stilliegende Hypothek tacit mortgage
Stillstand m deadlock n
stimmberechtigt adj entitled to vote
stimmberechtigte Aktie voting share
Stimmenmehrheit f majority of votes
Stimmenwerbung f canvass n
Stimmenzähler m scrutineer n
Stimmkarte f voting card
Stimmrecht n voting right
Stimmrechtsaktien f pl voting shares
stimmrechtslose Aktien non-voting shares
Stimmungsbarometer n trend indicator
Stockdividende f (Dividende in Form von Aktien) stock dividend
stocken v stagnate v
Stockmaster m (Börseninformationsgerät) stockmaster
Stockung f deadlock n
Stockwerkeigentum n flat property (GB)
Stopp-loss-Auftrag m stop-loss order
Stopppreis m controlled price
stornierbar adj cancellable adj
stornieren v cancel v; ~ v counterorder v, countermand v; ~ v (Buchung) reverse v
Stornierung f cancellation n; ~ f counterorder n; ~ f (Rückbuchung) reversal n
Storno m cancellation, contra entry, reversal
Stornobeleg m reversal voucher
Stornoumsatz m reversal entry
Straight-Anleihe f (Festzinsanleihe) straight bond
streichen v delete v
Streichung f deletion n; **~ der amtlichen Notierung** removal from the stock exchange list
Streifbanddepot n jacket deposit of securities
Streikbrecher m blackleg n
streng adj stringent adj
Strenge f stringency n
Streubesitz m widely spread share holdings
strittig adj disputable adj
Strohmann m dummy n
Struktur f structure n, organization n

Stück *n* piece, unit, item
Stückdividende *f* dividend per share
Stückelung *f* denomination *n*
Stückgebühr *f* charge per item
Stückpreis *m* piece price
Stückverzeichnis *n* bordereau *n*
Stückzinsen *m pl* bond interest accrued, accrued interest (on securities), broken-period interests
Stufenplan *m* multi-stage plan
Stufenswap *m* step-up swap
stunden; *eine Zahlung -* grant a respite in payment, accord a respite in payment
Stundung *f* deferment of payment, moratorium
Stundungszinsen *m pl* moratorium interest
stürzen *v* (Kurs, Preis) plunge *v*
stützen; *durch Staatsgelder -* subsidize *v*
Stützungskauf *m* pegging purchase, supporting purchase
Stützungskäufe *m pl* (Börse) backing *n*; **- *der Poolbeteiligten*** pool support
Stützungskredit *m* emergency credit, emergency loan
Stützungsmaßnahmen *f pl* support-measures
Subfonds *m* subfund
Submissionsofferte *f* tender *n*
subskribieren *v* (neue Aktien zeichnen) subscribe
Subskription *f* (Zeichnungsangebot für neue Aktien) subscription *n*
Substanzverlust *m* loss of assets, real asset loss, depletion *n*
Substanzwert *m* real value, breakdown value, material value, intrinsic value
subtrahieren *v* subtract *v*
Subtraktion *f* subtraction *n*
Subunternehmer *m* subcontractor
Subvention *f* subvention *n*, subsidy *n*

subventionieren *v* subventionize *v*
subventioniert *adj* subsidized *adj*, subventioned *adj*
Subventionierung *f* subsidizing, subsidization *n*
Summe *f* sum *n*, amount *n*; **- *f* (Gesamt-)** total *n*
Superdividende *f* bonus *n*, surplus dividend, superdividend *n*, special dividend
Swap *m* (Devisen- oder Währungstausch) swap *n*, arrangement whereby two companies lend to each other on different terms; **- *mit einer Laufzeitverlängerungsoption*** callable swap; **- *mit vorzeitigem Kündigungsrecht*** callable swap; **- *mit Prolongationsoption*** extendable swap; ***kündbarer -*** puttable swap
swapen *v* swap
Swapgeschäft *n* swap *n*
Swapgeschäfte *n pl* swap operations
Swapsatz *m* swap rate
Swaption *f* swaption, option on a swap
Swing *m* swing *n* (US)
switschen *v* switch *v*
Switschgeschäft *n* switch *n*; ***ein - machen*** switch *v*
Syndikat *n* syndicate *n*
Syndikus *m* company lawyer
syndizierter Kredit (Konsortialkredit) syndicated loan
Synergieeffekt *m* synergie
Systemausfall *m* systems failure
Systeme; *elektronische -* electronic systems
Systementwicklung *f* systems development
Szenario *n* scenario, background
Szenenwechsel *m* change of scene, scene shifting

T

Tabelle f table n, chart n, list n, schedule n, diagram m
Tabellenform f table format
Tabellensuchzeit f table search time, table look-up time
Tafelgeschäft n over the counter business
Tageberichtsbuch n blotter n
tagen v sit v, meet
Tagesauszug m daily statement of account
Tagesbilanz f daily balance sheet, today's balance
Tagesdurchschnitt m daily average
Tagesgeld n call money, money at call, day-to-day money, demand money; **Markt für -** call money market; **Satz für -** call rate
Tagesgeldzinssatz m call rate
Tagesgeschäft n day-to-day business
Tageskasse f counter cash
Tageskurs m current rate, today's rate, market price, day's rate, rate of the day, current price
Tagesordnung f agenda n
Tagespreis m market price
Tagesrohbilanz f today's tentative balance
Tagessatz m current rate, today's rate, market price, day's rate, rate of the day, current price
Tagesumsatzliste f daily transaction register
Tageswert m value on the day
Tageszinsen m pl daily interest
tagfertig buchen post up
täglich fällig at sight, on demand; **- kündbar** subject to call
tägliche Kasse counter cash
täglicher Saldo daily balance
tägliches Geschäft daily business
Tagung f meeting n, session n
Talon m renewal coupon, counterfoil n
Tankscheck m filling-station check
Tantieme f bonus n; **- f** (Autoren-) royalty n, share of profits
Tantiemenauszahlung f bonus payment
Tarif m scale n (e.g. of charges); **- m** tariff n

tarifbesteuerte Schuldverschreibungen bonds subject to normal tax rates
Tarifgruppe f wage group
Tariflohn m standard wage
Tastatur f keyboard n
Tastenfeld n keyboard n
tätig adj active adj
tätigen v effect n
Tätigkeit f action n; **- f** (Aufgabengebiet) activity n
tatsächlich adj actual adj
Tausch m exchange, barter
tauschen v (Tauschhandel betreiben) barter v; **- v** exchange v, change v; **- v** (Swapgeschäft durchführen) swap v
tauschfähig adj barterable adj
Tauschgeschäft n bartering n; **- n** (Börse) swap n
Tauschhandel m bartering n
Tauschhändler m barterer n
Tauschmittel n medium of exchange
Taxator m appraiser n, appreciator n, valuar n (GB), valuator n (US)
Taxe f tax, fee, charge
taxieren v value, rate, appraise
Taxierung f valuation, rating, appraisal
Taxpreis m put up price
Taxwert m appraised value
technische Analyse technical analysis; **- Kontoüberziehung** technical overdraft; **- Reaktion** technical reaction
technisieren v automate
Technisierung f automation n
Technologiewerte m pl (Börse) technology stocks
Teil m part n; **- m** (Verhältnis) proportion n
Teilabschnitt m portion n, instalment n
Teilakzept n partial acceptance
teilbar adj divisible adj
Teilbarkeit f divisibility n
Teilbetrag m partial amount
Teileigentum n part ownership
teilen v divide, share, split
Teilgutschein m fractional certificate
teilhaben v participate v

Teilhaber *m* joint proprietor, copartner *n*, partner *n*; ***geschäftsführender -*** managing partner, acting partner; ***nicht aktiver*** - nominal partner (GB); ***stiller -*** sleeping partner (GB), silent partner (US), dormant partner; ***unbeschränkt haftender -*** associated partner, general partner
Teilhaberschaft *f* partnership *n*
Teilhaberversicherung *f* partnership assurance (GB), partnership insurance, business life insurance
Teilhabervertrag *m* contract of copartnery
Teilnahme *f* participation *n*
Teilnehmer *m* participant *n*
Teilschuldverschreibung *f* bond, debenture, fractional debenture, debenture stock
Teilung *f* splitting *n*
teilweiser Schulderlaß abatement of debts
Teilwert *m* fractional value, part value
Teilzahlung *f* part payment; ***- in Anerkennung einer Verpflichtung*** token payment; ***eine - auf Aktien leisten*** pay a call
Teilzahlungsbank *f* instalment credit institute (bank)
Teilzahlungsbedingungen *f pl* instalment credit terms
Teilzahlungsfinanzierung *f* instalment financing
Teilzahlungsgeschäft *n* instalment business, instalment transaction, instalment lending business, instalment buying
Teilzahlungskredit *m* instalment credit
Teilzahlungssystem *n* instalment plan, deferred payment system
Teilzahlungsverkauf *m* instalment sale
Teilzahlungsvertrag *m* instalment agreement
Teilzahlungswechsel *m* instalment sale financing bill
Telebanking *n* telebanking, banking via telecommunication systems
Telefon-Marketing banking by phone, telephone-banking
telegrafieren *v* cable *v*
Telegrammschlüssel *m* telegraphic code, telegraphic key
telegrafische Auszahlung (Kurs) cable transfer rate, telegraphic transfer rate
Telescheckanlage *f* telecheck unit
Telex *n* telex *n*
Telquelkurs *m* tel quel rate (GB)
Tendenz *f* trend *n*, tendency *n*; ***steigende -*** buoyancy *n*
tendenziell *adj* having a tendency
tendenzlos sein (Börse) mark time
Tenderofferte *f* self tender (US); ***zweiteilige -*** two-tier tender (US)
Tenderverfahren *n* tender procedure, issue through a tender system
Termin *m* deadline *n*, expiry of a term, date *n*
Terminbörse *f* futures exchange
Terminbörsenfonds futures funds
Terminbuch *n* diary *n*
Termindevisen *plt* forward exchange
Termindollar *m* forward dollar
Termineinlage *f* time deposit, fixed deposit
Terminengagement *n* commitment for future delivery
Termingeld *n* term money, time deposit
Termingeldgeschäft *n* time money business
Termingeldmarkt *m* time money market
termingerecht *adj* on time, on due date
Termingeschäft *n* forward deal, forward transaction, futures contract, future transaction, forward dealing
Terminhandel *m* forward trading, futures and options trading
terminieren *v* set a date, time
terminiert *adj* at fixed term
Terminierung *f* timing
Terminkalender *m* diary *n*
Terminkontrakt *m* contract on futures; ***- auf eine Bundesanleihe*** Bund-future; ***- auf USD-Staatswechsel*** bill future; ***Einschußzahlung auf -*** futures margin
Terminkurs *m* forward rate (at forward exchange), forward price (of silver), future price
Terminlieferung *f* future delivery
Terminmarkt *m* forward market, futures market
Terminnotierung *f* forward price
Terminpreis *m* forward price

Terminsätze *m pl* forward rates
Terminsicherung *f* forward rate fixing
Terminspekulation *f* speculation in futures
Terminverkauf *m* forward sale, future sale
Terminvertrag *m* contract for futures
Testament *n* will *n*, testament *n*, last will; *ein ~ anfechten* dispute a will; *ein ~ errichten* draw up a will; *ein ~ gerichtlich bestätigen lassen* probate *v*, prove a will; *gegenseitiges ~* mutual testament, mutual will, double will; *nicht durch ~ verfügt* intestate *adj*; *unverständliches ~* mystic will
testamentarisch *adj* testamentary *adj*; *~ hinterlassen* bequeath *v*
testamentarische Verfügung testation *n*; *~ Zuwendung* legacy *n*, legate *n*, bequest *n*
Testamentsbestätigung; gerichtliche ~ und Erbscheinerteilung probate *n*
Testamentsbestimmung *f* clause of a will
Testamentserbe *m* devisee *n*
Testamentshinterlegungsstelle *f* probate register
Testamentsvollstrecker *m* (gerichtlich bestellt) administrator *n*; *~ m* executor *n*; *~ m* (mit der Befugnis der Vermögensverwaltung) executor trustee
Testator *m* bequeather *n*, devisor *n*, testator *n*, legator *n*
Testbetrieb *m* (EDV) test mode, test operation
Testdaten *plt* (EDV) test data
testen *v* test, check, analyse, survey
testierbar *adj* devisable *adj*
testierfähig *adj* testable *adj*
Testierfähigkeit *f* testacy *n*, ability to make a will
Testprogramm *n* test programme
teuer *adj* expensive *adj*
Teuerung *f* price increase
teures Geld close money, dear money
Textschlüssel *m* text key
thesaurierender Fonds cumulative fund
Thesaurierung *f* reinvestment *n*, hoarding *n*
Thesaurierungsfonds *m* reinvesting fund
Tick *m* tick (0.01%), base point, point
Ticker *m* ticker
Tickerdienst *m* ticker service (US)

Tiefstand *m* low, bottom *n*
Tiefstwert *m* lowest value, all-time low, rock-bottom
tilgbar *adj* redeemable *adj*
Tilgbarkeit *f* redeemableness *n*
tilgen *v* redeem, amortize; *eine Hypothek ~* extinguish a mortgage
Tilgung *f* repayment *n*, redemption *n*, amortization *n*; *~ von Vorzugsaktien* capital redemption
Tilgungsabkommen *n* redemption agreement
Tilgungsanleihe *f* redemption bond, sinking-fund loan, sinking-fund bond
Tilgungsbescheinigung *f* certificate of redemption
Tilgungsdarlehen *n* redeemable loan
Tilgungsfond *m* sinking fund
Tilgungshypothek *f* amortization mortgage, redemption mortgage
Tilgungskurs *m* redemption rate
Tilgungsleistung *f* amortization payment, redemption payment
Tilgungsplan *m* redemption table, repayment plan, amortization schedule, sinking fund table
Tilgungsrate *f* repayment rate, redemption rate, amortization rate
Tilgungsrücklage *f* redemption reserve, sinking fund
Tilgungsstock *m* amortization fund
Tilgungszeitpunkt *m* redemption date
tippen *v* typewrite *v*
Titel *m* (Wertpapier) security *n*, paper *n*
Tochtergesellschaft *f* affiliated company (GB), affiliated corporation (US), subsidiary *n*, subsidiary company, affiliate *n*, associated company
Tonne *f* (Gewicht) ton
Totalverlust *m* dead loss
totes Kapital dead capital, dead money, barren money, dormant capital, dormant money, idle capital; *~ Konto* dormant account, inoperative account (GB), broken account, dead account
tragen *v* carry; *~ v* (Gewinn abwerfen) yield
Tranche *f* tranche, portion *n* (of a loan)
Transaktion *f* transaction *n*
Transfer *m* transfer *n*
transferfähig *adj* transferable *adj*

Transfergebühr f transfer fee
transferierbar adj transferable adj
transferieren v transfer v
Transferierung f transfer n
Transferrisiko n transfer risk
Transit m transit n
Transithandel m transit trade, merchant trade
transitorische Posten prepaid items;
 - (auf der Aktivseite) prepaid expenses;
 - (auf der Passivseite) prepaid income
transitorisches Konto suspended account, suspense account
Transitschein m transit bill
Transitzoll m transit duty
Transport m transport n, transportation n, carriage n
transportierbar adj conveyable adj, transportable adj
transportieren v transport, convey
Transportkosten plt cost of transport, carriage, haulages (shipping) charges, freight charges
Transportschwierigkeiten f pl transportation difficulties
Transportunternehmen n common carrier (US)
Transportunternehmer m transport operator, carrier
Trassant m maker n, drafter n, drawer n
Trassat m drawee n
Trassieren n drawing n
trassieren v draw a bill
Trassierung f drawing n
Tratte f draft n; *- des Verladers* shipper's draft; *- ohne Dokumente* clean draft
Trattenkredit m acceptance credit
Travellerscheck m circular cheque (GB), traveler's check, traveller's cheque (GB)
Trennbankensystem n dual banking system
trennen v detach v; *- von* (sich) part with
Tresor m safe, vault, strong room
Tresorabteilung f safe deposit department
Tresorfach n safe deposit box
Tresorraum m safety vault

Treugeber m trustor, trust creator, settler, grantor
Treugut n trust property
Treuhandabteilung f trust department
Treuhandbank f trust company
Treuhänder m trustee n, custodian trustee, fiduciary n; *- von hinterlegten Dokumenten* escrow agent; ***beim - hinterlegte Gelder*** escrow funds
Treuhänderdienst m fiduciary service
treuhänderisch adj fiduciary adj
Treuhänderschaft f trusteeship n
Treuhandgebühren f pl trust fees
Treuhandgeschäft n trust transaction, trust operation
Treuhandgesellschaft f trust company
Treuhandgut n trust estate, trust fund, estate trust
Treuhandkonto n trust account
Treuhandkredit m fiduciary loan, escrow loan (US)
Treuhandschein m trust letter
Treuhandurkunde f trust deed
Treuhandverbindlichkeiten f pl liabilities incurred as trustee
Treuhandvermögen n assets held in trust, trust assets, trust estate, trust fund, estate trust
Treuhandvertrag m trust instrument, trust deed, trust agreement
Treuhandverwaltung f trusteeship n; ***lebenslängliche -*** living trust (US)
Treunehmer m fiduciary debtor
Trust m combine n; *- m* (Unternehmensorganisation) trust n; *- mit beschränkter Kapitalanlage* rigid trust
Trustbank f finance company
tüchtig adj capable adj, efficient adj, able adj
Tüchtigkeit f efficiency n
Turbulenzen f pl turmoil
Turnus m rotation
Typ m type
typisieren standardise the types
Tz-Bank f instalment credit bank
Tz-Geschäft n instalment financing business

U

U-Schätze siehe *unverzinsliche Schatzanweisungen*
überbelasten v overcharge v, overdebit v
überbesetzt adj overstaffed
überbewerten v overvalue v, overprice v
überbewertet adj top-heavy adj
Überbewertung f overvaluation n
überbezahlt adj overbought adj
überbieten v overbid v, outbid v
Überbringer m bearer n
Überbringerscheck m check to bearer
Überbrückungskredit m accommodation loan, stand-by credit, bridging loan
Überdeckung f excess cover
überdurchschnittlich adj above average
übereinstimmen v agree v; - v conform v; - v correspond v; - v (Konten) tally v
übereinstimmend adj in conformity with, identical, concurrent
Übereinstimmung f agreement n; - f conformity n; *in - bringen* reconcile v
Übererlös m surplus proceeds
überfällig adj overdue adj
überfälliger Betrag amount overdue; *- Scheck* overdue check; *- Wechsel* overdue bill
Überfinanzierung f overfinancing
Überfluß m surplus earnings (US), surplus profits (US)
Übergabe f surrender n, delivery n
Übergangshaushalt m interim budget
Übergangskonto n transit account
Übergangsposten m pl suspense items
übergeben v hand over, transfer v; *zu getreuen Händen -* place in escrow; *zwecks Umtausch -* surrender for exchange
Übergeber m surrenderer n, surrenderor n
übergeordnet adj higher, senior adj
Übergewinn m excess profit
Übergewinnsteuer f excess profit tax
überhöht adj excessive
überhöhte Miete rack-rent n
Überkapazität f excess capacity
überkapitalisieren v over-capitalize v
Überkapitalisierung f overcapitalisation

überkreditieren v overcredit v
Überkreuzbeteiligung f cross shareholding
Überkreuzverkauf m cross-selling
Überliegezeit f demurrage n
übermäßige Abschreibung overdepreciation n; *- Investition* overinvestment n
Übernahme f take-over, purchase, acquisition; *- f (Rechte, Pflichten)* assumption n; *- f taking over*; *- einer Mehrheitsbeteiligung* overtaking a controlling interest; *- eines Unternehmens* takeover, buyout; *- von Versicherungen* underwriting n; *abgewehrte -* defended takeover; *feindliche -* hostile takeover; *fremdfinanzierte -* leveraged buy-out
Übernahmeabwehr f takeover defence; *- durch Abfindung der Konzernleitung des Übernahmekandidaten* golden parachute (US); *- durch Abfindungen* greenmailing (US); *- durch Aktienrückkauf* greenmailing (US); *- durch Beteiligung eines Fusionspartners* white knight (US); *- durch gesellschaftsvertragliche Regelungen* shark repellants; *- durch Wandlung von Anleihen in Aktien* poison pills (US)
Übernahmeangebot n takeover bid; *fremdfinanziertes -* leveraged bid; *- mit Barabfindung* cash bid
Übernahmebetrag m subscription quota, amount subscribed
Übernahmefinanzierung f takeover financing
Übernahmekandidat m takeover candidate
Übernahmekonnossement n received bill of lading, receipt for shipment bill of lading
Übernahmekonsortium n purchase syndicate (group), underlying syndicate (US), board company; *- für Obligationen* (Pfandbriefe) bonding underwriter
Übernahmepreis m takeover price

Übernahmeprovision f underwriting commission
Übernahmeschein m certificate of receipt
Übernahmesyndikat n original syndicate
Übernahmevertrag m indenture of assumption
übernehmen v (z.B. Verpflichtungen) assume v; ~ v take over
Überpari-Emission f issue over par
Überpari-Kurs m over-par price
Überpreis m overprice n
Überproduktion f overproduction n, surplus production
überprüfen v examine, verify, check
Überprüfung f check, examination, review
überschätzen v overvalue v, overprice v
überschneiden v overlap
Überschneidung f overlapping
überschreiten v exceed v; *das Limit* ~ go beyond the limit, exceed the limit
Überschrift f title n
überschuldet overborrowed
Überschuldung f over-indebtedness
Überschuß m surplus earnings (US), surplus profits (US); *buchmäßiger* ~ book surplus
überschüssige *Reserven* excess reserve (US); ~ *Sicherheit* excess security
Überseetratte f bill on overseas drawee
übersenden v send, forward, remit, consign; *in bar* ~ make a remittance
Übersender m sender, remitter n
Übersetzer m translator n
Übersicherung f over-securing
Übersicht f (Bericht) review n; ~ f survey n
übersteigen v exceed v
übersteigern v overbid v, outbid v
Überstunden f pl overtime n
Übertrag m (Buchführung) carry over, carry forward
übertragbar adj assignable adj; ~ adj transferable adj, conveyable adj
übertragbare Wertpapiere transferable securities
übertragbares Akkreditiv transferable documentary credit
Übertragbarkeit f transferability, assignability
übertragen v assign v, convey v; ~ v (Buchführung) carry forward, carry over v; ~ v (von Grundbesitz) demise v; ~ (Recht, Vermögen) transfer v
Übertragung f assignment n, assignation n, cession n; ~ *durch Giro* transfer by means of indorsement
Übertragungsanweisung f transfer order (GB)
Übertragungsbescheinigung f certification of transfer
Übertragungsfehler m transmission error
Übertragungsnetz n network n
Übertragungsschwierigkeit f transmission difficulties
Übertragungssicherung f (EDV) protection of transmitted data
Übertragungsurkunde f deed of assignment, deed of conveyance, deed of release, deed of transfer
übertreffen v beat, exceed
Überversicherung f over-insurance n
überwachen v control n
überwälzen v pass on, allocate v
überweisen v remit v; ~ v transfer v
überweisende Bank remitting bank
Überweisung f transfer, remittance n
Überweisungsabteilung f transfer department, giro transfer department
Überweisungsauftrag m transfer order, payment order, remittance order
Überweisungsbuch n book of remittances
Überweisungsempfänger m beneficiary, remittee
Überweisungsformular n transfer voucher (slip), remittance form
Überweisungsgebühr f transfer charges, remittance fee
Überweisungskonto n remittance account
Überweisungsscheck m transfer check
Überweisungsspesen pl t transfer fee
Überweisungsträger m transfer voucher, remittance slip
Überweisungsverkehr m money transfer business
Überweisungsvordruck m transfer form
Überzahlung f overpayment n
überzeichnen v oversubscribe v
Überzeichnung f oversubscription n, subscription in excess; ~ *einer Emission* stagging
überziehen v overdraw v, overcheck v

Überziehung

Überziehung f overdraft n
Überziehungsbetrag m overdraft n, amount overdrawn
Überziehungskredit m overdraft facility
Überziehungsliste f overdraft list
Überziehungsprovision f commission on overdraft
Überziehungsrecht n overdraft facility
Überziehungsscheck m overcheck n
überzogenes Konto overdrawn account
üblich adj usual, customary adj
üblicher Zins conventional interest
übriges Geld spare cash
Ultimo m end-of-month, closing of the month
Ultimofinanzierung f end-of-month financing
Umbrellafonds m umbrella fund, funds consisting of several subfonds
umbuchen v account transfer
Umbuchung f book transfer
umdisponieren v rearrange, redispose
Umdisposition f rearrangement n, shift n
Umfang m (Reichweite) range n, scope n; ~ m size n, extent n
umfinanzieren v refinance
Umfinanzierung f refinancing
umgekehrter Floater (zinsvariabler Schuldschein) reverse floater (FRN)
Umladung f transhipment n
Umlageverfahren n adjustable-contribution procedure
Umlauf m circulation n; *außer* ~ *setzen* withdraw from circulation; *in* ~ outstanding adj; *in* ~ *befindlich* (Banknoten) circulating adj; ~ (Kapital, Effekten) floating adj; *in* ~ *bringen* put into circulation; *in* ~ *setzen* (Effekten) float v
umlaufen v float v
Umlaufkapital n floating capital, circulating capital, current capital, rolling capital, trading capital, working capital
Umlaufvermögen n floating assets, current assets, circulating assets, current funds, current receivables, fluid assets (US), liquid assets, revolving assets
umleiten v redirect, rechannel
Umleitung f redirection
Umorganisation f reorganization n
umprägen v recoin v

Umprägung f recoinage n
Umprogrammierung f reprogramming
umrechnen v convert v
Umrechnungskurs m conversion rate, rate of exchange, exchange rate, commercial rate of exchange (US), foreign exchange rate; *fester* ~ direct exchange
Umrechnungssatz m conversion rate
Umsatz m (Bewegung auf einem Konto) movement n; ~ m turnover n, sales n pl (US)
Umsatzband n transaction tape
Umsatzeingabe f transaction input
Umsatzliste f transaction list
umsatzloser Saldo dormant balance
umsatzloses *Guthaben* dormant balance; ~ *Konto* dormant account, inoperative account (GB), broken account, dead account
Umsatzprovision f turnover commission, sales commission
umsatzreiches Konto working account
Umsatzrendite f profit-sales ratio
umsatzschwache Börse dead market
umsatzstarkes Konto active account
Umsatzstatistik f transaction statistics
Umsatzsteuer f turnover tax
Umschichtung von Wertpapierbeständen portfolio turnover
Umschlag m turnover n, sales n pl (US)
Umschlagskapital n working capital
Umschreibegebühr f transfer fee
umschreiben v transfer v (e.g. registered shares)
Umschreibung f transfer, conveyance
umschulden v reschedule, convert a debt
Umschuldung f rescheduling, conversion of a debt, debt conversion
Umschuldungsanleihe f conversion bond; ~ *für Entwicklungsländer* exit bond
Umschulung f retraining n
Umschwung am Markt turn in the market
umsetzen v turn over
umsonst adv free of charge, cost-free adv
Umstrukturierung f restructuring
Umtausch m exchange, conversion
Umtauschanleihe f conversion bond
umtauschbar adj convertible adj
umtauschen v exchange, switch, convert, change

Umtauschkosten *plt* cost of exchange
Umtauschkurs *m* convertion price, rate of exchange, exchange rate, commercial rate of exchange (US), foreign exchange rate
Umtauschrecht *n* (bei Investmentanteilen) exchange privilege
Umtauschverhältnis *n* exchange rate; *- zweier Fremdwährungen* cross rate
umwandelbar *adj* convertible *adj*
Umwandelbarkeit *f* convertibility *n*
Umwandlung von Krediten in Anleihen mit Zins- oder Kapitalabschlag collaterised bond exchange; *- von Bankforderungen in Beteiligungskapital* debt equity swap
umwandeln *v* convert, change
Umwechselkurs *m* exchange rate
umwechseln *v* exchange
unabhängig independent; *finanziell -* self-supporting
unablösbar *adj* irredeemable *adj*
unangebracht *adj* inopportune *adj*
unausgefertigt *adj* blank *adj*
unausgeglichen *adj* unbalanced *adj*
unausgeschrieben *adj* blank *adj*
unbar *adj* cashless, non-cash
Unbarposten *m* non-cash item
Unbedenklichkeitsbescheinigung *f* clearance certificate
unbedingte Verpflichtung unconditional commitment
unbedruckt *adj* blank *adj*
unbefristet *adj* for an unlimited period
unbeglaubigt *adj* uncertified *adj*
unbelastet *adj* unencumbered, unmortgaged
unbelastetes Grundstück unmortgaged property
unberechenbar *adj* incalculable *adj*
Unberechenbarkeit *f* incalculability *n*
unbeschränkt haftender Gesellschafter unlimited partner
unbeschränkte Garantie general guarantee; *- Konvertierbarkeit* full convertibility; *- Vollmacht* carte blanche
unbeschränkter Eigentümer absolute owner
unbeschränktes Eigentumsrecht absolute ownership; *- Indossament* absolute endorsement
unbesicherte Anleihe unsecured bond
unbesichertes Darlehen unsecured loan
unbewegliches Vermögen immovables *n pl*, immovable property, real estate, real property
unbewegte Konten (kurze Zeit) inactive accounts; *- (lange Zeit)* dormant accounts
unbewegtes Konto dormant account, inoperative account (GB), broken account, dead account
unbezahlbarer Kupon outstanding coupon
unbezahlt *adj* unpaid *adj*
unbezahlte Ausgaben outstanding expenses
unbezahlter Restbetrag arrearage *n*
Und-Konto *n* joint account
unecht *adj* false
unedles Metall base metal
uneinbringbar *adj* irrecoverable *adj*
uneinbringliche Schuld bad debt
uneingeschränkter Eigentümer freeholder *n*
uneinheitlicher Markt sick market (US)
unelastisch *adj* rigid *adj*
unerfahrener Spekulant lamb *n*
unerledigte Aufträge outstanding orders
Unfallversicherung *f* accident insurance
unfrankiert *adj* unpaid *adj*
unfreie Aktie non-free share
unfreiwillige Hinterlegung involuntary bailment
unfreiwilliger Konkurs involuntary bankruptcy
unfundierte Schuld floating debt, unfunded debt
ungedeckt *adj* uncovered *adj*
ungedeckte Anleihe fiduciary bond; *- Kauf-/Verkaufsoption* *f* uncovered call-/put-option; *- Notenausgabe* fiduciary issue
ungedeckter Personalkredit unsecured personal loan; *- Scheck* check without provision, bad check, kite check, rubber check (US), uncovered check
ungedecktes Engagement open position
ungekreuzter Scheck open check, uncrossed check

ungekündigte Anleihe uncalled bond
ungemünzt *adj* uncoined *adj*
ungemünztes Edelmetall bullion *n*
Ungenauigkeit *f* (z. B. einer Übersetzung) inaccuracy *n* (e.g. of a translation)
ungenügende Kontoguthaben n.s.f. (abbreviation for »not sufficient fund«), N/F (abbreviation for »no funds«)
ungeprägt *adj* uncoined *adj*
ungeprüft *adj* unchecked *adj*
ungesetzlich *adj* illegal, unlawful
ungesetzlicher Zins illegal interest
ungesichert *adj* unsecured
ungesicherte *Obligationen* plain bonds; **- *Schuldverschreibung*** debenture bond, unsecured loan (US)
ungesicherter Gläubiger unsecured creditor
ungewiß *adj* uncertain, doubtful
ungiriert *adj* unindorsed *adj*, unendorsed *adj*
Ungleichheit *f* inequality, disparity *n*
ungültig *adj* invalid *adj*; **- *erklären*** reverse *v*
ungültige Obligationen disabled bonds (GB)
Universalbank *f* universal bank, all-purpose bank, full service bank, one-stop banking
universelles Banksystem all-purpose banking system
unkaufmännisch *adj* unbusinesslike *adj*
Unkosten siehe ***Kosten***
unkündbar *adj* uncallable, irredeemable *adj*
unkündbare Wertpapiere uncallable (irredeemable) stock
unlimitiert *adj* unlimited *adj*
unlimitierter Börsenauftrag unlimited order
Unmündige *f u. m* infant *n*, minor *n*
unnotiert *adj* unlisted *adj* (US)
unproduktive Anlagen dead assets
unrealisierte Gewinne paper profits (US)
unrechtmäßig *adj* unlawful, illegal; **- *verwenden*** misappropriate
unrechtmäßige Verwendung misappropriation *n*
unredlich *adj* dishonest, mala fide
unreeller Börsenmakler bucketeer *n* (US)
unregelmäßiges Depot irregular deposit
unrentabel *adj* unprofitable *adj*

unschätzbar *adj* invaluable *adj*
unsicher *adj* dubious *adj*, uncertain *adj*
unsicheres Darlehen precarious loan
unsichtbare Erträge invisible earnings
unsolide *adj* unsound
Unstimmigkeit *f* difference, discrepancy *n*
unter dem Strich below the line
unter pari below pari
Unterbeteiligung *f* subparticipation *n*
unterbewerten *v* undervalue *v*, underestimate *v*
Unterbewertung *f* undervaluation *n*, underestimation *n*
Unterbilanz *f* negative net worth, adverse balance
unterbrechen *v* interrupt, discontinue *v*, suspend *v*
Unterbrechung *f* (EDV) interruption *n*
unterbringen *v* place; **-** *v* (Kapital) invest *v*; **-** *v* (Wechsel, Anleihen) negotiate *v*
Unterbringung *f* placing
Unterbringungskommission *f* placing commission
Unterdeckung *f* cover shortage, deficient cover
Unterdirektor *m* sub-manager *n*
unterdisponieren *v* order less than normal
unterdurchschnittlich *adj* below average
unterer Goldpunkt gold import point
Unterfinanzierung *f* underfinancing
untergliedern *v* break down, classify
Untergliederung *f* breakdown, classification
Unterhalt *m* maintenance *n*, up-keep
Unterhaltsfonds *m* spendthrift trust
Unterhändler *m* go-between *n*, mediator *n*, negotiator *n*, intermediary *n*
unterkapitalisieren *v* undercapitalize *v*
Unterkapitalisierung *f* undercapitalization *n*
Unterkonsorte *m* sub-underwriter
Unterkonto *n* sub-account *n*
Unterkontonummer *f* subaccount number
Unterlagen *f pl* records *n pl*, documents *n pl*; ***statistische*** **-** statistics
Unterlassung *f* omission, default *n*
Untermiete *f* sublease *n*
unternehmen *v* undertake *v*
Unternehmen *n* business, corporation *n*, firm *n*, enterprise *n*, company *n*, con-

cern n; - n undertaking n; - **mittlerer Größe** medium-sized company; **beherrschtes** - controlled company; **börsennotiertes** - quoted company; **gemeinwirtschaftliches** - public company (GB); **geschäftliches** - business enterprise; **gut fundiertes** - well-established enterprise; **gut gehendes** - going concern; **innovative** - sunrise industries; **international operierendes** - global player; **kleine und mittlere** - small caps, small and medium-sized enterprises (SME); **riskantes** - speculative venture; **veraltete** - sunset industries
unternehmend adj enterprising adj
Unternehmensaufkäufer; agressiver - raider
Unternehmensberatung f management consultancy, business counselling
Unternehmensberichte m pl company comments
Unternehmensentscheidung f management decision
Unternehmensertrag m business earnings, business profit, corporate earnings
Unternehmensfinanzierung f corporate financing
Unternehmensforschung; betriebliche - operations research
Unternehmensführung f business management
Unternehmensgestaltung; ergebnisorientierte - business reengeneering
Unternehmenskredite f pl corporate lendings
Unternehmensübernahme f company takeover, takeover; **- durch das eigene Management** management buyout (MBO); **- durch ein fremdes Management** management buying; **- durch Kauf des Anlagevermögens** asset deal; **- durch Kauf der Anteile** share deal; **fremdfinanzierte** - leveraged buyout (LBO)
Unternehmensverkehrswert m going concern value
Unternehmer m business man, industrialist, company owner, entrepreneur
unternehmerisch adj managerial, enterprising, entrepreneurial

unternehmerische Initiative business initiative
Unternehmerkredit m contractor loan
Unternehmung f enterprise n
Unterpacht f sublease n
unter pari below par
Unterpari-Emission f issue under par, issue below par
unterrichten v (in Kenntnis setzen) inform v, notify v, advise v, communicate v; **- v** (instruieren) instruct v, direct v
unterscheiden (sich) v differ from, differentiate, distinguish
Unterschied m difference n
unterschiedlich behandeln discriminate v
unterschlagen v embezzle v, defalcate v
Unterschlagung f embezzlement n, defalcation n, peculation n
Unterschlagungsversicherung f fidelity insurance
unterschreiben v sign v
unterschrieben; ordnungsgemäß - duly signed
Unterschrift f signature n
Unterschriftenverzeichnis n signature book
Unterschriftsbeglaubigung f certification of signature, confirmation of signature
unterschriftsberechtigt adj entitled to sign
Unterschriftskarte f signature card
Unterschriftsprobe f specimen signature
Unterschriftsprüfung f signature verification
Unterschriftsvollmacht f authority to sign
unterstützen v support, assist, aid, subsidize
unterstützt; durch Staatszuschüsse - subsidized adj, subventioned adj
Unterstützung f assistance, aid, support n; **staatliche** - subvention n, subsidy n
Unterstützungsfonds m aid fund, relief fund
Unterstützungsverein m benefit association, benefit society, beneficiary association, benefit club
Untersuchung f investigation, examination n; **- über Verbrauchergewohnheiten** habit survey

Unterverfrachter m underfreighter n
untervermieten v sublease v, sublet v
Untervermietung f sublease n
unterverpachten v sublease v, sublet v
Unterverpachtung f sublease n
unterweisen v instruct v, direct v
Unterweisung f instruction n; *programmierte -* programmed instruction (PI)
unterzeichnen v sign v
Unterzeichnung f signature n; - f (Vorgang) signing n
untilgbar adj irredeemable adj
untilgbare Schuldverschreibung irredeemable debenture
unübertragbar adj non-transferable adj
unveränderliche Anleihe closed issue
unverbriefter Kredit unsecured credit
unverfälscht adj unfalsified, genuine adj, true adj
unverkäufliche Waren dead stock
unverkäufliches Wertpapier unmarketable title
unverkauft adj remaining adj
unvermögend adj without means, destitute adj, impecunious adj, moneyless adj
unverpfändet adj unpledged adj
unversichert adj uninsured adj
unverständliches Testament mystic will
unverteilter Reingewinn unappropriated profits (US), undivided profits, unappropriated earned surplus (US)
unverzinslich adj interest-free adj, bearing no interest, non-interest-bearing adj
unverzinsliche *Schatzanweisungen* treasury discount notes; *- Schuld* passive debt; *- Schuldverschreibung* passive bond, non-interest-bearing bond, discount bond (US)
unverzollt adj duty unpaid
unvorhergesehene Nebenausgaben contingencies n pl
unwiderruflich adj irrevocable adj
unwiderrufliche Stiftung irrevocable trust

unwiderruflicher Treuhandfonds irrevocable trust fund
unwiderrufliches *Abkommen* binding agreement; *- bestätigtes Akkreditiv* irrevocable confirmed letter of credit (US); *- Dokumentenakkreditiv* irrevocable documentary credit
unwiederbringlich verloren sein be past recovery
unwirksam adj not affecting, void adj; *- machen* invalidate v
unwirtschaftlich adj unprofitable, uneconomical adj
unzeitgemäß adj inopportune adj
unzuverlässig adj unreliable adj
Urheberrecht n copyright n
urheberschutzfähig adj copyrightable adj
Urkunde f (gesiegelte oder förmliche) deed n; - f document n
Urkunden; *Vorlage von - verlangen* call for production of documents
Urkundenbeglaubigung f attestation of a deed
Urkundenbeweis m documentary proof
Urkundenfälscher m counterfeiter n, falsifier n
Urkundenkassette f deed box
urkundlich documentary, by deed; *- übertragen* deed v
urkundlicher Rechtstitel document of title
Urschrift f original n
Ursprungszeugnis n certificate of origin
Urteil; *rechtskräftiges -* final judg(e)ment
Urtext m original n
Usance f custom, usage n, usance n, practice n
Usancekurs m cross rate
usancegemäß according to custom
usancemäßig adj customary adj
Usancen der Börse rules of the stock exchange, stock exchange regulations
USD-Anleihen *für schweizer Anleger* alpine bonds; *festverzinsliche -* dollar straights

V

vagabundierende Gelder erring funds
Validität f (Rechtsgültigkeit) validity
Valoren plt (Wertpapiere) securities n pl
Valorennummer f securities number
Valorenregister n security numbering system
Valorenversicherung f valuables insurance
Valuta f (Datum) availability date (US), value date; ~ f currency n
Valutaanleihe f foreign currency bond
Valutaforderung f foreign currency claim
Valutageschäft n foreign currency transaction, business in foreign notes and coin (US), currency exchange business, exchange business
Valutaklausel f foreign currency clause
Valutakonto n foreign currency account, foreign exchange account
Valutakredit m foreign currency loan
Valutarisiko n exchange risk
Valutasaldo m foreign exchange balance
Valutawechsel m currency bill
valutieren v fix the value date
Valutierungstag m value date
variabel adj variable; ~ *verzinsliche Anleihe* floating-rate bond (FRB); ~ *verzinslicher Schuldschein* m floating-rate note, floater (FRN)
variable Geschäftskosten operating expenses (US); ~ *Satzlänge* (EDV) variable record length
variabler Teil (bei Bestandssätzen) variable portion; ~ *Zinssatz* variable interest rate
variables Zinsänderungsrisiko floating rate risk
Venture Capital n (Risikokapital) venture capital
Verabredung f appointment n; *geschäftliche* ~ business appointment
Veränderung f alteration n, modification n, change n
veranlagen v assess, tax v
veranlagt adj assessed adj
Veranlagungsbescheid m tax assessment

Veranlagungskosten plt assessment costs
Veranlagungsperiode f assessment period
veranschlagen v value, evaluate, estimate v
Veranschlagung f estimation n
verantwortlich adj responsible adj
Verantwortlichkeit f responsibility n
Verarbeitungszeit f processing time
verarmt adj destitute adj, impecunious adj, moneyless adj
verausgaben v spend v
Veräußerer m seller, disposer n
veräußerlich adj saleable, alienable adj
Veräußerlichkeit f alienability n
veräußern v (meist Grundbesitz) alienate v; ~ v sell v; *Aktien* ~ realize shares
Veräußerung f sale, selling off, alienation n
Veräußerungsgewinn m gain of sale
Verbalbeschreibung f narrative n, narrative description
Verband m association n; ~ m federation n
verbessern v correct v, rectify v
Verbesserung f correction n, adjustment n
verbilligen v abate v, lower v, reduce v, cut the price of
Verbilligung f abatement n, reduction n
verbinden (sich) v associate v; ~ v connect v
verbindlich adj binding, firm
verbindliche Kursnotierung firm quotation
Verbindlichkeit f commitment n; *langfristige* ~ capital liability
Verbindlichkeiten f pl liabilities, debts; ~ *eingehen* assume obligations; ~ *erfüllen* cover liabilities; ~ *gegenüber Kreditinstituten* liabilities to anks; *gegenüber Kunden* liabilities to customers; *andere* ~ other liabilities; *kurzfristige* ~ current liabilities, short-term liabilities; *laufende* ~ current liabilities; *schwebende* ~ unadjusted liabilities; *seinen* ~ *nachkommen* meet one's liabilities; *verbriefte* ~ securitised liabilities, certificated liabilities
Verbindung f connection n; *sich in* ~ *setzen mit* contact v

verboten

verboten *adj* forbidden, prohibited, illicit *adj*
Verbrauch *m* consumption *n*
verbrauchen *v* consume *v*
Verbraucher *m* consumer *n*
Verbrauchergewohnheit *f* consumer habit
Verbrauchergruppe *f* consumer group
Verbraucherkredit *m* consumer credit
Verbraucherschutz *m* consumer protection
Verbrauchsgüter *n pl* consumer goods
Verbrauchsgütermarkt *m* consumer market
Verbrauchsrichtung *f* consumption trend
verbriefen *v* securitize
verbrieft *adj* chartered *adj*
verbriefte Rechte chartered rights
verbriefter Kredit securitised loan
Verbriefungstendenz *f* securitization
verbuchen *v* book *v*, enter *v*
Verbuchung *f* entry, entering, associated, posting *n*
verbunden *adj* associated, connected *adj*
Verbundfinanzierung *f* joint financing
Verdichtungsmethode *f* packing method
verdienen *v* earn, gain
Verdienst *m* (Arbeitslohn) earnings *n pl*; ~ *m* profit *m*
Verdienstspanne *f* profit margin
verdiente Abschreibungen amount of depreciation earned
veredeln *v* improve, finish, refine
Veredelungsindustrie *f* finishing industry
vereidigter Makler sworn broker
Verein *m* association, union society
vereinbaren *v* agree on, arrange
Vereinbarung *f* agreement *n*; ***vertragliche*** ~ contractual arrangement
vereinheitlichen *v* standardize, harmonize
Vereinheitlichung *f* harmonization, standardization *n*
vereinigen (sich) *v* associate *v*; ~ *v* consolidate *v*
Vereinigung *f* association *n*; ~ *f* (Zusammenlegung) consolidation *n*; ~ *f* federation *n*
vereinnahmen *v* receive *v*, show as revenue
Vereinssparen *n* association saving
Vereinzelungslauf *m* (beim Belegleser) single-digit sort
vererblich *adj* devisable *adj*

Verfahren *n* method *n*, procedure *n*
Verfall *m* (durch Zeit) expiration *n*, expiry *n*; ***bei*** ~ at maturity, when due; ***mittlerer*** ~ average due time
Verfallbuch *n* maturity index, maturity tickler (US)
Verfalldatum *n* expiry date
verfallen *v* expire, lapse, fall due; ***für*** ~ ***erklären*** foreclose *v*
verfallende Option expired option
verfallener Scheck overdue check
Verfallkartei *f* maturity file
Verfalltag *m* due date, due day, date of expiration, date of maturity, maturity date, accrual date
Verfallzeit *f* expiry date
verfälschen *v* counterfeit *v*, falsify *v*, forge *v*; ~ *v* (Münzen) debase *v*
Verfälscher *m* forger *n*, counterfeiter *n*, faker *n*, falsificator *n*
Verfälschung *f* counterfeit *n*, fake *n*, falsification *n*, forgery *n*
Verfrachter *m* shipper, transport agent
verfügbar *adj* available *adj*; ***direkt*** ~ on-line
verfügbare Gelder disposable funds; ~ ***Mittel*** available funds
verfügbares Einkommen disposable income
Verfügbarkeit *f* availability, disposability
verfügen über dispose of
Verfügung *f* disposal *n*; ~ will *n*, testament *n*, last will; ***letztwillige*** ~ (über Grundbesitz) devise *n*; ***testamentarische*** ~ testation *n*
Verfügungsmacht *f* authority to dispose, right of disposal
vergeben *v* place, award, extent
Vergebung *f* (Amt) appointment
vergesellschaften *v* socialize *v*, communize *v*
Vergleich *m* comparison, (mit Gläubigern) composition *n*, settlement *n*, arrangement *n*; ~ *m* (außergerichtlich) settlement *n*
Vergleichsanmeldung *f* declaration of insolvency
Vergleichsquote *f* composition dividend
Vergleichsschuldner *m* compounding debtor

172

Vergleichsurkunde f deed of arrangement, letter of license
Vergleichsverfahren n composition proceedings; *außergerichtliches* - settlement out of court
Vergleichsvertrag m composition agreement n
Vergnügungssteuer f amusement tax, admission tax (US)
Vergünstigung f benefit n, privilege n
vergüten v pay, remunerate v, reimburse v, refund v, compensate v
Vergütung f payment, remuneration n; *gegen* - remunerated adj
Vergütungsauftrag f bank payment order
Verhältnis n proportion, ratio n; *- der flüssigen Aktiva zu den laufenden Verbindlichkeiten* working capital ratio (US); *- der veränderlichen Geschäftsunkosten zur Roheinnahme* operating ratio (US); *- des Aktienkurses zum Reingewinn* price-earning ratio; *- des Umlaufvermögens zu den laufenden Verbindlichkeiten* quick ratio; *im* - ratable adj; *nach* - pro rata, proportionate adj
Verhaltensregeln f pl code of conduct
verhältnismäßig adj proportional adj
Verhältniszahl f ratio n
Verhältnisziffer f proportion n
verhandeln v negotiate v
Verhandlung f negotiation, talks
verjähren v become statute-barred, become prescribed
verjährt adj statute-barred adj (GB)
verjährte Schuld barred debt
verjährter Scheck stale check (US)
Verjährung f limitation of action, prescription n, statute of limitations
Verjährungsfrist f period of prescription, period of limitation
Verjährungsgesetz n statute of limitation
Verjährungsrecht n prescriptive right
Verkauf m sale, selling; *- ohne Deckung* short sale; *- unter Eigentumsvorbehalt* bailment lease
Verkäufe m pl (zwischen Konzerngesellschaften) intercompany sales

verkaufen v sell v; *auf Kredit* - sell on credit; *auf Termin* - sell forward; *leer* - to sell short; *mit Verlust* - sell at a disadvantage, slaughter v; *über den Bestand* - oversell v
Verkäufer m (Beruf) salesman n (US); - m seller n, vender n, vendor n; *- einer Kaufoption* call writer
verkäufliche Wertpapiere negotiable instruments
Verkaufsabteilung f distribution department
Verkaufsanalyse f sales analysis
Verkaufsauftrag m selling order
Verkaufsbedingungen f pl conditions of sale
Verkaufsbuch n cash book
Verkaufserlös m sale proceeds
verkaufsfähig adj merchantable adj
Verkaufsförderung f sales promotion
Verkaufsgenossenschaft f cooperative credit association
Verkaufskonto n trading account
Verkaufskurs m drawing rate
Verkaufsoption f put n, put option; *- auf einen Terminkontrakt* futures put option; *Ausübung einer* - put exercise; *Inhaber einer* - put holder; *Kauf (Erwerb) einer* - buying a put option; *Stillhalter (Verkäufer) einer* - put writer; *ungedeckte* - uncovered put option; *Verkauf einer* - putwriting, selling a put option; *Verkäufer einer* - put writer
Verkaufsoptionsschein m put warrant
Verkaufspreis m sales price
Verkaufsprovision f sales commission
Verkaufspunkt m = **POS** point of sale (POS)
Verkaufsvertrag m selling agreement, agreement for sale
Verkaufswert m sal(e)able value
Verkehr; *aus dem - ziehen* immobilize v, recall from circulation
Verkehrsflugzeug n airliner n
Verkehrshypothek f conventional mortgage, common mortgage
Verkehrsunternehmen n transport undertaking, common carrier (US)

Verkehrswert m market value; ~ m (Versicherung) sound value; **~ eines Unternehmens** going concern value
verklagen v take legal action, sue v
Verladedokumente n pl shipping documents
verladen v load, lade n
Verladeschein m certificate of receipt
Verladung f loading, shipping n
Verlangen n demand n; **auf ~** at call; **auf ~ zahlbar** due on demand
verlangen v demand v
verlängern v (Kredit) extend, renew (loan)
Verlängerung f prolongation n, extension n, renewal n
verlängerungsfähig adj renewable adj
Verlängerungsklausel f renewal clause
Verlängerungsstück n addendum
verlassen v abandon v
verleihen v (Titel) bestow v; ~ (Geld) lend v
Verleiher m lender n, credit grantor
Verleihung f lending n
verletzen v violate, (Vertrag) infringe v
Verletzung f violation, infringement n
verlieren v lose v
Verlosung f drawing
Verlosungsliste f list of drawings
Verlust m loss n; **~ tragen** bear a loss
Verlustanzeige f notice of loss
Verlustausgleich m loss offsetting
Verlustbegrenzung f limitation of losses
Verlustbegrenzungsauftrag m stop-loss order
Verlustbilanz f balance that shows a deficit
Verluste erleiden incur losses; **~ haben** be in the red (US)
Verlustkonto n deficiency account, deficit account
Verlustrisiko n exposure to loss
Verlustsaldo m adverse balance
Verlustübernahme f loss takeover, assumption of loss
Verlustvortrag m loss carried over, loss carried forward
vermachen v bequeath v; ~ v (Grundbesitz) devise v
Vermächtnis n (über Grundbesitz) devise n; ~ n legacy n, legate n, bequest n; ~ (nach Abzug der Nachlaßverbindlichkeiten) residuary legacy

Vermächtnisnehmer m (von Grundbesitz) devisee n; ~ m legatee n; ~ m taker n (US)
vermeidbar adj avoidable adj
vermeiden v avoid v
Vermeidung f avoidance n
Vermerk m entry n
vermietbar adj rentable adj
vermieten v let v, lease v
Vermieten n leasing n
Vermieter m leaser n, lessor n
vermietet adj rented adj
Vermietung f leasing n; **~ von Einrichtungsgegenständen** equipment leasing
vermindern v abate v, lower v; ~ v curtail v, cut down, cut v, impair v; ~ (sich) v diminish v
Verminderung f diminution n
vermitteln v intervene v, mediate v
Vermittler m go-between n, mediator n, negotiator n, intermediary n
Vermittlung f brokerage, settlement, mediation n
Vermittlungsgebühr f agency fee, commission n
Vermittlungsgeschäft n brokerage n, brokerage business, broking n
Vermögen n assets n pl; ~ n fortune n; ~ n property n; **bewegliches ~** movable estate, movable goods, movables n pl, goods movable; **bewegliches und unbewegliches ~** movables and immovables
Vermögensabgabe f property levy
Vermögensanlage f investment, assets invested; **~ in Industriewerten** industrial investment
Vermögensaufstellung f statement of affairs
Vermögensbeschlagnahme f attachment of property
Vermögensbetrag m amount of assets
Vermögensbildung f capital formation, capital accumulation
Vermögenserklärung f declaration of property
Vermögensertrag m property income, revenue from capital employed
Vermögensgegenstand m asset n

Vermögenshöhe f amount of assets
Vermögenslage f financial condition, financial situation
Vermögenslosigkeit f indigence n
Vermögensmasse f estate n
Vermögensreserve f property reserve
Vermögensschaden m damage to property
Vermögenssperre f blocking of property
Vermögensstand m net asset position
Vermögensstatus m property statement, asset and liability statement
Vermögenssteuer f general property tax
Vermögensübersicht f abstract of balance sheet
Vermögensübertragung f property transfer, capital transfer
Vermögensverhältnisse n pl financial circumstances
Vermögensverwalter m custodian n; ~ m trustee n, custodian trustee, fiduciary n
Vermögensverwaltung f asset management, property management, administration of assets, fund management; *~ für institutionelle Investoren* asset management; *Bank für Anlageberatung und ~* trust bank; *Vollmachtsvertrag einer ~* investment management agreement
Vermögensverwaltungsdepot n managed securities safe custody account
Vermögensverwaltungsgesellschaft f investment (portfolio) management company
Vermögenswerte m pl assets n pl; *immaterielle ~* intangible assets; *materielle ~* physical assets, tangible assets; *verschleierte ~* concealed assets
vermögenswirksames Sparen capital savings
Vermögenszuwachs m asset growth, accession of property
vernünftiger Preis reasonable price
verordnen v order, decree
Verordnung f order, decree, regulation n
verpachtbar adj rentable adj
verpachten v lease, let on lease
Verpachten n leasing n

Verpächter m leaser n, lessor n
verpachtet adj rented adj
Verpachtung f lease n; ~ f leasing n
verpfändbar adj mortgageable adj
verpfänden v pawn v, pledge v, put in pledge, impawn v, hock v
Verpfänder m pledger n (GB), pledgor n (US)
verpfändete Aktien pawned stock (GB)
Verpfändung f hypothecation n; ~ f pledge n, pledging
Verpfändungsklausel; *negative ~* negative pledging clause
Verpfändungsurkunde f letter of lien
Verpfändungsvertrag m contract of pledge
verpflichten v oblige, commit, obligate, contract, engage v
Verpflichtete f u. m obligor n, obligator n
Verpflichtung f obligation, commitment n; ~ f engagement n; *unbedingte ~* unconditional commitment
Verpflichtungen *aus geleisteten Akzepten* contingent liability in respect of acceptances; *~ einer Gesellschaft* partnership liabilities, partnership obligations; *~ eingehen* contract liabilities; *~ erfüllen* meet commitments; *~ nachkommen* cover liabilities; *~ übernehmen* incur liabilities; *andere ~* other commitments; *geschäftliche ~* business commitments; *sonstige ~* other liabilities
Verpflichtungserklärung f letter of undertaking
Verpflichtungskredit m guarantee credit
Verpflichtungsschein m certificate of obligation
verrechnen (sich) v miscalculate v
verrechnete Gemeinkosten absorbed overheads
Verrechnung f clearing n, settlement n, sett-off
Verrechnungsabkommen n clearing agreement, offset agreement
Verrechnungseinheit f unit of account
Verrechnungskonto n clearing account, settlement account

Verrechnungskurs m clearing rate
Verrechnungsland n agreement country
Verrechnungsposten m clearing item
Verrechnungssaldo m clearing balance
Verrechnungsscheck m check only for account, crossed check, collecting-only check; *- für Ausgleichsbeträge* redemption check (US)
Verrechnungsschlüssel m clearing ratio
Verrechnungsschuld f clearing debt
Verrechnungsstelle f clearing house, clearing center
Verrechnungssteuer f withholding tax
Verrechnungssystem n giro transfer system
Verrechnungswährung f clearing currency
verringern v diminish v, decrease v, reduce v
versammeln (sich) v meet, assemble v
Versammlung f meeting, assembly n; *eine - vertagen* adjourn a meeting; *einer - beiwohnen* attend a meeting
Versand m dispatch, delivery, shipment
Versandabteilung f delivery department
Versandartschlüssel m mailing code, shipping code
Versandhandel m mail-order business
Versandkosten plt cost of delivery
Versandpapiere n pl shipping documents
Versandschein m certificate of shipment
Versäumnisurteil n default judgement, decree in absence
verschicken v send v, dispatch v
verschieben v postpone v
Verschiedene n sundries n pl
Verschiedenheit f disparity n
Verschiffer m shipper n
Verschiffung f shipping n
Verschiffungsbescheinigung f certificate of shipment
Verschiffungspapiere n pl shipping documents; *nicht rechtzeitig eingereichte -* stale shipping documents
verschlechtern v worsen; *- (sich)* v deteriorate v
verschleiern v hide, (Bilanzen) conceal v; *eine Bilanz -* cook a balance sheet
verschleierte Bücher cooked accounts; *- Vermögenswerte* concealed assets
verschleudern v squander v, slaughter v (US)
Verschleuderung f slaughter n (US), dumping n
verschließen v seal v
verschlossen adj sealed adj
verschlossenes Depot sealed deposit
Verschluß m lock n
verschlüsseln v code v
verschmelzen v merge v, fuse v
Verschmelzung f amalgamation n, fusion n, merger n
verschuldet adj indebted, indebt
Verschuldung f debt n, indebtedness n
Verschuldungsgrenze f debt limit
verschwenden v waste v
Verschwiegenheit f discretion n
versehen adj (mit) furnished adj (with), provided adj (with)
Versehen n error n, mistake n
versenden v send, forward, dispatch, consign v
Versender m consigner n, consignor n; *- m* shipper n
Versendung f dispatch, shipping n
versetzen v transfer, move; *- v* (Personal) transfer v; (verpfänden) pawn
Versetzung f (Personal) transfer n
versicherbar adj insurable adj, assurable adj
versicherbarer Wert insurable value; *- Zins* insurable interest
versicherbares Risiko insurable risk
Versicherer m insurer n, assurer n
versichern v assure v, insure v
Versicherte f u. m insured n, assured n, insured n, insuree n
Versicherung f assurance n (GB), insurance n; *- für einen befristeten Zeitraum* time policy; *- mit Gewinnbeteiligung* participating insurance; *eine - abschließen* assure v, insure v
Versicherungsagentur f insurance agency
Versicherungsaktie f insurance share
Versicherungsbeleihung f policy loan
Versicherungsberechtigte f u. m beneficiary of insurance

Versicherungsdarlehen n loan from insurance company
Versicherungsfachmann m insurance expert
versicherungsfähig adj insurable adj, assurable adj
Versicherungsfähigkeit f insurability n
Versicherungsfonds m insurance fund; **- auf Gegenseitigkeit** benefit fund
Versicherungsgeber m insurer n, assurer n
Versicherungsgebühr f insurance fee
Versicherungsgesellschaft f insurance company, insurance corporation (US)
Versicherungsleistung f insurance benefit
Versicherungsmakler m insurance broker
Versicherungsmathematiker m actuary n
versicherungsmathematisch adj actuarial adj
Versicherungsnehmer m insurant n, assured n, insured n, insuree n
Versicherungspolice f insurance policy, policy of insurance
Versicherungsprämie f insurance premium
Versicherungsschein m insurance policy, certificate of insurance; **verzinslicher -** interest policy
Versicherungsschutz m insurance coverage
versicherungstechnisch adj actuarial adj
Versicherungsverein auf Gegenseitigkeit benefit association, benefit society, beneficiary association, benefit club
Versicherungswechsel m insurance draft (US)
Versicherungswert m insured value, policy value
Versicherungszweig m insurance branch
versiegeln v seal v
versiegelt adj sealed adj
versiert adj experienced adj
Versilberung f (bildlich) realization n
Versorgung f supply n
Versorgungsbetriebe m pl utilities n pl
Versorgungswerte m pl (Börse) utilities n pl
verspätete Zahlung delated payment

verspäteter Protest retarded protest
Versprechen f promise n; **formloses -** assumpsit n
verstaatlichen v nationalize v
verstärken v intensify, reinforce, strengthen v, fortify v
versteifen (sich) v stiffen v, harden v
Versteigerer; öffentlicher - auctioneer n
versteigern v auction v, sell at auction, sell by auction
Versteigerung f auction n; **öffentliche -** public sale
Verstempeln n stamping n
Verstorbene f u. m deceased n
Verstoß m violation, infringement n
verstümmelt adj (Telegramm) mutilated adj
Verstümmelung f mutilation n
vertagte Schuld deferred debt
verteilen v deal out; **-** v distribute v
verteilt adj divided adj
verteilter Gewinn distributed profits
Verteilung f distribution n
vertikaler Konzern lateral combination
Vertrag m agreement n; **-** m contract n; **-** m (Staats-) treaty n; **auf Grund eines -es** under an indenture; **beurkundeter -** contract under seal; **einen - abschließen** contract v; **gegenseitiger -** reciprocal contract
vertraglich adj contractual adj; **- abgesichert** covered by contract; **- verpflichtet** covenanted adj
vertragliche Vereinbarung contractual arrangement
Verträglichkeit f compatibility n
Vertragsabschluß m conclusion of contract, negotiation n
Vertragsanspruch m contract claim
Vertragsbedingungen f pl contract terms, conditions of a contract
Vertragsbestimmungen f pl (schriftlich) articles of agreement; **- f pl** provisions of a contract
Vertragsbrecher m convenient breaker
Vertragsbruch m break of contract
vertragschließender Teil contractant n, contracting party, stipulator n
Vertragsentwurf m draft of a contract; **-** m (erster, konzeptartiger) rough draft of contract

Vertragsfähigkeit

Vertragsfähigkeit f contractual capacity, ability to contract
vertragsgemäß *adj* contractual *adj*
vertragsgemäßer Zinssatz conventional interest
Vertragsgrundlage f basis of agreement
Vertragspartei f contractant n, contracting party, stipulator n; ~ counter party
Vertragsperiode f contractual period
Vertragspreis m contract price
Vertragspunkte m pl articles of agreement
Vertragsrecht n law of contracts
Vertragsrechte n pl contractual rights
Vertragsschuld f contract debt
Vertragsspediteur m contract carrier
Vertragsstempel m contract stamp
Vertragsurkunde f deed, indenture n
Vertragsverhältnis n contractual relation
Vertragsverletzung f contract violation
Vertrauen n confidence n
Vertrauensbruch m break of confidence
Vertrauensmann m confidant n
Vertrauensschadenversicherung f fidelity insurance
vertrauenswürdig *adj* trustworthy *adj*, reliable *adj*
vertraulich *adj* confidential *adj*
vertrauliche Information confidential information
Vertreter m representative, agent n
Vertreterprovision f agent's commission
Vertretervertrag m contract of agency
Vertretung f representation, agency n; ~ f (Ersatz) substitution n; **in** ~ by proxy
Vertretungsbefugnis f authority to represent, agent's authority
Vertretungsvollmacht f power of attorney, procura
Vertrieb m sale, distribution
Vertriebsabteilung f distribution department
Vertriebskredit m sales credit
Vertriebslehre f marketing n
veruntreuen v embezzle v, defalcate v
Veruntreuer m embezzler n
Veruntreuung f embezzlement n, defalcation n, fraud
Veruntreuungsversicherung f fidelity insurance
verurteilen v codemn v

Verurteilung f condemnation n
vervielfältigen v make copies v
Vervielfältigungsapparat m duplicator n
vervollständigen v complete, complement v
Verwahrbank f depository bank
Verwahrer m depository n, custodian n
Verwahrung f custodianship n; *sichere* ~ safekeeping n (US)
Verwahrungsgebühr f custody fee
Verwahrungsstelle f depository n, custodian n
verwaltbar *adj* manageable *adj*
verwalten v administer v; ~ v (Gelder) manage v
Verwalter m administrator n; ~ m trustee n, custodian trustee, fiduciary n
Verwaltung f management, administration n; ~ f custodianship n; ~ *der Unternehmensaktiva* asset management; ~ *der Unternehmenspassiva* liability management
Verwaltungs- (in Zus.) administrative *adj*
Verwaltungsakt m administrative action
Verwaltungsaufwand m operating expenses
Verwaltungsbeirat m advisory board, advisory council
Verwaltungsbezirk m county n
Verwaltungsdepot n management account
Verwaltungsgebühr f management fee
Verwaltungskosten plt administrative expenditures, cost of management
Verwaltungsmaßnahme f administrative action
Verwaltungsrat m board of directors, advisory board, administrative board
Verwaltungsratsmitglied n member of the board, director n
Verwaltungsrecht n administrative law; ~ *des Ehemannes* (über das Eigentum der Ehefrau) marital control (GB)
Verwaltungssitz m head office
Verwaltungsvollmacht f power to manage, management authorization
verwandte Industrien allied industries
verwässertes Aktienkapital watered capital, watered stock (US)

Verwässerung f dilution; **- von Aktienkapital** (Grundkapital) stock watering
verweigern v refuse v, turn down; **die Annahme -** refuse acceptance
verwenden v use, utilize
Verwendung des Gegenwerts application of proceeds
verwertbar adj realizable adj
Verwertung f use, realization, utilization n; **- von Kreditsicherheiten** realization of collaterals; **zwangsweise - von Kreditsicherheiten** forced sale of collaterals
verwirken v forfeit v
Verwirkung f forfeiture n
Verwirkungsklausel f forfeiture clause
verzeichnen v post, score; **einen Kursgewinn -** score an advance
Verzeichnis n list, table, schedule, register n
verzeihen v excuse v, forgive v, pardon v
Verzeihung f forgiveness, pardon, condonation n
Verzicht m waiver, disclaimer, abandonment n; **- m** renouncement n, quitclaim n; **- auf Sicherheit** abandonment of security; **- leisten** renounce v, quitclaim v
verzichten v waive, renounce v, quitclaim v; **auf einen Rechtsanspruch -** waive a claim
Verzichtserklärung f waiver n
Verzichtsklausel f waiver clause
Verzichtsleistung f renouncement n, quitclaim n
verzinsen v pay interest, yield interest
verzinslich adj interest-bearing adj, interest-yielding adj; yielding interest
verzinslicher Versicherungsschein interest policy
Verzinsung f yield n; **laufende -** running yield (GB)
verzögern v delay v, defer v
Verzögerung f delay n
verzollt adj duty paid
Verzollung f customs clearance n
Verzollungspapiere n pl clearance papers
Verzug m default n; **in - geraten** default v; **mit den Zahlungen in - kommen** default in payment
Verzugstage m pl days of grace
Verzugszinsen m pl default interest, interest for default, interest fine, penal interest, interest on overdue amounts
Vier-Augen-Prinzip n principle of dual control
vierteljährlich adj quarterly adj
Vinkulation f limitation of transfer, restricted transferability
Vizedirektor m Assistant Manager (GB), Second Vice President (US)
Volatilität f (Schwankungsintensität) volatility
Volksaktie f people's share
Volkswirt m economist n
Volkswirtschaft f economics plt, national economy
volkswirtschaftlich adj economical adj, economic adj
volkswirtschaftliche Entwicklung economic process
voll eingezahlte Aktie fully paid share, fully paid-up share; **- eingezahltes Kapital** fully paid-up capital; **- integriertes Datenverarbeitungssystem** fully integrated data processing system; **- und ganz besitzen** own outright
volle Bezahlung full payment; **- Haftung** full liability; **- Zahlung** payment in full
volleingezahlte Police paid-up policy
voller Betrag full amount
volles Konnossement full bill of lading; **- Wechselgiro** special endorsement, special indorsement, direct indorsement (US)
Vollgiro n special endorsement, special indorsement, direct indorsement (US)
Vollindossament n unqualified endorsement, full endorsement, full indorsement
Volljährige f u. m major n, adult n
Vollkasko n comprehensive coverage
Vollmacht f power, power of attorney, authority n; **- f** procuratory n (US); **- f** proxy n; **- erteilen** empower v; **- für einen Rechtsanwalt** warrant of attorney in; **- by proxy**; **mit - ausstatten** invest with power of attorney; **mit gehöriger - versehen** duly authorized; **unbeschränkte -** carte blanche
Vollmachtbesitzer m proxy holder

Vollmachtgeber *m* donor, principal *n*, mandator *n*
Vollmachtsindossament *n* procuration endorsement
Vollmachtsstimmrecht *n* proxy voting right
Vollmachtsurkunde *f* proxy deed, certificate of authority
vollständig *adj* complete, full
vollständige Abrechnung full settlement
vollständiges Indossament full endorsement, full indorsement
vollstreckbar *adj* enforceable *adj*
vollstrecken *v* execute *v*
Vollstreckung *f* execution *n*
Vollstreckungsgläubiger *m* judg(e)ment creditor, execution creditor
Vollstreckungsschuldner *m* judg(e)ment debtor, execution debtor
vollziehen *v* execute *v*, perform *v*
Vollziehung *f* fulfillment, execution
Volontär *m* trainee *n*
voraus; im - bezahlen pay in advance, make a payment beforehand
vorausbezahlen *v* prepay *v*
vorausbezahlt *adj* prepaid *adj*
Vorausempfang *m* (Erbrecht) advancement *n*
vorausgehend *adj* prior *adj*, former *adj*
Vorausschau über die finanzielle Lage eines Unternehmens financial forecasting
voraussichtlicher Kunde prospective customer
Vorauszahlung *f* advance payment, prepayment *n*
Vorauszahlungskredit *m* advance payment credit
Vorbehalt *m* reservation *n*; **unter üblichem -** under usual reserve
vorbehalten *v* reserve *v*
vorbehaltloses Akzept clean acceptance
Vorbehaltsgut *n* separate estate
Vorbehaltsklausel *f* saving clause, proviso clause
Vorbehaltspreis *m* upset price
vorbereitende Buchungsmaßnahmen vouching *n*

Vorbörse *f* premarket, unofficial dealings before official hours
vorbörslich *adj* before the trading session
vorbörslicher Kurs pre-market price
vordatieren *v* postdate *v*; **einen Scheck -** postdate a check
vordatiert *adj* postdated *adj*
vordatierter Scheck postdated check
Vorderseite *f* face *n*
Vordruck *m* form *n*, blank *n*
Vorfinanzierung *f* prefinancing, preliminary financing
Vorfinanzierungszusage *f* assurance of interim credit
Vorgirant *m* previous endorser
vorhanden *adj* existing, present, available *adj*
vorherrschend *adj* prevailing *adj*
Vorhersage *f* forecast *n*
Vorjahr *n* previous year
Vorjahresmonat *m* corresponding month in the previous year
Vorjahresvergleich *m* comparison with the previous year
Vorkasse *f* advance payment, prepayment *n*
Vorkauf *m* buying in advance, forward purchase, preemption
Vorkaufsrecht *n* preemption right, right of preemption
Vorkehrungen *f pl* dispositions *n pl*
Vorlage *f* presentation, presentment; **- zum Akzept** presentation for acceptance; **- zur Annahme** presentation for acceptance; **- zur Zahlung** presentment for payment
vorläufig *adj* temporary *adj*, provisional *adj*, pro tempore
vorläufige Deckungszusage cover note (GB), covering note; **- Posten** suspense items
vorläufiger Kredit bridge-over loan
vorläufiges Konto suspended account, suspense account
Vorlaufkarte *f* lead card
Vorleger *m* (Scheck) (check) presenter
vormerken *v* book *v* (e.g. an order)
Vormund *m* guardian *n*
Vormundschaft *f* guardianship *n*
vormundschaftlich *adj* custodial *adj*

Vorprämiengeschäfte n pl trading in calls
Vorrang m priority n, seniority, preference n
Vorranghypothek f senior mortgage, underlying mortgage (US)
vorrangig adj prior-ranking, prior, senior adj
Vorrat m stock, store, supply, reserve
Vorräte m pl inventories n pl, stock in hand, supplies n pl
Vorratsaktie f disposable share, own share
Vorrecht n privilege n (priority)
Vorruhestand m early retirement
Vorschaltgesellschaft f holding company
Vorschaltkonto n preliminary account
vorschießen v advance v
vorschlagen v propose, suggest, nominate v
vorschreiben v prescribe v
Vorschrift f instruction n
Vorschuß m advance n, loan (US); *-* m (Anwaltsgebühren) retaining fee; *- nehmen* anticipate salary
Vorschüsse an den Exporteur (Akkreditivbevorschussung) anticipatory credit
Vorschüsse zahlen advance funds
Vorschußkonto n advance account
Vorschußverein m lending society
Vorschußwechsel m advance bill
Vorschußzins m advance interest
vorsichtige Schätzung conservative estimate
Vorsitz m chairmanship n
Vorsitzende f u. m chairman n; *-(r) des Vorstands* Chairman of the Board of Management; *stellvertretende(r) -(r)* deputy chairman
Vorsitzer m chairman, president
Vorsorge f provision n
Vorstand m Board of Management, Board of Managing Directors, Board of Managers, Board of Directors, the Board
Vorstandsaktien f pl management shares
Vorstandsmitglied n Board Member, Member of the Board, Managing Director
Vorstandssitzung f Board meeting
Vorstandsvorsitzende f u. m Chairman of the Board (of Management), Chief General Manager (GB), Chief Executive Officer
Vorsteckeinrichtung f (für Sparbücher) passbook chute

Vorsteher m manager n
vortäuschen v simulate v, feign, fake
Vorteil m advantage n; *- m* benefit n, privilege n
vorteilhaft adj advantageous adj
Vortrag auf neue Rechnung balance carried forward (B/F), balance brought forward (B/F), account carried forward
vortragen v carry forward v, carry over v
Vortragsposten m item carried forward
Vortragssaldo m balance carried forward (B/F), balance brought forward (B/F), account carried forward
vorübergehende Einstellung suspension n
Vorverkauf m advance sale
vorverkaufen v selling in advance
Vorverkaufsklausel f clause of preemption
Vorverkaufsvertrag m forward sale contract
Vorwegnahme f anticipation n
vorwegnehmen v discount, anticipate v
vorwegnehmend adj anticipatory adj
Vorzug m priority n; *mit einem - ausgestattet* preferential adj
Vorzugsaktie *mit Umtauschrecht* convertible preferred stock; *- ohne Stimmrecht* non-voting preference share
Vorzugsaktien f pl preference shares (GB), preference stocks (US), priority shares, preferred stocks (US), preferences n pl; *- mit besonderer Dividendenberechtigung* cumulative participating preference shares; *- - mit variabler Dividende* adjustable rate preferred stocks; *- mit zusätzlicher Gewinnbeteiligung* participating preference shares (GB), participating preferred stocks (US); *- zweiter Klasse* second preferred stock (US); *kumulative -* cumulative preference stocks; *kündbare - * redeemable preferred stock; *Tilgung von -* capital redemption
Vorzugsdividende f preference dividend, preferred dividend
Vorzugsgläubiger m preferential creditor (GB), preferred creditor (US)

Vorzugsobligation f preference bond, preferred bond, senior bond
Vorzugspreis m bargain price
Vorzugsrecht n preference right, privilege n
Vorzugsstammaktie f preferred ordinary share, privileged common stock
Vorzugszahlung f preferential payment
Vostrokonto n vostro account
Votum n vote n
Vreneli n (Schweizer 20-Franken-Goldmünze) Vreneli (20 Swiss Franc gold coin)

W

Wachstum n growth
Wachstum der Industrie industrial growth
Wachstumsaktie f growth stock, growth share
Wachstumsanleihe f bond repayable at a premium
Wachstumsfond m growth fund
Wachstumsmärkte m pl emerging markets (e.g. Asia)
Wachstumspotential n growth potential
wachstumsschwach adj slowgrowing
wachstumsstark adj fast-growing
Wachstumswert m (Börse) growth stock
Wachstumswerte m pl (Börse) growth stocks
wagen v risk v
Wagenladung f carload n (US)
Waggonladung f carload n (US)
Waggonsendung f carloading n
Wagnis n risk n, (Neugründung) venture n
Wagnisfinanzierungsfonds venture (capital) fund
Wagniskapital n venture capital; **Expansionsfinanzierung mit -** expansion stage financing, later stage financing; **Gründungsfinanzierung mit -** early stage financing
Wagniskapitalgeber m venture capitalist
Wählbarkeit f eligibility n
wählen v elect v; ~ v (durch Abstimmung) vote v
Währung f currency n; **manipulierte -** managed currency; **notleidende -** depreciated currency; **weiche -** soft currency
Währungsabteilung f foreign exchange department
Währungsabwertung f currency devaluation (depreciation)
Währungsarbitrage f exchange arbitration
Währungsaufwertung f currency revaluation
Währungsausgleichsfonds m stabilization fund
Währungsbank f currency issuing bank
Währungsbarkredit m currency advance

Währungsbehörden f pl monetary authorities
Währungsblock m monetary block
Währungsbuchhaltung f foreign exchange accounting, foreign exchange accounting department
Währungsdollar m paper dollar
Währungseinheit f currency unit, unit of currency
Währungsfonds m currency fund; **Internationaler -** (IWF) International Monetary Fund (IMF)
Währungsgebiet n currency area
Währungsgeld n legal tender money
Währungsgeschäft n foreign exchange business, dealings in foreign exchange
Währungsgesetz n currency law
währungsgleicher Zinsswap single-currency interest rate swap
Währungsgold n monetary gold
Währungsguthaben n currency balance
Währungshoheit f monetary sovereignty
Währungsklausel f currency clause, exchange clause, foreign currency clause
Währungskonto n foreign currency account, foreign exchange account
Währungskontrolle f exchange control, currency control
Währungskredit m currency loan, foreign loan
Währungsoption f currency option
Währungsoptionsschein m currency warrant
Währungsparität f monetary parity
Währungspolitik f monetary policy, currency policy
währungspolitische Zusammenarbeit monetary cooperation
Währungsposition; ungesicherte - unhedged currency exposure
Währungsreform f currency reform
Währungsreserve f monetary reserve
Währungsrisiko n currency risk, exchange risk
Währungsscheck m foreign currency check

Währungsschlange f (Europäische W.) European Currency Snake
Währungsschuldner m foreign currency debtor
Währungssicherung f safeguarding of the currency
Währungssicherungsklausel f currency safeguarding clause
Währungsspekulant m currency operator
Währungsstabilisierung f currency stabilization
Währungsstandard m monetary standard
währungsstarke Länder countries having a strong currency
Währungssystem n currency system
Währungsumstellung f currency conversion
Währungsunion f monetary union
Währungsverfall m currency erosion
Währungsverfassung f currency constitution
Währungswert m currency value
Waise f u. m orphan n
Wandelanleihe f convertible bond
wandelbare Wertpapiere convertible securities
Wandelgenußschein m convertible profit-sharing certificate
Wandelobligation f convertible bond
Wandelparität f conversion parity
Wandelprämie f conversion premium
Wandelpreis m conversion price
Wandelrecht n conversion right, warrant
Wandelschuldverschreibung f convertible debenture, convertible bond; *- mit geringem Aufgeld* busted convertible
Wandlungsgenußschein m convertible profit-sharing certificate
Ware f commodity, goods, merchandise
Waren f pl goods n pl; *gepfändete -* distrained goods; *unter Zollverschluß liegende -* goods in bond; *unverkäufliche -* dead stock
Warenakkreditiv n commercial letter of credit
Warenakzept n trade acceptance
Warenanlagefonds siehe *Rohstoff-Fonds*
Warenausfuhr f export n, exportation n

Warenbegleitschein m waybill n
Warenbestand m goods on hand
Warenbestände m pl inventories n pl, stock in hand, supplies n pl
Warenbezeichnung f description of goods
Warenbörse f commodity exchange
Warendividende f commodity dividend (US)
Warendokument n trade document
Wareneinstandspreis m cost price
Warenempfangsschein m delivery receipt
Warenhandel m trade in goods, merchandise trade
Warenhaus n department store
Warenkorb m basket of commodities
Warenkredit m commodity credit, commodity loan, credit in goods, commercial loan
Warenkreditbank f instalment credit institution
Warenkreditbrief m commercial letter of credit
Warenkreditgenossenschaft f consumer credit cooperative
Warenkreditversicherung f commercial credit insurance
Warenlager n inventories
Warenlombard m advance (lending) on goods, advances against merchandise, commodity collateral advance
Warenoption f commodity option
Warenpapier n trade document
Warenpreise m pl commodity prices
Warenrembourskredit m commercial acceptance credit
Warenschuld f commercial debt
Warenskonto n trade allowance
Warenterminbörse f commodity futures exchange
Warenterminkontrakt m commodity future
Warenterminoption f commodity option
Warenumschlag m turnover of goods
Warenumschlagskredit m goods turnover financing credit
Warenwechsel m commercial draft, commercial note, commercial bill, trade bill
Warenwert m commodity value
Warenzeichen n trademark n

Warnung f caution n
Wasserkraftanleihe f hydro-electric bond
Wechsel m bill of exchange, bill; *- auf kurzfristige Sicht* short-term bill; *- auf London* bill on London; *- auf uns* bills on us; *- gegen Dokumente* bill against documents; *- in mehrfacher Ausfertigung* bill in a set; *- zum Inkasso* bill for encashment; *akzeptierter -* acceptance n, bill of acceptance; *auf Grund von Getreidelieferungen gezogener -* grain bill; *avalierter -* backed bill; *bankfähiger -* discountable bill; *bundesbankfähiger -* rediscountable (eligible) bill of exchange at the Deutsche Bundesbank; *diskontierbarer -* bank bill; *echter -* real bill (US); *ein Satz -* set of exchange; *einen - akzeptieren* accept a bill; *einen - einlösen* cash a bill, clear a bill, discharge a bill, draw in a bill, retire a bill, take up a bill, honor a bill, answer a bill of exchange; *einen - mit Akzept versehen* provide a bill with acceptance; *einen - mit Sichtvermerk versehen* sight a bill; *einen - vor Verfall einlösen* anticipate a bill; *einen - ziehen* draw a bill; *einen - zum Akzept vorlegen* sight a bill; *einen - zu Protest gehen lassen* allow a bill to be protested; *eingelöster -* discharged bill; *erstklassiger -* prime bill, first-class paper; *fällige -* notes payable (US), bills payable; *Fälligkeit eines -s* date of a bill; *fauler -* query bill; *in Kürze fällig werdender -* bill about to mature; *indossierter -* made bill (GB); *langfristiger -* long-term bill; *laufender -* bill to mature; *nicht vollständig ausgefüllter -* inchoate bill (GB); *notleidender -* bill in distress, dishonoured bill, overdue bill; *prima -* prime bill, first-class paper; *protestierter -* protested bill; *überfälliger -* overdue bill; *umlaufende -* bills in circulation; *zur Annahme geschickter -* bill out for acceptance

Wechselabrechnung f discount liquidation
Wechselabteilung f discount department, bill department
Wechselagent m bill broker
wechselähnliche Anweisung bill-like payment order
Wechselakzept n bill acceptance, acceptance of a bill
Wechselakzeptant m acceptor of a bill
Wechselarbitrage f exchange arbitration
Wechselaussteller m drawer of a bill; *bankrotter -* bankrupt drawer
Wechselausstellung f drawing of a bill
Wechselbank f exchange bank
Wechselbestand m bill portfolio, bill holdings, bills in portfolio, bills in hand
Wechselbeteiligte f u. m party to a bill
Wechselbetrag m face amount (of bill)
Wechselblankett n blank bill
Wechselbuch n discount register, draft book (GB), bill copying book, bill book, bill diary, bill discount ledger, bill ledger, acceptance maturity tickler, bills payable book; *- für Inkassowechsel* bill for collection book
Wechselbürge m bill guarantor
Wechselbürgschaft f bill guarantee, guarantee of a bill, aval n; *Kredit gegen -* accommodation endorsement loan
Wechselcourtage f bill brokerage
Wechseldeckung f bill cover
Wechseldiskontierer m bill discounter
Wechseldiskontierung f bill discounting
Wechseldiskontierungsspesen plt bill discounting charges
Wechseldiskontkredit m discount credit
Wechseldiskontsatz m bill discount (GB), bill discount rate
Wechselduplikat n duplicate bill
Wechseleingangsbuch n bill register
Wechseleinlösung f payment of a bill
Wechseleinnehmer m payer of a bill
Wechseleinreicher m presenter of a bill
Wechseleinzug m bill collection
Wechselfälscher m bill forger
Wechselfälschung f bill forgery
Wechselforderung f bill-based claim, claim arising from a bill
Wechselforderungen f pl trade notes receivable, bills receivable
Wechselformular n bill form
Wechselgeber m maker n, drafter n, drawer n

Wechselgeld

Wechselgeld *n* change *n*
Wechselgeschäft *n* bill business, discount business
Wechselgeschäfte *n pl* bill transactions
Wechselgiro; volles - special endorsement, special indorsement, direct indorsement (US)
Wechselgläubiger *m* bill creditor
Wechselhaftung *f* liability on a bill
Wechselhandel *m* bill brokerage
Wechselhändler *m* bill broker, discount broker
Wechselindossament *n* endorsement on bill
Wechselinhaber *m* holder of a bill, bill holder
Wechselinkasso *n* bill collection, collection of bills, draft collection
Wechselinkassobüro *n* bill collector
Wechselklage *f* action on a bill of exchange
Wechselkosten *plt* exchange charges
Wechselkredit *m* discount credit, bill credit, acceptance credit
Wechselkurs *m* rate of exchange, exchange rate, commercial rate of exchange (US), foreign exchange rate
Wechselkursanpassung in kleinen Schritten crawling peg
Wechselkurse; - in verschiedenen Fremdwährungen cross rates; **multiple -** multiple exchange rates
Wechselkursrisiko *n* currency risk
Wechselkurssatz *m* par exchange rate
Wechsellaufzeit *f* currency of a bill
Wechsellombard *m* lending on bills
Wechselmakler *m* bill broker, discount broker
Wechselmarkt *m* discount market, bill market
wechseln *v* exchange v, change v
Wechselnehmer *m* payee of a bill
Wechselobligo *n* liability on bills, bill commitments
Wechselparität *f* par of exchange
Wechselpension *f* loan against pledged bill
Wechselportefeuille *n* bill case, bill holdings, bill portfolio
Wechselpräsentierung *f* presentment of a bill

Wechselprolongation *f* bill prolongation
Wechselprotest *m* protest a bill, bill protest
Wechselprovision *f* exchange commission
Wechselrechnung *f* bill account
Wechselrecht *n* bill of exchange law
Wechselreiter *m* bill jobber, jobber in bills (GB), bill doer
Wechselreiterei *f* bill jobbing, jobbing in bills, cross firing (GB), cross acceptance, kite flying
Wechselrembours *m* documentary acceptance credit
Wechselrückgabe *f* return of a bill to drawer
Wechselschuld *f* bill debt
Wechselschulden *f pl* bills and notes payable
Wechselschuldner *m* bill debtor
Wechselspesen *plt* discount charges, discount expenses, bill charges
Wechselstelle *f* exchange bureau, exchange office
Wechselstempelmarke *f* bill stamp
Wechselsteuer *f* bill tax, tax on notes and bills of exchange
Wechselsteuermarke *f* bill stamp
Wechselstrenge *f* summary bill enforcement procedure
Wechselstube *f* exchange office
Wechselübertragung *f* endorsement of a bill
Wechselumlauf *m* circulation of bills
Wechsel-und-Scheck-Bestand *m* (Bilanzposten) drafts and checks in hand, bills and checks
Wechselverbindlichkeiten *f pl* bill commitments, bills payable
Wechselverpflichtete *f u. m* bill debtor
Wechselverzeichnis *n* draft register
Wechselvordruck *m* bill form
Wechselvorlage *f* presentation of a bill
Wechselwucher *m* bill usury
Wechselzahlung *f* payment by bill
Wechselziehung *f* drawing of a bill
weich *adj* soft *adj*
weiche Währung soft currency
Weichwährung *f* weak currency
Weigerung *f* refusal *n*
Weißbuch *n* White paper

Weisung f instruction n
Weisungen; gegen - handeln disregard instructions
Weiterbelastung f on-debiting
weitergeben v discount, rediscount, pass on
Weiterleitungskredit m pass-through loan, transmitted loan
Weiterverarbeitung; maschinelle - subsequent machine processing
Weiterverfrachter m underfreighter n
weiterverkaufen v resell v
weiterverpfänden v rehypothecate v
weiterzahlen v continue to pay
Weiterzahlung f continuation of payment
Weltbank f World Bank
weltpolitisch adj world politics, international adj
Weltspartag m Word Savings Day
Weltwährungsfonds; Internationaler - (IWF) International Monetary Fund (IMF)
weltweit tätige Bank internationally operating bank
weniger minus, less
Werbeabteilung f advertising department, publicity department
Werbeagentur f advertising agency
Werbeerfolg m advertising result, advertising success
Werbeetat m advertising budget
Werbefachmann m ad man
Werbefeldzug m advertising campaign
Werbeforschung f advertising research
Werbefunk m radio advertising
Werbegeschenkartikel m advertising gift
Werbemotto n advertising slogan
werben v advertise v
Werbeprospekt m hand bill
Werbesendung f (Rundfunk, Fernsehen) commercial n
Werbeslogan m advertising slogan
Werbespot m spot n
Werbetext m advertising copy
Werbewesen n publicity n
Werbewettbewerb m advertising competition
Werbung f advertising n
Werbungtreibende f u. m advertiser n
Werdegang m career n

Werft f dockyard n, shipyard n
Werk n plant n
Werkanlage f company plant
Werkssparen n industrial savings
Werkzeuge und Geräte tools and implements
Wert m (Datum) availability date (US), value date; **- m** worth n, value n; **- zum Einzug** value for collection; **- zum Inkasso** value for collection; **berichtigter -** absorption value; **dem - nach** ad valorem; **effektiver -** real value; **steuerbarer -** taxable value, value for tax purposes; **steuerpflichtiger -** taxable value, value for tax proposes
Wertangabe f declared valuation, declaration of value
Wertansatz m valuation n
Wertberichtigung f value adjustment, valuation reserve
Wertberichtigungsaktien f pl bonus shares
Wertberichtigungskonto n absorption account
wertbeständig adj stable, of stable value
Wertbeständigungsklausel f stable value clause
Wertbestimmung f valuation, appraisement n
Wertbrief m insured letter
Werte m pl values n pl, securities n pl; **- abstoßen** shake out; **an der Börse notierte -** listed securities; **nicht einziehbare -** write-offs n pl (US); **zurückzahlbare -** redeemable stock
Wertentwicklung f (eines Investmentfonds) performance n (of a mutual fund)
Wertermittlung f valuation n
Wertfaktor m price-earnings ratio (PER)
Wertfeststellung f assessment n
Wertgegenstände m pl valuables n pl
Wertkarte f prepaid card (electronic purse)
wertlos adj worthless, of no value
wertlose Sicherheit dead security
Wertmarke f token coin, token money
Wertmaßstab m bench mark, standard of rate, measure of value
Wertmesser m standard of rate, measure of value

Wertminderung f (Metallgeld) defacement n; ~ f depreciation n

Wertpapier n security n; **nicht diskontfähiges** ~ ineligible paper (US); **per Kasse gekauftes** ~ purchased paper; **quasi begebbares** ~ quasi-negotiable instrument; **quasi übertragbares** ~ quasi-negotiable instrument; **schwerfälliges** ~ lame duck (US); **unverkäufliches** ~ unmarketable title

Wertpapierabteilung f securities department

Wertpapieranalyse f securities research, securities analysis

Wertpapieranalyst m (der Charts) chartist

Wertpapieranlage f securities investment, investment in securities

Wertpapieranlageberatung f investment counseling

Wertpapierart f security category

Wertpapieraufstellung f statement of securities

Wertpapierbeleihung f lending against (on) securities

Wertpapierberatung f investment advice, investment counselling

Wertpapierbereich m trust area

Wertpapierbesitz m security ownership, investment portfolio, portfolio n

Wertpapierbestand m securities holdings, securities investment portfolio, portfolio n

Wertpapierbezeichnung f securities description

Wertpapierbilanz f balance of securities

Wertpapierbörse f stock exchange n, securities exchange, stock market

Wertpapierclearing n securities clearing

Wertpapierdepot n securities deposit, securities portfolio, stock deposit

Wertpapiere n pl (Bilanz) investments n pl (balance sheet); ~ n pl securities n pl; ~ **abstoßen** (Panikverkäufe) sell out stocks; ~ **auf Kreditbasis kaufen** buy securities on margin; ~ **aufnehmen** absorb stocks; ~ **besitzen** carry securities; ~ **die nicht den rechtlichen Vorschriften entsprechen** non-legals; ~ **mit kurzer Laufzeit am Euromarkt** revolving underwriting facilities (RUF); ~ **ohne Rückkaufsrecht** irredeemable stock; ~ **von Bergwerksunternehmen** mining securities; **Abteilung für festverzinsliche** ~ bond department (US); **begebbare** ~ negotiable papers, negotiable securities; **beliehene, lombardierte** ~ collateral securities; **bevorrechtigte** ~ senior securities; **börsengängige** ~ stock exchange securities, marketable securities, realizable stock; **durch Vermögensrechte gesicherte** ~ asset-backed securities; **effektiv im Besitz befindliche** ~ long stock (GB); **erstklassige** ~ gilt-edged (first-class) bills; **festverzinsliche** ~ fixed interest bearing securities, fixed income securities, fixed interest issues; **festverzinsliche, hypothekarisch gesicherte** ~ Government National Mortgage Association (Ginnie Mae); **gut renommierte** ~ seasoned securities; **im Sammeldepot hinterlegte** ~ assented securities; **international gehandelte** ~ international securities, international stocks (US), internationals n pl; **mündelsichere** ~ legal investments (US), gilt-edged securities, gilt-edged investment, savings securities, widow and orphan stock (US); **nicht an der Börse notierte** ~ outside securities; **registrierte** ~ registered securities (US); **Ordnungsnummer für** ~ security number; **Scheingeschäft mit** ~ n wash sale, washing; **übertragbare** ~ transferable securities; **verkäufliche** ~ negotiable instruments; **wandelbare** ~ convertible securities; **wertlose** ~ valueless securities; **zweitklassige** ~ second-class papers

Wertpapieremission; Leitbank einer weltweiten ~ joint global coordinator

Wertpapierfonds m securities investment trust, security fund

Wertpapiergattungsaufnahme f securities listing by categories

Wertpapiergeschäft n securities business

Wertpapierhandel m security trading, securities trading, securities business, securities operations

Wertpapierinformationssystem n securities information system
Wertpapierkennummer f security identification number, security number
Wertpapierkonto n securities account
Wertpapierkredit m loan to purchase shares (stocks)
Wertpapiermarkt m securities market, security market, stock market
Wertpapierpensionsgeschäft n securities repurchase agreement
Wertpapierportefeuille n investment portfolio, securities portfolio
Wertpapiersammeldepot n collective security deposit
Wertpapiersteuer f securities tax
Wertpapierterminhandel m security futures trading
Wertpapierverwaltung f securities administration
Wertpapierzins m security interest
Wertsachen f pl valuables n pl
Wertschätzung f estimation n
Wertsendung f consignment of valuables
Wertsendungsversicherung f insurance of value
Wertsicherungsklausel f stable value clause
Wertsteigerung f increase in value, appreciation value
Wertstellung f availability date (US), value date
Wertverhältnis n ratio n
Wertverlust m depreciation n
Wertzoll m ad valorem duty
Wertzuwachs m increment value; **- eines Grundstücks** appreciation of real estate; **- für Aktionäre** shareholder value
Wertzuwachssteuer f tax on increment value, betterment tax
wesentlicher Rückgang material recession
Wettbewerb m competition n; - m contest n
Wettbewerber m competitor n
Wettbewerbsaufsichtsbehörde f Federal Trade Commission (US)
Wettbewerbsklausel f competition clause
Wettbewerbssituation f competitive position
Wette f bet n

wetteifern v compete n
wetten v bet v
Wettpolice f wager policy
Wichtigkeit f importance n; - f weight n
widerrechtlich adj illegal adj
Widerruf m withdrawal, countermand n; - m revocation n; **bis auf** - till cancelled, until cancelled, until recalled
widerrufen v withdraw, counterorder v, countermand v; - v revoke v
widerrufgültiger Börsenauftrag revocable stock order
widerruflicher Kredit revocable credit
widerrufliches Akkreditiv revocable letter of credit; **- Dokumentenakkreditiv** revocable documentary credit
wieder; - **anlegen** reinvest v; - **ausgebbare Banknoten** reissuable notes; - **begeben** reissue v; - **in Kurs setzen** remonetize v; - **übertragen** reassign v; - **einführen** reimport v; - **einzahlen** redeposit v; - **verpfänden** rehypothecate v
Wiederabtretung f re-assignment n
Wiederanlage f reinvestment n
Wiederanlagerabatt m reinvestment discount
Wiederanlaufprogramm n restart programme
Wiederanlaufroutine f (EDV) restart routine
Wiederaufbau m reconstruction n
wiederaufnehmen; ein Geschäft - reopen business; **Zahlungen** - resume payments
Wiederausgabe f reissue n; - **eines Wechsels** reissue of a bill of exchange
wiederbegebbar adj renegotiable adj
wiederbegeben v renegotiate v
Wiederbeschaffungskosten plt replacement costs
Wiedereinfuhr f reimportation n
Wiedereinfuhrgenehmigung f bill of store (US)
Wiedereinfuhrschein m bill of store (US)
wiedereinsetzen v reinstate v
Wiedereinsetzung f reinstatement n
wiedererlangen v recover v
wiedereröffnen; ein Geschäft - reopen business

wiedererstatten v reimburse v, refund v
Wiedererstattung f refunding, restitution n
wiedergutgebracht adj re-credited adj
Wiedergutmachung f reparation n
wiederkehrende Zahlungen revolving payments
wiederprägen v recoin v
Wiederverkauf m reselling n
wiederverkaufen v resell v
Wiederverkäufer m reseller n
wiederverkäuflich adj renegotiable adj
wiedervermieten v re-lease v
wiederverwertbar adj renegotiable adj
wiederverwerten v renegotiate v
wiedervorlegen v present again
Wiegenote f bill of weight
wilder Spekulant wild catter
Wille; *letzter* - will n, testament n, last will
willkürlich adj arbitrary adj
Winkelbörse f bucket-shop n (US)
wirklich adj actual adj; **- vorhanden** effective adj
wirklicher Wert equity n
wirksam werden take effect
wirkungslos adj inefficient adj
Wirkungslosigkeit f inefficiency n
Wirtschaft f economy, trade and industry; ***Ankurbelung der* -** reflation
Wirtschaft-auf-Bank-Ziehung f trader-on-bank-bill
Wirtschaft-auf-Wirtschaft-Ziehung f trader-on-trader bill
wirtschaftlich adj economical adj, economic adj
wirtschaftliche *Hilfsquellen* (Aktiva) economic resources; **- *Kräfte*** economic forces; **- *Stabilität*** economic stability; **- *Unterstützung*** economic support
wirtschaftliches Eigentum beneficial ownership
Wirtschaftlichkeit f economy n, profitability n, efficiency n
Wirtschaftlichkeitsuntersuchung f economic feasibility study
Wirtschafts- (in Zus.) economic adj
Wirtschaftsanalytiker m business analyst
Wirtschaftsbelebung f business recovery, business revival

Wirtschaftsberater m business consultant
Wirtschaftseinheit f economic entity
wirtschaftsfeindlich adj anticommercial adj
Wirtschaftsgebiet n economic area, economic territory
Wirtschaftsgeographie f economic geography
Wirtschaftsgrad m efficiency n
Wirtschaftsgüter; *abnutzbare* - wasting assets; ***körperliche* -** tangible assets; ***kurzlebige* -** wasting assets
Wirtschaftsindikatoren m pl economic indicators
Wirtschaftsjahr n financial year (GB), fiscal year
Wirtschaftskreise m pl business circles, economic circles
Wirtschaftskrise f economic crisis
Wirtschaftslage f economic situation
Wirtschaftsministerium n Ministry of Economics
Wirtschaftsplanung f economic planning
Wirtschaftsprüfer m certified public accountant, auditor n, chartered accountant, public accountant
Wirtschaftssituation f economic situation, economic condition
Wirtschaftstheorie f economic theory
Wirtschaftsunion f economic union
Wirtschaftsvereinigung f business syndicate
Wirtschaftswachstum n economic growth
Wirtschaftswerbung f business advertising
Wirtschaftswissenschaft f economics plt, national economy
Wirtschaftswissenschaftler m economist n
Wirtschaftszahlen f pl economic data
Wirtschaftszeitung f financial paper
Wirtschaftszweig m branch of the economy
wöchentliche Kündigung seven day's notice
wohlerworbene Rechte acquired rights, vested rights
Wohlfahrtsfonds m welfare fund
Wohlstand m prosperity n, wealth n
Wohltätigkeitsfonds m benefit fund

Wohlwollenserklärung f letter of comfort
Wohnblock m apartment house, block of flats
Wohnort m domicile n, residence n
Wohnsitz m residence, domicile
Wohnung f flat n, apartment n
Wohnungsbau m home building
Wohnungsbaudarlehen n housing loan
Wohnungsbaufinanzierung f housing finance
Wohnungsbauhypothek f mortgage loan for housing
Wohnungseigentum n residential property
Wortlaut m wording n
Wrack n wreck n

Wucher m usury n
Wucherer m usurer n, loan shark
wucherisch adj usurious adj
Wucherpreis m cut-throat price
Wucherzinsen m pl illegal interest
Wuchsaktie f growth stock
Wuchswerte m pl (Börse) growth stock
Wunschbild n rosy illusion
Wunschdenken n wishful thinking
wünschen v wish, desire, request
wunschgemäß adv according to your request
würdigen v acknowledge, appreciate
Würdigung f appraisal n
Wurzelaktie f downward-growing-share

Yankee-Anleihe f (USD-Anleihe) Yankee bond, USD bond issued in the US by a non-US borrower

Yen m (japanische Währungseinheit) yen

Yuan m (chinesische Währungseinheit) yuan

Z

Zahl f figure n
zahlbar adj payable, due; **~ an Order** payable to order; **~ bei Lieferung** cash on delivery (C.O.D.); **~ bei Vorlage** payable on presentation; **~ stellen** domicile v, domiciliate v; **bei Sicht ~** payable on demand, payable at sight
zählbar adj countable adj
Zahlbarstellung f domiciliation, making payable
zahlen v pay v
zählen v count v
Zahlen vergleichen check figures
Zahlenfolge f numerical order
Zahlenmaterial n figures, data
Zahler m payer n; **säumiger ~** defaulter n
Zahlkarte; integrierte ~ smart card
Zahlschein m payment slip
Zahlstelle f sub-branch, place of payment
Zahlstellenwechsel m domociled bill
Zahltag m day of payment
Zahlung f payment, settlement; **~ beantragen** apply for payment; **~ in Hartgeld** specie payment; **~ leisten** effect payment; **Dokumente gegen ~** documents against payment, cash against documents; **gegen ~ von** upon payment of; **mangels ~** for want of payment; **rückständige ~** overdue payment; **verspätete ~** delated payment; **volle ~** payment in full; **vor Fälligkeit geleistete ~** anticipating payment, anticipated payment; **zur ~ auffordern** demand payment; **zur ~ mahnen** demand payment
Zählung f counting n
Zäsur f turnaround
Zahlungen einstellen stop payment; **~ wiederaufnehmen** resume payments
Zahlungsabkommen n payments agreement
Zahlungsabwicklung f making (handling) payments
Zahlungsadresse f domicile n, residence n

Zahlungsansprüche befriedigen meet demands for payment
Zahlungsanweisung f money order, payment order; **~ im Postscheckverkehr** postal payment order
Zahlungsanzeige f advice of payment
Zahlungsart f type of payment
Zahlungsaufforderung f demand for payment
Zahlungsaufforderungsschein m call ticket
Zahlungsaufschub m deferring payment, moratorium, delay of payment, payment deferral
Zahlungsauftrag m payment order
Zahlungsausgang m outpayment
Zahlungsausgleich m payment, repayment, settlement, clearance of payments
Zahlungsbedingungen f pl terms of payment
Zahlungsbefehl m payment order, order to pay
Zahlungsbereitschaft f solvency, willingness to pay
Zahlungsbewilligung f payment permit
Zahlungsbilanz f balance of payments
Zahlungseingang m receipt of payment, inpayment
Zahlungseinstellung f stoppage of payments, failure n; **~ f** insolvency n
Zahlungsempfänger m payee n
Zahlungsermächtigung f payment authorization
zahlungsfähig adj solvent adj
zahlungsfähiger Schuldner solvent debtor
Zahlungsfähigkeit f solvency n
Zahlungsfrist f period allowed for payment, term of payment
Zahlungsgarantie f guarantee of payment
Zahlungsgewohnheiten f pl payment habits, paying practices
Zahlungsland n country of payment
Zahlungsmittel n pl means of payment, payment media; **bargeldlose ~** deposit

Zahlungsmitteleinheit

currency (US), money in account, deposit money, bank money, check book money (US); **zum gesetzlichen ~ machen** monetize v
Zahlungsmitteleinheit f currency unit
Zahlungsmittelversorgung f currency supply
Zahlungsmodalitäten f pl terms of payment, payment procedures
Zahlungsort m place of payment
Zahlungspflichtige debtor n, party liable for payment
Zahlungsrückstände m pl payment arrears, arrears of payment
Zahlungsscheck m cashable check
Zahlungsschwierigkeiten f pl financial difficulties
Zahlungssperre f stoppage of payment
Zahlungsstelle f paying agent
Zahlungsstopp m payments stop
Zahlungssystem n payment system
Zahlungstag m day of payment
Zahlungstermin m date for payment; **durchschnittlicher ~** equation of payments; **mittlerer ~** average due date
zahlungsunfähig adj insolvent adj
Zahlungsunfähige f u. m insolvent n
zahlungsunfähiger Schuldner bad debtor
Zahlungsunfähigkeit f illiquidity, insolvency n
Zahlungsverbot an den Drittschuldner garnishment n; **~ erlassen** garnish v
Zahlungsvereinbarung f payments agreement
Zahlungsverkehr m payments, monetary transactions, payment transactions; **bargeldloser ~** cashless transactions; **belegloser ~** paperless payments; **elektronischer ~** wire transfer, electronic fund transfer (EFT); **Internationale Kommunikationssystem für den ~** n Society for Worldwide Interbank Financial Telecommunication (SWIFT)
Zahlungsverpflichtung f obligation to pay
Zahlungsverweigerung f refusal to pay
Zahlungsverzug m default of payment
Zahlungsweise f form of payment
Zahlungsziel n period of payment

Zedent m assignor n, cedent n, transferor n
zedieren v assign, cede
Zehn-Cent-Stück n dime n
Zehnerklub m Group of Ten
Zehntelwert m decile n
Zeichen n mark, sign
Zeichenerkennung; optische ~ optical character recognition (OCR)
Zeichenkombination f code configuration, code combination
zeichnen v (Unterschrift leisten) sign v; **~** v (z. B. Anleihen) subscribe v
Zeichner m underwriter n; **~** m (z. B. einer Anleihe) subscriber n; **~ von Effekten** applicant n
Zeichnung f (z. B. einer Anleihe) subscription n; **~ von Aktien** subscription for shares
Zeichnungsangebot n public offering; **erstmaliges ~ von Stammaktien** initial public offering (IPO) (US)
Zeichnungsbedingungen f pl underwriting conditions
Zeichnungsberechtigung f authority to sign
Zeichnungsbetrag m subscription money, amount subscribed
Zeichnungsbogen m subscription list
Zeichnungsformular n subscription blank (US), subscription form
Zeichnungsfrist f subscription period
Zeichnungsgrenze f writing limit
Zeichnungskurs m subscription price
Zeichnungsliste f subscription list
Zeichnungsofferte f public offering
Zeichnungsprospekt m subscription prospectus, offering prospectus
Zeichnungsschein m subscription blank (US), subscription form
Zeichnungsvollmacht f signing authority, power of signature
Zeit f time n; **auf ~** forward
Zeitbedarf m time requirement, time required
Zeitfaktor m timing factor
Zeitfrachtvertrag m time charter
Zeitgelder n pl time deposits
Zeitgeschäft n forward deal, forward transaction, futures contract, forward operation

Zeitgewinn m gain of time, pick-up of time
Zeitkontrolleur m timetaker n, timekeeper n
Zeitrente f temporary annuity
Zeitverlust m loss of time
Zeitvorteil m time advantage
Zeitwechsel m time bill, time draft, time certificate of deposit
Zeitwert m market value, time value
Zentralbank f central bank; ~ f (z. B. die Federal Reserve Banken in den USA) Banker's bank (US); *- als Kreditgeber für Banken in Liquiditätskrisen* lender of last resort
zentralbankfähig adj eligible at the Central Bank
Zentralbankgeld n central bank money
Zentralbankgeldschaffung f central bank money creation
Zentralbankgesetz n central bank law
Zentralbankrat m Central Bank Council
Zentralbanksystem n central banking system
Zentralbankwesen n central banking
Zentrale f central office, head office
Zentralkartei f central file
Zentralnotenbank f central bank
Zentralobligo n central commitments file
Zentralstelle f central agency, headquarters
Zertifikat n certificate n, unit n, share n
Zertifikatbesitzer m certificate holder
Zession f assignment n, assignation n, cession n; *stille -* undisclosed assignment
Zessionar m assignee n, cessionary n, transferee n
zessionsfähig adj assignable adj
Zessionskredit m loan against assignment of receivables
Zessionsschuldner m assigned debtor
Zessionsurkunde f instrument of assignment, transfer deed
Zessionsverbot n prohibition of assignment
Zettel m ticket n
zeugen v witness n
Zeugnis n certificate n
ziehen v draw n; *einen Saldo -* strike the balance

Ziehen n drawing n
Ziehung; *einschließlich -* cum drawing
Ziehungsrechte n pl (IWF) drawing rights
Ziel n target n; *auf - gekauft* bought on credit
Zielkonflikt m conflict of goals
Zielkorridor m target range
Ziffer f (Stelle) digit n; *~ f* figure n
Zins m interest n; *- zum Satz von ...* interest at the rate of ...; *aufgelaufener -* broken-period interest; *üblicher -* conventional interest; *ungesetzlicher -* illegal interest
Zinsabkommen n interest rates agreement
Zinsabrechnung f interest statement
Zinsabschnitt m interest coupon
Zinsabzug m interest deduction; *im voraus vorgenommener -* prepaid interest
zinsähnlich adj interest like
Zinsänderungsrisiko n floating rate risk
Zinsarbitrage f interest rate arbitrage
Zinsaufwendungen f pl interest expenditures, interest expense, interest charge
Zinsausfall m interest loss
Zinsausgleich m adjustment of interest
Zinsauszahlungsschein m interest warrant
Zinsbegrenzung nach oben und unten interest rate collar
Zinsbegrenzungsgebühr f cap fee
Zinsbelastung f interest expenditures, interest expense, interest charge
Zinsberechnung f calculation of interest, computation of interest
Zinsbogen m interest coupon sheet
Zinsbuckel m interest hump
Zinsdivisor m interest divisor
Zinseingänge m pl interest receipts
Zinseinnahmen f pl interest earnings, interest income, interest revenue
Zinsen m pl interest n; *- auf der Basis von 365 Tagen* exact interest; *- berechnen* charge interest; *- bringen* bear interest, earn interest, yield interest; *- einbringen* carry interest; *- errechnen* ascertain

interest; *fällige* - interest due; **laufende** - current interest; **mit - belasten** charge interest; *ohne* ~ ex interest
Zinsenaufstellung f interest statement
Zinsendienst m interest service, interest expenditures, interest expense, interest charge
Zinsenkonto n interest account
Zinsertrag m interest received, interest earnings, interest income, interest revenue
Zinseszinsen m pl compound interest
Zinseszinsrechnung f compound computation of interest
Zinsformel f interest formula
zinsfrei adj interest-free adj, bearing no interest, non-interest-bearing adj
Zinsfuß m rate of interest, interest rate; *interner* - *eines festverzinslichen Wertpapiers* yield to maturity
Zinsgarantie f interest guarantee
Zinsgeschäft n interest-related operations, bank operation on which interest is earned
Zinsgewinn m net interest earnings
zinsgünstig adj low interest
Zinshöhe f amount of interest
Zinsinversion f inverse interest
Zinskapitalisierung f amortization of interest
Zinskappe f cap
Zinskonditionen f pl terms of interest
Zinskorridor m collar
Zinskupon m interest coupon
Zinslast f interest expenditures, interest expense, interest charge
zinslos adj interest-free adj, bearing no interest, non-interest-bearing adj
zinslose Anleihe zero bond, interest free bond
zinsloser Kredit interest-free loan
zinsloses Bankguthaben free balance; - *Darlehen* zero-interest loan
Zinsmarge f interest margin
Zinsnachlaß m interest rebate
Zinsnebenkosten plt interest rate incidentals (charges)
Zinsniveau n interest rate level
Zinsobergrenze f interest rate ceiling, interest rate cap
Zinsoption f interest rate option

Zinsoptionsschein m interest warrant
Zinspapier n interest-bearing security
Zinsperiode f interest paying period
zinspflichtig adj interest-bearing adj
Zinspolitik f interest rate policy
Zinsrate f interest instalment
Zinsrechnung f calculation of interest, computation of interest; **permanente** - continuous interest calculation
Zinsrendite f interest yield
Zinsrückstände m pl arrears of interest
Zinssaldo m interest balance
Zinssatz m rate of interest, interest rate; *gesetzlicher* - legal interest, legal rate of interest, statutory interest; **normaler** - standard interest; **vertragsgemäßer** - conventional interest
Zinssatzänderung f change in interest rate
Zinsschein m interest coupon; - *nach Trennung von Mantel und Kupon* coupon issue
Zinsscheinbogen m interest coupon sheet
Zinsscheininkasso n bond coupon collection
Zinssenkung f interest rate reduction
Zinsspanne f interest margin, interest differential
Zinsspiegel m interest rate level
Zinsstaffel f day-to-day interest statement, interest calculation list
Zinssteuerfreiheit f freedom from tax on interest
Zinsstruktur; *inverse* - reverse yield curve
Zinsswap m interest swap; **währungsgleicher** - single-currency interest rate swap
Zinstabelle f interest table
Zinstermin m interest date
Zinstermingeschäft n forward rate agreement (FRA)
Zinsterminkontrakt m interest rate future
zinstragend adj interest-bearing adj, interest-yielding adj; - *anlegen* invest interest-bearing
zinstreibend adj interest rate-raising
Zinsüberschuß m net interest received
Zinsuntergrenze f (interest) floor
zinsvariable Anleihe floating rate bond, floater; - *Anleihe mit verbrieften*

Wandlungsrechten convertible floating rate bond; **- Anleihe ohne Laufzeitbegrenzung** perpetual floating rate note; **-r Schuldtitel** floating debt, countdown floater; **-r Schuldtitel mit einer Zinsobergrenze** maxi floating rate note, capped floater; **-r Schuldtitel mit einer Zinsuntergrenze** floored floater; **-r Schuldtitel mit Höchst- und Mindestsatz** mini-maxi floating rate bond (loan); **-s Darlehen** floating rate loan
Zinsverbilligungsmaßnahmen f pl interest-subsiding measure
Zinsverlust m interest loss
Zinszahlen f pl interest numbers (red), red numbers
Zinszahlungen f pl interest payments
Zinszahlungstermin m interest payment date, interest date
Zinszuschlag m additional interest
Zinszuschuß m subsidy for interest
Zirkaauftrag m near-order, approximate-limit order
Zirkapreis m approximate price
Zirkularkreditbrief m circular letter of credit
Zivilprozeß m suit n
Zivilrecht n civil law
Zoll m customs n pl
Zollabfertigung f customs clearing
Zollabfertigungsschein m bill of clearance
Zollabgabe f customs duty
Zollager n customs warehouse
Zollamt n customhouse n
zollamtliche Erlaubnis customs permission
Zollaufseher m customs inspector
Zollaval n customs guarantee
Zollbeamte m customs official
Zollbegleitschein m bond note, customs bond note
Zollbehörde f customs n pl, customs authorities
Zollbescheinigung f clearance certificate
Zollbürgschaft f customs guarantee
Zolldeklaration f customs declaration
Zolleinfuhrschein m bill of entry
Zolleinlagerer m bonder n
Zolleinlagerung f bonding n

Zollerklärung f customs entry
Zollfahndung f customs investigation
Zollformalitäten f pl customs formalities
zollfrei adj duty free
Zollfreiheit f free trade, exemption from customs duty
Zollfreischein m permit n
Zollgebühr f customs duty
Zollgebührenrechnung f bill of customs
Zollgewicht n customs weight, customs tare
Zollhaus n customhouse n
zollpflichtig adj customable adj
Zollpflichtigkeit f ratability n, rateability n
Zollquittung f certificate of the customhouse, customhouse receipt
Zollrückgabeschein m debenture certificate, debenture n (customs)
Zollrückvergütung f customs draw back
Zollsatz m rate of customs; - m rate of duty (GB)
Zollschein m customs receipt
Zollschranke f tariff wall, tariff barrier
Zollschutz m tariff protection
Zollsenkung f tariff reduction
Zollstundung f duty deferment
Zolltarif m customs tariff
Zollunion f tariff union, customs union
Zollvergehen n customs offence
Zollverordnungen f pl customs acts
Zollverschluß m customs bond; **unter - lagernd** bonded adj; **unter - liegende Waren** goods in bond; **Waren unter -** bonded goods
Zollverschlußlager n locked warehouse, bonded warehouse
Zollverwaltungszone f customs authorities zone; - f area n
Zollvormerkschein m customs note
Zollwesen n customs n pl
Zubehörpfandrecht n appurtenance lien
Zuerkennung f awarding n
Zufallauswahlverfahren n random selection process
Zug-um-Zug-Geschäft n contingent order
Zugang m access; m **- (Bilanz)** accrual n, addition n, increase n; **- m** (zu einem Datenbestand) file addition; **- zum Kapitalmarkt** access to the capital market

zugeben v concede v, admit v
zugehörig adj belonging (to the group), appropriate adj
Zugeständnis n concession n
zugestehen v concede; *eine Fristverlängerung -* grant a delay
zugeteilt adj allotted adj
zugunsten von in favor of (US), in favour of (GB)
Zukauf m additional purchase
zukünftiger Kunde prospect n
zulassen v admit v; *~ v* allow v, grant v
zulässig adj allowable adj, admissible
Zulassung f admission n; *~ von Effekten zum Börsenhandel* admission of securities; *offizielle ~ zum Börsenhandel* official listing (US)
Zulassungsanspruch m right of admission
Zulassungsgebühr f admission fee
Zulassungsstelle f office for the admission of securities to quotation
Zulieferant m supplier, subcontractor
zumessen v apportion v
zunehmen v increase v
zurückbehalten v retain v, keep back, withhold v
zurückbehaltene Gewinne retained earnings, retained profits
zurückbehaltenes Einkommen retained income
Zurückbehaltungsrecht n right of retention, right to retain, retaining lien; *~ der Bank* bank lien, banker's lien; *bevorrechtigtes ~* prior lien; *erstrangiges ~* first lien
zurückbelasten v charge back, redebit
zurückbuchen v write back, reverse an entry
zurückdatieren v date back
zurückerhalten v recover v
zurückerstatten v reimburse v, refund v
zurückfordern v redemand v
zurückgehen v decline v; *~ v (Preise)* drop v
zurückgehend adj declining adj
zurückgesandt adj returned adj
zurückkaufen v buy back; *Anleihestücke ~* retire a loan
zurückkehren v return v
Zurücknahme f revocation n

zurückrechnen v count back
zurücksenden v return v
zurückstellen v (Zahlung) delay v, defer v; *~ v* reserve v
Zurückstufung f down-grading
zurückübertragen v retransfer, reassign v, re-convey
zurückweisen v reject v, refuse v
zurückzahlbar adj redeemable adj
zurückzahlbare Werte (Börse) redeemable stock
zurückzahlen v repay v, pay back
Zurückzahlung f repayment, refund n, reimbursement n
zurückziehen v withdraw v
Zurückziehung f withdrawal, revoking n
Zusage f promise n, commitment, assurance n
Zusageprovision f commitment commission
Zusammenarbeit f cooperation n, collaboration n; *währungspolitische ~* monetary cooperation
zusammenarbeiten v cooperate v
Zusammenbruch m breakdown, collapse, crash, failure n
zusammenbündeln v bundle v
Zusammenfassung pooling; *~ von Bankleistungen zu einem neuen Produkt* bundling
Zusammenfassung von Hypotheken bunching of mortgages
zusammenlegen v consolidate v
Zusammenlegung des Aktienkapitals consolidation of shares
zusammenrechnen v sum up, add up
zusammenschließen v merge v, fuse v
Zusammenschluß m amalgamation n, fusion n, merger n
zusammenstellen v compile, collect, put-together
zusammentreten v meet v, convene v
zusammenzählen v add up
zusammenziehen v consolidate v
Zusatzaktie f bonus share
Zusatzdividende f surplus dividend, extra dividend
Zusatzhypothek f wraparound mortgage
zusätzlich adj additional adj

zusätzliche Kosten additional charges; **~ Leistungen** fringe benefits; **~ Sicherheit** collateral security
Zusatzrendite f extra yield
Zuschlag erteilen accept the tender
zuschlagen v add, allocate v
Zuschuß m allowance n; **staatlicher ~** subvention n, subsidy v
zusetzen v (Geld) lose v
zusichern v assure v, insure v
Zusicherung f guarantee n, assurance n
Zustand m condition n
zustandebringen v negotiate v
zuständig adj competent adj
zuständiger Beamter officer in charge
Zuständigkeit f competence n
Zustellgebühr f delivery charge
Zustellung f delivery n
Zustellungsadresse f mailing adress
Zustellungsbeamte m bailiff n (law)
Zustellungsurkunde f notice of delivery (US)
zustimmen v agree v; ~ v assent v
Zustimmung f agreement n; ~ f approval n, assent n, consent n
Zustrom von Auslandskapital inflow of foreign capital
zuteilen v allot v, allocate v; **Aktien voll ~** allocate shares to all applicants
Zuteilung f allotment n, allocation n; **~ bei einer überzeichneten Emission** subscribed allotment
Zuteilungsanzeige f allotment certificate (US), allotment letter (GB), letter of allotment (GB)
Zuteilungsausschuß m allocation committee
Zuteilungsbetrag m allotment money
Zuteilungskurs m allotment rate
Zuteilungsplan m allocation scheme
Zuteilungsschein m allotment certificate (US), allotment letter (GB), letter of allotment (GB)
Zuteilungsverfahren n allotment system
zuverlässig adj trustworthy adj, reliable adj
Zuverlässigkeit f reliability n
zuviel Kredit gewähren overcredit v
Zuwachs m growth, increase, gain n
Zuwachsrate f growth rate
zuweisbar adj assignable adj

zuweisen v allot v, allocate v
Zuweisung f allotment n, allocation n
zuwenden v contribute, allocate v
Zuwendung f contribution n; **~ aus dem Reingewinn** allocation out of profits
zuwiderhandeln v contravene v
Zuwiderhandlung f contravention n
zuzüglich adj additional adj
Zwang zu Deckungskäufen squeeze n
Zwangsanleihe f forced loan
Zwangskurs m forced rate of exchange
Zwangsliquidation f compulsory liquidation, compulsory windingup
Zwangspreis m controlled price
Zwangssparen n forced savings
Zwangsvergleich m composition in bankruptcy, enforced liquidation
Zwangsverkauf m forced sale, forced selling
Zwangsversteigerung f forced sale, forced selling; **~ auf Grund einer Hypothek** foreclosure sale
Zwangsverwalter m sequestrator n, receiver n
Zwangsverwaltung f administrative receivership n (US)
Zwangsvollstreckung f execution n; **eine ~ aus einer Hypothek betreiben** foreclose a mortgage
Zwangswährung f forced currency
zweckbestimmtes Konto earmarked account
Zweckbestimmung von Zahlungen appropriation of payments
zweckdienlich adj appropriate adj
zweckgebunden adj earmarked for specific purposes
zweckgebundene Rücklage surplus reserve (US)
Zweckmäßigkeit f expediency n
zwecks in order to
Zweckvermögen n special-purpose fund
zweifacher Gläubiger double creditor
zweifelhaft adj dubious adj, uncertain adj
zweifelhafte Zinszahlung doubtful interest
zweifelhafter Anspruch doubtful claim
zweigeteilter Markt two-tier market
Zweigniederlassung f branch n

Zweigstelle f branch n, branch office; ~ f (einer Bank) subbranch n, sub-office n
Zweigstellennetz n branch network
zweijährig adj biennal adj
zweimonatlich adj bi-monthly adj
zweiseitig adj bilateral adj
Zweitausfertigung f duplicate, second copy
zweite Hypothek second mortgage, junior mortgage; ~ *Wechselausfertigung* second bill of exchange
zweiteilige Emission two-tranche issue
zweiter; aus ~ Hand second-hand adj, used adj
zweitklassige Wertpapiere second-class papers
Zweitmarkt m secondary market
Zweitplazierung f secondary offering
Zweitschrift f duplicate n; ~ *einer Urkunde* duplicate document
zweitstellige Hypothek junior mortgage, second mortgage
Zwillingsaktien f pl twin shares
Zwischenabschluß m interim accounts
Zwischenaktie f interim share, interim stock certificate (US)
Zwischenanlagen f pl parked funds
Zwischenbankgelder n pl interbank funds
Zwischenbankgeschäfte n pl interbank business
Zwischenbilanz f interim balance sheet, interim accounts, interim statement
Zwischendividende f dividend on account, interim dividend
zwischenfinanzieren v finance at interim
Zwischenfinanzierung f bridge loan, bridge-over financing, interim financing

Zwischenfinanzierungskredit m bridging advance, bridge-over loan
Zwischengewinn m mid-way profit
Zwischenhandel m transit n
Zwischenkonto n interim account
Zwischenkredit m interim credit, interim loan, intermediate credit
Zwischenmakler m jobber n, stockjobber n
zwischenschalten v interpose
Zwischenschaltung eines Kreditinstituts use of a credit institution as intermediary
Zwischenschein m scrip, interim certificate (US); ~ *für eine Obligation* provisional bond; ~ *für eine Obligation bzw. Aktie* provisional certificate
Zwischenspeichern n (EDV) temporary storage
zwischenstaatlich adj international adj; ~ adj (zwischen den einzelnen US-Bundesstaaten) interstate adj
zwischenstaatlicher Handel (zwischen den einzelnen US-Bundesstaaten) interstate commerce
Zwischensumme f subtotal, intermediate total
Zwischenumsatz m intercompany sales, internal sales
Zwischenverwahrer m intermediate depositary (custodian)
zwischenzeitlich adj interim
Zwischenzins m intermediary's interest
zyklisch adj cyclical adj
zyklische Werte (Börse) cyclical stocks
zyklusverstärkend adj procyclical
Zylinder m (Daten) cylinder n

Englisch–Deutsch

A

A US-Bezeichnung für Börsenwerte guter Qualität
AA-double A US-Bezeichnung für Börsenwerte erster Qualität
AAA-triple A US-Bezeichnung für Börsenwerte allererster Qualität
abandon v verlassen v, ausbuchen v, übergeben v, überlassen v
abandonment n Verzicht m, Aufgabe f, Ausbuchung f, Überlassung f; *- clause* Abandonklausel f, Verzichtsklausel f; *- of security* Verzicht auf Sicherheit; *- of the gold standard* Aufgabe des Goldstandards; *- of the option money* Prämienaufgabe f
abate v herabsetzen v (Preise), ermäßigen v, verbilligen v, vermindern v
abatement n Herabsetzung f, Ermäßigung f, Verbilligung f, Abschlag m, Berichtigung f, Abnahme f, Abzug m, Preisermäßigung f, Steuernachlaß m, Zollerlaß m; *- in fees* Gebührenermäßigung f; *- of debts* teilweiser Schulderlaß; *- of purchase money* Kaufpreisherabsetzung f, Kaufpreisminderung f
abbreviated adj abgekürzt adj, gekürzt adj, gerafft adj
abeyance n Schwebezustand m, Anwartschaft f, Unentschiedenheit f; *fall into -* zeitweilig außer Kraft treten
abide by anerkennen v (Recht, Urteil)
ability to contract Vertragsfähigkeit f; *- to inherit* Erbfähigkeit f; *- to make a will* Testierfähigkeit f
able adj tüchtig adj, fähig adj
abolish v abschaffen v, widerrufen v
abolition n Abschaffung f, Aufhebung f
above par über pari; *- the line* Posten des ordentlichen Haushalts, normale Werbemaßnahmen
abridge v abkürzen v, verkürzen v
abridgement n Kürzung f (Abriß), Auszug m, Verkürzung f
abrogate v außer Kraft setzen, aufheben v, für ungültig erklären

abrogation n (of a law) Widerrufung f, Aufhebung f
absconding debtor unbekannt verzogener Schuldner, flüchtiger Schuldner
absence; *decree in -* Versäumnisurteil n
absolute assignment Forderungsabtretung f; *- endorsement* unbeschränktes Indossament; *- monopoly* unumschränktes Monopol; *- owner* unbeschränkter Eigentümer; *- ownership* unbeschränktes Eigentumsrecht
absolutely void null und nichtig
absorb buying power Kaufkraft abschöpfen; *- stocks* Wertpapiere aufnehmen
absorbed expenses verrechnete Gemeinkosten
absorbing company aufnehmende Gesellschaft
absorption account Wertberichtigungskonto n; *- value* berichtigter Wert
abstract n Auszug m, Abriß m, Katasterauszug für Immobilien (US); *- of account* Kontoauszug m, Rechnungsauszug m; *- of balance sheet* Vermögensübersicht f
abuse; *credit -* Kreditmißbrauch m
academic training akademische Ausbildung
accede v einwilligen v, zustimmen v
accelerated depreciation Sonderabschreibung f
acceleration clause Fälligkeitsklausel f; *- note* Schuldscheinverpflichtung mit dem Recht vorzeitiger Rückzahlung
accept v annehmen v, entgegenkommen v; *- a bill* Wechsel akzeptieren; *- bills for collection* Wechsel zum Einzug hereinnehmen; *- bills for discount* Wechsel zum Diskont hereinnehmen; *- in blank* blanko akzeptieren; *- the tender* Zuschlag erteilen
acceptable as collateral beleihbar adj, lombardfähig adj; *- paper* rediskontfähiges Papier

acceptance

acceptance n Akzept n, akzeptierter Wechsel; ~ n Annahme f (eines Wechsels); **~ account** Akzeptkonto n; **~ against documents** Annahme gegen Dokumente; **~ bank** Akzeptbank f; **~ bill** Dokumentenwechsel m; **~ charge** Akzeptgebühr f; **~ commitments** Akzeptumlauf m; **~ credit** Akzeptkredit m, Rembourskredit m; **~ creditor** Akzeptgläubige; **~ debtor** Akzeptschuldner m; **~ house** Akzeptbank f; **~ ledger** Akzeptbuch n, Oligoverzeichnis n; **~ liability** Akzeptverbindlichkeit f, Wechselobligo n; **~ line** Akzeptkreditlinie f, Akzeptlimit n, Akzeptkreditrahmen m; **~ maturity tickler** Wechselkopierbuch n, Wechsellogierbuch n, Wechselbuch n, Wechselobligo n (Buch), Wechselverfallbuch n; **~ price** Übernahmepreis m; **~ register** Obligobuch n; **~ under rebate** (GB) vor Fälligkeit bezahltes Akzept; **accommodation** ~ Gefälligkeitsakzept n; **against** ~ gegen Annahme; **anticipated** ~ vor Fälligkeit bezahltes Akzept; **bank** ~ Bankakzept n, Bankwechsel m; **bill out for** ~ zur Annahme geschickter Wechsel; **blank** ~ Blankoakzept n, Blankoannahme f; **clean** ~ bedingungsloses Akzept, reines Akzept, vorbehaltloses Akzept; **commercial ~ credit** Warenrembourskredit m; **commission for** ~ Akzeptprovision f; **conditional** ~ bedingtes Akzept, bedingte Annahme; **cross** ~ Wechselreiterei f; **decline** ~ Annahme verweigern; **documentary ~ credit** dokumentärer Akzeptkredit, Rembours m; **documents against** ~ Dokumente gegen Akzept; **partial** ~ Teilakzept n; **provide a bill with** ~ Wechsel mit Akzept versehen; **qualified** ~ bedingtes Akzept, bedingte Annahme; **rebated** ~ (US) vor Fälligkeit bezahltes Akzept; **trade** ~ Handelsakzept n, Kundenakzept n, Warenakzept n

accepted adj akzeptiert adj, mit Akzept versehen

acceptilation n Erlaß einer geringfügigen Schuld, Schulderlaß m

accepting commission Akzeptprovision f; **~ house** Akzeptbank f

acceptor n Akzeptant m; **~ for honour** Ehrenakzeptant m; **~ of a bill** Wechselakzeptant m; **bankrupt** ~ bankrotter Akzeptant

access to the capital market Zugang zum Kapitalmarkt

accession n Zuwachs m, Zustimmung f, Beitritt m; **~ of property** Vermögenszuwachs m

accident insurance Unfallversicherung f

accommodation n finanzielle Unterstützung, Gefallen m, Gefälligkeit f, Kulanz f; **~ acceptance** Gefälligkeitsakzept n; **~ bill** Gefälligkeitswechsel m, Finanzwechsel m, Kellerwechsel m; **~ draft** Gefälligkeitstratte f; **~ endorsement** Gefälligkeitsdossament n; **~ endorsement loan** Kredit gegen Wechselbürgschaft; **~ loan** Überbrückungskredit m; **~ maker** Gefälligkeitsaussteller m; **~ note** Gefälligkeitswechsel m, Finanzwechsel m, Kellerwechsel m; **~ paper** Gefälligkeitspapier n; **credit ~** Kreditgewährung f

accomodate v gefällig sein; **~ with money** Geld ausleihen

accompanying documents Begleitpapiere n pl

accord a commission eine Provision gewähren; **~ a respite in payment** eine Zahlung stunden

according to nach, laut, gemäß

account v Rechnung ablegen; **~** n Konto n, Rechnung f (Bank), Kontobestätigung f; **~ analysis** Kontoanalyse f, Kontountersuchung f; **~ book** Kontobuch n; **~ card** Kontokarte f; **~ carried forward** Vortrag auf neue Rechnung, Saldovortrag m, Vortragssaldo m; **~ classification** Kontenaufgliederung f; **~ close** Kontoschließung f; **~ current creditors** Kreditoren in laufender Rechnung; **~ day** (GB) Lieferungstag m (Börse), Zahltag m; **~ deposits** Kontoguthaben n pl; **~ files** Kontounterlagen f pl; **~ form** Kontoblatt n; **~ holder** Kontoinhaber m; **~ in bank** Bankkonto n; **~ ledger sheet** Kontoblatt n; **~ maintenance charge**

account

Kontoführungsgebühr f (US); ~ **manager** Kontoführer m; ~ **mandate** Kontovollmacht f; ~ **move** Kontenbewegung f; ~ **number** Kontonummer f; ~ **numbering system** Kontonummernsystem n; ~ **of charges** Spesenkonto n, Unkostenkonto n; ~ **of exchange** Wechselkonto n; ~ **of expenses** Spesenkonto n, Unkostenkonto n; ~ **of payee** für Rechnung des Remittenten (Kreuzung auf Schecks); ~ **of redraft** Rückwechselkonto n; ~ **of settlement** Abschlußrechnung f, Schlußabrechnung f; ~ **opening** Kontoeröffnung f; ~ **payee only** nur zur Verrechnung; ~ **settled** bezahlte Rechnung; ~ **statement** Bankkontoauszug m; ~ **subject to notice** Kündigungskonto n; ~ **title** Kontobezeichnung f; ~ **turnover** Kontoumsatz m; **absorption** ~ Wertberichtigungskonto n; **abstract of** ~ Kontoauszug m, Rechnungsauszug m; **acceptance** ~ Akzeptkonto n; **active** ~ umsatzstarkes Konto; **adjunct** ~ Hilfskonto n; **adjustment** ~ Berichtigungskonto n; **advance** ~ Vorschußkonto n; **agency** ~ Filialkonto n; **agio** ~ Aufgeldkonto n; **alimentation of an** ~ Dotierung eines Kontos; **appropriation** ~ Bereitstellungsfonds m, Rückstellungskonto n, Konto, aus dem die Reingewinnverwendung ersichtlich ist; **approval of** ~ Kontoanerkennung f; **assets** ~ Bestandskonto n; **assigned** ~ abgetretenes Konto (US), Garantiekonto n; **assignment of** ~ Kontoabtretung f; **assignment of** ~ **receivable** Forderungsabtretung f; **attached** ~ (US) blockiertes Konto; **aval** ~ Avalrechnung f; **balance** ~ Ausgleichskonto n; **balance an** ~ Konto abschließen, saldieren v (Konto); **bank** ~ Bankkonto n; **bank premises** ~ Grundstückskonto n (einer Bank); **bear** ~ Baisseposition f; **bill** ~ Wechselrechnung f; **blocked** ~ blockiertes Konto, eingefrorenes Konto, gesperrtes Konto, Sperrkonto n; **blocking of** ~ Kontensperre f; **bonds** ~ Aberdepot n; **bonus** ~ Prämienkonto n; **branch** ~ Filialkonto n; **broken** ~ umsatzloses Konto,

unbewegtes Konto, totes Konto; **budgetary** ~ Haushaltskonto n; **building** ~ Gebäudekonto n; **bull** ~ Hausseposition f; **business** ~ Geschäftskonto n; **capital** ~ Kapitalkonto n; **carriage** ~ Frachtkonto n; **cash** ~ Kassenkonto n, Kassakonto n, Kassekonto n; **cashier's** ~ Kassenkonto n, Kassakonto n, Kassekonto n; **certificate of** ~ (US) Bestätigung vom Buchprüfer; **change of** ~ Kontoänderung f; **charge** ~ Kundenkonto n; **charge an** ~ ein Konto belasten; **Christmas Club** ~ (US) Sparkonto für Weihnachtseinkäufe; **clearing** ~ Verrechnungskonto n; **clearing of an** ~ Kontoglattstellung f; **collection** ~ Inkassokonto n; **commercial** ~ Geschäftskonto n; **commission** ~ Provisionskonto n; **community** ~ Gemeinschaftskonto n; **compensation** ~ Ausgleichskonto n; **consignment** ~ Kommissionskonto n; **contingent** ~ (GB) Reservekonto n, Reservefonds für unvorhergesehene Verluste; **continuing** ~ Kontokorrentkonto n; **contra** ~ Gegenkonto n; **control** ~ Kontrollkonto n, Hauptbuchsammelkonto n; **controlling** ~ Kontrollkonto n, Hauptbuchsammelkonto n; **counter** ~ Gegenkonto n; **credit** ~ kreditarisches Konto, laufendes Konto mit Kreditsaldo; **credit an** ~ ein Konto erkennen; **creditor** ~ Guthabenkonto n; **current** ~ Kontokorrentkonto n, laufendes Konto, Konto in laufender Rechnung, offenes Konto; **custodian** ~ Depot n; **custodianship** ~ Depot n (bei Bank), Depotkonto n; **dead** ~ umsatzloses Konto, unbewegtes Konto, totes Konto; **del credere** ~ Delkrederekonto n; **deposit** ~ (US) Einlegerkonto n, Despositenkonto n, Festgeldkonto n, Sparkonto n; **discharge an** ~ ein Konto ausgleichen; **dividend on** ~ Abschlagsdividende f, Zwischendividende f, Interimsdividende f; **dormant** ~ umsatzloses Konto, unbewegtes Konto, totes Konto; **earmarked** ~ zweckbestimmtes Konto; **earned surplus** ~ aus Reingewinn gebildete Reserven; **extract of** ~ Kontoauszug m, Rechnungsauszug m; **for**

accountancy

your ~ and at your risk für Ihre Rechnung und Gefahr; **foreign currency** ~ Währungskonto n, Valutakonto n; **frozen** ~ blockiertes Konto, eingefrorenes Konto, gesperrtes Konto, Sperrkonto n; **giro** ~ Girokonto n; **inoperative** ~ umsatzloses Konto, unbewegtes Konto, totes Konto (GB); **keep an** ~ Konto unterhalten; **on** ~ **of** für Rechnung von; **open** ~ Kontokorrentkonto n, laufendes Konto, Konto in laufender Rechnung, offenes Konto; **public** ~ (GB) Staatskonto n; **revenue** ~ Gewinn- und-Verlust-Konto n; **semiannual** ~ halbjährlicher Kontoauszug

accountancy n Buchführung f, Buchhaltung f, Rechnungswesen n; ~ **office** Buchungsstelle f

accountant n Buchhalter m, Buchführer m; **bank** ~ Bankbuchhalter m; **chartered** ~ Wirtschaftsprüfer m, Buchprüfer m, Rechnungsprüfer m, Revisor m; **chief** ~ Hauptbuchhalter m; **public** ~ Bücherrevisor m, Wirtschaftsprüfer m, Buchprüfer m, Rechnungsprüfer m, Revisor m

accountant's certificate Prüfungsvermerk m

account-holding bank kontoführende Bank

accounting n Buchführung f, Buchhaltung f, Rechnungswesen n; ~ **axioms** Bilanzierungsgrundsätze m pl, Bilanzierungsrichtlinien f pl; ~ **department** Buchhaltungsabteilung f; ~ **expert** Bilanzexperte m; ~ **machine** Buchungsmaschine f; ~ **method** Buchführungsmethode f; ~ **period** Bilanzierungsperiode f; ~ **policy** Bilanzpolitik f; ~ **practitioner** Bilanzexperte m; ~ **principles** Bilanzierungsgrundsätze m pl, Bilanzierungsrichtlinien f pl; ~ **process** Buchführungsvorgang m; ~ **records** Buchführungsunterlagen f pl, Buchführungsbelege m pl; ~ **statement** Rechnungsaufstellung f; ~ **supervisor** Buchhaltungschef m; ~ **system** Buchhaltungssystem n; ~ **transaction** Buchhaltungsvorgang m; ~ **value** Buchwert m; ~ **voucher** Buchungsbeleg m, Buchhaltungsbeleg m; ~ **year** Geschäftsjahr n; **action for** ~ Klage auf Rechnungslegung; **bank** ~ Bankbuchhaltung f; **budgetary** ~ Finanzplanung f

account-only check Verrechnungscheck m

accounts closing day Buchungsschnitt m; ~ **opened and closed book** (US) Kontenverzeichnis n; ~ **payable** Kreditoren m pl (aus Buchlieferantenschulden); ~ **receivable** Außenstände m pl, ausstehende Forderungen, Debitoren m pl, Buchforderungen f pl; ~ **receivable financing** Finanzierung durch Abtretung der Debitoren; ~ **receivable loan** Debitorenkredit m; ~ **receivable statement** Debitorenaufstellung f; ~ **with creditors** Gläubigerkonten n pl; ~ **with customers** Kundenkonten n pl; **activity of** ~ Kontenbewegung f; **adjust** ~ Konten bereinigen; **age** ~ Konten nach Ihrer Fälligkeit aufgliedern; **agree** ~ Konten abstimmen; **audit the** ~ Bücher überprüfen; **balance of** ~ Bilanz f, Rechnungsabschluß m, Kontenabschluß m; **balancing of** ~ Konto- oder Bücherabschluß, Rechnungsabschluß m, Bilanzierung f; **book of** ~ Kontobuch n; **borrowing on** ~ **receivable** Kreditaufnahme durch Abtretung von Debitoren; **checking of** ~ Buchprüfung f, Bilanzprüfung f, Bücherrevision f, Rechnungsprüfung f, Revision f; **cooked** ~ frisierte Bücher, verschleierte Bücher; **cooking of** ~ Bücherfälschung f; **Kontofälschung f; **dissection of** ~ Kontenaufgliederung f; **overextended** ~ (US) nicht genügend gedeckte Konten; **systematic chart of** ~ Kontenrahmen m; **systematic schedule of** ~ Kontenrahmen m

accredit v akkreditieren v, gutschreiben v, beglaubigen v

accreditee n Akkreditierte f u. m, Akkreditivinhaber m

accrete den Wert steigern

accretion n Zuwachs m, Wertsteigerung f

accrual n Auflaufen n, Zuwachs m, Zugang m (Bilanz); ~ **date** Verfalltag m, Fälligkeitstermin m, Fälligkeitstag m; ~ **of dividends** Dividendenanfall m

accrue v auflaufen v, entstehen v

accrued adj aufgelaufen adj, angewachsen adj; **~ charges** aufgelaufene Kosten; **~ depreciation** Abschreibungsreserve f, Abschreibungsfonds m, Abschreibungsrücklage f; **~ expenses** antizipative Posten (auf der Passivseite), Rechnungsabgrenzungsposten m pl; **~ income** antizipative Posten (auf der Aktivseite), Rechnungsabgrenzungsposten m pl; **~ interest** (on securities) Stückzinsen m pl; **~ liabilities** transitorische Passiva; **~ rents** Mietrückstände m pl

accumulate v anhäufen v, ansammeln v, auflaufen v

accumulated adjustment register akkumulierte Nachtragliste; **~ credit activity** akkumulierte Habenumsätze; **~ debit activity** akkumulierte Sollumsätze; **~ surplus** Gewinnvortrag m

accumulation n Akkumulierung f, Anhäufung f, Ansammlung f, Auflaufen n; **~ of reserves** Reservebildung f; **~ of savings** Spareinlagenbildung f; **~ schedule** Kapitalbildungsplan m

accustomed; average ~ Havarie nach Seebrauch

achieve v erlangen v, erzielen v

acid-test ratio Liquiditätsgrad m, Liquiditätsverhältnis n

acknowledge v anerkennen v, quittieren v, beurkunden v, notariell beglaubigen, bescheinigen v, bestätigen v (Empfang); **~ receipt** den Empfang bestätigen

acknowledgement n Anerkenntnis f, Empfangsbescheinigung f, urkundliche Anerkennung, notarielle Beglaubigung, Bestätigung f (Empfang); **~ of debt** Schuldanerkenntnis f; **~ of receipt** Empfangsbescheinigung f, Quittung f; Empfangsbestätigung f

acquire v erwerben v, erlangen v, beschaffen v

acquired rights wohlerworbene Rechte

acquirer n Erwerber m

acquisition n (of data) Erfassung f (von Daten); **~** n Erwerbung f, Erwerb m, Ankauf m, Anschaffung f; **~ of property** Eigentumserwerb m; **~ value** Anschaffungswert m, Erwerbswert m

acquisitive adj; erwerbstüchtig adj, auf Erwerb gerichtet; **~ company** übernehmende Gesellschaft f

acquit v entlasten v (von Verbindlichkeiten)

acquittance n Quittung f, Schulderlaß m, Entlastung f

ACT = advance corporation tax Körperschaftsteuervorrauszahlung f

act v handeln v (tätig sein), fungieren v, auftreten v, dienen v; **~** n Akte f, Gesetz n, Handlung f, Urkunde f; **~ of bankruptcy** Konkursordnung f, Konkursvergehen n; **~ of God** höhere Gewalt; **~ of honour** Ehreneintritt m, Intervention f; **~ of protest** Protesterhebung f, Protesturkunde f; **~ of transfer** Abtretungserklärung f; **bankruptcy ~** Konkursgrund m, Konkurshandlung f

acting adj stellvertretend adj, tätig adj, verantwortlich adj, geschäftsführend adj; **~ partner** geschäftsführender Gesellschafter, geschäftsführender Teilhaber

action n (at law) Rechtsstreit m, Prozeß m; **~** n Tätigkeit f, Handlung f; **~ for accounting** Klage auf Rechnungslegung; **~ for damages** Schadenersatzklage f; **~ for payment** Klage auf Zahlung; **~ on a bill of exchange** Wechselklage f; **administrative ~** Verwaltungsakt m, Verwaltungsmaßnahme f; **bankruptcy ~** Konkursverfahren n

actionable adj klagbar adj, prozeßfähig adj

active adj aktiv adj, tätig adj, rührig adj, lebhaft adj; **~ account** umsatzstarkes Konto; **~ balance** Aktivsaldo m (Handelsbilanz); **~ bonds** (GB) festverzinsliche Obligationen; **~ capital** flüssiges Kapital, arbeitendes Kapital; **~ circulation** (GB) Banknotenumlauf m; **~ debts** Außenstände m pl, ausstehende Forderungen, Debitoren m pl, Buchforderungen f pl; **~ partner** Komplementär f, persönlich haftender Gesellschafter; **~ securities** täglich an der Börse gehandelte Wertpapiere; **~ side** Aktivseite f; **~ stock** gängige Aktie; **~ trade balance** aktive Handelsbilanz

activity

activity n Tätigkeit f (Aufgabengebiet); **~ charge** Bankgebühren f pl, Bankspesen pl/t; **~ of accounts** Kontenbewegung f, Bankspesen pl/t; **banking ~** Banktätigkeit f; **business ~** Geschäftsverkehr m

acts; customs ~ Zollverordnungen f pl

actual adj effektiv adj, tatsächlich adj wirklich adj; **~ amount** Ist-Bestand m, Effektivbestand m; **~ assets** Reinvermögen n; **~ balance** effektiver Saldo; **~ costs** Selbstkosten pl/t, Gestehungskosten pl/t; **~ market value** Marktwert m; **~ price** Marktpreis m; **~ profit** echter Gewinn; **~ value** effektiver Wert

actuarial adj versicherungsmathematisch adj, versicherungstechnisch adj, versicherungsstatistisch adj;

actuary n Versicherungsmathematiker m

ACU = Asian Currency Unit Asiatische Währungseinheit f

acumen; business ~ Geschäftssinn m

acute liquidity shortage Liquiditätsmangel m

ad n Anzeige f (Werbung), Annonce f, Inserat n; **~ man** Werbefachmann m; **~ valorem** dem Werte nach; **~ valorem duty** Wertzoll m

adapted adj angepaßt adj, bereinigt adj

add v addieren v, hinzurechnen v, hinzuzählen v, vergrößern v; **~ on interest** aufzinsen v; **~ up** zusammenrechnen v, addieren v, aufrechnen v

addendum n Anhang m, Allonge f, Verlängerungsstück n

adding machine Addiermaschine f

addition n Addition f, Zusammenrechnung f; **~ n** Zugang m (Bilanz); **in ~ to** zusätzlich

additional adj zuzüglich adj, zusätzlich adj; **~ charges** zusätzliche Kosten, Mehrkosten pl/t; **~ fee** Gebührenzuschlag m; **~ insurance** Nachversicherung f; **~ payment** Nachzahlung f; **call for ~ cover** Nachschußzahlung fordern

address v adressieren v; **~ n** Adresse f, Anschrift f, Ansprache f, Anrede f; **~ file** Adreßdatei f; **~ in case of need** Notadresse f; **~ tape** Adreßdatei f

addressed bill Domizilwechsel m

addressee n Empfänger m, Adressat m

addresser n Aussteller m, Adressant m

addressing n Adressierung f; **~ method** Adressierungsverfahren n; **~ technique** Adressierungsverfahren n

addressograph n Adrema f, Adressiermaschine f

adds and outs Ein- und Ausgänge

adhesive stamp Stempelmarke f

adjourn a meeting eine Versammlung vertagen

adjournable adj aufschiebbar adj, hinausschiebbar adj

adjudication of bankruptcy Konkurseröffnung f

adjunct account Hilfskonto n

adjust v ausgleichen v, angleichen v, anpassen v, regulieren v, abwickeln v, beilegen v, schlichten v; **~ accounts** Konten bereinigen

adjustable rate peferred stock Vorzugsaktie mit variabler Dividende

adjustable-contribution procedure Umlageverfahren n, Kapitaldeckungsverfahren n

adjusted for inflation inflationsbereinigt adj

adjuster n Schadenssachverständiger

adjuster; average ~ Dispacheur m, Havarievertreter m, Havarieagent m; **claim ~** Schadenschätzer m, Schadenregulierer m

adjusting journal entry Berichtigungsbuchung f

adjustment n Ausgleichung f, Angleichung f, Regulierung f, Richtigstellung f, Berichtigung f (Werte, Preise), Abwicklung f, Beilegung f, Sanierung f, Schlichtung f; **~ account** Berichtigungskonto n; **~ bond** Sanierungsanleihe f; **~ entry** Berichtigungseintragung f; **~ income bond** (US) Schuldverschreibung mit Zinsen auf Einkommensbasis; **~ of capital** Kapitalberichtigung f; **~ of claims** Schadensfestsetzung f; **~ of interest** Zinsausgleich m; **accumulated ~ register** akkumulierte Nachtragsliste

administer v verwalten v, als Nachlaßverwalter tätig sein, handhaben v, regulieren v

208

administration n Verwaltung f; **- expenses** Verwaltungsaufwendungen f pl; **- of an estate** Nachlaßverwaltung f; **- of assets (property -)** Vermögensverwaltung f; **- of property** Vermögensverwaltung f; **business -** Betriebswirtschaft f, Betriebswirtschaftslehre f; **customs -** Zollverwaltung f

administrative adj Verwaltungs- (in Zus.); **- action** Verwaltungsakt m, Verwaltungsmaßnahme f; **- expenditures** Verwaltungskosten plt; **- law** Verwaltungsrecht n

administrator n Verwalter m, Kurator m, Sequester m, Nachlaßverwalter m, Nachlaßpfleger m, Testamentvollstrecker m (gerichtlich bestellt)

admission n Zulassung f, Aufnahme f; **- fee** Zulassungsgebühr f; **- of securities** Zulassung von Effekten zum Börsenhandel; **- tax** (US) Vergnügungssteuer f

admit v zulassen v, zugeben v, anerkennen v

ADR siehe **American depositary receipt**

adult n Volljährige, Mündige

advance v vorschießen v, bevorschussen v, steigen v, erhöhen v (sich); **-** n Vorschuß m, Kredit m, Darlehen n, Anzahlung f, Beförderung f, Aufschlag m, Überschuß m, Kursgewinn m; **- a claim** Anspruch erheben, Anspruch geltend machen; **- account** Vorschußkonto n; **- against documents** Dokumentenvorschuß m; **- bill** Vorschußwechsel m; **- commitment** Kreditzusage f; **- corporation tax = ACT** Körperschaftsteuervorrauszahlung f; **- credit** Vorauszahlungskredit m; **- funds** Vorschüsse zahlen, Mittel vorschießen; **- interest** Vorschußzins m; **- loan** Vorschaltdarlehen n; **- money** Geld vorstrecken; **- of salary** Gehaltsvorschuß m; **- on current account** Kontokorrentkredit m, offener Kredit; **- on wages** Lohnvorschuß m; **- payment** Vorauszahlung f, Vorkasse f; **- payment guarantee** Auszahlungsgarantie f; **- the price** Kurs heraufsetzen; **- the rate** Kurs heraufsetzen; **banker's -** Bankdarlehen n, Bankkredit m; **blank -** Blankokredit m, Blankovorschuß m; **cash -** Barvorschuß m; **collateral -** Lombardvorschuß m; **secured -** gedecktes Darlehen

advance-decline-index n Aufwärts-Abwärts-Index m, Index der Bewegungen des Aktienmarktes

advancement n Vorausempfang m (Erbrecht); **-** (US) Vorschuß m, Kredit m, Darlehen n, Anzahlung f, Beförderung f, Aufschlag m, Überschuß m, Kursgewinn m

advances against merchandise Warenlombard m; **- against securities** Effektenbeleihung f, Effektenlombard m, Effektenlombardkredit m; **- on securities** Effektenbeleihung f, Effektenlombard m, Effektenlombardkredit m

advancing market feste Börse

advantage n Vorteil m, Nutzen m, Gewinn m, Profit m

advantageous adj vorteilhaft adj, günstig adj, gewinnbringend adj

adventitious property Erbschaftsvermögen n

adventure n Risikogeschäft n, Spekulationsgeschäft n, Risiko n

adverse adj defizitär, ungünstig, nachteilig; **- balance** Unterbilanz f, Verlustsaldo m

advertise v werben v, annoncieren v, inserieren v, Werbung betreiben

advertisement n Anzeige f (Werbung), Annonce f, Inserat n; **joint -** Gemeinschaftswerbung f

advertiser n Werbungtreibende, Inserent m

advertising n Werbung f, Reklame f; **- agency** Werbeagentur f, Werbebüro n; **- budget** Werbeetat m; **- campaign** Werbefeldzug m; **- competition** Werbewettbewerb m; **- copy** Werbetext m; **- department** Werbeabteilung f; **- gift** Werbegeschenkartikel m; **- rates** Anzeigentarif m; **- research** Werbeforschung f; **- result** Werbeerfolg m; **- slogan** Werbeslogan m, Werbemotto n; **- success** Werbeerfolg m; **commercial -** Wirtschaftswerbung f

advise

advise v beraten v, anzeigen v, raten v, unterrichten v, informieren v; ~ n Bekanntmachung f (förmlich), Mitteilung f, Notifikation f, Benachrichtigung f; ~ n Ratschlag m; ~ **note** Buchungsanzeige f; ~ **of collection** Inkassoanzeige f; ~ **of deal** Ausführungsanzeige f; ~ **of dishonour** Protestanzeige f; **credit** ~ Gutschrift f, Gutschriftsanzeige f

advised; ill ~ schlecht beraten

adviser (advisor) n Berater m, Ratgeber m

advisory board Beirat m

aerospace issue Aktien der Raumfahrtindustrie

affairs; banking ~ Bankangelegenheiten f pl; **course of** ~ Geschäftsgang m; **trend of** ~ Geschäftsgang m

affect v sich auswirken auf, betreffen, beeinflussen

affidavit n eidesstattliche Erklärung, Affidavit n; ~ **of means** Offenbarungseid m

affiliate n Konzerngesellschaft f, Tochtergesellschaft f

affiliated company (GB) Konzerngesellschaft f, Tochtergesellschaft f; ~ **corporation** (US) Konzerngesellschaft f, Tochtergesellschaft f

affiliates n pl Konzernfirmen f pl

affluent adj wohlhabend adj, reich adj

affreight v chartern v, befrachten v

affreightment n Befrachtung f, Schifffrachtvertrag m

à-forfait paper Forfaitierungsmaterial n

after acceptance spätere Annahme; ~ **account** neue Rechnung; ~ **costs** nachträgliche Kosten; ~ **hours** nachbörslich adj; ~ **market** nachbörslich adj; ~ **price** nachträglicher Kurs; ~ **tax** nach Steuerabzug

after-date bill Datowechsel m

after-hours trading Nachbörse f

aftermarket n Nachbörse f

afternoon trade Nachmittagshandel m

after-sight bill Nachsichtwechsel m

against all risks gegen alle Risiken

age accounts Kosten nach ihrer Fälligkeit aufgliedern

agency n Agentur f, Vertretung f, Filiale f, Depositenkasse f, Geschäftsstelle f; ~ **account** Filialkonto n; ~ **draft** Inkassotratte f; ~ **report** (US) Kreditauskunfteibericht m; **advertising** ~ Werbeagentur f, Werbebüro n; **commercial** ~ (US) Auskunftei f; **contract of** ~ Vertretervertrag m; **credit** ~ Kreditvermittlungsbüro n, Kreditauskunftei f; **mercantile** ~ (US) Handelsauskunftei f

agenda n Tagesordnung f, Programm n

agent n Agent m, Vertreter m, Handelsagent m, Bevollmächtigte f u.m, Zwischenhändler m; ~ **of necessity** Geschäftsführer ohne Auftrag; **average** ~ Dispacheur m, Havarievertreter m, Havarieagent m; **bank** ~ Bankvertreter m; **claim** ~ Schadengutachter m, Schadenregulierer m; **closing** ~ Abschlußagent m; **escrow** ~ Treuhänder von hinterlegten Dokumenten; **mercantile** ~ Handelsvertreter m

agent's authority Vertretungsbefugnis f; ~ **commission** Vertreterprovision f

aggregate v sich belaufen, im ganzen betragen; ~ **amount** Gesamtsumme f; ~ **face value** Gesamtnennwert m; ~ **loan facility** Gesamtkredit m

aging schedule Debitorenliste nach Fälligkeit

agio n Agio n, Aufgeld n; ~ **account** Aufgeldkonto n; **bank** ~ Bankprovision f

agiotage n Agiotage f, Börsenspiel n, Wechselgeschäft n, Aktienspekulation f

agree v übereinstimmen v, abmachen v, vereinbaren v, zustimmen v, einwilligen v; ~ **accounts** Konten abstimmen; ~ **the books** Bücher abstimmen

agreed price vereinbarter Preis

agreement n Abkommen n, Übereinstimmung f, Abmachung f, Vereinbarung f, Vertrag m, Zustimmung f, Einwilligung f; ~ **country** Verrechnungsland n; ~ **for sale** Verkaufsvertrag m; ~ **of consolidation** Fusionsvertrag m; ~ **of interests** Interessenabstimmung f; **area** ~ Bereichsabkommen n; **articles of** ~ Vertragspunkte m pl, Vertragsbestimmungen f pl (schriftlich); **basis of** ~ Vertragsgrundlage f; **binding** ~ unwiderrufliches Abkommen; **cartel** ~

210

Kartellvertrag m; **clearing** ~ Verrechnungsabkommen n; **compensation** ~ Kompensationsabkommen n; **composition** ~ Vergleichsvertrag m; **continuing** ~ (US) Kreditvertrag mit gleichbleibenden Sicherheiten; **credit** ~ Kreditabkommen n; **trade** ~ Handelsabkommen n, Handelsvertrag m; **underwriting** ~ Konsortialvertrag m
agricultural bank Landwirtschaftsbank f; ~ **cooperative credit society** (GB) Raiffeisenkasse f; ~ **loan** Landwirtschaftskredit m, landwirtschaftliches Darlehen, Agrarkredit m
AIBOR = Amsterdam Interbank Offered Rate Amsterdamer Interbanken-Angebotszinssatz
aid fund Unterstützungsfonds m, Hilfsfonds m, Unterstützungskasse f
air cargo Luftfracht f; ~ **cargo carrier** Luftfrachtgesellschaft f; ~ **carriage** Luftfracht f; ~ **freight** Luftfracht f; ~ **receipt** Lufttransportbescheinigung f
aircraft n Flugzeug n; ~ **mortgage** Flugzeughypothek f
aircrafts n pl (stock exchange) Luftfahrtwerte m pl, Flugzeugwerte m pl (Börse)
airline n Luftverkehrsgesellschaft f, Fluglinie f
airliner n Verkehrsflugzeug n
airmail n Luftpost f, Flugpost f; ~ **transfer** Auslandszahlungsauftrag m
airport n Flughafen m
airway bill Luftfrachtbrief m
alien n Ausländer m, Fremde f u. m; ~ adj ausländisch adj; ~ **corporation** (US) ausländische Gesellschaft; ~ **property** Ausländervermögen n
alienability n Veräußerlichkeit f, Übertragbarkeit f, Abtretbarkeit f
alienable adj (of property) veräußerlich adj, übertragbar adj, abtretbar adj
alienate v veräußern v (meist Grundbesitz), übertragen v, abtreten v; ~ **capital** Kapital abziehen; ~ **customers** Kunden abwerben
alienation n Veräußerung f, Übertragung f; ~ **of capital** Kapitalabzug m
alienator n Veräußerer m
alienee n Erwerber m

alimentation of an account Dotierung eines Kontos
All Ordinaries Index Preisindex an der australischen Börse
allied company Konzerngesellschaft f, Schwestergesellschaft f; ~ **industries** verwandte Industrien
all-in costs Gesamtkosten plt
all-loss insurance Gesamtschadensversicherung f, Globalversicherung f
all-money debenture Gesamtsicherungspfandrecht n
allocable adj aufteilbar adj
allocate v zuwenden v, zuschlagen v, zuweisen v, zuteilen v; ~ **shares to all applicants** Aktien voll zuteilen
allocated account Einzelkonto n, Streifbandverwahrung f
allocation n Zuweisung f, Zuteilung f, Verteilung f, Repartierung f, Lieferung f, Zuschlag m; ~ **committee** Zuteilungsausschuß m; ~ **of currency** Devisenzuteilung f; ~ **of funds** Geldbewilligung f; ~ **of shares** Aktienzuteilung f; ~ **scheme** Zuteilungsplan m; ~ **system** Bewirtschaftungssystem n
allodial adj zinsfrei adj, erbeigen adj
allodium n Erbgut n
allonge Anhang m, Allonge f
all-or-none underwriting (US) Emission f, die bei fehlender Vollplazierung eingestellt wird
allot v zuweisen v, zuteilen v, verteilen v, repartieren v, quotieren v, liefern v
allotment n Zuweisung f, Zuteilung f, Verteilung f, Repartierung f, Lieferung f, Zuschlag m; ~ **certificate** (US) Zuteilungsanzeige f, Zuteilungsschein m, Bezugsrechtzuteilung f; ~ **letter** (GB) Zuteilungsanzeige f, Zuteilungsschein m, Bezugsrechtzuteilung f; ~ **money** Zuteilungsbetrag m; ~ **rate** Zuteilungskurs m; ~ **sheet** Aktienzeichnungsliste f; ~ **system** Zuteilungsverfahren n; **application for** ~ **of shares** Zeichnung von Aktien, Antrag auf Zuteilung von Aktien
allotted adj zugeteilt adj
allottee n Bezugsberechtigte f u. m, Zeichner m

allow

allow v erlauben v, gestatten v, gewähren v, zulassen v, bewilligen v, anrechnen v, einräumen v; *- a bill to be protested* Wechsel zu Protest gehen lassen; *- a credit* Kredit einräumen, Kredit gewähren; *- a discount* Diskont einräumen, Nachlaß gewähren; *- for sums paid in advance* Anzahlungen verrechnen

allowable adj zulässig adj, statthaft adj, abziehbar adj

allowance n Bewilligung f, Zuschuß m, Vergütung f, Entschädigung f, Abzug m, Nachlaß m, Rabatt m, Zuteilung f, Deputat n, Steuerfreibetrag m; *- for bad debts* Dubiosenrückstellung f; *- for depreciation* Abschreibungsreserve f, Abschreibungsfonds m, Abschreibungsrücklage f; *- for wear and tear* Absetzung für Abnutzung; *- in money* Geldzuweisung f; **trade** *-* Warenskonto n, Großhandelsrabatt m, Rabatt für Wiederverkäufer

alloy n Legierung f, Feingehalt m, Münzzusatz m

all-risk cover volle Deckung f; *- insurance* Gesamtrisikenversicherung f, Globalversicherung f

All-Share Index Aktienindex der Financial Times m

all-time high Höchstkurs m; *- low* Niedrigstkurs m

alpha securities umsatzstärkste Werte (London Stock Exchange)

alpine bonds USD-Anleihe für schweizer Anleger

alteration n Änderung f, Veränderung f, Abänderung f; *- of checks* Scheckfälschung f

alternate deposit Gemeinschaftsdepot (wobei jeder einzelne verfügungsberechtigt ist)

alternative drawee Alternativbezogene f u. m; *- obligation* Alternativverpflichtung f; *- payee* Alternativbegünstigte f u. m

amalgamation n Verschmelzung f, Zusammenschluß m, Fusion f

amendment n Änderung f, Ergänzung f; *- of stock laws* Aktienrechtsreform f

American Bankers Association (US) Amerikanische Banken- und Bankiervereinigung; *- Depository Receipt = ADR* ADR m, Zertifikat einer US-Bank für hinterlegte ausländische Aktien; *- market* (GB) Markt für amerikanische Werte; *- option* Amerikanische Option f (jederzeit ausübbare Option); *- rails* (GB) amerikanische Eisenbahnwerte; *- Stock Exchange (NYSE)* Größte US-Börse nach der New York Stock Exchange; **sponsored** *- level-I* US-Freiverkehrswert, dessen US-Emittent durch die AG bestimmt wird; **sponsored** *- level-II/III* NYSE notierter ADR, bei der die ausländische AG die US-Bilanzierungsrichtlinien unter SEC-Kontrolle erfüllt; **unsponsored** *-* US-Freiverkehrswert, dessen US-Emittent ohne Information und Unterstützung der ausländischen AG emittiert

amicable adj freundschaftlich adj, außergerichtlich adj

amortizable adj amortisierbar adj

amortization n Amortisation f, Tilgung f, Schuldentilgung f, Abschreibung f; *- and depreciation of intangible and tangible fixed assets* Abschreibungen und Wertberichtigungen auf immaterielle Anlagewerte und Sachanlagen (Bilanzposten); *- charges* Abschreibungslasten f pl; *- fund* Tilgungsstock m; *- instalment* Amortisationsquote f; *- mortgage* Amortisationshypothek f; *- of a loan* Anleihetilgung f; *- of interest* Zinskapitalisierung f; *- payment* Amortisationszahlung f, Tilgungsleistung f; *- rate* Tilgungsrate f; *- reserve* Rückstellung für Amortisationen; *- schedule* Tilgungsplan m

amortize v amortisieren v, tilgen v, abschreiben v

amortized cost Kosten nach Abschreibungen; *- mortgage* Tilgungshypothek f

amount n Betrag m, Summe f; *- in cash* Kassenbestand m, Bargeld n; *- of assets* Vermögenshöhe f, Vermögensbetrag m; *- of capital* Kapitalhöhe f,

Kapitalbetrag m; **~ of compensation** Abfindungssumme f; **~ of depreciation earned** verdiente Abschreibungen; **~ of income** Einkommensbetrag m; **~ of interest** Zinshöhe f; **~ of premium** Prämienhöhe f; **~ of redemption** Ablösesumme f; **~ of risk** Risikobetrag m; **~ of stock** Kapitalanteil m; **~ of the documentary credit** Akkreditivbetrag m; **~ of the debt** Schuldsumme f; **~ overdrawn** Überziehungsbetrag m; **~ overdue** überfälliger Betrag; **~ to** betragen v, (sich) belaufen auf; **actual ~** Istbestand m; Effektivbestand m; **bond ~** Anleihebetrag m; **clear ~** Nettobetrag m, Reinbetrag m

amounts transferred to other earnings reserves Einstellungen in andere Gewinnrücklagen (Bilanzposten)

ample security genügende Sicherheit

Amsterdam Interbank Offered Rate = AIBOR Amsterdamer Interbanken-Angebotszinssatz

Amsterdam Stock Exchange Amsterdamer Börse

amusement tax Vergnügungssteuer f

analog computer Analogrechner m

analyse v analysieren v

analysis n Aufgliederung f, Analyse f; **~ department** Analysenabteilung f, Finanzstudienabteilung f; **~ of cyclical trends** Konjunkturanalyse f; **~ sheet** Bilanzaufgliederungsbogen m; **account ~** Kontoanalyse f, Kontountersuchung f; **certificate of ~** Prüfungsbescheinigung f (für Waren)

analyst; business ~ Wirtschaftsanalytiker m

ancillary ergänzend, zusätzlich adv; **~ industry** Zulieferungsindustrie f; **~ letter of credit** Hilfskreditbrief m; **~ market** Nebenmarkt m; **~ papers** Beiakten f pl

annex n Anhang m; **~** n Anlage f, Beilage f

annexed adj anliegend adj, anhängend adj

announce v bekanntmachen v, ankündigen v, anzeigen v; **~ shares** Aktien auflegen

announcement n Bekanntmachung f, Ankündigung f, Anzeige f, Veröffentlichung f

annual n Jahrbuch n; **~** adj jährlich adj; **~ accounts** Jahresrechnung f; **~ balance sheet** Jahresbilanz f, Jahresabschluß m; **~ financial statement** Jahresabschluß m, Jahresrechnung f; **~ general meeting** Jahreshauptversammlung f; **~ income** Jahreseinkommen n; **~ instalment** Jahresrate f; **~ meeting** Hauptversammlung f, Generalversammlung f, Aktionärsversammlung f; **~ meeting of shareholders** (GB) ordentliche Hauptversammlung der Aktionäre; **~ meeting of stockholders** (US) ordentliche Hauptversammlung der Aktionäre; **~ output** Jahresproduktion f; **~ percentages** effektiver Jahreszins; **~ production** Jahresproduktion f; **~ report** Jahresbericht m; jährlicher Geschäftsbericht; **~ return** (GB) Jahresrendite f, jährlicher Geschäftsbericht; **~ sheet** Jahresbilanz f, Jahresabschluß m; **~ statement** Jahresausweis m; **~ turnover** Jahresumsatz m

annually adj jährlich adj

annuitant n Rentner m

annuities n pl Renten f pl, Jahreszinsen m pl

annuity n Annuität f, Rente f, Jahresrente f, Jahreszahlung f; **~ bond** Rententitel m, Rentenschuldverschreibung f; **~ certificate** Rentenschein m; **~ coupon** Rentenschein m; **~ department** Rentenabteilung f; **~ option** Rentenwahlrecht n; **~ value** Rentenbarwert m, Rentenrückkaufswert m; **clear ~** steuerfreie Rente; **contract of ~** Leibrentenvertrag m, Rentenvertrag m; **deferred ~** hinausgeschobene Annuität; **immediate ~** sofort fällige Rente; **life ~** lebenslängliche Rente, Lebensrente f, Leibrente f; **nonapportionable ~** Leibrente ohne Zahlung im Todesfall; **participating ~** Rente mit Gewinnbeteiligung; **perpetual ~** lebenslängliche Rente, Lebensrente f, Leibrente f

annul v annullieren v, aufheben v, widerrufen v, für nichtig erklären

annullable adj annullierbar adj, aufhebbar adj

annulment n Annullierung f, Aufhebung f, Abschaffung f

answer v antworten v, beantworten v, entgegnen v; ~ n Antwort f, Beantwortung f, Gegenerklärung f; **~ a bill of exchange** einen Wechsel einlösen, einen Wechsel honorieren; **~ for a debt** für eine Schuld einstehen

answerable adj haftbar adj, verantwortlich adj

answer-back Rückmeldung f

antedate v zurückdatieren v, nachdatieren v

antedated check nachdatierter Scheck

anti legislation Kartellgesetzgebung f

anti-capitalism n Antikapitalismus m

anti-capitalistic adj antikapitalistisch adj

antichresis n Antichrese f, Nutzungspfandrecht n

anticipate v vorwegnehmen v, erwarten v, im voraus bezahlen; **~ a bill** Wechsel vor Verfall einlösen; **~ salary** Vorschuß nehmen

anticipated *acceptance* vor Fälligkeit bezahltes Akzept; **~ *payment*** Vorauszahlung f, vor Fälligkeit geleistete Zahlung

anticipating payment Vorauszahlung f, vor Fälligkeit geleistete Zahlung

anticipation n Vorwegnahme f, Erwartung f, Vorauszahlung f, Abschlagszahlung f, Vorausdatierung f

anticipatory adj vorwegnehmend adj; **~ credit** Anzahlung (Vorschuß) für den Exporteur

anti-commercial adj wirtschaftsfeindlich adj

anti-inflationary adj inflationsfeindlich adj

anti-trust adj kartellfeindlich adj

apartment n (US) Etagenwohnung f; **~ block** Wohnblock m; **~ building** Mietshaus n; **~ house** Mietshaus n

APCS = Association of Payment Clearing Services Dachverband des Londoner Clearingsystems m

apparel manufactures Konfektionsindustrie f

appeal n Anziehungskraft f, Einspruch m, Berufung f

appear v erscheinen v, herauskommen v

appendix n Anhang m

applicant n Bewerber m, Stellenbewerber m, Anwärter m, Antragsteller m, Zeichner von Effekten; **credit ~** Kreditantragsteller m

application n Bewerbung f, Antrag m, Gesuch n, Anwendung f; **~ blank** Antragsformular n, Zeichnungsschein m; **~ for a mortgage** Hypothekenantrag m; **~ for allotment of shares** Zeichnung von Aktien, Antrag auf Zuteilung von Aktien; **~ for listing** (US) Antrag auf offizielle Einführung an der Börse, Antrag auf Börsenzulassung; **~ for payment** Zahlungsaufforderung f; **~ form** Antragsformular n, Zeichnungsschein m; **~ of proceeds** Verwendung des Gegenwertes; **business ~** Antrag auf Geschäftseröffnung

apply for beantragen v; **~ for payment** Zahlung beantragen, mahnen v

appoint v ernennen v, festsetzen v, bestellen v (Amt), berufen v (Amt)

appointee n Bestellte f u. m, Ernannte f u. m, Beauftragte f u. m

appointment n Verabredung f, Ernennung f, Anstellung f, Bestimmung f; **business ~** geschäftliche Verabredung, Geschäftssitzung f

apportion v zumessen v, repartieren v, verteilen v, zuteilen v

apportionable adj aufteilbar adj

apportionment n Aufteilung f, Zuteilung f, verhältnismäßige Aufteilung, Repartierung f

appraisable adj abschätzbar adj, taxierbar adj

appraisal n Schätzung f, Taxierung f; **cost of ~** Schätzungskosten plt; **staff ~** Personalbeurteilung f

appraise v abschätzen v, taxieren v, bewerten v

appraised value Schätzwert m, Taxwert m

appraisement n Wertbestimmung f, Schätzung f, Taxierung f, Taxwert m

appraiser n Schätzer m, Taxator m

appreciable adj nennenswert adj, spürbar adj

appreciate v bewerten v, schätzen v, im Werte steigen

appreciation n Wertschätzung f, Wertzuwachs m, Schätzung f; *- of real estate* Wertzuwachs eines Grundstücks; *- value* Wertsteigerung f; *capital -* Kapitalwerterhöhung f

appreciator n Schätzer m, Taxator m

apprentice n Lehrling m; *- training* Lehrlingsausbildung f

apprenticeship n Lehre f, Lehrzeit f

apprise v benachrichtigen v, in Kenntnis setzen

appropriate v aneignen v (sich), Besitz ergreifen, zuweisen v, bewilligen v, in Beschlag nehmen, verwenden v; *-* adj zugehörig adj, passend adj, zweckdienlich adj, sachdienlich adj

appropriation n Aneignung f, Inbesitznahme f, Zuweisung f, Verwendung f; *- account* Bereitstellungsfonds m, Rückstellungskonto n, Konto n (aus dem die Reingewinnverwendung ersichtlich ist); *- of funds* Geldzuweisung f; *- of net profit* (GB) Verwendung des Reingewinns; *- of payments* Zweckbestimmung von Zahlungen; *- of surplus* Reservebildung f

approval n Zustimmung f, Genehmigung f, Billigung f; *- of account* Kontoanerkennung f; *- of acts of directors* Entlastung des Vorstands; *- of profit and loss account* Genehmigung der Gewinn-und-Verlust-Rechnung; *- of the balance sheet* Genehmigung der Bilanz

approve v zustimmen v, genehmigen v, billigen v

approved adj anerkannt adj bewährt adj; *- securities* lombardfähige Wertpapiere f pl (GB)

approximate *value* Annäherungswert m; *- price* Zirkakurs m

approximate-limit order Zirkaauftrag m

approximation n Annäherung f, Näherung f

appurtenance lien Zubehörpfandrecht n

apron n Talon m, Erneuerungsschein m, Allonge f

APTS = automated pit trading system elektronisches Handelssystem der London International Financial Futures Exchange (LIFFE)

arbiter n Schiedsrichter m, Schlichter m

arbitrable adj schiedsgerichtsfähig adj

arbitrage v schlichten v, durch Schiedsspruch entscheiden; *- n* Arbitrage f, schiedsgerichtliche Entscheidung, Schiedsverfahren n

arbitrager n Arbitrageur m

arbitragist n Arbitrageur m

arbitral adj schiedsgerichtlich adj

arbitrary adj willkürlich adj, schiedsgerichtlich adj

arbitration n Arbitrage f, schiedsgerichtliche Entscheidung, Schiedsverfahren n; *board of -* Schlichtungsausschuß m

arbitrational adj schiedsgerichtlich adj

arbitrator n Schiedsrichter m, Schlichter m

arbitratorship n Schiedsrichteramt n

archives n pl Archiv n

area n Bereich m (Gebiet); *- agreement* Bereichsabkommen n; *- of speciality* Sachgebiet n; *built-up -* bebautes Gebiet; *currency -* Währungsgebiet n

armament *industry* Rüstungsindustrie f; *- order* Rüstungsauftrag m; *- securities* Rüstungswerte m pl (Börse)

armchair decision Entscheidung am grünen Tisch

arrange v arrangieren v, anordnen v (ordnen), regeln v, erledigen v, schlichten v

arrangement n, Anordnung f (Ordnung), Regelung f, Erledigung f, Schlichtung f; *- fee* Bereitstellungsprovision f, Vermittlungsgebühr f; *- in bankruptcy* Zwangsvergleich m; *- with creditors* Gläubigerausgleich m; *blocking -* Stillhalteabkommen n; *contractual -* vertragliche Vereinbarung; *credit -* Kreditvereinbarung f; *credit sales -* Abzahlungsvertrag m; *deed of -* Vergleichsurkunde f, Vergleichsvertrag m

arrearage n Restsumme f, unbezahlter Restbetrag, Rückstand m

arrears n Zahlungsrückstände m pl; *- of interest* Zinsrückstände m pl; *- of payment* Zahlungsrückstände m pl, *interest on -* n Verzugszinsen m pl

arrest n Arrest m, Pfändung f, Beschlagnahme f

arrestee n Pfandschuldner m

arrester n Pfandgläubiger m

arrestment n Pfändung f, Beschlagnahme f, Arrest m

article n Artikel m, Ware f, Posten m, Gegenstand m; **branded ~** Markenartikel m

articles of agreement Vertragspunkte m pl, Vertragsbestimmungen f pl (schriftlich); **~ of association** (GB) Satzung f (einer Gesellschaft), Statut n, Statuten n pl; **~ of incorporation** (US) Gründungsvertrag m (einer Gesellschaft)

artificial adj künstlich adj; **~ person** juristische Person

as if and when per Erscheinen (der Wertpapiere)

ascending order aufsteigende Reihenfolge; **~ sequence** aufsteigende Reihenfolge

ascertain v feststellen v, ermitteln v; **~ interest** Zinsen errechnen

ascertainment of loss Schadenfeststellung f

Asian Currency Unit = ACU Asiatische Währungseinheit f; **~ dollar** Asien-Dollar m

asked adj angeboten adj (Börse), geforderter Preis (Börse), Brief m (Börse); **~ price** Briefkurs m; **~ quotation** Briefkurs m

asking price geforderter Preis m

assemble v versammeln v (sich), einberufen v, zusammenrufen v, vorladen v

assembly n Versammlung f

assent v zustimmen v, einwilligen v; **~ n** Zustimmung f, Einwilligung f

assented securities im Sammeldepot hinterlegte Wertpapiere

assess v steuerlich veranlagen, besteuern v, belasten v, bewerten v, abschätzen v, taxieren v; **~ a building** Gebäude abschätzen; **~ damages** Schaden feststellen, Entschädigungssumme bestimmen

assessable adj steuerbar adj, steuerpflichtig adj, schätzbar adj, taxierbar adj

assessed n Besteuerter f u. m; **~ adj** veranlagt adj; **~ value** Einheitswert m, Steuerwert m

assessment n Besteuerung f, Wertfeststellung f, Belastung f, Bewertung f, Schätzung f, Taxierung f; **~ company** Gegenseitigkeitsverein m; **~ costs** Veranlagungskosten plt; **~ period** Veranlagungsperiode f; **board of ~** Steuerbehörde f

assessor n Steuerschätzer m, sachverständiger Beisitzer

asset n Aktivposten m, Aktivum n, Vermögensgegenstand m; **~ allocation** Asset Allocation f, Kapitalverteilung auf unterschiedliche Investitionsobjekte; **~ backed securities** durch Vermögensrechte gesicherte Wertpapiere; **~ deal** Unternehmensübernahme durch Kauf des Anlagevermögens; **~ management** Verwaltung der Unternehmensaktiva, Anlageverwaltung f, Vermögensverwaltung für institutionelle Investoren; **~ stripping** gezielter Verkauf der Aktiva

assets n pl Aktivseite f, Aktiva plt, Aktiven plt, Aktivmasse f, Betriebsvermögen n, Vermögen n, Vermögenswert m; **~ account** Bestandskonto n; **~ and liabilities** Aktiva und Passiva; **~ at disposal** freie Aktive; **~ held intrust** Treuhandvermögen n; **~ mortgage** Aktivhypothek f; **~ of a bank** Bankvermögen n; **~ of a partnership** Gesellschaftsvermögen n (einer OHG); **~ purchases** Anlagekäufe m pl; **~ side** Aktivseite f; **~ status** Anlagestatus m; **~ valuation** Anlagebewertung f; **~ value** Aktivwert m; **amount of ~** Vermögenshöhe f, Vermögensbetrag m; **available ~** jederzeit greifbare Aktiva; **bank ~** Vermögenswerte einer Bank; **business ~** Geschäftsvermögen n; **capital ~** Kapitalanlagen f pl; **concealed ~** verschleierte Vermögenswerte; **corporate ~** Gesellschaftsvermögen n (einer AG); **current ~** Umlaufvermögen n, flüssige Aktiva, flüssige Mittel; **dead ~** unproduktive Anlagen, ertragsloses Kapital; **floating ~** Umlaufvermögen n, flüssige Aktiva, flüssige Mittel; **fluid ~** (US) Umlaufvermögen n, flüssige Aktiva, flüssige Mittel; **frozen ~** blockierte Guthaben; **intangible ~** immaterielle Aktiva; nicht greifbare Aktien; **operating ~** Betriebsvermögen n; **partnership ~** Gesellschaftsvermögen n (einer OHG); **quick**

assumable mortgage

~ leicht realisierbare Aktiva (z. B. Kasse, Bank, Postscheckguthaben, börsengängige Wertpapiere, Außenstände), Umlaufvermögen n; **real** ~ Immobilien f pl, Grundbesitz m, Grund und Boden, Grundeigentum n, Grundstückseigentum n, Liegenschaften f pl; **revolving** ~ Umlaufvermögen n, flüssige Aktiva, flüssige Mittel; **sticky** ~ schwer verwertbare Aktiva; **tangible** ~ Sachanlagevermögen n, körperliche Wirtschaftsgüter; **wasting** ~ abnutzbare Wirtschaftsgüter, kurzlebige Wirtschaftsgüter

assign v übertragen v, zedieren v, abtreten v, anweisen v, zuweisen v, übereignen v

assignability n Abtretbarkeit f, Übertragbarkeit f

assignable adj abtretbar adj, übertragbar adj, zuweisbar adj, zessionsfähig adj; ~ **credit** übertragbarer Kredit m

assignation n Abtretung f, Übertragung f, Zession f; ~ **of shares** Aktienübertragung f, Aktienumschreibung f

assigned account abgetretenes Konto (US), Garantiekonto n; ~ **writer** Optionsverkäufer m (Stillhalter)

assignee n Zessionar m, Forderungsübernehmer m

assigneeship n Pflegschaft f, Treuhandverwaltung f

assigner n Zedent m, Abtretender m

assignment n Abtretung f, Übertragung f, Zession f; ~ **credit** Zessionskredit m; ~ **in blank** Blankoindossament n, Blankogiro n; ~ **of a right** Rechtsübertragung f; ~ **of account** Kontoabtretung f; ~ **of account receivable** Forderungsabtretung f; ~ **of claim** Forderungsabtretung f; ~ **of debt** Forderungsabtretung f; ~ **of interest** Anteilsübertragung f; ~ **of mortgage** Hypothekenabtretung f; ~ **of stock** Aktienübertragung f, Aktienumschreibung f; **absolute** ~ Forderungsabtretung f; **declaration of** ~ Abtretungserklärung f; **deed of** ~ Abtretungsurkunde f, Übertragungsurkunde f; **mortgage** ~ Hypothekenabtretung f; **undisclosed** ~ stille Zession

assignor n Zedent m, Abtretender m

assistant n Mitarbeiter m, Gehilfe m, Stellvertreter m, Hilfs- (in Zus.); ~ **manager** stellvertretender Direktor; **bank** ~ Bankangestellter m, Bankbeamter m

Assistant; ~ **Manager** (GB) Chefprokurist m; ~ **Treasurer (Officer)** Handlungsbevollmächtigter m; ~ **Vice President** Prokurist m

associate v verbinden v (sich), vereinigen v (sich), assoziieren v; ~ n Genosse m, Kollege m, Gesellschafter m, Teilhaber m, Beteiligungsgesellschaft f; **business** ~ Geschäftspartner m

associated banks (US) Clearingbanken f pl; ~ **company** (GB) nahestehende Gesellschaft, Tochtergesellschaft f; ~ **partner** unbeschränkt haftender Teilhaber

associateship n Teilhaberschaft f

association n Vereinigung f, Verband m, Genossenschaft f, Gesellschaft f, Syndikat n; ~ **of banks** Bankvereinigung f; **bankers** ~ Bankvereinigung f, Bankiervereinigung f; Bankverein m; **banking** ~ Bankvereinigung f; Bankverein m; **beneficiary** ~ Versicherungsverein auf Gegenseitigkeit, Unterstützungsverein m; **benefit** ~ Versicherungsverein auf Gegenseitigkeit, Unterstützungsverein m; **building and loan** ~ Bausparkasse f; **cooperative** ~ Erwerbsgenossenschaft f; **industrial** ~ Industrieverband m

Association of Payment Clearing Services = APCS Dachverband des Londoner Clearingsystems m

assort v assortieren v, sortieren v

assorted adj sortiert, adj, ausgewählt adj

assortment n Sortiment n, Kollektion f, Auswahl f

assume v übernehmen v (z. B. Verpflichtungen); ~ **debts** Schulden übernehmen; ~ **obligations** Verbindlichkeiten eingehen; ~ **ownership** Eigentum übernehmen

assumable mortgage übernehmbare Hypothek

assumed bond mit zusätzlicher Dividendengarantie ausgestattetes Wertpapier

assuming of a mortgage Hypothekenübernahme f

assumpsit n formloses Versprechen

assumption n Annahme f (Rechte, Pflichten), Übernahme f (Rechte, Pflichten); **~ agreement** Schuldübernahmevertrag m

assurable adj versicherungsfähig adj, versicherbar adj

assurance n Zusage f, Garantie f, Gewährleistung f, Versicherung f, Assekuranz f; Zusicherung f; **life ~** (GB), Lebensversicherung f; **partnership ~** (GB) Teilhaberversicherung f

assure v versichern v, zusichern v, Versicherung abschließen, sich versichern lassen

assured n Versicherungsnehmer m, Versicherter m

assurer n Versicherungsgeber m, Versicherer m

at best bestens adj (Börse); **~ call** auf Abruf, auf Sicht; **~ limit** limitierter Wertpapierauftrag m; **~ par** zum Nennwert; **~ sight** bei Sicht; **~ the market** zum Marktpreis bestens, billigst adj; **~ the money** zum Kassakurs

ATM = **automatic teller machine** Bankautomat für Geldausgabe und andere Funktionen

attach v anheften v, beschlagnahmen v, beilegen v, beifügen v, pfänden v, mit Beschlag belegen

attachability n Pfändbarkeit f

attachable adj pfändbar adj, beschlagnahmefähig adj, einziehbar adj

attached adj beigefügt adj, angeschlossen adj; **~ account** (US) blockiertes Konto

attachment n Pfändung f, Beschlagnahme f, Arrest m; **~ of debts** Forderungspfändung f; **~ of property** Vermögensbeschlagnahme f; **~ order** Pfändungsanordnung f

attend v Dienst leisten, dienen v, bedienen v; **~ a meeting** einer Versammlung beiwohnen; **~ to the collection of a bill** das Inkasso eines Wechsels besorgen

attendance fees Sitzungsgelder n pl

attention; due ~ gebührende Sorgfalt

attest v beglaubigen v, bezeugen v, bestätigen v, bescheinigen v

attestation n Beglaubigung f, Bestätigung f, Bescheinigung f; **~ of a deed** Urkundenbeglaubigung f

attested adj beglaubigt adj

attestor n Beglaubiger m, Zeuge m

attitude; bearish ~ Baissehaltung f

attorney n Jurist m, Rechtsanwalt m, Anwalt m; **~ n (at law)** (US) Rechtsanwalt m, Rechtsvertreter m, Rechtsbeistand m; **power of ~** Vertretungsvollmacht f, Handlungsvollmacht f, Prozeßvollmacht f

attorney's fee Anwaltsgebühren f pl

attributable profits zurechenbare Gewinne

auction v versteigern v; **~ n** Auktion f, Versteigerung f; **buy by ~** auf einer Auktion kaufen; **purchase at ~** ersteigern v; **sell at ~** versteigern v; **sell by ~** versteigern v

auctioneer n Auktionator m, öffentlicher Versteigerer

audit v revidieren v, Rechnungen prüfen; **~ n** Buchprüfung f, Bilanzprüfung f, Bücherrevision f, Rechnungsprüfung f, Revision f; **~ book** Revisionsbuch n; **~ certificate** Prüfungsvermerk m; **~ report** Buchprüfungsbericht m, Revisionsbericht m; **~ standards** Revisionsrichtlinien f pl; **~ the accounts** Bücher überprüfen; **balance sheet ~** Bilanzprüfung f; **cash ~** Kassenrevision f

audited balance sheet geprüfte Bilanz

auditing n Revisionswesen n, Prüfungswesen n; **~ company** Revisionsgesellschaft f; **~ department** Revisionsabteilung f; **~ expert** Buchsachverständige f u. m; **~ of accounts** Buchprüfung f, Bilanzprüfung f, Bücherrevision f, Rechnungsprüfung f, Revision f

auditor n Bücherrevisor m, Wirtschaftsprüfer m, Buchprüfer m, Rechnungsprüfer m, Revisor m; **bank ~** Bankrevisor m

auditor's report Buchprüfungsbericht m, Revisionsbericht m

Aussie-bonds Australische Anleihen *f pl*
Austrian Schilling Österreichische Schilling *m*
Australian Stock Exchange australische Börse
authenticate *v* beglaubigen *v* (Echtheit, Gültigkeit), beurkunden *v*
authentication *n* Beglaubigung *f* (der Echtheit, Gültigkeit), Beurkundung *f*
authority *n* Autorität *f*, Amtsgewalt *f*, Machtbefugnis, *f*, Befugnis *f*, Vollmacht *f*, Ermächtigung *f*, Bevollmächtigung *f*; **- to dispose** Verfügungsmacht *f*; **- to purchase** Ankaufsermächtigung *f*; **- to sign** zeichnungsberechtigt, Unterschriftsvollmacht *f*; **agent's -** Vertretungsbefugnis *f*; **certificate of -** Vollmachtsurkunde *f*; **public -** Behörde *f*
authorization *n* Autorisation *f*, Ermächtigung *f*, Bevollmächtigung *f*
authorize *v* autorisieren *v*, ermächtigen *v*, bevollmächtigen *v*, genehmigen *v*
authorized *adj* autorisiert *adj*, ermächtigt *adj*, bevollmächtigt *adj*, befugt *adj*; **- bank** ermächtigte Bank *f*; **- capital** für eine Kapitalerhöhung genehmigtes Aktienkapital, genehmigtes Kapital (GB); **- signature** berechtigte Unterschrift; **- stock** (US) genehmigtes Kapitel
automate *v* automatisieren *v*
automated pit trading system = APTS elektronisches Handelssystem der LIFFE (siehe *LIFFE*)
automatic reinvestment automatische Wiederanlage; **- teller machine (ATM)** Schalterautomat *m*
automation *n* Automation *f*, Automatisierung *f*
automatization *n* Automation *f*, Automatisierung *f*
automatize *v* automatisieren *v*
auxiliary accounting department Nebenbuchhaltung *f*; **- routine** Hilfsprogramm *n*
avail oneself of Gebrauch machen von
availability date (US) Wert *m* (Datum), Valuta *f* (Datum), Wertstellung *f*, Wertstellungszeitpunkt *m*; **- surplus** nicht zweckgebundener Gewinn

available *adj* verfügbar *adj*, vorhanden *adj*, erhältlich *adj*, disponibel *adj*; **- assets** jederzeit greifbare Aktiva; **- funds** liquide Mittel; **make -** bereitstellen *v*
avails *n pl* (US) Gewinn *m*, Ertrag *m*, Nutzen *m*, Vorteil *m*; **net -** (US) Nettoerlös *m*, Gegenwert *m*
aval *n* Aval *n*, Wechselbürgschaft *f*; **- account** Avalrechnung *f*
average *n* Durchschnitt *m*, Durchschnitts- (in Zus.), Havarie *f*, Seeschaden *m*; **- accustomed** Havarie nach Seebrauch; **- adjuster** Dispacheur *m*, Havarievertreter *m*, Havarieagent *m*; **- agent** Dispacheur *m*, Havarievertreter *m*, Havarieagent *m*; **- balance** Durchschnittssaldo *m*; **- bill** Havarierechnung *f*; **- bond** Havarieschein *m*; **- charges** Haveriegelder *n pl*; **- clause** Freizeichnungsklausel *f*, Havarieklausel *f*; **- due date** mittlerer Zahlungstermin; **- due time** mittlerer Verfall (Fälligkeit); **- expenses** Havariegelder *n pl*; **- money** Havariegelder *n pl*; **- stater** Dispacheur *m*, Havarievertreter *m*, Havarieagent *m*; **- term** mittlere Laufzeit *f*
averager *n* Kapitalanleger der nach dem Prinzip »averaging« vorgeht
averages Durchschnittskurs *m* (US)
averaging *n* ein Wertpapier zu verschiedenen Kursen kaufen, um zu einem Durchschnittskurs zu gelangen
aviation *n* Luftfahrt *f*; **- stocks** Luftfahrtaktien *f pl*
avoid *v* vermeiden *v*, entgehen *v*, ungültig machen, annullieren *v*
avoidable *adj* vermeidbar *adj*, annullierbar *adj*, anfechtbar *adj*
avoidance *n* Vermeidung *f*, Aufhebung *f*, Nichtigkeitserklärung *f*, Widerruf *m*
avouch *v* erklären *v*, zusichern *v*
avouchment *n* Zusicherung *f*
award *n* Preis *m*, Prämie *f*, Belohnung *f*, Zuerkennung *f*, Zubilligung *f*, Schiedsspruch *m*; **- a contract** Liefer- oder Fabrikationsauftrag erteilen; **- a loan** Anleihe gewähren
axiom *n* Grundsatz *m*

B

baby bonds Wertpapiere mit geringem Nominalwert, Obligationen mit kleiner Stückelung; *- stock* (US) neu ausgegebene Aktie

back v indossieren v, girieren v; *- n* Rückseite eines Wechsels oder Schecks; *- charges* Rückspesen plt; *- instalment* rückständige Rate; *- interest* rückständige Zinsen; *date - v* zurückdatieren v

backbond n Rückbürgschaft f, Gegenbürgschaft f

backed bill avalierter Wechsel; *- by gold* gedeckt durch Gold

backer n Wechselbürge m, Indossierer m

backing n Indossament n, Giro n, Stützungskäufe m pl (Börse)

backlog (of orders) n Auftragsbestand m

back-to-back credit (US) Gegenakkreditiv n, Gegenkredit m, gegenseitige Kreditgewährung zweier Geschäftsparteien

back-up *facilities* Back-up-Fazilitäten f pl, Kredite zur Übernahme nicht plazierter Emissionen; *- services* ergänzende Dienstleistungen

backvalue (an entry) v eine Buchung mit Rückvaluta vornehmen; *- n* Rückvaluta f

backwardation n (GB) Deport m, Kursabschlag m; *- business* (GB) Deportgeschäft n; *- rate* Deportkurs m

BACS = British Association of Payment Clearing System Dachverband des Londoner Clearingsystems

bad *bargain* schlechtes Geschäft; *- check* ungedeckter Scheck; *- debt* uneinbringliche Schuld; *- debt reserve* Rückstellungen für uneinbringliche Forderungen; *- debtor* zahlungsunfähiger Schuldner; *- delivery* schlechte Lieferung; *- money* Falschgeld n; *- title* mangelhafter Rechtstitel; *allowance for - debts* Dubiosenrückstellung f

bail v Kaution leisten, Kaution stellen; *- n* Bürgschaft f, Kaution f, Sicherheitsleistung f, Bürge m; *- bond* Bürgschaftsschein m, Bürgschaftskunde f

bailable adj bürgschaftsfähig adj, kautionsfähig adj

bailee n Verwahrer m, Depositar m

bailer n Bürge m, Treugeber m, Hinterleger m

bailiff n (law) Gerichtsvollzieher m, Zustellungsbeamter m

bailment n Verwahrung f, Bürgschaftsleistung f, Kautionsleistung f; *- lease* Verkauf unter Eigentumsvorbehalt; *involuntary -* unfreiwillige Hinterlegung

bailor n Bürge m, Treugeber m, Hinterleger m

bailout plan Sanierungsplan m

bailsman n Bürge m, Treugeber m, Hinterleger m

balance v bilanzieren v, abschließen v (Konten), saldieren v; *-* v einen Saldo ziehen; *- n* Saldierung f, Berechnung f; *- n* Saldo m, Bilanz f, Abschluß m; *- account* Ausgleichskonto n; *- an account* Konto abschließen, saldieren v (Konto); *- at the bank* Bankguthaben m; *- books* Bücher abschließen; *- brought forward (B/F)* Vortrag auf neue Rechnung, Saldovortrag m, Vortragssaldo m; *- carried forward (B/F)* Vortrag auf neue Rechnung, Saldovortrag m, Vortragssaldo m; *- date* Bilanzstichtag m; *- entry* Ausgleichsbuchung f; *- in cash* Kassenbestand m, Bargeld m; *- in hand* Barüberschuß m; *- notification* Saldomitteilung f; *- of accounts* Bilanz f, Rechnungsabschluß m, Kontenabschluß m; *- of payments* Zahlungsbilanz f; *- of securities* Wertpapierbilanz f; *- of the bank* Bankausweis m; *- of trade* Handelsbilanz f; *- sheet* Bilanz f, Bilanzaufstellung f, Bilanzbogen m; *- sheet audit* Bilanzprüfung f; *- sheet book* Bilanzbuch n; *- sheet clerk* Bilanzbuchhalter m; *- sheet figures* Bilanzziffern f pl; *- sheet item* Bilanzposten m; *- sheet term* bilanztechnischer Ausdruck; *- sheet total* Bilanzsumme f (Bilanzvolumen); *- value* Bilanzwert m; *with home and foreign bankers* Nostroguthaben bei in- und ausländischen Banken; *abstract of - sheet* Vermögensübersicht f; *active - Aktivsaldo* m (Handelsbilanz); *actual - effektiver* Saldo; *adverse -* Unterbilanz f, Verlustsaldo m; *approval of the - sheet* Genehmigung der Bilanz; *audited - sheet* geprüfte Bilanz; *average - Durchschnittssaldo* m; *bank -* Bankguthaben n; *blocked -* gesperrtes Guthaben; *clean up a - sheet* eine Bilanz bereinigen; *clear a -* einen Saldo ausgleichen; *clearing -* Verrechnungssaldo m; *condensed - sheet* Bilanzauszug m, verkürzte Bilanz; *consolidated - sheet* Fusionsbilanz f, Konzernbilanz f, konsolidierte Bilanz, Fusionsbilanz f; *cook a - sheet* eine Bilanz frisieren, eine Bilanz verschleiern; *credit -* Guthaben n, Habensaldo m, Kreditsaldo m, Aktivsaldo m, Haben n; *credit - with other banks* Nostroguthaben n; *credit by -* per Saldo gutschreiben; *dormant -* umsatzloser Saldo; *draw up a -* eine Bilanz aufstellen; *leave a - of* einen Saldo von ausweisen; *monthly - sheet* monatlicher Bilanzaufgliederungsbogen; *trial -* Probebilanz f, provisorische Bilanz; *ultimate -* letzte Bilanz

balances *in postal giro accounts* Guthaben bei Postgiroämtern; *- with central banks* Guthaben bei Zentralnotenbanken

balancing n (of accounts) Abstimmung f (von Konten); *- n* Bilanzziehung f, Saldieren n; *- of accounts* Konto- oder Bücherabschluß m, Rechnungsabschluß m, Bilanzierung f; *- of the books* Bilanzabschluß m, Buchabschluß m

bale n Ballen m (Ware)

balloon v Wertpapiere künstlich in die Höhe treiben; *- loan* endfälliger Kredit; *- payment* Endfälligkeitstilgung f

ballot vote geheime Abstimmung

Baltic Futures Exchange Baltische Terminbörse f

Bancomat Bancomat m, Geldausgabeautomat m

band n Bandbreite f; *- of fluctuation* Schwankungsbreite f

bang the market (slang) den Markt durch anhaltende Verkäufe drücken

banger n Spekulant, der durch anhaltende Verkäufe auf den Markt drückt

bank v Banktätigkeit ausüben, ein Bankgeschäft betreiben, mit einer Bank arbeiten, ein Bankkonto unterhalten; *- n* Bank f, Bankgeschäft n; *- acceptance* Bankakzept n, Bankwechsel m; *- account* Bankkonto n; *- accountant* Bankbuchhalter m; *- accounting* Bankbuchhaltung f; *- advertising* Bankwerbung f; *- agent* Bankvertreter m; *- agio* Bankprovision f; *- assets* Vermögenswerte einer Bank; *- assistant* Bankangestellter m, Bankbeamter m; *- auditor* Bankrevisor m; *- automation* Bankautomation f; *- balance* Bankguthaben n; *- balance sheet* Bankbilanz f; *- bill* Banknote f, Bankwechsel m, diskontierbarer Wechsel; *- book* Sparbuch n, Einlageheft n; *- building* Bankgebäude n; *- burglary insurance* Bankeinbruchsversicherung f; *- card* Bankkarte f, Kreditkarte f; *- cashier* Bankkassierer m; *- charges* Bankspesen plt, Bankgebühren f pl; *- check* (US) Bankscheck m; *- cheque* (GB) Bankscheck m; *- clearing* Bankenclearing n, Bankgiro m; *- clerk* Bankangestellter m; *- collateral* Banksicherheit f; *- commission* Bankenkommission f; *- confirmation* Bankbestätigung f, Bestätigung des Kontoauszugs; *- crash* Bankkonkurs m, Bankkrach m, Bankzusammenbruch m; *- credit* Bankkredit m, Bankdarlehen m; *- credit transfer* Banküberweisung f; *- currency* (US) Banknotensätze auf der Debetseite; *- customer* Bankkunde m; *- debit* Kontobelastung f; *- debits* (US) Bankumsätze auf der Debetseite; *- debts* Bankschulden f pl; *- deposit* Bankeinlage f; *- deposit insurance* Einlagenversicherung f, Depositenversicherung f; *- depositor* Einleger m, Einzahler m, Depositeninhaber m, Hinterleger m, Deponent m; *- direc-*

tor (US) Bankaufsichtsratmitglied n, Bankdirektor m; **- discount** Bankdiskont m; **- draft** Bankwechsel m, Banktratte f; **- employee** Bankangestellter m, Bankbeamter m; **- examination** (US) Bankrevision f; **- examiner** (US) Bankrevisor m; **- facilities** Bankfazilitäten f pl; **- failure** Bankkonkurs m, Bankkrach m, Bankzusammenbruch m; **- for cooperatives** (US) Genossenschaftsbank f

Bank for International Settlements = BIS Bank für Internationalen Zahlungsausgleich f (BIZ)

bank funds Bankkapital n; **- giro** Bankgiro n; **- guarantee** Bankgarantie f; **- guaranty** (US) Bankgarantie f; **- holding company** (US) Gesellschaft mit Mehrheitsbesitz an einer Bank oder an mehreren Banken; **- holiday** Bankfeiertag m; **- identification number** Bankleitzahl f; **- inquiry** Bankauskunft f; **- inspector** Bankrevisor m; **- law** Bankgesetz n; **- ledger** Bankhauptbuch n; **- lien** Pfandrecht der Bank, Zurückbehaltungsrecht der Bank; **- liquidity** Bankliquidität f; **- loan** Bankkredit m, Bankdarlehen n; **- management** Bankvorstand m, Bankleitung f; **- manager** Bankdirektor m; **- merger** Bankenfusion f; **- messenger** Bankbote m, Kassenbote m; **- money** Buchgeld n, Giralgeld n, bargeldlose Zahlungsmittel; **- money order** Bankanweisung f, Zahlungsanweisung f, Banküberweisung f; **- note** Banknote f; **- note circulation** Banknotenumlauf m; **- note printing** Banknotendruck m; **- of circulation** Notenbank f; **- of deposit** Depositenbank f; **- of discount** Diskontbank f

Bank of England (GB) Bank von England f; **- of England minimum leding rate** Diskrensatz der Bank von England; **- of England Return (GB)** wöchentlicher Ausweis der Bank von England

bank of issue Notenbank f; **- official** Bankangestellter m, Bankbeamter m; **- operation on which interest is earned or paid** Zinsgeschäft n; **- overdraft** Überziehungskredit m; **- paper** bankfähiges Papier; **- payment order** Zahlungsauftrag m; **- payment slip** Bankeinzahlungsschein m; **- policy** Diskontpolitik f; **- post bill** (GB) Bankwechsel der Bank von England; **- post remittance** Postüberweisung im Auftrag der Bank; **- premises** Bankgrundstück n, Bankgebäude n; **- premises account** Grundstückskonto n (einer Bank); **- publicity** Bankwerbung f; **- rate** (of discount) Diskontsatz der Notenbank; **- rate for loans** Lombardzins m; **- receipt** Bankquittung f; **- receiver** Bankkassierer m; **- reconciliation statement** Kontoabrechnung f; **- records** Bankbelege m pl; **- reference** Bankauskunft f; **- report** Bankausweis m; **- reserve** Bankreserve f; **- resources** Aktiva einer Bank; **- roll** (US) Banknotenbündel n; **- secrecy** Bankgeheimnis n; **- security** Banksicherheit f; **- share** Bankaktie f; **- shareholder** Bankaktionär m; **- stamp** Bankindossament n; **- statement** Bankauszug m; **- stock** Bankaktien f pl; **- teller** Bankkassierer m; **- transfer** Banküberweisung f; **- vault** Banktresor m; **- withdrawal** Bankabhebung f; **acceptance** - Akzeptbank f; **agricultural** - Landwirtschaftsbank f; **assets of a** - Bankvermögen n; **balance at the** - Bankguthaben n; **balance of the** - Bankausweis m; **Banker's** - (US) Zentralbank (z. B. die 12 regionalen »Federal Reserve Banks« in USA); **big** - Großbank f; **borrower's** - Hausbank f; **branch** - Filialbank f, Bankfiliale f; **cash in** - Bankguthaben n; **central** - Zentralnotenbank f; **chartered** - (GB) priviligierte Bank, konzessionierte Bank; **circulating - notes** Banknotenumlauf m; **clearing** - Clearingbank f, Girobank f; **collecting** - Inkassobank f, einziehende Bank; **commercial** - Geschäftsbank f, Gewerbebank f, Handelsbank f; **cooperative** - genossenschaftliches Kreditinstitut; **correspondent** - Korrespondenzbank f; **country** - (GB) Provinzbank f; **credit at the** -

Bankguthaben n; **deposit** - Depositenbank f; **drawee** - bezogene Bank; **drive-in** - Bank mit Autoschalter; **large** - Großbank f; **major** - Großbank f; **member** - (US) dem Clearingsystem angehörende Bank, Mitgliedsbank f (des Federal Reserve Systems); **merchant** - Handelsbank f; **mortgage** - Hypothekenbank f; **municipal** - Kommunalbank f; **national** - (US) mit der Genehmigung der Bundesregierung im Rahmen eines Nationalbankgesetzes gegründete Bank, Nationalbank f, Staatsbank f; **nonmember** - Bank außerhalb des Clearingsystems; **non-par** - Bank außerhalb des Clearingsystems; **parent** - Stammbank f; **proprietor of a** - Bankinhaber m, Bankier m; **regional** - Regionalbank f, Landesbank f; **specialized** - Spezialbank f

bankable adj diskontierbar adj, diskontfähig adj, bankfähig adj; - **bill** diskontfähiger Wechsel; - **security** bankmäßige Sicherheit

banker n Bankier m, Mitarbeiter einer Bank; **merchant** - Handelsbank f

bankers association Bankenvereinigung f, Bankverein m; - **balance with home and foreign** Nostroguthaben bei in- und ausländischen Banken

banker's acceptance Bankakzept n, Bankwechsel m; - **acceptance credit** Akzeptkredit m, Rembourskredit m; - **advance** Bankdarlehen n, Bankkredit m

Banker's bank (US) Zentralbank (z. B. die Federal Reserve Banken in USA)

banker's buying rate Geldkurs m, Kaufkurs m; - **check** Bankscheck m; - **clearing house** (GB) Bankabrechnungsstelle f; - **commission** Bankprovision f; - **deposit** Bankeinlage f; - **deposit rate** Einlagenzinssatz m; - **discount** Bankdiskont m; - **discretion** Bankgeheimnis n; - **draft** (US) Bankwechsel m; - **guarantee** Bankgarantie f; - **guaranty** (US) Bankgarantie f; - **lien** Pfandrecht der Bank, Zurückbehaltungsrecht der Bank; - **order** (GB) Bankauftrag m; - **payment**

Bankzahlung f, Bankanweisung f; - **receipt** Depotschein m; - **reference** Bankauskunft f

banking Bankwesen n, Bankbetrieb m, Bankgeschäft n, Kreditgewerbe n, Abwicklung von Bankgeschäften; - **account** Bankkonto n; - **activity** Banktätigkeit f; - **affairs** Bankangelegenheiten f pl; - **association** Bankvereinigung f, Bankverein m; - **business** Bankwesen n, Bankgeschäft n, Bankbetrieb m, Kreditgewerbe n, Bankgewerbe n; - **center** Bankplatz m; - **charges** Provisionssätze m pl; - **circles** Bankkreise m pl; - **combine** Bankkonzern m; - **connection** Bankverbindung f; - **crisis** Bankenkrise f; - **department** Bankabteilung f; - **facilities** Bankfazilitäten f pl; - **failure** Bankkonkurs m, Bankzusammenbruch m; - **group** Bankkonzern m; - **hall** Schalterhalle f; - **hours** Schalterstunden f pl; - **house** Bankhaus n; - **institution** Bankinstitut n; - **interest** Bankanteil m; - **law** Bankrecht n

Banking Law Bankgesetz n

banking matters Bankangelegenheiten f pl; - **office** Bankgeschäftsstelle f; - **operations** Bankgeschäfte n pl; - **place** Bankplatz m; - **practice** Bankpraxis f, Bankusancen f pl; - **reserve** Bankreserve f; - **secrecy** Bankgeheimnis n; - **statistics** Bankstatistik f; - **support** Bankenstützungsaktion f, Bankenintervention f; - **syndicate** Bankenkonsortium n; - **system** Banksystem n; - **trade** n Bankwesen n, Bankgeschäft n, Bankbetrieb m, Kreditgewerbe n, Bankgewerbe n; - **transactions** Bankgeschäfte n pl; - **usage** Bankpraxis f, Bankusance f; - **world** Bankwelt f; **branch** - Filialbanksystem n; **co-operative** - genossenschaftliches Bankwesen; **deposit** - Depositengeschäft n, Einlagengeschäft n; **deposit** - **division** Depositenabteilung f, Einlagenabteilung f, Kreditorenabteilung f

banknotes; counterfeiter of - Banknotenfälscher m

bankrupt

bankrupt v zum Konkurs treiben; ~ n Konkursschuldner m, Bankrotteur m; ~ adj bankrott adj, insolvent adj, in Konkurs; ~ **acceptor** bankrotter Akzeptant; ~ **drawee** bankrotter Bezogener; ~ **drawer** bankrotter Wechselaussteller; ~ **firm** in Konkurs gegangene Firma; ~ **partner** in Konkurs gegangener Teilhaber; ~ **person** Konkursschuldner m, Bankrotteur m; ~ **surety** in Konkurs gegangener Bürge; ~ **trustee** in Konkurs gegangener Treuhändler; **become** ~ in Konkurs gehen, in Konkurs geraten; **go** ~ in Konkurs gehen, in Konkurs geraten

bankruptcy n Konkurs m, Bankrott m; ~ **act** Konkursordnung f; ~ **action** Konkursverfahren n; ~ **examination** Konkursverfahren n; ~ **fraudulent** betrügerischer Bankrott; ~ **law** Konkursrecht n; ~ **notice** Konkurserklärung f, Konkursanmeldung f, Bankrotterklärung f; ~ **petition** Konkursantrag m; ~ **proceedings** Konkursverfahren n; ~ **rules** Konkursbestimmungen f pl; ~ **statute** Konkursordnung f; **act of** ~ Konkursvergehen n; **adjudication of** ~ Konkurseröffnung f; **composition in** ~ Zwangsvergleich m, Konkursvergleich m; **court of** ~ Konkursgericht n; **declaration of** ~ Konkurserklärung f, Konkursanmeldung f, Bankrotterklärung f; **decree in** ~ Konkurseröffnungsbeschluß m; **discharge in** ~ (US) Rehabilitierung eines Konkursschuldners; **involuntary** ~ unfreiwilliger Konkurs, durch Gläubigerantrag herbeigeführter Konkurs; **prove a claim in** ~ Konkursforderung anmelden

bankrupt's certificate Konkursvergleich m; ~ **creditor** Konkursgläubiger m; ~ **estate** Konkursmasse f

banks Banken f pl, Bankaktien f pl; **associated** ~ (US) Clearingbanken f pl; **association of** ~ Bankvereinigung f; **consolidation of** ~ Bankenfusion f; **consortium of** ~ Bankenkonsortium n

bar n Hindernis n, Hemmnis n; ~ v ausnehmen v, ausschließen n

bar-bell Wertpapierportefeuille mit sehr kurz- oder langfristiger Laufzeit

bargain v handeln v, vereinbaren v, feilschen v, den Preis herunterhandeln; ~ n Gelegenheitskauf m, Geschäft n, Handel m, Übereinkunft f; ~ **basement prices** Ausverkaufspreise m pl, Spottpreise m pl; ~ **book** Schlußnotenregister n; ~ **counter** Effektenschalter m; ~ **hunter** Börsenspekulant m; ~ **hunting** Effektenspekulation f; ~ **money** Draufgeld n, Handgeld n; ~ **penny** Draufgeld n, Handgeld n; ~ **price** Vorzugspreis m, Ausverkaufspreis m; ~ **sale** Ausverkauf m (Verkauf zu herabgesetzten Preisen); **bad** ~ schlechtes Geschäft; **blind** ~ Geschäft, bei dem die »Katze im Sack« gekauft wird; **conclusion of a** ~ Geschäftsabschluß m; **contract a** ~ einen Handel abschließen

bargainee n Käufer m

bargainer n Verkäufer m, Feilscher m, Schacherer m

bargaining Verhandeln, Aushandeln

bargainor Verkäufer m

barometer stocks (US) Standardwerte m pl

barred debt verjährte Schuld

barren money totes Kapital, brachliegendes Kapital

barter v tauschen v (Tauschhandel betreiben); ~ n Tausch m; ~ **transaction** Kompensationsgeschäft n, Gegenseitigkeitsgeschäft n

barterable adj tauschfähig adj

barterer n Tauschhändler m

bartering n Tauschgeschäft n, Tauschhandel m

base coin (GB) falsche Münze, (US) Scheidemünze f ; ~ **gold** Gold von geringem Feingehalt; ~ **metal** unedeles Metall

basic analysis Fundamentalanalyse f; ~ **industry** Grundstoffindustrie f; ~ **price** Grundpreis m; ~ **rate of interest** Eckzins m; ~ **savings deposit rate** Spareckzins m; ~ **training** Grundausbildung f; ~ **value** Einheitswert m (eines Grundstücks)

basis n Basis f, Grundlage f; ~ **of agreement** Vertragsgrundlage f; ~ **of calcu-**

lation Berechnungsgrundlage f; *- point* Basispunkt m (0,01 Prozent), Tick m; *- rate* Basissatz m, Eckzins m; *- savings rate* Sparekzins m; *- swap* Tausch von Zinsverpflichtungen; *business -* Geschäftsgrundlage f

basket currency Korbwährung f

batch program Stapelprogramm n

batch-processing program Stapelprogramm n

bear v auf Baisse spekulieren, fixen v; *- n* Baissespekulant m, Baissier m, Fixer m; *- a loss* Verlust tragen; *- account* Baisseposition f; *- covering* Deckungskauf m; *- interest* Zinsen bringen; *- market* Baissemarkt m; *- operation* Baissespekulation f; *- position* Baisseposition f, Baisseengagement n; *- raid* Baissemanöver f pl; *- raiding* Leerverkäufe f pl; *- rumours* Baissegerüchte n pl; *- seller* Baissespekulant m, Baissier m, Fixer m; *- speculation* Baissespekulation f; *- the market* Baisse herbeiführen, Kurse drücken; *- the stocks* Baisse herbeiführen, Kurse drücken; *sell a -* auf Baisse spekulieren, fixen v; *stale -* geschlagener Baissier

bearer n Überbringer m, Inhaber m; *- bond* Inhaberobligation f, Inhaberschuldverschreibung f; *- certificate* Inhaberzertifikat n; *- check* Inhaberscheck m; *- debenture* Inhaberobligation f, Inhaberschuldverschreibung f; *- instrument* Inhaberpapier n; *- loan* Inhaberanleihe f; *- mortgage note* Inhaberschuldbrief m; *- of a bill* Wechselinhaber m; *- of a check* Scheckinhaber m; *- securities* Inhaberpapiere n pl, Inhabereffekten plt; *- share* Inhaberaktie f; *- stock* Inhaberaktie f; *- warrant issue* Inhaberoptionsanleihe f; *bill to -* Inhaberwechsel m; *bond to -* Inhaberobligation f, Inhaberschuldverschreibung f; *check to -* Überbringerscheck m, Inhaberschein m; *in - form* auf den Inhaber lautend

bearing Verkauf auf Baisse; *- interest* verzinslich adj

bearish adj auf Baisse ausgerichtet; *- attitude* Baissehaltung f; *- market* Baissemarkt m; *- operation* Baissespekulation f; *- tendency* Baissetendenz f

beat down drücken v (Preise), herunterhandeln v; *- the gun* (US) Aktien vor öffentlicher Auflegung zum Verkauf anbieten

become due fällig werden

before hours Vorbörse f

behalf; on - and for account of im Auftrag und für Rechnung; *on - of* im Namen von, zugunsten von

behindhand im Rückstand

bellwether bond marktgerechte Anleihe

below par unter pari, unter dem Nennwert; *- the line* »unter dem Strich«

bench mark Orientierungsgröße f, Wertmaßstab m, Richtgröße f, Performancemaß f

beneficial adj vorteilhaft adj, günstig adj, nutzbringend adj; *- enjoyment* Nutznießungsrecht n, Nießbrauchsrecht n; *- estate* Nießbrauch an einem Vermögen; *- interest* Nießbrauch m, Nutznießung f; *- occupant* Nießbrauchberechtigter m; *- owner* Nutznießer m, materieller Eigentümer; *- ownership* materielles Eigentum, wirtschaftliches Eigentum, Nießbrauchsrecht n; *- property* Nießbrauch an einem Vermögen; *- right* Nießbrauch m, Nutznießung f

beneficially entitled legatsberechtigt adj, eigentumsberechtigt adj

beneficiary n Begünstigter m, Nießbraucher m, Nutznießer m; *- association* Versicherungsverein auf Gegenseitigkeit, Unterstützungsverein m; *- clause* Begünstigungsklausel f; *- heir* auf das Nachlaßverzeichnis beschränkter Erbe; *- of a letter of credit* Kreditbriefinhaber m, Akkreditivbegünstigter m; *- of provident fund* Bezugsberechtigter einer Versorgungsstiftung; *- owner* Nutznießer m, materieller Eigentümer

benefit v begünstigen v, Nutzen bringen; *- n* Nutzen m, Gewinn m, Vergünstigung f, Vorteil m; *- association* Versicherungsverein auf Gegenseitigkeit, Unterstützungsverein m; *- by* Nutzen ziehen

benefits

aus; *- by the exchange* Kursgewinne mitnehmen; *- club* Versicherungsverein auf Gegenseitigkeit, Unterstützungsverein m; *- fund* Versicherungsfonds auf Gegenseitigkeit, Wohltätigkeitsfonds m; *- of division* Ausgleichseinrede mehrerer Bürgen; *- of inventory* Recht des Erben auf Nachlaßbeschränkung; *- society* Versicherungsverein auf Gegenseitigkeit, Unterstützungsverein m; *death -* Sterbegeld n; *disability -* Invaliditätsrente f, Invaliditätsunterstützung f

benefits; *social insurance -* Sozialversicherungsleistungen f pl

bequeath v vermachen v, testamentarisch hinterlassen

bequeathable adj hinterlassungsfähig adj

bequeather n Erblasser m, Testator m

bequest n Legat n, Vermächtnis n, testamentarische Zuwendung

best *selling* meistverkauft adj; *at -* bestens, bestmöglich (Börse)

best-efforts underwriting Emissionsübernahmegeschäft ohne Plazierungsrisikoübernahme

bestow v geben v, schenken v, verleihen v (Titel)

bestowal n Gabe f, Schenkung f, Verleihung f

bestowment n Gabe f, Schenkung f, Verleihung f

bet v wetten v; *- n* Wette f

better fester adj (Börse)

betterment tax Wertzuwachssteuer f

beverage tax Getränkesteuer f

beverages Getränkeindustrieaktien f pl

bi-monthly adj zweimonatlich adj

biannual adj halbjährlich adj

bid v bieten v, Gebot machen; *- n* Angebot n, Gebot n, Offerte f; *- and asked quotations* Geld- und Briefkurs; *- bond* Bietungsgarantie f; *- for* (sich) bewerben um; *- price* Geldkurs m, gebotener Preis; *- talk* Übernahmegerüchte f pl; *- value* Rücknahmewert m; *closing -* Höchstgebot n

bidder n Bieter m, Bietender m, Bewerber m

bidding n Gebot n, Bieten n; *- company* bietende Gesellschaft f; *- syndicate* Bietungskonsortium n

bids and offers Käufe und Verkäufe

biennial adj zweijährig adj

Big Bang Neuordnung des britischen Wertpapiermarktes f (27.10.1986)

big bank Großbank f; *- shareholder* Großaktionär m

Big Board (US) New Yorker Börse, Anzeigesystem der New Yorker Börse; *- Four* (GB) die 4 britischen Großbanken (früher »Big Five«)

bilateral adj zweiseitig adj

bilateralism n Gegenseitigkeitsprinzip n

bill v fakturieren v, in Rechnung stellen; *- n* Urkunde f, Rechnung f, Faktura f, Wechsel m, Dokument n, Banknote f, Kontoauszug m, Tratte f, Papiergeld n, Bescheinigung f, Gesetzesvorlage f, Gesetzesantrag m; *- about to mature* in Kürze fällig werdender Wechsel; *- account* Wechselrechnung f; *- after date* Datowechsel m; *- against documents* Wechsel gegen Dokumente; *- at interim* Interimswechsel m; *- at par* Pariwechsel m; *- at sight* Sichtwechsel m; *- book* Wechselkopierbuch n, Wechsellogierbuch n, Wechselbuch n, Wechselobligo n (Buch), Wechselverfallbuch n; *- broker* Wechselmakler m, Wechselhändler m; *- brokerage* Wechselhandel m, Wechselcourtage f; *- case* Wechselportefeuille n, Wechselbestand m; *- charges* Wechselspesen plt; *- collector* Wechselinkassobüro n; *- commission* Wechselcourtage f; *- copying book* Wechselkopierbuch n, Wechsellogierbuch n, Wechselbuch n, Wechselobligo n (Buch), Wechselverfallbuch n; *- cover* Wechseldeckung f; *- credit* Wechselkredit m; *- creditor* Wechselgläubiger m, Wechselinhaber m; *- debt* Wechselverbindlichkeit f, Wechselschuld f; *- debtor* Wechselschuldner m, Wechselverpflichteter m; *- department* Wechselabteilung f; *- diary* Wechselkopierbuch n, Wechsellogierbuch n, Wechselbuch n, Wechselobligo n (Buch), Wechselverfallbuch n; *- discount* (GB) Wechseldiskontsatz m; *- discount ledger* Wechselkopierbuch n, Wechsellogierbuch n, Wechselbuch n, Wechselobligo n (Buch), Wechselverfallbuch n; *- discount rate*

Wechseldiskontsatz m; *- discounter* Wechseldiskontierer m; *- discounting* Wechseldiskontierung f; *- file* Wechselregistratur f; *- for collection* Inkassowechsel m; *- for collection book* Wechselbuch für Inkassowechsel m; *- for encashment* Wechsel zum Inkasso; *- forger* Wechselfälscher m; *- forgery* Wechselfälschung f, Banknotenfälschung f; *- form* Wechselvordruck m; *- guaranty* Wechselbürgschaft f; *- holder* Wechselinhaber m; *- holdings* Wechselportefeuille n, Wechselbestand m; *- in distress* notleidender Wechsel; *- in foreign currency* Auslandswechsel m, Wechsel in ausländischer Währung; *- in full settlement* Ausgleichswechsel m; *- in pension* Depotwechsel m, Pensionswechsel m; *- jobber* Wechselreiter m; *- jobbing* Wechselreiterei f; *- ledger* Wechselkopierbuch n, Wechsellogierbuch n, Wechselbuch n, Wechselobligo n (Buch), Wechselverfallbuch n; *- market* Diskontmarkt m, Wechselmarkt m; *- of acceptance* Akzept n, akzeptierter Wechsel; *- of bottomry* Bodmereibrief m, Schiffsverpfändung f; *- of carriage* Frachtbrief m (Bahn); *- of clearance* Zollabfertigungsschein m; *- of consignment* Frachtbrief m, Speditionsrechnung f; *- of conveyance* Speditionsrechnung f; *- of costs* Spesenrechnung f, Anwaltsgebührenrechnung f; *- of course of exchange* Kurszettel m (Devisen), Kursbericht m (Devisen), Devisenkursliste f; *- of customs* Zollgebührenrechnung f; *- of debt* Schuldschein m, Schuldanerkennung f; *- of delivery* Lieferschein m, Begleitschein m; *- of discount* Diskontnote f; *- of emption* Kaufvertrag m, Kaufbrief m; *- of entry* Zolleinfuhrschein m, Zolldeklaration f; *- of exchange* Wechsel m, Tratte f; *- of freight* Frachtbrief m; *- of lading* Konnossement n, Seefrachtbrief m, Frachtbrief m (US); *- of protest* Protesturkunde f; *- of receipts and expenditures* Einnahmen-und-Ausgaben-Rechnung f; *- of sale* Kaufvertrag m, Kaufbrief m; *- of security* Garantie f, Sicherheitswechsel m; *- of sight* Zollerlaubnisschein m; *- of store* (US) Wiedereinfuhrgenehmigung f, Wiedereinfuhrschein m; *- of sufferance* Erlaubnis zollfreier Warenausfuhr von Hafen zu Hafen; *- of taxes* Steuerbescheid m; *- of the exchequer* Schatzanweisung f; *- of weight* Gewichtsschein m, Wiegenote f; *- on customers* Kundenwechsel m; *- on demand* Sichtwechsel m; *- on deposit* Depotwechsel m, Pensionswechsel m; *- on London* Wechsel auf London; *- out for acceptance* zur Annahme geschickter Wechsel; *- protest* Wechselprotest m; *- receivable* einzulösender Wechsel; *- register* Wechseleingangsbuch n, Wechselregister n, Wechsellogierbuch n; *- stamp* Wechselsteuermarke f, Wechselstempelmarke f; *- surety* Wechselbürge m; *- tax* Wechselsteuer f; *- to bearer* Inhaberwechsel m; *- to mature* laufender Wechsel; *- transactions* Wechselgeschäfte n pl; *- under one's own band* Schuldschein m, Schuldanerkennung f; *- usury* Wechselwucher m; *- with document attached* Wechsel mit anhängenden Papieren; **accept a** *-* einen Wechsel akzeptieren; **acceptance** *-* Dokumentenwechsel m; **acceptor of a** *-* Wechselakzeptant m; **accommodation** *-* Gefälligkeitswechsel m, Finanzwechsel m, Kellerwechsel m; **action on a** *- of exchange* Wechselklage f; **addressed** *-* Domizilwechsel m; **advance** *-* Vorschußwechsel m; **allow a** *- to be protested* einen Wechsel zu Protest gehen lassen; **answer a** *- of exchange* einen Wechsel einlösen, einen Wechsel honorieren; **anticipate a** *-* einen Wechsel vor Verfall einlösen; **average** *-* Havarierechnung f; **backed** *-* avalierter Wechsel; **bank** *-* Banknote f, Bankwechsel m, diskontierbarer Wechsel; **bank post** *-* (GB) Bankwechsel der Bank von England; **banker's** *-* Bankwechsel m; **bearer of a** *-* Wechselinhaber m; **blank** *-* Blankowechsel m, Wechselblankett n; **cash a** *-* einen Wechsel einlösen, einen Wechsel honorieren; **certified ~ of lading** beglaubigtes Konnossement; **claim arising from a ~** Wechselforderung f; **clean ~ of lading** reines Konnossement, Konnossement ohne Einschränkung; **clear a ~** einen Wechsel einlösen, einen Wechsel honorieren; **collateral ~** Lombardwechsel m; **collective ~ of lading** Sammelkonnossement n; **commercial ~** Handelswechsel m, Warenwechsel m; **continuation ~** (GB) Prolongationswechsel m ; **country ~** (GB) Provinzwechsel m ; **cover a ~** Deckung für einen Wechsel anschaffen; **credit ~** Kreditwechsel m; **cross ~** Rückwechsel m, Gegenwechsel m; **currency ~** Wechsel in ausländischer Währung; **currency of a ~** Wechselaufzeit f, Laufzeit eines Wechsels; **customer's ~** Kundenwechsel m; **date of a ~** Fälligkeit eines Wechsels; **discharge a ~** einen Wechsel einlösen, einen Wechsel honorieren; **discharged ~** eingelöster Wechsel; **discountable ~** bankfähiger Wechsel; **dishonoured ~** notleidender Wechsel; **documentary ~** Dokumentenwechsel m; **domestic ~** Inlandswechsel m; **domiciled ~** Domizilwechsel m; **draw a ~** einen Wechsel ziehen; **draw in a ~** einen Wechsel einlösen, einen Wechsel honorieren; **duplicate ~** Wechselduplikat n; **grain ~** auf Grund von Getreidelieferungen gezogener Wechsel; **noting of a ~** Protestaufnahme f; **on-board ~ of lading** Bordkonnossement n; **overdue ~** überfälliger Wechsel, notleidender Wechsel; **party to a ~** Wechselbeteiligte f u. m, Wechselverpflichtete f u. m; **prime ~** erstklassiger Wechsel, prima Wechsel; **protested ~** protestierter Wechsel; **protesting of a ~** Protestaufnahme f; **queery ~** fauler Wechsel; **raised ~** durch Werterhöhung gefälschte Banknote (US); **real ~** echter Wechsel (US); **short ~** Inkassowechsel m; **sight ~** Sichtwechsel m; **straight ~ of lading** Namenskonnossement n (US); **trade ~** Handelswechsel m, Warenwechsel m; **unclean ~ of lading** fehlerhaftes Konnossement

billback Rückbelastung f

billed adj berechnet adj, in Rechnung gestellt

billing n Fakturierung f, Etat einer Werbeagentur f; **~ department** Fakturierabteilung f; **~ machine** Fakturiermaschine f

billings in Rechnung gestellte Beträge f

billion n Billion f (1.000.000.000.000) (GB); **~ n** Milliarde f (1.000.000.000) (US)

bill-like payment order wechselähnliche Anweisung

bills and checks Wechsel- und Scheckbestand (Bilanzposten); **~ and money** Brief und Geld; **~ eligible for discount** Diskontmaterial n; **~ in a set** Wechsel in mehrfacher Ausfertigung; **~ in circulation** umlaufende Wechsel; **~ in hand** Wechselportefeuille n, Wechselbestand m; **~ in portfolio** Wechselportefeuille n, Wechselbestand m; **~ of exchange** Wechsel m (Bilanzposten); **~ on us** Wechsel auf uns; **~ payable** fällige Wechsel, Wechselverbindlichkeit f, Wechselschulden f pl; **~ payable book** Wechselkopierbuch n, Wechsellogierbuch n, Wechselbuch n, Wechselobligo n (Buch), Wechselverfallbuch n; **~ receivable** Kundenwechsel m pl (Bilanz), Wechselforderungen f pl; **accept ~ for collection** Wechsel zum Einzug hereinnehmen; **accept ~ for discount** Wechsel zum Diskont hereinnehmen; **circulation of ~** Wechselumlauf m; **collection of ~** Wechselinkasso f; **discount ~** Diskontwechsel m, Diskonten m pl; **gilt-edged ~** erstklassige Wertpapiere; **sort ~ away in the bill case** Wechsel in das Wechselportefeuille einsortieren

bimetallism n Bimetallismus m, Doppelwährungssystem n

binder n Deckungszusage f (Versicherung), Vorverkaufsvertrag m (Grundstückskauf)

binding adj bindend adj; **~ agreement** unwiderrufliches Abkommen; **~ effect** bindende Wirkung; **~ receipt** Deckungszusage f; **legally ~** rechtsverbindlich adj

BIS = Bank for International Settlements Bank für Internationale Zahlungsausgleich f (BIZ)

B/L = bill of lading Konnossement n, Seefrachtbrief m

black book schwarze Liste, Insolventenliste f, Verzeichnis unsicherer Kunden; **- bourse** schwarze Börse

Black Friday schwarzer Freitag (erster Börsenkrach am 24. Sept. 1869)

black list schwarze Liste, Insolventenliste f, Verzeichnis unsicherer Kunden; **- market** Schwarzmarkt m

Black Monday schwarzer Montag (Börsenkrach am 19. Okt. 1987)

blackleg n Streikbrecher m

blacklist v auf die schwarze Liste setzen

blackmail n Erpressung f

blank n Blankoformular n; **-** Formular n, Formblatt, Vordruck m; - adj blanko adj, Blanko-(in Zus.), unausgefertigt adj, unausgeschrieben adj, unbedruckt adj; **- acceptance** Blankoakzept n, Blankoannahme f; **- advance** Blankokredit m, Blankovorschuß m; **- bill** Blankowechsel m, Wechselblankett n; **- certificate** Blankopapier n; **- check** Blankoscheck m; **- credit** Blankokredit m, Blankoindossament n; **- endorsement** Blankoindossament n, Blankogiro n; **- form** Blankett n, Blankoformular n; **- paper** Blankopapier n; **- policy** Generalpolice f; **- power of attorney** Blankovollmacht f; **- signature** Blankounterschrift f; **- transaction** Blankogeschäft n; **- transfer** Blankogiro n

blanket adj General- (in Zus.), Gesamt-(in Zus.), generell adj, allgemeingültig adj; **- assignment** Globalzession f; **- bond** sicherungsweise abgetretene Hypothek; **- clause** Generalklausel f; **- mortgage** Gesamthypothek f; **- order** Blankoauftrag m; **- policy** Generalpolice f; **- waybill** Kollektivfrachtbrief m

blended fund zur Versilberung bestimmter Nachlaß (GB)

blind bargain Geschäft, bei dem die »Katze im Sack« gekauft wird

blip n kurzfristiger Wirtschaftseinbruch

block v blockieren v, sperren v; **- n** Block m, Paket n, Partie f, Häuserblock m, Geschäftsblock m; **- factor** Blockungsfaktor m (EDV); **- gap** Blocklücke f (EDV); **- length** Blocklänge f (EDV); **- of shares** Aktienpaket n

blocked account blockiertes Konto, eingefrorenes Konto, gesperrtes Konto, Sperrkonto n; **- balance** gesperrtes Guthaben; **- currency** nicht frei konvertierbare Devisen; **- deposit** Sperrdepot n; **- foreign exchange** eingefrorene Devisen, blockierte Devisen; **- period** Sperrfrist f; **- securities** Sperrstücke n pl

blocking n (of an account) Sperre f (eines Kontos); **- arrangement** Stillhalteabkommen n; **- factor** Blockungsfaktor m (EDV); **- of account** Kontensperre f; **- of property** Vermögenssperre f; **- period** Sperrfrist f

blotter n Tageberichtsbuch n, Orderbuch n, Kladde f, Strazze f

blue chip stock Standardwerte m pl, Spitzenwerte m pl, erstklassige Wertpapiere; **- chips** Standardwerte m pl, Spitzenwerte m pl, erstklassige Wertpapiere

Blue-Sky-Laws (US) einzelstaatliche Gesetze gegen betrügerische Effektenemissionen

board n Ausschuß m, Behörde f, Ministerium n; **- company** Übernahmekonsortium n; **- lot** feste Stückzahl für den Handel; **- member** Aufsichtsratsmitglied n; **- of arbitration** Schlichtungsausschuß m; **- of assessment** Steuerbehörde f; **- of brokers** Maklersyndikat m; **- of creditors** Gläubigerausschuß m; **- of directors** Verwaltungsrat m

Board of Directors (the Board) Vorstand m, Direktorium n: **- of the Exchequer** (GB) Finanzministerium n; **- of Trade** (US) Handelskammer f, (GB) Handelsministerium n, Wirtschaftsministerium n

board room Börsensaal m, Sitzungssaal des Direktoriums; **advisory -** Beirat m; **first -** erste Kursnotierung; **member of the -** Vorstandsmitglied n

boatage n Frachtgebühr für Beförderung auf Booten
body n Körper m, Körperschaft f, Vereinigung f; *corporate* - Körperschaft f, juristische Person
boilerplate (informal) (US) Allgemeine Geschäftsbedingungen
bona fide gutgläubig *adj*, in gutem Glauben; *- fide creditor* gutgläubiger Forderungsinhaber; *- fide holder* gutgläubiger Besitzer, gutgläubiger Inhaber; *- fide transaction* gutgläubiger Erwerb
bonanza n unerwarteter großer Gewinn (US)
bond n Anleihe f (= Obligation), Obligation f, Schuldverschreibung f, Anleihepapier n, Schuldschein m, Garantie f, Kaution f; *- v* verbriefen v; *- amount* Anleihebetrag m; *- broker* (US) Fondsmakler m; *- capital* Anleihekapital n; *- certificate* Interimsschein für eine Inhaberschuldverschreibung; *- circular* Prospekt über die Ausgabe von Obligationen; *- circulation* Anleiheumlauf m; *- conversion* Anleihekonversion f; *- coupon* Zinsschein m; *- coupon collection* Zinsscheininkasso n; *- creditor* Obligationsinhaber m, Pfandbriefgläubiger m, Pfandbriefinhaber m; *- cum warrant* Anleihe mit Optionsschein; *- debt* Anleiheschuld f; *- debtor* Obligationenschuldner m, Pfandbriefschuldner m; *- department* Abteilung für festverzinsliche Wertpapiere (US); *- discount* Obligationsagio n, Pfandbriefagio n; *- dividend* Dividende in Form eigener Obligationen; *- ex warrant* Anleihe ohne Optionsschein; *- fund* Obligationenfonds m, Pfandbrieffonds m, Rentenfonds m; *- holder* Obligationsinhaber m, Pfandbriefgläubiger m, Pfandbriefinhaber m; *- holdings* Obligationenbesitz m, Pfandbriefbesitz m; *- house* Pfandbriefinstitut n; *- indenture* Schuldverschreibungsurkunde f; *- interest* Obligationszinsen m pl; *- interest accrued* Stückzinsen m pl; *- investment fund* Rentenfonds m, Anleihefonds m; *- issue* Pfandbriefemission f, Pfandbriefausgabe f, Emission von Obligationen; *- issue in default* notleidende Anleihe; *- issue with monetary option* Anleihe mit Währungsoption; *- issue without fixed maturity* ewige Rente; *- market* Obligationsmarkt m, Rentenmarkt m, Pfandbriefmarkt m, Anleihemarkt m; *- note* Zollbegleitschein m; *- of indebtedness* Schuldschein m, Schuldanerkennung f; *- of indemnity* (US) Ausfallbürgschaft f, schriftliche Garantieerklärung, Schadenersatzerklärung f; *- of obligation* Schuldverschreibung f, Schuldschein m; *- premium* Obligationsagio n, Pfandbriefagio n; *- price* Obligationenkurs m, Rentenkurs m; *- rating* Schätzung des Nettowertes festverzinslicher Wertpapiere, Bonitätsprüfung von Anleiheschuldnern; *- redemption* Obligationstilgung f; *- register* Obligationsbuch n; *- sinking fund* Amortisationsfonds für Obligationen; *- to bearer* Inhaberobligation f, Inhaberschuldverschreibung f; *- trading* Obligationshandel m, Pfandbriefhandel m; *- trading department* Pfandbriefabteilung f, Abteilung für festverzinsliche Wertpapiere; *- valuation* Wertberechnung einer Obligation; *- warrants* Anleiheoptionsscheine m pl; *- with surety* Schuldverschreibung mit zusätzlicher Bürgschaft; *- with warrants* Optionsanleihe f; *annuity* - Rententitel m, Rentenschuldverschreibung f; *assumed* - mit zusätzlicher Dividendengarantie ausgestattetes Wertpapier; *average* - Havarieschein m; *bail* - Bürgschaftsschein m, Bürgschaftsurkunde f; *bearer* - Inhaberobligation f, Inhaberschuldverschreibung f; *bid* - Bietungsgarantie f; *blanket* - sicherungsweise abgetretene Hypothek; *bottomry* - Bodmereibrief m; *clean* - (US) auf den Inhaber laufende Obligation ohne Giro- oder Stempelvermerk; *coupon* - (US) Inhaberobligation f, Inhaberschuldverschreibung f; *currency* - Obligation in ausländischer Währung; *debenture* - ungesicherte Schuldverschreibung; *deferred* - Obligation mit hinausgescho-

bener Verzinsung; **discharge a** ~ einen Schuldschein einlösen; **discount** ~ unverzinsliche Schuldverschreibung, Abzinsungstitel m, Anleihe mit Abschlag vom Nennwert; **drawn** ~ ausgeloste Obligation; **endorsed** ~ durch Wechsel garantierte Schuldverschreibung, durch einen weiteren Verpflichteten garantierte Schuldverschreibung; **guaranteed** ~ garantierte Anleihe; **indorsed** ~ durch Wechsel garantierte Schuldverschreibung, durch einen weiteren Verpflichteten garantierte Schuldverschreibung; **mortgage** ~ Hypothekenpfandbrief m, Hypothekenbrief m; **non-interest-bearing** ~ unverzinsliche Schuldverschreibung; **passive** ~ zinslose Schuldverschreibung; **payment** ~ Zahlungsbürgschaft f; **personal** ~ persönliche Garantie; **preference** ~ Vorzugsobligation f, Obligation mit Vorzugsrecht; **preferred** ~ Vorzugsobligation f, Obligation mit Vorzugsrecht; **provisional** ~ Zwischenschein für eine Obligation; **secured** ~ hypothekarisch gesicherte Obligation, hypothekarisch gesicherte Schuldverschreibung; **senior** ~ Vorzugsobligation f, Obligation mit Vorzugsrecht; **trust** ~ Schuldverschreibung über eine bevorrechtigte Forderung

bonded adj durch Obligationen gesichert, durch Schuldverschreibungen gesichert, mit Schulden belastet, verpfändet adj, unter Zollverschluß lagernd; **~ debt** Anleiheschuld f; fundierte Schuld; **~ goods** Waren unter Zollverschluß; **~ indebtedness** Anleiheschuldenlast f; **~ warehouse** Zollverschlußlager n

bonder n Zolleinlagerer m

bondholder n Anleiheinhaber, Pfandbriefinhaber

bonding n Zolleinlagerung f; **~ company** Kautionsversicherungsgesellschaft f; **~ underwriter** Übernahmekonsortium für Obligationen (Pfandbriefe)

bonds account Aberdepot n; **~ and notes** Anleihen und Schuldverschreibungen (Bilanzposten); **~ and other interests** Beteiligungen und andere Wertpapiere; **~ equipment** (US) Schuldverschreibungen zum Ankauf von Ausrüstungsgegenständen; **active** ~ (GB) festverzinsliche Obligationen; **baby** ~ Wertpapiere mit geringem Nominalwert, Obligationen mit kleiner Stückelung; **certificate of** ~ (GB) Bescheinigung über die Registrierung von Namensobligationen; **city** ~ (US) Stadtanleihe f; **civil** ~ (US) Schuldverschreibungen der öffentlichen Hand; **classified** ~ in verschiedenen Serien ausgegebene Schuldverschreibungen; **collateral trust** ~ durch Effektenlombard gesicherte Obligationen; **continued** ~ (US) prolongierte Obligationen; **convertible** ~ Wandelschuldverschreibungen f pl; **corporate** ~ (US) Schuldverschreibungen von Aktiengesellschaften; **county** ~ Kommunalobligationen f pl; **defaulted** ~ notleidende Obligationen; **digested** ~ (US) fest plazierte Obligationen; **disabled** ~ (GB) ungültige Obligationen; **first mortgage** ~ durch erststellige Hypotheken gesicherte Pfandbriefe; **government** ~ Staatspapiere n pl; **junior** ~ durch nachstehende Hypothek oder nachstehendes Pfandrecht sichergestellte Obligationen; **optional** ~ (US) kündbare Obligationen; **participating** ~ (US) Obligationen mit Gewinnbeteiligung; **plain** ~ ungesicherte Obligationen; **profitsharing** ~ Obligationen mit Gewinnbeteiligung; **public** ~ Staatsanleihe f, Staatspapiere f pl; **real estate** ~ (US) Grundkreditpfandbriefe m pl, Grundstücksobligationen f pl; **redeemable** ~ auflösbare Obligationen; **redemption** ~ neufundierte Obligationen; **registered** ~ Namensschuldverschreibungen f pl; **small** ~ Obligationen mit kleiner Stückelung; **straight** ~ Obligationen ohne Konversions- oder Bezugsrechte; **underlying** ~ (US) durch Vorranghypothek gesicherte Obligationen

bondsman n Bürge m, Treugeber m, Hinterleger m

bonus v durch Prämie fördern; n Bonus m, Extradividende f, Sonderdividende f, Superdividende f, außerordentliche Dividende; Gratifikation f, Tantieme f, Prämie f

BONUS = borrower's options for notes and underwritten standby

bonus

Fremdkapitalaufnahmeoption für Eurowährungsinhaberschuldscheine oder US-Schuldtitel

bonus *account* Prämienkonto n; *- earnings* Prämienverdienst m; *- fund* Dividendenfonds m; *- issue* Prämiengewährung f, Ausgabe von Gratisaktien (Kapitalberechtigungsaktien); *- payment* Tantiemeauszahlung f; *- plan* Prämiensystem n; *- reserve* Prämienreserve f, Dividendenreserve f; *- right* Gratisrecht n; *- share* (GB) Gratisaktie f, Kapitalberechtigungsaktie f, Bonusaktie f; *- stock* Gratisaktie f, Kapitalberechtigungsaktie f (US); **capital** *- Gratisaktie f, Kapitalprämie f; **cash** - cash* Sonderbonus in bar, Barbonus m, Bardividende f

book v buchen v, verbuchen v, eintragen v, aufzeichnen v, notieren v; *- n* Journal n, Bestand n, Portefeuille n; *- claim* Buchforderung f; *- cost* Buchwert m; *- credit* Buchkredit m; *- creditor* Buchgläubiger m; *- debt* Buchschuld f; *- debtor* Buchschuldner m; *- figures* Buchwerte m pl; *- in conformity* gleichlautend buchen; *- keeper* Konsortialführer m; *- of accounts* Kontobuch n; *- of receipts and expenditures* Einnahmen-und-Ausgaben-Buch; *- of remittances* Überweisungsbuch n; *- omitted items* Posten nachtragen; *- position* Sollstellung f; *- profit* Buchgewinn m; *- runner* Konsortialführer m; *- surplus* buchmäßiger Überschuß; *- transfer* Umbuchung f; *- value* Buchwert m, Bilanzwert m; *account -* Kontobuch n; *accounts opened an closed -* Kontenverzeichnis n (US); *audit -* Revisionsbuch n; *balance sheet -* Bilanzbuch n; *bargain -* Schlußnotenregister n; *bill for collection -* Wechselbuch für Inkassowechsel; *black -* schwarze Liste, Insolventenliste f, Verzeichnis unsicherer Kunden; *cash payments -* Kassenausgangsbuch m; *cashier's -* Kassenbuch n; *coupon -* Kuponkonto n

book-building Preisermittlung bei der Neuemission von Aktien

booking n Buchung f (Tätigkeit); *- item* Buchungsposten m; *- terminal* Buchungsplatz m; *- voucher* Buchungsbeleg m, Buchhaltungsbeleg m

bookkeeper n Buchhalter m, Buchführer m; **general** *-* Hauptbuchhalter m

bookkeeping n Buchführung f, Buchhaltung f, Rechnungswesen n; *- by double entry* doppelte Buchführung; *- by single entry* einfache Buchführung; *- department* Buchhaltungsabteilung f; *- entry* Buchungsposten m; *- expense* Buchhaltungskosten plt; *- form* Buchungsformular n; *- loss* Buchungsverlust m; *- machine* Buchungsmaschine f; *- method* Buchungsverfahren n; *- records* Buchungsunterlagen f pl; *- work* Buchführungsarbeit f; *commercial -* kaufmännische Buchführung; **double entry** *-* doppelte Buchführung; **tabular** *-* amerikanische Buchführungsmethode

books of corporations Geschäftsunterlagen f pl; *agree the -* Bücher abstimmen; *balancing of the -* Bilanzabschluß m, Buchabschluß m; *check the -* Bücher revidieren; *closing of -* Bücherabschluß m

book-squaring Glattstellen von Positionen

boom v rapide ansteigen v (Preise, Kurse), in die Höhe gehen; *- n* Hausse f, Konjunktur f, plötzliche Kurssteigerung, kräftige Geschäftsbelebung; *- conditions* Haussebedingungen f pl, Hochkonjunktur f; *- market* Haussemarkt m; *- price* Haussekurs m; *- profit* Konjunkturgewinn m; *- the market* Kurse steigern; *- year* Konjunkturjahr n

booming adj (US) Aufschwung nehmend, im Aufschwung begriffen

boost v ankurbeln v, fördern v; *- n* Aufschwung m, Förderung f

bordereau n Bordereau n, Strazze f, Kladde f, Stückverzeichnis n, Sortenzettel m, Sonderzettel m

borrow v borgen v, leihen v, entleihen v, entlehnen v; *- money* Kredit aufnehmen

borrowed adj geborgt adj, geliehen adj; *- capital* Fremdkapital n, Leihkapital n, Kreditkapital n; *- money* geliehenes Geld, aufgenommener Kredit

borrower n Kreditnehmer m, Darlehensnehmer m, Anleiheschuldner m

borrower's bank Hausbank f; **- note** Schuldschein m; **- options for notes and underwritten standby = BONUS** Fremdkapitalaufnahmeoption für Eurowährungsinhaberschuldscheine oder US-Schuldtitel

borrowing n Leihen n, Borgen n, Kreditaufnahme f; **- demand** Kreditbedarf m, Kreditwunsch m; **- facilities** Kreditaufnahmemöglichkeiten f pl; **- on accounts receivable** Kreditaufnahme durch Abtretung von Debitoren; **- power** Kreditwürdigkeit f, Kreditfähigkeit f; **- rate** Kreditzinssatz m, Darlehenszinssatz m, Ausleihungssatz m; **- requirements** Mittelbedarf m

borrowings Kreditverbindlichkeiten f pl

borsa n italienische Börse

bottom n Tiefstand m, niedrigster Stand; **- of the bear market** Tiefpunkt der Baisse; **- price** niedrigster Kurs, niedrigster Preis

bottomry n Bodmerei f, Bodmereibrief m; **- bandholder** Bodmereigläubige f u. m; **- debt** Bodmereischuld f; **bill of -** Bodmereibrief m

bought adj gekauft adj; **- deal** festes Bankangebot an den Emittenten im Emissionsgeschäft; **- for cash** gegen Kasse gekauft, bar gekauft; **- note** Schlußnote f, Schlußschein m; **- on credit** auf Ziel gekauft

bounty n Bonus m, Prämie f, Ausfuhrprämie f, Subvention f

bourse n Börse f; **black -** schwarze Börse; **continental -** Festlandbörse f

Bourse (the Bourse) Pariser Börse f

Brady Bonds (South American debt crisis) Anleihen, mit Rückzahlungs-, aber ohne Tilgungsgarantie

brain trust Sachverständigenrat m, Expertenrat m

branch n Niederlassung f, Zweigstelle f, Filiale f, Nebenstelle f, Depositenkasse f, Geschäftsstelle f; **- account** Filialkonto n; **- bank** Filialbank f, Bankfiliale f; **- banking** Filialbanksystem n; **- banking activities** Filialbankwesen n; **- manager** Filialleiter m; **- network** Filialnetz n, Geschäftsstellennetz n; **- office** Niederlassung f, Zweigstelle f, Filiale f, Nebenstelle f, Depositenkasse f, Geschäftsstelle f; **- profitability** Branchenrendite f; **- statistics** Branchenstatistik f; **business -** Geschäftszweig m, Geschäftssparte f; **city -** Stadtfiliale f, Stadtkasse f; **country -** (GB) Provinzfiliale f; **main -** Hauptfiliale f; **network of - offices** Filialnetz n, Geschäftsstellennetz n

branchlet n kleine Zweigstelle

branch-of-business classification Branchengliederung f

brand n Marke f (Handelsmarke), Warenzeichen n

branded article Markenartikel m

brassage n Münzgebühr f, Münzgewinn m

break n Bruch m, Unterbrechung f, Trendwende f; **- v** Konkurs machen, bankrott machen; **- even** Geschäft ohne Gewinn oder Verlust machen; **- in prices** Kurseinbruch m, Kurssturz m; **- in the market** Kursumschwung m, Marktwende f

breakdown n Aufgliederung f, Analyse f

break-down by size Größenklassengliederung f

break-even-point Rentabilitätsgrenze f, Rentabilitätsschwelle f

Bretton Woods Agreement Bretton-Woods-Übereinkommen 1944 (Gründung der Weltbank und des Internationalen Währungsfonds (IWF))

breweries n pl (US) Brauereiaktien f pl

bribe n Schmiergeld n, Bestechung f

bribery n Bestechung f

bridge loan Zwischenfinanzierung f

bridge-over financing Vorfinanzierung f, Zwischenfinanzierung f

bridging loan Überbrückungskredit m; **- advance** Zwischenfinanzierungskredit m

bring up to date auf den neuesten Stand bringen

brisk

brisk *adj* lebhaft *adj*
Britannia Britania (englische Goldmünze; 100 £ Nominalwert)
British Association of Payment Clearing System = BACS Clearing-System-Dachverband des Londoner Clearingsystems
broad market aufnahmefähiger Markt
broadcasting stocks Aktien von Rundfunkanstalten und Fernsehgesellschaften
broadly diversified portfolio breit gestreute Wertpapieranlage
broken *adj* bankrott *adj*, ruiniert *adj*; *- account* umsatzloses Konto, unbewegtes Konto, totes Konto; *- lot* (US) Effekten unter 1000 Dollar Nominalwert;
broken-period interest Stückzins *m*, aufgelaufener Zins *m*, pro-rate Zins *m*
broker *n* Makler *m*, Agent *m*, Zwischenhändler *m*; *bill -* Wechselmakler *m*, Wechselhändler *m*; *bond -* (US) Fondsmakler *m*; *bullion -* Makler im Edelmetallhandel; *certified -* amtlich zugelassener Makler; *commission -* Börsenkommissionsfirma *f*, Kommissionsmakler *m*; *curb -* Freiverkehrsmakler *m*; *curbstone -* Freiverkehrsmakler *m*; *discount -* Wechselmakler *m*, Wechselhändler *m*, spesengünstiger Wertpapierhändler; *exchange -* Devisenmakler *m*, Wechselmakler *m*, Börsenmakler *m*; *inside -* (GB) amtlich zugelassener Makler; *money -* Geldmakler *m*; *nonmember -* freier Makler, nicht zur offiziellen Börse zugelassener Makler; *outside -* freier Makler, nicht zur offiziellen Börse zugelassener Makler; *put and call -* (US) Prämienmakler *m*; *real estate -* (US) Grundstücksmakler *m*, Immobilienmakler *m*; *sworn -* vereidigter Makler; *unofficial -* Freiverkehrsmakler *m*
brokerage *n* Maklergebühr *f*, Maklerprovision *f*, Courtage *f*; *- n* Maklergeschäft *n*, Vermittlungsgeschäft *n*; *- business* Maklergeschäft *n*, Vermittlungsgeschäft *n*; *- concern* Maklerfirma *f*; *- field* Maklerwesen *n*; *- firm* Maklerfirma *f*; *- house* Maklerfirma *f*; *- office* Maklerfirma *f*; *- practices* Maklerusancen *f pl*; *bill -* Wechselhandel *m*, Wechselcourtage *f*
brokers; board of *-* Maklersyndikat *n*
broker's business Börsenkommissionsgeschäft *n*; *- commission* Maklergebühr *f*, Maklerprovision *f*, Courtage *f*; *- fee* Maklergebühr *f*, Maklerprovision *f*, Courtage *f*; *- loan* Maklerdarlehen *n*, Kredit an Börsenmakler unter Beleihung von Wertpapieren; *- memorandum* Schlußnote *f*, Schlußschein *m*; *- note* Schlußnote *f*, Schlußschein *m*; *- ticket* Börsenabrechnung *f*
broking *n* Maklergeschäft *n*, Vermittlungsgeschäft *n*
brought-in capital Kapitaleinzahlung *f*, Kapitaleinlage *f*
buck *n* (US-Slang) Dollar *m*
bucket-shop *n* (GB) Büro eines Freiverkehrsmaklers; *- n* (US) Winkelbörse *f*
bucketeer *n* (US) unreeller Börsenmakler
bucketing *n* (US) Betreiben unreeller Maklergeschäfte
budget *v* einen Haushaltsplan aufstellen; *- n* Budget *n*, Etat *m*, Haushalt *m*, Staatshaushalt *m*; *- position* Sollstellung *f*; *advertising -* Werbeetat *m*
budgetary *adj* etatmäßig *adj*, haushaltsmäßig *adj*, budgetmäßig *adj*; *- account* Haushaltskonto *n*; *- accounting* Finanzplanung *f*; *- reform* Haushaltsreform *f*
budgeting *n* Haushaltsaufstellung *f*, Etatplanung *f*, Geschäftsplanung *f*, Planrechnung *f*
buffer *n* Pufferung *f* (EDV); *- stocks* Pufferbestände *m pl*, Ausgleichslager für Rohstoffe
buffering *n* Pufferung *f* (EDV)
building account Gebäudekonto *n*; *- and loan association* Bausparkasse *f*; *- capital* Baukapital *n*; *- estate* Baugrundstück *n*, baureifes Grundstück; *- ground* Bauplatz *m*; *- lease* Erbpachtvertrag *m*, Baupachtrecht *n*; *- loan* Baudarlehen *n*; *- loan contract* Bausparvertrag *m*; *- management* Gebäudeverwaltung *f*; *- market*

Baumarkt m; *- society* (GB) Bausparkasse f; *- society loans* Bankdarlehen der Bausparkasse; *- society savings agreement* Bausparvertrag m; *- stocks* (US) Bauaktien f pl; *assess a -* Gebäude abschätzen; *intermediate - credit* Bauzwischenkredit m
buildings Bauaktien f pl
build-up area bebautes Gebiet
bulk n Hauptanteil m, Gesamtheit f, Masse f, Ladung f, Volumen m, Umfang m; *- buying* Mengeneinkauf m; *- of one's business* Hauptgeschäft n; *in -* in großen Mengen
bulky goods Sperrgut n
bull v auf Hausse spekulieren, im Hinblick auf eine Hausse kaufen; *-* n Haussespekulant m, Haussier m; *- account* Hausseposition f; *- buying* Haussekauf m; *- campaign* Angriff der Haussepartei f; *- clique* Haussepartei f; *- market* Haussemarkt m; *- movement* Haussebewegung f; *- operation* Haussespekulation f; *- pool* Haussegruppe f; *- purchase* (US) Haussekauf m; *- speculation* Haussespekulation f; *stale -* geschlagener Haussier; *- transactions* Haussegeschäft n; *- trap* Bullenfalle f;
bulldog bond Pfund-(Sterling-)Auslandsanleihe f
bullet *bond* unkündbare Anleihe f; *- loan* Kredit, der in einem Betrag zurückgezahlt wird
bulling Kauf auf Hausse
bullion n Goldbarren m, Silberbarren m, ungemünztes Edelmetall; *- broker* Makler im Edelmetallhandel; *- coin* Goldmünze mit geringem Agio; *- point* Goldpunkt m; *- reserve* Goldreserve f, Gold-und-Silber-Bestand m; *- value* Gold- oder Silberwert einer Münze
bullish adj haussierend adj, steigend adj, in Hausse; *- market* Haussemarkt m; *- report* Haussenachricht f; *- tendency* Haussetendenz f
bullishness n Haussetendenz f
bumping Personalabbau nach dem LIFO Prinzip (last in first out)
bunched adj (US) fortlaufend notiert
Bund Bundesanleihe f (deutsche B.)

Bundesbank Act Bundesbankgesetz n
Bund-future Terminkontrakt auf eine Bundesanleihe
bundle v zusammenbündeln v, einpacken v; *- of notes* Banknotenbündel n
bundling Bündelung von Bankdienstleistungen, Zusammenfassung von Bankleistungen zu einem neuen Produkt
bunny bonds Euroanleihen mit Zinswiederanlageoption
buoyancy n steigende Tendenz
buoyant adj steigend adj, sehr fest (Kurse); *- market* feste Börse
burden v besteuern v, belasten v; *-* n Last f, Belastung f; *- of financing* Finanzierungslast f; *- of taxation* Steuerlast f; *- sharing* Lastenverteilung f, Umschuldung f
burdened *estate* belastetes Grundstück; *- with mortgages* mit Hypotheken belastet
bureau; *credit -* Kreditvermittlungsbüro n Kreditauskunftei f
burglary insurance Einbruchversicherung f
business n Geschäft n, Gewerbe n, Geschäftszweig m, Handel m, Handelsbetrieb m, Handelsunternehmen n, Firma f; *- account* Geschäftskonto n; *- activity* Geschäftsverkehr m; *- acumen* Geschäftssinn m; *- administration* Betriebswirtschaft f, Betriebswirtschaftslehre f; *- analyst* Wirtschaftsanalytiker m; *- application* Antrag auf Geschäftseröffnung; *- appointment* geschäftliche Verabredung, Geschäftssitzung f; *- assets* Geschäftsvermögen n; *- associate* Geschäftspartner m; *- basis* Geschäftsgrundlage f; *- branch* Geschäftszweig m, Geschäftssparte f; *- capital* Geschäftskapital n; *- card* Geschäftskarte f; *- circles* Wirtschaftskreise m pl; *- commitments* geschäftliche Verpflichtungen; *- concern* Geschäftsunternehmen n; *- conference* geschäftliche Besprechung; *- connections* Geschäftsverbindung f, Geschäftsbeziehungen f pl; *- consultant* Wirtschaftsberater m; *- corporation* (US)

Geschäftsunternehmen n; **~ counselling** Unternehmensberatung f; **~ custom** Geschäftsgebrauch m, Geschäftssitte f; **~ customer** Firmenkunde m; **~ cycle** Konjunkturzyklus m, Konjunkturverlauf m; **~ debts** Geschäftsschulden f pl, Betriebsschulden f pl; **~ decline** Geschäftsrückgang m; **~ department** Akquisitionsabteilung f, Kundenwerbeabteilung f; **~ economics** Betriebswirtschaft f, Betriebswirtschaftslehre f; **~ enterprise** geschäftliches Unternehmen; **~ expenses** Geschäftskosten plt; **~ failure** Zahlungseinstellung f, Konkurs m, Bankrott m; **~ finance** Betriebsfinanzen plt; **~ fluctuations** Geschäftsschwankungen f pl, Konjunkturschwankungen f pl; **~ for own account** Eigengeschäft n; **~ forecasting** Konjunkturdiagnose f; **~ forecasting service** Nachrichtendienst für Wirtschaftsprognosen; **~ friend** Geschäftsfreund m, Korrespondent m; **~ hours** Geschäftszeit f; **~ in securities** Effektengeschäft n; **~ income** Geschäftseinkommen n; **~ initiative** unternehmerische Initiative; **~ interest** Geschäftsbeteiligung f; **~ interruption insurance** Betriebsunterbrechungsversicherung f; **~ inventory** Geschäftsinventar n, Firmeninventar n, Betriebsinventar n; **~ investment** betriebliche Investition; **~ letter** Geschäftsbrief m; **~ liabilities** Geschäftsschulden f pl, Betriebsschulden f pl; **~ life insurance** Teilhaberversicherung f; **~ line** Geschäftszweig m, Geschäftssparte f; **~ loan** Geschäftskredit m, Betriebskredit m, Firmenkredit m; **~ management** Betriebsführung f; **~ office** Geschäftslokal n, Geschäftsräume m pl; **~ on joint account** Konsortialgeschäft n; **~ outlook** Geschäftsaussichten f pl; **~ paper** Warenwechsel m; **~ participation** Geschäftsbeteiligung f; **~ plan** Business-Plan m, Geschäftsplan m, Unternehmensplan m; **~ premises** Geschäftslokal n, Geschäftsräume m pl; **~ proceeds** Geschäftsertrag m, Betriebsertrag m; **~ profit** Geschäftsgewinn m; **~ property** Geschäftsgrundstück n, Betriebsgrundstück n; **~ prospects** Geschäftsaussichten f pl; **~ prosperity** Geschäftskonjunkturauftrieb m, Hochkonjunktur f; **~ recession** Rezession f, Geschäftskonjunkturrückgang m; **~ records** Geschäftsbücher n pl; **~ recovery** Konjunkturbelebung f, Wirtschaftsbelebung f; **~ reference** geschäftliche Empfehlung, geschäftliche Referenz; **~ relations** Geschäftsverbindung f, Geschäftsbeziehungen f pl; **~ report** Geschäftsbericht m; **~ reputation** geschäftliches Ansehen; **~ research** Konjunkturforschung f; **~ revival** Konjunkturbelebung f, Wirtschaftsbelebung f; **~ savings** geschäftliche Einsparungen, betriebliche Einsparungen; **~ school** Handelsschule f; **~ secret** Geschäftsgeheimnis n, Betriebsgeheimnis n; **~ set-up loan** Starthilfekredit m; **~ struggle** Konkurrenzkampf m; **~ style** Firmierung f; **~ syndicate** Wirtschaftsvereinigung f; **~ transaction** Geschäftsvorfall m; **~ unit** Geschäftsstelle f; **~ usages** Handelsbräuche m pl, Usancen f pl; **~ volume** Geschäftsumfang m; **~ with corporate customers** Firmenkundengeschäft n; **~ year** Geschäftsjahr n; **backwardation ~** (GB) Deportgeschäft n; **banking ~** Bankwesen n, Bankgeschäft n, Bankbetrieb m, Kreditgewerbe n, Bankgewerbe n; **brokerage ~** Maklergeschäft n, Vermittlungsgeschäft n; **broker's ~** Börsenkommissionsgeschäft n; **class of ~** Geschäftszweig m, Geschäftssparte f; **collecting ~** Inkassogeschäft n; **commencement of ~** Geschäftsbeginn m; **commercial ~** Handelsgeschäft n; **commission ~** Kommissionsgeschäft n, Kommissionshandel m; **compensation ~** Kompensationsgeschäft n; **current ~** laufende Geschäfte; **foundation of a ~** Geschäftsgründung f; **place of ~** Geschäftssitz m

businesslike adj geschäftsmäßig adj, geschäftlich adj
businessman n Geschäftsmann m
businesswoman n Geschäftsfrau f
bust adj (US-Slang) bankrott adj

busted *bond* historisches Wertpapier; *- convertible* Wandelschuldverschreibung mit geringem Aufgeld

buy *v* kaufen *v*, einkaufen *v*, erwerben *v*, erstehen *v*, ersteigern *v*, beziehen *v*, abnehmen *v*; *- n* Kauf *m*, Ankauf *m*, Einkauf *m*, Anschaffung *f*, Erwerb *m*; *- and sell* handeln *v* (Handel treiben); *- at a loss* mit Verlust verkaufen; *- at a premium* über pari kaufen; *- at first hand* aus erster Hand kaufen; *- back* zurückkaufen *v*; *- by auction* auf einer Auktion kaufen; *- for cash* gegen bar kaufen; *- for ready money* gegen bar kaufen; *- for the rise* auf Hausse spekulieren, im Hinblick auf eine Hausse kaufen; *- forward* auf Lieferung kaufen; *- on credit* auf Kredit kaufen; *- on time* auf Kredit kaufen; *- on trust* auf Kredit kaufen; *- outright* (US) per Kasse gegen sofortige Lieferung kaufen; *- securities on margin* Wertpapiere auf Kreditbasis kaufen; *- up* aufkaufen *v*

buyable *adj* käuflich *adj*

buy-back agreement Pensionsgeschäft *n*

buyer *n* Käufer *m*

buyers *n pl* (stock exchange) Geld *n* (Börse)

buyer's *market* Käufermarkt *m*; *- monopoly* Käufermonopol *n*; *- option* Kaufoption *f*; *- rate* Geldkurs *m*

buyer-up *n* Aufkäufer *m*

buying *n* Kauf *m*, Ankauf *m*, Einkauf *m*, Anschaffung *f*, Erwerb *m*; *- attention* Käuferinteresse *n* (Börse); *- back* Eindeckung *f*, Rückkauf *m*; *- for a rise* Kauf auf Hausse; *- on margin* Effektenkauf mit Einschuß *f*; *- order* Kaufauftrag *m*; *- out* Auszahlung *f*, Abfindung *f*; *- price* Kaufpreis *m*, Ausgabekurs *m*; *- rate* Geldkurs *m*, Kaufkurs *m*; *- surge* Kaufwelle *f* (Börse); *- up* Aufkauf *m*; *absorb - power* Kaufkraft abschöpfen; *bulk* - Mengeneinkauf *m*; *bull* - Haussekauf *m*; *cash* - Kassakauf *m*; *cooperative - association* Einkaufsgenossenschaft *f*; *credit* - Kreditkauf *m*; *outright* - (US) Kassakauf *m*

bylaws; corporate - Satzung *f* (einer Gesellschaft), Statut *n*, Statuten *n pl*

bypass *v* umgehen *v*; *banking* - Bankumgehung *f*

by-product *n* Nebenprodukt *n*

byte *n* (storage unit in a computer) Byte *n*

c = comptant in bar, Lieferung gegen Kasse

cable v kabeln v, telegrafieren v; ~ n Depesche f, Telegramm n; **~ order** Kabelauftrag m; **~ transfer** Kabelüberweisung f, telegrafische Auszahlung; telegrafische Geldüberweisung; **~ transfer rate** Kabelauszahlung f (Kurs), telegrafische Auszahlung (Kurs)

cadastral adj Kataster- (in Zus.), Grundbuch- (in Zus.)

cadastre n Grundbuch n, Kataster m

cage (US) Abwicklungsstelle f, Wertpapierabteilung f

calculability n Berechenbarkeit f

calculable adj berechenbar adj

calculate v rechnen v, berechnen v, kalkulieren v

calculating n Rechnen n, Rechnung f, Zählung f; **~ machine** Rechenmaschine f

calculation n Rechnung f (Berechnung), Kalkulation f, Ausrechnung f; **~ of cost** Selbstkostenrechnung f; **~ of earning power** Rentabilitätsberechnung f; **~ of exchange** Devisenkursberechnung f; **~ of interest** Zinsberechnung f, Zinsrechnung f; **~ of profits** Gewinnberechnung f, Rentabilitätsberechnung f; **basis of ~** Berechnungsgrundlage f

calculator n Taschenrechner m

calendar n Kalender m; **~ day** Kalendertag m

call v rufen v, aufrufen v, einberufen v, fordern v, auffordern v; ~ n Ruf m, Aufruf m, Schlußnote f, Schlußschein m, Nachfrage f, Differenzgeschäft n, Zeitgeschäft n, Prämiengeschäft auf Abnahme, Antrag m, Forderung f; **~ a meeting of shareholders** eine Hauptversammlung einberufen; **~ a meeting of stockholders** eine Hauptversammlung einberufen; **~ an option** ein Prämiengeschäft eingehen; **~ date** Kündigungstermin m; **~ deposits** Sichteinlagen f pl; **~ facility** Abrufkredit m; **~ for** anfordern v; **~ for additional cover** eine Nachschußzahlung fordern; **~ for production of documents** eine Vorlage von Urkunden verlangen; **~ for redemption** Kündigung f (einer Anleihe); **~ in** einziehen v, kündigen v, außer Kurs setzen; **~ leger** Einzahlungsaufforderung f; **~ loan** (GB) kurzfristiges Darlehen, täglich fälliges Geld, Tagesgeld n; **~ money** Tagesgeld n, täglich fälliges Geld; **~ money market** Markt für Tagesgeld; **~ money rate** Satz für Tagesgeld; **~ of more** Nochgeschäft n (Börse); **~ on shares** Aufforderung zur Einzahlung auf Aktien; **~ option** Kaufoption f; **~ premium** Kündigungsaufgeld n; **~ price** Rücknahmekurs m (Investitionsanleihe); **~ protection** Zahl der kündigungsfreien Jahre; **~ provision** Bestimmung, nach der die Obligationen jederzeit zurückgezahlt werden können; **~ rate** Tagesgeldzinssatz m, Satz für Tagesgeld; **~ right** Kündigungsrecht für Aktien; **~ ticket** Zahlungsaufforderungsschein m; **~ warrant** Kaufoptionsschein m; **~ writer** Verkäufer einer Kaufoption; **~ writing** Erwerb von Kaufoptionen; **at ~** auf Verlangen; **margin ~** (US) Effektengeschäft mit Einschuß; **pay a ~** eine Teilzahlung auf Aktien leisten

callable adj abrufbar adj, kündbar adj, einziehbar adj; **~ bond** Tilgungsanleihe f, kündbare Anleihe; **~ preferred stock** (US) rückzahlbare Vorzugsaktien f pl; **~ swap** Swap mit vorzeitigem Kündigungsrecht, Swap mit Laufzeitverlängerungsoption

called adj gekündigt adj, zur Rückzahlung aufgerufen f; **~ up capital** eingefordertes Kapital

calling Aufforderung f, Einberufung f (Versammlung); **~ bank** anfragende Bank

calls Optionsrechte zum Kauf von Effekten; **trading in ~** Vorprämiengeschäfte n pl

calm market ruhiger Markt
cambist n Devisenhändler m, Spezialist für ausländische Währungsarbitrage
campaign n Werbefeldzug m, Werbekampagne f; **advertising ~** Werbefeldzug m; **bull ~** Angriff der Haussepartei
canal freight Kanalfracht f
cancel v stornieren v, aufheben v, streichen v, für nichtig erklären
cancellable adj stornierbar adj, aufhebbar adj, annullierbar adj
cancellation n Stornierung f, Aufhebung f, Storno n, Annullierung f; **~ clause** Kündigungsklausel f
cancelled adj annulliert adj, aufgehoben adj; **~ check** entwerteter Scheck
canvass n Kundenwerbung f, Stimmenwerbung f
canvasser n Akquisiteur m
canvassing n Akquisition f
cap Zinskappe f, Höchstzinssatz m; **~ fee** Zinsbegrenzungsgebühr f
capable adj tüchtig adj, fähig adj; **~ of being financed** finanzierungsfähig
capacity n Kapazität f, Leistungsfähigkeit f, Qualifikation f, Fähigkeit f, Befähigung f; **contractual ~** Vertragsfähigkeit f; **credit ~** Kreditkapazität f
capita; per ~ pro Kopf
capital n Kapital n, Geldmittel n pl, Eigenkapital n; **~ account** Kapitalkonto n; **~ accumulation** Kapitalbildung f, Vermögensbildung f, Kapitalansammlung f; **~ adjustment** Kapitalberichtigung f; **~ allowance** Abschreibung f; **~ and retained earnings** Eigenkapital und Rücklagen; **~ appreciation** Kapitalwerterhöhung f; **~ assets** Kapitalanlagen f pl, Kapitalvermögen n; **~ base** Kapitalbasis f; **~ bonus** Gratisaktie f, Kapitalprämie f; **~ brought in** eingebrachtes Kapital; **called up ~** eingefordertes Kapital n; **~ charges** Kapitalkosten plt; **~ commitments** Kapitalverpflichtungen f pl; **~ cost** Kapitalaufwand m; **~ demand** Kapitalbedarf m; **~ depreciation** Kapitalabschreibung f; **~ disbursements** Kapitalaufwendungen f pl; **~ distribution**
Kapitalausschüttung f; **~ duty** Emissionssteuer f, Vermögensabgabe f; **~ earnings rate** Kapitalverzinsung f; **~ employed** investiertes Kapital; **~ endowment** Kapitalausstattung f; **~ equipment** Anlagen f pl; **~ exodus** Kapitalflucht f; **~ expenditure** in ein Unternehmen investiertes Kapital; **~ export** Kapitalausfuhr f; **~ flight** Kapitalflucht f; **~ formation** Kapitalbildung f, Vermögensbildung f, Kapitalansammlung f; **~ fund** Grundkapital n, Stammkapital n; **~ gain** Kapitalgewinn m, Kapitaleinkommen n; **~ gains tax** Kapitalgewinnsteuer f, Kapitalzuwachssteuer f; **~ goods** Kapitalgüter n pl, Investitionsgüter n pl; **~ grant** Kapitalzuschuß m; **~ growth** Kapitalzuwachs m; **~ increase** Kapitalerhöhung f; **~ interest** Kapitalbeteiligung f; **~ investment** langfristige Kapitalanlage; **~ investment company** Kapitalanlagegesellschaft f; **~ investment grant** Investitionsbeihilfe f; **~ investment loan** Investitionskredit m; **~ issue** Effektenemission f; **~ levy** Kapitalsteuer f, Vermögensabgabe f; **~ liability** Kapitalverbindlichkeit f, langfristige Verbindlichkeit; **~ loan** Betriebsmittelkredit m; **~ loss** Kapitalverlust m; **~ market** Kapitalmarkt m; **~ movement** Kapitalverkehr m; **~ needs** Kapitalbedarf m; **~ net worth** Eigenkapital n; **~ note** Schuldschein m; Kapitalmarkt m; **~ outlay** Kapitalaufwand m; **~ project** Investitionsvorhaben n; **~ projects** Investitionsplanung f, langfristige Anlagevorhaben n; **~ property** Kapitalvermögen n; **~ rating** Kapitalbewertung f; **~ ratio** Kapitalverhältnis n; **~ redemption** Tilgung von Vorzugsaktien; **~ reduction** Kapitalherabsetzung f, Kapitalzusammenlegung f; **~ requirements** Kapitalbedarf m; **~ reserves** Kapitalrücklage f, Kapitalreserve f, Reservekapital n; **~ (equity) resources** Eigenkapital n, eigene Mittel; **~ resources rules** Eigenkapitalbestimmungen f pl; **~ return** Kapitalverzinsung f; **~ savings** vermögenswirksames Sparen; **~ share** Kapitalanteil m; **~ shor-**

tage Kapitalknappheit f; **~ stock** (US) Grundkapital n, Stammkapital n; **~ stock exchange offer** Aktienumtauschangebot n; **~ surplus** Kapitalreserven f pl, Kapitalüberschuß m; **~ tax** Kapitalvermögensteuer f; **~ transaction tax** Kapitalverkehrssteuer f; **~ transfer** Kapitaltransferierung f; **~ turnover** Kapitalumsatz m; **~ valuation** Kapitalbewertung f; **~ venture** Kapitalbeteiligung f, Investition f; **~ write-down** Kapitalschnitt m; **~ yield** Kapitalertrag m; **~ yield tax** Kapitalertragsteuer f; **active ~** flüssiges Kapital, arbeitendes Kapital; **adjustment of ~** Kapitalberichtigung f; **alienation of ~** Kapitalabzug m; **amount of ~** Kapitalhöhe f, Kapitalbetrag m; **authorized ~** für eine Kapitalerhöhung genehmigtes Aktienkapital, (GB) genehmigtes Kapital; **bond ~** Anleihekapital n; **borrowed ~** Fremdkapital n, Leihkapital n, Kreditkapital n; **brought-in ~** Kapitaleinzahlung f, Kapitaleinlage f; **building ~** Baukapital n; **business ~** Geschäftskapital n; **cash ~** Barkapital n; **circulating ~** Betriebskapital n, Umlaufvermögen n, Betriebsmittel n pl; **common ~ stock** (US) Stammkapital n, Stammaktien f pl; **concentration of ~** Kapitalkonzentration f; **conditional ~** bedingtes Kapital; **contribute ~** Kapital einbringen; **contributed ~** eingezahltes Grundkapital; **contribution to ~** Kapitaleinzahlung f, Kapitaleinlage f; **contributor of ~** Kapitaleinleger m; **convert into ~** kapitalisieren v, in Kapital umwandeln; **current ~** Betriebskapital n, Umlaufkapital n, Betriebsmittel n pl; **dead ~** totes Kapital, brachliegendes Kapital, **debenture ~** Obligationenerlös m; **declared ~** festgesetztes Kapital; **dormant ~** totes Kapital, brachliegendes Kapital; **employment of ~** Kapitalanlage f; **floating ~** Betriebskapital n, Umlaufkapital n, Betriebsmittel n pl; **fluid ~** (US) Umlaufkapital n; **idle ~** totes Kapital, brachliegendes Kapital; **issued ~** (GB) effektiv ausgegebenes Aktienkapital, effektiv ausgegebenes Kapital; **partnership ~** Gesellschaftskapital n (einer OHG); **registered ~** (GB) eingetragenes Kapital; **rolling ~** Betriebskapital n, Umlaufkapital n, Betriebsmittel n pl; **share ~** Gesellschaftskapital n (einer AG), Aktienkapital n; **stock ~** Gesellschaftskapital n (einer AG), Aktienkapital n; **trading ~** Betriebskapital n, Umlaufkapital n, Betriebsmittel n pl; **uncalled ~** nicht eingezahltes Kapital; **working ~** Betriebskapital n, Umlaufkapital n, Betriebsmittel n pl

capitalism n Kapitalismus m
capitalist n Kapitalist m
capitalistic adj kapitalistisch adj
capitalization n Kapitalisierung f, Kapitalausstattung f; **~ of earning** Kapitalisierungsfaktor m
capitalize v kapitalisieren v, in Kapital umwandeln
capitalized income Ertragswert m
capitation tax Kopfsteuer f
capped floater zinsvariabler Schuldtitel mit einer Zinsobergrenze; **~ floating rate note** nach oben begrenzter, zinsvariabler Schuldtitel; **~ note** Geldmarktpapier mit flexiblem, nach oben begrenztem Zinssatz; **~ warrant** Optionsschein mit Zinsobergrenze
caption (cap option) Option auf eine Zinsbegrenzungsvereinbarung
captive market monopolistischer Markt
carat n Karat n
card holder Karteninhaber m; **~ index system** Karteisystem n; **~ receiver** Ablagefach n; **~ stacker** Ablagefach n; **~ withdrawals** Geldabhebungen mit der Kreditkarte; **business ~** Geschäftskarte f; **store ~** Kundenkarte f
cardinal number Grundzahl f
career n Karriere f, Laufbahn f, Werdegang m, Entwicklungsgang m
carefulness n Sorgfalt f
careless adj nachlässig adj
carelessness n Nachlässigkeit f
cargo n Fracht f, Ladung f, Frachtgut n; **~ capacity** Ladefähigkeit f; **~ insurance** Frachtversicherung f, Güterversicherung f; **~ policy** Frachtpolice f; **~ ship** Frachtschiff n; **air ~** Luftfracht f
cargo-book n Ladebuch n

carload n (US) Wagenladung f, Waggonladung f

carloading n Waggonsendung f

carriage n Beförderung f, Transport m, Transportkosten plt, Frachtkosten plt, Fuhrgeschäft n, Transportgeschäft n, Frachtgeschäft n; **- account** Frachtkonto n; **- by rail** Eisenbahntransport m; **- by sea** Seetransport m; **- forward** (GB) Frachtkosten per Nachnahme; **- paid** (GB) frachtfrei, franko; **- receipt** Ladeschein m (Landtransport); **air -** Luftfracht f; **bill of -** Frachtbrief m (Bahn)

carrier n Frachtführer m, Verfrachter m, Transportunternehmer m, Spediteur m; **air cargo -** Luftfrachtgesellschaft f; **common -** (US) Verkehrsunternehmen n, Transportunternehmen n; **contract -** Vertragsspediteur m

carrier's charges Speditionsgebühr f

carry v tragen v, befördern v, transportieren v, überbringen v, übertragen v; **- forward** übertragen v (Buchführung), vortragen v, Rechnungsvortrag m; **- interest** Zinsen einbringen; **- out** abwickeln v, durchführen v, ausführen v; **- over** übertragen v (Buchführung), vortragen v, Übertrag m (Buchführung); **- securities** Wertpapiere besitzen; **- through** durchführen v, ausführen v

carry-back Verlustrücktrag m

carrying agent Spediteur m; **- charges** Lager- und Finanzierungskosten; **- over** (GB) Prolongation f, Reportierung f (Börse)

carrying-over business (GB) Prolongationsgeschäft n

cartage n Rollfuhr f, Rollgeld n, Anfuhrgebühren f pl; Fuhrgeld n

carte blanche Blankovollmacht f, uneingeschränkte Vollmacht, Blankoauftrag m

carted goods Rollgut n

cartel n Kartell n, Pool m, Ring m; **- agreement** Kartellvertrag m; **- regulations** Kartellbestimmungen f pl

cartelism n Kartellwesen n

cartelization n Kartellisierung f

cartelize v kartellisieren v

cartwheel n (US-Slang) US-Silberdollar m

case n Fall m, Rechtsfall m, Rechtssache f, Prozeß m; **- of need** Notadresse f bill **-** Wechselportefeuille n, Wechselbestand m

cash v einkassieren v, zu Geld machen, in bar einlösen, einziehen v, kassieren v; **-** n Kasse f, Bargeld n, Barmittel n pl, Kassenbestand m; **- a bill** einen Wechsel einlösen, einen Wechsel honorieren; **- a check** einen Scheck einlösen, einen Scheck kassieren; **- account** Kassenkonto n, Kassakonto n, Kassekonto n; **- advance** Barvorschuß m; **- against documents** Dokumente gegen Zahlung, Kasse gegen Dokumente; **- and carry** (slang) Barverkauf mit Selbstabholung (US); **- assets** Kassenbestand m, Bargeld n; **- at bankers** Bankguthaben n; **- at call** Sichteinlagen f pl; **- audit** Kassenrevision f; **- bid** Übernahmeangebot mit Barabfindung; **- bonus** Sonderbonus in bar, Barbonus m, Bardividende f; **- book** Verkaufsbuch n, Kassenbuch n; **- box** Geldkassette f; **- boy** Kassenbote m; **- buy back** Rückkauf einer Schuld (häufig mit Abschlag); **- buying** Kassakauf m; **- capital** Barkapital n; **- clerk** Kassierer m; **- credit** Barkredit m, Kassenkredit m, Kontokorrentkredit m; **- department** Kasse f (Abteilung); **- deposit** Bareinlage f, Barhinterlegung f; **- desk** Kassenschalter m; **- diary** Kassenkladde f; **- disbursement** Kassenauszahlung f; **- discount** Barrabatt m, Kassaskonto n; **- dispensing machine** Bargeldauszahlungsautomat m; **- dispenser** Geldausgabeautomat, Bancomat m; **- distribution** Barausschüttung f; **- dividend** Bardividende f; **- down** gegen Barzahlung; **- drawings** Barabhebungen f pl; **- earnings** Bareinnahmen f pl; **- equity** Bargeld n, Barmittel; **- flow** Finanzüberschuß eines Jahres, Gewinn zuzüglich Abschreibungen; **- forward transaction** Kassageschäft per Termin; **- funds** Barreserve f; **- holding** Kassenbestand m, Bargeld n; **- in bank** Bankguthaben n; **- in hand** Kassenbestand m, Bargeld n; **- in transit** durchlaufende Gelder; **- in**

value Rückkaufswert m; **~ in vault** Kassenbestand m, Bargeld n; **~ investment** Bareinlage f; **~ item** Kassenposten m; **~ less discount** bar abzüglich Diskont; **~ letter** Geldbrief m; **~ liquidity** Barliquidität f; **~ loan** Kassendarlehen n; **~ management** Planung, Steuerung und Kontrolle der Liquidität; **~ market** Geldmarkt m; **~ market price** Kassakurs m; **~ needs** Liquiditätsbedarf m; **~ note** (GB) Auszahlungsnachweis f, Kassenanweisung f; **~ offer** Barangebot n; **~ office** Kasse f (Abteilung); **~ on delivery (C.O.D.)** zahlbar bei Lieferung; **~ on shipment** zahlbar bei Verschiffung; **~ operation** Bargeschäft n, Kassageschäft n; **~ order** Barzahlungsauftrag m, (GB) Sichtwechsel m; **~ over** Kassenüberschuß durch Irrtümer in der Kassenführung; **~ parcel** Nachnahmepaket n; **~ payment** Barzahlung f, sofortige Zahlung f; **~ payments** Kassenausgänge m pl; **~ payments book** Kassenausgangsbuch n; **~ position** Barposition f, Liquidität f, Kassenbestand m, Barbestand m; **~ price** Barpreis m, Kassakurs m; **~ proceeds** Barerlös m; **~ purchase** Barkauf m; **~ rate** Scheckkurs m, Kassakurs m; **~ receipt** Kassenquittung f; **~ receipts** Bareinnahmen f pl; **~ record** Kassenbeleg m; **~ refund** Barvergütung f; **~ register** Registrierkasse f; **~ remittance** Barüberweisung f; **~ report** Kassenbericht m; **~ reserve** Kassenreserve f, Barreserve f; **~ resources** Kassenmittel n pl; **~ sale** Barverkauf m; **~ settlement** Barausgleich m; **~ short** Kassendefizit n, Kassenfehlbetrag m; **~ surplus** Kassenüberschuß durch Irrtümer in der Kassenführung; **~ surrender value** Rückkaufwert m (einer Versicherungspolice); **~ system** Barzahlungssystem n; **~ transaction** Bargeschäft n, Kassageschäft n; **~ turnover** Kassenumsatz m; **~ value** Barwert m; **~ voucher** Kassenbeleg m; **~ with order** Barzahlung bei Auftragserteilung; **amount in ~** Kassenbestand m, Bargeld n; **balance in ~** Kassenbestand m, Bargeld n; **bought for** ~ gegen Kasse gekauft, bar gekauft; **buy for** ~ gegen bar kaufen; **convert into** ~ realisieren v, flüssig machen, versilbern v, verkaufen v, veräußern v; **counter** ~ tägliche Kasse, Tageskasse f; **deatings for** ~ Kassageschäfte n pl; **in** ~ bar adv; **petty** ~ Portokasse f, kleine Kasse

cashable adj einkassieren adj, einlösbar adj, eintreiben adj, einziehbar adj

cash-card Geldautomatenkarte f

cash-card service Geldausgabeautomat m, Bankomat m

cash-down payment Barzahlung f, sofortige Zahlung

cashier n (US) Hauptkassierer m; ~ n Kassierer m; **~ in charge of operations** Hauptkassierer m; **bank** ~ Bankkassierer m; **chief** ~ Hauptkassierer m

cashier's account Kassenkonto n, Kassakonto n, Kassekonto n; **~ book** Kassenbuch n; **~ check** (US) Bankscheck m; **~ department** Kasse f (Abteilung); **~ desk** Kassenschalter m; **~ receipt** Kassenquittung f

cashing n Kassieren n, Einziehen n Inkasso n

cashless adj bargeldlos adj; **~ society** bargeldlose Gesellschaft; **~ transactions** bargeldloser Zahlungsverkehr

cast v einen Saldo ziehen; **~ n** Saldierung f, Berechnung f

casual work Aushilfsarbeit f

casualty insurance Schadenversicherung f

catculator n Rechenmaschine f

category of securities Effektengattung f

cats and dogs (US) billige Spekulationspapiere

CATS = certificates of accrual on treasury securities (US) Inhaberobligationen, die nur außerhalb der USA an Nichtamerikaner verkauft werden dürfen

caution n Warnung f, Bürge m, Bürgschaft f, Kaution f

cautioner n Bürge m

CD = certificate of deposit Geldmarktpapier n, Einlagenzertifikat n

cede v zedieren v, überlassen v

cedent n Zedent m, Abtretende f u. m

ceiling n Höchstgrenze f, Höchstbetrag m; *- price* Höchstpreis m

cent n (= one hundredth of a dollar) Cent m

center of commerce Markt m, Handelszentrum n; *banking -* Bankplatz m

central bank Zentralnotenbank f; *- bank money* Notenbankgeldmenge f; *- commitments file* Zentralobligo f; *- file* Zentralkartei f, Kundenkartei f; *- management* Hauptverwaltung f; *- office* Zentrale f; *- rate* Leitkurs m

certificate v bescheinigen v (durch Zeugnis); *- n* Bescheinigung f, Beglaubigung f, Zertifikat n, Zeugnis n, Urkunde f, Anteilschein m; *- of account* (US) Bestätigung vom Buchprüfer; *- of analysis* Prüfungsbescheinigung f (für Waren); *- of authority* Vollmachtsurkunde f; *- of bonds* (GB) Bescheinigung über die Registrierung von Namensobligationen; *- of charge* (GB) Grundschuldbrief m; *- of deposit* Depositenschein m, Einlagenschein m, Hinterlegungsschein m; *- of guarantee* Garantieschein m; *- of incorporation* Urkunde über die Eintragung in das Handelsregister; *- of indebtedness* (US) Schuldschein m, Schatzanweisung f; *- of insurance* Versicherungsschein m, Police f; *- of origin* Ursprungszeugnis n, Herkunftsbescheinigung f; *- of pledge* Pfandschein m; *- of posting* Postquittung f, Einlieferungsschein bei der Post; *- of protest* Protesturkunde f; *- of purchase* Grunderwerbsbescheinigung f; *- of receipt* Übernahmeschein m, Verladeschein m; *- of redemption* Tilgungsbescheinigung f; *- of shipment* Ladeschein m, Verschiffungsbescheinigung f, Versandschein m; *- of stock* (US) Aktienzertifikat n, Aktienanteilschein m, Aktienschein m; *- of the customhouse* Zollquittung f; *accountant's -* Prüfungsvermerk m; *allotment -* (US) Zuteilungsanzeige f, Zuteilungsschein m, Bezugsrechtzuteilung f; *annuity -* Rentenschein m; *audit -* Prüfungsvermerk m; *bankrupt's -* Konkursvergleich m; *bearer -* Inhaberzertifikat n; *blank -* Blankopapier n; *bond -* Interimsschein für eine Inhaberschuldverschreibung; *clearance -* Zollbescheinigung f, Seebrief m, Unbedenklichkeitsbescheinigung f, *collateral trust -* (US) Investmentzertifikat n, Wertpapier eines Investment-Trusts; *currency -* (US) Schatzanweisung f; *debenture -* Zollrückgabeschein m; *ownership -* Bescheinigung über das Eigentum (an einem bestimmten Wertpapier); *provisional -* Zwischenschein für eine Obligation oder Aktie; *registered -* Namenspapier n

certificated bankrupt Konkursschulden f pl; *- liabilities* verbriefte Verbindlichkeiten

certification department Scheckbestätigungsabteilung f; *- of signature* Unterschriftsbeglaubigung f; *- of transfer* Übertragungsbescheinigung f

certified adj bescheinigt adj, beglaubigt adj, beurkundet adj; *- bill of lading* beglaubigtes Konnossement; *- broker* amtlich zugelassener Makler; *- check* bankbestätigter Scheck; *- financial statement* Bilanz mit Prüfungsvermerk; *- public accountant* (US) beeidigter Wirtschaftsprüfer

certifier n Aussteller einer Bescheinigung, Ausstellung einer Beglaubigung, Aussteller einer Urkunde

certify v bescheinigen v, beglaubigen v, beurkunden v; *- a check* einen Scheck bestätigen; *this is to -* hiermit wird bescheinigt, daß

cessation n Einstellung f (Beendigung)

cession n Abtretung f, Übertragung f, Zession f

cessionary n Zessionar m, Forderungsübernehmer m

c & f = cost and freight Kosten und Fracht

CFTC = Commodity Futures Trading Commission Aufsichtsbehörde für das Warentermingeschäft in den USA

chain n Kette f, Zusammenschluß m; *- address* Anschlußadresse f (bei Großspeicherdateien); *- banking* Filialbankwesen n; *- banking system* Filialbanksystem n; *- store* Handelskettenladen m

chaining address Anschlußadresse f (bei Großspeicherdateien)

chair

chair n Präsidium n, Vorsitz m

chairman n Präsident m (eines Gremiums), Vorsitzende f u. m, Vorsitzer m; **- of the supervisory board** Aufsichtsratsvorsitzende f u. m; **deputy** ~ stellvertretende(r) Vorsitzende(r)

chairmanship n Vorsitz m, Präsidentenamt n

challenge v bestreiten v, abstreiten v

Chamber of Commerce (GB) Handelskammer f

Chancellor of The Exchequer (GB) Schatzkanzler m, Finanzminister m

change v ändern v, tauschen v, umtauschen v, wechseln v, umwechseln v, einwechseln v; ~ n Änderung f, Kleingeld n, Wechselgeld n, Scheidemünze f; **- a partnership to a corporation** eine Personalgesellschaft in eine juristische Person umwandeln; **- hands** in andere Hände übergehen; **- hands at** gehandelt werden zu: **- in interest rate** Zinssatzänderung f; **- in liquidity** Liquiditätsumschichtung f; **- of account** Kontoänderung f; **- of ownership** Besitzwechsel m, Eigentumswechsel m; **- of rates** Kursänderung f; **- of title** Besitzwechsel m, Eigentumswechsel m

changer n Geldwechsler m

channel v in eine bestimmte Richtung lenken

characteristic n Merkmal n

charge v belasten v (Konto), berechnen v, in Rechnung stellen, anschreiben v; ~ n Last f, Belastung f; **- account** Kundenkonto n; **- an account** ein Konto belasten; **- an extra** v aufschlagen v; **- back** zurückbelasten v; **- commission** Provision berechnen; **- freight** Fracht berechnen; **- interest** Zinsen berechnen, Zinsen belasten; **- off** abschreiben v (Schuld oder Forderung); **- purchase** Kreditkauf m; **- sale** Kreditverkauf m; **- ticket** (US) Belastungsanweisung f; **- up against** anrechnen auf; **acceptance -** Akzeptgebühr f; **activity -** Bankgebühren f pl, Bankspesen pIt, **registered -** Grundschuld f; **without -** kostenlos

chargeable adj belastbar adj, anrechenbar adj, besteuerbar adj; **- to** zu Lasten von

charge-off n Abschreibung f (Schuld oder Forderung), Ausfall m, Abbuchung f

charges n pl Gebühren f pl, Spesen pIt; **- for postal services** Postgebühren f pl; **- on credits** Kreditkosten pIt; **- paid in advance** Kostenvorschuß m; **account of** ~ Spesenkonto n, Unkostenkonto n; **accrued -** aufgelaufene Kosten; **additional -** zusätzliche Kosten, Mehrkosten pIt; **amortization -** Abschreibungslasten f pl; **average -** Havariegelder n pl; **back -** Rückspesen pIt; **bank -** Bankspesen pIt, Bankgebühren f pl; **banking -** Provisionssätze m pl; **bill -** Wechselspesen pIt; **carriers' -** Speditionsgebühr f; **collecting -** Inkassogebühren f pl, Inkassospesen pIt, Einzugsspesen pIt; **collection -** Inkassogebühren f pl, Inkassospesen pIt, Einzugsspesen pIt; **other -** sonstiger Aufwand

charging lien Sicherungsrecht n (mit Besitz nicht verbunden)

chart n Tabelle f, Börsenkursgrafik f

charter v chartern v, befrachten v; ~ n Satzung f, Konzession f, Privileg n, Chartervertrag m, Befrachtung f, Verfrachtung f; **- contract** Frachtvertrag m, Chartervertrag m

charterable adj befrachtbar adj

charterage n Charterung f

chartered adj gechartert adj, befrachtet adj, verbrieft adj; **- accountant** Bücherrevisor m, Wirtschaftsprüfer m, Buchprüfer m, Rechnungsprüfer m, Revisor m; **- bank** (GB) Geschäftsbank f, konzessionierte Bank; **- company** privilegierte Gesellschaft, konzessionierte Gesellschaft; **- rights** verbriefte Rechte; **- ship** gechartertes Schiff

charterer n Charterer m, Befrachter m

chartering agency n Zulassungsstelle f

charterpark n Frachtvertrag m, Chartervertrag m

charting n Auswerter von Tabellen und Schaubildern

chartist n am graphischen Kursverlauf orientierter Wertpapieranalyst

chattel mortgage Mobiliarhypothek f

chattels n pl bewegliches Eigentum, Mobilien plt; **~ personal** bewegliches Eigentum, Mobilien plt

cheap money billiges Geld, billige Geldsätze

cheapen verbilligen v

cheapening of money Herabsetzen der Geldsätze

cheat v betrügen v, übervorteilen v

check v kontrollieren v, überprüfen v, abhaken v, nachrechnen v; **~** n Kontrolle f (Überprüfung), Nachprüfung f, Revision f; **~** n (US) Scheck m, Bankanweisung f; **~ account depositor** Scheckkontoinhaber m; **~ an entry** einen Buchungsposten abstreichen; **~ and bill transactions** (GB) Scheck-und-Wechsel-Verkehr m; **~ book** Scheckbuch n, Scheckheft n; **~ book money** (US) Buchgeld n, Giralgeld n, bargeldlose Zahlungsmittel; **~ card** Scheckkarte f; **~ clearing system** Scheckverrechnungsverkehr m; **~ collection** Scheckeinzug m, Scheckinkasso n; **~ currency** Buchgeld n, Giralgeld n (US) **~ department** Scheckabteilung f; **~ desk** (US) Buchhaltungsabteilung f; **~ digit** Prüfziffer f (EDV); **~ digit calculation** Prüfziffernrechnung f (EDV); **~ digit method** Prüfziffernverfahren n (EDV); **~ ending number** Scheckendnummer f; **~ figures** Zahlen vergleichen; **~ form** (US) Scheckformular n; **~ in collection** Scheckinkasso n; **~ made out to cash** Barscheck m; **~ number** Schecknummer f; **~ payment at face value** gebührenlose Scheckeinlösung; **~ protecting device** (US) Scheckschutzvorrichtung f, Apparat zur Verhütung von Fälschungen; **~ rate** Scheckkurs m; **~ register** Scheckliste f; **~ routing symbol** Scheckleitzahl f; **~ stamp** Scheckstempel m; **~ the books** Bücher revidieren; **~ to bearer** Überbringerscheck m, Inhaberschein m; **~ to order** Orderscheck m; **~ with deferred credit** zum Inkasso hereingenommener Scheck; **~ without provision** ungedeckter Scheck; **bad ~** ungedeckter Scheck; **banker's ~** Bankscheck m; **bearer ~** Inhaberscheck m; **bearer of a ~** Scheckinhaber m; **blank ~** Blankoscheck m; **cancelled ~** entwerteter Scheck; **cash a ~** einen Scheck einlösen, einen Scheck kassieren; **cashier's ~** (US) Bankscheck m; **certified ~** bankbestätigter Scheck; **certify a ~** einen Scheck bestätigen; **collect a ~** einen Scheck einziehen, einen Scheck einkassieren; **collection ~** Inkassoscheck m; **counter ~** Kassenscheck m; **coupon ~** (US) Kuponscheck m; **dishonoured ~** notleidender Scheck; **draw a ~ upon an account** einen Scheck auf ein Konto ziehen; **drawer of a ~** Scheckaussteller m; **duplicate ~** Scheckduplikat n; **kite ~** ungedeckter Scheck; **marked ~** besonders gekennzeichneter Scheck zur Verhinderung von Fälschungen; **overdue ~** überfälliger Scheck, verfallener Scheck; **postdate a ~** einen Scheck vordatieren; **protested ~** protestierter Scheck; **raised ~** (US) durch Werterhöhung gefälschter Scheck; **rubber ~** (US) ungedeckter Scheck; **stale ~** (US) verjährter Scheck; **uncovered ~** ungedeckter Scheck

checking n Kontrolle f (Überprüfung), Nachprüfung f, Revision f; **~ account** (US) Kontokorrentkonto n; **~ balances** (US) Guthaben auf Kontokorrentkonto; **~ deposits** Sichteinlagen f pl, Kontokorrentguthaben n pl; **~ information** Kontrollinformation f; **~ of accounts** Buchprüfung f, Bilanzprüfung f, Bücherrevision f, Rechnungsprüfung f, Revision f; **~ of books** Abstimmung der Bücher; **credit ~** Kreditprüfung f

check-kiting Scheckreiterei f

checks; bills and ~ Wechsel-und-Scheckbestand m (Bilanzposten)

cheerful tone freundliche Stimmung (Börse)

chemicals Chemieaktien f pl

cheque n (GB) Scheck m, Bankanweisung; **~ account** (GB) Scheckkonto n; **~ (guarantee) card** Scheckkarte f; **~ collection** (GB) Inkasso von Schecks; *~ cover* (GB) Scheckdeckung *f*; *~ form* (GB) Scheckformular *n*; *~ ledger* (GB) Buch, das etwa der Primanota entspricht; *~ in hand* (GB) Scheckbestand *m*; *~ money* (GB) Buchgeld *n*; *~ proceeds* (GB) Scheckerlös *m*; *~ to order* (GB) Orderscheck *m*; *~ without cover* (GB) ungedeckter Scheck *m*; *circular ~* (GB) Reisescheck *m*, Travellerscheck *m*; *marked ~* (GB) bestätigter Scheck

chequelet *n* (GB) Bankquittungsheft *n*

cheques held over (GB) erst am folgenden Tag zum Clearing gehende eingereichte Schecks

chicken feed (slang) Kleckerbeträge *m pl*, kleine Beträge

chief accountant Hauptbuchhalter *m*; *~ cashier* Hauptkassierer *m*; *~ creditor* Hauptgläubige *f u. m*; *~ executive officer* Generaldirektor *m*, Vorstandsvorsitzende *f u. m*; *~ dealer* Chefhändler *m*

China B-shares in Shenzhen und Schanghai börsennotierte Aktien nichtchinesischer Gesellschaften; *~ H-shares* in Hongkong börsennotierte Aktien chinesischer Gesellschaften, *~ N-shares* in New York börsennotierte Aktien chinesischer Gesellschaften; *~ plays* in Hongkong oder an anderen Börsen notierte Aktien nichtchinesischer Gesellschaften mit starken Wirtschaftsinteressen in China; *~ Red Chips* in Hongkong börsennotierte Gesellschaften ohne Genehmigung der Republik China; *~ shares* chinesische Aktien

Chinese walls (slang) innere Abschottung

chip *n* (computer chip) Computerchip *m*

choice *n* Auswahl *f*

choose *v* auswählen *v*

Christmas Club account (US) Sparkonto für Weihnachtseinkäufe

church rate (GB) Kirchensteuer *f*

cif = cost, insurance and freight Kosten, Versicherung und Fracht (siehe *Incoterm*)

circles; banking ~ Bankkreise *m pl*; *business ~* Wirtschaftskreise *m pl*

circular capital Umlaufkapital *n*; *~ cheque* (GB) Reisescheck *m*, Travellerscheck *m*; *~ letter of credit* Zirkularkreditbrief *m*, Reisekreditbrief *m*; *bond ~* Prospekt über die Ausgabe von Obligationen

circulating *adj* in Umlauf befindlich (Banknoten); *~ assets* Umlaufvermögen *n*, flüssige Aktiva, flüssige Mittel; *~ bank notes* Banknotenumlauf *m*; *~ capital* Betriebskapital *n*, Umlaufkapital *n*

circulation *n* Umlauf *m*; *~ of bank notes* Banknotenumlauf *m*; *~ of bills* Wechselumlauf *m*; *~ of money* Geldumlauf *m*; *active ~* (GB) Banknotenumlauf *m*; *bank note ~* Banknotenumlauf *m*; *bank of ~* Notenbank *f*; *bills in ~* umlaufende Wechsel; *bond ~* Anleiheumlauf *m*; *put into ~* in Umlauf bringen

city bonds (US) Stadtanleihe *f*; *~ branch* Stadtfiliale *f*, Stadtkasse *f*; *~ man* Geschäftsmann *m*

civil bonds (US) Schuldverschreibungen der öffentlichen Hand; *~ commotion insurance* Aufruhrversicherung *f*; *~ corporation* Gesellschaft des bürgerlichen Rechts; *~ law* Zivilrecht *n*, bürgerliches Recht; *~ loan* (US) öffentliche Anleihe, öffentlicher Kredit; *~ service* öffentlicher Dienst, Beamtenschaft; *~ stock* Schuldverschreibungen der öffentlichen Hand

claim *v* fordern, *v* beanspruchen *v*, reklamieren *v*, beanstanden *v*; *~ n* Anspruch *m*, Forderung *f*, Versicherungsanspruch *m*, Beanstandung *f*; *~ a title* Eigentum beanspruchen; *~ adjuster* Schadenschätzer *m*, Schadenregulierer *m*; *~ against the estate* Masseanspruch *m*; *~ agent* Gutachter *m*, Schadenregulierer *m*; *~ arising from a bill* Wechselforderung *f*; *~ for damages* Schadenersatzanspruch *m*; *~ for loss* Schadenersatzanspruch *m*; *~ of exemption* (US) Aussonderungsanspruch *m*; *~ reserve* Schadenreserve *f*; *~ settlement* Schadenregulierung *f*; *~ to inheritance* Erbberechtigung *f*, Erbschaftsanspruch *m*; *advance*

a - einen Anspruch erheben, einen Anspruch geltend machen; ***assignment of*** - Forderungsabtretung f; ***book*** - Buchforderung f; ***collect a*** - eine Forderung eintreiben; ***contract*** - Vertragsanspruch m; ***damage*** - Schadenersatzanspruch m; ***doubtful*** - zweifelhafter Anspruch; ***file a*** - einen Anspruch anmelden; ***lodge a*** - einen Anspruch erheben, einen Anspruch geltend machen; ***raise a*** - einen Anspruch erheben, einen Anspruch geltend machen

claimable *adj* einforderbar *adj*, reklamierbar *adj*

claims on banks Forderungen an Kreditinstitute; ***on customers*** Forderungen an Kunden; ***adjustment of*** - Schadenfestsetzung f

class *v* klassifizieren *v*, rangieren *v*, gruppieren *v*; ***of business*** Geschäftszweig m, Geschäftssparte f

classification *n* Klassifizierung f; ***by size*** Größenklassengliederung f; ***criterion*** Ordnungsbegriff m; ***key*** Ordnungsbegriff m; ***account*** Kontenaufgliederung f

classified *adj* klassifiziert *adj*, geheim *adj*; ***bonds*** in verschiedenen Serien ausgegebene Schuldverschreibungen; ***stocks*** in verschiedenen Serien ausgegebene Schuldverschreibungen

classify *v* klassifizieren *v*, rangieren *v*, gruppieren *v*

clause *n* Klausel f, Bedingung f; ***of a will*** Testamentsbestimmung f; ***of pre-emption*** Vorverkaufsklausel f; ***of warranty*** Garantieklausel f; ***blanket*** - Generalklausel f; ***cancellation*** - Kündigungsklausel f; ***competition*** - Wettbewerbsklausel f; ***currency*** - Währungsklausel f

claw back rückfordern *v*, sich zurückholen

clean *adj* einwandfrei *adj*, fehlerfrei *adj*; ***acceptance*** bedingungsloses Akzept, reines Akzept, vorbehaltloses Akzept; ***bill of lading*** reines Konnossement, Konnossement ohne Einschränkung; ***bond*** (US) auf den Inhaber lautende Obligation ohne Giro- oder Stempelvermerk; ***credit*** nicht durch Dokumente gesicherter Kreditbrief; ***draft*** Tratte ohne Dokumente; ***floating (float)*** v sauberes Floaten (einer Währung); ***letter of credit*** Akkreditiv ohne Dokumente; ***payment*** Blancozahlung f; ***up a balance sheet*** eine Bilanz bereinigen

clear *v* klären *v*, kompensieren *v*, verrechnen *v*, abrechnen *v*, verzollen *v*, entlasten *v*, verdienen *v*; ***a balance*** einen Saldo ausgleichen; ***a bill*** einen Wechsel einlösen, einen Wechsel honorieren; ***amount*** Nettobetrag m, Reinbetrag m; ***annuity*** steuerfreie Rente; ***estate*** unbelastetes Grundstück; ***gain*** Reingewinn m, Nettogewinn m; ***loss*** Nettoverlust m; ***of charges*** spesenfrei, gebührenfrei; ***off a debt*** Schulden begleichen; ***profit*** Reingewinn m, Nettogewinn m; ***text*** Klartext m; ***value*** Nettowert m

clearance *n* Zollabfertigung f, Verzollung f; ***certificate*** Zollbescheinigung f, Seebrief m, Unbedenklichkeitsbescheinigung f; ***item*** Abrechnungsposten m; ***of payments*** Zahlungsausgleich m; ***papers*** Verzollungspapiere *n pl*; ***sale*** Ausverkauf m (Räumungsverkauf); ***bill of*** - Zollabfertigungsschein m

cleared *adj* verzollt *adj*

clearing *n* Clearing n, Abrechnungsverfahren n; ***account*** Verrechnungskonto n; ***agreement*** Verrechnungsabkommen n; ***balance*** Verrechnungssaldo m; ***bank*** Clearingbank f, Girobank f; ***center*** Clearingstelle f, Clearinghaus n, Clearinginstitut n, Verrechnungsstelle f; ***currency*** Verrechnungswährung f; ***debt*** Verrechnungsschuld f; ***house*** Clearingstelle f, Clearinghaus n, Clearinginstitut n, Verrechnungsstelle f; ***item*** Verrechnungsposten m, Abrechnungsposten m; ***of an account*** Kontoglattstellung f; ***operations*** Giroverkehr m; ***rate*** Verrechnungskurs m; ***ratio*** Verrechnungsschlüssel m; ***sale*** Ausverkauf m (Räumungsverkauf); ***system*** Abrechnungssystem n; ***system for settling***

security transactions Effektengiroverkehr m; **banker's - house** (GB) Bankabrechnungsstelle f; **check - system** Scheckverrechnungsverkehr m

Clearing; Credit - House (US) Vermittlungsstelle für Kreditauskünfte

clearing-office Abrechnungsstelle f

clerk n Sachbearbeiter m, Büroangestellte f u. m; **balance sheet -** Bilanzbuchhalter m; **bank -** Bankangestellte f u. m, Bankbeamte m; **cash -** Kassierer m; **collecting -** Kassenbote m; **commercial -** Handlungsgehilfe m; **managing -** Geschäftsführer m, Prokurist m

client n Kunde m, Mandant m, Klient m

clientele n Kundenkreis m, Kundschaft f

climate for investment Anlageklima n

clique n Interessengemeinschaft zwecks Erzielung gemeinschaftlicher Erfolge

close n Abschluß m (Börse), Schluß m (Börse); **- a position** Glattstellen einer Position; **- an account** v ein Konto auflösen; **- books** Bücher abschließen; **- corporation** Aktiengesellschaft f (deren Aktien sich in festem Besitz einiger weniger Personen befinden und nicht in den Verkehr gelangen); **- down business** ein Geschäft aufgeben; **- money** teures Geld; **- of exchange** Börsenschluß m; **- out a position** Bestandsglattstellung (Börse)

closed issue unveränderliche Anleihe; **- mortgage** abgelöste Hypothek

closed-end fund Investmentfonds mit geschlossenem Anlageportefeuille; **- investment company** Investmentgesellschaft mit geschlossenem Anlageportefeuille

closing agent Abschlußagent m; **- bid** Höchstgebot n; **- date** Schlußtermin m; **- department** Abschlußabteilung f; **- entry** Abschlußbuchung f; **- of accounts** Kontenabschluß m; **- of books** Bücherabschluß m; **- of the month** (Monats)Ultimo m; **- price** Schlußkurs m; **- statement** Abschlußbericht m, Kontoabschluß m; **- stock** Schlußbestand m; **- unit** Schlußeinheit f

club; benefit - Versicherungsverein auf Gegenseitigkeit, Unterstützungsverein m

cocktail swap Kombination verschiedener Swaps

co-creditor n Mitgläubige f u. m

C.O.D (cash on delivery) Barzahlung bei Lieferung

code v verschlüsseln v, chiffrieren v; **- n** Code m, Geheimschrift f, Schlüssel m; **- combination** Zeichenkombination f; **- configuration** Zeichenkombination f; **- of conduct** Verhaltensregeln f pl; **- selector** Codiergerät n; **- structure** Coderahmen m; **- word** Kennwort n; **commercial -** Handelsgesetzbuch n

codebtor n Mitschuldner m, Solidarschuldner m

coded fine Codierzeile f

coder n Codiergerät n

codetermination n Mitbestimmung f

codification n Kodifizierung f, Verschlüsselung f

codify v kodifizieren v

coding line Codierzeile f

co-finance mitfinanzieren v

cognovit note schriftliche Schuldanerkenntnis

coheir n Miterbe m

coheritage n Miterbschaft f, gemeinsame Erbschaft

coin v münzen v, prägen v; **- n** Münze f, Hartgeld n, Geldstück n; **base -** (GB) falsche Münze, (US) Scheidemünze f; **common -** gängige Münze; **current -** gängige Münze; **defaced -** abgenutzte Münze; **divisional -** Scheidemünze f; **foreign notes and -** ausländische Banknoten und Münzen, Sorten f pl; **subsidiary -** Scheidemünze f

coinage n Prägung f (von Münzen), Münzen f pl, Hartgeld n, Münzsystem n; **- prerogative** Münzregal n, Münzhoheit f

coiner n Münzer m, Falschmünzer m

coins in circulation Münzumlauf m; **deficiency of -** Münzverschlechterung f

coinsurance n Mitversicherung f

co-lead manager Mitführer in einem Konsortium

collaboration *n* Zusammenarbeit *f*, Mitarbeit *f*, Mitwirkung *f*
collapse of the market Börsenzusammenbruch *m*
collar Zinskorridor *m*, Zinsbegrenzung *f*
collateral *n* Sicherheit *f*, Besicherung *f*, Sicherungsgegenstand *m*; - *adj* zusätzlich *adj*; - *advance* Lombardvorschuß *m*; - *assignment* Sicherungsübereignung *f*; - *bill* Lombardwechsel *m*, Kautionswechsel *m*; - *bonds* (US) Obligationen mit zusätzlichen Sicherheiten; - *credit* Lombardkredit *m*, Lombarddarlehen *n*, abgesicherter Kredit; - *debt* Lombardschuld *f*; - *loan* Lombardkredit *m*, Lombarddarlehen *n*, abgesicherter Kredit; - *mortgage bonds* Obligationen, für die vom Schuldner verpfändete Hypotheken als Sicherheit dienen; - *note* Verpflichtungsschein über erfolgte Hinterlegung von Effekten zwecks Deckung eines Kredits; - *securities* beliehene Wertpapiere, lombardierte Wertpapiere; - *security* zusätzliche Sicherheit; - *security margin* Sicherheitsmarge *f*; - *trust bonds* durch Effektenlombard gesicherte Obligationen, (US) Obligationen mit Sicherung durch Aktienbesitz des Schuldners; - *trust certificate* (US) Investmentzertifikat *n*, Wertpapier eines Investmenttrusts; - *trust notes* pfandrechtlich gesicherte Obligationen; - *value* Beleihungswert *m*, Lombardwert *m*; *acceptable as* - beleihbar *adj*, lombardfähig *adj*; *commodity* - *advance* Warenlombard *m*
collaterised bond exchange Umwandlung von Krediten in Anleihen mit Zins- oder Kapitalabschlag
collateralize *n* Sicherheitsleistung *f*
colleague *n* Mitarbeiter *m*, Kollege *m*
collect *v* einziehen *v*, sammeln *v*, kassieren *v*, einkassieren *v*, einlösen *v*, vereinnahmen *v*, erheben *v*, eintreiben *v*, betreiben *v*; - *a check* einen Scheck einziehen, einen Scheck einkassieren; - *a claim* eine Forderung eintreiben
collectible *adj* einkassierbar *adj*, einlösbar *adj*, eintreibbar *adj*, einziehbar *adj*

collecting agency Inkassobüro *n*; - *bank* Inkassobank *f*, einziehende Bank; - *business* Inkassogeschäft *n*; - *charges* Inkassogebühren *f pl*, Inkassospesen *pl t*, Einzugsspesen *pl t*; - *clerk* Kassenbote *m*; - *commission* Inkassogebühren *f pl*, Inkassospesen *pl t*, Einzugsspesen *pl t*; - *rates* Inkassotarif *m*; *commission for* - Einzugsprovision *f*
collecting-only check Verrechnungsscheck *m*
collection *n* (of data) Erfassung *f* (von Daten); - *n* Inkasso *n*, Einkassierung *f*, Einzug *m*, Einziehung *f*, Eintreibung *f*; - *account* Inkassokonto *n*; - *at source* Quellenbesteuerung *f*; - *authority* Inkassovollmacht *f*; - *by hand* (US) Selbstabholung *f*, Inkasso durch Boten; - *by the customer* Selbstabholung *f*, Inkasso durch Boten; - *charges* Inkassogebühren *f pl*, Inkassospesen *pl t*, Einzugsspesen *pl t*; - *check* Inkassoscheck *m*; - *credit* Sammelgutschrift *f*; - *department* Inkassoabteilung *f*; - *fee* Inkassogebühren *f pl*, Inkassospesen *pl t*, Einzugsspesen *pl t*; - *of bills* Wechselinkasso *n*; - *of debts* Forderungseinziehung *f*; - *of documents* Dokumenteninkasso *n*; - *of letters* Postabholung *f*; - *of rents* Mietinkasso *n*; - *order* Inkassoauftrag *m*; - *procedure* Einzugsweg *m*; - *teller* Schalterbeamter für den Inkassoverkehr; - *window* Einziehungsschalter *m*; *attend to the* - *of a bill* das Inkasso eines Wechsels besorgen; *bill for* - Inkassowechsel *m*; *bond coupon* - Zinsscheininkasso *n*; *check in* - Scheckinkasso *n*; *cheque* - (GB) Inkasso von Schecks; *coupon* - *teller* (US) Kuponkassierer *m*; *par* - Inkasso zu pari; *value for* - Wert zum Einzug, Wert zum Inkasso

collective account Sammelkonto *n*; - *bill of lading* Sammelkonnossement *n*; - *custody* Girosammelverwahrung *f*; - *insurance* Gruppenversicherung *f*; - *liability* Gesamtschuld *f*; - *order* Sammelauftrag *m*; - *ownership* Gemeinschaftseigentum *n*

collector

collector n Inkassobeamte m, Steuereinnehmer m; **bill ~** Wechselinkassobüro n
co-maker (US) Mitbürge m, Mitunterzeichner m
co-manager Mitglied der Führungsgruppe, Mitkonsorte (einer Emission)
combination n Kombination f, Verbindung f, Interessengemeinschaft f, Konzern m, Trust m, Pool m
combine n Konzern m, Trust m, Pool m, Kartell n
combined *bill of lading* Sammelladungskonnossement n; **~ *policy*** Sammelpolice f
come to betragen v, (sich) belaufen auf
coming-out price Emissionskurs m, Ausgabekurs m
command credit Überziehungskredit m
commencement of business Geschäftsbeginn m
comments; company ~ Unternehmensberichte m pl
commerce n Handel m, Handelsverkehr m
Commerce; *Chamber of* ~ (GB) Handelskammer f
commercial n Werbesendung f (Rundfunk, Fernsehen); ~ adj kommerziell adj, kaufmännisch adj; **~ *academy*** Handelshochschule f; **~ *acceptance credit*** Warenrembourskredit m; **~ *account*** Geschäftskonto n; **~ *advertising*** Wirtschaftswerbung f; **~ *agency*** (US) Auskunftei f; **~ *bank*** Geschäftsbank f, Gewerbebank f, Handelsbank f; **~ *bill*** Handelswechsel m, Warenwechsel m; **~ *bookkeeping*** kaufmännische Buchführung; **~ *business*** Handelsgeschäft n; **~ *clerk*** Handlungsgehilfe m; **~ *code*** Handelsgesetzbuch n; **~ *company*** Handelsgesellschaft f; **~ *concern*** Handelsfirma f, Geschäftshaus n; **~ *corporation*** Handelsgesellschaft f; **~ *correspondence*** Handelskorrespondenz f; **~ *court*** (GB) Handelsgericht n; **~ *credit*** Handelskredit m, Warenkredit m; **~ *credit company*** (US) Gesellschaft, die Forderungen von Herstellern und Händlern bevorschußt oder ankauft; **~ *debt*** Warenschuld f; **~ *draft*** Warenwechsel m, Handelswechsel m; **~ *failure*** Zahlungseinstellung f, Konkurs m, Bankrott m; **~ *finance company*** Finanzierungsgesellschaft f; **~ *firm*** Handelsfirma f, Geschäftshaus n; **~ *goods*** Handelsware f; **~ *insurance*** Garantieversicherung f; **~ *interests*** Handelsinteressen n pl; **~ *invoice*** Rechnung f (Warenrechnung), Faktura f, Nota f; **~ *law*** Handelsrecht n; **~ *letter of credit*** Warenkreditbrief m, Warenakkreditiv n; **~ *loan*** Warenkredit m; **~ *note*** Handelswechsel m, Warenwechsel m; **~ *paper*** kurzfristiger Schuldschein aus kommerziellen Transaktionen, ungesicherter kurzfristiger Schuldtitel m; **~ *papers*** Handelspapiere n pl; **~ *partnership*** Handelsgesellschaft f; **~ *practice*** Geschäftspraxis f; **~ *profit*** Geschäftsgewinn m; **~ *property*** Gewerbeimmobilie f; **~ *rate of exchange*** (US) Devisenkurs m, Umrechnungskurs m, Wechselkurs m, Umtauschkurs m; **~ *register*** Handelsregister n; **~ *survey*** Marktanalyse f; **~ *transaction*** Handelsgeschäft n; **~ *travel(l)er*** Handlungsreisende f u. m; **~ *treaty*** Handelsabkommen n, Handelsvertrag m

commercialization n Kommerzialisierung f
commercialize v kommerzialisieren v
commercially adj geschäftlich adj, gewerblich adj, kommerziell adj
commission n Provision f, Kommission f, Vermittlungsgebühr f; **~ *account*** Provisionskonto n; **~ *agent*** Kommissionär m; **~ *broker*** Börsenkommissionsfirma f, Kommissionsmakler m; **~ *business*** Kommissionsgeschäft n, Kommissionshandel m; **~ *charge*** Courtage f, Provision f; **~ *dealing*** Kommissionsgeschäft n, Kommissionshandel m; **~ *for acceptance*** Akzeptprovision f; **~ *for collecting*** Einzugsprovision f; **~ *for domiciling*** Domizilprovision f; **~ *house*** Maklerfirma f; **~ *income*** Provisionsüberschuß m; **~ *merchant*** Kommissionär m; **~ *on overdraft*** Überziehungsprovision f; **~*s paid*** Provisionsaufwendungen f pl; **~*s received*** Provisionserträge m pl; **accepting ~**

Akzeptprovision f; **accord a** ~ eine Provision gewähren; **agent's** ~ Vertreterprovision f; **bank** ~ Bankenkommission f; **banker's** ~ Bankprovision f; **bill** ~ Wechselcourtage f; **charge** ~ eine Provision berechnen; **collecting** ~ Inkassogebühren f pl, Inkassospesen plt, Einzugsspesen plt; **commitment** ~ Bereitstellungsprovision f; **rate of** ~ Provisionssatz m; **underwriting** ~ Provision aus Konsortialbeteiligungen, Konsortialprovision f

commissionable adj provisionspflichtig adj

commissioned adj beauftragt adj, bevollmächtigt adj

commissioner n Kommissar m, Bevollmächtigte f u. m, Kommissionsmitglied n

commissions paid Provisionsaufwand m; ~ **surplus** Provisionsertrag m

commit v übergeben v, überlassen v, anvertrauen v, begehen v, verüben v, verpflichten v, verbindlich machen

commitment n Verbindlichkeit f, Verpflichtung f, Engagement n (Börse), Auftrag m; ~ **commission** Bereitstellungsprovision f; ~ **fee** Bereitstellungsprovision f; ~ **for future delivery** Terminengagement n; **advance** ~ Kreditzusage f

commitments; acceptance ~ Akzeptumlauf m; **business** ~ geschäftliche Verpflichtungen; **capital** ~ Kapitalverpflichtungen f pl; **meet** ~ Verpflichtungen erfüllen

committee n Komitee n, Kommission f, Ausschuß m; ~ **of the stock exchange** Börsenvorstand m; **allocation** ~ Zuteilungsausschuß m; **creditors'** ~ Gläubigerausschuß m

commodity n Artikel m, Ware f, Rohstoff m, Posten m, Gegenstand m; ~ **collateral advance** Warenlombard m; ~ **credit** Warenkredit m

Commodity Credit Corporation (US) Rohstoff-Kredit-Gesellschaft f

commodity dividend (US) Warendividende f; ~ **exchange** Warenbörse f; ~ **fund** Rohstoffonds m; ~ **future** Warenterminkontrakt m

Commodity Futures Trading Commission = CFTC Aufsichtsbehörde für das Warentermingeschäft in den USA

commodity loan Warenkredit m; ~ **money** Indexwährung f; ~ **option** Warenoption f, Warenterminoption f; ~ **paper** (US) Dokumententratte f; ~ **prices** Warenpreise m pl; ~ **theory of money** Geldwerttheorie f; ~ **value** Warenwert m, Sachwert m

common adj gemeinsam adj, gemeinschaftlich adj, allgemein adj; ~ n Gemeinschaftseigentum n, Gemeinschafts-; ~ **carrier** (US) Verkehrsunternehmen n, Transportunternehmen n; ~ **coin** gängige Münze; ~ **debtor** Gemeinschuldner m

Common Market Gemeinsamer Markt

common mortgage Verkehrshypothek f; ~ **share** Stammaktie f; ~ **stock** (US) Stammaktie f

Commonwealth n Commonwealth n, Gemeinwesen n, Gemeinschaft f, Staat m

communal adj kommunal adj, gemeindlich adj; ~ **loan** Kommunalkredit m, Gemeindedarlehen n

communication system Verkehrssystem n, Verkehrsnetz n, Nachrichtensystem n, Nachrichtennetz n

community n Gemeinde f, Gemeinschaft f, Allgemeinheit f, Publikum n; ~ **account** Gemeinschaftskonto n; ~ **debt** Gesamtschuld f

Community of the Six Europäische Wirtschaftsgemeinschaft (EWG)

communization n Sozialisierung f, Überführung in Gemeineigentum

communize v sozialisieren v, vergesellschaften v

commute v umwandeln v

Companies Act (GB) Aktiengesetz n

company n Gesellschaft f, Genossenschaft f; ~ **borrowing** Kreditaufnahme der Unternehmen; ~ **comments** Unternehmensberichte m pl; ~ **financing** Unternehmensfinanzierung f; ~ **foundation** Firmengründung f, Gesellschaftsgründung f; ~ **law** Gesellschaftsrecht n; ~ **limited by guarantee** (GB)

company's surplus

Gesellschaft mit beschränkter Nachschußpflicht; **- meeting** Gesellschafterversammlung f; **- of merchants** Handelsgesellschaft f; **- plant** Werkanlage f; **- statement** Gesellschaftsbilanz f, Firmenbilanz f; **- take over** Unternehmen übernehmen (aufkaufen); **- tax** Körperschaftssteuer f; **absorbing -** aufnehmende Gesellschaft; **affiliated -** (GB) Konzerngesellschaft f, Tochtergesellschaft f; **assessment -** Gegenseitigkeitsverein m; **associated -** (GB) nahestehende Gesellschaft, Tochtergesellschaft f; **auditing -** Revisionsgesellschaft f; **bonding -** Kautionsversicherungsgesellschaft f; **chartered -** privilegierte Gesellschaft, konzessionierte Gesellschaft; **commercial -** Handelsgesellschaft f; **commercial credit -** (US) Gesellschaft, die Forderungen von Herstellern und Händlern bevorschußt oder ankauft; **controlled -** beherrschtes Unternehmen; **limited -** (GB) etwa: GmbH; **limited liability -** (GB) etwa: GmbH; **manufacturing -** Produktionsgesellschaft f; **operating -** aktive Geschäfte betreibende Gesellschaft; **registered -** eingetragene Handelsgesellschaft; **statutory -** Körperschaft des öffentlichen Rechts; **trading -** Handelsgesellschaft f, Erwerbsgesellschaft f; **trust -** Treuhandgesellschaft f, Treuhandbank f

company's surplus Gesellschaftsgewinn m

comparable adj vergleichbar adj

comparative valuation of deposited securities Depotwertvergleich m

compatibility n Verträglichkeit f

compensate v kompensieren v, ausgleichen v; - vergüten v, bezahlen v

compensating balance zinslose Sichteinlagen bei einer Korrespondenzbank; **- use tax** Umsatzsteuer f (US)

compensation n Entschädigung f, Abfindung f, Kompensation f, Ersatz m, Schadenersatz m, Vergütung f, Lohn m, Gehalt n; **- account** Ausgleichskonto n; **- agreement** Kompensationsabkommen n; **- business** Kompensationsgeschäft n; **- payment** Abfindungszahlung f; **- transaction** Kompensationsgeschäft n; **amount of -** Abfindungssumme f; **rate of -** Kompensationskurs m

compete v konkurrieren v, wetteifern v

competence n Kompetenz f, Befugnis f, Zuständigkeit f, Fähigkeit f, Befähigung f

competent adj fähig adj, kompetent adj, befugt adj, zuständig adj, berechtigt adj

competing adj konkurrierend adj

competition n Konkurrenz f, Wettbewerb m; **- clause** Wettbewerbsklausel f; **advertising -** Werbewettbewerb m

competitive adj konkurrenzfähig adj; **- bidding** Übernahmeangebot n; **- devaluation** (of a currency) Abwertung aus Wettbewerbsgründen (Währung); **- position** Wettbewerbssituation f; **- power** Konkurrenzfähigkeit f; **- price** Konkurrenzpreis m, konkurrenzfähiger Preis

competitiveness n Wettbewerbsfähigkeit f

competitor n Konkurrent m, Wettbewerber m

compile v zusammenstellen v, erstellen v

complain v (sich) beschweren v, reklamieren v

complaint n Beanstandung f, Beschwerde f, Reklamation f; **customer's -** Kundenbeschwerde f

complement v vervollständigen v, ergänzen v

complete adj vollständig adj, komplett adj

completed period alte Rechnung, abgeschlossene Rechnungsperiode

completion guarantee; - guaranty (US) Fertigstellungsgarantie f

compliance department bankinternes Aufsichtsorgan (z. B. zur Vermeidung von Insiderhandel); **- officer** Mitarbeiter m (der die Wertpapiergeschäfte der Angestellten überwacht)

compliant adj entgegenkommend adj

comply with nachkommen v (Anordnungen), erfüllen v, einhalten v

component n Bestandteil m

composite trading (US) Börsenauftrag zum bestmöglichen Kurs

composition n Vergleich m (mit Gläubigern); **- agreement** Vergleichsvertrag m; **- in bankruptcy** Zwangsvergleich m; **- proceedings** Vergleichsverfahren n; **- with creditors** Gläubigervergleich m

compound *computation of interest* Zinseszinsrechnung f; **- interest** Zinseszinsen m pl, Staffelzinsen m pl; **- with creditors** mit Gläubigern einen Vergleich schließen; **- yield** Gesamtrendite f

comprehensive account Komplettkonto n; **- coverage** Vollkasko n

compromise v einen Kompromiß schließen; **-** n Kompromiß m, gegenseitiges Zugeständnis, außergerichtlicher Vergleich

comptroller n (US) Kostenüberprüfung m, Bilanzprüfer m, Revisor m

Comptroller of the Currency (US) Bankaufsichtsbehörde für nationale (von der Bundesregierung genehmigte) Banken

compulsory liquidation Zwangsliquidation f; **- repurchase** zwangsweiser Rückkauf von Investmentfondsanteilen; **- saving** Zwangssparen n; **- winding-up** Zwangsliquidation f

computation n Berechnung f, Ausrechnung f; **- of costs** Kostenberechnung f, Kostenkalkulation f, Preisberechnung f, Rentabilitätsberechnung f; **- of interest** Zinsberechnung f, Zinsrechnung f; **compound - of interest** Zinseszinsrechnung f

computational effort Rechenaufwand m

compute v berechnen v

computer n Computer m, Rechner m, elektronische Rechenanlage; **- error** Computerfehler m; **- program** Computerprogramm n; **- readable** computerlesbar; **- trading system** Computerhandelssystem n

computer-assisted (aided) computergestützt

computerize v Umstellen auf Computer

computing speed Rechengeschwindigkeit f

conceal v verschleiern v (Bilanzen), verbergen v

concealed assets verschleierte Vermögenswerte

concede v bewilligen v, einräumen v, gewähren v

concentration n Konzentration f; **- of capital** Kapitalkonzentration f

concentrator network Konzentratornetz n

concern n Konzern m, Unternehmen n, Betrieb m, Firma f, Geschäft n; **brokerage -** Maklerfirma f; **business -** Geschäftsunternehmen n; **commercial -** Handelsfirma f, Geschäftshaus n

concerned adj beteiligt adj, interessiert adj

concerning adj betreffend adj

concerted action konzertierte Aktion (gemeinsames Vorgehen)

concession n Zugeständnis n, Konzession f, Genehmigung f, Bewilligung f, Vergünstigung f

concessionaire n Konzessionär m, Konzessionsinhaber m

concessionary n (US) Konzessionär m, Konzessionsinhaber m

concessioner n Konzessionär m, Konzessionsinhaber m

conciliation Vermittlung f, Schlichtung f

conclude v abschließen v (Geschäfte), folgern v

conclusion n Abschluß m (Vertrag, Geschäft), Beschluß m, Schlußfolgerung f; **- of a bargain** Geschäftsabschluß m

condemn v verurteilen v, beschlagnahmen v, einziehen v, konfiszieren v

condemnation n Verurteilung f, Beschlagnahme f, Konfiskation f

condensed adj abgekürzt adj, gekürzt adj, gerafft adj; **- balance sheet** Bilanzauszug m, verkürzte Bilanz; **- course** n Schnellkurs m

condition n Bedingung f, Voraussetzung f, Zustand m, Abmachung f, Vermögenslage f, Klausel f

conditional adj bedingt adj, vertragsgemäß adj; **- acceptance** bedingtes Akzept, bedingte Annahme; **- endorsement** beschränktes Giro, Rektaindossament n; **- order** bedingter Auftrag; **- sale** Verkauf mit Eigentumsvorbehalt m

conditions *of (a) contract* Vertragsbedingungen f pl; **- of sale** Verkaufsbedingungen f pl; **- of the documentary**

condominium ownership

credit Akkreditivbedingungen f pl; **boom ~** Haussebedingungen f pl, Hochkonjunktur f; **credit ~** Kreditbedingungen f pl, Kreditkonditionen f pl
condominium ownership (US) Miteigentum an Wohnungen
condonation n Vergebung f, Verzeihung f
condone v vergeben v
condor fund festverzinsliche Anleihe mit index-gekoppeltem Rückzahlungsbetrag
conduct of account Kontoführung f
confer v übertragen v, verhandeln v, verleihen v
conference n Konferenz f, Besprechung f, Beratung f, Sitzung f; **business ~** geschäftliche Besprechung
confidant n Vertrauensmann m
confidence n Vertrauen n, vertrauliche Mitteilung
confidential adj vertraulich adj; **~ information** vertrauliche Information
confirm v bestätigen v, ratifizieren v
confirmation n Bestätigung f; **~ note** Bestätigungsschreiben n; **~ of balance** Saldenanerkenntnis f; **~ of signature** Unterschriftsbeglaubigung f; **bank ~** Bankbestätigung f, Bestätigung des Kontoauszugs
confirmed authority Negoziierungsakkreditiv n (Trattenankaufzusage); **~ credit** bestätigter Kredit; **~ letter of credit** bestätigtes Akkreditiv
confirming bank Bestätigungsbank f
confiscate v beschlagnahmen v (Privateigentum), konfiszieren v
confiscation n Beschlagnahme f (Privateigentum), Konfiskation f
conflict of interests Interessengegensatz m, Interessenkonflikt m
conform v entsprechen v, übereinstimmen v; **~ with** nachkommen v (Anordnungen), erfüllen v, einhalten v
conformable adj übereinstimmend adj
conformity n Übereinstimmung f; **book in ~** gleichlautend buchen
conglomerate Mischkonzern m, Konglomerat n; **~ merger** anorganische Fusion
congress n Kongreß m
connect v verbinden v

connected adj verbunden adj
connection n Verbindung f, Anschluß m, Zusammenhang m
consecutive adj fortlaufend adj
consecutively numbered fortlaufend numeriert
consent n Zustimmung f, Einwilligung f
conservative estimate vorsichtige Schätzung
conservator n (US) Bankenkommissar für Nationalbanken, die sich in Schwierigkeiten befinden
consider v bedenken v, überlegen v
consideration n Überlegung f, Erwägung f, Entgelt n; **~ money** (GB) Effektenstempel m; **for a ~** entgeltlich adj; **nominal ~** (GB) formaler Gegenwert; **rate of ~** Prämiensatz m
consign v versenden v, übersenden v, einzahlen v, konsignieren v, hinterlegen v, in Kommission geben, übertragen v
consignation n (Scotish Law) Hinterlegung f, Deponierung f
consignee n Empfänger m, Konsignator m, Kommissionär m
consigner n Absender m, Konsignant m, Versender m, Zedent m
consignment n Versand m, Sendung f, Konsignation f, Hinterlegung f, Übertragung f, Deponierung f, Kommission f; **~ account** Kommissionskonto n; **~ contract** Kommissionsvertrag m; **~ note** Frachtbrief m; **~ of valuables** Wertsendung f; **bill of ~** Frachtbrief m
consignor n Absender m, Konsignant m, Versender m, Zedent m
consolidate v konsolidieren v, vereinigen v, zusammenziehen v, zusammenlegen v
consolidated balance sheet Konzernbilanz f, konsolidierte Bilanz, Fusionsbilanz f; **~ debt** konsolidierte Schuld; **~ financial statement** Konzernbilanz f, konsolidierte Bilanz, Fusionsbilanz f; **~ group** Konzerngruppe f; **~ loan** konsolidierte Anleihe; **~ mortgage** (US) Gesamthypothek f; **~ profit and loss statement** konsolidierte Gewinn-und-Verlust-Rechnung; **~ stock** (GB) konsolidierte Papiere; **~ surplus** (GB) Konzernüberschuß m

consolidation n Konsolidierung f, Vereinigung (Zusammenlegung) f, Fusion f, Verschmelzung f; **~ of banks** Bankenfusion f; **~ of shares** Zusammenlegung des Aktienkapitals; **agreement of ~** Fusionsvertrag m

consols n pl (GB) Konsols m pl (britische Staatsanleihe, britische Staatspapiere)

consortial adj konsortial adj

consortium n Konsortium n; **~ loan** Konsortialkredit m; **~ of banks** Bankenkonsortium m

constant adj gleichbleibend adj, dauernd adj, konstant adj

constitution; decree of ~ Feststellungsurteil n

construction n Bau m, Konstruktion f, Anlage f, Gebäude n, Bauwerk n; **~ financing** Baufinanzierung f; **~ loan** Baukredit m; **~ mortgage** Bauhypothek f; **cost of ~** Baukosten pl t

constructions Bauaktien f pl, Bauwerte m pl

consul n Konsul m; **~ general** Generalkonsul m

consular adj konsularisch adj; **~ fees** Konsulargebühren f pl; **~ invoice** Konsulatsfaktura f; **~ service** Konsulatsdienst m; **~ status** Konsularstatus m

consulate n Konsulat n; **~ general** Generalkonsulat n

consult v konsultieren v, um Rat fragen

consultant n Berater m, Ratgeber m; **business ~** Wirtschaftsberater m

consultary adj gutachtlich adj

consultation n Konsultation f, Beratung f

consultative adj beratend adj

consume v verbrauchen v, konsumieren v, aufbrauchen v

consumer n Konsument m, Verbraucher m, Abnehmer m; **~ credit** Kundenkredit m, Konsumentenkredit m; **~ goods** Verbrauchsgüter n pl, Konsumgüter n pl; **~ group** Verbrauchergruppe f; **~ habit** Verbrauchergewohnheit f; **~ loan** Konsumentenkredit m; **~ loan company** Teilzahlungskreditinstitut n; **~ market** Verbrauchsgütermarkt m; **~ protection** Verbraucherschutz m; **~ purchasing power** Konsumentenkaufkraft f

consumption n Konsum m, Verbrauch m, Absatz m, Bedarf m; **~ credit** Kundenkredit m, Konsumentenkredit m; **~ trend** Verbrauchsrichtung f, Konsumtrend m

consumptive power Konsumkraft f

contact v sich in Verbindung setzen mit

container n Behälter m

contango business Reportgeschäft n; **~ rate** (GB) Reportsatz m, Reportprämie f, Kurszuschlag m

contest v bestreiten v, abstreiten v; **~** n Wettbewerb m, Streitfall m

contested takeover angefochtene Übernahme

continental bourse Festlandbörse f; **~ rates** (GB) Sorten- und Devisenkurse bei Banken des europäischen Kontinents

contingencies n pl unvorhergesehene Nebenausgaben

contingency n ungewisses Ereignis; **~ fund** außerordentlicher Reservefonds; **~ insurance** Risikoversicherung f; **~ lending** Kreditvergabe mit beweglichem Kreditrahmen; **~ reserve** Sicherheitsrücklage f, Delkredererückstellung f, Rückstellung für unvorhergesehene Ausgaben

contingent n Kontingent n, Anteil m, Quote f; **~ account** (GB) Reservekonto n, Reservefonds für unvorhergesehene Verluste; **~ claim** Eventualforderung f; **~ estate** Erbanwartschaft f; **~ fund** (US) Sicherheitsrücklage f, Delkredererückstellung f, Rückstellung für unvorhergesehene Ausgaben; **~ liability** Eventualverbindlichkeit f, Eventualverpflichtung f; **~ liability in respect of acceptances** Verpflichtungen aus geleisteten Akzepten; **~ order** Zug-um-Zug-Geschäft n; **~ profit** noch nicht realisierter Gewinn; **~ property** Reservekapital n; **~ receivables** ungewisse Forderungen, bedingte Forderungen; **~ reserve** Sicherheitsrücklage f, Delkredererückstellung f, Rückstellung für unvorhergesehene Ausgaben; **~ right** Anwartschaftsrecht n

continuable adj prolongationsfähig adj

continuation Fortsetzung f; **~ bill** (GB) Prolongationswechsel m; **~ rate** (GB) Reportsatz m, Reportprämie f, Kurszuschlag m

continued bonds (US) prolongierte Obligationen

continuing *account* Kontokorrentkonto n; **~ agreement** (US) Kreditvertrag mit gleichbleibenden Sicherheiten; **~ guaranty** (US) Kreditbürgschaft f, Dauergarantie f; **~ security** Kreditbürgschaft f, Dauergarantie f

continuous *interest calculation* permanente Zinsrechnung; **~ paper tape** Endlospapierstreifen m; **~ trading** permanenter Handel

contomat Geldausgabeautomat m, Bankomat m

contra *account* Gegenkonto n; **~ item** Gegenposten m

contract v einen Vertrag abschließen, kontrahieren v, sich verpflichten v; ~ n Vertrag m, Vereinbarung f, Kontrakt m; **~ a bargain** einen Handel abschließen; **~ a loan** einen Kredit aufnehmen; **~ book** Schlußscheinbuch n; **~ carrier** Vertragsspediteur m; **~ claim** Vertragsanspruch m; **~ debt** Vertragsschuld f; **~ debts** Schulden machen; **~ for futures** Terminvertrag m; **~ for sale** Kaufvertrag m, Verkaufsvertrag m; **~ liabilities** Verpflichtungen eingehen; **~ note** Schlußnote f, Schlußschein m; **~ of agency** Vertretervertrag m; **~ of annuity** Leibrentenvertrag m, Rentenvertrag m; **~ of copartnery** Gesellschaftsvertrag m, Teilhabervertrag m; **~ of guaranty** Bürgschaftsvertrag m; **~ of indemnity** Garantievertrag m; **~ of lease** Mietvertrag m, Pachtvertrag m; **~ of pledge** Verpfändungsvertrag m; **~ of purchase** Kaufvertrag m; **~ of sale** Kaufvertrag m; **~ of suretyship** Bürgschaftsvertrag m; **~ on futures** Terminkontrakt m; **~ price** Vertragspreis m; **~ sheet** Abrechnung des Börsenmaklers; **~ stamp** Vertragsstempel m, Schlußscheinstempel m; **~ terms** Vertragsbedingungen f pl; **~ trading** Terminhandel m; **~ under seal** beurkundeter Vertrag; **~ violation** Vertragsverletzung f; **ability to ~** Vertragsfähigkeit f; **award a ~** einen Liefer- oder Fabrikationsauftrag erteilen; **building loan ~** Bausparvertrag m; **conditions of (a) ~** Vertragsbedingungen f pl; **consignment ~** Kommissionsvertrag m; **covered by ~** vertraglich abgesichert; **draft of a ~** Vertragsentwurf m; **employment ~** Dienstvertrag m; **provisions of a ~** Vertragsbestimmungen f pl; **reciprocal ~** gegenseitiger Vertrag

contractant n Kontrahent m, vertragsschließender Teil, Vertragspartei f

contracting party Kontrahent m, vertragsschließender Teil, Vertragspartei f

contraction; credit ~ Kreditschrumpfung f

contractor n Auftragnehmer m, Unternehmer m, Lieferant m, Vertragspartei f; **~ loan** Unternehmerkredit m

contractual adj vertraglich adj, vertragsgemäß adj; **~ arrangement** vertragliche Vereinbarung; **~ capacity** Vertragsfähigkeit f; **~ incapacity** Geschäftsunfähigkeit f; **~ period** Vertragsperiode f; **~ relation** Vertragsverhältnis n; **~ rights** Vertragsrechte n pl

contravene v zuwiderhandeln v

contravention n Zuwiderhandlung f, Verstoß m

contribute v beitragen v, beisteuern v; **~ capital** Kapital einbringen

contributed capital eingezahltes Grundkapital

contribution n Beitrag m, Zuwendung f, Spesen plt, Quote f, Verlustanteil m, Schadenanteil m; **~ agreement** Einbringungsvereinbarung (z. B. bei joint ventures); **~ procedure** Umlageverfahren bei Rentenzahlungen; **~ to capital** Kapitaleinzahlung f, Kapitaleinlage f

contributor of capital Kapitaleinleger m

contributory mortgage für mehrere Gläubiger bestellte Hypothek

control v lenken v, kontrollieren v, beaufsichtigen v, überwachen v, überprüfen v, beherrschen v; ~ n Kontrolle f (Einflußnahme), Steuerung f, Lenkung f; ~

n Kontrolle f (Überwachung); **~ account** Kontrollkonto n, Hauptbuchsammelkonto n; **~ character** Steuerzeichen n; **~ stock** Sperrminorität f; **credit ~** Kreditkontrolle f (staatliche); **currency ~** Devisenbewirtschaftung f, Devisenkontrolle f, Währungskontrolle f; **exchange ~** Devisenbewirtschaftung f, Devisenkontrolle f, Währungskontrolle f; **marital ~** (GB) Verwaltungsrecht des Ehemannes (über das Eigentum der Ehefrau)

controlled company beherrschtes Unternehmen; **~ price** Stoppreis m, gebundener Preis

controller *n* Controller m, Kontrolleur m, Aufseher m, Leiter des Rechnungswesens; **~** *n* (US) Rechnungsprüfer m

controlling account Kontrollkonto n, Hauptbuchsammelkonto n; **~ company** Obergesellschaft f, Muttergesellschaft f, herrschendes Unternehmen; **~ interest** Mehrheitsbeteiligung f, maßgebendes Kapitalinteresse

convene *v* einberufen v, zusammentreten v

convention *n* Abkommen n (Konvention)

conventional interest üblicher Zins, vertragsgemäßer Zinssatz; **~ lien** Vertragspfand n

convergence *n* Annäherung f, Konvergenz f

conversion *n* Konvertierung f, Tausch m, Umtausch m, Umwandlung f, Umstellung f; **~ loan** Umschuldungsanleihe f, Konvertierungsanleihe f; **~ offer** Umtauschangebot n; **~ parity** Wandlungsparität f; **~ premium** Wandlungsprämie f; **~ price** Umrechnungskurs m, Wandlungskurs m; **~ right** Wandelrecht n; **bond ~** Anleihekonversion f; **rate of ~** Konversionssatz m

convert *v* umtauschen v (Wertpapiere), konvertieren v; **~ into capital** kapitalisieren v, in Kapital umwandeln v; **~ into cash** realisieren v, flüssig machen, versilbern v, verkaufen v, veräußern v

convertibility *n* Konvertibilität f, Konvertierbarkeit f, Umwandelbarkeit f; **full ~** unbeschränkte Konvertierbarkeit; **limited ~** beschränkte Konvertierbarkeit

convertible *adj* konvertierbar adj, umtauschbar adj, umwandelbar adj; **~ bonds** Wandelschuldverschreibungen f pl; **~ currency** konvertierbare Währung; **~ debenture** Wandelschuldverschreibung f; **~ financing** Finanzierung durch Ausgabe von Wandelschuldverschreibungen; **~ floating rate bond** zinsvariable Anleihe mit verbrieften Wandlungsrechten; **~ loan** Wandelanleihe f, Wandelobligation f; **~ money** in Gold einlösbares Papiergeld; **~ paper currency** konvertierbares Papiergeld; **~ preferred stock** Vorzugsaktie mit Umtauschrecht, Wandelvorzugsaktien f pl; **~ profit-sharing certificate** Wandelgenußschein m; **~ securities** wandelbare Wertpapiere

convey *v* transportieren v, befördern v; **~** übertragen v, zedieren v, abtreten v, anweisen v, zuweisen v, übereignen v

conveyable *adj* transportierbar adj, beförderungsfähig adj; **~** *adj* übertragbar adj

conveyance *n* Übertragung f, Beförderung f, Beförderungsmittel n; **~ of property** Eigentumsübertragung f; **~ of title** Rechtsübertragung f; **bill of ~** Speditionsrechnung f

conveyancer *n* Notar m (der Eigentumsübertragungsurkunden ausstellt)

cook a balance sheet eine Bilanz frisieren, eine Bilanz verschleiern

cooked accounts frisierte Bücher, verschleierte Bücher

cooking of accounts Bücherfälschung f, Kontofälschung f

cooperate *v* zusammenarbeiten v, mitarbeiten v, mitwirken v

cooperation *n* Zusammenarbeit f, Mitarbeit f, Mitwirkung f

cooperative *n* Genossenschaft f; **~ association** Erwerbsgenossenschaft f, Genossenschaftsverband m; **~ bank** genossenschaftliches Kreditinstitut; **~ banking** genossenschaftliches Bankwesen; **~ buying association** Einkaufsgenossenschaft f; **~ credit association** Verkaufsgenossenschaft f; **~ credit union** Kreditgenossenschaft f; **~ savings organization** Kreditgenossenschaft f; **~ stock** Genossenschaftskapital n; **agricultural ~ credit society** (GB) Raiffeisenkasse f; **credit ~** Kreditgenossenschaft f

cooperatives; bank for ~ (US) Genossenschaftsbank f

cooperator n Mitarbeiter m

coordinate v koordinieren v, gleichordnen v

coordination n Koordinierung f, Gleichordnung f

coowner n Miteigentümer m

coownership n Miteigentum n

coparcenary n Miterbschaft f, gemeinsame Erbschaft

coparcener n Miterbe m, Miteigentümer m (von ererbtem Grundbesitz)

coparceny n Miterbschaft f, gemeinsame Erbschaft

copartner n Mitinhaber m, Mitbesitzer m, Teilhaber m, Partner m

copartnership n Teilhaberschaft f

copartnery; contract of ~ Gesellschaftsvertrag m, Teilhabervertrag m

copied adj nachgemacht adj (imitiert)

copper coin Kupfergeld n, Kupfermünze f

coppers n pl Kupfermünzen f pl

coproperty Miteigentum n

coproprietor Miteigentümer m

copy v kopieren v, abschreiben v; ~ n Kopie f, Durchschlag m, Duplikat n, Abschrift f, Muster n, Exemplar n

copyhold deed Zinsbrief m

copyright n Urheberrecht n

copyrightable adj urheberschutzfähig adj

core activity Kerngeschäft n; **~ business** Kerngeschäft f, Hauptgeschäft f; **~ deposit** Bodensatz m (Einlagen); **~ dump** Kernspeicherabzug m

corn exchange Getreidebörse f

corporate adj korporativ adj, körperschaftlich adj, gesellschaftlich adj; **~ assets** Gesellschaftsvermögen n (einer AG); **~ banking** Firmengeschäft n (der Banken); **~ body** Körperschaft f, juristische Person; **~ bonds** (US) Schuldverschreibungen von Aktiengesellschaften; **~ borrowings** Industriekredite m pl; **~ business** Firmenkundengeschäft n (Bank); **~ customer** Firmenkunde m (Bank); **~ debt issue** Industrieschuldverschreibung f; **~ department** Firmenkundenabteilung f (Bank); **~ finance** Unternehmensfinanzen plt; **~ financing** Unternehmensfinanzierung f; **~ form** Gesellschaftsform f; **~ funds** Gesellschaftsmittel n pl; **~ housekeeping activities** gesellschaftlicher Finanzhaushalt; **~ identity** Erscheinungsbild n (eines Unternehmens); **~ income tax** Körperschaftssteuer f; **~ liabilities** Verbindlichkeiten einer Gesellschaft; **~ liability** Gesellschaftshaftung f, Firmenhaftung f; **~ loan** Firmenkundenkredit m, Industrieschuldverschreibung f; **~ loans** Organkredite m pl; **~ management** Gesellschaftsleitung f; **~ meeting** Vorstandssitzung f; **~ net profit** Gesellschaftsreingewinn m; **~ power** Gesellschaftsbefugnisse n pl; **~ profit** Gesellschaftsgewinn m; **~ property** Gesellschaftseigentum n, Gesellschaftsvermögen n; **~ raider** (US) (professioneller) Unternehmensaufkäufer m pl (mit häufig feindlicher Übernahmeabsicht); **~ report** Geschäftsbericht m, Gesellschaftsbericht m; **~ statement** Gesellschaftsbilanz f, Firmenbilanz f

corporately adj korporativ adj, solidarisch adj (z. B. haften)

corporates Industrieschuldverschreibungen f pl

corporation n Körperschaft f, juristische Person; **~ n** (US) Korporation f, Gesellschaft f, Kapitalgesellschaft f; **~ bill** Handelswechsel m; **~ bond** Industrieschuldverschreibung f, Industrieobligation f; **~ financing** (US) Finanzierung von Aktiengesellschaften; **~ income tax** Körperschaftssteuer f; **~ law** (US) Aktiengesetz n; **~ loan** (GB) Kommunalschuldverschreibungen f pl, Stadtanleihe f, Kommunalanleihe f, Kommunalobligationen f pl; **~ paper** (US) begebbares Papier einer Aktiengesellschaft; **~ report** Geschäftsbericht m, Gesellschaftsbericht m; **~ stocks** (GB) Kommunalschuldverschreibungen f pl, Stadtanleihe f, Kommunalanleihe f, Kommunalobligationen f pl; **~ tax** Körperschaftssteuer f; **alien** ~ (US) ausländische Gesellschaft; **books of** ~ Geschäftsunterlagen f pl; **business** ~ (US) Geschäftsunternehmen n; **civil** ~ Gesellschaft des bürgerlichen Rechts; **close** ~ Aktiengesellschaft f (deren Aktien sich in festem Besitz einer weniger Personen befinden und nicht in den Verkehr gelangen); **commercial** ~ Handelsgesellschaft f

Corporation; *Commodity Credit* ~ (US) Rohstoff-Kredit-Gesellschaft f

corporation; **moneyed** ~ (US) Gesellschaft, die bank- oder versicherungsmäßige Geschäfte betreibt; **non-profit** ~ gemeinnützige Gesellschaft; **statutory** ~ Körperschaft des öffentlichen Rechts; **trading** ~ Handelsgesellschaft f, Erwerbsgesellschaft f

corpus n (US) Kapital und Eigentum eines Trusts

correct v korrigieren v, berichtigen v, verbessern v, abändern v; ~ adj einwandfrei adj, fehlerfrei adj

correcting entry Berichtigungsbuchung f

correction n Korrektur f, Berichtigung f, Verbesserung f

correspond v korrespondieren v, übereinstimmen v, entsprechen v

correspondence n Korrespondenz f, Schriftwechsel m, Geschäftsverbindung f; ~ **check** Korrespondenzscheck m

correspondent n Korrespondent m, Geschäftsfreund m; ~ **bank** Korrespondenzbank f

corruption n Bestechung f

co-signer Mitunterzeichner m, Mithaftende f u. m

cost v kosten v, kalkulieren v; ~ n Kosten plt, Geschäftskosten plt, Spesen plt, Preis m; ~ **account** Kostenkonto n; ~ **accountant** Kostenrechner m, Kalkulator m; ~ **accounting** Kostenrechnung f, Betriebskalkulation f; ~ **allocation** Kostenaufteilung f; ~ **analysis** Kostenanalyse f; ~ **and freight = c & f** Kosten und Fracht (siehe **Incoterms**); ~ **averaging** Verwendung fester Beträge zum Kauf bestimmter Wertpapiere f; ~ **budget** Kostenplan m; ~ **center** Kostenstelle f, Kostenträger m; ~ **control** Kostenkontrolle f; ~ **data** Kostenunterlagen f pl, Kostenangaben f pl; ~ **department** Kalkulationsabteilung f; ~ **increase** Kostensteigerung f; ~ **insurance and freight (c.i.f.)** Kosten, Versicherung, Fracht (c.i.f.); ~ **keeping** Kostenrechnung f; ~ **method** Kostenrechnungsmethode f; ~ **of appraisal** Schätzungskosten plt; ~ **of borrowing** Kreditkosten plt; ~ **of construction** Baukosten plt; ~ **of delivery** Lieferkosten plt, Versandkosten plt; ~ **of exchange** Umtauschkosten plt; ~ **of finance** Finanzierungskosten plt; ~ **of financing** Finanzierungskosten plt; ~ **of living** Lebenshaltungskosten plt; ~ **of management** Verwaltungskosten plt; ~ **of operating** Betriebskosten plt; ~ **of production** Herstellungswert m; ~ **of promotion** Gründungskosten plt; ~ **price** Kostenpreis m, Wareneinstandspreis m; ~ **push inflation** Kosteninflation f; ~ **record** Kostenbeleg m, Spesenzettel m; ~ **reduction** Kostensenkung f; ~ **saving** Kostenersparnis f; ~ **standard** Kalkulationsnorm f; ~ **structure** Kostengefüge n; ~ **unit** Kosteneinheit f; ~ **value** Anschaffungswert m, Erwerbswert m; **amortized** ~ Kosten nach Abschreibungen; **book** ~ Buchwert m; **calculation of** ~ Selbstkostenrechnung f; **capital** ~ Kapitalaufwand m; **credit** ~ Kreditkosten plt; **prime** ~ Selbstkosten plt, Gestehungskosten plt

cost-benefit analysis Kosten-Nutzen Analyse f

cost-cutting Kostensenkung f

cost-effective kostenwirksam

cost-free adj kostenlos adj, kostenfrei adj

costing n Kostenberechnung f, Kostenkalkulation f, Preisberechnung f, Rentabilitätsberechnung f

cost-of-living index Lebenshaltungsindex m

costs n pl Kosten plt, Geschäftskosten plt, Spesen plt, Preis m; **actual** ~ Selbstkosten plt, Gestehungskosten plt; **assessment** ~ Veranlagungskosten plt; **bill**

of ~ Spesenrechnung f, Anwaltsgebührenrechnung f; **computation of** ~ Kostenberechnung f, Kostenkalkulation f, Preisberechnung f, Rentabilitätsberechnung f; **fixed** ~ fixe Kosten
co-surety Mitbürge m
cotton exchange Baumwollbörse f
counsel n Rat m, Anwalt m, Rechtsberater m, Berater m, Beirat m; ~ **bill** (GB) kurzfristige Schatzanweisung; ~ **draft** (GB) kurzfristige Schatzanweisung
counsel's fee Anwaltsgebühren f pl; ~ **opinion** Gutachten n (eines Rechtssachverständigen)
counsellor n Berater m, Ratgeber m; ~ n Rat m, Anwalt m, Rechtsberater m, Beirat m
count v zählen v, rechnen v; ~ **again** nachzählen v, durchzählen v; ~ **back** zurückrechnen v; ~ **over** nachzählen v, durchzählen v; ~ **up** zusammenzählen v, addieren v
countable adj zählbar adj, berechenbar adj
countdown floater zinsvariabler Schuldtitel
counter Wert m, Wertpapier n, Schalter m; ~ **account** Gegenkonto n; ~ **bid** Gegenangebot n; ~ **cash** n tägliche Kasse, Tageskasse f; ~ **check** Kassenscheck m; ~ **error** Ausgleichsfehler m; ~ **hall** Kassenraum m; ~ **offer** Gegenangebot n; ~ **purchase (c. trade)** Kompensationsgeschäft n; ~ **requirements** Zahlungsanforderungen am Kassenschalter; **bargain** ~ Effektenschalter m; **over the** ~ über den Bankschalter, außerbörslich adj (Handel mit nicht notierten Wertpapieren)
counterbalance v kompensieren v, ausgleichen v; ~ n Gegensaldo m, Gegengewicht n
counterbalanced by saldiert durch
counterbill n Rückwechsel m, Gegenwechsel m
counterbond n Rückbürgschaft f, Gegenbürgschaft f
counterclaim n Gegenforderung f, Gegenrechnung f
counterclerk n Schalterangestellte f u. m, Schalterbeamte f u. m

counterfeit coins Falschmünzen f pl; ~ **money** Falschgeld n
counterfeit v fälschen v (Geld, Wechsel), verfälschen v, nachdrucken v, nachahmen v, nachmachen v; ~ n Fälschung f, Verfälschung f, Falsifikat n
counterfeit(ed) adj nachgemacht adj (gefälscht)
counterfeiter n Fälscher m, Verfälscher m; ~ n Falschmünzer m, Urkundenfälscher m; ~ **of banknotes** Banknotenfälscher m
counterfeiting n Falschmünzerei f, Banknotenfälscherei f, Fälschung f
counterfoil n Kontrollabschnitt m, Kupon m, Talon m
countermand v absagen v, abbestellen v, stornieren v, widerrufen v; ~ n Absage f, Widerruf m
counteroffer n Gegenofferte f, Gegenangebot n
counterorder v absagen v, abbestellen v, stornieren v, widerrufen v; ~ n Gegenauftrag m, Gegenorder f, Stornierung f
counterparty n Gegenpartei f; ~ **risk** Adressenausfallrisiken n pl
counterreckoning n Gegenrechnung f
counterremittance n Gegendeckung f
countersale n Gegenverkauf m
countersecurity n Rückbürgschaft f, Gegenbürgschaft f
countersign v gegenzeichnen v, mitunterzeichnen v
countersignature n Gegenzeichnung f, Mitunterzeichnung f
countersigner n Gegenzeichner m
counterstock n Talon m, Erneuerungsschein m, Allonge f
countertally n Talon m, Erneuerungsschein m, Allonge f
countertrade n Gegengeschäft f
countervailing credit Gegenakkreditiv n
countervalue n Gegenwert m
counting n Zählung f
countries having a strong currency währungsstarke Länder
country bank (GB) Provinzbank f; ~ **bill** (GB) Provinzwechsel m; ~ **branch** (GB) Provinzfiliale f; ~ **of destination**

Bestimmungsland n; **~ risk** Länderrisiko n; **~ shipper** Inlandsspediteur m; **agreement ~** Verrechnungsland n; **undeveloped ~** Entwicklungsland n

county n Verwaltungsbezirk m; **~ bonds** Kommunalobligationen f pl; **~ fund** Kommunalvermögen n; **~ stocks** (GB) Papiere der verschiedenen englischen Grafschaften

coupon n Kupon m, Zinsschein m, Gewinnanteilschein m; **~ bond** (US) Inhaberobligation f, Inhaberschuldverschreibung f; **~ book** Kuponkonto n; **~ check** (US) Kuponscheck m; **~ collection department** Kuponabteilung f; **~ collection teller** (US) Kuponkassierer m; **~ date** Kupontermin m; **~ holder** Kuponinhaber m; **~ issue** Zinsschein nach Trennung von Mantel und Kupon; **~ service** Kuponeinlösung f; **~ sheet** Kuponbogen m, Zinsscheinbogen m; **~ teller** Kuponkassierer m; **annuity ~** Rentenschein m; **bond ~** Zinsschein m; **current ~** laufender Kupon; **dividend ~** Dividendenschein m, Gewinnanteilschein m; **outstanding ~** unbezahlbarer Kupon, ausstehender Kupon; **overdue ~** notleidender Kupon; **registered ~ bonds** Namenspapiere mit Zinsschein

coupons paying department Kuponkasse f; **detached ~** abgetrennte Kupons

course n Kurs m (Ausbildung), Kursus m, Lehrgang m; **~ of affairs** Geschäftsgang m; **~ of exchange** (GB) Wechselkurs m; **~ of law** Rechtsgang m; **~ of training** Ausbildungskurs m; **bill of ~ of exchange** Kurszettel m (Devisen), Kursbericht m (Devisen), Devisenkursliste f

court composition Zwangsvergleich m; **~ of bankruptcy** Konkursgericht n; **~ of trade** Kammer für Handelssachen f, Gerichtsverfahren n; **commercial ~** (GB) Handelsgericht n; **decree of ~** Gerichtsbeschluß m

co-user Mitbenutzer m

covenant n Formalversprechen n, Abkommen n (förmlich), Abmachung f (förmlich), Satzung f, Statut n, Vertragsklausel f, Vertrag m; **~ breaker** Vertragsbrecher m; **general ~** allgemeine Abmachung

covenanted adj vertraglich verpflichtet

covenantee n Vertragsberechtigte f u. m

covenantor n Vertragspartei f (verpflichtete, versprechende)

covenants Klauseln im Kreditvertrag

cover v decken v, Deckung anschaffen, ausgleichen v; **~** n Briefumschlag m (Kuvert); **~** n Deckung f, Gelddeckung f, Notendeckung f, Sicherheit f; **~ a bill** Deckung für einen Wechsel anschaffen; **~ debts** Schulden abdecken; **~ fund** Deckungsstock m, Deckungsfonds m; **~ letter** Begleitbrief m, Begleitschreiben n; **~ liabilities** Verbindlichkeiten erfüllen, Verpflichtungen nachkommen; **~ note** (GB) vorläufige Deckungszusage; **~ ratio** Deckungsverhältnis n; **~ shortage** Unterdeckung f; **bill ~** Wechseldeckung f

coverage Deckung f, Versicherungsschutz m; **~ capital** Deckungskapital n; **~ requirement** Eindeckungspflicht f; **comprehensive ~** Vollkasko n

covered by contract vertraglich abgesichert; **~ warrant** gedeckte Option f

covering n Deckung f, Abdeckung f, Absicherung f; **~ deed** Treuhandurkunde f; **~ funds** Deckungsmittel n; **~ letter** Begleitbrief m, Begleitschreiben n; **~ note** vorläufige Deckungszusage; **~ order** Deckungsauftrag m; **~ purchase** Deckungskauf m; **bear ~** Deckungskauf m

craft n Handwerk n

craftsman n Handwerker m

crash Börsenkrach m

crawl in parity Paritätsänderung f

crawling peg Wechselkursanpassung in kleinen Schritten

create gründen, errichten, ausgeben, schöpfen v; **~ money** Geld schöpfen

creation of bank money Giralgeldschöpfung f; **~ of a mortgage** Hypothekenbestellung f; **~ of reserves** Reservebildung f

creative accounting Bilanzkosmetik f

credit

credit n Kredit m, Darlehen f, Akkreditiv n, Kreditwürdigkeit f, Guthaben n, Gutschrift f; **~ v** gutschreiben v, kreditieren v, verrechnen v, verbuchen v, leihen v, borgen v, Kredit gewähren; **~** Ruf m, Zuverlässigkeit f; **~ abuse** Kreditmißbrauch m; **~ accommodation** Kreditgewährung f; **~ account** kreditorisches Konto, laufendes Konto mit Kreditsaldo; **~ advice** Gutschrift f, Gutschriftanzeige f; **~ agency** Kreditvermittlungsbüro n, Kreditauskunftei f; **~ agreement** Kreditabkommen n; **~ an account** ein Konto erkennen; **~ and debit** Soll und Haben; **~ applicant** Kreditantragsteller m; **~ approval** Kreditzusage f; **~ arrangement** Kreditvereinbarung f; **~ at the bank** Bankguthaben n; **~ balance** Guthaben n, Habensaldo m Kreditsaldo m, Aktivsaldo m, Haben n; **~ balance with other banks** Nostroguthaben n; **~ bank** Kreditbank f, Darlehenskasse f; **~ barometrics** Kreditmaßstäbe m pl; **~ basis** Kreditbasis f; **~ bill** Kreditwechsel m; **~ broker** Finanzmakler m, Kreditvermittler m; **~ bureau** Kreditvermittlungsbüro n, Kreditauskunftei f; **~ bureau report** Kreditauskunft f; **~ buying** Kreditkauf m; **~ by balance** per Saldo gutschreiben; **~ capacity** Kreditkapazität f; **~ card** Kreditkarte f; **~ check** Bonitätsprüfung f; **~ checking** Kreditprüfung f; **~ ceiling** Kreditgrenze f, Kreditplafond m; **~ commission** Kreditkommission f; **~ conditions** Kreditbedingungen f pl, Kreditkonditionen f pl; **~ contraction** Kreditschrumpfung f; **~ control** Kreditkontrolle f (staatliche); **~ cooperative** Kreditgenossenschaft f; **~ cost** Kreditkosten plt; **~ creation** Kreditschöpfung f; **~ crisis** Kreditkrise f; **~ department** Kreditabteilung f, Kreditbüro n; **~ element** Kreditfaktor m; **~ enquiry** Kreditauskunftsanfrage f, Bitte um Kreditauskunft; **~ expansion** Kreditausweitung f; **~ expert** Kreditfachmann m; **~ facilities** Kreditfazilitäten f pl; **~ folder** Kreditakte f; **~ for collected item(s)** Sammelgutschrift f; **~ form** (US) Kreditformular n, Kreditantragsformular n, Kreditantrag m; **~ given flat** zinsloser Kredit; **~ grantor** Kreditgeber m, Darlehensgeber m, Anleihegeber m, Ausleiher m, Verleiher m; **~ guarantee** Kreditbürgschaft f; **~ in current account** Buchkredit m; **~ in goods** Warenkredit m; **~ in use** in Anspruch genommener Kredit; **~ information** Kreditauskunft f; **~ inquiry agency** Handelsauskunftei f; **~ institution** Kreditinstitut n, Kreditanstalt f; **~ instrument** Kreditmittel n; **~ insurance** Kreditversicherung f; **~ interchange** gegenseitige Kreditauskunft; **~ interest** Habenzinsen m pl, Passivzinsen m pl; **~ item** Habenposten m, Gutschrift f; **~ ledger** Kreditregister n; **~ life insurance** Risikolebensversicherung f; **~ limit** Kreditlimit n; Kreditlinie f, Kreditrahmen m, Kreditbetrag m, eingeräumter Kredit, Höchstkredit m; **~ line** Kreditlinie f, Kreditrahmen m, Kreditbetrag m, eingeräumter Kredit, Höchstkredit m; **~ loss** Kreditausfall m; **~ loss insurance** Warenkreditversicherung f; **~ man** Kreditbearbeiter m; **~ management** Kreditmanagement n; **~ maturity** Kreditlaufzeit f (US); **~ memorandum** Gutschrift f, Gutschriftsanzeige f; **~ note** Gutschrift f, Gutschriftsanzeige f; **~ offer** Kreditangebot n; **~ officer** Kreditsachbearbeiter m; **~ on real estate** Realkredit m; **~ on securities** Lombardkredit m, Lombarddarlehen n, abgesicherter Kredit; **~ operations** Kreditgeschäfte n pl; **~ order** Kreditauftrag m; **~ period** Laufzeit eines Kredits; **~ policy** Kreditpolitik f; **~ principles** Kreditgrundsätze m pl; **~ rate** Habenzinsen m; **~ rating** Bonitätsbeurteilung f, (US) Kreditwürdigkeitsprüfung f, Einschätzung der Kreditfähigkeit; **~ report** Kreditauskunft f; **~ requirement** (US) Kreditbedürfnis n; **~ resources** Kreditquellen f pl; **~ restriction** Krediteinschränkung f, Kreditrestriktion f; **~ risk** Kreditrisiko n; **~ rob-**

bery Kreditbetrug m; **~ rules** Kreditrichtlinien f pl; **~ sale** Kreditverkauf m; **~ sales arrangement** Abzahlungsvertrag m; **~ service organization** Kreditauskunftsorganisation f; **~ situation** kreditpolitische Situation; **~ slip** Einzahlungsbeleg n; **~ society** Kreditgesellschaft f; **~ solvency** Bonität f; **~ squeeze** Kreditknappheit f; **~ standards** Kreditrichtlinien f pl; **~ standing** Kreditwürdigkeit f, Kreditfähigkeit f; **~ strain** Kreditanspannung f; **~ stringency** Kreditknappheit f; **~ surplus** Aktivüberschuß m; **~ system** Kreditwesen n; **~ terms** Kreditbedingungen f pl, Kreditkonditionen f pl; **~ the proceeds to an account** den Gegenwert einem Konto gutschreiben; **~ tranche** Kredittranche f (IMF); **~ undertaking** Kreditzusage f; **~ union** Kreditverein m, Kreditgenossenschaft f, Volksbank f; **~ volume** Kreditvolumen n; **~ with a savings bank** Sparkassenguthaben n; **acceptance ~** Akzeptkredit m, Rembourskredit m; **accumulated ~ activity** akkumulierte Habenumsätze; **allow a ~** einen Kredit einräumen, einen Kredit gewähren; **back-to-back ~** (US) Gegenakkreditiv n; **bank ~** Bankkredit m, Bankdarlehen n; **banker's acceptance ~** Akzeptkredit m, Rembourskredit m; **bill ~** Wechselkredit m; **book ~** Buchkredit m; **bought on ~** auf Ziel gekauft; **buy on ~** auf Kredit kaufen; **cash ~** Barkredit m, Kassenkredit m, Kontokorrentkredit m; **clean ~** nicht durch Dokumente gesicherter Kreditbrief; **collateral ~** Lombardkredit m, Lombarddarlehen n, abgesicherter Kredit; **commercial ~** Handelskredit m, Warenkredit m; **commodity ~** Warenkredit m; **confirmed ~** bestätigter Kredit; **cooperative ~ association** Verkaufsgenossenschaft f; **cooperative ~ union** Kreditgenossenschaft f; **countervailing ~** Gegenakkreditiv n; **current account ~** Kontokorrentkredit m, offener Kredit; **deferred ~** aufgeschobener Kredit; **deflation of ~** Kreditrestriktion f; **documentary ~** Dokumentenkredit m, Dokumentenakkreditiv n; **documented ~** Dokumentenkredit m, **draft ~** Rembourskredit m; **emergency ~** Stützungskredit m; **establish a ~** einen Kredit einrichten, einen Kredit eröffnen; **evergreen ~** unbefristeter Kredit; **farm ~** Landwirtschaftskredit m, landwirtschaftliches Darlehen n, Agrarkredit m; **frozen ~** eingefrorener Kredit; **investment ~** Investitionskredit m; **open ~** Kontokorrentkredit m, offener Kredit; **open a ~** ein Akkreditiv stellen; **public ~** öffentliche Anleihe, öffentlicher Kredit; **revocable ~** widerrufbarer Kredit; **revolving ~** revolvierender Kredit, sich automatisch erneuernder Kredit; **rural ~** landwirtschaftlicher Kredit; **stand-by ~** Kreditzusage f, Beistandskredit m; **standing ~** laufender Kredit; **working ~** Betriebskredit m

creditability n Kreditwürdigkeit f, Kreditfähigkeit f

creditable adj kreditwürdig adj, kreditfähig adj, glaubwürdig adj

creditor n Gläubiger m, Kreditor m, Forderungsberechtigte f u. m; **~ account** Guthabenkonto n; **acceptance ~** Akzeptgläubige; **bankrupt's ~** Konkursgläubiger m; **bill ~** Wechselgläubiger m, Wechselinhaber m; **bona fide ~** gutgläubiger Forderungsinhaber; **bond ~** Obligationsinhaber m, Pfandbriefgläubiger m, Pfandbriefinhaber m; **book ~** Buchgläubiger m; **chief ~** Hauptgläubiger m; **double ~** zweifacher Gläubiger; **fellow ~** Mitgläubiger m; **joint ~** Mitgläubiger m; **paid off ~** abgefundener Gläubiger; **partnership ~** Gesellschaftsgläubiger m; **preferential ~** (GB) Vorzugsgläubiger m, bevorrechtigter Gläubiger, bevorzugter Gläubiger; **preferred ~** (US) Vorzugsgläubiger m, bevorrechtigter Gläubiger, bevorzugter Gläubiger; **public ~** Staatsgläubiger m, öffentlicher Gläubiger; **trade ~** Gläubiger aus Kontokorrentgeschäften; **unsecured ~** ungesicherter Gläubiger

creditors Kreditoren m pl, Lieferverbindlichkeiten f pl; **accounts with ~** Gläubigerkonten n pl; **arrangement with ~** Gläubigerausgleich m; **board of ~** Gläubi-

gerausschuß m; **composition with ~** Gläubigervergleich m
creditors' committee Gläubigerausschuß m; **~ ledger** Kreditorenbuch n; **~ meeting** Gläubigerversammlung f; **~ petition** Konkurseröffnungsantrag eines Gläubigers; **~ protection agency** Schufa f (Schutzgemeinschaft für allgemeine Kreditsicherung)
creditress n Gläubigerin f
Credit Swisse Index Preisindex der Börse in Zürich
creditworthiness n Kreditwürdigkeit f
creeping inflation schleichende Inflation
crisis n Krise f; **banking ~** Bankenkrise f
cross v kreuzen v, querschreiben v; **~ acceptance** Wechselreiterei f; **~ bill** Rückwechsel m, Gegenwechsel m; **~ default clause** wechselseitige Verzugsklausel; **~ entry** Gegenbuchung f; **~ exchange** (GB) Wechselarbitrage über mehrere Plätze; **~ firing** (GB) Wechselreiterei f; **~ hedge** Sicherung einer Kassaposition durch einen Terminkontrakt; **~ liability** gegenseitige Haftung; **~ order** Kompensationsorder f; **~ out** ausstreichen v; **~ rate** Wechselkurs zweier Fremdwährungen zueinander, Usancekurs m, Cross-Rate f; **~ shareholding** Überkreuzbeteiligung f; **~ trade** Börsenkompensationsgeschäft n
cross-border listing Wertpapier das zum Handel in mehreren Ländern zugelassen ist
crossed check Verrechnungsscheck m, gekreuzter Scheck
crossing n (GB) Querschreiben n
cross-selling Überkreuzverkauf m
crown n Krone f; **~ jewels** besonders wertvolle Vermögensteile
CRT (Cathode Ray Tube) **terminal** Datensichtgerät n
crumbling price nachgebender Kurs
cum mit, inklusive; **~ dividend** mit Dividende; **~ drawing** einschließlich Ziehung; **~ interest** mit Stückzinsen; **~ new** mit Bezugsrecht auf neue Aktien; **~ rights** mit Bezugsrecht, mit Optionsrecht
cumulative adj kumulativ adj, sich anhäufend; **~ dividend** kumulative Dividende; **~ fund** thesaurierender Fonds; **~ participating preference shares** Vorzugsaktien mit besonderer Dividendenberechtigung; **~ preference stocks** kumulative Vorzugsaktien; **~ stocks** (US) kumulative Aktien
curb n Freiverkehrsbörse f, Freibörse f, Freiverkehrsmarkt m, Nachbörse f; **~ broker** Freiverkehrsmakler m; **~ exchange** Freiverkehrsbörse f, Freibörse f, Freiverkehrsmarkt m, Nachbörse f; **~ market** Freiverkehrsbörse f, Freibörse f, Freiverkehrsmarkt m, Nachbörse f; **~ market price** nachbörslicher Kurs, außerbörslicher Kurs; **~ stocks** (US) im Freiverkehr gehandelte Wertpapiere
curbstone broker Freiverkehrsmakler m
currency n Währung f, Valuta f, Geld n, Geldumlauf m, Laufzeit f Gültigkeit f; **~ agreement** Währungsabkommen n; **~ arbitrage** Devisenarbitrage f; **~ area** Währungsgebiet n; **~ assets** Devisenguthaben n; **~ bill** Wechsel in ausländischer Währung; **~ bond** Obligation in ausländischer Währung; **~ call option** Devisenkaufoption f; **~ certificate** (US) Schatzanweisung f; **~ clause** Währungsklausel f; **~ control** Devisenbewirtschaftung f, Devisenkontrolle f, Währungskontrolle f; **~ dealer** Devisenhändler m; **~ declaration** Devisenerklärung f; **~ depreciation** Währungsabwertung f; **~ draft** Valutawechsel m; **~ exchange standard** Devisenwährung f; **~ exposure** (GB) Währungs-, Wechselkursrisiko; **~ fund** Währungsfonds m; **~ futures** (contract) Devisenterminkontrakt m; **~ hedge** Wechselkurssicherung f; **~ holdings** Devisenbestände m pl; **~ law** Währungsgesetz n; **~ of a bill** Wechsellaufzeit f, Laufzeit eines Wechsels; **~ offense** Devisenvergehen n; **~ operator** Währungsspekulant m; **~ option** Währungsoption f; **~ policy** Währungspolitik f; **~ principle** Golddeckungsprinzip n; **~ put option** Devisenverkaufsoption f; **~ racket** Devisenschiebung f; **~ rates** (GB) in Pfund Sterling notierte Devisenkurse; **~ reform** Währungsreform f; **~ regulations** Devisenbestimmungen f pl; **~ restrictions**

Devisenbeschränkungen f pl; **- revaluation** Währungsaufwertung f; **- risk** Währungsrisiko n; **- stabilization** Währungsstabilisierung f; **- supply** Zahlungsmittelversorgung f; **- system** Währungssystem n; **- unit** Zahlungsmitteleinheit f; **- value** Währungswert m; **allocation of -** Devisenzuteilung f; **bank -** (US) Banknoten der amerikanischen Nationalbanken; **blocked -** nicht frei konvertierbare Devisen; **clearing -** Verrechnungswährung f

Currency; *Comptroller of the -* (US) Bankenaufsichtsbehörde für nationale (von der Bundesregierung genehmigte) Banken

currency; *depreciated -* entwertetes Geld, notleidende Währung; ***managed -*** manipulierte Währung; ***national -*** Landeswährung f; ***standard -*** Einheitswährung f

current adj laufend adj, kursierend adj, zirkulierend adj, marktfähig adj, verkehrsfähig adj, kursfähig adj; **- account** Kontokorrentkonto n, laufendes Konto, Konto in laufender Rechnung, offenes Konto; **- account credit** Kontokorrentkredit m, offener Kredit; **- account ledger** Kontokorrentbuch n; **- assets** Umlaufvermögen n, flüssige Aktiva, flüssige Mittel; **- business** laufende Geschäfte; **- capital** Betriebskapital n, Umlaufkapital n, Betriebsmittel n pl; **- coin** gängige Münze; **- coupon** laufender Kupon; **- funds** Umlaufvermögen n, flüssige Aktiva, flüssige Mittel; **- income** laufende Erträge; **- interest** laufende Zinsen; **- investment** vorübergehende Anlage; **- liabilities** kurzfristige Verbindlichkeiten, laufende Verbindlichkeiten; **- on exchange** börsengängig adj; **- price** Tageskurs m, Tagessatz m, Marktpreis m; **- rate** Tageskurs m, Tagessatz m, Marktpreis m; **- ratio** Liquiditätsgrad m, Liquiditätsverhältnis n; **- receivables** Umlaufvermögen n, flüssige Aktiva, flüssige Mittel; **- value** Marktwert m; **- yield** laufender Ertrag, laufender Gewinn, laufende Rendite; **account - creditors** Kreditoren in laufender Rechnung; **advance on - account** Kontokorrentkredit m, offener Kredit

curriculum vitae (US) Resümee n, Lebenslauf m

curtail v kürzen, v einschränken v, schmälern v, vermindern v

curtailment n Kürzung f, Einschränkung f, Schmälerung f, Verminderung f

cushion bond Anleihe mit überdurchschnittlicher Rendite

custodial adj vormundschaftlich adj

custodian n Hinterlegungsstelle f, Verwahrungsstelle f, Verwahrer m; **- n** Vormund m, Vermögensverwalter m, Treuhänder m; **- account** (US) Depot n (bei einer Bank), Depotkonto n; **- bank** Depotbank f; **- fee** Depotgebühr m; **- trustee** Vermögensverwalter m, Treuhänder m, Bevollmächtigte f u. m, Verwalter m, Pfleger m

custodianship n Effektenverwaltung durch Banken (US), Treuhänderschaft f, Verwahrung f, Verwaltung f; **- account** Depot n (bei einer Bank), Depotkonto n

custodianships n pl (US) Depotgeschäft n

custody n Gewahrsam m, Obhut f, Aufbewahrung f; **- account** Depotkonto n; **- bill of lading** Lagerhalterkonnossement n; **- fee** Verwahrungsgebühr f; **- receipt** Depotquittung f, Depotschein m

custom n Gewohnheit f, Usance f, Kundschaft f; **according to -** usancegemäß adj; **business -** Geschäftsgebrauch m, Geschäftssitte f, Geschäftsusance f

customable adj zollpflichtig adj

customary adj gebräuchlich adj, üblich adj, usancegemäß adj; **- freehold** Erbpachtgut n; **- right** Gewohnheitsrecht n

customer n Kunde m; **- advisor** Kundenberater m; **- deposits** Publikumsgelder n pl, Kundengelder n pl; **- recommendation** Kundenempfehlung f; **- waiting time** Kundenwartezeit f; **- bank** Bankkunde m; **collection by the -** Selbstabholung f, Inkasso durch Boten; **prospective -** voraussichtlicher Kunde

customer-operated terminal Selbstbedienungsterminal m

customer-oriented *adj* kundennah *adj*

customers; accounts with ~ Kundenkonten *n pl*; **alienate ~** Kunden abwerben; **bill on ~** Kundenwechsel *m*; **draw away ~** Kunden abwerben

customer's bill Kundenwechsel *m*; **~ complaint** Kundenbeschwerde *f*; **~ loan** Kundenkredit *m*, Konsumentenkredit *m*; **~ needs** Kundenbedürfnis *n*; **~ note** Kundenwechsel *m*; **~ order** Kundenauftrag *m*; **~ security department** Depotabteilung *f*; **~ wishes** Kundenwünsche *m pl*

customs *n pl* Zoll *m*, Zollwesen *n*; **~ acts** Zollverordnungen *f pl*; **~ administration** Zollverwaltung *f*; **~ authorities** Zollbehörde *f*; **~ bond note** Zollbegleitschein *m*; **~ duty** Zollabgabe *f*, Zollgebühr *f*; **~ entry** Zollerklärung *f*; **~ formalities** Zollformalitäten *f pl*; **~ house** Zollamt *n*; **~ inspector** Zollaufseher *m*; **~ note** Zollvormerkschein *m*; **~ official** Zollbeamte *m*; **~ penny** Rückzoll *m*; **~ permission** zollamtliche Erlaubnis; **~ receipt** Zollschein *m*; **~ tare** Zollgewicht *n*; **~ tariff** Zolltarif *m*; **~ union** Zollunion *f*; **~ warehouse** Zollager *n*; **~ weight** Zollgewicht *n*; **bill of ~** Zollgebührenrechnung *f*; **rate of ~** Zollsatz *m*, Steuersatz *m*

cut *v* kürzen *v*, einschränken *v*, schmälern *v*, vermindern *v*; **~ n** Zinskupon *m*, Kapitalherabsetzung *f*, (US) Summe von Schecks; **~ down** kürzen *v*, einschränken *v*, schmälern *v*, vermindern *v*; **~ statement** Zwischenbilanz *f*

cut-off *n* (US) Scheckbilanz für Kontrollzwecke

cut-throat price Wucherpreis *m*

cycle; business ~ Konjunkturzyklus *m*, Konjunkturverlauf *m*

cyclical *adj* zyklisch *adj*, konjunkturell *adj*; **~ depression** Konjunkturbaisse *f*; **~ influence** Konjunktureinfluß *m*; **~ policy** Konjunkturpolitik *f*; **~ recovery** konjunkturelle Erholung; **~ trend** Konjunkturtendenz *f*

cylinder *n* Zylinder *m* (Daten); **~ option** Kauf einer Kaufoption und Verkauf einer Verkaufoption

D

DA (D/A) = documents against acceptance Dokumente gegen Akzept
dabbler n Börsendilettant m
daily average Tagesdurchschnitt m; **- balance** täglicher Saldo; **- balance interest calculation** Staffelmethode f; **- business** tägliches Geschäft; **- interest** Tageszinsen m pl; **- transaction register** Tagesumsatzliste f
damage v schaden v, beschädigen v, Schaden zufügen, benachteiligen v; **- n** Schaden m, Beschädigung f; **- claim** Schadenersatzanspruch m; **- report** Schadenbericht m; **- to property** Sachschaden m, Vermögensschaden m
damages n pl Schadenersatz m, Entschädigungssumme f, Schadenersatzsumme f; **action for -** Schadenersatzklage f; **assess -** Schaden feststellen, Entschädigungssumme bestimmen; **claim for -** Schadenersatzanspruch m
damp down abschwächen v, dämpfen v (Nachfrage)
dandy note (GB) Zollfreigabeschein m
Danish Krone Dänische Krone f
data n pl Daten plt; **- acquisition** Datenerfassung f; **- acquisition system** Datensammelsystem n; **- bank** Datenbank f; **- base** Datenbestand m; **- codification** Datenverschlüsselung f; **- collection** Datenerfassung f; **- communication** Datenaustausch m; **- compression** Datenkomprimierung f; **- gathering system** Datensammelsystem n; **- medium for temporary storage** Datenzwischenträger m; **- traffic** (as opposed to voice traffic) Datenverkehr m; **- transfer** Datentransport m; **- transmission** Datenübertragung f; **- transmission line** Datenübertragungsleitung f
data-processing terminal Datenendgerät n, Datenendplatz m
date v datieren v; **- n** Datum n, Termin m, Frist f, Sicht f; **- in advance** im voraus datieren; **- of a bill** Fälligkeit eines Wechsels; **- of bill of lading** Konnossementsdatum n; **- of declaration** Erklärungstag m; **- of discount** Diskontierungstag m; **- of entry** Buchungsdatum n; **- of expiration** Verfalltag m, Fälligkeitstermin m, Fälligkeitstag m; **- of issue** Emissionstag m, Ausgabetag m; **- of maturity** Verfalltag m, Fälligkeitstermin m, Fälligkeitstag m; **- of receipt** Eingangsdatum n; **- of redemption** Rückzahlungstermin m; **- of repayment** Rückzahlungstermin m; **- stamp** Poststempel m, Datumstempel m; **balance -** Bilanzsuchtag m; **bill after -** Datowechsel m; **closing -** Schlußtermin m; **due -** Verfalltag m, Fälligkeitstermin m, Fälligkeitstag m
dated securities Wertpapiere mit festem Rückzahlungstermin
dating n Datierung f
DAX = German Stock Market Index Deutsche Aktienindex m (DAX)
DAX-future option Dax-Future-Option f
day loan Tagesgeld n, täglich fälliger Kredit; **- of account** Abrechnungstag m; **- of issue** Emissionstag m, Ausgabetag m; **- of payment** Zahlungstermin m, Zahltag m; **- order** Auftrag, der nur einen Tag Gültigkeit hat; **due -** Verfalltag m, Fälligkeitstermin m, Fälligkeitstag m
day-book n Journal n, Primanote f, Memorial n, Kladde f
day's high Tageshöchstkurs m; **- rate** Tageskurs m, Tagessatz m, Marktpreis m
day-to-day business Tagesgeschäft n
day-to-day loan (GB) Tagesgeld n, täglich fälliger Kredit
day-to-day money Tagesgeld n, täglich fälliges Geld
day-to-day money market Tagesgeldmarkt m
dead account umsatzloses Konto, unbewegtes Konto, totes Konto; **- assets**

deadline

unproduktive Anlagen, ertragloses Kapital; **~ capital** totes Kapital, brachliegendes Kapital; **~ loan** (GB) Anleihe ohne Verfallfrist; **~ loss** Totalverlust m; **~ market** lustlose Börse, umsatzschwache Börse; **~ money** totes Kapital, brachliegendes Kapital; **~ rent** (GB) Minimalpacht f, Bergregalabgabe f; **~ security** wertlose Sicherheit; **~ stock** unverkäufliche Waren

deadline n Fristablauf m, Termin m

deadlock n Stillstand m, Stockung f

deal v handeln v (Handel treiben); **~** n Handel m, Abschluß m, Vertrag m, Geschäft n; **~ on joint account** Metageschäft n; **~ on the stock exchange** Börsencoup m; **~ out** verteilen v, austeilen v

dealer n Händler m, Makler m, Kaufmann m; **~ commission** Händlerprovision f; **~ for own account** Eigenhändler m; **~ in stocks** (US) Effektenhändler m, Börsenhändler m; **~ position** Händlerposition f; **foreign exchange ~** Devisenhändler m; **money ~** Geldwechsler m; **real estate ~** Grundstücksmakler m, Immobilienmakler m; **wholesale ~** Grossist m, Großhändler m

dealer's engagement Händlerobligo n

dealing n (GB) Effektenhandel m, Geschäft n, Abschluß m, Handel m; **commission ~** Kommissionsgeschäft n, Kommissionshandel m

dealings Handel m, Umsatz m; **~ for cash** Kassageschäft n pl; **~ for the account** Termingeschäfte f pl; **~ in foreign exchange** Währungsgeschäft n, Devisengeschäft n, Devisenhandel m; **~ in foreign notes and coins** Sortenhandel m; **~ in futures** Terminhandel m; **~ in real estate** Immobilienhandel m; **~ in stocks** (US) Effektenhandel m, Börsenhandel m, Aktienhandel m; **~ in the over-the-counter (OTC) market** Freiverkehrshandel m

dear money teures Geld

death benefit Sterbegeld n; **~ duty** (GB) Erbschaftsteuer f, Nachlaßsteuer f

debase v verfälschen v (Münzen), verschlechtern v

debenture n Obligation f, Schuldverschreibung f, Schuldtitel m, Schuldschein m; **~** n Zollrückgabeschein m; **~ bond** ungesicherte Schuldverschreibung; **~ book** Rückzahlbuch n; **~ capital** Obligationenerlös m; **~ certificate** Zollrückgabeschein m; **~ holder** Obligationeninhaber m; **~ income bond** Schuldverschreibung ohne Zinsgarantie; **~ stock** (US) Vorzugsaktie f, hypothekarisch gesicherte Obligation, (GB) Obligation, die man in Teilbeträgen überweisen kann; **~ yield** Rendite einer Schuldverschreibung; **bearer ~** Inhaberobligation f, Inhaberschuldverschreibung f; **mortgage ~** hypothekarisch gesicherte Obligation, hypothekarisch gesicherte Schuldverschreibung; **naked ~** (GB) ungesicherte Obligation; **registered ~** Namensobligation f; **trust ~** Schuldverschreibung über eine bevorrechtigte Forderung

debentures; unissued ~ noch nicht ausgegebene Schuldverschreibungen

debit v berechnen v (Konto), in Rechnung stellen, belasten v, anschreiben v; **~** n Debet n, Soll n, Lastschrift f, Sollseite f; **~ account** Debitorenkonto n; **~ advice** Belastungsaufgabe f, Belastungsanzeige f; **~ balance** Debetsaldo m, Schuldensaldo m, Sollsaldo m; **~ charge procedure** Lastschriftverfahren n; **~ entry** Debetbuchung f, Belastung f (Buchung); **~ interest** Sollzinsen m pl, Aktivzinsen m pl; **~ item** Debetbuchung f, Belastung f (Buchung); **~ note** Belastungsaufgabe f, Belastungsanzeige f; **~ rate** Sollzinsrate f, Sollzinssatz m; **~ side** Sollseite f, Debetseite f; **~ ticket** Belastungsanweisung f; **~ voucher** Lastschriftbeleg m, Sollbeleg m; **accumulated ~ activity** akkumulierte Sollumsätze; **credit and ~** Soll und Haben

debitable adj belastbar adj

debits; bank ~ (US) Bankumsätze auf der Debetseite

deblock v entsperren v (Guthaben)

debt n Schuld f, Verschuldung f, Schuldtitel m; **~ and other fixed-income securities** Schuldverschreibungen und andere festverzinslichen Wertpapiere (Bilanzposten); **- balance** Debetsaldo m, Schuldensaldo m, Sollsaldo m; **- calendar** Emissionskalender m; **- ceiling** Kreditgrenze f; **- collecting business** Inkassobüro n; **- conversion** Umschuldung f; **- convertible bond** Wandelschuldverschreibung f; **- discount** Kreditdisagio n; **- equity swap** Umwandlung von Bankforderungen in Beteiligungskapital; **- financing** Finanzierung mittels Forderungsabtretung; **- issue** Schuldtitel m; **- limit** Verschuldungsgrenze f; **- load** Schuldenlast f; **- on mortgage** Hypothekarschuld f; **- owing** fällige Schuld; **- paid** getilgte Schuld; **- recovery** Einziehung von Forderungen f; **- recovery agency** Inkassobüro n; **- redemption** Schuldentilgung f; **- reduction** Schuldenabbau m; **- refunding** Umschuldung f; **- register claim** Schuldbuchforderung f; **- rescheduling** Umschuldung f; **- retirement** Schuldenabbau m; **- securities** Schuldscheine f pl; **- security** Geldmarktpapier n; **- service** Schuldendienst m; **- service fund** Tilgungsfonds m; **- to nature swap** Tausch von Auslandsschulden eines Entwicklungslandes gegen Naturschutzprojektfinanzierung; **acknowledgement of -** Schuldanerkenntnis f; **amount of the -** Schuldsumme f; **answer for a -** für eine Schuld einstehen; **assignment of -** Forderungsabtretung f; **bad -** uneinbringliche Schuld; **barred -** verjährte Schuld; **bill -** Wechselverbindlichkeit f, Wechselschuld f; **bill of -** Schuldschein m, Schuldanerkennung f; **bond -** Anleiheschuld f; **bonded -** Anleiheschuld f; fundierte Schuld; **book -** Buchschuld f; **bottomry -** Bodmereischuld f; **clearing -** Verrechnungsschuld f; **collateral -** Lombardschuld f; **commercial -** Warenschuld f; **community -** Gesamtschuld f; **consolidated -** konsolidierte Schuld; **contract -** Vertragsschuld f; **deferred -** vertagte Schuld; **discharge a -** eine Schuld begleichen; **funded -** fundierte Schuld; **liquidated -** festgestellte Schuld; **partnership -** Gesellschaftsschuld f; **passive -** unverzinsliche Schuld; **preferential -** bevorrechtigte Schuld, bevorrechtigte Forderung; **preferred -** bevorrechtigte Schuld, bevorrechtigte Forderung; **privileged -** bevorrechtigte Schuld, bevorrechtigte Forderung; **public -** Staatsschuld f, öffentliche Schuld; **secured -** bevorrechtigte Schuld, bevorrechtigte Forderung

debt-discounted bond Anleihe mit hohem Disagio und niedrigem Zins

debtee n Gläubiger m, Kreditor m, Forderungsberechtigter m

debtless adj schuldenfrei adj, unbelastet adj

debt-options trading Optionshandel m

debtor n Schuldner m, Kreditnehmer m, Debitor m; **- account** Debitorenkonto n, Schuldenkonto n; **- in default** säumiger Schuldner; **- interest rate** Sollzinssatz m; **- nation** Schuldnerland n; **- on mortgage** Hypothekengläubiger m; **- warrant** Besserungsschein m; **acceptance -** Akzeptschuldner m; **bad -** zahlungsunfähiger Schuldner; **bill -** Wechselschuldner m, Wechselverpflichteter m; **bond -** Obligationenschuldner m, Pfandbriefschuldner m; **book -** Buchschuldner m; **common -** Gemeinschuldner m; **principal -** Hauptschuldner m

debtors Debitoren f pl, Warenforderungen f pl

debtor's assets Konkursmasse f; **- petition** Konkurseröffnungsantrag eines Schuldners; **- statement of affairs** Konkursstatus m, Konkursbilanz f

debts founded on open account Kontokorrentforderungen f pl; **- of estate** Nachlaßschulden f pl; **abatement of -** teilweiser Schulderlaß; **active -** Außenstände m pl, ausstehende Forderungen, Debitoren m pl, Buchforderungen f pl; **assume -** Schulden übernehmen; **attachment of -** Forderungspfändung f; **bank -** Bankschulden f pl; **business -** Geschäftsschulden f pl, Betriebsschulden f pl; **collection**

of ~ Forderungseinziehung f; **contract** ~ Schulden machen; **cover** ~ Schulden abdecken; **ordinary** ~ Buchschulden f pl; **provable** ~ nachweisbare Schulden; **surviving** ~ Restschulden f pl

decartelization n Entkartellisierung f

decartelize v entflechten v

deceased n Erblasser m, Verstorbener m

deceased's estate Nachlaß m (Erbrecht), Erbschaft f

decedent's estate (US) Nachlaß m (Erbrecht), Erbschaft f

decelerate v verlangsamen v (Kursanstieg)

decile n Dezile f, Zehntelwert m

decimal adj dezimal adj; ~ **place** Dezimalstelle f

decimals n pl (GB) Zinsnummern f pl

decision table Entscheidungstabelle f

declaration n Deklaration f, Zolldeklaration f, Zollanmeldung f, Zollerklärung f, Erklärung f; ~ **day** Stichtag m; ~ **of assignment** Abtretungserklärung f; ~ **of bankruptcy** Konkurserklärung f, Konkursanmeldung f, Bankrotterklärung f; ~ **of dividends** Dividendenbekanntmachung f, Dividendenerklärung f; ~ **of guaranty** Bürgschaftserklärung f; ~ **of imports** Einfuhrerklärung f; ~ **of income** Einkommensteuererklärung f; ~ **of indemnity** Schadloserklärung f; ~ **of insolvency** Vergleichsanmeldung f; ~ **of options** Prämienerklärung f; ~ **of property** Vermögenserklärung f; ~ **of solvency** Liquidationsmeldung bei Gesellschaftsauflösung; ~ **of value** Wertangabe f, Deviserklärung f; **statutory** ~ eidesstattliche Erklärung, Affidavit n; **sworn** ~ eidesstattliche Erklärung, Affidavit n

declare v bekanntmachen v, ankündigen v, anzeigen v; erklären v, anmelden v, deklarieren v, verzollen v

declared adj deklariert adj, zollamtlich erklärt; ~ **capital** festgesetztes Kapital; ~ **dividend** festgesetzte Dividende; ~ **reserves** offene Reserven; ~ **valuation** Wertangabe f

decline v zurückgehen v, fallen v, abnehmen v, heruntergehen v; ~ n Rückgang m, Rückläufigkeit f, Baisse f, Verfall m, Kursrückgang m; ~ **acceptance** Annahme verweigern; ~ **in earnings** Ertragsminderung f; ~ **in price** Preisrückgang m; ~ **in prices** Nachgeben der Kurse; ~ **in sales** Umsatzrückgang m; ~ **in share prices** Rückgang der Aktienkurse m; ~ **of business** Geschäftsrückgang m

declining adj zurückgehend adj, rückläufig adj; ~ **costs** Kostendegression f; ~ **market** nachgebende Kurse

deconcentrate v entflechten v

deconcentration n Entflechtung f

decontrol v liberalisieren v; ~ **of imports** Einfuhrliberalisierung f

decontrolled adj liberalisiert adj, nicht mehr bewirtschaftet

decrease v abnehmen v, zurückgehen v; ~ n Abnahme f, Rückgang m, Verminderung f

decreasing adj abnehmend adj

decree in absence Versäumnisurteil n; ~ **in bankruptcy** Konkurseröffnungsbeschluß m; ~ **of constitution** Feststellungsurteil n; ~ **of court** Gerichtsbeschluß m; ~ **of registration** Anerkenntnisurteil n

deduct v abziehen v, absetzen v, abrechnen v

deductible adj abzugsfähig adj, abziehbar adj; ~ **loss** absetzbarer Verlust

deduction n Abzug m, Abschlag m, Absetzung f, Rabatt m, Nachlaß m; ~ **of tax at source** Quellenbesteuerung f

deed v urkundlich übertragen, durch Urkunde übertragen; ~ n Urkunde f (gesiegelte oder förmliche), Dokumente n, Schriftstück n; ~ **box** Urkundenkassette f; ~ **of amalgamation** Fusionsvertrag m; ~ **of arrangement** Vergleichsurkunde f, Vergleichsvertrag m; ~ **of assignment** Abtretungsurkunde f, Übertragungsurkunde f; ~ **of conveyance** Abtretungsurkunde f, Übertragungsurkunde f; ~ **of donation** Schenkungsurkunde f, Stiftungsurkunde f; ~ **of gift** Schenkungsurkunde f, Stiftungsurkunde f; ~ **of ownership** Erwerbsurkunde f,

Eigentumsurkunde f, Besitzurkunde f; **~ of property** Vermögensübertragung f; **~ of protest** Protesturkunde f; **~ of real estate** Grundstücksvertrag m; **~ of release** Abtretungsurkunde f, Übertragungsurkunde f; **~ of sale** Kaufvertrag m, Kaufbrief m; **~ of settlement** Abfindungsvertrag m; **~ of suretyship** Bürgschaftsschein m, Bürgschaftsurkunde f; **~ of transfer** Abtretungsurkunde f, Übertragungsurkunde f; **~ poll** einseitige Rechtserklärung f; **~ stock** Inhaberwertpapiere f pl; **attestation of a ~** Urkundenbeglaubigung f; **copy ~** Zinsbrief m; **covering ~** Treuhandurkunde f; **guarantee ~** Bürgschaftsschein m, Bürgschaftsurkunde f; **title ~** Erwerbsurkunde f, Eigentumsurkunde f, Besitzurkunde f; **trust ~** Treuhandvertrag m, Sicherungsübereignung f

deep discount Preisnachlaß m, Sonderrabatt m

defaced coin abgenutzte Münze

defacement n Wertminderung f (Metallgeld)

defacer n Entwertungsstempel m

defalcate v unterschlagen v, veruntreuen v

defalcation n Unterschlagung f, Veruntreuung f

default v nicht erfüllen, in Verzug geraten; ~ n Unterlassung f, Nichterfüllung f, Verzug m, Vertragsverletzung f; **~ fee** Säumnisgebühr f; **~ in payment** mit den Zahlungen in Verzug kommen; **~ interest** Verzugszinsen m pl

defaulted bonds notleidende Obligationen

defaulter n Schuldner m, säumiger Zahler

defaulting bond debtor zahlungsunfähiger Anleiheschuldner

defeasance n Annullierung f, Aufhebung f; **~ clause** Verwirkungsklausel f

defeasibility n Annullierbarkeit f, Anfechtbarkeit f, Aufhebbarkeit f

defeasible adj annullierbar adj, aufhebbar adj

defeat v für null und nichtig erklären; ~ n Niederlage f

defect of title Rechtsmangel m, Mangel im Recht

defective delivery schlechte Lieferung

defence stocks Rüstungsaktien f pl

defendant n Beklagter m

defended takeover abgewehrte Übernahme

defensive stocks Aktien mit einer gleichmäßigen Gewinnerzielung

defer v verzögern v, hinausschieben v, aufschieben v, zurückklassen v (Zahlung)

deferment n Aufschub m (auch Zurückstellung vom Militärdienst)

deferrable adj aufschiebbar adj, hinausschiebbar adj

deferred annuity hinausgeschobene Annuität; **~ bond** Obligation mit hinausgeschobener Verzinsung; **~ credit** aufgeschobener Kredit; **~ creditor** nachrangiger Gläubiger; **~ debt** vertagte Schuld; **~ dividends** Dividenden mit aufgeschobener Fälligkeit; **~ expenses** transitorische Posten (auf der Aktivseite), Rechnungsabgrenzungsposten m pl; **~ items** transitorische Posten (auf der Passivseite), Rechnungsabgrenzungsposten m pl; **~ payment** gestundete Ratenzahlung; **~ payment documentary credit** Akkreditiv mit aufgeschobener Zahlung; **~ payment system** Teilzahlungssystem n; **~ shares** Nachbezugsaktien (können erst nach Befriedigung der vorgehenden Aktien Dividende beanspruchen); **~ stock** Aktienkapital mit hinausgeschobener Zinszahlung; **~ stocks** (US) nicht bevorrechtigte Aktien (in bezug auf Dividendenzahlungen); **~ taxes** Steuervorauszahlungen f pl

deficiency n Mangel m, Defizit n, Unterbilanz f, Fehlbetrag m; **~ account** Verlustkonto n; **~ advances** (GB) Vorschüsse der Bank von England an das Schatzamt; **~ bills** (GB) kurzfristige Anleihe der Bank von England; **~ guarantee** Ausfallbürgschaft f; **~ of coins** Münzverschlechterung f; **~ payment** Ausfallzahlung f

deficit n Defizit n, Verlust m, Fehlbetrag m, Ausfall m; **~ account** Verlustkonto n; **~ spending** Ankurbelung der Volkswirtschaft durch staatliche Ausgaben; **cash ~** Kassendefizit n,

deflate the economy

Kassenfehlbetrag m; *cover a ~* ein Defizit decken; *make up a ~* ein Defizit decken
deflate the economy restriktive Wirtschaftspolitik betreiben
deflation n Deflation f; *~ of credit* Kreditrestriktion f
deflationary policy Deflationspolitik f
defraud v unterschlagen v, betrügen v, hinterziehen v
defraudation n Betrug m, Hinterziehung f, Unterschlagung f
defray costs Kosten übernehmen
degearing Reduzierung des Verschuldungsgrades
degression n Degression f, degressive Abnahme
degressive adj degressiv adj
del credere Delkredere n, Bürgschaft f; *~ credere account* Delkrederekonto n
delay v verzögern v, hinausschieben v, aufschieben v, zurückstellen v (Zahlung); *~ n* Verzögerung f, Verzug m, Aufschub m, Zeitverlust m; *~ of payment* Zahlungsaufschub m, Moratorium n
delayable adj aufschiebbar adj, hinausschiebbar adj
delayed delivery verzögerte Auslieferung (Börse)
del-credere risk Delkredererisiko n
delegate v delegieren v, bevollmächtigen v, beauftragen v, Vollmacht erteilen
delegation n Delegation f, Bevollmächtigung f
delete v tilgen v, streichen v
deletion n Tilgung f, Streichung f
delinquency notice Mahnung f; *~ procedure* Mahnwesen n
delinquent accounts unbezahlte Rechnungen; *~ receivables* zweifelhafte Forderungen; *~ taxes* rückständige Steuern
delist v Börsennotiz aufheben
deliver v liefern v, abliefern v, abgeben v, zustellen v, übergeben v
deliverable adj lieferbar adj
delivery n Lieferung f (Auslieferung), Ablieferung f, Zustellung f, Übergabe f; *~ charge* Zustellgebühr f; *~ date* Liefertermin m, Auslieferungstermin m; *~ department*

Versandabteilung f; *~ note* Lieferschein m, Begleitschein m; *~ order* Auslieferungsauftrag m; Lieferschein m, Begleitschein m; *~ place* Erfüllungsort m, Lieferort m; *~ receipt* Warenempfangsschein m; *~ ticket* Lieferungsanzeige f; *bill of ~* Lieferschein m, Begleitschein m; *cost of ~* Lieferkosten plt, Versandkosten plt; *notice of ~* (US) Zustellungsurkunde f, Empfangsbestätigung f; *terms of ~* Lieferbedingungen f pl, Lieferungsbedingungen f pl
demand v fordern v, verlangen v, beanspruchen v; *~ n* Nachfrage f, Bedarf m, Forderung f, Verlangen n; *~ account* Kontokorrentkonto n; *~ balances* Sichtguthaben f pl; *~ bill* Sichtwechsel m; *~ certificate of deposit* (US) Einzahlungsbescheinigung einer Bank, auf Sicht zahlbares Papier; *~ deposit* (US) Sichteinlage f; *~ deposits* Krediten auf Sicht, Sichteinlagen m pl; *~ draft* Sichttratte f; *~ instrument* Sichtpapier n; *~ loan* Tagesgeld n, täglich fälliger Kredit; *~ money* Tagesgeld n, täglich fälliges Geld; *~ note* Sichtpapier n; *~ paper* Sichtpapier n; *~ payment* zur Zahlung auffordern, zur Zahlung mahnen; *~ rate* Geldkurs m, Sichtkurs m (Devisenmarkt); *~ sterling* Sichtwechsel auf London; *bill on ~* Sichtwechsel m; *~ borrowing* Kreditbedarf m, Kreditwunsch m; *~ capital* Kapitalbedarf m; *due on ~* auf Verlangen zahlbar; *in ~* gesucht adj, gefragt adj; *slack ~* spärliche Nachfrage
demerger Konzernentflechtung f
demise v übertragen v (von Grundbesitz), vermachen v, verpachten v; *~ n* Grundstücksübertragung f, Vermächtnis n, Legat n, Abtretung f, Zession f
demonetization n Außerkurssetzung f
demonetize v außer Kurs setzen (Münzen), einziehen v (Münzen)
demoralized market sehr gedrückter Markt
demur v Einwendungen erheben, aufschieben v, vertagen v
demurrage n Überliegezeit f, Lagergeld n

272

demurrer n Einrede f, Rechtseinwand m, Einwand m; *interpose a* - einen Rechtseinwand vorbringen
denominate stückeln v
denomination n Benennung f, Stückelung f, Sorte f; *- unit* Abschnitt m (einer Anleihe); *- value* Nennwert m
denominational portraits (US) auf Banknoten aufgedruckte Porträts
department n Abteilung f, Ressort n, Referat n; *- manager* Abteilungsleiter m
Department of Commerce (US) Handelsministerium n, Wirtschaftsministerium n
department store Kaufhaus n, Warenhaus n; *accounting* - Buchhaltungsabteilung f; *advertising* - Werbeabteilung f; *analysis* - Analysenabteilung f, Finanzstudienabteilung f; *annuity* - Rentenabteilung f; *auditing* - Revisionsabteilung f; *banking* - Bankabteilung f; *bill* - Wechselabteilung f; *bond* - (US) Abteilung für festverzinsliche Wertpapiere; *bond trading* - Pfandbriefabteilung f, Abteilung für festverzinshohe Wertpapiere; *bookkeeping* - Buchhaltungsabteilung f; *business* - Akquisitionsabteilung f, Kundenwerbeabteilung f; *cash* - Kasse f (Abteilung); *cashier's* - Kasse f (Abteilung); *certification* - Scheckbestätigungsabteilung f; *check* - Scheckabteilung f; *closing* - Abschlußabteilung f; *collection* - Inkassoabteilung f; *coupon collection* - Kuponabteilung f; *coupons paying* - Kuponkasse f; *credit* - Kreditabteilung f, Kreditbüro n; *customer's security* - Depotabteilung f; *delivery* - Versandabteilung f; *deposit* - Depositenabteilung f, Einlagenabteilung f, Kreditorenabteilung f; *discount* - Wechselabteilung f; *distribution* - Verkaufsabteilung f, Vertriebsabteilung f; *foreign exchange* - Devisenabteilung f; *head of* - Abteilungsleiter m; *new business* - (US) Abteilung einer Bank zur Entwicklung neuer Dienstleistungen; *publicity* - Werbeabteilung f; *service* - Kundendienstabteilung f
dependent (dependant) (US) Angehörige f u. m, abhängige Person
deplete v erschöpfen v, abschreiben v

depletion n Erschöpfung f, Substanzverlust m, Abschreibung f
deponent n Aussagende f u. m, Abgeber einer eidesstattlichen Erklärung
deposit v einlegen v, deponieren v, hinterlegen v, einzahlen v, einlagern v; *-* n Einlage f, Depot n, Deponierung f, Aufbewahrung f, Verwahrung f, Anzahlung f; *- account* (US) Einlegerkonto n, Depositenkonto n, Festgeldkonto n, Sparkonto n; *- account credit* Einzahlungsbeleg m; *- account debit* Auszahlungsbeleg m; *- balance* Guthabenkonto n; *- bank* Depositenbank f; *- banking* Depositengeschäft n, Einlagengeschäft n; *- banking division* Depositenabteilung f, Einlagenabteilung f, Kreditorenabteilung f; *- base* Bodensatz von Einlagen; *- book* Bankbuch n, Einlageheft n, Einlagenbuch n, Kontobuch n, Depositenbuch n; *- business* Passivgeschäfte n; *- creation* Geldschöpfung f; *- currency* (US) Buchgeld n, Giralgeld n, bargeldlose Zahlungsmittel; *- dealings* Geldhandel einer Bank; *- department* Depositenabteilung f, Einlagenabteilung f, Kreditorenabteilung f; *- futures* Einlagenterminsgeschäfte fpl; *- in escrow* bedingte Einlage; *- insurance* Einlagenversicherung f, Depositenversicherung f; *- insurance fund* Einlagensicherungsfonds m, Feuerwehrfonds m (informal); *- ledger* (GB) Depositenkonto n, Einlagenkonto n, Depositenregister n; *- liabilities* Kontokorrentverbindlichkeiten f pl; *- line* (US) durchschnittlicher Einlagenbestand eines Kontos; *- money* Bankgeld n, Buchgeld n, Giralgeld n, bargeldlose Zahlungsmittel; *- rate* Habenzinssatz m; *- receipt* Depotquittung f, Depotschein m; *- rollover* Festgeldverlängerung f; *- slip* Depotquittung f, Depotschein m; *- ticket* Gutschriftsbeleg m, Einzahlungsbeleg m; *alternate* - Gemeinschaftsdepot (wobei jeder einzelne verfügungsberechtigt ist); *bank* - Bankeinlage f; *bank of* - Depositenbank f; *banker's* - Bankeinlage f; *banker's - rate* Einlagenzinssatz m; *bill*

on ~ Depotwechsel m, Pensionswechsel m; **blocked** ~ Sperrdepot n; **cash** ~ Bareinlage f, Barhinterlegung f; **certification of** ~ Depositenschein m, Einlagenschein m, Hinterlegungsschein m; **derivative** ~ (US) Einlage (die aus einem Kredit entstanden ist); **minimum** ~ Mindesteinlage f; **primary** ~ (US) Einlage (die nicht aus der Gutschrift eines eingeräumten Kredits entstanden ist); **sight** ~ Sichteinlage f; **specific** ~ Sonderdepot n; **thrift** ~ Spargelder n pl; **time** ~ befristete Einlage, Termineinlage f

depositary Depotstelle f, Treuhänder m; ~ **bank** Depotbank f

deposited funds Depositen plt, Einlagen f pl, Depositengelder n pl, Depositeneinlagen f pl

depositing Einzahlung f, Verwahrung f; ~ **business** Einlagengeschäft n

depositor n Einleger m, Einzahler m, Depositeninhaber m, Hinterleger m, Deponent m; ~ **protection** Einlegerschutz m; **bank** ~ Einleger m, Einzahler m, Depositeninhaber m, Hinterleger m, Deponent m; **check account** ~ Scheckkontoinhaber m

depositors' ledger Depositenkonto n, Einlagenkonto n, Depositenregister n

depository n Hinterlegungsstelle f, Verwahrungsstelle f, Verwahrer

deposits n pl Depositen plt, Einlagen f pl, Passivgelder n pl, Guthaben n, Kreditoren m pl; ~ **and borrowed funds** Fremdgelder n pl, Fremdmittel n pl; **account** ~ Kontoguthaben n pl; **government** ~ (US) Einlagen der Regierung, Einlagen der öffentlichen Hand

depot n Depot n, Lager n, Magazin n

depreciable adj abschreibungsfähig adj; ~ **amount** Abschreibungsbetrag m

depreciate v abschreiben v (Wert), entwerten v, im Wert fallen

depreciated currency entwertetes Geld, notleidende Währung

depreciation n Abschreibung f (Wert), Entwertung f, Wertminderung f, Wertverlust m; ~ **account** Abschreibungskonto n; ~ **fund** Abschreibungsreserve f, Abschreibungsfonds m, Abschreibungsrücklage f; ~ **of capital** Kapitalabschreibung f; ~ **of plant** Abschreibung auf Betriebsanlagen; ~ **rate** Abschreibungssatz m; ~ **reserve** Abschreibungsreserve f, Abschreibungsfonds m, Abschreibungsrücklage f; **accrued** ~ Abschreibungsreserve f, Abschreibungsfonds m, Abschreibungsrücklage f; **amount of** ~ **earned** verdiente Abschreibungen; **capital** ~ Kapitalabschreibung f; **currency** ~ Währungsabwertung f; **rate of** ~ Abschreibungssatz m; **straightline** ~ lineare Abschreibung

depressed adj gedrückt adj, flau adj, mißgestimmt adj

depression n Depression f, Konjunkturrückgang m, Baisse f; **cyclical** ~ Konjunkturbaisse f

deputy chairman stellvertretender Vorsitzender; ~ **manager** stellvertretender Direktor

deregister v im Handelsregister löschen

deregistration n Löschung im Handelsregister

deregulation Deregulierung f, Liberalisierung f

derivative deposit (US) Einlage (die aus einem Kredit entstanden ist); ~ **instruments** derivative Instrumente, abgeleitete Finanzprodukte

descend v abstammen v, durch Erbschaft zufallen

descendance n Abstammung f

descending order absteigende Reihenfolge; ~ **sequence** absteigende Reihenfolge

description of goods Warenbezeichnung f; ~ **of securities** Effektengattung f

descriptions n pl (GB) Wertpapiere n pl

design n Entwurf m

designate v bezeichnen v, ernennen v, bestimmen v

designation n Bezeichnung f, Ernennung f, Bestimmung f

desist from Abstand nehmen von

desk check Schreibtischtest m (von Programmen); **cash** ~ Kassenschalter m; **cashier's** ~ Kassenschalter m; **check** ~ (US) Buchhaltungsabteilung f

destination n Bestimmungsort m

destitute *adj* mittellos *adj*, unvermögend *adj*, verarmt *adj*
destitution *n* Geldmangel *m*, Mittellosigkeit *f*
detach *v* trennen *v*, abtrennen *v*
detachable abtrennbar *adj*, ablösbar *adj*
detached coupons abgetrennte Kupons
detail *v* detaillierten *v*, ausführlich beschreiben; **~** *n* Einzelheit *f*
deteriorate *v* (sich) verschlechtern *v*
determination clause Verfallsklausel *f*
detriment *n* Nachteil *m*, Verlust *m*, Beeinträchtigung *f*
detrimental *adj* nachteilig *adj*
devalorization *n* Abwertung *f*, Entwertung *f*
devalorize *v* abwerten *v*, entwerten *v*
devaluate *v* abwerten *v*, entwerten *v*
devaluation *n* Abwertung *f*, Entwertung *f*; **~ of a currency** Abwertung einer Währung; **~ rate** Abwertungssatz *m*; **competitive ~ (of a currency)** Abwertung aus Wettbewerbsgründen (Währung)
devalue *v* abwerten *v*, entwerten *v*
develop *v* entwickeln *v*
developing country Entwicklungsland *n*
development *n* Entwicklung *f*; **~ bank** Entwicklungsbank *f*; **~ lending** Entwicklungshilfekredite *m pl*; **~ loan** Investitionskredit *m*
deviation clause Abweichungsklausel *f*
devisable *adj* vererblich *adj*, testierbar *adj*
devise *v* vermachen *v* (Grundbesitz), hinterlassen *v* (Grundbesitz); **~** *n* Vermächtnis *n* (über Grundbesitz), letztwillige Verfügung (über Grundbesitz)
devisee *n* Testamentserbe *m*, Vermächtnisnehmer *m* (von Grundbesitz)
devisor *n* Erblasser *m*, Testator *m*
diagnostic program Fehlersuchprogramm *n*
diary *n* Terminkalender *m*, Terminbuch *n*, Verfallbuch *n*; **cash ~** Kassenkladde *f*
die testate unter Hinterlassung eines Testaments sterben
differ *v* abweichen *v*, (sich) unterscheiden *v*
difference *n* Differenz *f*, Unterschied *m*, Unterschiedsbetrag *m*; **~ account** (US) Differenzkonto *n*; **~ in price** Preisunterschied *m*; **~ in rates** Kursunterschied *m*

differences; speculate for ~ Differenzgeschäfte machen
difficulty *n* Schwierigkeit *f*
digested bonds (US) fest plazierte Obligationen
digit *n* Ziffer *f* (Stelle)
digital computer Digitalcomputer *m*
dilatory *adj* dilatorisch *adj*, aufschiebend *adj*
diligence; due ~ gebührende Sorgfalt
dilute equity *v* Eigenkapital verwässern
diluted verwässert *adj* (Börse)
dilution Kapitalverwässerung (Börse); **~ of shareholdings** Wertminderung von Aktien
dime *n* Zehncentstück *n*
diminish *v* (sich) vermindern *v*
diminuation *n* Verminderung *f*, Schrumpfung *f*, Kürzung *f*; **~ of profits** Gewinnschrumpfung *f*
dip *v* fallen *v*, sinken *v*, kurzfristiger Rückgang
direct *v* anweisen *v*, beauftragen *v*, unterweisen *v*, unterrichten *v* (instruieren); **~** *v* leiten *v*, anordnen *v*, adressieren *v*; **~ access** direkter Zugriff; **~ advertising** Direktwerbung *f*; **~ borrowings** Direktkredite *m pl*; **~ charge-off** Direktabbuchung *f*; **~ exchange** fester Umrechnungskurs; **~ financing** Direktkredite der Wirtschaft; **~ indorsement** (US) Vollgiro *n*, volles Wechselgiro, ausgefülltes Giro; **~ letter of credit** (GB) an eine bestimmte Bank gerichteter Kreditbrief; **~ mail advertising** Postversandwerbung *f*; **~ rates** (GB) in Pence notierte Devisenkurse; **~ reduction mortgage** Hypothek mit direkter Tilgung; **~ taxation** direkte Besteuerung; **~ underwriting** Festübernahme *f*
direction *n* Leitung *f*, Führung *f*, Lenkung *f*
director *n* Direktor *m*, Geschäftsführer *m*, Aufsichtsratsmitglied *n*, Verwaltungsratsmitglied *n*, Leiter *m*; **bank ~** (US) Bankaufsichtsratmitglied *n*, Bankdirektor *m*
directors; board of ~ Verwaltungsrat *m*
directorship *n* Aufsichtsratsposten *m*
dirty bill of lading unreines Konnossement; **~ floating** schmutziges Floaten

disability benefit Invaliditätsrente f, Invaliditätsunterstützung f; **~ fund** Invaliditätsversicherung f
disabled bonds (GB) ungültige Obligationen
disadvantage n Nachteil m, Verlust m
disagio n Disagio n, Abschlag m
disallow v nicht anerkennen, untersagen v
disappropriate v enteignen v
disappropriation n Enteignung f
disburse v ausgeben v (verauslagen), auszahlen v
disbursement n Ausgabe f, Auslage f, Auszahlung; **cash ~** Kassenauszahlung f
disbursements; capital ~ Kapitalaufwendungen f pl; **social ~** Sozialaufwendungen f pl
disbursing account Auszahlungskonto n
disc file organization (EDP) Plattenorganisation f (EDV)
discharge v entlasten v, entlassen v, entladen v, ausladen v, quittieren v, bezahlen v, tilgen v, einlösen v; **~** n Entlastung f, Entlassung f, Ausladen n, Entladen n, Tilgung f, Bezahlung f, Quittung f; **~ a bill** einen Wechsel einlösen, einen Wechsel honorieren; **~ a bond** einen Schuldschein einlösen; **~ a debt** eine Schuld begleichen; **~ an account** ein Konto ausgleichen; **~ in bankruptcy** (US) Rehabilitierung eines Konkursschuldners
discharged bill eingelöster Wechsel
disclaim v nicht anerkennen, bestreiten v, verzichten v; **~ an estate** eine Erbschaft ausschlagen
disclose v offenbaren v, anzeigen v
disclosed profit ausgewiesener Gewinn
disclosure Offenlegung f, Veröffentlichung f
discontinue v unterbrechen v, einstellen v, abbestellen v, aufhören v
discount v diskontieren v, skontieren v, abziehen v, vorwegnehmen v; **~** n Abschlag m, Skonto m, Rabatt m, Preisabschlag m, Zinsabzug m, Disagio n, Diskontsatz m; **~ bank** Diskontbank f; **~ bills** Diskontwechsel m pl, Diskonten n pl; **~ bond** (US) unverzinsliche Schuldverschreibung, (US) Abzinsungsanleihe f; **~ broker** Wechselmakler m, Wechselhändler m, (US) Diskontbroker m,

Direktanlagebank f; **~ business** Wechselgeschäft n; **~ charges** Wechselspesen plt; **~ company** Diskontbank f; **~ credit** Diskontkredit m; **~ days** Diskonttage m pl; **~ department** Wechselabteilung f; **~ earned** Diskonterlös m; **~ expenses** Wechselspesen plt; **~ for cash** Barzahlungsrabatt m; **~ holdings** Bestand an Diskontwechseln m; **~ house** Diskontbank f; **~ in advance** v eskomptieren v (abzinsen v); **~ ledger** Diskontwechselbuch n, Wechselobligo n; **~ liquidation** Wechselabrechnung f; **~ market** Diskontmarkt m, Wechselmarkt m; **~ rate** Diskontsatz m; **~ register** Wechselkopierbuch n, Wechsellogierbuch n, Wechselbuch n, Wechselobligo n (Buch), Wechselverfallbuch n; **~ terms** Diskontbedingungen f pl; **~ without recourse** Wechselkauf ohne Rückgriff, Diskont à forfait; **allow a ~** Diskont einräumen, Nachlaß gewähren; **bank ~** Bankdiskont m; **bank of ~** Diskontbank f; **banker's ~** Bankdiskont m; **bill ~ rate** Wechseldiskontsatz m; **bill of ~** Diskontnote f; **bills eligible for ~** Diskontmaterial n; **bond ~** Obligationsagio n, Pfandbriefagio n, **cash ~** Barrabatt m, Kassaskonto n; **cash less ~** bar abzüglich Diskont; **debt ~** Kreditdisagio n; **quantity ~** Mengenrabatt m; **rate of ~** Diskontsatz m; **take on ~** diskontieren v; **unearned ~** im voraus gemachter Abzug

discountability n Diskontierbarkeit f

discountable adj diskontierbar adj, diskontfähig adj, bankfähig adj; **~ bill** bankfähiger Wechsel

discounted adj diskontiert adj; **~ note** abgezinster Schuldschein; **~ receivables** abgetretene Forderungen; **~ value** Diskontwert m

discounter n Diskontierer m, Wechselmakler m; **~ without recourse** Diskontierung ohne Regreß; **bill ~** Wechselkontierer m

discounting n Diskontgeschäft n, Diskontieren n, Diskontierung f; **bill ~** Wechseldiskontierung f

discounts n pl Diskontwechsel m pl, Diskonten m pl; **~ received** Diskonterträge m pl

discredit v diskreditieren v, in Mißkredit bringen; ~ n Mißkredit m, schlechter Ruf

discrepancy n Diskrepanz f, Abweichung f, Unstimmigkeit f

discretion n Gutdünken n, Ermessen n, Verschwiegenheit f

discretionary adj beliebig adj, mit Ermessensspielraum; **~ clause** Kannvorschrift f

discriminate v diskriminieren v, unterschiedlich behandeln; **~ against** v benachteiligen v

discrimination n Benachteiligung f, Diskriminierung f

disencumber v (an estate) entschulden v (Grundstück)

disencumbrance n Entschuldung f

dishonour v nicht einlösen, nicht bezahlen, nicht akzeptieren; ~ n Nichteinlösung f

dishonoured bill notleidender Wechsel; **~ check** notleidender Scheck

disinflation n Inflationsbekämpfung f

disinherit v enterben v

disinheritance n Enterbung f

disintermediation n Industrieclearing

disk n Disk f, Diskette f; **hard ~** Festplatte f

diskette n Diskette f

disinvest v desinvestieren v

dismiss v entlassen v

dismissal n Entlassung f

disparity n Disparität f, Verschiedenheit f, Ungleichheit f

dispatch v expedieren v, absenden v, verschicken v, abschicken v, befördern v; ~ n Expedition f, Versand m, Beförderung f

dispatching Versand m

dispense v befreien v, entbinden v

displaced shares nicht notierte Aktien

displacement of funds anderweitige Kapitalverwendung

display unit Anzeigegerät n

disposable adj, verfügbar adj, disponibel adj; **~ funds** verfügbare Gelder; **~ income** verfügbares Einkommen

disposal n Disposition f; ~ n Verfügung f, Verkauf m, Übergabe f; **~ of trade investments** Verkauf von Beteiligungen

disposals Abgänge m pl (Bilanz)

dispose v verkaufen, veräußern v; **~ of** verfügen über, beseitigen v; **authority to ~** Verfügungsmacht f

disposer n Veräußerer m, Verkäufer m

dispositions n pl Anordnungen f pl, Vorkehrungen f pl

dispossess v enteignen v

dispossession n Enteignung f

disproportion n Mißverhältnis n

disputable adj strittig adj

dispute v bestreiten v, abstreiten v; **~ a will** ein Testament anfechten

disqualification Ausschluß m

disqualified from voting nicht stimmberechtigt

disregard instructions gegen Weisungen handeln

disrepute n Mißkredit m, schlechter Ruf

dissection of accounts Kontenaufgliederung f

dissolution n Auflösung f, Liquidation f

dissolve v auflösen v, liquidieren v

distrain v pfänden v

distrained goods gepfändete Waren

distrainee n Pfändungsschuldner m, Vollstreckungsschuldner m

distrainer n Pfänder m

distraint n Pfändung f, Beschlagnahme f, Arrest m

distress n Notlage f, Seenot f, Pfändung f, Beschlagnahme f, gepfändeter Gegenstand, Steuerpfändung f; **bill in ~** notleidender Wechsel

distressed adj gepfändet adj

distributable profit (ausgeschütteter) Bilanzgewinn m; **~ property** Konkursmasse f

distribute v aufteilen v, verteilen v, vertreiben v, absetzen v; **~ a dividend** eine Dividende ausschütten; **~ by lots** auslösen v

distributed profits ausgeschütteter Gewinn, verteilter Gewinn

distribution n Verteilung f, Ausschüttung f; **~ department** Verkaufsabteilung f, Vertriebsabteilung f; **~ fund**

distributor

Ausschüttungsfonds m; **- of profits** Gewinnverteilung f; **- of risk** Risikoverteilung f; **capital -** Kapitalausschüttung f; **cash -** Barausschüttung f
distributor n Verteiler m, Händler m, Wiederverkäufer m
district n Bezirk m; **- office** Bezirksagentur f
disturbed market bewegte Börse
diversification Diversifikation f, Verteilung f, Streuung f; **- of investments** Anlagestreuung f
diversify v diversifizieren, verteilen, streuen v
divide v teilen v, verteilen v, dividieren v
divided adj geteilt adj, verteilt adj
dividend n Dividende f, Gewinnanteil m; **- account** Dividendenkonto n; **- balance** Restdividende f; **- bonds** (US) Obligationen f pl (die mit Dividendenberechtigung ausgestattet sind); **- book** Aktionärsverzeichnis n; **- check** Dividendenscheck m; **- coupon** Dividendenschein m, Gewinnanteilschein m; **- disbursement** Dividendenausschüttungen f pl; **- forecast** Dividendenvoraussage f; **- fund** Dividendenfonds m; **- guarantee** Dividendengarantie f; **- income** Dividendeneinnahme f; **- omission** Dividendenausfall m; **- on** (US) einschließlich Dividende; **- on account** Abschlagsdividende f, Zwischendividende f, Interimsdividende f; **- payment** Dividendenzahlung f; **- rate** Dividendensatz m; **- recommendation** Dividendenvorschlag m; **- reserve fund** Dividendenrücklage f; **- requirements** Ausschüttungsbedarf m; **- rights** Dividendenrechte n pl; **- warrant** Dividendenschein m, Gewinnanteilschein m; **- yield** Dividendenrendite f, Dividendenertrag m; **bond -** Dividende in Form eigener Obligationen; **cash -** Bardividende f; **commodity -** (US) Warendividende f; **cumulative -** kumulative Dividende; **declared -** festgesetzte Dividende; **distribute a -** eine Dividende ausschütten; **ex -** nach Dividendenausschüttung; **noncumulative -** nicht kumulative Dividende; **omit a -** eine Dividende ausfallen lassen; **participating -** Vorzugsdividende f; **preferred -** Vorzugsdividende f; **sham -** Scheindividende f, fiktive Dividende; **share -** Aktiendividende f; **special -** Bonus m, Extradividende f, Sonderdividende f, Superdividende f, außerordentliche Dividende; **strike a -** eine Dividende ausschütten; **surplus -** Bonus m, Extradividende f, Sonderdividende f, Superdividende f, außerordentliche Dividende
dividend-bearing securities Dividendenwerte f pl
dividend-paying stock Dividendenpapiere n pl
dividend-right certificate Genußschein m
dividends; accrual of - Dividendenanfall m; **declaration of -** Dividendenausschreibung f, Dividendenerklärung f; **deferred -** Dividenden mit aufgeschobener Fälligkeit
divisibility n Teilbarkeit f
divisible adj teilbar adj; **- surplus** ausschüttbarer Gewinn
division n Abteilung f; **- of labour** Arbeitsteilung f; **benefit of -** Ausgleichseinrede mehrerer Bürgen
divisional coin Scheidemünze f
DM-bond issuer DM-Anleiheemittent m
dock charges Dockgebühren f pl, Dockgeld n, Löschgeld n, Landungszoll m
dockage n Dockgebühren f pl, Dockgeld n, Löschgeld n, Landungszoll m, Kaigeld n
dockyard n Werft f
document n Dokument n, Urkunde f, Schriftstück n; **- flow** Belegfluß m; **- of title** urkundlicher Rechtstitel; **- preparation** Belegaufbereitung f; **- sorter** Belegsortiermaschine f; **- transport** Belegtransport m; **bill with - attached** Wechsel mit anhängenden Papieren
documentary acceptance credit dokumentärer Akzeptkredit, Rembours m; **- bill** Dokumentenwechsel m; **- collection** Dokumenteninkasso n; **- credit** Dokumentenkredit m, Dokumentenakkreditiv n; **- credit transactions** Akkreditivgeschäfte n pl; **- draft** Dokumententratte f; **- letter of credit**

Dokumentenkredit m, Dokumentenakkreditiv n; **- proof** Urkundenbeweis m; **revocable - credit** widerrufliches Dokumentenakkreditiv

documentation n Dokumentation f

documented credit Dokumentenkredit m

documents n pl Dokumente n pl, Verschiffungspapiere n pl; **- against acceptance** Dokumente gegen Akzept; **- against payment** Dokumente gegen Zahlung, Kasse gegen Dokumente; **bill against -** Wechsel gegen Dokumente; **call for production of -** eine Vorlage von Urkunden verlangen; **cash against -** Dokumente gegen Zahlung, Kasse gegen Dokumente; **collection of -** Dokumenteninkasso n; **shipping -** Verladedokumente n pl, Verschiffungspapiere n pl

dollar n Dollar m; **- acceptance** (US) auf Dollar lautender Wechsel; **- area** Dollarblock m, Dollarraum m; **- bond issued in the US by a non-US borrower (yankee bond)** Yankee-Anleihe f, in den USA emittierte Anleihe eines Nicht-US Schuldners; **- drain** Dollarschwund m; **- gap** Dollarlücke f; **- loan** Dollaranleihe f; **- stock** britischer Ausdruck für US Aktien; **- straights** festverzinsliche USD-Anleihe

domestic adj inländisch adj, Inlands- (in Zus.), Binnen- (in Zus.); **- bill** Inlandswechsel m; **- bond issue** Inlandsanleihe f; **- business** Inlandsgeschäft n; **- investments** Inlandsbeteiligungen f pl; **- market** Inlandsmarkt m; **- sales** Inlandsabsatz m; **- trade** Binnenhandel m; **- travellers letter of credit** (US) Inlandsreisekreditbrief m

domicile v domizilieren v, zahlbar stellen; **- n** Domizil n, Zahlungsadresse f, Wohnort m, Zahlstelle f; Gesellschaftssitz m

domiciled bill Domizilwechsel m

domiciliate v domizilieren v, zahlbar stellen

domiciliation n Domizilierung f, Zahlbarstellung f

domiciling; commission for - Domizilprovision f

donate v spenden v, schenken v

donation n Spende f, Stiftung f, Schenkung f; **deed of -** Schenkungsurkunde f, Stiftungsurkunde f

donator n Spender m, Stifter m, Schenker m

done gehandelt (Börse)

donee n Schenkungsempfänger m

donor n Spender m, Stifter m, Schenker m

door-to-door market Hausverkauf m

dormant account umsatzloses Konto, unbewegtes Konto, totes Konto; **- accounts** unbewegte Konten (lange Zeit); **- balance** umsatzloser Saldo; **- capital** totes Kapital, brachliegendes Kapital; **- money** totes Kapital, brachliegendes Kapital; **- partner** Geldgeber m (in einer GmbH oder Kommanditgesellschaft), stiller Teilhaber, Kommanditist m; **- partnership** stille Gesellschaft

dos-a-dos accreditif (US) Gegenakkreditiv n

dossier n Dossier n

dot n Mitgift f, Aussteuer f

dotal property Mitgift f, Aussteuer f

dotation n Dotierung f, Schenkung f, Aussteuer f

double n Doppel n, Duplikat n; **- bottom** (US) äußerster Tiefstand des Marktes (Börse); **- creditor** zweifacher Gläubiger; **- eagle** Goldmünze der USA (20 Dollar); **- entry bookkeeping** doppelte Buchführung; **- option** Stellagegeschäft n; **- receipt** Doppelquittung f; **- standard** Doppelwährung f; **- taxation** Doppelbesteuerung f; **- will** gegenseitiges Testament, Berliner Testament

double-taxation agreement Doppelbesteuerungsabkommen n

doubtful claim zweifelhafter Anspruch; **- debts provision** Rückstellung für Dubiosa; **- debts, notes and accounts** (US) dubiose Forderungen

Dow-Jones-Index n Index der New Yorker Börse (Durchschnittskurs einer Auswahl Aktien)

down payment Anzahlung f; **- swing** Abschwung m

down-grading Bonitätszurückstufung f

downstairs members Kursmakler *m pl* (US-Börse); **- merger** Fusion der Mutter- mit der Tochtergesellschaft

downward movement Abwärtsbewegung *f*; **- trend** Abschwächungstendenz *f*

dowry *n* Mitgift *f*, Aussteuer *f*

DP (D/P)= documents against payment Dokumente gegen Zahlung

draft *n* Tratte *f*, Entwurf *m*, Wechsel *m*, Beleg *m*, Zahlungsanweisung *f*; **-** *v* entwerfen *v*, aufsetzen *v*, abfassen *v*; **- after date** nach dato zahlbar gestellter Wechsel; **- at sight** Sichttratte *f*; **- book** (GB) Wechselkopierbuch *n*, Wechselobligierbuch *n*, Wechselbuch *n*, Wechseloblige *n* (Buch), Wechselverfallbuch *n*; **- collection** Wechselinkasso *n*; **- credit** Rembourskredit *m*; **- of a contract** Vertragsentwurf *m*; **- register** Wechselverzeichnis *n*; **accommodation -** Gefälligkeitstratte *f*; **agency -** Inkassotratte *f*; **bank -** Banktratte *f*; **banker's -** (US) Bankwechsel *m*; **clean -** Tratte ohne Dokumente; **currency -** Valutawechsel *m*; **demand -** Sichttratte *f*; **documentary -** Dokumententratte *f*; **sight -** Sichttratte *f*

drafter *n* Aussteller *m* (Wechsel), Wechselgeber *m*, Wechselaussteller *m*, Trassant *m*

drafts and checks in hand Wechsel-und-Scheck-Bestand *m* (Bilanzposten)

drain *n* Abfluß *m* (von Geldern in das Ausland); **- of bullion** (GB) Goldabfluß *m*, Kapitalflucht *f*, Geldabfluß *m*; **- of gold** Goldabfluß *m*, Kapitalflucht *f*, Geldabfluß *m*; **- of money** Geldabfluß *m*

drains Abflüsse vom Geldmarkt

draw *v* ziehen *v*, trassieren *v*, ausstellen *v*, abheben *v*; **- a bill** einen Wechsel ziehen; **- a check upon an account** einen Scheck auf ein Konto ziehen; **- by lot** auslosen *v*; **- in a bill** einen Wechsel einlösen, einen Wechsel honorieren; **- in a loan** einen Kredit kündigen; **- lots** losen *v*; **- out money from the bank** Geld von der Bank abheben; **- up a balance** eine Bilanz aufstellen; **- up a will** ein Testament errichten

drawable auslosbar *adj* (Wertpapiere)

drawback *n* Rückzoll *m*

drawee *n* Trassat *m*, Bezogene *f u. m*; **- bank** bezogene Bank; **alternative -** Alternativbezogene *f u. m*; **bankrupt -** bankrotte Bezogene

drawer *n* Aussteller *m* (Wechsel), Wechselgeber *m*, Wechselaussteller *m*, Trassant *m*; **- of a check** Scheckaussteller *m*; **bankrupt -** bankrotter Wechselaussteller

drawing *n* Ziehen *n*, Trassieren *n*, Trassierung *f*, Ausstellen *n*, Entnahme *f*; **- account** Kontokorrentkonto *n*, Girokonto *n*; **- of kites** Wechselreiterei *f*; **- on an account** Verfügung über ein Konto; **- rate** Verkaufskurs *m*, Briefkurs *m* (Devisen); **- rights** Ziehungsrechte *n pl* (IWF); **- under a letter of credit** Akkreditivziehungen *f pl*

drawings *n pl* Abhebungen *f pl*

drawn bond ausgeloste Obligation

drayage *n* Frachtkosten *pl*, Rollgeld *n*

drive *n* (US) Baisseangriff *m*

drive-in bank Bank mit Autoschalter; **- window** Autoschalter *m*

drop *v* fallen *v*, zurückgehen *v* (Preise), sinken *v*; **-** *n* Baisse *f*, Fallen *n*, Rückgang *m*; **- in prices** Preisrückgang *m*

drop lock bonds variable verzinsliche Wertpapiere mit Zinsuntergrenze

drugs Aktien der Pharmaindustrie

dual *adj* doppelt *adj*, zweierlei *adj*; **- banking system** Trennbankensystem *n*; **- currency bond (loan)** Doppelwährungsanleihe *f*

dubious *adj* zweifelhaft *adj*, unsicher *adj*

duck zahlungsunfähiger Spekulant

dud check ungedeckter Scheck; **- loan** ungedeckter Kredit

due *n* Schuld *f*, Verpflichtung *f*, Anspruch *m*; **-** *adj* fällig *adj*, gebührend *adj*, angemessen *adj*, zahlbar *adj*; **- date** (of a loan) Rückzahlungstermin *m* (eines Kredits), Verfalltag *m*, Fälligkeitstermin *m*, Fälligkeitstag *m*; **- day** Verfalltag *m*, Fälligkeitstermin *m*, Fälligkeitstag *m*; **- diligence** gebührende Sorgfalt; **- from banks on demand** Bankdebitoren auf Sicht; **- from banks on time** Bankdebitoren auf Zeit; **- on**

demand auf Verlangen zahlbar; **~ to banks on demand** Bankkreditoren auf Sicht; **~ to banks on time** Bankkreditoren auf Zeit; **become ~** fällig werden; **fall ~** fällig werden; **on ~ date** termingerecht *adj*; **repayment on ~ date** fristgemäße Rückzahlung; **when ~** bei Verfall

dull *n* flau *adj*, matt *adj*, lustlos *adj*, geschäftslos *adj*, still *adj*; **~ market** flauer Markt, flaue Börse

dullness *n* Flaute *f*, Börsenflaute *f*

duly *adv* ordnungsgemäß *adv*, pünktlich *adv*; **~ authorized** mit gehöriger Vollmacht versehen; **~ signed** ordnungsgemäß unterschrieben

dummy *n* Strohmann *m*; **~ transaction** Scheingeschäft *n*

dump *v* Dumping betreiben, ins Ausland zu Schleuderpreisen verkaufen

dumping *n* Dumping *n*, Schleuderverkauf ins Ausland

dun *v* mahnen *v*

dunning *n* Mahnung *f*; **~ letter** Mahnbrief *m*

duopoly *n* Marktkontrolle durch zwei Firmen

duplicate *n* Duplikate *n*, Zweitschrift *f*; **~ bill** Wechselduplikat *n*; **~ check** Scheckduplikat *n*; **~ document** Zweitschrift einer Urkunde, Zweitausfertigung einer Urkunde

duplicating book Kopierbuch *n*

duplicator *n* Vervielfältigungsapparat *m*

duration *n* (average time) Durchschnittslaufzeit *f* (eines Anleihendepots), Laufzeit *f*, Gültigkeit *f*, Dauer *f*

duress *n* Nötigung *f*, Zwang *m*

Dutch Guilder Holländische Gulden *m*

dutiable *adj* zollpflichtig *adj*, steuerabgabepflichtig *adj*

duty *n* Zollgebühr *f*, Steuer *f*, Abgabe *f*, Gebühr *f*, Verpflichtung *f*; **~ free** zollfrei *adj*, steuerfrei *adj*, gebührenfrei *adj*; **~ paid** verzollt, versteuert; **ad valorem ~** Wertzoll *m*; **customs ~** Zollabgabe *f*, Zollgebühr *f*; **death ~** (GB) Erbschaftssteuer *f*, Nachlaßsteuer *f*; **export ~** Ausfuhrzoll *m*, Ausfuhrabgabe *f*; **rate of ~** (GB) Steuerrate *m*, Zollsatz *m*

dwindling earnings schrumpfende Erträge

dynamic hedging dynamische Anpassung an die Marktverhältnisse

E

Eagle n (10 Dollar) Goldmünze der USA
early profit taking Gewinnmitnahme bei Börsenbeginn; **~ stage financing** Gründungsfinanzierung mit Beteiligungskapital
earmark n Kennzeichen n, Eigentumszeichen n; **~ a check** einen Scheck sperren
earmarked account zweckbestimmtes Konto
earmarking of funds Bereitstellung von Geldern (für einen bestimmten Zweck)
EARN = expected to accrue return on nominal warrant Kurskanal-Optionsschein m, Hamster-Optionsschein m
earn v verdienen v, erwerben v, gewinnen v, als Lohn erhalten; **~ interest** Zinsen bringen
earned surplus Betriebsgewinn m; **~ surplus account** aus Reingewinn gebildete Reserven; **unappropriated ~ surplus** (US) unverteilter Reingewinn
earning assets Aktivgeschäft einer Bank, verzinsliche Aktivposten; **~ capacity** Ertragkraft f, Ertragsfähigkeit f, Erwerbsfähigkeit f, Rentabilität f; **~ power** Ertragkraft f, Ertragsfähigkeit f, Erwerbsfähigkeit f, Rentabilität f; **calculation of ~ power** Rentabilitätsberechnung f; **capitalization of ~ power** Kapitalisierung der Ertragsfähigkeit eines Unternehmens; **monthly ~** monatlicher Ertrag
earnings n pl Einkommen n, Ertrag m, Einkünfte f pl; **~** n pl erarbeiteter Gewinn, Verdienst m (Arbeitslohn); **~ before interests and taxes = EBIT** Ergebnis vor Steuern und Zinsen; **~ per share** Gewinn je Aktie; **~ power** Ertragkraft f; **~ report** Ertragsbericht m; **~ reserves** Gewinnrücklagen f pl; **~ statement** Erfolgsrechnung f, Gewinn-und-Verlust-Rechnung f, Ertragsaufstellung f, Ertragsrechnung f; **~ yield** Gewinnrendite f (d. h. Prozentsatz des Aktienkurswertes, der auf diese Aktie bei restloser Auszahlung entfallen würde); **bonus ~** Prämienverdienst m; **cash ~** Bareinnahmen f pl; **decline in ~** Ertragsminderung f; **cross ~** Gesamteinkommen n; **net ~** Nettoverdienst m; **price ~ ratio** (P/E ratio) Kurs-Gewinn-Verhältnis f; **retained ~** zurückbehaltene Gewinne, nicht ausgeschüttete Gewinne; **surplus ~** (US) Gewinnüberschuß m, Überschuß m, Überfluß m, unverteilter Reingewinn
earnings/cost-ratio Erlös-Kosten-Verhältnis n
ease v erleichtern v, abbröckeln v (Kurse); **~ off** abschwächen v (Kurse)
easily marketable assets leicht verwertbare Aktiva
easing in money rates Erleichterung am Geldmarkt, Abschwächung der Geldsätze
easing-off n Sinken n, Abflauen n, Abschwächung f
easy money billiges Geld, billige Geldsätze
easy-money policy Niedrigzinspolitik f
ec = eurocheque Euroscheck m
EC = European Community Europäische Gemeinschaft f (EG)
ec-card ec-Karte f (Euroscheckkarte)
economic adj wirtschaftlich adj, volkswirtschaftlich adj, sparsam adj, ökonomisch adj; **~ agreement** Handelsabkommen n; **~ condition** Wirtschaftslage f; **~ crisis** Wirtschaftskrise f; **~ data** Wirtschaftszahlen f pl, **~ entity** Wirtschaftseinheit f; **~ feasibility study** Wirtschaftlichkeitsuntersuchung f; **~ forces** wirtschaftliche Kräfte f; **~ geography** Wirtschaftsgeographie f; **~ growth** Wirtschaftswachstum n; **~ indicators** Wirtschaftsindikatoren m pl; **~ planning** Wirtschaftsplanung f; **~ policy** Konjunkturpolitik f; **~ process** volkswirtschaftliche Entwicklung; **~ resources** wirtschaftliche Hilfsquellen (Aktiva); **~ situation** Wirtschaftssituation f; **~ stability** wirtschaftliche Stabilität; **~ support** wirtschaftliche Unterstützung; **~ theory**

Wirtschaftstheorie f; **~ union** Wirtschaftsunion f

economical adj wirtschaftlich adj, volkswirtschaftlich adj, sparsam adj, ökonomisch adj

economics plt Wirtschaftswissenschaft f, Nationalökonomie f, Volkswirtschaft f

economies n pl Einsparungen f pl

economist n Wirtschaftswissenschaftler m, Volkswirt m, Nationalökonom m

economize n sparen v, sparsam wirtschaften, haushalten v

economy n Wirtschaft f, Ökonomie f, Sparsamkeit f; **~ n** Wirtschaftlichkeit f; **managed ~** Planwirtschaft f; **planned ~** Planwirtschaft f

ECP = eurocommercial paper Euro-Schuldtitel mit kurzfristigen Laufzeiten (1, 3, 6 oder 12 Monate)

ECU = European Currency Unit Europäische Währungseinheit f

ECU-bond Euroanleihe in ECU-Währung

edition n Ausgabe f, Auflage f

education n Erziehung f; **~ (student) loan** Ausbildungskredit m

effect n Effekt m, Auswirkung f; **~ v** ausführen v, tätigen v; **~ payment** Zahlung leisten

effective adj wirklich vorhanden; **~ yield** Effektivverzinsung f; **become ~** in Kraft treten

effectual adj rechtsgültig adj, bindend adj

efficiency n Leistungsfähigkeit f, Tüchtigkeit f, Wirtschaftsgrad m

efficient adj tüchtig adj, fähig adj

EFT = electronic fund transfer elektronischer Zahlungsverkehr

elaborate v ausarbeiten v

elastic limit dehnbares Limit, dehnbare Grenze

elasticity of supply and demand Elastizität von Angebot und Nachfrage

elect v wählen v, auswählen v, erwählen v, designieren v

election of the supervisory board Aufsichtsratswahl f

electronic banking elektronische Abwicklung von Bankgeschäften; **~ cash terminal** elektronische Kasse; **~ counter** elektronischer Schalter; **~ data processing (EDP)** elektronische Datenverarbeitung (EDV); **~ delivery system** elektronisches Übertragungssystem; **~ fund transfer = EFT** elektronischer Zahlungsverkehr; **~ money** elektronische Geld; **~ purse** (prepaid card) elektronische Zahlkarte, Geldkarte f; **~ stock exchange** elektronische Börse; **~ systems** elektronische Systeme

eligibility n Wählbarkeit f, Befähigung f; **~ for rediscount** Rediskontierungsfähigkeit f

eligible as collateral beleihbar adj, lombardfähig adj; **~ bill** rediskontierbarer Wechsel; **~ investment** (US) besonders sichere Anlage

eliminate v ausschalten v, ausschließen v, ausscheiden v; **~ an account** ein Konto auflösen

elimination of risk Risikoausschluß m

embargo v einem Embargo unterwerfen, in Beschlag nehmen, den Handelsverkehr sperren, beschlagnahmen v; **~ n** Handelsverbot n, Beschlagnahme f, Embargo n, Hafensperre f

embark v (sich) einschiffen, an Bord gehen

embarkation n Einschiffung f, Verladung f

embarrassed adj in Zahlungsschwierigkeiten, in Geldverlegenheit

embarrassment n Zahlungsschwierigkeit f

embezzle v unterschlagen v, veruntreuen v

embezzlement n Unterschlagung f, Veruntreuung f

embezzler n Veruntreuer m

emergency n Notfall m, Notstand m, dringende Notlage f; **~ credit** Stützungskredit m; **~ loan** Stützungskredit m; **~ money** Notgeld n

emerging markets Wachstumsmärkte m pl

emit v ausgeben v (Wertpapiere), emittieren v, in Umlauf setzen

emitter n Emittent m, Aussteller m, Ausgeber m

emoluments n pl Bezüge m pl

employe n (US) Angestellte f u. m, Arbeitnehmer m, Gehaltsempfänger m

employed adj beschäftigt adj, angestellt adj

employee n Angestellte f u. m, Arbeitnehmer m, Gehaltsempfänger m; **~ stock**

employer

Belegschaftsaktien f pl; **~ stock ownership plan (ESOP)** (US) Belegschaftsaktienausgabe f; **bank ~** Bankangestellter f u. m, Bankbeamte m

employer n Arbeitgeber m, Unternehmer m, Auftraggeber m

employment n Tätigkeit f, Anstellung f, Beruf m, Geschäft n, Dienstverhältnis n, Arbeitsverhältnis n; **~ contract** Dienstvertrag m; **~ of capital** Kapitalanlage f; **~ of funds** Kapitalverwendung f; **~ tax** Lohnsteuer f

empower v ermächtigen v, Vollmacht erteilen, berechtigen v, bevollmächtigen v

empowered adj autorisiert adj, ermächtigt adj, bevollmächtigt adj, befugt adj

empowerment n Bevollmächtigung f

en nom participation Emissionsbeteiligung mit Namensnennung im Prospekt

enable v befähigen v, berechtigen v, ermächtigen v

enact v verordnen v

enactment n Erlaß eines Gesetzes, gesetzliche Bestimmung

encash v (GB) einkassieren v, zu Geld machen, in bar einlösen, einziehen v, kassieren v

encashment n Inkasso n, Einkassieren f, Einzug m, Einziehung f, Eintreibung f; **~ credit** Überziehungskredit m; **bill for ~** Wechsel zum Inkasso

enclose v beifügen v, beilegen v

enclosure n Anlage f, Beilage f

encoder n Codiergerät n

encoding machine Codiergerät n

encumber v hypothekarisch belasten, verpfänden v, mit einer Hypothek belasten, dinglich belasten

encumbered adj dinglich belastet, hypothekarisch belastet

encumbrance n Hypothekenbelastung f, Belastung f, Last f, Grundpfandrecht n

encumbrancer n Hypothekengläubiger m, Pfandgläubiger m, Hypothekenpfandgläubiger m

endeavor n (US) Bemühung f, Anstrengung f

endeavour n (GB) Bemühung f, Anstrengung f

endorsable adj indossierbar adj, girierbar adj, begebbar adj, indossabel adj

endorse v indossieren v, girieren v, begeben v, bestätigen v, mit Giro versehen, durch Indossament übertragen

endorsed adj giriert adj, mit Giro versehen, mit Indossament versehen; **~ bond** durch Wechsel garantierte Schuldverschreibung, durch einen weiteren Verpflichteten garantierte Schuldverschreibung; **~ in blank** blanko giriert

endorsee n Indossatar m, Indossat m, Girat m, Wechselübernehmer m

endorsement n Indossament n, Indossierung f, Giro n, Bestätigung f; **~ in blank** Blankoindossament n, Blankogiro n; **~ without recourse** (GB) Indossament ohne Obligo; **absolute ~** unbeschränktes Indossament; **accommodation ~** Gefälligkeitsindossament n; **blank ~** Blankoindossament n, Blankogiro n; **conditional ~** beschränktes Giro, Rektaindossament n; **qualified ~** bedingtes Indossament; **restrictive ~** beschränktes Giro, Rektaindossament n; **special ~** Vollgiro n, volles Wechselgiro, ausgefülltes Giro

endorser n Indossant m, Girant m, Wechselbürge m, Begebender m

endorsing n Indossament n, Indossierung f, Giro n, Bestätigung f

endow v dotieren v, ausstatten v

endowment n Stiftung f (Ausstattung mit Vermögensgütern), Dotation f; **~ capital** Dotationskapital n, Stiftungskapital n; **~ insurance policy** Aussteuerversicherungspolice f; **~ mortgage** durch Lebensversicherung abgesicherter Hypothekenkredit

enforce payment eine Zahlung eintreiben

enforceable adj erzwingbar adj, betreibbar adj, vollstreckbar adj

enforced liquidation Zwangsvergleich m

engage v verpflichten v, engagieren v, (sich) verpflichten v, bestellen v

engaged adj beschäftigt adj

engagement n Verbindung f, Verpflichtung f, Verabredung f, Engagement n, Börsenengagement n

engross v aufkaufen v

enjoyment; beneficial - Nutznießungsrecht n, Nießbrauchrecht n

enquiry agent Auskunftei f; **credit -** Kreditauskunftsanfrage f, Bitte um Kreditauskunft

enrich v bereichern v

enrichment n Bereicherung f

enrol v registrieren v, verzeichnen v

ensue v (from) (sich) ergeben v (aus)

enter v buchen v, eintragen v, registrieren v, kontrahieren v; **- in conformity** gleichlautend buchen; **- in the books** in die Bücher eintragen; **- into a contract** einen Vertrag abschließen; **- into relations with** Beziehungen aufnehmen mit; **- protest of draft** einen Wechsel protestieren lassen

enterprise n Geschäft n, Unternehmen n, Unternehmung f; **business -** geschäftliches Unternehmen; **trading -** Handelsunternehmen n

enterprising adj unternehmend adj; unternehmerisch adj

entertainment expenses Bewirtungsspesen plt

entertainments Aktien der Unterhaltungsindustrie

entitle v berechtigen v

entitled adj berechtigt adj, ermächtigt adj; **- to vote** stimmberechtigt adj

entitlement n Anspruch m, Berechtigung f; **holiday -** Urlaubsanspruch m

entity; legal - juristische Person

entrepôt n Lagerplatz m, Stapelplatz m

entrepreneur n Unternehmer m

entrepreneurial adj unternehmerisch adj

entrust v anvertrauen v, betrauen v

entruster Treugeber m

entry n Buchung f, Zolldeklaration f, Deklaration f, Eintragung f, Vermerk m; **- advice** Buchungsaufgabe f; **- legend** Buchungstext m; **- pass** Eingangssortieren n (beim Beleglesen); **- permit** Einreiseerlaubnis f; **- ticket** Buchungsbeleg m, Buchhaltungsbeleg m; **adjustement -** Berichtigungseintragung f; **bill of -** Zolleinfuhrschein m, Zolldeklaration f; **bookkeeping -** Buchungsposten m; **check an -** einen Buchungsposten abstreichen; **closing -** Abschlußbuchung f; **correcting -** Berichtigungsbuchung f; **cross -** Gegenbuchung f; **customs -** Zollerklärung f; **upon -** nach Eingang

enumerate v aufzählen v

envelope n Briefumschlag m (Kuvert)

environmental share Aktie aus dem Umweltbereich

equal adj gleich adj, gleichmäßig adj, gleichwertig adj

equalization fund Ausgleichsfonds m

equalizing dividend Ausgleichsdividende f; **- duty** Ausgleichszoll m

equation of payments durchschnittlicher Zahlungstermin

equipment n Ausrüstung f, Ausstattung f, Einrichtung f (Gerät); **- and material cost** Sachkosten plt; **- bonds** (US) Schuldverschreibungen zum Ankauf von Ausrüstungsgegenständen; **- leasing** Vermietung von Einrichtungsgegenständen

equitable mortgage Billigkeitspfand n

equities n pl Dividendenpapiere n pl; **- n pl** (GB) Eisenbahnobligationen f pl; **- market** Aktienmarkt m

equity n Billigkeitsrecht n, Billigkeit f; **- n** Realwert m, wirklicher Wert, Differenz zwischen Veräußerungswert und hypothekarischen Belastungen eines Grundstücks; **- banking** Beteiligungsgeschäft der Bank; **- capital** Eigenkapital n, Beteiligungskapital n; **- dilution** Verwässerung des Aktienkapitals; **- offering** Aktienmission f; **- of redemption** Hypothekenablösungsrecht n; **- participation** Aktienbeteiligung n; **- portfolio** Aktienportefeuille n; **- price** Aktienpreis m, Aktienkurs m; **- ratio** Eigenfinanzierungsgrad m; **- securities** Dividendenpapiere n pl, Aktien n pl, Dividendenwerte f pl; **- share** Stammaktie f; **- sweetener** (informal) Optionsrechte auf Aktien; **- trading** Aktienhandel m; **- proprietary** Barbetrag aus einem Grundbesitz; **shareholders' -** Eigenkapital n (Bilanz); **stockholders' -** (US) Eigenkapital n (Bilanz)

equity-linked issue

equity-linked issue Anleihe mit Optionsschein auf Aktien
equivalent *n* Gegenwert *m*
erring funds vagabundierende Gelder
erroneous *adj* irrtümlich *adj*
error *n* Irrtum *m*, Versehen *n*; *- correction* Fehlerkorrektur *f*; *- frequency* Fehlerhäufigkeit *f*; *- probability* Fehlerwahrscheinlichkeit *f*; *counter -* Ausgleichsfehler *m*
errors and omissions excepted (E. and O.E.) Irrtümer und Auslassungen vorbehalten
escalator clause Indexklausel *f*, Gleitklausel *f*
escape clause Rücktrittsklausel *f*
escheat *n* Heimfall *m*; *- v* anheimfallen *v*
escrow treuhänderisch halten, zu getreuen Händen hinterlegtes Dokument; *- agent* Treuhänder von hinterlegten Dokumenten; *- funds* beim Treuhänder hinterlegte Gelder; *deposit in -* bedingte Einlage; *place in -* zu getreuen Händen übergeben
escrower Treuhändler *m*
essential goods lebenswichtige Güter
essentials *n pl* wichtige Punkte, lebenswichtige Güter
establish a credit einen Kredit einrichten, einen Kredit eröffnen
establishment *n* Betrieb *m*, Unternehmen *n*, Einrichtung *f*, Geschäft *n*, Gründung *f*
estate *n* (Grund-)Eigentum *n*, (Grund-)Besitz *m*, Vermögen *n*, Nachlaß *m*, Erbmasse *f*, Konkursmasse *f*, Landgut *n*; *- administration* Nachlaßverwaltung *f*; *- administrator* Nachlaßpfleger *m*, Nachlaßverwalter *m*; *- distribution* Erbteilung *f*; *- duty* (GB) Erbschaftssteuer *f*, Nachlaßsteuer *f*; *- trust* Treuhandvermögen *n*, Treuhandgut *n*, Stiftungsvermögen *n*, Mündelgelder *n pl*; *administration of an -* Nachlaßverwaltung *f*; *bankrupt's -* Konkursmasse *f*; *beneficial -* Nießbrauch an einem Vermögen; *building -* Baugrundstück *n*, baureifes Grundstück; *burdened -* belastetes Grundstück; *claim against the -* Masseanspruch *m*; *clear -* unbelastetes Grundstück; *contingent -* Erbanwartschaft *f*; *deceased's -* Nachlaß *m* (Erbrecht), Erbschaft *f*; *decedent's -* (US) Nachlaß *m* (Erbrecht), Erbschaft *f*; *disclaim an -* eine Erbschaft ausschlagen; *party to an -* Miterbe *m*, Miterbin *f*; *personal -* Besitz an beweglichem Vermögen; *real -* Immobilien *pl*, Grundbesitz *m*, Grund und Boden, Grundeigentum *n*, Grundstückseigentum *n*, Liegenschaften *f pl*; *separate -* Vorbehaltsgut *n*, Sondervermögen, eingebrachtes Gut; *several -* Sondervermögen *n*; *trust -* Treuhandvermögen *n*, Treuhandgut *n*, Stiftungsvermögen *n*, Mündelgelder *n pl*
estates; separation of - Gütertrennung *f*
estimate *v* veranschlagen *v*, schätzen *v*, bewerten *v*; *- of expenditure* Ausgabenschätzung *f*; *- of profits* Gewinnschätzung *f*, Ertragsschätzung *f*; *conservative -* vorsichtige Schätzung
estimated value Schätzwert *m*
estimation *n* Schätzung *f*, Veranschlagung *f*, Wertschätzung *f*, Bewertung *f*
eurobond (euroloan) Euroanleihe *f*; *- market* Euroanleihemarkt *m*
eurocapital market Eurokapitalmarkt *m*
Eurocard Eurocard *f*, Eurokreditkarte *f*
eurocheque = ec Euroscheck *m*
Euroclear (CEDEL) Clearingsystem für Euroanleihen
eurocommercial kurzfristige Schuldverschreibung am Euromarkt; *- paper = ECP* Euroschuldtitel mit kurzfristigen Laufzeiten (1, 3, 6 oder 12 Monate)
eurocredit Eurokredit *m*; *- market* Eurokreditmarkt *m*
eurocurrency Eurowährung *f*; *- deposits* Eurowährungseinlagen *f pl*; *- loan* Eurowährungskredit *m*; *- market* Eurowährungsmarkt *m*
eurodeposit *n* Euroeinlage *f*
eurodollar *n* Eurodollar *m*; *- market* Eurodollarmarkt *m*
euro-equities Euroaktien *f pl*
euroloan *n* Euroanleihe *f*, Euroemission *f*
euromarket *n* Euromarkt *m*, europäischer Währungsmarkt
euromoney market Eurogeldmarkt *m*
euronote *n* kurzfristiger Eurowährungsinhaberschuldschein

euro-option Eurooption f
European *Bank for Reconstruction and Development (EBRD)* Europäische Bank für Wiederaufbau und Entwicklung f; **- *Community = EC*** Europäische Gemeinschaft f (EG)
european currency loan europäischer Währungskredit
European *Currency Snake* Europäische Währungsschlange f; **- *Currency Unit (ECU)*** Europäische Währungseinheit f; **- *Economic Community (EEC)*** Europäische Wirtschaftsgemeinschaft f (EWG); **- *Free Trade Association (EFTA)*** Europäische Freihandelsgemeinschaft f; **- *Fund for Monetary Cooperation*** Europäische Fonds für Währungspolitische Zusammenarbeit m; **- *Investment Bank (EIB)*** Europäische Investitionsbank f
european monetary policy europäische Währungspolitik
European Monetary System (EMS) Europäische Währungssystem n
european option europäische Option (zum vereinbarten Termin ausübbare O.)
European *Recovery Program (ERP)-loans* ERP-Kredite m pl; **- *Regional Development Fund (ERDF)*** Europäische Fonds für währungspolitische Entwicklung m; **- *Union (EU)*** Europäische Union f (EU);
european unit of account europäische Rechnungseinheit
European Unit of Account(ing) Europäische Rechnungseinheit f
euroyen Euro-Yen m
evaluate v bewerten v, berechnen v, einschätzen v
evaluation Bewertung f, Wertbestimmung f; **job** - Arbeitsplatzbewertung f
evergreen credit (US) unbefristeter Kredit
evidence n Beweismaterial n
ex ohne, ausschließlich, exklusive; **- *interest*** ohne Zinsen; **- *new*** ohne Bezugsrecht; **- *scrip issue*** Ex-Gratis-(Berichtigungs)aktien f pl
exact adj genau adj, pünktlich adj; **- interest** Zinsen auf der Basis von 365 Tagen
exaction n Beitreibung f

ex-allotment Ex-Bezugsrecht n (Börse)
examination n Untersuchung f, Prüfung f; **bank** - (US) Bankrevision f; **bankruptcy** - Konkursverfahren n
examine v prüfen v, kontrollieren v; **- *closely*** eingehend prüfen
examiner; bank - (US) Bankrevisor m
example n Beispiel n, Vorbild n, Muster n
exceed v übertreffen v, überschreiten v, übersteigen v; **- *in*** (sich) auszeichnen v; **- *the limit*** das Limit überschreiten
excepted risks ausgenommene Risiken
excerpt n Auszug m, Extrakt m
excess n Überschuß m, Mehrbetrag m; **- *profits tax*** Übergewinnsteuer f; **- *reserve*** (US) überschüssige Reserve; **- *security*** überschüssige Sicherheit
exchange v wechseln v, tauschen v, austauschen v, umtauschen v; - n Börse f, Devisen f pl, Währung f, Valuta f, Tausch m, Austausch m, Umtausch m; **- *agent*** Börsenvertreter m; **- *arbitrage*** Währungsarbitrage f, Devisenarbitrage f, Wechselarbitrage f; **- *bank*** Devisenbank f, Wechselbank f; **- *board*** Kursanzeigetafel f; **- *broker*** Devisenmakler m, Wechselmakler m, Börsenmakler m; **- *charges*** Wechselkosten pl t; **- *clause*** Währungsklausel f; **- *commission*** Wechselprovision f; **- *control*** Devisenbewirtschaftung f, Devisenkontrolle f, Währungskontrolle f; **- *control regulations*** Devisenbestimmungen f pl; **- *cover*** Devisendeckung f; **- *cross rate*** Usancekurs m; **- *dealer*** Devisenhändler m; **- *embargo*** Devisensperre f; **- *instruments*** Devisen f pl; **- *list*** Kurszettel m (Devisen), Kursbericht m (Devisen), Devisenkursliste f; **- *of acknowledgement signals*** Quittungsaustausch m; **- *of data carriers*** Datenträgeraustausch m (DTA); **- *of data media*** Datenträgeraustausch m; **- *office*** Wechselstube f; **- *parity*** Kursparität f; **- *permit*** Devisengenehmigung f; **- *price*** Börsenkurs m, Kurswert m; **- *privilege*** Umtauschrecht n (bei Investmentanteilen); **- *profit*** Börsengewinn m; **- *rate*** Devisenkurs m,

Umrechnungskurs m, Wechselkurs m, Umtauschkurs m; **- rate guarantee** Kursgarantie f; **- regulations** Devisenbestimmungen f pl; **- restrictions** Devisenbeschränkungen f pl; **- risk** Kursrisiko n, Währungsrisiko n; **account of -** Wechselkonto n; **bill of -** Wechsel m, Tratte f; **calculation of -** Devisenkursberechnung f; **close of -** Börsenschluß m; **commodity -** Warenbörse f; **corn -** Getreidebörse f; **cost of -** Umtauschkosten plt; **cotton -** Baumwollbörse f; **course of -** (GB) Wechselkurs m; **cross -** (GB) Wechselarbitrage über mehrere Plätze; **curb -** Freiverkehrsbörse f, Freibörse f, Freiverkehrsmarkt m, Nachbörse f; **currency - standard** Devisenwährung f; **current on -** börsengängig adj; **multiple - rates** multiple Wechselkurse f; **pegged -** künstlich gehaltener Devisenkurs; **rate of -** Devisenkurs m, Umrechnungskurs m, Wechselkurs m, Umtauschkurs m; **sight -** Sichtwechsel m; **triangular -** Devisenarbitrage in drei verschiedenen Währungen

exchanges n pl Zahlungsausgleich zwischen Banken

exchequer n (GB) Fiskus m, Schatzamt n, Staatsschatz m; **- account** Schatzkonto n; **- bill** (GB) Schatzwechsel m (kurzfristig); **- bonds** (GB) Schatzanweisungen f pl (langfristig); **bill of the -** Schatzanweisung f

Exchequer; Board of the - (GB) Finanzministerium n; **Chancellor of the -** (GB) Schatzkanzler m, Finanzminister m

ex-claims Ex-Bezugsrecht n (Börse)

exclude v ausschließen v

exclusive agent Alleinvertreter m; **- sale** Alleinverkauf m, Alleinvertrieb m

excuse v verzeihen v

ex-date Ex-Tag m

ex-dividend Ex-Dividende f (Börse)

execute v vollstrecken v, ausführen v, durchführen v, ausüben v; **- an order** einen Auftrag ausführen

execution n Durchführung f, Ausführung f, Vollstreckung f, Pfändung f, Zwangsvollstreckung f; **- creditor** Vollstreckungsgläubiger m, gerichtlich anerkannter Gläubiger; **- debtor** Vollstreckungsschuldner m; **- of a will** Testamentsvollstreckung f; **- sale** Zwangsversteigerung f

executive n Exekutive f, leitende(r) Angestellte(r); **- board** Vorstand m; **- vice president** stellvertretender geschäftsführender Direktor

executives n pl Führungskräfte f pl

executor n Testamentsvollstrecker m; **- and trustee department** Treuhandabteilung f; **- trustee** Testamentsvollstrecker mit der Befugnis der Vermögensverwaltung

exempt from withholding tax quellensteuerfrei

exemption n Steuerfreibetrag m, Freibetrag m, pfändungsfreier Betrag; **claim of -** (US) Aussonderungsanspruch m

exercise v ausüben v, geltend machen; **- of option** Ausübung des Prämienrechts

exhaust v erschöpfen v

exhibition n Ausstellung f

exit bond Umschuldungsanleihe für Entwicklungsländer

exodus of capital Kapitalflucht f

expand v ausdehnen v, erweitern v

expansion n Ausdehnung f, Erweiterung f; **credit -** Kreditausweitung f; **- stage financing** Expansionsfinanzierung mit Wagniskapital

expected to accrue return Hamster-Optionsschein m, Kurskanal-Optionsschein m

expediency n Zweckmäßigkeit f, Ratsamkeit f

expenditure; capital - in einem Unternehmen investiertes Kapital

expenditure(s) Ausgaben f pl, Spesen plt, Unkosten plt, Aufwendungen f pl, Kostenaufwand m

expenditures; administrative - Verwaltungskosten plt

expense n Kosten plt, Aufwand m, Spesen plt; **- account** Spesenkonto n, Unkostenkonto n; **bookkeeping -** Buchhaltungskosten plt

expenses n pl Ausgaben f pl, Spesen pl t, Unkosten pl t, Aufwendungen f pl, Kostenaufwand m; **absorbed ~** verrechnete Gemeinkosten; **account of ~** Spesenkonto n, Unkostenkonto n; **accrued ~** antizipative Posten (auf der Passivseite), Rechnungsabgrenzungsposten m pl; **amount of ~** Unkostenbetrag m; **average ~** Havariegelder n pl; **business ~** Geschäftsunkosten pl t; **cutting down of ~** Unkostenherabsetzung f; **deferred ~** transitorische Posten (auf der Aktivseite), Rechnungsabgrenzungsposten m pl; **extraordinary ~** außerordentliche Aufwendungen; **incidental ~** Nebenkosten pl t; **outstanding ~** unbezahlte Ausgaben; **petty ~** kleine Unkosten; **working ~** Betriebskosten pl t

expensive adj teuer adj, kostspielig adj

experience n Erfahrung f; **~ v** erfahren v, erleben v

experienced adj erfahren adj, versiert adj, bewandert adj

expert n Fachmann m; **~ opinion** n Gutachten n (eines Rechtssachverständigen); **auditing ~** Buchsachverständiger m; **credit ~** Kreditfachmann m

expiration n Ablauf m, Verfall m (durch Zeit), Ende n

expire v verfallen v, erlöschen v, ablaufen v

expired option verfallene Option

expiring adj ablaufend adj

expiry n Ablauf m, Verfall m (durch Zeit), Ende n; **~ date** Verfallzeit f, Verfalltag m, Verfalldatum n; **~ of a term** Fristablauf m, Termin m

export v exportieren v, ausführen v; **~ n** Export m, Warenausfuhr f, Ausfuhr f; **~ bank** Außenhandelsbank f; **~ certificate** Exportbescheinigung f, Ausfuhrbescheinigung f; **~ credit** Exportkredit m, Ausfuhrkredit m; **~ credit insurance** Ausfuhrkreditversicherung f; **~ department** Exportabteilung f; **~ drive** Exportfeldzug m; **~ duty** Ausfuhrzoll m, Ausfuhrabgabe f; **~ earnings** Ausfuhrerlöse m pl; **~ financing** Exportfinanzierung m, Außenhandelsfinanzierung f; **~ financing credit** Exportfinanzierungskredit m; **~ firm** Exportfirma f, Exporthaus n; **~ industry** Exportindustrie f; **~ letter of credit** Exportakkreditiv n; **~ licence** Ausfuhrgenehmigung f, Ausfuhrbewilligung f, Exportbewilligung f; **~ order** Exportauftrag m; **~ permit** Ausfuhrgenehmigung f, Ausfuhrbewilligung f, Exportbewilligung f; **~ quota** Exportkontingent n; **~ regulations** Ausfuhrbestimmungen f pl; **~ surplus** Ausfuhrüberschuß m; **~ tariff** Ausfuhrzolltarif m; **~ trade** Exporthandel m, Ausfuhrhandel m; **capital ~** Kapitalausfuhr f

exportable adj ausführbar adj, ausfuhrfähig adj

exportation n Export m, Warenausfuhr f, Ausfuhr f

exporter n Exporteur m, Exportfirma f

exports n pl Exporte m pl, Exportwaren f pl

exposition n (US) Ausstellung f

exposure Verlustrisiko n (Verlustpotential)

expromission n Schuldabtretung f

expromissor n Schuldübernehmer m

expropriate v enteignen v

expropriation n Enteignung f

ex-right Ex-Anrecht n

ex-rights Ex-Bezugsrechte n pl (Börse)

extend v ausbauen v, verlängern v, prolongieren v, erweitern v

extendable bond Anleihe mit Verlängerungsrecht

extended credit langfristiger Kredit

extension n Prolongation f, Verlängerung f; **~ of a contract** Vertragsverlängerung f; **~ of a loan** Verlängerung des Kredits; **~ to the cover** Erweiterung der Deckungszusage

extent n Umfang m; **to the ~ of** bis zum Betrag von

external account Auslandskonto n; **~ bond (loan)** Auslandsanleihe f; **~ debt** Auslandsverschuldung f; **~ finance** Fremdkapital n; **~ financing** Fremdfinanzierung f, Außenfinanzierung f; **~ loan** Auslandsanleihe f; **~ trade surplus** Außenhandelsüberschuß m; **~ value** (of a currency) Außenwert m (einer Währung)

extinguish v löschen v; *- a mortgage* eine Hypothek tilgen

extortion n Erpressung f

extra adj extra adj, Sonder- (in Zus.), Extra- (in Zus.); *- charges* Extraspesen plt, Kostenzuschlag m; *- dividend* Zusatzdividende f; *- yield* Zusatzrendite f

extract n Auszug m, Extrakt m; *- of account* Kontoauszug m, Rechnungsauszug m

extraordinary expenses außerordentliche Aufwendungen; *- income* Sondererträge m pl

ex-warrant bond ohne Optionsschein gehandelte Anleihe

F

fabrication n Fabrikation f, Herstellung f, Fertigung f

face n Vorderseite f; *- amount (of bill)* Wechselbetrag m; *- rate* Nettosatz m; *- value* Nennwert m, Nominalwert m, Pariwert m

facilities n pl Einrichtungen f pl, Möglichkeiten f pl, Fazilitäten f pl; *borrowing -* Kreditaufnahmemöglichkeiten f pl; *credit -* Kreditfazilitäten f pl

facility n Einrichtung f, Möglichkeit f, Kredit m, Fazilität f

facsimile n Faksimile n, getreue Nachbildung

factor n Faktor m, eine Person oder Firma, die das Factoringgeschäft betreibt; *- n* Kommissionär m; *cost -* Kostenfaktor m

factoring n Forderungsankauf m, Debitorenverkauf m, Factoring n; *- company* Factoring-Gesellschaft f

factory n Fabrik f, Betrieb m, Handelsniederlassung f; *- extension* Betriebserweiterung f

fail v Bankrott machen, Konkurs machen

failing payment mangels Zahlung

failure n Bankrott m, Konkurs m, Zusammenbruch m, Fehlschlag m, Zahlungseinstellung f; *- to pay* Nichtzahlung f; *bank -* Bankkonkurs m, Bankkrach m, Bankzusammenbruch m; *banking -* Bankkonkurs m, Bankkrach m, Bankzusammenbruch m; *commercial -* Zahlungseinstellung f, Konkurs m, Bankrott m

fair n Messe f, Ausstellung f, Markt m; *- price* angemessener Preis

faith; in good - gutgläubig adj, in gutem Glauben

fake n Fälschung f, Verfälschung f, Falsifikat n; *- a balance sheet* eine Bilanz fälschen

faked adj falsch adj, unecht adj

faker n Fälscher m, Verfälscher m

fall n Fallen n, Kurssturz m, Kurseinbruch m, Rückgang m; *- due* fällig werden

false adj falsch adj, fehlerhaft adj

falsification n Fälschung f, Verfälschung f, Falsifikat n

falsificator n Fälscher m, Verfälscher m

falsifier n Falschmünzer m, Urkundenfälscher m

falsify v fälschen v (Geld, Wechsel), verfälschen v, nachdrucken v, nachahmen v, nachmachen v

family company Familienunternehmen n; *- savings* Ersparnisse der privaten Haushalte

fancy stocks unsichere Spekulationspapiere

fare n Fahrgeld n

farm credit Landwirtschaftskredit m, landwirtschaftliches Darlehen, Agrarkredit m; *- loan* Landwirtschaftskredit m, landwirtschaftliches Darlehen, Agrarkredit m; *- mortgage* landwirtschaftliche Hypothek

fas = free alongside ship frei bis zum Schiff

fault n Fehler m

faulty adj falsch adj, fehlerhaft adj

favo(u)r v begünstigen v, Nutzen bringen; *balance in one's -* Guthabensaldo m; *in - of* zugunsten von

favo(u)rable adj aktiv adj (Zahlungsbilanz)

FAZ-stock-index FAZ-Index der Frankfurter Allgemeinen Zeitung

feasibility study Durchführbarkeitsstudie f

feature n Merkmal n

federal agency Bundesbehörde f; *- aid* Bundeshilfe f, Bundeszuschuß m

Federal bond syndicate Bundesanleihekonsortium n

federal debt Staatsschuld f

Federal *Deposit Insurance Corporation* (US) US-Bundesversicherungsbehörde für Kundeneinlagen (Einlagensicherungsfonds der Banken); *- Farm Credit Bank* (US) Agrarkreditanstalt f; *- Financing Bank* (US) Bundesfinanzierungsbank f

federal funds Bankguthaben bei der Zentralbank; *- government bond*

Federal

Bundesanleihe f; **- government futures** Bundestermingeschäfte n pl; **- government guarantee** Bundesbürgschaft f; **- government securities** Bundeswertpapiere n pl
Federal Home Loan Bank (US) Bausparkassenzentralbank f; **- Home Loan Mortgage Corp.** (US) Bundeshypothekenkreditanstalt f
federal income tax Bundeinkommensteuer f
Federal Post Office bond Bundespostanleihe f; **- Railway bond** Bundesbahnanleihe f; **- Reserve Banks** (US) US-Zentralbanken f pl; **- Reserve Board** (US) US-Zentralbankrat des US-Zentralbanksystems; **- Reserve System** (US) US-Zentralbanksystem n; **- savings bond** Bundesschatzbrief m; **- securities** (US) US-Staatspapiere n pl; US-Staatstitel m pl; **- treasury bill** Bundesschatzwechsel m; **- treasury note** Bundesschatzanweisung f
federation n Verband m, Vereinigung f
fee n Gebühr f, Honorar n, Tantieme f; **additional -** Gebührenzuschlag m; **admission -** Zulassungsgebühr f; **collection -** Inkassogebühren f pl, Inkassospesen pl/t, Einzugsspesen pl/t; **completion -** Abschlußgebühr f; **counsel's -** Anwaltsgebühren f pl; **custody -** Verwahrungsgebühr f; **result -** Erfolgshonorar n; **transfer -** Transfergebühr f, Umschreibegebühr f, Überweisungsspesen pl/t
fees; abatement in - Gebührenermäßigung f; **consular -** Konsulargebühren f pl; **notarial -** Notariatsgebühren f pl
feign v vortäuschen v, simulieren v, fingieren v
fellow creditor Mitgläubiger m; **- debtor** Mitschuldner m, Solidarschuldner m
FIBOR = Frankfurt Interbank Offered Rate Frankfurter Interbanken-Angebotszinssatz
fiction n gefälschte Unterschrift
fictitious adj fingiert adj, fiktiv adj; **- account** Pseudokonto n; **- instrument** gefälschte Urkunde

fiddle n (informal) Schiebung f, Manipulation f; **- v** frisieren v, tricksen v
fidelity insurance Veruntreuungsversicherung f, Unterschlagungsversicherung f
fiduciary n Vermögensverwalter m, Treuhänder m, Bevollmächtigter m, Verwalter m, Pfleger m; **- adj** fiduziarisch adj, treuhänderisch adj; **- company** Treuhandgesellschaft f; **- contract** Treuhandvertrag m; **- debtor** Treunehmer m; **- issue** ungedeckte Notenausgabe; **- loan** ungedeckte Anleihe; **- management** Treuhandverwaltung f; **- service** Treuhänderdienst m; **- transactions** Treuhandgeschäfte n pl
field of application Sachgebiet n
figure n Betrag m, Zahl f, Ziffer f, Preis m
figures; book - Buchwerte m pl
file v ablegen v; **- n** Akte f, Aktenstück n, Verzeichnis n, Liste f; **- a claim** Anspruch anmelden; **- addition** Zugang m (zu einem Datenbestand); **- format** Dateiaufbau m; **- maintenance** Änderungsdienst m, Fortschreibung f; **- maintenance code** Änderungsschlüssel m; **- maintenance notice** Änderungsmitteilung f; **- number** Geschäftszeichen n; **- organization** Dateiorganisation f; **- reorganization** Reorganisationsablauf m (bei Großspeicherdateien); **- bill -** Wechselregistratur f; **central -** Zentralkartei f, Kundenkartei f
filed for record abgelegt adj
files account Kontounterlagen f pl
fill v (aus)füllen v, (Börsenordner) ausführen v; **- or cancel (kill)** Börsenauftrag sofort annullieren, sofern (Kauf oder Verkauf) zum vorgegebenen Kurs nicht möglich
final judg(e)ment rechtskräftiges Urteil; **- dividend** Schlußdividende f; **- sort pass** Ausgangssortierung f (beim Beleglesen)
finance v finanzieren v, Kapital beschaffen, kapitalisieren v; **- n** Geldwesen n, Finanzen pl/t, Finanzwirtschaft f, Finanzwesen n; **- bill** Finanzierungswechsel m, Mobilisierungswechsel m; **- charge** Finanzierungskosten pl/t; **- company**

292

Finanzgesellschaft f; **~ department** Finanzabteilung f; **~ division** Finanzabteilung f; **~ loan** Finanzierungskredit m; **~ market** Finanzmarkt m; **~ notes** Finanzierungsschätze m pl; **~ requirements** Finanzbedarf m; **~ resources** Finanzierungsquellen f pl; **~ stamp** (GB) Effektenstempel m; **business** ~ Betriebsfinanzen plt; **commercial ~ company** Finanzierungsgesellschaft f; **cost of** ~ Finanzierungskosten plt; **public ~** staatliches Finanzwesen, öffentliches Finanzwesen

financial adj finanziell adj, geldlich adj, finanztechnisch adj; **~ aid** Kredithilfe f; **~ analysis** Finanzanalyse f; Geldvermögen n; **~ area** Finanzraum m; **~ arrangement** Finanzierungsplan m; **~ assets** Finanzanlagevermögen n, Finanzanlagen f pl; **~ backing** finanzielle Unterstützung; **~ bill** Finanzwechsel m; **~ boutique** Allfinanzanbieter für Firmenkunden m; **~ centre** Bankzentrum n, Finanzzentrum n; **~ circumstances** Vermögensverhältnisse n pl; **~ condition** Finanzlage f, Vermögenslage f, finanzielle Lage; **~ control** Finanzkontrolle f; **~ difficulties** finanzielle Schwierigkeiten; **~ engineering** Finanzierungstechnik f; **~ failure** finanzieller Zusammenbruch; **~ forecasting** Vorausschau über die finanzielle Lage eines Unternehmens; **~ futures** Finanzterminkontrakte m pl; **~ house** Geldinstitut n, Finanzierungsinstitut n; **~ income** Finanzerträge m pl; **~ innovations** Finanzinnovationen f pl; **~ insolvency** Zahlungsunfähigkeit f; **~ institution** Geldinstitut n, Finanzierungsinstitut n; **~ instrument** Kreditinstrument n; **~ interests** Kapitalinteressen n pl; **~ interrelation** Kapitalverflechtung f; **~ investments** Finanzanlagen f pl; **~ loan** Finanzkredit m; **~ markets** Finanzmärkte f pl; **~ needs** Finanzierungsbedarf m; **~ operations** Finanzgeschäfte n pl; **~ paper** Börsenblatt n, Wirtschaftszeitung f; **~ plan** Finanzierungsplan m; **~ position** Finanzlage f; **~ quarters** Finanzkreise m pl; **~ rating** finanzieller Stand; **~ records** finanzielle Unterlagen; **~ requirements** Kapitalbedarf m; **~ responsibility** finanzielle Haftung; **~ services** Finanzleistungen f pl, Finanzdienstleistungen f pl; **~ situation** Finanzlage f, Vermögenslage f, finanzielle Lage; **~ solvency** Zahlungsfähigkeit f; **~ squeeze** finanzieller Engpaß m; **~ supermarket** Finanzsupermarkt m, Universalbank f; **~ statements** Finanzstatus m, Jahresabschluß m; **~ study** Finanzstudie f; **~ swap** Finanzswap m; **~ syndicate** Finanzierungskonsortium n; **~ world** Finanzwelt f; **~ year** (GB) Geschäftsjahr n, Finanzjahr n, Wirtschaftsjahr n, Rechnungsjahr n, Betriebsjahr n, Steuerjahr n; **annual ~ statement** Jahresabschluß m, Jahresrechnung f; **certified ~ statement** Bilanz mit Prüfungsvermerk; **consolidated ~ statement** Konzernbilanz f, konsolidierte Bilanz, Fusionsbilanz f

Financial Times FT-Index (GB) Financial-Times-Aktienindex m

financier n Finanzier m, Finanzmann m, Geldgeber n

financing n Finanzierung f; **~ company** Finanzierungsgesellschaft f; **~ methods** Finanzierungsmethoden f pl; **~ of the monthend needs** Ultimofinanzierung f, Finanzierungsbedarf m; **~ with building society funds** Bausparfinanzierung f; **accounts receivable ~** Finanzierung durch Abtretung der Debitoren; **burden of ~** Finanzierungslast f; **construction ~** Baufinanzierung f; **convertible ~** Finanzierung durch Ausgabe von Wandelschuldverschreibungen; **corporation ~** (US) Finanzierung von Aktiengesellschaften; **cost of ~** Finanzierungskosten plt; **real estate ~** Immobilienfinanzierung f

fine v bestrafen v, strafen v, eine Geldstrafe verhängen; ~ n Geldstrafe f, Buße f; **~ gold content** Feingoldgehalt m; **~ sort** Feinsortierung f (beim Beleglesen); **~ trade bill** erstklassiger Handelswechsel

fineness n Feingehalt m

finishing industry Veredelungsindustrie f

Finnish Markka Finnmark f

fire *insurance* Feuerversicherung f; **- *underwriters*** Feuerversicherungsgesellschaft f

fireworks n pl (US) plötzliche Hausse

firm n Firma f, Unternehmen n, Betrieb m, Handelshaus n; - adj fest adj; **- *commitment*** Festübernahme von Wertpapieren; **- *market*** feste Börse; **- *name*** Firmenname m, Firmenbezeichnung f; **- *offer*** festes Verkaufsangebot; **- *order*** Fixauftrag m; **- *quotation*** verbindliche Kursnotierung; **- *sale*** fester Verkauf; **- *stock*** gehaltene Werte; **- *underwriting*** Festübernahme f; **bankrupt -** in Konkurs gegangene Firma; **brokerage -** Maklerfirma f; **commercial -** Handelsfirma f, Geschäftshaus n

firming up of prices Anziehen der Kurse

first *board* erste Kursnotierung; **- *lien*** erstrangiges Zurückbehaltungsrecht, erstrangiges Pfandrecht; **- *mortgage*** erste Hypothek, erststellige Hypothek; **- *mortgage bonds*** durch erststellige Hypotheken gesicherte Pfandbriefe; **- *mortgage loan*** erststellige Hypothekendarlehen; **- *of exchange*** Primawechsel m; **- *paper*** erstklassiger Wechsel, prima Wechsel; **- *rank*** erststellig adj; **buy at - hand** aus erster Hand kaufen

first-class adj erstrangig adj

First Vice President (VP) stellvertretender Direktor

fiscal n Geschäftsjahr n, Finanzjahr n, Wirtschaftsjahr n, Rechnungsjahr n, Betriebsjahr n, Steuerjahr n; **- *report*** Geschäftsbericht m (Finanzbericht); **- *year*** Geschäftsjahr n, Finanzjahr n, Wirtschaftsjahr n, Rechnungsjahr n, Betriebsjahr n, Steuerjahr n

fives n pl (US) fünfprozentige Papiere

fixed adj festgesetzt adj, ausgemacht adj; **- *advance*** fester Vorschuß m; **- *assets*** Anlagevermögen n; **- *capital*** Anlagekapital n; **- *charges*** Generalunkosten plt, feste Ausgaben; **- *costs*** fixe Kosten; **- *debt*** feste Schulden; **- *debt option*** Option auf Tausch zinsvariabler in Festsatz-Obligationen; **- *deposit*** befristete Einlage, Termineinlage f; **- *exchange rate*** fester Wechselkurs m; **- *income*** festes Einkommen; **- *income securities*** festverzinsliche Wertpapiere; **- *interest bearing*** festverzinslich adj; **- *interest bearing securities*** festverzinsliche Wertpapiere; **- *interest issues*** festverzinsliche Wertpapiere; **- *loan*** Kredit mit fester Laufzeit; **- *portion*** fixer Teil (bei Bestandssätzen); **- *price*** Festpreis m; **- *rate deal*** Festzinssatzemission f; **- *term*** fester Termin; **- *trust*** Investmenttrust (dessen Anlagen schon bei der Gründung festgelegt werden); **- *value*** Nennwert m, Festwert m

fixed-date mortgage Festhypothek f

fixed-dated bill Nachsichtwechsel m

fixed-interest security festverzinsliches Wertpapier

fixed-rate tender Mengentender m

fixed-term deposits Festgeldanlagen f pl

fixed-yield festverzinslich adj

fixing Fixing n, Festlegung amtlicher Kurse

fixtures n pl Mobiliar eines Unternehmens

flat n Wohnung f; - adj flau adj, matt adj, lustlos adj, geschäftslos adj, still adj; **- *credit*** zinsloser Kredit m; **- *market*** lustloser Markt; **- *property*** (GB) Stockwerkeigentum n; **- *rate*** Pauschalsatz m

flawless adj einwandfrei adj, fehlerfrei adj

flexible *exchange rate* flexibler Wechselkurs m; **- *limit*** dehnbares Limit, dehnbare Grenze; **- *trust*** Investmenttrust (dessen Verwaltung bei Vornahme von Kapitalanlagen Bewegungsfreiheit hat)

flight *capital* Fluchtgelder f pl; **- *of capital*** Kapitalflucht f

float v (f. the exchange rate) umlaufen v, in Umlauf setzen (Effekten), floaten v (Wechselkurs); - n (US) im Einzug befindliche Schecks; **- *a bond issue*** eine Anleihe auflegen, eine Anleihe begeben; **- *a loan issue*** eine Anleihe aufgeben, eine Anleihe begeben; **- *profit*** Floatgewinn m; **- *the exchange rate*** den Wechselkurs floaten

floatation n Inumlaufsetzen n, Begebung f, Auflegung f

floater = **(FRN)** variabel verzinslicher Schuldschein, Floater m

floaters n pl (GB) erstklassige Inhaberpapiere

floating n (of a currency) Freigabe des Wechselkurses (einer Währung); ~ adj schweben adj, in Umlauf befindlich (Kapital, Effekten); **~ assets** Umlaufvermögen n, flüssige Aktiva flüssige Mittel; **~ capital** Betriebskapital n, Umlaufkapital n, Betriebsmittel n pl; **~ charge** (GB) Höchstbetragshypothek f; **~ debt** schwebende Schuld, unfundierte Schuld, zinsvariabler Schuldtitel; **~ exchange rates** freie Wechselkurse, flexible Wechselkurse; **~ money** Geld (das infolge schlechter Geldmarktlage nicht gewinnbringend angelegt werden kann); **~ mortgage** Gesamthypothek f; **~ policy** gleitende Neuwertversicherung, Pauschalversicherung f; **~ rate bond** = **FRB** variabel verzinsliche Anleihe; **~ rate issue** Obligation mit variabler Verzinsung; **~ rate loan** zinsvariables Darlehen; **~ rate note (floater)** = **FRN** variabel verzinslicher Schuldschein; **~ rate risk** Zinsänderungsrisiko

floor n Börsensaal m, Parkett n (Börse), Mindestzinssatz m, Zinsuntergrenze f; **~ broker** auf eigene Rechnung arbeitender Makler; **~ trader** (US) Börsenmitglied (das für eigene Rechnung spekuliert), Eigenhändler m

floored floater zinsvariabler Schuldtitel mit einer Zinsuntergrenze

flop n Reinfall m, Pleite f

flotation n Gründung einer Gesellschaft, Auflegung f (einer Anleihe), Freigabe des Wechselkurses, Börseneinführung f, Emission f

flow back Rückfluß m (internationaler Aktien an die Heimatbörse); **~ of funds** Kapitalfluß m

fluctuation margin; band of permitted fluctuation Bandbreite f

fluctuations; business ~ Geschäftsschwankungen f pl, Konjunkturschwankungen f pl

fluid adj flüssig adj; **~ assets** (US) Umlaufvermögen n, flüssige Aktiva, flüssige Mittel; **~ capital** (US) Umlaufkapital n

flurry n (US) kurzfristige Belebung des Effektenmarktes

flux of money Geldumlauf m

fly-by-night n (US) Unternehmen von zweifelhafter Natur

fob = **free on board** alle Kosten bis zur Verladung der Ware eingeschlossen

follow-up issue Nachemission f

following adj nachfolgend adj, folgend adj

foods Aktien von Nahrungsmittelproduzenten

for deposit only nur zur Verrechnung

forbearance n Stundung f

force majeure höhere Gewalt

forced; ~ currency Zwangswährung f; **~ loan** Zwangsanleihe f; **~ rate of exchange** Zwangskurs m; **~ sale** Zwangsverkauf m, Zwangsversteigerung f; **~ sale of collaterals** zwangsweise Verwertung von Kreditsicherheiten f; **~ savings** Zwangssparen n; **~ selling** Zwangsverkauf m, Zwangsversteigerung f

forecast n Vorhersage f

forecaster n Konjunkturbeobachter m

forecasting n Geschäftsprognose f; **business ~** Konjunkturdiagnose f; **business ~ service** Nachrichtendienst für Wirtschaftsprognosen; **financial ~** Vorausschau (über die finanzielle Lage eines Unternehmens)

foreclosable kündbar, vollstreckbar adj

foreclose v für verfallen erklären; **~ a mortgage** Zwangsvollstreckung aus einer Hypothek betreiben

foreclosure proceedings Zwangsvollstreckungsverfahren n: **~ sale** Zwangsversteigerung f

foreign adj ausländisch adj, Auslands-; **~ assets** Auslandsaktiven f pl; **~ balances** Auslandsguthaben n; **~ bank** Auslandsbank f; **~ bank notes** ausländische Banknoten f pl; **~ bill** Auslandswechsel m, Wechsel in ausländischer

Währung; **~ bond issue** Auslandsanleihe f; **~ bonds** ausländische Obligationen; **~ business** Auslandsgeschäft n; **~ business corporation** im Ausland arbeitende Gesellschaft; **~ currency** Devisen f pl, Fremdwährung f, ausländische Währung; **~ currency account** Devisenkonto n; Währungskonto n, Valutakonto n; **~ currency allocation** Devisenzuteilung f; **~ currency clause** Währungsklausel f, Valutaklausel f; **~ currency debt** Fremdwährungsschuld f; **~ currency holdings** Devisenbestand m; **~ currency loan** Devisenkredit m; Fremdwährungsanleihe f; **~ currency reserve** Devisenbestand m; **~ currency reserves** Devisenreserven f pl; **~ department** Auslandsabteilung f; **~ DM-bond** DM-Auslandsanleihe f; **~ exchange** (US) Devisen f pl, Fremdwährung f, ausländische Währung; **~ exchange account** Währungskonto n, Valutakonto n; **~ exchange accounting** Währungsbuchhaltung f; **~ exchange accounting department** Währungsbuchhaltung f; **~ exchange balance** Valutensaldo m; **~ exchange broker** Devisenmakler m; **~ exchange business** Währungsgeschäft n, Devisengeschäft n, Devisenhandel m; **~ exchange (forex) control** Devisenkontrolle f; **~ exchange dealer** Devisenhändler m; **~ exchange (forex) dealings** Devisenhandel m; **~ exchange department** Devisenabteilung f; **~ exchange market** Devisenmarkt m; **~ exchange (forex) option** Devisenoption f; **~ exchange position** Devisenlage f, Devisenposition f; **~ exchange rate** Devisenkurs m, Umrechnungskurs m, Wechselkurs m, Umtauschkurs m; **~ exchange restrictions** Devisenbeschränkungen f pl; **~ exchanges** (GB) Devisen f pl, Fremdwährung f, ausländische Währung; **~ investment** Auslandsanlage f; **~ liabilities** Auslandspassiven f pl; **~ notes and coin** ausländische Banknoten und Münzen, Sorten f pl; **~ postal money order** Auslandspostanweisung f; **~ securities** Auslandswertpapiere n pl, Auslandswerte m pl; **~ security clearing association** Auslandskassenverein m; **~ shareholdings** Auslandsbeteiligungen f pl; **~ stock** Auslandswertpapiere n pl, Auslandswerte m pl; **~ trade** Außenhandel m; **~ trade bank** Außenhandelsbank f; **~ trade financing** Außenhandelsfinanzierung f, Export-und-Import-Finanzierung f; **~ transaction** Auslandsgeschäft n; **bill in ~ currency** Auslandswechsel m, Wechsel in ausländischer Währung; **blocked ~ exchange** eingefrorene Devisen, blockierte Devisen; **losses on ~ exchange** Devisenverluste m pl

foreigner n Ausländer m, Fremder m

forestaller n Aufkäufer m

forex = foreign exchange Devisen f pl, Devisenhandel m, Devisenmarkt m, Fremdwährung f, Geldwechsel m

forfaiting n Forfaitierung f, Ankauf von Forderungen; **~ company** Forfaitierungsgesellschaft f, Forderungskäufer m

forfeit v verwirken v, einbüßen v

forfeiture n Verwirkung f, Verlust m, Verfall m; **~ of shares** Kaduzierung von Aktien

forge v fälschen v (Geld, Wechsel), verfälschen v, nachdrucken v, nachahmen v, nachmachen v

forged adj gefälscht adj; **~ check** gefälschter Scheck; **~ transfer** gefälschte Überweisung

forger n Fälscher m, Verfälscher m; **bill ~** Wechselfälscher m

forgery n Fälschung f, Verfälschung f, Falsifikat n; **bill ~** Wechselfälschung f, Banknotenfälschung f

forgive v verzeihen v

form n Formular n, Formblatt n, Vordruck m; **~ n** Schema n; **~ a company** eine Gesellschaft gründen; **~ feeding track** Formularbahn f; **~ of application** Antragsformular n, Zeichnungsschein m; **~ of payment** Zahlungsweise f; **bill ~** Wechselvordruck m; **blank ~** Blankoformular n; **bookkeeping ~** Buchungsformular n; **credit ~** (US) Kreditformular n, Kreditantragsformular n, Kreditantrag m

formalities; customs - Zollformalitäten f pl
formation n Gründung f; **- of coverage capital** Kapitaldeckungsverfahren n
former adj früher adj, vorausgehend adj
forms lay-out Formulargestaltung f
fortnightly settlement Halbmonatsabrechnung f
fortune n Vermögen n
forward v expedieren v, absenden v, verschicken v, abschicken v, befördern v; - adv auf Zeit; **- cover** Kurssicherung durch Devisentermingeschäft; **- deal** Termingeschäft n, Zeitgeschäft n; **- dollar** Termindollar m; **- exchange** Termindevise f; **- exchange transactions** Devisenterminhandel m, Devisentermingeschäft n pl; **- interest rate** heute fixierter Zinssatz für ein zukünftiges Kreditgeschäft; **- market** Terminmarkt m; **- operation (transaction)** Termingeschäft n, Zeitgeschäft n; **- price** Terminpreis m, Terminnotierung f; **- rate agreement = FRA** Zinstermingeschäft ohne Einschußzahlung; **- rates** Terminsätze m pl; **- sale** Terminverkauf m; **- trading** Terminhandel m; **- transaction** Termingeschäft n, Zeitgeschäft n; **buy -** auf Lieferung kaufen; **carry -** v übertragen v (Buchführung), vortragen v
forwardation (contango) Kassakurs ist niedriger als Terminkurs
forwarder n Spediteur m
forwarder's receipt Spediteurempfangsschein m
forwarding agent Spediteur m
foundation n Basis f, Grundlage f; - n Stiftung f, Schenkung f, Fonds m; **- charter** Stiftungsurkunde f; **- of a business** Geschäftsgründung f; **- syndicate** Gründungskonsortium n; **company -** Firmengründung f, Gesellschaftsgründung f
founder n Stifter m, Gründer m
founders' preference rights Gründungsrechte n pl; **- shares** Gründungsaktien f pl
FRA = forward rate agreement Zinstermingeschäft n
fraction Börsenabschluß, der kleiner als marktüblich ist

fractional certificate Teilgutschein m; **- right** Bezugsrecht (das nicht zur Zeichnung einer neuen Aktie ausreicht)
franchise n Franchise f, Vorrecht n, Alleinverkaufsrecht n; - n (US) Konzession f
franchising Lizenzerteilung f
franchisor Franchise-Geber m
Frankfurt Interbank Offered Rate = FIBOR Frankfurter Interbanken-Angebotszinssatz; **- Stock Exchange** Frankfurter Wertpapierbörse f
fraud n Betrug m
fraudulent adj betrügerisch adj; **- bankruptcy** betrügerischer Bankrott
FRB = floating rate bond Anleihe mit variablem Zinssatz
free adj franko, frei adj, befreit adj; **- and clear** unbelastet, freiverfügbar adj; **- alongside ship (f a s)** frei bis zum Schiff; **- assets** frei verfügbare Vermögenswerte; **- balance** zinsloses Bankguthaben; **- capital ratio** Eigenkapital zur Bilanzsummenkennzahl; **- flow of capital** freier Kapitalverkehr; **- items** (US) spesenfreie Inkassi; **- market** freier Markt, offener Markt; **- movement of capital** freier Kapitalverkehr; **- of charge** spesenfrei, gebührenfrei; **- of stamp** börsenumsatzsteuerfrei adj; **- on board** (f.o.b.) frei an Bord; **- reserves** freie Reserven; **- surplus** freie Rücklagen
freehold n (GB) freier Grundbesitz, freies Grundeigentum; **customary -** Erbpachtgut n
freeholder n uneingeschränkter Eigentümer, freier Grundbesitzer
freely convertible frei konvertierbar; **- fluctuating exchange rates** freie Wechselkurse, flexible Wechselkurse
free-tier gold market freier Goldmarkt
freeze v blockieren v, sperren v
freight v (e.g. ship, plane) befrachten v; - n Fracht f, Frachtkosten pl t; **- bill** Frachtbrief m; **- collect** Fracht wird eingezogen; **- forward** Fracht gegen Nachnahme; **- forwarder** Spediteur m; **- paid**

freightage

frachtfrei, franko; *- prepaid* Lieferung ohne Spesen; *- rates* Frachttarif m; *air -* Luftfracht f; *bill of -* Frachtbrief m; *canal -* Kanalfracht f; *charge -* Fracht berechnen

freightage n Frachtkosten plt

freighter Spediteur m, Transportunternehmer m

freighting Frachtgeschäft n, Betrachtung f

French Franc Französischer Franke m

fresh issue Neuemission f

friend; business - Geschäftsfreund m, Korrespondent m

fringe banking Teilzahlungskreditgeschäft n; *- benefits* zusätzliche Leistungen, Leistungsanreize m pl (Pensionszusagen, Firmenwagen)

FRN = floating rate note variabel verzinslicher Schuldschein, Floater m

front running deals Vorgeschäfte n pl

front-end load Ausgabeaufschlag m

frozen adj eingefroren adj, blockiert adj; *- account* blockiertes Konto, eingefrorenes Konto, gesperrtes Konto, Sperrkonto n; *- assets* blockierte Guthaben; *- credit* eingefrorener Kredit; *- loan* eingefrorener Kredit

fulfill v erfüllen v, vollziehen v

fulfillment n Erfüllung f, Vollziehung f

full amount voller Betrag, Gesamtbetrag m; *- bill of lading* volles Konnossement; *- convertibility* unbeschränkte Konvertierbarkeit; *- endorsement* Vollindossament n, vollständiges Indossament; *- indorsement* Vollindossament n, vollständiges Indossament; *- legal tender coin* Kurantmünze f; *- liability* volle Haftung; *- payment* volle Bezahlung; *- service bank* Universalbank f; *- set* vollständiger Satz für ein Konnossement; *- settlement* vollständige Abrechnung

fully diluted earnings per share Ertrag je Aktie; *- funded* voll abgesichert, voll finanziert adj; *- integrated processing system* vollintegriertes Datenverarbeitungssystem; *- paid share* voll eingezahlte Aktie; *- paid-up capital* voll eingezahltes Kapital; *- paid-up share* voll eingezahlte Aktie; *- subscribed loan* vollständig gezeichnete Anleihe

fund v finanzieren v, refinanzieren v, umschulden v, konsolidieren v; *- n* Kapital n, Kapitalvermögen n, Geldsumme f, Fonds m, Anlagefonds m; *- for general banking risks* Fonds für allgemeine Bankrisiken; *- investing in an individual industry* Branchenfonds m; *- investing in an specific country* Länderfonds m; *- investing in environment protecting industries* Ökofonds m; *investment -* Investmentfonds m; *- management* Vermögensverwaltung f; *- of funds* Investmentfonds mit auswechselbarem Portefeuille; *- raising* Kapitalbeschaffung f; *amortization -* Tilgungsstock m; *benefit -* Versicherungsfonds auf Gegenseitigkeit, Wohltätigkeitsfonds m; *blended -* (GB) zur Versilberung bestimmter Nachlaß; *bond -* Obligationenfonds m, Pfandbrieffonds m; *bonus -* Dividendenfonds m; *capital -* Grundkapital n, Stammkapital n; *closed-end -* Investmentfonds mit geschlossenem Anlageportefeuille; *contingency -* außerordentlicher Reservefonds; *contingent -* (US) Sicherheitsrücklage f, Delkredererücksstellung f, Rückstellung für unvorhergesehene Ausgaben; *county -* Kommunalvermögen n; *cumulative -* thesaurierender Fonds; *depreciation -* Abschreibungsreserve f, Abschreibungsfonds m, Abschreibungsrücklage f; *disability -* Invaliditätsfonds m; *mutual -* Investmentgesellschaft mit offenem Anlageportefeuille; *offshore -* Investmenttrust in einem steuerbegünstigten Land; *open-end -* Investmentgesellschaft mit offenem Anlageportefeuille; *pension -* Pensionskasse f; *provident -* Fürsorgefonds m, Pensionsfonds m; *provident reserve -* Spezialreserve f, außerordentliche Reserve; *relief -* Unterstützungsfonds m, Hilfsfonds m, Unterstützungskasse f; *semi-fixed -* Investmentfonds mit begrenzt auswechselbarem Portefeuille; *sinking -* Amortisationsfonds m, Ablösungsfonds m

fundable adj kapitalisierbar adj

funded adj kapitalisiert adj, fundiert adj;
 ~ **debt** fundierte Schuld
funding bonds kurzfristige Verbindlichkeiten, die in eine neue Anleihe umgewandelt werden
funds n pl Gelder n pl, Kapital n, Mittel plt, Staatspapiere n pl (GB); **advance** ~ Vorschüsse zahlen, Mittel vorschießen; **allocation of** ~ Geldbewilligung f; **appropriation of** ~ Geldzuweisung f; **available** ~ liquide Mittel; **bank** ~ Bankkapital n; **covering** ~ Deckungsmittel n pl; **current** ~ Umlaufvermögen n, flüssige Aktiva, flüssige Mittel; **deposited** ~ Depositen plt, Einlagen f pl, Depositengelder n pl, Depositeneinlagen f pl; **displacement of** ~ anderweitige Kapitalverwendung; **disposable** ~ verfügbare Gelder; **employment of** ~ Kapitalverwendung f; **escrow** ~ beim Treuhänder hinterlegte Gelder; **fund of** ~ Dachgesellschaft f; **government** ~ Staatspapiere n pl; **public** ~ Staatsgelder n pl, öffentliche Gelder; **raise** ~ Geldmittel auftreiben; **unappropriated** ~ nicht verteilte Mittel; **unfreeze** ~ Guthaben freigeben
fungible adj fungibel adj, handelbar adj, vertretbar adj, austauschbar adj; ~ **securities** verwertbare Sicherheiten

furnish a guarantee Garantie leisten, Garantie übernehmen; ~ **a person with full power** jemanden mit Generalvollmacht ausstatten
furnished adj (with) versehen adj (mit)
further margin Nachschußzahlung f, zusätzliche Deckung
fuse v fusionieren v, verschmelzen v zusammenschließen v
fusion n Fusion f, Verschmelzung f
future cable rate (US) Kabelsatz für Devisenterminegeschäfte; ~ **delivery** Terminlieferung f; ~ **sale** Terminverkauf m; ~ **transaction** Termingeschäft m, Zeitgeschäft m
futures Futures m pl, börsengehandelte Termingeschäfte; ~ **call option** Kaufoption auf Terminkontrakte; ~ **contract** Termingeschäft n, Zeitgeschäft n; ~ **funds** Terminbörsenfonds; ~ **margin** Einschußzahlung auf Terminkontrakt; ~ **market** Terminmarkt m; ~ **option** Option auf Terminkontrakte
Futures & Options Exchange (FOX) Londoner Warenterminbörse f
futures put option Verkaufsoption auf einen Terminkontrakt; ~ **rate** (US) Kurs für Termingeschäfte; ~ **trading** Terminhandel m, Futureshandel m; **contract for** ~ Terminvertrag m

G

gain v gewinnen v, erwerben v, verdienen v; ~ n Gewinn m (Zuwachs), Vorteil m; ~ **of time** Zeitgewinn m; **clear** ~ Reingewinn m, Nettogewinn m

gains on securities Wertpapiergewinne f pl

gain-sharing Gewinnbeteiligung f

galloping inflation galoppierende Inflation

gap Lücke f; ~ **in the market** Marktlücke f

garnish v pfänden v (Forderung beim Drittschuldner), Zahlungsverbot erlassen

garnishee n Drittschuldner m

garnisher n Forderungsgläubiger m, Pfändungsgläubiger m, Pfandgläubiger m

garnishment n (US) Zahlungsverbot an den Drittschuldner, Lohn- oder Gehaltspfändungsbeschluß

GATT = General Agreement on Tariffs and Trade Allgemeine Zoll- und Handelsabkommen n

gearing n Fremdverschuldung f, Fremdkapitalanteil n; **equity** ~ Verhältnis: Fremdkapital/Eigenkapital

general adj General- (in Zus.), Gesamt- (in Zus.), generell adj, allgemeingültig adj; ~ **account** Hauptkonto n; ~ **accounting** Hauptbuchhaltung f; ~ **accounting department** Hauptbuchhaltung f

General Agreement to Borrow (GAB) Allgemeine Kreditvereinbarungen

general assembly Generalversammlung f; ~ **bookkeeper** Hauptbuchhalter m; ~ **conditions of the bank** Allgemeine Geschäftsbedingungen (AGB) einer Bank; ~ **covenant** allgemeine Abmachung; ~ **creditor** Gesamtgläubiger m; ~ **expenses** allgemeine Betriebsaufwendungen f; ~ **guarantee** unbeschränkte Garantie; ~ **ledger** Hauptbuch n; ~ **licence** Sammelausfuhrgenehmigung f; ~ **loan loss reserves** Pauschalwertberichtigung f; ~ **manager** Generaldirektor m; ~ **meeting** Generalversammlung f; ~ **mortgage** Gesamthypothek f; ~ **partner** unbeschränkt haftender Teilhaber; ~ **power** Generalvollmacht f

gentlemen's agreement auf gegenseitiges Vertrauen begründete Vereinbarung

genuine adj echt adj, unverfälscht adj, authentisch adj; ~ **signature** echte Unterschrift

geographic code Ortsschlüssel m

German Banking Act Deutsche Kreditwesengesetz n (KWG); ~ **bond market index** Deutsche Rentenindex m (REX); ~ **futures and options exchange** Deutsche Terminbörse f (DTB); ~ **Options and Financial Futures Exchange Ltd. = GOFFEX** Deutsche Terminbörse f (DTB); ~ **stock market index** Deutsche Aktienindex m (DAX)

Germany's official brokers information system Makler-Tele-Informationssystem n (MATIS)

gift n Schenkung f, Geschenk n; ~ **tax** Schenkungssteuer f

gilt-edged adj erstklassig adj (Wertpapiere, Kapitalanlagen); ~ **bills** erstklassige Wertpapiere; ~ **investment** mündelsichere Anlagepapiere, mündelsichere Wertpapiere, mündelsichere Papiere; ~ **securities** mündelsichere Anlagepapiere, mündelsichere Wertpapiere, mündelsichere Papiere

gilts (GB) mündelsichere britische Staatsanleihen

Ginnie Maes = Government National Mortgage Association (US) festverzinsliche, hypothekarisch gesicherte Wertpapiere

giro account Postscheckkonto n; ~ **system** bargeldloser Zahlungsverkehr m; ~ **transfer** Banküberweisung f, Postscheküberweisung f

give an order einen Auftrag erteilen

give-away n Gutschein m, Prämie f

giver of the rate Prämienzahler m; ~ **to the option** Optionsgeber m

giving way Nachgeben n (von Kursen)

glamour stocks Wachstumsaktie mit stark spekulativem Einschlag

gliding *bands* gleitende Bandbreiten; *- rates* Gleitzoll *m*

global *bill of lading* Sammelladungskonnossement *n*; *- certificate* Sammelzertifikat *n*; *- player* international operierendes Unternehmen; *- warrant* Sammeloptionsschein *m*

gloomy *adj* gedrückt *adj*, flau *adj*, mißgestimmt *adj*

go bankrupt Bankrott machen, Konkurs machen; *- beyond the limit* ein Limit überschreiten

go-between *n* Unterhändler *m*, Vermittler *m*

GOFFEX = German Options and Financial Futures Exchange Ltd. Deutsche Terminbörse *f* (DTB)

go-go fund Anlagefonds mit spekulativer Anlagepolitik

going *concern* gut gehendes Unternehmen; *concern value* Unternehmensverkehrswert *m*; *- price* Marktpreis *m*, Tageskurs *m*; *- public* Publikumsöffnung *f*, Börsengang eines Unternehmens; *- public warrant issue (option loan)* Going-Public-Optionsanleihe *f*, Anleihe mit Optionsrecht im Falle des Börsenganges des Emittenten

gold backing requirements Golddeckungsvorschriften *f pl*; *- bar* Goldbarren *m*; *- bonds* (US) Goldobligationen *f pl*; *- bullion standard* Goldwährung *f*; *- card* goldene Kreditkarte (für vermögende Privatkunden); *- clause* Goldklausel *f*; *- coin* Goldmünze *f*; Goldstück *n*; *- coverage* Golddeckung *f*; *- cover requirements* Golddeckungsvorschriften *f pl*; *- credit* Goldkredit *m*; *- exchange standard* Golddevisenwährung *f*; *- export point* oberer Goldpunkt; *- holdings* Goldbestand *m*; *- import point* unterer Goldpunkt; *- loan* Goldkredit *m*; *- libor* Interbankenangebotssatz für Gold in London; *- mine* *n* Goldmine *f*; *- option* Goldoption *f*; *- parity* Goldparität *f*; *- piece* Goldstück *n*; *- point* Goldpunkt *m*; *- reserves* Goldreserven *f pl*, Goldbestand *m*; *- standard* Goldstandard *m*, Goldwährung *f*; *- tranche* Goldtranche (IMF); *abandonment of the - standard* Aufgabe des Goldstandards; *base -* Gold von geringem Feingehalt; *pure -* Feingold *n*; *standard -* Feingold *n*; *sterling -* echtes Gold; *two-tier - system* gespaltener Goldpreis

Gold Pool Goldpool *m*

golden *parachute* (US) hohe Abfindungen für die Konzernleitung im Übernahmefall *f pl*; *- rule of banking* goldene Bankregel *f* (z. B. Deckungsgleichheit langfristiger Aktiva mit Passiva)

good *adj* kreditfähig *adj*, sicher *adj*; *- delivery* (stock exchange) gut lieferbar (Börse); *- faith taker* gutgläubiger Erwerber

goods *n pl* Waren *f pl*; bewegliches Vermögen, Güterladung *f*, Fracht *f*; *- in bond* unter Zollverschluß liegende Waren; *- movable* bewegliches Vermögen, Mobiliarvermögen *n*; *- on hand* Warenbestand *m*; *bonded -* Waren unter Zollverschluß; *bulky -* Sperrgut *n*; *capital -* Kapitalgüter *n pl*, Investitionsgüter *n pl*; *carted -* Rollgut *n*; *consumer -* Verbrauchsgüter *n pl*, Konsumgüter *n pl*; *credit in -* Warenkredit *m*; *distrained -* gepfändete Waren

goodwill *n* Firmenwert *m*, Geschäftswert *m*, Goodwill *m*

government bonds Staatspapiere *n pl*; *- deposits* (US) Einlagen der Regierung, Einlagen der öffentlichen Hand; *- funds* Staatspapiere *n pl*; *- loan* Staatsanleihe *f*; *- official* Regierungsbeamte *m*; *- securities* Staatspapiere *n pl*; *- sponsored* staatlich gefördert

grace *n* (period) Nachfrist *f*; *days of -* Respekttage *m pl*, Verzugstage *m pl*, Fristtage *m pl*

graduate *n* Akademiker *m*, Hochschulabgänger *m*; *- school of banking* (US) Bankakademie in den USA

graduated interest loan Schuldverschreibung mit gestaffeltem Zinssatz

graft *n* (US) Schmiergeld *n*, Bestechung *f*

grain bill auf Grund von Getreidelieferungen gezogener Wechsel

grand total Endsumme f

grant v erlauben v, gestatten v, gewähren v, zulassen v, bewilligen v, anrechnen v, einräumen v; ~ n Gewährung f, Bewilligung f, Zuschuß m, Subvention f, Beihilfe f, Stipendium n; ~ *a delay* eine Fristverlängerung zugestehen; ~ *a respite in payment* eine Zahlung stunden; *capital* ~ Kapitalzuschuß m

grantee Kreditnehmer m, Grundstückskäufer m

granting of credit Kreditgewährung

grantor n Kreditgeber m, Darlehensgeber m, Anleihegeber m, Ausleiher m, Verleiher m

gratuity n Gratifikation f, Abfindungssumme f

graveyard n Flaute f; ~ *market* Kurssturz m

Greek Drachme Griechische Drachme f

green card (GB) grüne Versicherungskarte, (US) Arbeitserlaubnis f; ~ *clause credit* Kreditvorschuß gegen dingliche Sicherheit; ~ *shoe* (option) Option der Emissionsbank auf höhere Zuteilung; ~ *warrants* Optionsschein auf einen Aktienkorb

greenback Dollar m (US)

greenbacks n pl (US) US-Banknoten f pl

greenmailing (US) Übernahmeabwehr durch Aktienrückkauf oder Abfindungszahlungen

grey market grauer Markt, inoffizieller Handel

gross amount Bruttobetrag m; ~ *earnings* Gesamteinkommen n; ~ *interest return* Bruttoverzinsung f; ~ *margin* Handelsspanne f, Bruttospanne f; ~ *plant* feste Anlagen; ~ *proceeds* Rohertrag m, Bruttoertrag m; ~ *profit* Bruttogewinn m, Rohgewinn m; ~ *property* feste Anlagen; ~ *sales* Bruttoumsatz m; ~ *gross spread* Bruttospanne f; ~ *working capital* Umlaufvermögen n; ~ *yield* Bruttorendite f

Gross National Product (G.N.P.) Bruttosozialprodukt n

ground; *building* ~ Bauplatz m

group Konzern m; ~ *balance sheet* Konzernbilanz f; ~ *banking* Filialbankwesen n; ~ *collection* Sammelinkasso n; ~ *discount* Mengenrabatt m; ~ *of banks* Bankenkonsortium n; ~ *of companies* Konzern m ~ *sales* Konzernumsatz m

Group of Ten Zehnerklub m

group; consolidated ~ Konzerngruppe f; **consumer** ~ Verbrauchergruppe f

grouping of shares Zusammenlegung von Aktien

growth stock Wachstumsaktie f; *capital* ~ Kapitalzuwachs m; *economic* ~ Wirtschaftswachstum n

guarantee v garantieren v, Bürgschaft leisten, Gewähr leisten, bürgen v; ~ n (GB) Garantie f, Bürgschaft f, Sicherheit f, Sicherstellung f, Gewährleistung f; ~ *agreement* Garantievertrag m; ~ *bank* Bürgschaftsbank f; ~ *coupon* Garantieschein m; ~ *credit* Avalkredit m, Kautionskredit m; ~ *deed* Bürgschaftsschein m, Bürgschaftsurkunde f; ~ *fund* Garantiefonds m; ~ *insurance* (GB) Kautionsversicherung f; ~ *of a bill of exchange* Aval n, Wechselbürgschaft f; ~ *with direct liability as co-debtor* selbstschuldnerische Bürgschaft; *banker's* ~ Bankgarantie f; *certificate of* ~ Garantieschein m; *company limited by* ~ (GB) Gesellschaft mit beschränkter Nachschußpflicht; *credit* ~ Kreditbürgschaft f; *furnish a* ~ Garantie leisten, Garantie übernehmen; *joint and several* ~ gesamtschuldnerische Bürgschaft; *stand* ~ *for* haften für

guaranteed bond garantierte Anleihe; ~ *letter of credit* garantiertes Akkreditiv, garantierter Kreditbrief; ~ *mortgage bond* Hypothekenpfandbrief m; ~ *stocks* Aktien mit garantierter Dividendenzahlung

guarantor n Bürger m, Bürgin f, Garant m, Gewährsmann m

guaranty n (US) Garantie f, Bürgschaft f, Sicherheit f, Sicherstellung f, Gewährleistung f; ~ *deposit* Garantiehinterlegung f; ~ *funds* Garantiefonds m pl, Garantiemittel n pl; ~ *of payment*

Zahlungsgarantie f; **- stock** Sicherheitshinterlegung von Aktien f; **- stock savings and loan association** Bausparkasse f; **bank -** (US) Bankgarantie f; **bill** - Wechselbürgschaft f; **continuing -** (US) Kreditbürgschaft f, Dauergarantie f; **contract of -** Bürgschaftsvertrag m; **declaration of -** Bürgschaftserklärung f; **letter of -** Garantiebrief m; **specific -** (US) Garantievertrag m;

guardian n Vormund m, Pfleger m

guardianship n Vormundschaft f, Pflegschaft f

guess n Schätzung f; **- estimate** grobe Schätzung

guide v führen v; - n Führer m, Ratgeber m

gun; beat the - (US) Aktien vor öffentlicher Auflegung zum Verkauf anbieten

gunning for stocks (US) Börsenmanöver der Baisse-Partei

gyrating exchange rates stark schwankende Wechselkurse

H

habit *survey* Untersuchung über Verbrauchergewohnheiten; *consumer* ~ Verbrauchergewohnheit f

haggler n Feilscher m, Schacherer m

haircut n Sicherheitsmarge f, Differenz zwischen Marktwert und Beleihungsgrenze

half-years figures Halbjahresbilanzzahlen f pl

halt v einstellen v, aussetzen v; ~ n Einstellung f, Stopp n (Börsenhandel)

hand *bill* Werbeprospekt m, Reklamezettel m, Handzettel m; ~ *notes* entwertete Banknoten; *collection by* ~ (US) Selbstabholung f, Inkasso durch Boten

handbook n Leitfaden m, Handbuch n, Führer m

handicraft n Handwerk n

handle v behandeln v, erledigen v

handling charges Bearbeitungsgebühren f pl

Hang Seng Index Index der Börse in Hongkong

hard *cash* (US) Hartgeld n; ~ *currency* Hartwährung f; ~ *currency countries* Hartwährungsländer f pl; ~ *money* Hartgeld n; ~ *prices* feste Kurse

harden v fester werden, (sich) versteifen v

hardening of prices das Anziehen der Preise

haulage n Transportkosten plt (Straßenverkehr); ~ *business* Straßengüterverkehr m; ~ *trade* Speditionsgewerbe n

haven n Zufluchtsort m; *tax* ~ Steueroase f

head *of department* Abteilungsleiter m; ~ *office* Hauptgeschäftssitz m; Zentrale f; ~ *teller* Hauptkassierer m

headhunter n Headhunter m, Talentsucher m

head-hunting Personalabwerbung f, Kopfjäger m

hearing n Anhörung f, Verhandlung f, gerichtlicher Termin

heaven and hell bond (informal) Doppelwährungsanleihe f

heavily-traded lebhaft gehandelt

heavy *drop in prices* Kurseinbruch m; ~ *industrials* Aktien der Schwerindustrie; ~ *market* gedrückter Markt

hedge n Deckungsgeschäft n, Sicherungsgeschäft n; ~ *against inflation* Inflationsschutz m; ~ *against price risks* Kurssicherung von Wertpapieren

hedging n Kurssicherungsgeschäft f, Abschluß von Deckungsgeschäften, Hedgegeschäft n, Absicherung f

heir n Erbe m; *beneficiary* ~ auf das Nachlaßverzeichnis beschränkter Erbe

hereditary adj erblich adj

heritable adj erbfähig adj

heritage n Erbschaft f, Nachlaß m, Hinterlassenschaft f

HIBOR = Hongkong Interbank Offered Rate Hongkonger Interbanken-Angebotszinssatz

hidden *assets* stille Reserven; ~ *reserves* stille Reserven

high Höchstkurs m; ~ *finance* (US) Hochfinanz f; ~ *flyers* von der Börse stark favorisierte Aktien; ~ *interest rate policy* Hochzinspolitik f; ~ *quotation* (stocks) Höchstkurs m; ~ *rate* (money) Höchstkurs m; ~ *shares* schwere Papiere; ~ *yielders* hochverzinsliche Wertpapiere

high-coupon loan hochverzinsliche Anleihe; ~ *securities* hochverzinsliche Wertpapiere

higher bid höheres Gebot

highest *bid* Meistgebot n, Höchstgebot n; ~ *bidder* Meistbietender m; ~ *level* Höchststand m

high-grade investments erstklassige Kapitalanlagen

high-priced securities schwere Wertpapiere

high-return on capital hohe Kapitalverzinsung

high-tech companies High-Tech-Unternehmen, Hochtechnologiewerte m pl

hike in interest rates Zinserhöhung f

hint *n* Börsentip *m*, Ratschlag *m*, vertrauliche Information

hire *n* Mieten *n*, Leihen *n*; *- v* mieten *v*, vermieten *v*, einstellen *v*; *- and fire* einstellen und entlassen

hire agreement Teilzahlungsvertrag *m*, Ratenkreditvertrag *m*; *- finance house* Teilzahlungskreditinstitut *n*; *- loan* Teilzahlungskredit *m*, Ratenkredit *m*

hire-purchase Teilzahlungsgeschäft *n*, Ratenkredit *m*

hoard *v* horten *v*

hoarding *n* Thesaurierung *f*; *- purchase* Hortungskauf *m*

hock *v* verpfänden *v*, versetzen *v*

hold *v* besitzen *v*, innehaben *v*; *- in pledge* als Pfand unterhalten; *- overs* (US) infolge von Formfehler nicht einlösbare Papiere (Schecks, Wechsel usw.)

holder *n* Inhaber *m*, Besitzer *m*; *- in due course* gutgläubiger Besitzer, gutgläubiger Inhaber; *- on trust* Treuhänder *m*; *account -* Kontoinhaber *m*; *bill -* Wechselinhaber *m*; *bona fide -* gutgläubiger Besitzer, gutgläubiger Inhaber; *bond -* Obligationeninhaber *m*, Pfandbriefgläubiger *m*, Pfandbriefinhaber *m*; *coupon -* Kuponinhaber *m*; *debenture -* Obligationeninhaber *m*; *policy -* Versicherungsnehmer *m*, Policeninhaber *m*; *title -* Eigentümer *m*

holding *n* Holding *f*, Besitz *m*, Bestand *m*, Aktienbesitz *m*; *- charge* Depotgebühr *f*; *- company* Holdinggesellschaft *f*, Dachgesellschaft *f*; *- gains* Wertzuwachs *m* (Wertpapiere); *- of securities* Wertpapierbestand *m*; *- period* Sperrfrist *f*; *- the market* (US) Marktstützung *f*

holdings *n pl* Besitz *m* (Wertpapiere, Land); *bill -* Wechselportefeuille *n*, Wechselbestand *m*; *bond -* Obligationenbesitz *m*, Pfandbriefbesitz *m*

holiday on interest and capital repayments zins- und tilgungsfreie Jahre

hologram *n* Hologramm *n*, dreidimensionales Bild zur Sicherung einer Service-Karte

home improvement loan Modernisierungsdarlehen *n*; *- loan* Wohnungsbaudarlehen *n*; *- market* Inlandsmarkt *m*; *- securities* Inlandswerte *f pl*

home-banking Home-Banking *n*, Abwicklung von Bankgeschäften über Datennetze

home-country control Kontrolle durch das Heimatland

homecroft *n* (GB) Heimstätte *f*, Arbeitersiedlung *f*

homecrofter *n* (GB) Heimstättenbesitzer *m*

homeowner *n* (US) Eigenheimbesitzer *m*

homestead *n* (US) Eigenheim *n*; *- association* Bausparkasse *f*

home-trade bill Inlandswechsel *m*

Hongkong Interbank Offered Rate = HIBOR Hongkonger Interbanken-Angebotszinssatz

honor *v* (US) einlösen *v* (z. B. einen Scheck oder einen Wechsel), annehmen *v*, honorieren *v*; *- a bill* einen Wechsel einlösen, einen Wechsel honorieren

honorarium *n* Honorar *n*

honour *v* (GB) einlösen *v* (z. B. einen Scheck oder einen Wechsel), annehmen *v*, honorieren *v*; *acceptor for -* Ehrenakzeptant *m*; *act of -* Ehreneintritt *m*, Intervention *f*

horizontal merger horizontale Fusion

hostile takeover feindliche Übernahme

hot card heiße (gestohlene) Kreditkarte; *- issues* heiße Aktien; *- money* spekulatives Geld, heißes Geld

hotel financing Hotelfinanzierung *f*

hours of business Geschäftszeit *f*; *banking -* Schalterstunden *f pl*; *business -* Geschäftszeit *f*

house bills auf die eigene Geschäftsstelle gezogene Wechsel; *acceptance -* Akzeptbank *f*; *accepting -* Akzeptbank *f*; *bond -* Pfandbriefinstitut *n*; *brokerage -* Maklerfirma *f*

House; The - (London) Londoner Börse *f*

house-building financing Wohnungsbaufinanzierung *f*; *- loan* Wohnungsbaukredit *m*

housekeeping; corporate - activities gesellschaftlicher Finanzhaushalt

housing loan Wohnungsbaudarlehen n
hunter; *bargain* - Börsenspekulant m
hunting; *bargain* - Effektenspekulation f
hurdle rate Mindestertragsrate eines Projektes
hyperinflation Hyperinflation f, rasende Inflation

hypothecary adj hypothekarisch adj;
   - ***value*** Beleihbarkeit f, Lombardwert m
hypothecate v hypothekarisch belasten, verpfänden v, mit einer Hypothek belasten, dinglich belasten
hypothecation n Verpfändung f, Beleihung f, Lombardierung f; - ***value*** Beleihungswert m

I

IBRD = International Bank for Reconstruction and Development (World Bank) Weltbank f
identification card Pesonalausweis m, Ausweiskarte f; **~ papers** Personalausweis m, Ausweiskarte f
identity n Identität f; **~ card** Personalausweis m, Ausweiskarte f; **prove one's ~** (sich) legitimieren v
idle capital totes Kapital, brachliegendes Kapital; **~ money** freies Kapital, nicht angelegtes Kapital
ill advised schlecht beraten
illegal adj ungesetzlich adj, unrechtmäßig adj, gesetzwidrig adj, rechtswidrig adj, widerrechtlich adj; **~ interest** ungesetzlicher Zins, Wucherzinsen m pl; **~ trade** Schmuggel m, Schleichhandel m
illicit adj verboten adj
illiquid adj illiquide adj, nicht flüssig
illiquidity Illiquidität f; Zahlungsunfähigkeit f
image n Bild n (eines Unternehmens in der Öffentlichkeit)
IMF = International Monetary Fund Internationale Weltwährungsfonds m (IWF)
imitate v nachmachen v
imitated adj nachgemacht adj (imitiert)
immediate access Sofortzugriff m (EDV); **~ annuity** sofort fällige Rente
immigrate v einwandern v
immigration n Einwanderung f
immobilization of capital Kapitalfestlegung f
immobilize v aus dem Verkehr ziehen
immovable property Immobilien plt, unbewegliches Vermögen
immovables n pl Immobilien plt, unbewegliches Vermögen
impact n Wirkung f, Auswirkung f; **~ v** beeinflussen v
impair v kürzen v, einschränken v, schmälern v, vermindern v
impeachment of waste Mängelklage f, Haftung für Schäden aus Mietgegenstand

impecuniosity n Geldmangel m, Mittellosigkeit f
impecunious adj mittellos adj, unvermögend adj, verarmt adj
impersonal account Sachkonto n
import v importieren v, einführen v; **~ n** Import m, Einfuhr f; **~ certificate** Einfuhrschein m; **~ credit** Importkredit m, Einfuhrkredit m; **~ cuts** Einfuhrbeschränkungen f pl, Importbeschränkungen f pl; **~ deposit** (GB) Einfuhrabgabe f; **~ duty** Einfuhrzoll m, Einfuhrabgabe f; **~ excise tax** (US) Einfuhrsteuer f, Einfuhrverbrauchsabgabe f; **~ letter of credit** Einfuhrkreditbrief m; **~ licence** Einfuhrerlaubnis f, Einfuhrlizenz f; **~ permit** Einfuhrerlaubnis f, Einfuhrlizenz f; **~ restrictions** Einfuhrbeschränkungen f pl, Importbeschränkungen f pl; **~ surplus** Einfuhrüberschuß m; **~ tariff** Einfuhrzoll m, Einfuhrabgabe f; **~ trade** Importhandel m, Importgeschäft n, Einfuhrhandel m, Einfuhrgeschäft n; **articles of ~** Importware f
importance n Wichtigkeit f
importation n Import m, Einfuhr f
importer n Importeur m
imports n pl Importartikel m pl, Einfuhrwaren f pl; **declaration of ~** Einfuhrerklärung f; **decontrol of ~** Einfuhrliberalisierung f
impose v erheben v, belegen mit, verhängen v, auferlegen v
impost n Abgabe f, Steuer f
impound v beschlagnahmen, pfänden v
imprest Vorschuß m, Darlehen n; **~ fund** Sonderfonds m, Spesenkasse f
improve v verbessern v, bessern v, (sich) im Kurs steigen
improvement bonds (US) Kommunalanleihen f plt (die der Verbesserung öffentlicher Anlagen dienen)
impulse purchase Spontankauf m, Impulskauf m
imputation system of taxation steuerliches Anrechnungsverfahren

inaccuracy

inaccuracy n (e.g. of a translation) Ungenauigkeit f (z. B. einer Übersetzung)
inactive accounts unbewegte Kosten (kurze Zeit); **- funds** zinslose Gelder; **- market** lustlose Börse
inadequate collateral unzureichende Sicherheit
incalculability n Unberechenbarkeit f
incalculable adj unberechenbar adj
incapacitation n Entmündigung f
incapacity to contract Geschäftsunfähigkeit f
incentive n Anreiz m; **- fee** Erfolgshonorar n; **- payment** Gratifikation f, Erfolgsprämie f
inchoate bill (GB) nicht vollständig ausgefüllter Wechsel; **- check** (US) nicht vollständig ausgefüllter Scheck; **- cheque** (GB) nicht vollständig ausgefüllter Scheck; **- instrument** Blankoakzept n
incidental expenses Nebenkosten plt
in-clearer n (GB) Bankbevollmächtigter im Clearinghaus
include v einschließen v, einbeziehen v
inclusive adj einschließlich adj; **- sum** Pauschale f, Gesamtgebühr f
income n Einkommen n, Ertrag m, Einkünfte f pl; **- account** Ertragskonto n; **- bonds** (US) Gewinnschuldverschreibung f pl; **- bracket** Einkommensstufe f; **- debentures** Obligationen mit Gewinnbeteiligung; **- engineering** (US) Aufstellung des Budgets; **- from investments** Ergebnis aus Beteiligungen; **- from profit pooling** Erträge aus Gewinngemeinschaften; **- from revaluations of investments** Erträge aus der Zuschreibung von Beteiligungen; **- from the writing back of special items with partial reserve character** Erträge aus der Auflösung von Sonderposten mit Rücklageanteil; **- fund** Investmentfonds mit hoher Ausschüttung; **- return** (US) Rendite f; **- statement** (US) Erfolgsrechnung f, Gewinn-und-Verlust-Rechnung f, Erträgnisaufstellung f, Ertragsrechnung f; **- sum** Pauschale f, Gesamtgebühr f; **- tax** Einkommensteuer f; **- tax return** (GB) Einkommensteuererklärung f; **- tax statement** (US) Einkommensteuererklärung f; **- taxes** Steuern vom Einkommen und Ertrag; **accrued -** antizipative Posten (auf der Aktivseite), Rechnungsabgrenzungsposten m pl; **adjustment - bond** (US) Schuldverschreibung mit Zinsen auf Einkommensbasis; **amount of -** Einkommensbetrag m; **annual -** Jahreseinkommen n; **business -** Geschäftseinkommen n; **declaration of -** Einkommensteuererklärung f; **deferred -** transitorische Posten (auf der Passivseite), Rechnungsabgrenzungsposten m pl; **extraordinary -** Sondererträge m pl; **fixed -** festes Einkommen; **net -** Nettoeinkommen n, Reinertrag m; **other -** sonstige Erträge; **property -** Einkommen aus Grundbesitz; **rent -** Mieteinkommen n, Pachteinkommen n; **retained -** zurückbehaltenes Einkommen, Gewinnrücklage f; **settled -** festes Einkommen; **taxable -** steuerpflichtes Einkommen; **unappropriated -** nicht vorkalkulierter Ertragsüberschuß
incoming exchanges (US) Schecks (die bei einer Bank von einer Clearingstelle eingehen); **- orders** Auftragseingang m
incompetent adj geschäftsunfähig adj
inconvertible adj nicht einlösbar, nicht konvertierbar
incorporate v eingliedern v, verbinden v, integrieren v; **- adj** amtlich eingetragen
Incorporated (Inc) adj als Gesellschaft amtlich eingetragen
incorporated bank Aktienbank f; **- company** Aktiengesellschaft f
incorporation n amtliche Eintragung einer Gesellschaft; **certificate of -** Urkunde über die Eintragung in das Handelsregister
incorporator Gründer m, Gründungsmitglied n
Incoterms = International Commercial Terms Internationale Handelsbedingungen (Incoterms)
increase v erhöhen v, zunehmen v, aufschlagen v; **- n** Zugang m (Bilanz); **- in the bank rate** Diskonterhöhung f; **- in the discount rate** Diskonterhöhung f; **- of capital** Kapitalerhöhung f; **- of value**

Wertsteigerung f; *- the original capital by ...* das Grundkapital um ... erhöhen; *capital -* Kapitalerhöhung f
increment value Wertzuwachs m
incumbrance n Hypothekenbelastung f, Belastung f, Last f, Grundpfandrecht n
incur *liabilities* Verpflichtungen übernehmen; *- losses* Verluste erleiden
indebted *adj* verschuldet *adj*
indebtedness n Schuld f, Verschuldung f; *bond of -* Schuldschein m, Schuldanerkennung f; *bonded -* Anleiheschuldenlast f; *certificate of -* (US) Schuldschein m, Schatzanweisung f
indemnification n Schadenersatz m, Entschädigung f, Abfindung f, Ausgleich m
indemnify v entschädigen v, schadlos halten
indemnitee n Entschädigungsempfänger m, Entschädigungsnehmer m
indemnitor n Entschädiger m
indemnity n Schadenersatz m, Entschädigung f; *- benefits* Entschädigungsgewinn m, Entschädigungsvorteil m; *- bond* Garantie auf Schadloshaltung; *- contract* Entschädigungsvertrag m; *- insurance* Schadenersatzversicherung f; *bond of -* (US) Ausfallbürgschaft f, schriftliche Garantieerklärung, Schadenersatzerklärung f; *contract of -* Garantievertrag m
indenture n Anleihevertrag m, Verpfändungsurkunde f, Hypothekenurkunde f, Vertragsurkunde f; *- of assumption* Übernahmevertrag m; *bond -* Schuldverschreibungsurkunde f; *under an -* auf Grund eines Vertrages
indeterminate bonds (US) Anleihen ohne bestimmtes Fälligkeitsdatum
index n Index m, Sachregister n, Namensverzeichnis n; *- arbitrage* Indexarbitrage f; *- clause* Indexklausel f, Gleitklausel f; *- fund* Indexfonds m; *- futures* Indexfutures m pl; *- of number of securities* Effektenindex m; *maturity -* Verfallbuch n; *purchasing power -* Kaufkraftindex m
indexation n Indexbindung f, Indexierung f
indexational lease deed indexierter Mietvertrag

indexed *bond (loan)* indexgebundene Anleihe; *- currency option note (ICON)* Euroanleihe mit Bindung an den Index der Anleihenwährung
index-linked bond issue (indexed b.) Indexanleihe f
index-linked guarantee Indexgarantie f
indigence n Vermögenslosigkeit f, Armut f
indigent *adj* bedürftig *adj*, arm *adj*
indirect *business tax* indirekte Steuer f; *- cost* Gemeinkosten *pl t*
individual n natürliche Person; *- banker* (US) Privatbank f, Privatbankier m; *- deposits* (US) Einlagen bei Banken von Privatpersonen und Firmen; *- income* persönliches Einkommen; *- loan* Personaldarlehen n; *- property* Privatvermögen n
indorsable *adj* indossierbar *adj*, girierbar *adj*, begebbar *adj*, indossabel *adj*
indorsation n Indossament n, Indossierung f, Giro m, Bestätigung f
indorse v indossieren v, girieren v, begeben v, bestätigen v, mit Giro versehen, durch Indossament übertragen
indorsed *adj* giriert *adj*, mit Giro versehen, mit einem Indossament versehen; *- bond* durch Wechsel garantierte Schuldverschreibung, durch einen weiteren Verpflichteten garantierte Schuldverschreibung; *- in blank* blanko giriert
indorsee n Indossatar m, Indossat m, Girat m, Giratar m
indorsement n Indossament n, Indossierung f, Giro n, Bestätigung f; *- in blank* Blankoindossament n, Blankogiro n; *- required* Fehlen eines Indossaments; *- without recourse* Indossament ohne Verbindlichkeit; *special -* Vollgiro n, volles Wechselgiro, ausgefülltes Giro; *transfer by means of -* Übertragung durch Giro
indorser n Indossant m, Girant m, Wechselbürge m, Begebender m
indorser's liability Wechselhaftung f
inducement to invest Investitionsanreiz m
industrial *adj* industriell *adj*, gewerblich *adj*; *- n* Gewerbetreibender, Industrieller m; *- accident* Betriebsunfall m,

industrialist

Fabrikunfall m; **- association** Industrieverband m; **- bank** Industriebank f, Gewerbebank f; **- bill** Industrieakzept n; **- bonds** Industrieanleihe m pl, Industrieobligationen f pl; **- capacity** Industriekapazität f; **- capital** Industriekapital n, Gewerbekapital n; **- centre** Industriezentrum n; **- collateral** (US) Sicherheit durch Hinterlegung von Industrieaktien; **- combination** Industriekonzern m; **- company** Industrieunternehmen n; **- concern** Industrieunternehmen n; **- country** Industriestaat m; **- development** Industrieentwicklung f; **- enterprise** Industrieunternehmen n; **- equipment** Betriebsausrüstung f; **- growth** Wachstum der Industrie; **- income** gewerbliches Einkommen; **- investment** Vermögensanlage an Industriewerten; **- issues** Industrieemissionen f pl; **- loan** Industriekredit m; **- loan company** gewerbliche Kreditgenossenschaft; **- management** Betriebsführung f; **- output** Industrieproduktion f; **- production** Industrieproduktion f; **- prosit** Betriebsgewinn m, gewerblicher Gewinn; **- relations** Arbeitgeber-Arbeitnehmerverhältnis n; **- revenue bond = IRB** (US) US-bundesstaatliche Anleiheemission für Industrieunternehmen; **- risk** Branchenrisiko n; **- savings** Betriebssparen n, Werkssparen n; **- securities** Industriepapiere n pl, Industriewerte m pl; **- shares** Industriepapiere n pl, Industriewerte m pl; **- state** Industriestaat m; **- stocks** Industriepapiere n pl, Industriewerte m pl; **- trust** (US) Finanzierungsgesellschaft für Industriebedarf; **- undertaking** Industrieunternehmen n; **- wealth** Industrievermögen n; **- worker** Fabrikarbeiter m

industrialist n Industrieller m

industrialization n Industrialisierung f

industrialize v industrialisieren v

industrials n pl Industriepapiere n pl, Industriewerte m pl

industries; allied - verwandte Industrien

industry n Industrie f, Gewerbe n, Industriezweig m; **armament** - Rüstungsindustrie f; **basic** - Grundstoffindustrie f

inefficiency n Wirkungslosigkeit f

inefficient adj wirkungslos adj

ineligible paper (US) nicht diskontfähiges Wertpapier

infant n Minderjähriger m, Unmündiger m

inflate v aufblähen v

inflation n Inflation f, Geldentwertung f; **- boom** inflationistische Konjunktur; **- danger** Inflationsgefahr f; **- peril** Inflationsgefahr f

inflationary adj inflationistisch adj; **- period** Inflationszeit f; **- rate** Inflationsrate f

inflow of foreign currency Devisenzufluß m; **- of orders** Auftragseingang m

influence; cyclical - Konjunktureinfluß m

influx of capital Kapitalzufluß m

inform v informieren v, mitteilen v, unterrichten v (in Kenntnis setzen), benachrichtigen v

informal adj formlos adj

informality n Formlosigkeit f

informatic network Informatiknetzwerk n

information n Information f, Auskunft f, Nachricht f, Benachrichtigung f; **- bureau** Auskunftsbüro n; **- content** Informationsgehalt m; **- flow** Informationsfluß m; **- volume** Informationsvolumen n; **credit -** Kreditauskunft f

infringe v übertreten v, verstoßen v, verletzen v (Vertrag)

infringement n Verstoß m, Verletzung f

ingot n Barren m

inherit v erben v

inheritable adj erblich adj

inheritance n Erbschaft f, Nachlaß m, Hinterlassenschaft f, Erbe n; **- tax** (US) Erbschaftsteuer f, Nachlaßsteuer f; **claim to -** Erbberechtigung f, Erbschaftsanspruch m; **law of -** Erbrecht n; **right of -** Erbberechtigung f, Erbschaftsanspruch m

inherited adj ererbt adj

inheritor n Erbe m

inheritress n Erbin f

initial capital Anfangskapital n, Anschaffungskapital n; **- cost** Anschaffungspreis m, Anlaufkosten p/t; **- dividend**

(GB) Abschlagsdividende f (erste); *~ margin* Sicherheitsmarge f (S. bei Eröffnung einer Terminposition); *~ offering price* Erstausgabepreis m; *~ parity* Anfangsparität f (IMF); *~ public offering = IPO* (US) erstmaliges Zeichnungsangebot von Stammaktien (US)

initialed check Scheck mit geprüfter Unterschrift

initiative n Initiative f (z. B. vom Datenplatz aus); *business ~* unternehmerische Initiative

injunction n richterliche Verfügung

inland n Inland n, Binnenland n; *~ bill* Inlandswechsel m; *~ revenue office* (GB) Finanzamt n, Steueramt n; *~ waterway* Binnenschiffahrtsweg m

inner reserves stille Reserven

inofficial dealings Freiverkehr m; *~ market* Freiverkehrsbörse f, Freibörse f, Freiverkehrsmarkt m, Nachbörse f

inoperative account umsatzloses Konto, unbewegtes Konto, totes Konto

inopportune adj unangebracht adj, unzeitgemäß adj

input error Eingabefehler m (EDV)

inquire v nachfragen v, (sich) erkundigen v

inquiry n Nachforschung f, Nachfrage f, Erhebung f (Umfrage), Erkundigung f, Anfrage f; *~ facilities* Abfragemöglichkeit f; *~ terminal* Abfragestation f; *bank ~* Bankauskunft f; *credit ~ agency* Handelsauskunftei f

ins and outs of a matter alle Einzelheiten einer Sache

insane adj geisteskrank adj, geistesgestört adj

insanity n Geisteskrankheit f

inscribed adj eingetragen adj, registriert adj, auf den Namen lautend; *~ stock* (GB) Namensaktie f

inside betriebsintern, innen; *~ n* Innen n; *~ broker* (GB) amtlich zugelassener Makler; *~ information* Informationen f pl (über ein Unternehmen, die nur einem begrenzten Personenkreis zugänglich sind)

insider Insider m (Mitarbeiter eines Unternehmens der über interne, vertrauliche Informationen verfügt); *~ trading* Insiderhandel m

insiders n pl eingeweihte Kreise

insolvency n Insolvenz f, Zahlungsunfähigkeit f, Zahlungseinstellung f; *declaration of ~* Vergleichsmeldung f

insolvent n Zahlungsunfähiger m; *~ adj* insolvent adj, zahlungsunfähig adj

inspect v besichtigen v, beaufsichtigen v, kontrollieren v

inspection n Prüfung f, Kontrolle f, Untersuchung f, Inspektion f, Beaufsichtigung f, Aufsicht f

inspector; bank ~ Bankrevisor m; *customs ~* Zollaufseher m

instalment n Rate f, Ratenzahlung f, Abschlagszahlung f, Abzahlung f, Teilzahlung f; *~ bonds* serienweise rückzahlbare Obligationen; *~ business* Abzahlungsgeschäft n, Ratenzahlungsgeschäft n, Teilzahlungsgeschäft n; *~ buying* Abzahlungsgeschäft n, Ratenzahlungsgeschäft n, Teilzahlungsgeschäft n; *~ credit* Abzahlungskredit m, Teilzahlungskredit m; *~ lending business* Abzahlungsgeschäft n, Ratenzahlungsgeschäft n, Teilzahlungsgeschäft n; *~ loan* Ratenkredit m; *~ mortgage* Amortisationshypothek f; *~ plan* Teilzahlungssystem n; *~ sale* Teilzahlungsverkauf m; *~ transaction* Abzahlungsgeschäft n, Ratenzahlungsgeschäft n, Teilzahlungsgeschäft n; *amortization ~* Amortisationsquote f; *annual ~* Jahresrate f

institute v einsetzen v, einleiten v

Institute of Bankers (GB) Bankiersvereinigung

institution n Anstalt f, Institut n, Einrichtung f, Stiftung f; *banking ~* Bankinstitut n; *credit ~* Kreditinstitut n, Kreditanstalt f

institutional investor Kapitalsammelstelle f, institutioneller Kapitalanleger (der große Summen fremder Mittel anzulegen hat)

instruct v anweisen v, beauftragen v, unterweisen v, unterrichten v (instruieren)

instruction n Anordnung f, Instruktion f, Unterweisung f, Vorschrift f, Weisung f, Anweisung f

instructions; disregard ~ gegen Weisung handeln

instrument n Dokument n, Urkunde f, Schriftstück n; **~ of acceptance** Annahmeurkunde f; **~ of assignment** Zessionsurkunde f; **~ payable to bearer** Inhaberpapier n; **~ payable to order** Orderpapier n; **bearer ~** Inhaberpapier n; **credit ~** Kreditmittel n; **fictitious ~** gefälschte Urkunde; **quasi-negotiable ~** quasi begebbares Wertpapier, quasi übertragbares Wertpapier; **trust ~** Treuhandvertrag m, Sicherungsübereignung f

instruments; negotiable ~ verkäufliche Wertpapiere

insurability n Versicherungsfähigkeit f

insurable adj versicherungsfähig adj, versicherbar adj; **~ interest** versicherbarer Zins; **~ risk** versicherbares Risiko; **~ value** versicherbarer Wert

insurance n Versicherung f, Assekuranz f; **~ against loss by redemption** Kursverlustversicherung f; **~ agency** Versicherungsagentur f; **~ bank** Versicherungsanstalt f; **~ benefit** Versicherungsleistung f; **~ branch** Versicherungszweig m; **~ broker** Versicherungsmakler m; **~ company** Versicherungsgesellschaft f; **~ corporation** (US) Versicherungsgesellschaft f; **~ coverage** Versicherungsschutz m; **~ draft** (US) Versicherungswechsel m; **~ expert** Versicherungsfachmann m; **~ fee** Versicherungsgebühr f; **~ fund** Versicherungsfonds m; **~ of value** Valorenversicherung f, Wertsendungsversicherung f; **~ option** Kapital- oder Rentenzahlung nach Wahl (Versicherung); **~ policy** Versicherungspolice f; **~ premium** Versicherungsprämie f; **accident ~** Unfallversicherung f; **additional ~** Nachversicherung f; **bank burglary ~** Bankeinbruchversicherung f; **bank deposit ~** Einlagenversicherung f, Depositenversicherung f; **beneficiary of ~** Versicherungsberechtigte f u. m; **burglary ~** Einbruchversicherung f; **business interruption ~** Betriebsunterbrechungsversicherung f; **business life ~** Teilhaberversicherung f; **cargo ~** Frachtversicherung f, Güterversicherung f; **casualty ~** Schadenversicherung f; **certificate of ~** Versicherungsschein m, Police f; **civil commotion ~** Aufruhrversicherung f; **collective ~** Gruppenversicherung f; **commercial ~** Garantieversicherung f; **credit ~** Kreditversicherung f; **deposit ~** Einlagenversicherung f, Depositenversicherung f; **disability ~** Invalidenversicherung f; **endowment ~ policy** Aussteuerversicherungspolice f; **export credit ~** Ausfuhrkreditversicherung f; **fidelity ~** Veruntreuungsversicherung f, Unterschlagungsversicherung f; **fire ~** Feuerversicherung f; **guarantee ~** (GB) Kautionsversicherung f; **indemnity ~** Schadenersatzversicherung f; **legal liability ~** Haftpflichtversicherung f (gesetzlich); **life ~** Lebensversicherung f; **loan ~** Kreditversicherung f; **marine ~** Seeschadenstransportversicherung f, Seeversicherung f; **participating ~** Versicherung mit Gewinnbeteiligung; **partnership ~** Teilhaberversicherung f; **sea ~** Seeschadenstransportversicherung f, Seeversicherung f; **social ~** Sozialversicherung f; **theft ~** Diebstahlversicherung f; **third party ~** Haftpflichtversicherung f

insurant n Versicherungsnehmer m, Versicherter m

insure v versichern v, zusichern v, Versicherung abschließen, sich versichern lassen

insured n Versicherungsnehmer m, Versicherter m

insuree n Versicherungsnehmer m, Versicherter m

insurer n Versicherungsgeber m, Versicherer m

intangible assets immaterielle Aktiva, nicht greifbare Aktiva

intangibles immaterielle Güter

integrated financial area integrierter Finanzraum

intensify v intensivieren v

intent n Absicht f; **letter of ~** Absichtserklärung f

intention n Absicht f; **notice of ~** (US) Antrag auf Erteilung einer Bankkonzession

inter company leasing Leasing zwischen Konzernunternehmen in verschiedenen Ländern; *- dealer broker* (GB) Makler am Londoner Bankmarkt

interbank balances gegenseitige Bankverpflichtungen; *- business* Interbankengeschäft n; *- deposits* gegenseitige Bankguthaben; *- forex (foreign exchange) market* Interbankdevisenmarkt m; *- loans* Bank-an-Bank-Kredite m pl; *- rate* Interbankenzinssatz m; *- transactions* Interbankgeschäfte n pl

interblock gap Blocklücke f (EDV); *- space* Blocklücke f (EDV)

interbourse securities (US) international gehandelte Wertpapiere

intercede for somebody für jemanden eintreten

interchange v austauschen v (gegenseitig), auswechseln v; *- n* Austausch m; *credit -* gegenseitige Kreditauskunft

interchangeable adj auswechselbar adj

intercompany profits Konzerngewinne m pl; *- sales* Verkäufe zwischen Konzerngesellschaften; *- participation* Schachtelbeteiligung f

interest n Zins m, Zinsen m pl, Anteil m, Interesse n, Verzinsung f, Beteiligung f; *- account* Zinsenkonto n; *- accruals* Zinssollstellung f; *- accrued* aufgelaufene Zinsen; *- arbitrage* Zinsarbitrage f; *- at the rate of* Zins zum Satz von; *- balance* (US) Saldo m (der für die tägliche Berechnung der Zinsen benützt wird), Zinssaldo m; *- cap* Zinsobergrenze f; *- charge* Zinsaufwendungen f pl, Zinsendienst m, Zinslast f, Zinsbelastung f; *- collar* Zinskorridor m; *- coupon* Zinskupon m, Obligationenkupon m, Zinsschein m; *- date* Zinstermin m, Zinszahlungstermin m; *- deduction* Zinsabzug m; *- divisor* Zinsdivisor m; *- due* fällige Zinsen; *- earned* Aktivzins m; *- earnings* Zinsertrag m, Zinseinnahmen f pl, Zinserträge m pl

Interest Equalization Tax amerikanische Zinsausgleichssteuer auf Käufe ausländischer Wertpapiere

interest expenditures Zinsaufwendungen f pl, Zinsendienst m, Zinslast f, Zinsbelastung f; *- expenses* Zinsaufwendungen f pl, Zinsendienst m, Zinslast f, Zinsbelastung f; *- fine* Verzugszinsen m pl; *- floor* Zinsuntergrenze f; *- for default* Verzugszinsen m pl; *- formula* Zinsformel f; *- hump* Zinsbuckel m; *- income* Zinsertrag m, Zinseinnahmen f pl, Zinserträge m pl; *- instalment* Zinsrate f; *- loss* Zinsverlust m, Zinsausfall m; *- margin* Zinsspanne f; *- numbers* Zinszahlen f pl; *- on arrears* n Verzugszinsen m pl; *- on overdue amounts* Verzugszinsen m pl; *- paid* Passivzins m; *- payable* Habenzinsen m pl, Passivzinsen m pl; *- paying period* Zinsperiode f; *- payment date* Zinszahlungstermin m; *- payments* Zinszahlungen f pl; *- policy* verzinslicher Versicherungsschein; *- rate* Zinssatz m, Zinsfuß m; *- rate cap* Höchstzinssatz m; *- rate collar* Zinsbegrenzung nach oben und unten; *- rate option* Zinsoption f; *- rebate* Zinsnachlaß m; *- receipts* Zinseingänge m pl; *- receivable* Sollzinsen m pl, Aktivzinsen m pl; *- revenue* Zinsertrag m, Zinseinnahmen f pl, Zinserträge m pl; *- share* Beteiligungsquote f; *- statement* Zinsabrechnung f, Zinsenaufstellung f; *- subsidies* Zinszuschüsse m pl; *- surplus* Zinsüberschuß m; *- swap* Zinsswap m; *- table* Zinstabelle f; *- warrant* Zinsschein m, Zinsoptionsschein m, Zinsauszahlungsschein m; *- yield* Zinsertrag m; **adjustment of** *-* Zinsausgleich m; **amount of** *-* Zinshöhe f; **arrears of** *-* Zinsrückstände m pl; **ascertain** *-* Zinsen errechnen; **assignment of** *-* Anteilsübertragung f; **banking** *-* Bankanteil m; **bear** *-* Zinsen bringen; **bearing no** *-* zinsfrei adj, zinslos adj, unverzinslich adj; **beneficial** *-* Nießbrauch m, Nutznießung f; **bond** *-* Obligationszinsen m pl; **bond - accrued** Stückzinsen m pl; **business** *-* Geschäftsbeteiligung f; **calculation of** *-* Zinsberechnung f, Zinsrechnung f; **capital** *-* Kapitalbeteiligung f; **carry** *-* Zinsen einbringen; **charge** ~ Zinsen berechnen, Zinsen belasten; **compound** ~ Zinseszinsen m pl, Staffelzinsen m pl; **computation of** ~ Zinsberechnung f, Zinsrechnung f; **controlling** ~ Mehrheitsbeteiligung f, maßgebendes Kapitalinteresse; **conventional** ~ üblicher Zins, vertragsgemäßer Zinssatz; **credit** ~ Habenzinsen m pl, Passivzinsen m pl; **current** ~ laufende Zinsen; **debit** ~ Sollzinsen m pl, Aktivzinsen m pl; **earn** ~ Zinsen bringen; **ex** ~ ohne Zinsen; **exact** ~ Zinsen m pl (auf der Basis von 365 Tagen); **illegal** ~ ungesetzlicher Zins, Wucherzinsen m pl; **legal** ~ gesetzlicher Zinssatz; **legal rate of** ~ gesetzlicher Zinssatz; **majority** ~ Mehrheitsbeteiligung f, maßgebendes Kapitalinteresse; **minority** ~ Minderheitsbeteiligung f; **net** ~ Nettozinsen m pl; **ordinary** ~ Zinsen m pl (berechnet auf der Basis von 360 Tagen); **prepaid** ~ im voraus vorgenommener Zinsabzug; **pure** ~ Nettozinsen m pl; **rate of** ~ Zinssatz m, Zinsfuß m; **reversionary** ~ Anwartschaftsrecht n; **simple** ~ Kapitalzinsen m pl; **standard** ~ normaler Zinssatz; **statutory** ~ gesetzlicher Zinssatz; **yield** ~ Zinsen bringen

interest-bearing adj verzinslich adj, zinstragend adj

interested adj beteiligt adj, interessiert adj; ~ adj (in) beteiligt adj (an); ~ **parties** Interessenten m pl

interest-free adj zinsfrei adj, zinslos adj, unverzinslich adj

interest-free bond zinslose Anleihe f, Nullkuponanleihe f

interest-free loan zinsloses Darlehen n

interests in equity shares Aktienkapitalbeteiligungen f pl; **agreement of** ~ Interessenabstimmung f; **commercial** ~ Handelsinteressen n pl; **conflict of** ~ Interessengegensatz m, Interessenkonflikt m; **secure** ~ Beteiligungen erwerben

interest-yielding adj verzinslich adj, zinstragend adj

interface n Nahtstelle f (EDV), Schnittstelle f (EDV)

interim account Zwischenkonto n, Interimskonto n; ~ **balance sheet** Zwischenbilanz f; ~ **certificate** (US) Zwischenschein m; ~ **credit** Zwischenkredit m; ~ **data files** Datenzwischenträger; ~ **dividend** Abschlagsdividende f, Zwischendividende f, Interimsdividende f; ~ **financing** Zwischenfinanzierung f; ~ **loan** Zwischenkredit m; ~ **share** Zwischenaktie f; ~ **statement** Zwischenbilanz f; ~ **stock certificate** (US) Zwischenaktie f; **bill at** ~ Interimswechsel m

interior bank (US) Provinzbank f

interlocking stock-ownership Kapitalverflechtung f

intermediary n Unterhändler m, Vermittler m

intermediate building credit Bauzwischenkredit m; ~ **credit** Zwischenkredit m; ~ **data medium** Datenzwischenträger m; ~ **loan** mittelfristiger Kredit m; ~ **total** Zwischensumme f

internal adj inländisch adj, Inlands (in Zus.), Binnen- (in Zus.); ~ **account** Inlandskonto n; ~ **bonds** Inlandsschuldverschreibungen f pl, Inlandsanleihen f pl; ~ **commerce** (US) Binnenhandel m; ~ **currency** Inlandswährung f; ~ **financing** Innenfinanzierung f; ~ **loan** Inlandsanleihe f; ~ **market** Binnenmarkt m; ~ **revenue office** (US) Steuerbehörde f; ~ **sources** Eigenmittel f pl; ~ **tariff** Binnenzoll m; ~ **value of a currency** Binnenwert m (B. einer Währung)

international adj international adj, zwischenstaatlich adj, weltpolitisch adj

International Bank for Reconstruction and Development (IRBD) Internationale Bank für Wiederaufbau und Entwicklung f

international banking internationales Bankwesen

International Banking Facilities (IBF) Internationale Bankgeschäftsbedingungen

international branch banking Bankfilialeneröffnung im Ausland

International Chamber of Commerce Internationale Handelskammer f

international check (US) Reisescheck m

International Commercial Terms = Incoterms Internationale Handelsbedingungen; **~ Development Association (IDA)** Internationale Entwicklungsbank f; **~ Finance Corporation** Internationale Finanzgesellschaft f; **~ Future Market of France** Marché à Terme International de France (MATIF), französischer Terminmarkt

international market Markt für international gehandelte Wertpapiere

International Monetary Fund (IMF) Weltwährungsfonds m

international monetary system Weltwährungssystem n; **~ money order** internationale Zahlungsanweisung; **~ placement of shares** internationale Aktienplatzierung; **~ securities international** gehandelte Effekten, international gehandelte Papiere, international gehandelte Wertpapiere

International Securities-Dealers Market Association (ISMA) internationale Vereinigung der Wertpapierhändler

international stocks (US) international gehandelte Effekten, international gehandelte Papiere, international gehandelte Wertpapiere

International Swap and Derivative Association, Inc. = ISDA internationale Vereinigung für Swaps und derivative Instrumente; **Bank for ~ Settlements** Bank für internationalen Zahlungsausgleich f

internationally operating bank weltweit tätige Bank

internationals n pl international gehandelte Effekten, international gehandelte Papiere, international gehandelte Wertpapiere

interpret v dolmetschen v, auslegen v, interpretieren v

interpreter n Dolmetscher m

interrogation facilities Abfragemöglichkeit f

interrupt n Unterbrechung f (EDV)

interstate adj (US) zwischenstaatlich adj (zwischen den einzelnen US-Bundesstaaten); **~ commerce** (US) zwischenstaatlicher Handel (zwischen den einzelnen US-Bundesstaaten)

intervene v vermitteln v, intervenieren v

intervention n Intervention f, Einmischung f, Eingriff m; **~ currency** Interventionswährung f; **~ points** Interventionspunkte m pl; **~ rate** Interventionskurs m; **~ rates** Interventionskurse m pl

intestacy n Fehlen eines Testaments, Sterben ohne Hinterlassung eines Testaments

intestate adj nicht durch Testament verfügt, ohne Testament

intrinsic adj innerlich adj, eigentlich adj, wirklich adj; **~ value** innerer Wert, Sachwert m

introduce v einführen v; **~ shares on the market** Aktien an der Börse einführen

introduction on the stock exchange Börseneinführung f

invalid adj ungültig adj, nichtig adj, kraftlos adj

invalidate v unwirksam machen, für ungültig erklären, für nichtig erklären

invalidation n Aufhebung f, Annullierung f, Ungültigkeitserklärung f, Entwertung f

invaluable adj unschätzbar adj

invariable dividend gleichbleibende Dividende

inventories n pl Vorräte m pl, Lagerbestände m pl, Warenbestände m pl

inventory n Inventar m, Bestand m, Warenbestand m, Bestandsverzeichnis n, Nachlaßverzeichnis n, Nachlaßaufnahme f; **~ rate** Inventarkurs m; **~ sheet** Inventarverzeichnis n; **~ value** Inventarwert m; **~ write-downs** Abschreibungen auf Inventar; **benefit of ~** Recht des Erben auf Nachlaßbeschränkung; **business ~** Geschäftsinventar n, Firmeninventar n, Betriebsinventar n

inverse interest Zinsinversion f; **~ interest rate structure** inverse Zinsstruktur

invest v investieren v, anlegen v, unterbringen v (Kapital); **~ advantageously** zinstragend investieren, zinstragend anlegen; **~ with power of attorney** mit Vollmacht ausstatten

invested capital Anlagekapital n; **~ money** investiertes Geld, angelegtes Geld

investigation n Nachforschung f, Nachfrage f, Erhebung f (Umfrage),

investigations

Erkundigung f, Anfrage f; **~ of a company's affairs** Revision der Geschäfte einer Gesellschaft; **credit ~** Kreditwürdigkeitsprüfung f, Einschätzung der Kreditfähigkeit
investigations; make ~ Erhebungen anstellen
investing public Anlagepublikum n
investment n Investition f, Vermögensanlage f, Kapitalanlage f, Beteiligung f (Kapital); **~ abroad** Auslandsanlage f; **~ account** Beteiligungskonto n; **~ adviser** Anlageberater m; **~ advisory service** Anlageberatung f; **~ analysis** Finanzanalyse f; **~ bank** Emissionshaus n; **~ banking** (US) Emissionsgeschäft n; **~ business** Anlagegeschäft n; **~ company** Investmentgesellschaft f; **~ consultant** Anlageberater m; **~ counselling** Wertpapieranlageberatung f; **~ credit** Investitionskredit m; **~ fund** Anlagefonds m, Investmentfonds m; **~ fund for shares** Aktienfonds m; **~ income** (US) Kapitalertrag m; **~ loan** Investitionskredit m; **~ management agreement** Vollmachtsvertrag m (V. einer Vermögensverwaltung); **~ management company** Vermögensverwaltungsgesellschaft f; **~ media** (US) Anlagemöglichkeiten f pl; **~ paper** Anlagepapier n; **~ plan** Anlageplan m, Investmentplan m; **~ policy** Anlagepolitik f; **~ portfolio** Effektenportefeuille n, Wertpapierbesitz m, Wertpapierbestand m, Effektenbestand m; **~ rating** (US) Anlagebewertung f; **~ ratio** Investitionsquote f; **~ recommendations** Anlageempfehlungen f pl; **~ reserve** Kapitalreserve f, Reservekapital n; **~ return** Kapitalverzinsung f; **~ revenue** Kapitalverzinsung f; **~ risk guarantee** Investitionsrisikogarantie f; **~ securities** Anlagepapiere n pl; **~ standards** Anlagegrundsätze m pl; **~ stocks** Anlagepapiere n pl; **~ trust** Kapitalanlagegesellschaft f, Investmenttrust m; **~ trust securities** Effekten eines Investmenttrusts, Anlagefonds-Anteilscheine m pl; **~ value** Anlagewert eines Wertpapiers (auf Grund der Rendite); **business ~** betriebliche Investition; **capital ~** langfristige Kapitalanlage; **cash ~** Bareinlage f; **closed-end ~ company** Investmentgesellschaft mit geschlossenem Anlageportefeuille; **current ~** vorübergehende Anlage; **eligible ~** (US) besonders sichere Anlage; **gilt-edged ~** mündelsichere Anlagepapiere, mündelsichere Wertpapiere, mündelsichere Papiere; **misdirected ~** Fehlinvestition f; **original ~** Gründungseinlage f; **rate of ~** Investitionsrate f; **real ~** Sachanlage f; **real estate ~** Immobilienanlage f, Grundbesitzanlage f; **safe ~** sichere Anlage
investment-grade bonds Anleihen erster Bonität (Baa und besser)
investments n pl (balance sheet) Effekten pl t (Bilanz), Wertpapiere n pl (Bilanz); **~ in affiliated enterprises** Anteile an verbundenen Unternehmen; **~ in associated enterprises** Anteile an assoziierten Unternehmen; **~ in companies** Beteiligungen an Gesellschaften; **~ in non-affiliated enterprises** Beteiligungen (Bilanzposten); **high-grade ~** erstklassige Kapitalanlagen; **~ on the euro market** Euroanlagen f pl; **property ~** Anlagevermögen n; **trustee ~** (GB) mündelsichere Kapitalanlage
investor n Kapitalanleger m, Kapitalgeber m
investors n pl Anlagepublikum n; **~ relations** betriebliche Einrichtung zur Aktionärspflege; **~ risk** Anlegerrisiko n
invisible earnings unsichtbare Erträge
invisibles unsichtbare Ein- oder Ausfuhren
invite tenders zur Abgabe von Zeichnungsangeboten auffordern
invoice v fakturieren v, in Rechnung stellen; **~ n** Rechnung f (Warenrechnung), Faktura f, Nota f; **~ amount** Rechnungsbetrag m; **~ value** Fakturawert m, Rechnungswert m; **consular ~** Konsulatsfaktura f; **proforma ~** Proformarechnung f
invoicing Fakturierung f, Rechnungsstellung f
involuntary bailment unfreiwillige Hinterlegung; **~ bankruptcy** unfreiwilliger Konkurs, durch Gläubigerantrag herbeigeführter Konkurs; **~ lending** unfreiwillige Kreditvergabe
involvement n finanzielle Schwierigkeiten

inward *bill of lading* Importkonnossement *n*; **~ *duty*** Einfuhrzoll *m*
IOU = I owe you Schuldschein *m*, Schuldanerkennung *f*, Schuldanerkenntnis *f*
IPO = initial public offering (US) erstmaliges Zeichnungsangebot von Stammaktien
IRB = industrial revenue bond (US) US-bundesstaatliche Anleiheemission für Industrieunternehmen
Irish Punt (Pound) Irische Pfund *n*
irrecoverable *adj* uneinbringbar *adj*
irredeemable *adj* untilgbar *adj*, unkündbar *adj*, unablösbar *adj*; **~ *debenture*** untilgbare Schuldverschreibung; **~ *stock*** unkündbare Wertpapiere, Wertpapiere ohne Rückkaufsrecht
irregular *deposit* unregelmäßiges Depot; **~ *endorsement*** regelwidriges Indossament
irrevocable *adj* unwiderruflich *adj*; **~ *confirmed letter of credit*** bestätigtes unwiderrufliches Akkreditiv; **~ *documentary credit*** unwiderrufliches Dokumentenakkreditiv; **~ *trust*** unwiderrufliche Stiftung; **~ *trust fund*** unwiderruflicher Treuhandfonds
ISDA = International Swap and Derivate Association, Inc. Internationale Vereinigung für Swaps und derivative Instrumente *f*
issuance fees Emissionsgebühren *f pl*
issue *v* ausgeben *v* (Wertpapiere), emittieren *v*, in Umlauf setzen; **~ *n*** Ausgabe *f* (von Wertpapieren), Begebung *f*, Emission *f*; **~ *at par*** Pariemission *f*; **~ *bank*** Notenbank *f*; **~ *banknotes*** Banknoten in Umlauf setzen; **~ *department*** Emissionsabteilung *f*; **~ *of bonus shares*** Ausgabe von Gratisaktien; **~ *of stock*** (US) Aktienausgabe *f*; **~ *par*** (GB) Emissionskurs *m*, Ausgabekurs *m*; **~ *price*** Emissionskurs *m*, Ausgabekurs *m*, Emissionspreis *m*; **~ *prospectus*** Emissionsprospekt *n*; **~ *yield*** Emissionsrendite *f*; **~ *bank of*** Notenbank *f*; **~ *bond*** Pfandbriefemission *f*, Pfandbriefausgabe *f*, Emission von Obligationen; **~ *bonus*** Prämiengewährung *f*, Ausgabe von Gratisaktien (Kapitalberichtigungsaktien); **~ *capital*** Effektenemission *f*; **~ *closed*** unveränderliche Anleihe; **~ *date of*** Emissionstag *m*, Ausgabetag *m*; **~ *day of*** Emissionstag *m*, Ausgabetag *m*; **~ *fiduciary*** ungedeckte Notenausgabe; **~ *rate of*** Emissionskurs *m*, Ausgabekurs *m*
issued *capital* (GB) effektiv ausgegebenes Aktienkapital, effektiv ausgegebenes Kapital; **~ *stock*** (US) effektiv ausgegebenes Aktienkapital, effektiv ausgegebenes Kapital; **~ *to*** lautend auf
issuer *n* Emittent *m*, Aussteller *m*, Ausgeber *m*
issues; *fixed interest* ~ festverzinsliche Wertpapiere; ***shipping* ~** Schiffahrtsaktien *f pl*, Schiffswerte *m pl*
issuing *n* (of securities) Ausgabe *f* (von Wertpapieren), Begebung *f*; **~ *bank*** Emissionsbank *f*; **~ *broker*** Emissionsbroker *m*; **~ *company*** Emissionshaus *n*; **~ *creditor*** Emissionsgläubiger *m*; **~ *debtor*** Emissionsschuldner *m*; **~ *house*** (GB) Emissionshaus *n*; **~ *premium*** Emissionsaufgeld *n*, Emissionsagio *n*; **~ *price*** Emissionskurs *m*, Ausgabekurs *m*; **~ *proceeds*** Emissionserlös *m*; **~ *prospectus*** Emissionsprospekt *n*; **~ *share*** Konsortialquote *f*; **~ *transaction*** Emissionsgeschäft *n*
Italian Lira Italienische Lira *f*
item *n* Artikel *m*, Ware *f*, Posten *m*, Gegenstand *m*; **~ *n*** Rechnungsposten *m*, Posten *m*, Position *f*, Buchungsposten *m*; **~ *carried forward*** Vortragsposten *m*; **~ *in transit*** Durchgangsposten *m*; **~ *booking*** Buchungsposten *m*; ***cash* ~** Kassenposten *m*; ***credit* ~** Habenposten *m*, Gutschrift *f*
itemization *n* Aufgliederung *f*, Einzelaufstellung *f*
itemize *v* einzeln aufführen, spezifizieren *v*, nach Posten gliedern
items *in transit* Inkassopapiere *f pl*; ***book omitted* ~** Posten nachtragen; ***sight* ~** Sichtpapiere *n pl*; ***suspense* ~** vorläufige Posten, Übergangsposten *m pl*, Schwebeposten *m pl*

J

Japanese *stock price index (NIKKEI)* Index der Tokioter Börse; *- Yen* Japanischer Yen *m*

job *n* Beruf *m*, Arbeitsplatz *m*, Stellung *f*; *- sharing* Arbeitsplatzteilung *f* (mit Teilzeitkräften)

jobber *n* Börsenmakler *m*, Kursmakler *m*, Effektenhändler *m*, Fondshändler *m*; *- in bills* (GB) Wechselreiter *m*; *bill -* Wechselreiter *m*; *money -* Geldhändler *m*

jobber's turn (GB) Gewinn des Börsenmaklers (Börsenjobbers)

jobbing Effektenhandel *m*, Börsenspekulation *f*; *- in bills* Wechselreiterei *f*; *bill -* Wechselreiterei *f*

jobless *adj* arbeitslos *adj*

joint *adj* gemeinsames Konto, Und-Konto *n*, (GB) Gemeinschaftskonto *n*; *- advertisement* Gemeinschaftswerbung *f*; *- and several* gesamtschuldnerisch *adj*; *- and several guarantee* gesamtschuldnerische Bürgschaft, Solidarbürgschaft *f*, selbstschuldnerische Bürgschaft; *- and several liabilities* Gesamtschuldnerschaft *f*; *- auditing body* Revisionsverband *m* (der Bausparkassen); *- contract* Gemeinschaftsvertrag *m*; *- creditor* Mitgläubiger *m*; *- current account* gemeinschaftliches Kontokorrentkonto; *- custody* Gemeinschaftsdepot *n*; *- debtor* Mitschuldner *m*, Solidarschuldner *m*; *- deposit* Gemeinschaftsdepot *n*; *- financing* Gemeinschaftsfinanzierung *f*, Ko-Finanzierung *f*; *- global coordinator* führende Bank bei Plazierung einer weltweiten Wertpapieremission; *- guarantor* Solidarbürge *m*; *- heir* Miterbe *m*; *- holder* Mitinhaber *m* *- liability* Solidarhaftung *f*, gesamtschuldnerische Haftung *f*, Solidarschuld *f*; *- policy* Gesamtpolice *f*; *- property* Gesamteigentum *n*; *- proprietor* Mitinhaber *m*, Mitbesitzer *m*, Teilhaber *m*, Partner *m*; *- stock bank* (GB) Aktienbank *f*; *- transaction* Metageschäft *n*; *- surety* Mitbürge *m*, Gesamtbürgschaft *f*; *- venture* Interessengemeinschaft *f*; Gemeinschaftsunternehmen *n*; *business on - account* Konsortialgeschäft *n*; *deal on - account* Metageschäft *n*

jointly and severally kooperativ *adj*, solidarisch *adv* (z. B. haften)

joint-stock company (GB) Aktiengesellschaft *f*

journal *n* Journal *n*, Primanote *f*, Memorial *n*, Kladde *f*

judg(e)ment *creditor* Vollstreckungsgläubiger *m*, gerichtlich anerkannter Gläubiger; *- debt* gerichtlich anerkannte Schuld; *- debtor* Vollstreckungsschuldner *m*; *- note* Schuldschein mit Unterwerfungsklausel; *final -* rechtskräftiges Urteil

judge *v* beurteilen *v*; *- n* Richter *m*

judicial arbitration gerichtlicher Schiedsspruch; *- sale* (US) Zwangsversteigerung *f*

jumbo issue Großemission *f*, Jumboemission *f*

jump in price Hausse *f*, starker Kursanstieg (Börse)

junior *adj* nachrangig *adj*; *- bonds* durch nachstehende Hypothek oder nachstehendes Pfandrecht sichergestellte Obligationen; *- creditor* nachrangiger Gläubiger; *- issue* Ausgabe geringeren Ranges; *- lien* nachstehendes Pfandrecht; *- mezzanine debt* nachrangiges Darlehen; *- mortgage* nachrangige Hypothek, zweitstellige Hypothek, zweite Hypothek; *- securities* nachrangige Sicherheiten

junk *n* Plunder *m*, Trödel *m*; *- bond* Risikoanleihe *f*

juridical person juristische Person

jurisdiction *n* Gerichtsstand *m*, Gerichtsbarkeit *f*, Rechtsprechung *f*; *- clause* Zuständigkeitsklausel *f*

just price angemessener Preis

justifiable risk vertretbares Risiko

justify *v* rechtfertigen *v*, begründen *v*

K

Kaffirs südafrikanische Bergbauaktien
keep *an account* Konto unterhalten; *- back* zurückbehalten v, einbehalten v; *- the minutes* Protokoll führen
kerb market Freiverkehrsbörse f, Freibörse f, Freiverkehrsmarkt m, Nachbörse f
key n Schlüssel m, Kennziffer f; *- account* Großkunde m; *- currency* Leitwährung f; *- figures* Eckdaten plt; *- industry* Schlüsselindustrie f; *- of ratings* Schlüssel für eine Bewertung von Unternehmen und Wertpapieren; *- rate* Leitzins m
keyboard n Tastenfeld n, Bedienungsfeld n, Tastatur f
keyborder n Datentypist /-in
keying *error* Eintastfehler m; *- speed* Eintastgeschwindigkeit f
kicker n Anreiz m, Vergünstigung f; ***equity*** *-* Gewährung einer Kapitalbeteiligung, Beteiligung am Zuwachs des Unternehmenswertes (Spezialfinanzierung)

killing n (US) hoher Spekulationsgewinn
kite n Gefälligkeitswechsel m, Kellerwechsel m, Reitwechsel m; *- check* ungedeckter Scheck; *- checks* (US) nicht (voll) gedeckte Schecks in Umlauf bringen; *- flying* Wechselreiterei f
kiting of stocks (US) Hinauftreiben von Aktienkursen
Kiwi-bond Auslandsanleihe in neuseeländischer Währung
knock *down* v drücken (Kurse, Preise) v; *- bid* n Mindestangebot n; *- off* v herunterhandeln v; *- price* n Mindestpreis m
knocking down Zuschlag m (Versteigerung)
know-how-agreement Lizenzvertrag m
Krona Krone f (Währung in Schweden und Island)
Krone Krone f (Währung in Dänemark und Norwegen)
Krugerrand Krügerrand m (südafrikanische Goldmünze; 1 Unze Gold)

L

labo(u)r n (US) Arbeit f, Arbeiter m, Arbeitskräfte f pl, Belegschaft f; **- bank** (US) Arbeiterbank f, Gewerkschaftsbank f; **- conflict** Lohnstreitigkeiten f pl; **- costs** Lohnkosten; **- disputes** Arbeitskämpfe m pl; **- force** Arbeitskräfte f pl, Belegschaft f; **- relations** Arbeitgeber-Arbeitnehmer-Verhältnis n; **- turnover** Personalfluktuation f

lack n Mangel m; **- of money** Geldknappheit f; **- of capital** Kapitalmangel m

lackluster trading lustlose Börsenstimmung

lade v laden v, beladen v, verladen v

lading; bill of - Konnossement n, Seefrachtbrief m, Frachtbrief m (US); **port of -** Ladehafen m

lamb n unerfahrener Spekulant

lame duck (US) schwerfälliges Wertpapier, unrentable Firma

land bank Hypothekenbank f; **- bonds** (US) Pfandbriefe m pl; **- charge** Grundschuld f; **- charge claim** Grundschuldforderung f; **- charge deed** Grundschuldbrief m; **- development** Geländeerschließung f; **- mortgage bank** Bodenkreditbank f; **- owner** Grundeigentümer m; **- register** Grundbuch n, Kataster m; **- registration office** Grundbuchamt n

Land Registry (GB) Grundbuchamt n

land registry fees Grundbuchgebühren f pl; **- rent** Grundpacht f; **- speculation** Grundstücksspekulation f; **- tax** (GB) Grundsteuer f; **- tenure** Grundstückspacht f; **- value** Grundstückswert m, Bodenwert m

landed property Immobilien pl t, Grundbesitz m, Grund und Boden, Grundeigentum n, Grundstückseigentum n, Liegenschaften f pl

landing certificate Löschungsschein m; **- charges** Löschungsgebühren f pl; **- place** Landeplatz m

landlord n Vermieter m, Grundeigentümer m

lapse v ablaufen, erlöschen, verfallen v

lapsed policy abgelaufene Versicherung

large bank Großbank f; **- corporate customer** Großkunde m; **- volume loan** Großkredit m

large-scale check payment system Massenzahlungsverkehr m

last in first out (LIFO) LIFO-Personalpolitik f, LIFO-Abschreibungsmethode f

last will Testament n, letztwillige Verfügung, letzter Wille

late quotation Schlußnotierung f

latent inflation schleichende Inflation; **- partner** stiller Gesellschafter; **- reserves** stille Reserven

later adj später adj; **- stage financing** Expansionsfinanzierung mit Wagniskapital; **- will** später abgefaßtes Testament

lateral combination vertikaler Konzern

latest date Schlußtermin m

launch a loan eine Anleihe auflegen, eine Anleihe begeben; **- date** Auflegungsdatum n

launching cost Anlaufkosten pl t

law n Gesetz n, Recht n (objektives Recht); **- adjective** formelles Recht; **- charges** Prozeßkosten pl t; **- of contracts** Schuldrecht n, Vertragsrecht n; **- of inheritance** Erbrecht n; **administrative -** Verwaltungsrecht n; **banking -** Bankrecht n; **bankruptcy -** Konkursrecht n; **civil -** Zivilrecht n, bürgerliches Recht; **company -** Gesellschaftsrecht n; **course of -** Rechtsgang m; **currency -** Währungsgesetz n

lawful adj rechtmäßig adj; **- money** (US) gesetzliche Zahlungsmittel

lawsuit n Rechtsstreit m, Prozeß m

lawyer n Jurist m, Rechtsanwalt m, Anwalt m

lawyer's fee Anwaltsgebühren f pl

L/C = letter of credit Akkreditiv n

lead v leiten v, führen v; ~ n Führung f, Spitze f; **- card** Vorlaufkarte f; **- management** Federführung f (z. B. bei Emissionen); **- management fee** Führungsprovision f; **- manager** Konsortialführer m, Lead Manager; **- time** Lieferzeit f

leader n Marktführer m, Spitzenreiter m

leaders Spitzenwerte f pl, Standardaktien f pl

leading adj führen adj; **- bank** führende Bank, maßgebende Bank; **- currency** Leitwährung f; **- group** Spitzengruppe f

lean banking schlanke Bankorganisation; **- management** schlankes Management

learner n Anlernling m

lease v vermieten v, verpachten v; ~ n Miete f (Mietverhältnis), Pacht f, Verpachtung f, Mietvertrag m, Pachtvertrag m; **- agreement** Leasingvertrag m; **- deed** Mietvertrag m, Pachtvertrag m; **- bailment** Verkauf unter Eigentumsvorbehalt; **building -** Erbpacht f, Baupachtrecht n; **contract of -** Mietvertrag m, Pachtvertrag m; **sale and - back** Verkauf und Rückmiete

leasehold n Pachtvertrag m, Mietvertrag m (Pacht-, Mietbesitz)

leaseholder n Mieter m, Pächter m

leaseholds Pachtgrundstücke f pl

leaser n Verpächter m, Vermieter m

leasing n Vermieten n, Verpachten n, Vermietung f, Verpachtung f, Leasing n; **- company** Leasinggesellschaft f; **equipment -** Vermietung von Einrichtungsgegenständen

leave a margin einen Gewinn abwerfen; **- a profit** einen Gewinn abwerfen

ledger n Journal n, Buchhaltungsbuch n, Hauptbuch n, Register n; **- clerk** Hauptbuchführer m; **- fee** (GB) Kontoführungsgebühr f; **- machine** Buchhaltungsmaschine f; **- records** Hauptbücher n pl; **acceptance -** Akzeptbuch n, Obligoverzeichnis n; **bank -** Bankhauptbuch n; **branches -** Filialenhauptbuch n; **cheque -** (GB) Buch, das etwa der Primanota entspricht; **credit -** Kreditregister n; **creditors' -** Kreditorenbuch n; **current account** ~ Kontokorrentbuch n; **depositors'** ~ Depositenkonto n, Einlagenkonto n, Depositenregistern; **payroll -** Lohn- und Gehaltsliste f; **share** ~ (GB) Aktienbuch n; **shareholders' -** Aktionärsbuch n, Aktionärsverzeichnis n; **stockholders'** ~ Aktionärsbuch n, Aktionärsverzeichnis n; **subscription -** Aktienzeichnungsbuch n

legacy n Legat n, Vermächtnis n, testamentarische Zuwendung; **- duty** Erbschaftssteuer f (US); **- hunting** Erbschleicherei f; **- residuary** ~ Restvermächtnis n, Vermächtnis nach Abzug der Nachlaßverbindlichkeiten

legal adj gesetzlich adj; **- adviser** Rechtsbeistand m; **- capacity** Rechtsfähigkeit f; **- claim** Rechtsanspruch m, Rechtstitel m; **- department** Rechtsabteilung f; **- entity** juristische Person; **- form** Rechtsform f; **- incapacity** Geschäftsunfähigkeit f; **- interest** gesetzlicher Zinssatz; **- investments** (US) mündelsichere Anlagepapiere, mündelsichere Wertpapiere, mündelsichere Papiere; **- liability insurance** Haftpflichtversicherung f (gesetzlich); **- mortgage** rechtsgültige Hypothek, gesetzliche Hypothek; **- person** juristische Person; **- personality** Rechtspersönlichkeit f; **- position** Rechtslage f; **- provisions** Rechtsvorschriften f pl; **- rate of interest** gesetzlicher Zinssatz; **- reserve** gesetzliche Rücklage, gesetzlich vorgeschriebene Reserve; **- securities** mündelsichere Wertpapiere f pl (US); **- settlement** Zwangsvergleich m (US); **- status** Rechtspersönlichkeit f; **- successor** Rechtsnachfolger m; **- tender** gesetzliche Zahlungsmittel

legal lien gesetzliches Pfandrecht

legalization n Legalisierung f, amtliche Beglaubigung

legalize v legalisieren v, amtlich beglaubigen

legalized; have a document - ein Dokument beglaubigen lassen

legate v vermachen v; ~ n Legat n, Vermächtnis n, testamentarische Zuwendung

legatee n Vermächtnisnehmer m; **residuary -** Nachvermächtnisnehmer m
legator n Erblasser m, Testator m
legislation n Gesetzgebung f; **antitrust -** Kartellgesetzgebung f
legitimate adj ehelich adj; **-** adj rechtmäßig adj
lend v ausleihen v, verleihen (Geld), Darlehen gewähren
lender n Kreditgeber m, Darlehensgeber m, Gläubiger m, Geldgeber m, Ausleiher m, Verleiher m
lender of last ressort Zentralbanken als Kreditgeber für Banken in Liquiditätskrisen
lending n Kredit m, Kreditforderung f, Kreditgewährung f; **- authority** Kreditvollmacht f; **- bank** kreditgebende Bank; **- business** Kreditgeschäft n; **- limit** Kreditgrenze f, Beleihungsgrenze f; **- policy** Kreditpolitik f; **- power** Kreditpotential n; **- rate** (US) Lombardsatz m; **- society** Vorschußverein m; **- without recourse** Kreditgewährung ohne Rückgriffsmöglichkeit auf den Schuldner
length of notice Kündigungsfrist f
less adj weniger adj, abzüglich adj; **- developed countries** Entwicklungsländer f pl
lessee n Mieter m, Pächter m
lessor n Verpächter m, Vermieter m
let v vermieten v, verpachten v; **-** n Vermietung f; **offices to -** Büroräume zu vermieten
let-out clause Rücktrittsklausel f
letter of allotment (GB) Zuteilungsanzeige f, Zuteilungsschein m, Bezugsrechtszuteilung f; **- of awareness** Patronatserklärung f; **- of charge** (GB) Dokument über die Hinterlegung von Inhaberpapieren zur Besicherung eines Darlehens; **- of consent** Einverständniserklärung f; **- of conveyance** Frachtbrief m; **- of credit** Akkreditiv n, Kreditbrief m; **- of credit opening** Akkreditiveröffnung f; **- of delegation** Inkassovollmacht f; **- of deposit** Hinterlegungsurkunde f; **- of guaranty** Garantiebrief m; **- of hypothecation** (US) Verpfändungsurkunde für Verschiffung gegen Wechsel; **- of indemnity** (GB) Ausfallbürgschaft f, schriftliche Garantieerklärung, Schadenersatzerklärung f; **- of inquiry** Auskunftersuchen n; **- of intent** Absichtserklärung f; **- of introduction** Einführungsschreiben n; **- of licence (license)** (GB) Vergleichsurkunde f, Vergleichsvertrag m; **- of lien** Sicherungsübereinigungsvertrag m, Verpfändungsurkunde f; **- of protection** Moratorium n, Moratoriumsurkunde f; **- of respite** Moratorium n, Moratoriumsurkunde f; **- of undertaking** Verpflichtungserklärung f; **- stocks** nicht börsengängige Aktien (US); **allotment -** (GB) Zuteilungsanzeige f, Zuteilungsschein m, Bezugsrechtszuteilung f; **ancillary - of credit** Hilfskreditbrief m; **beneficiary of a - of credit** Kreditbriefinhaber m, Akkreditivbegünstigte f u. m; **business -** Geschäftsbrief m; **call -** Einzahlungsaufforderung f; **cash -** Geldbrief m; **circular - of credit** Zirkularkreditbrief m, Reisekreditbrief m; **clean - of credit** Akkreditiv ohne Dokumente; **commercial - of credit** Warenkreditbrief m, Warenakkreditiv n; **cover -** Begleitbrief m, Begleitschreiben n; **covering -** Begleitbrief m, Begleitschreiben n; **direct - of credit** (GB) an eine bestimmte Bank gerichteter Kreditbrief; **documentary - of credit** Dokumentenkredit m, Dokumentenakkreditiv n; **domestic travellers - of credit** (US) Inlandsreisekreditbrief m; **irrevocable confirmed - of credit** bestätigtes unwiderrufliches Akkreditiv; **revocable - of credit** widerrufliches Akkreditiv; **revolving - of credit** automatisch sich erneuerndes Akkreditiv; **straight - of credit** bestätigtes unwiderrufliches Akkreditiv; **trust -** Treuhandschein m; **unconfirmed - of credit** nicht bestätigtes Akkreditiv
letterhead n Briefkopie m
letters despatched book (GB) Kontrollbuch über die ausgehenden Briefe; **- testamentary** Testamentsvollstreckerzeugnis n; **collection of -** Postabholung f
level n Ebene f, Stand m, Niveau n; **- of prices** Kursniveau n, Preisniveau n

leverage Verhältnis zwischen Eigen- und Fremdkapital; **~ fund** Investmentfonds mit Leihkapital

leveraged adj mit Fremdkapital finanziert, fremdfinanziert adj; **~ bid** fremdfinanziertes Übernahmeangebot; **~ buy-out** fremdfinanzierte Übernahme; **~ corporate acquisition** fremdfinanzierter Firmenkauf; **~ stock** mit Fremdkapital finanzierte Aktien

levy n Steuererhebung f, Erhebung f; **~ v** erheben v, einziehen v, belasten v; **capital ~** Kapitalsteuer f, Vermögensabgabe f

liabilities n pl Passiva plt, Verbindlichkeiten f pl, Schulden f pl; **~ incurred as trustee** Treuhandverbindlichkeiten f pl; **~ payable at sight** Sichtverbindlichkeiten f pl; **~ to banks** Verbindlichkeiten gegenüber Kreditinstituten; **~ to customers** Verbindlichkeiten gegenüber Kunden (Bilanzposition); **~ to depositors** Verbindlichkeiten aus Einlagen; **assets and ~** Aktiva und Passiva; **business ~** Geschäftsschulden f pl, Betriebsschulden f pl; **contract ~** Verpflichtungen eingehen; **cover ~** Verbindlichkeiten erfüllen, Verpflichtungen nachkommen; **current ~** kurzfristige Verbindlichkeiten, laufende Verbindlichkeiten; **deposit ~** Kontokorrentverbindlichkeiten f pl; **joint and several ~** Gesamtschuldnerschaft f; **meet one's ~** seinen Verbindlichkeiten nachkommen; **other ~** sonstige Verpflichtungen; **partnership ~** Verpflichtungen einer Gesellschaft, Gesellschaftsverpflichtungen f pl; **quick ~** kurzfristig zurückzahlbare Schulden; **secondary ~** Eventualverbindlichkeiten f pl; **suspense ~** transitorische Passiva; **unadjusted ~** schwebende Verbindlichkeiten

liability n Schuld f, Verbindlichkeit f, Haftung f, Verantwortlichkeit f; **~ accounting** Obligoführung f; **~ for prospectus** Prospekthaftung f; **~ management** Verwaltung der Unternehmenspassiva; **~ of partners** Haftung der Gesellschafter; **~ on a bill** Wechselhaftung f; **~ on a guarantee** Haftung aus einer Bürgschaft; **~ on acceptances** Wechselhaftung; **~ on bills of exchange** Wechselobligo n; **~ on payments guaranteed** Avaloblige n; **acceptance ~** Akzeptverbindlichkeit f, Wechselobligo n; **capital ~** Kapitalverbindlichkeit f, langfristige Verbindlichkeit f; **collective ~** Gesamtschuld f; **contingent ~** Eventualverbindlichkeit f, Eventualverpflichtung f; **contingent ~ in respect of acceptances** Verpflichtungen aus geleisteten Akzepten; **corporate ~** Gesellschaftshaftung f, Firmenhaftung f; **cross ~** gegenseitige Haftung; **reserve ~** Nachschußpflicht f

liable adj haftbar adj, haftpflichtig adj, verantwortlich adj; **~ capital** Haftkapital n, haftendes Eigenkapital; **~ to recourse** regreßpflichtig adj; **to be ~ for** haften für

liberalization of imports Einfuhrliberalisierung f; **~ of capital markets** Liberalisierung des Kapitalverkehrs

liberalize v liberalisieren v

liberate capital Kapital flüssig machen

LIBID = London Interbank Bid Rate Londoner Interbanken-Nachfragezinssatz (Geldkurs)

LIBOR = London Interbank Offered Rate Londoner Interbanken-Angebotszinssatz (Briefkurs); **~ flat** Londoner Interbanken-Angebotszinssatz ohne Aufschlag

licence (license) n Lizenz f, Erlaubnis f, Genehmigung f, Verkaufsrecht n, Konzession f; **~ v** konzessionieren v, genehmigen v, zulassen v, lizensieren v; **~ fee** Lizenzgebühr f

licensee Lizenznehmer m

licenser Lizenzgeber m

lien n Pfandrecht n, Zurückbehaltungsrecht n; **~ creditor** Pfandgläubiger m, Inhaber eines Zurückbehaltungsrechts; **~ upon real estate** Grundpfandrecht n; **bank ~** Pfandrecht der Bank, Zurückbehaltungsrecht der Bank; **banker's ~** Pfandrecht der Bank, Zurückbehaltungsrecht der Bank; **charging ~** Sicherungsrecht n (mit Besitz nicht verbunden); **conventional ~** Vertragspfand n; **first ~** erstrangiges Zurückbehaltungsrecht, erstrangiges Pfandrecht; **junior ~** nachstehendes Pfandrecht; **prior**

lienee

~ bevorrechtigtes Pfandrecht, bevorrechtigtes Zurückbehaltungsrecht; **second** ~ nachrangiges Pfandrecht; **special** ~ Zurückbehaltungsrecht n (an einem bestimmten Gegenstand); **specific** ~ Zurückbehaltungsrecht n (an einem bestimmten Gegenstand)

lienee n Pfandschuldner m

lienor n Pfandgläubiger m, Inhaber eines Zurückbehaltungsrechts

life n Leben n, (of a contract) Laufzeit f (eines Vertrags); ~ **annuity** lebenslängliche Rente, Lebensrente f, Leibrente f; ~ **assurance** (GB) Lebensversicherung f; ~ **assurance company** Lebensversicherungsgesellschaft f; ~ **insurance** Lebensversicherung f; ~ **interest** lebenslängliche Nutznießung; ~ **of a loan** Laufzeit einer Anleihe, Dauer einer Anleihe; ~ **policy** Lebensversicherungspolice f

LIFFE = London International Financial Futures Exchange Londoner Börse für Finanzterminkontrakte f

LIMEAN = London Interbank Mean Rate Londoner mittlerer Geldmarktzinssatz zwischen LIBID und LIBOR

limit v beschränken v, einschränken v; ~ n Grenze f, Limit n; ~ **of credit** Kreditgrenze f, Beleihungsgrenze f; ~ **order** Preisgrenze für den An- und Verkauf von Wertpapieren; **exceed the** ~ das Limit überschreiten; **go beyond the** ~ das Limit überschreiten

limitation n Begrenzung f; ~ **of action** Verjährung f; ~ **of losses** Verlustbegrenzung f

limited adj beschränkt adj, limitiert adj, begrenzt adj; ~ **cheque** (GB) Scheck von begrenzter Höhe; ~ **company** (GB) etwa: GmbH; ~ **convertibility** beschränkte Konvertierbarkeit; ~ **liability company** (GB) etwa: GmbH; ~ **order** limitierter Auftrag (Börse), begrenzter Kauf- oder Verkaufsvertrag; ~ **partner** Kommanditist m, beschränkt haftender Gesellschafter, beschränkt haftender Teilhaber m; ~ **partnership** Kommanditgesellschaft f; ~ **partnership agreement** Kommanditvertrag m; ~ **preferred stocks** Vorzugsaktien mit festgelegter Dividende; ~ **recourse financing** Finanzierung mit eingeschränktem Rückgriff

limping standard hinkende Währung

line of acceptance Akzeptkreditlinie f, Akzeptlimit n, Akzeptkreditrahmen m; ~ **of code** Kodierzeile f; ~ **of credit** Kreditlinie f, Kreditrahmen m, Kreditbetrag m, eingeräumter Kredit, Höchstkredit m; ~ **of deposit** (US) durchschnittlicher Saldo eines Einlagenkontos; ~ **speed** Leitungsgeschwindigkeit f; ~ **width** Schreibbreite f (eines Schnelldruckers); **acceptance** ~ Akzeptkreditlinie f, Akzeptlimit n, Akzeptkreditrahmen m; **below the** ~ »unter dem Strich«; **business** ~ Geschäftszweig m, Geschäftssparte f; **credit** ~ Kreditlinie f, Kreditrahmen m, Kreditbetrag m, eingeräumter Kredit, Höchstkredit m

link address Anschlußadresse f (bei Großspeicherdateien)

linked business fondsgebundene Versicherungsabschlüsse

linking address Anschlußadresse f (bei Großspeicherdateien)

liquid adj flüssig adj; ~ **assets** Umlaufvermögen n, flüssige Aktiva, flüssige Mittel; ~ **capital** Umlaufkapital n; ~ **funds** liquide Mittel, greifbare Mittel; ~ **investments** liquide Anlagen; ~ **reserves** flüssige Mittel, flüssige Reserven; ~ **resources** flüssige Mittel, flüssige Reserven

liquidate v liquidieren v, abwickeln v, auflösen v

liquidated assets veräußerte Vermögenswerte; ~ **collateral** verwertete Sicherheit; ~ **debt** festgestellte Schuld

liquidating dividend Liquidationsrate f, Liquidationsanteil m; ~ **value** Liquidationswert m

liquidation n Liquidation f, Abwicklung f, Glattstellung f; ~ **by arrangement** gütliche Liquidation, außergerichtliche Liquidation; **compulsory** ~ Zwangsliquidation f; **enforced** ~ Zwangsvergleich m

liquidator n Liquidator m, Masseverwalter m; ~ **in bankruptcy** Konkursverwalter m

liquidity n Liquidität f, Flüssigkeit f, Liquiditätsstatus m, Geldflüssigkeit f; **~ ratio** Liquiditätsgrad m, Liquiditätsverhältnis n; **~ reserve** Liquiditätsreserve f; **~ statement** Liquiditätsausweis m; **cash ~** Barliquidität f; **change in ~** Liquiditätsumschichtung f; **overall ~** Gesamtliquidität f; **strain on ~** Liquiditätsanspannung f

lira Lire f (Währung in Italien und Türkei)

list n (US) die an der Börse eingeführten Effekten; **~** n Liste f, Aufstellung f; **~ of balances** Saldenliste f; **~ of deposited securities** Depotübersicht f; **~ of drawings** Verlosungsliste f; **~ of foreign exchanges** (GB) Devisenkursblatt n; **~ of quotations** Börsenkursblatt n; **~ of shareholders** Aktionärsverzeichnis n; **~ structure** Listenbild n; **black ~** schwarze Liste, Insolventenliste f, Verzeichnis unsicherer Kunden; **subscription ~** Zeichnungsliste f, Zeichnungsbogen m, Zeichnungsschein m

listed adj (US) an der Börse eingeführt; **~ securities** an der Börse notierte Werte; **~ shares** (bonds) börsennotierte Aktien (Anleihen); **~ stock** (US) amtlich eingeführte Aktie

listing procedure Börsenzulassungsverfahren f; **~ prospectus** Börsenzulassungsprospekt m; **application for ~** (US) Antrag auf offizielle Einführung an der Börse, Antrag auf Börsenzulassung; **official ~** (US) offizielle Zulassung zum Börsenhandel; **Stock Exchange ~** amtliche Notierung an der Börse

listless market lustlose Börse

litigation n Rechtsstreit m, Prozeß m

lively market lebhafte Börse

living trust (US) lebenslängliche Treuhandverwaltung; **cost of ~** Lebenshaltungskosten plt

Lloyd's (of London) Londoner Versicherungsbörse

load v laden v, beladen v, verladen v, befrachten v; **~** n Belastung f, Last f, Aufwand m, Ladung f, Fracht f, Abschlußgebühr f, Provisionsbelastung f (beim Kauf von Investmentanteilen)

loaded adj befrachten adj

loading Beladen n, Verladen n

loan v leihen v, ausleihen v; **~** n Kredit m, Darlehen n, Anleihe f, Vorschuß m; **~ account** Kreditkonto n, Darlehenskonto n, Anleihekonto n; **~ against a promissory note** Schuldscheindarlehen n; **~ against pledge** Faustpfandkredit m; **~ agreement** Kreditvertrag m, Darlehensvertrag m, Anleihevertrag m; **~ amount** Kreditsumme f; **~ application** Kreditantrag m, Kreditgesuch m; **~ balance** Kreditsaldo m; **~ bank** Kreditbank f, Darlehensbank f; **~ capital** Anleihekapital n; **~ certificate** Anleiheschein m, Darlehensschein m; **~ contract** Kreditvertrag m, Darlehensvertrag m, Anleihevertrag m; **~ conversion** Anleihekonversion f; **~ crowd** (US) Makler m pl (die entweder Aktien borgen oder ausleihen); **~ department** Kreditabteilung f, Kreditbüro n; **~ insurance** Kreditversicherung f; **~ interests** Kreditzinsen m pl, Darlehenszinsen m pl, Anleihezinsen m pl; **~ officer** Kreditsachbearbeiter m; **~ on overdraft** Kontokorrentkredit m, offener Kredit; **~ rate** Kreditzinssatz m, Darlehenszinssatz m, Ausleihungssatz m; **~ secured by a personal guarantee** verbürgtes Darlehen; **~ service** Anleihedienst m, Anleiheverzinsung f; **~ shark** Kredithai m (Wucherer); **~ subscriber** Anleihezeichner m; **~ subscription price** Anleihezeichnungskurs m; **~ sub-participation** Kreditunterbeteiligung f; **~ syndicate** Anleihekonsortium n, Kreditkonsortium n; **~ teller** Sachbearbeiter in der Kreditabteilung; **~ terms** Anleihebedingungen f pl; **~ to purchase shares (stocks)** Wertpapierkredit m, Effektenkredit m; **~ undertaking** Kreditzusage f; **~ underwriting** Anleiheübernahme f, Kreditaufnahme f; **~ upon collateral security** (US) Lombardkredit m, Lombarddarlehen n, abgesicherter Kredit; **~ value** Beleihungswert m, Lombardwert m; **accommodation ~** Überbrückungskredit m; **accommodation endorsement ~** Kredit gegen Wechselbürgschaft; **accounts receivable ~** Debitorenkredit m; **amortization**

of a - Anleihetilgung f; **award a** - Anleihe gewähren; **bank** - Bankkredit m, Bankdarlehen n; **bearer** - Inhaberanleihe f; **broker's** - Maklerdarlehen n, Kredit an Börsenmakler unter Beleihung von Wertpapieren; **building** - Baudarlehen n; **business** - Geschäftskredit m, Betriebskredit m; **call** - (GB) kurzfristiges Darlehen, täglich fälliges Geld, Tagesgeld n; **cash** - Kassendarlehen n; **civil** - (US) öffentliche Anleihe, öffentlicher Kredit; **collateral** - Lombardkredit m, Lombarddarlehen n, abgesicherter Kredit; **commercial** - Warenkredit m; **commodity** - Warenkredit m; **communal** - Gemeinschaftsdarlehen n; **consolidated** - konsolidierte Anleihe; **contract a** - einen Kredit aufnehmen; **conversion** - Umschuldungsanleihe f, Konvertierungsanleihe f; **convertible** - Wandelanleihe f, Wandelobligation f; **corporation** - (GB) Kommunalschuldverschreibungen f pl, Stadtanleihe f, Kommunalanleihe f, Kommunalobligationen f pl; **customer's** - Kundenkredit m, Konsumentenkredit m; **day-to-day** - (GB) Tagesgeld n, täglich fälliger Kredit; **dead** - (GB) Anleihe ohne Verfallfrist; **draw in a** - einen Kredit kündigen; **emergency** - Stützungskredit m; **farm** - Landwirtschaftskredit m, landwirtschaftliches Darlehen, Agrarkredit m; **fiduciary** - ungedeckte Anleihe; **frozen** - eingefrorener Kredit; **government** - Staatsanleihe f; **housing** - Wohnungsbaudarlehen n; **investment** - Investitionskredit m; **launch a** - eine Anleihe auflegen, eine Anleihe begeben; **local authority** - (GB) Kommunalschuldverschreibungen f pl, Stadtanleihe f, Kommunalanleihe f, Kommunalobligationen f pl; **margin** - (US) Effektenbeleihung f, Effektenlombard m, Effektenlombardkredit m; **money** - Kassendarlehen n; **mortgage** - Hypothekardarlehen n, Hypothekendarlehen n; **ninety days** - Dreimonatsgeld n; **oversubscribe a** - eine Anleihe überzeichnen; **participating** - Konsortialkredit m; **pledge** - Pfandanleihe f; **precarious** - unsicheres Darlehen; **public** - öffentliche Anleihe, öffentlicher Kredit; **redeemable** - Tilgungsdarlehen n; **share** - Effektenbeleihung f, Effektenlombard m, Effektenlombardkredit m; **sinking-fund** - Tilgungsanleihe f; **stock** - Effektenbeleihung f, Effektenlombard m, Effektenlombardkredit m; **straight** - nicht handelbare Anleihe; **syndicate** - (US) Konsortialkredit m; **tax-free** - steuerfreie Anleihe; **term** - befristetes Darlehen; **time** - befristetes Darlehen; **undersubscribed** - nicht in voller Höhe gezeichnete Anleihe; **unsecured** - unbesichertes Darlehen, unbesicherte Anleihe; **war** - Kriegsanleihe f; **working capital** - Betriebsmittelkredit m

loans on bonds Beleihung von festverzinslichen Wertpapieren; **bank rate for** - Lombardzins m; **state** - Staatskredite m pl, staatliche Kreditmittel

local authority loan (GB) Kommunalschuldverschreibungen f pl, Stadtanleihe f, Kommunalanleihe f, Kommunalobligation f; **~ bank** Lokalbank f; **~ bill** Platzwechsel m; **~ cheque** (GB) Platzscheck m; **~ currency** Inlandswährung f; **~ custom** Platzusance f; **~ draft** Platzwechsel m; **~ government** Kommune f; **~ time** Ortszeit f

locally drawn check Platzscheck m

lock n Schloß n, Verschluß m; **~** v schließen v; **~ box** Schließfach n; **~ up agreement** (US) Absicherungsmaßnahme einer Fusion; **~ up capital** Kapital festlegen

locked warehouse Zollverschlußlager n

locker n Schrankfach n, Safe m

locking up (e.g. of capital) Festlegung f

lock-up note verlängerter (erneuerter) Schuldschein

lodg(e)ment n Hinterlegung f, Einlieferung f, Einreichung f

lodge v anbringen v, einreichen v, hinterlegen v; **~ a claim** Anspruch erheben, Anspruch geltend machen; **~ a credit with** bei jemandem einen Kredit eröffnen; **~ securities** Effekten hinterlegen

log n Bestandsverzeichnis n (eines Wertpapierhändlers), Protokoll n (Informationsverarbeitung)
lombard loan Lombardkredit m, Lombarddarlehen n, abgesicherter Kredit
Lombard Street Finanzviertel von London
London Bullion Market Londoner Edelmetallmarkt m; **- Commodity Exchange (LCE)** Londoner Rohstoffbörse f; **- Debt Agreement** Londoner Schuldabkommen n; **- equivalent** Londoner Parität; **- Futures and Options Exchange (FOX)** Londoner Termin- und Optionsbörse f; **- Interbank Bid Rate (LIBID)** Londoner Interbanken-Nachfragezinssatz (Geldkurs); **- Interbank Mean Rate (LIMEAN)** Londoner mittlerer Geldmarktzinssatz zwischen LIBID und LIBOR; **- Interbank Offered Rate (LIBOR)** Londoner Interbanken-Angebotszinssatz (Briefkurs); **- International Financial Futures Exchange = LIFFE** Londoner Börse für Finanzterminkontrakte f; **- Metal Exchange (LME)** Londoner Metallbörse f; **- Stock Exchange (LSE)** Londoner Börse f; **- Traded Options Market (LTOM)** Londoner Optionsmarkt m
long n langfristiges Wertpapier, Langläufer m, Käufer m, Haussier m, Hausse-Spekulant m, Haussier m; **- and short positions** Hausse- und Baisse-Positionen f pl; **- bill** Wechsel mit Laufzeit von mindestens 3 Monaten, langfristiger Wechsel; **- credit** langfristiger Kredit; **- debt** langfristige Schulden; **- futures position** Futures-Verkaufsposition f; **- hedges** Termin und Deckungsgeschäfte n pl; **- investment** langfristige Anlage; **- loan** langfristiges Darlehen; **- maturities** Langläufer f pl; **- obligations** langfristige Verpflichtungen; **- position** Hausse-Position, langfristige Anlage; **- pull** (US) Spekulation auf lange Sicht; **- side** Hausse-Partei f; **- stock** (US) effektiv im Besitz befindliche Aktien, (GB) effektiv im Besitz befindliche Wertpapiere; **- stocks** Langläufer f pl; **to be - of stock** (US) mit Aktien eingedeckt sein

long-dated adj langfristig adj
longs Langläufer f pl
long-sighted loan langfristiges Darlehen
long-term debt langfristige Verbindlichkeiten
loose change Kleingeld m
loose-leaf format Loseblattform f
loro account Lorokonto n; **- securities** Loroeffekten f pl
lose v verlieren v, einbüßen v, zusetzen v
loss n Verlust m, Schaden m (Einbuße), Ausfall m, Wertminderung f; **- and gain account** Gewinn-und-Verlust-Rechnung f (US); **- carried forward** Verlustvortrag m; **- carried over** Verlustvortrag m; **- in assets** Anlageabgänge m pl; **- of earnings** Ertragsausfall m; **- of time** Zeitverlust m; **- on exchange** Kursverlust m; Wechselkursverlust m; **- rate** Kreditausfallquote f; **ascertainment of -** Schadenfeststellung f; **bear a -** Verlust tragen; **bookkeeping -** Buchverlust m; **buy at a -** mit Verlust kaufen; **claim for -** Schadenersatzanspruch m; **clear -** Nettoverlust m; **credit -** Kreditausfall m; **trading -** Betriebsverlust m
losses n pl Verluste m pl, Abgänge m pl; **- on receivables** Debitorenverluste m pl
lot v parzellieren v, auslosen v; **- n** (US) Grundstücksparzelle f, Bauplatz m, Teil m, Anteil m, Posten m, Los m; **- trading** Blockhandel m; **board -** feste Stückzahl für den Handel; **broken -** (US) Effekten (unter 1000 Dollar Nominalwert); **draw by -** auslosen v
lots; draw - losen v
lottery n Lotterie f; **- bond** Prämienanleihe f, Losanleihe f
low adj niedrig adj, gering adj; **- n** Tiefstand m; **- exercise price option (LEPO)** Kaufoptionsschein mit niedrigem Ausübungspreis; **- quotation** (stock) Niedrigstkurs m; **- rate** (money) Niedrigstkurs m
lower v senken v, herabsetzen v (Preise), ermäßigen v, verbilligen v, vermindern v; **- bid** niedrigstes Gebot
lowering of interest rates Zinssenkung f

low-interest loan niedrig verzinslicher Kredit (Anleihe)

low-prices shares Kleinaktien f pl, Aktien mit geringem Kurswert

low-rated share niedrig bewertete Aktie

loyalty bonus Loyalitätsbonus m

lucrative adj lukrativ adj, gewinnbringend adj, rentabel adj, einträglich adj

lucrum cessans entgangener Gewinn

lull n Flaute f

lump *sum* einmalige Summe, Pauschalbetrag m; **- *sum payment*** Pauschalzahlung f; **- *rate*** Pauschalsatz m

Luxembourg Interbank Offered Rate = LUXBOR Luxemburger Interbanken-Angebotszinssatz

luxury *goods* Luxusgüter; **- *tax*** Luxussteuer f

LYON = Liquid Yield Option Note Nullkuponanleihe mit Wandelrecht in Aktien

M

M&A = mergers and acquisitions Fusionen und Übernahmen von Firmen, Beteiligungsvermittlung f
machine posting maschinelle Buchhaltung; **- run** Maschinendurchlauf m; **subsequent - processing** maschinelle Weiterverarbeitung
machinery n Maschinen f pl, maschinelle Anlagen
made bill (GB) indossierter Wechsel; **- out to** lautend auf
Madrid interbank offered rate = MIBOR Madrider Interbanken-Angebotszinssatz
magnetic tape clearing Datenträgeraustausch im Zahlungsverkehr
mail n Post f; **- v** mit der Post senden; **- box** Briefkasten; **- credit** Postlaufkredit m; **- order** Postauftrag m; **- teller** Kassier für postalisch eingehende Überweisungen; **- transfer** Postüberweisung f; **registered -** Einschreibesendung f
mailing address Postanschrift f; **- code** Versandartschlüssel m
main branch Hauptfiliale f; **- office** Hauptniederlassung f
maintain v unterhalten v, (er)halten v
maintained behauptet (Börse)
maintenance n Unterhalt m, Unterstützung f; **- charges** Kontoführungsgebühren f pl (US); **- costs** Unterhaltungskosten plt
major n Volljähriger m, Mündiger m; **- bank** Großbank f; **- shareholder** Großaktionär m; **- swing** (US) Marktentwicklung über einen größeren Zeitraum
majority interest Mehrheitsbeteiligung f, maßgebendes Kapitalinteresse; **- of shares** Aktienmehrheit f; **- of stock** Aktienmehrheit f; **- of votes** Stimmenmehrheit f
majors Großunternehmen
make v fertigen v, ein Angebot machen, abschließen v; **- n** Erzeugnis n, Produkt n, Fabrikat n; **- an additional charge** nachbelasten v; **- an offer** ein Angebot unterbreiten; **- copies** vervielfältigen v; **- investigations** Erhebungen anstellen; **- out** ausstellen v, ausfertigen v; **- payable** zahlbar stellen
maker n Aussteller m (Wechsel), Wechselgeber m, Wechselaussteller m, Trassant m
making up day Prämienerklärungstag m
maladministration Mißwirtschaft f, schlechte Verwaltung
mala fide arglistig, unredlich, bösgläubig
manage v verwalten v (Gelder), leiten v, führen v, vorstehen v, behandeln v, beaufsichtigen v, bewerkstelligen v
manageable adj verwaltbar adj, lenkbar adj, leicht zu regulieren, zu bewältigen; **- risk** steuerbare Risiken
managed currency manipulierte Währung; **- economy** Planwirtschaft f; **- securities safe custody account** Vermögensverwaltungsdepot n
management n Geschäftsführung f, Betriebsführung f, Geschäftsleitung f, Direktion f, Vorstand m; **- account** Verwaltungsdepot n; **- authorization** Verwaltungsvollmacht f; **- by delegation** Unternehmensführung durch Delegation von Aufgaben; **- buyin** Unternehmensübernahme durch ein fremdes Management f; **- by motivation** Unternehmensführung durch Motivation der Mitarbeiter; **- by objectives** Unternehmensführung durch Zielvorgaben; **- buyout (MBO)** Management buyout n, Unternehmensübernahme durch das eigene Management; **- by results** Unternehmensführung durch Erfolgsmessung; **- company** Verwaltungsgesellschaft f; **- consultant** Unternehmensberater; **- fee** Verwaltungsgebühr f; **- group** Konsortium n; **- information system** Management-Informations-System n (MIS); **- of property** Vermögensverwaltung f; **- shares** Vorstandsaktien f pl; **- trust** Kapitalanlagegesellschaft

mit Anlageverwaltung; **bank** ~ Bankvorstand m, Bankleitung f; **building** ~ Gebäudeverwaltung f; **business** ~ Betriebsführung f; **central** ~ Hauptverwaltung f; **corporate** ~ Gesellschaftsleitung f; **cost of** ~ Verwaltungskosten plt; **industrial** ~ Betriebsführung f

manager n Direktor m Geschäftsführer m, Betriebsleiter m, Leiter m, Verwalter m, Vorsteher m; **~ in bankruptcy** Konkursverwalter m; **~ of a bank** Bankdirektor m; **assistant** ~ stellvertretender Direktor; **bank** ~ Bankdirektor m; **branch** ~ Filialleiter m; **deputy** ~ stellvertretender Direktor

managerial adj führend adj, unternehmerisch adj

managermental adj unternehmerisch adj

manager's commission Führungsprovision f

managership n Geschäftsführertätigkeit f, Managertum n

managing adj geschäftsführend adj; **~ clerk** Geschäftsführer m, Prokurist m; **~ director** Vorstandsmitglied n; **~ partner** geschäftsführender Gesellschafter, geschäftsführender Teilhaber

mandatary n Mandatar m, Bevollmächtigter m, Beauftragte f u. m

mandate n Mandat n, Vollmacht f, Auftrag m

mandator n Vollmachtgeber m, Auftraggeber m

mandatory adj verpflichtend adj, obligatorisch adj, verbindlich adj; ~ n Bevollmächtigte f u. m, Beauftragte f u. m; **~ payment** Pflichtzahlung f

manifold v vervielfältigen v

manipulation n Kursbeeinflussung f, Kursmanipulation f, Beeinflussung f

manpower Arbeitskraft f, Personal n

MANTIS = Market and Trading Information System Informationssystem an der Londoner Börse

manual n Leitfaden m, Handbuch n, Führer m

manufactory Fabrik f, Herstellungsbetrieb m, Werk n

manufacture v fabrizieren v, herstellen v; ~ n Fabrikation f, Herstellung f, Fertigung f

manufactured adj fabrikmäßig hergestellt

manufacturer n Fabrikant m, Hersteller m, Industrieller m, Fabrikbesitzer m, Erzeuger m, Produzent m

manufacturing company Produktionsgesellschaft f

map Katasterplan m; **~ records** Grundbuch n

Maple Leaf Maple Leaf m ($ 50; kanadische Goldmünze mit 1 Unze Feingehalt)

margin n Bruttogewinn m, Spanne f, Überschuß m, Marge f, Differenz f; **~ account** (US) Einschußkonto n; **~ business** (US) Effektendifferenzgeschäft n; **~ call** (US) Effektengeschäft mit Einschuß; **~ calls** Nachschußforderungen f pl; **~ loan** (US) Effektenbeleihung f, Effektenlombard m, Effektenlombardkredit m; Effektenkredit m; **~ of profit** Gewinnspanne f; **~ requirements** (US) Mindestbarzahlung bei Wertpapierenkäufen auf Kreditbasis; **buy securities on** ~ Wertpapiere auf Kreditbasis kaufen; **buying on** ~ Effektenkauf mit Einschuß; **initial** ~ Einschußmarge f; **leave a** ~ einen Gewinn abwerfen

marginable beleihbar adj (US)

marginal adj gerade noch rentabel, knapp adj, Grenz- (in Zus.); **~ account** (US) Einschußkonto n; **~ cost** Grenzkosten plt; **~ loan** risikobehafteter Kredit; **~ producer** Grenzbetrieb m; **~ utility** Grenznutzen m

marine insurance Seeschadenstransportversicherung f, Seeversicherung f; **~ insurance policy** Seeversicherungspolice f; **~ insurance underwriters** Seeversicherungsgesellschaft f

marital adj ehelich adj; **~ control** (GB) Verwaltungsrecht des Ehemannes (über das Eigentum der Ehefrau)

maritime lien Seepfandrecht n

mark n (stock exchange) Kursfestsetzung f; ~ n Marke f (Markierung), Zeichen n, Merkmal n, Stempel m; **~ down** im Preis herabsetzen; **~ time** tendenzlos sein (Börse); **~ up** anschreiben v, im Preis erhöhen

marked check (US) besonders gekennzeichneter Scheck zur Verhinderung von Fälschungen; **~ cheque** (GB) bestätigter Scheck

market m Markt m, Börse f, Marktpreis m; ~ n Markt m, Marktlage f, Absatzgebiet n; ~ v vertreiben v, handeln v; ~ *analysis* Marktanalyse f; ~ *average* Durchschnittskurs m, Durchschnittspreis m, Mittelkurs m; ~ *bid price* Geldkurs m; ~ *capitalization* Börsenkapitalisierung f; ~ *condition* Marktlage f; ~ *closing rate* Börsenkurs m; ~ *crash* Börsenkrach m; ~ *days* Börsentage f pl; ~ *dealings* Börsenhandel m; ~ *depression* Baisse f; ~ *discount rate* Privatdiskontsatz m; ~ *dullness* Börsenflaute f; ~ *economy* Marktwirtschaft f; ~ *forces* Marktkräfte f pl; ~ *forecast* Marktprognose f; ~ *hours* Börsensitzung f; ~ *leaders* führende Werte an der Börse; ~ *off* (US) Markt abgeschwächt, Kurse abgeschwächt; ~ *order* Bestensauftrag m, unlimitierter Börsenauftrag; ~ *overt* offener Markt; ~ *price* Börsenkurs m, Kurswert m; Tageskurs m, Tagessatz m, Marktpreis m; ~ *prime rate* (US) Privatdiskontsatz m; ~ *professionals* Börsianer m pl; ~ *quotation* Marktnotierung f, Börsennotierung f; ~ *rally* Markterholung f; ~ *rate* Börsenkurs m, Kurswert m; ~ *rates of interest* (US) Geldmarktsätze m pl; ~ *ratio* (US) Marktverhältnis n; ~ *report* Börsenbericht m; ~ *requirement* Markterfordernis n; ~ *research* Marktforschung f; ~ *rigging* Kurstreiberei f, Börsenmanöver n; ~ *sentiment* Börsenstimmung f; ~ *share* Marktanteil m; ~ *shares* abgestempelte Aktien m pl; ~ *swing* (US) Konjunkturbewegung am Markt; ~ *theories* Börsentheorien f pl; ~ *value* (GB) Diskontsatz der Londoner Banken und Wechselmakler; ~ *value* Marktwert m, Börsenwert m; *actual* - *value* Marktwert m; *american* - (GB) Markt für amerikanische Werte; *at the* - bestens (Ausführungsbedingung für einen Börsenauftrag, d. h. ohne Preislimit); *bear* - Baissemarkt m; *bear the* - Baisse herbeiführen, Kurse drücken; *bearish* - Baissemarkt m; *bill* - Diskontmarkt m, Wechselmarkt m; *black* - Schwarzmarkt m; *bond* - Obligationsmarkt m, Rentenmarkt m, Pfandbriefmarkt m, Anleihemarkt m; *boom* - Hausse-Markt m; *building* - Baumarkt m; *bull* - Hausse-Markt m; *bullish* - Hausse-Markt m; *buyer's* - Käufermarkt m; *call money* - Markt für Tagesgeld; *capital* - Kapitalmarkt m; *cash* - Geldmarkt m; *collapse of the* - Börsenzusammenbruch m

Market; *Common* - Gemeinsame Markt m

market; *consumer* - Verbrauchsgütermarkt m; *curb* - Freiverkehrsbörse f, Freibörse f, Freiverkehrsmarkt m Nachbörse f; *dead* - lustlose Börse, umsatzschwache Börse; *demoralized* - sehr gedrückter Markt; *discount* - Diskontmarkt m, Wechselmarkt m; *disturbed* - bewegte Börse; *domestic* - Inlandsmarkt m; *door-to-door* - Hausverkauf m; *dull* - flauer Markt, flaue Börse; *foreign exchange* - Devisenmarkt m; *growth* - Wachstumsmarkt m; *in line with the* - marktkonform; *inofficial* - Freiverkehrsbörse f, Freibörse f, Freiverkehrsmarkt m, Nachbörse f; *international* - Markt für international gehandelte Wertpapiere; ~ *maker* Marktmacher m; *money* - Geldmarkt m; *open* - freier Markt, offener Markt; *over the counter* - Markt im Telefonverkehr und am Schalter; *parallel* - Parallelmarkt m, freier Devisenmarkt; *pegged* - (US) in engem Rahmen gehaltener Markt; *real estate* - Immobilienmarkt m; *sagging* - abgeschwächter Markt; *secondary* - Markt zweiter Ordnung; *securities* - Effektenbörse f, Effektenmarkt m, Wertpapiermarkt m; *sensitive* - leicht reagierende Börse, empfindlich reagierende Börse; *seller's* - Verkäufermarkt m; *share* - Aktienmarkt m; *sick* - (US) uneinheitlicher Markt, lustloser Markt; *stale* - flauer Markt, flaue Börse; *stock* - Börse f; *tendencies of the* - Börsenentwicklung f; *thin* - schwacher Markt; *to be in and out of the* - ein kurzfristiges Börsengeschäft machen; *turn in the* - Umschwung am Markt; *undersell the*

marketability

~ eine erwartete Baisse am Markt im voraus berücksichtigen; **unofficial** ~ (GB) Freiverkehrsbörse f, Freibörse f, Freiverkehrsmarkt m, Nachbörse f; **weak** ~ schwacher Markt
marketability n Marktfähigkeit f, Börsenfähigkeit f
marketable adj marktfähig adj, börsenfähig adj, absatzfähig adj; kurant; ~ **collaterals** verkehrsfähige Sicherheiten; ~ **securities** börsengängige Wertpapiere, Börsenwerte m pl
marketing n Absatzförderung f, Absatzmethode f, Vertriebslehre f; ~ **mix** Marketing-Mix m; ~ **research** Marktforschung f
market-to-market settlement börsentägliche Abrechnung (z. B. von Gewinnen/Verlusten aus Termingeschäften)
markings Börsenumsätze f pl
Markka Markka f (Währung in Finnland)
marriage settlement Ehevertrag m
mart n Markt m, Handelszentrum n
mass business Massengeschäft n; ~ **production** Massenproduktion f, Massenerzeugnis n, Massenherstellung f, Massenfabrikation f; ~ **purchasing power** Massenkaufkraft f
master record (EDP) Bestandssatz m (EDV), Hauptsatz m (EDV); ~ **tape** (EDP) Bestandsband n (EDV)
matched order (US) Börsenauftrag m (zum Kauf und Verkauf des gleichen Wertpapiers)
material asset (intrinsic) value Substanzwert m; ~ **recession** beträchtlicher Rückgang, wesentlicher Rückgang; ~ **value clause** Sachwertklausel f
matrimonial adj ehelich adj
matters; banking ~ Bankangelegenheiten f pl
mature v fällig werden; **bill about to** ~ in Kürze fällig werdender Wechsel; **bill to** ~ laufender Wechsel
maturity n Fälligkeit f, Verfallzeit f; ~ **cap** Laufzeitbegrenzung f; ~ **code** Fälligkeitsschlüssel m; ~ **date** Verfalltag m, Fälligkeitstermin m, Fälligkeitstag m; ~ **file** Verfallkartei f; ~ **index** Verfallbuch n; ~ **tickler** (US)

Verfallbuch n; **at** ~ bei Verfall; **date of** ~ Verfalltag m, Fälligkeitstermin m, Fälligkeitstag m; **prior to** ~ vor Fälligkeit
maxi floating rate note zinsvariabler Schuldtitel mit einer Zinsobergrenze
maximization of profits Gewinnmaximierung f
maximum spread höchste Spanne zwischen Geld- und Briefkurs; ~ **term** (e.g. of loan) Höchstlaufzeit f
mean due date mittlerer Verfalltag; ~ **price** Mittelkurs m; ~ **rate of exchange** Mittelkurs m; ~ **value** Mittelwert m
means n pl Geldmittel n pl, Kapital n, Vermögen n, Geld n; ~ **of payment** Zahlungsmittel n pl; ~ **of transport** Beförderungsmittel n
measure n Maß n, Maßnahme f; ~ **a company's performance** Leistung eines Unternehmens bewerten; ~ **of value** Wertmaßstab m, Wertmesser m
medaillon Medaille, Münzprägung ohne Nennwert
medal n Medaille f
median bid and ask quotation Mittelkurs zwischen Geld- und Briefkurs
mediate v schlichten v, durch Schiedsspruch entscheiden
mediation n Vermittlung f
mediator n Unterhändler m, Vermittler m
medium of exchange Valuta f, Tauschmittel n
medium-sized company Unternehmen mittlerer Größe
medium-term mittelfristig adj
medium-term loan mittelfristiger Kredit
medium-term note = MTN Schuldverschreibung mit mittlerer Laufzeit
meet v eine Sitzung abhalten, tagen v; ~ v nachkommen v (Verpflichtungen), befriedigen v, bezahlen v; ~ **commitments** Verpflichtungen erfüllen; ~ **demands for payment** Zahlungsansprüche befriedigen; ~ **one's liabilities** seinen Verbindlichkeiten nachkommen
meeting n Sitzung f, Versammlung f, Tagung f; ~ **of creditors** Gläubigerversammlung f; ~ **of shareholders** (GB)

Hauptversammlung f, Generalversammlung f, Aktionärsversammlung f; **- of stockholders** (US) Hauptversammlung f, Generalversammlung f, Aktionärsversammlung f; **- of the executive board** Verwaltungsratssitzung f; **- of the supervisory board** Aufsichtsratssitzung f; **adjourn a -** eine Versammlung vertagen; **annual -** Hauptversammlung f, Generalversammlung f, Aktionärsversammlung f; **annual - of shareholders** (GB) ordentliche Hauptversammlung der Aktionäre; **annual - of stockholders** (US) ordentliche Hauptversammlung der Aktionäre; **attend a -** einer Versammlung beiwohnen; **call a - of shareholders** eine Hauptversammlung einberufen; **call a - of stockholders** Hauptversammlung einberufen; **company -** Gesellschafterversammlung f; **corporate -** Vorstandssitzung f; **creditors' -** Gläubigerversammlung f; **shareholders' -** Hauptversammlung f, Generalversammlung f, Aktionärsversammlung f; **stockholders' -** Hauptversammlung f, Generalversammlung f, Aktionärsversammlung f

mega issue Großemission f (z. B. Deutsche Telekom)

melon n (US) außerordentliche Dividende; **cutting the -** (US-Slang) Ausschüttung einer außerordentlichen Dividende

member n (of a syndicate) Konsorte m; **- bank** (US) dem Clearingsystem angehörende Bank, Mitgliedsbank f (d. Federal Reserve System); **- of the board** Vorstandsmitglied n; **- of the executive board** Verwaltungsratsmitglied n; **- of the supervisory board** Aufsichtsratsmitglied n; **syndicate -** Konsortialmitglied n

members' liability Haftung der Gesellschafter; **- shareholdings** Anteile der Gesellschafter

memorandum check (US) vordatierter Scheck; **- of association** (GB) Gründungsvertrag m (einer Gesellschaft); **- of deposit** (GB) Hinterlegungsurkunde f

memory card Kreditkarte mit elektronischem System; **- capacity** Speicherkapazität f (EDV); **- size** Speicherkapazität f (EDV)

mental incapacity Handlungsunfähigkeit f

mentally deranged geisteskrank adj, geistesgestört adj

mercantile adj merkantil adj, kaufmännisch adj, Handels- (in Zus.); **- agency** (US) Handelsauskunftei f; **- agent** Handelsvertreter m; **- credit** Warenkredit m, Lieferantenkredit; **- law** Handelsrecht n; **- paper** Wechselmaterial n

merchandise v handeln v (Handel treiben); **-** n Handelsware f; **advances against -** Warenlombard m

merchant n Kaufmann m, Händler m; **- bank** Handelsbank f; **- banker** Handelsbank f; **- class** Handelsstand m, Handel m

merchantable adj verkaufsfähig adj, absatzfähig adj

merchants n pl Handelsstand m, Handel m; **company of -** Handelsgesellschaft f

merge v zusammenschließen v, fusionieren v, verschmelzen v

merger n Verschmelzung f, Zusammenschluß m, Fusion f; **bank -** Bankenfusion f; **downstairs -** Fusion der Mutter mit der Tochtergesellschaft

mergers and acquisitions = M&A Beteiligungsvermittlung f

message format Nachrichtenaufbau m

messenger n Bote m, Kassenbote m, Bürodiener m; **- service** Botendienst m

metal; base - unedles Metall; **precoins -** Edelmetall n

metayer contract Naturalpachtvertrag m

method n Verfahren n; **- of identification** Identifikationsmethode f; **bookkeeping -** Buchungsverfahren n; **cost -** Kostenrechnungsmethode f

metropolitan cheque (GB) Scheck einer Bank in Groß-London

mezzanine finance Mezzanine f, nachrangige Finanzierung

micro-film Mikrofilm m

microprocessor Mikroprozessor m

middle price

middle price Durchschnittskurs *m*, Durchschnittspreis *m*, Mittelkurs *m*
middleman *n* Zwischenhändler *m*
mid-month Medio *m*, Monatsmitte *f*
mid-way profit Zwischengewinn *m*
mid-year movements of funds Kapitalbewegungen zum Semesterultimo
mid-year settlement Halbjahresrechnung *f*, Halbjahresabschluß *m*
milking *n* (US) Ausbeutung eines Unternehmens, Ausnutzung eines Unternehmens
mines *n* Bergbauaktien *f pl*
minimax bonds variable Zinstitel mit Mindest- und Höchstzinssätzen
mini-max floating rate note zinsvariabler Schuldtitel mit Höchst- und Mindestzinssatz
minimum *deposit* Mindesteinlage *f*; *- lending rate* Mindestzinssatz der Bank von England; *- reserve* Mindestreserve *f*
mining company share Kux *f*; *- securities* Wertpapiere von Bergwerksunternehmen
Ministry of Economics Wirtschaftsministerium *n*
minor *adj* unbedeutend *adj*, unwichtig *adj*, minderjährig *adj*; *- n* Minderjähriger *m*, Unmündiger *m*
minority *interest* Minderheitsbeteiligung *f*; *- interests* Ausgleichsposten für Anteile anderer Gesellschaften (Bilanzposten); *- shareholder rights* Minderheitsrechte des Aktionärs
mint *n* Münze *f* (Prägeanstalt), Münzamt *n*, Münzstätte *f*; *- par* Münzparität *f*; *- price* Anzahl der Münzen (die aus einer bestimmten Menge von Metall geschlagen werden kann)
mintage *n* Ausprägung *f*, Ausmünzung *f*
minting *n* Münzprägung *f*
minus weniger, abzüglich
minute *n* Bericht *m*, Entwurf *m*, Notiz *f*, Vermerk *m*; *- book* Protokollbuch *n*
minutes *n pl* Protokoll *n* (einer Sitzung), Sitzungsbericht *m*; **keep the** *-* Protokoll führen
mirror contract (GB) Gegengeschäft *n*
misapplication *n* Unterschlagung *f*, Veruntreuung *f*

misapply *v* falsch verwenden, unterschlagen *v* (Gelder)
misappropriate *v* veruntreuen *v*, unrechtmäßig verwenden
misappropriation *n* Veruntreuung *f*, unrechtmäßige Verwendung
miscalculate *v* falsch berechnen, verrechnen *v* (sich)
miscalculation *n* Rechenfehler *m*, Kalkulationsfehler *m*
miscellaneous market Markt für verschiedene Werte
misdirected investment Fehlinvestition *f*
misinvestment Fehlinvestition *f*
mismanagement Mißwirtschaft *f*
mismatch floating rate note zinsvariabler Schuldtitel, Floater ohne Deckungsgleichheit von Zinsfeststellung und Zinszahlung
mispriced bond Anleihe mit nicht marktgerechter Ausstattung
miss *v* fehlen *v*
mistake *n* Fehler *m*; *- n* Irrtum *m*, Versehen *n*
mixed *investment trust* gemischter Anlagefonds; *- loan (credit)* Mischkredit *m*; *- to lower* einheitlich bis schwächer (Börse)
mobilize *v* mobilisieren *v*; *- capital* Gelder flüssig machen
mode of payment Zahlungsweise *f*
modification *n* Änderung *f*, Veränderung *f*, Abänderung *f*; *- code* Änderungsschlüssel *m*; *- notice* Änderungsmitteilung *f*; *- service* Änderungsdienst *m*
module *n* Modul *m*
MOFF = multiple option financing facility Finanzierung mit Wahlrecht zwischen verschiedenen Währungen
monetary *adj* geldlich *adj*, finanziell *adj*, Geld- (in Zus.), Münz- (in Zus.); *- agreement* Zahlungsabkommen *n*; *- arrangements* Gelddisposition *f*; *- authorities* Währungsbehörden *f pl*; *- base* monetäre Basis; *- cooperation* währungspolitische Zusammenarbeit *f*; *- policy* Währungspolitik *f*; *- reserve* Währungsreserve *f*; *- sovereignty* Währungshoheit *f*; *- standard* Münzfuß *m*,

Währungsstandard m, Währungseinheit f; **- stock** (US) gesamter Geldbestand; **- system** Geldsystem n, Währungssystem n; **- theory** Geldtheorie f; **- transactions** Zahlungsverkehr m; **- union** Währungsunion f; **- unit** Geldeinheit f, Münzeinheit f, Währungseinheit f; **- value** Geldwert m; **- wealth** Geldvermögen n

Monetary; International - Fund (IMF) Internationale Währungsfonds m (IWF)

monetization n Münzprägung f

monetize v ausprägen v, zum gesetzlichen Zahlungsmittel machen, Münzfuß festsetzen

money n Geld n; **- at call** Tagesgeld n, täglich fälliges Geld; **- box** Sparbüchse f; **- broker** Geldmakler m; **- dealer** Geldwechsler m; **- holdings** gesamter Geldbestand; **- in account** Buchgeld n, Girogeld n, bargeldloses Zahlungsmittel; **- in cash** Kassenbestand m, Bargeld n - **in hand** Kassenbestand m, Bargeld n; **- jobber** Geldhändler m; **- lender** Geldgeber m, Geldverleiher m; **- lent and lodged book** (GB) Kontokorrentbuch n; **- loan** Kassendarlehen n;; **- market** Geldmarkt m; **- market paper** Geldmarktpapier n; **- office** Kassenabteilung f; **- order** (MO) Postanweisung f; **- parcel** Geldpaket n, Geldrolle f; **- pinch** zeitweilige Geldknappheit am Geldmarkt; **- rate** Geldsatz m; **- supply** Geldversorgung f; **- transfer** Geldüberweisung f; **- transfer business** Überweisungsverkehr m; **- vault** Kassenschrank m; **accommodate with** - Geld ausleihen; **advance** - Geld vorstrecken; **allotment** - Zuteilungsbetrag m; **allowance in** - Geldzuweisung f; **amount of** - Geldsumme f; **average** - Havariegelder n pl; **bad** - Falschgeld n; **bank** - Buchgeld n, Giralgeld n, bargeldloses Zahlungsmittel; **bargain** - Draufgeld n, Handgeld n; **barren** - totes Kapital, brachliegendes Kapital; **bills and** - Brief und Geld; **borrow** - Kredit aufnehmen; **borrowed** - geliehenes Geld, aufgenommener Kredit, **call** - Tagesgeld n,

täglich fälliges Geld; **cheap** - billiges Geld, billige Geldsätze; **cheapening of** - Herabsetzen der Geldsätze; **check book** - (US) Buchgeld n, Giralgeld n, bargeldloses Zahlungsmittel; **circulation of** - Geldumlauf m; **close** - teures Geld; **commodity** - Indexwährung f; **convertible** - in Gold einlösbares Papiergeld; **counterfeit** - Falschgeld n; **create** - Geld schöpfen; **day-to-day** - Tagesgeld n, täglich fälliges Geld; **dead** - totes Kapital, brachliegendes Kapital; **demand** - Tagesgeld n, täglich fälliges Geld; **deposit** - Buchgeld n, Giralgeld n, bargeldloses Zahlungsmittel; **dormant** - totes Kapital, brachliegendes Kapital; **drain of** - Geldabfluß m; **easy** - billiges Geld, billige Geldsätze; **flux of** - Geldumlauf m; **idle** - freies Kapital, nicht angelegtes Kapital; **public** - Staatsgelder n pl, öffentliche Gelder; **ready** - Bargeld n, bares Geld, flüssige Mittel; **rent** - Mietgeld n, Pachtgeld n; **spare** - Notgroschen m, erübrigtes Geld; **token** - Wertmarke f; **trust** - Mündelgeld n

moneyage n Münzgerechtigkeit f

moneyed corporation (US) Gesellschaft (die bank- oder versicherungsmäßige Geschäfte betreibt)

money-laundering Geldwäscherei f

moneyless adj mittellos adj, unvermögend adj, verarmt adj

money-making gewinnbringend adj, einträglich adj

money-market fund Geldmarktfonds m

money-spinner Kassenschlager m

monometallism n Monometallismus m, Einzelwährung f

monopolize v monopolisieren v, Monopol besitzen, alleinbeherrschen v

monopoly n Monopol n, Alleinhandel m, Alleinvertrieb m; **buyer's** - Käufermonopol n

month-end n Monatsultimo m; **- settlement** Ultimofinanzierung f

monthly adj monatlich adj; **- account** Monatskonto n; **- balance** Monatsbilanz f; **- balance sheet** monatlicher Bilanzaufgliederungsbogen f; **- earning** monatlicher Ertrag; **- return** (GB)

Monatsausweis *m*; **- statement** Monatsausweis *m*
moonlight Schwarzarbeiten *f pl*
moral suasion Seelenmassage *f*
moratorium *n* Zahlungsaufschub *m*, Moratorium *n*
mortgage *v* hypothekarisch belasten, verpfänden *v*, mit einer Hypothek belasten, dinglich belasten; - *n* Hypothek *f*, hypothekarische Belastung, Hypothekenbrief *m*; **- assignment** Hypothekenabtretung *f*; **- bank** Hypothekenbank *f*; **- bond** Hypothekenpfandbrief *m*, Hypothekenbrief *m*; **- business** Hypothekengeschäft *n*; **- debenture** hypothekarisch gesicherte Obligation, hypothekarisch gesicherte Schuldverschreibung; **- deed** Hypothekenpfandbrief *m*, Hypothekenbrief *m*; **- interest** Hypothekenzins *m*; **- loan** Hypothekardarlehen *n*, Hypothekendarlehen *n*; **- note** Schuldbrief *m*, hypothekarisch gesicherter Schuldschein; **- with fixed interest** Festzinshypothek *f*; **amortization -** Amortisationshypothek *f*; **application for a -** Hypothekenantrag *m*; **assets -** Aktivhypothek *f*; **assignment of -** Hypothekenabtretung *f*; **assuming of a -** Hypothekenübernahme *f*; **blanket -** Gesamthypothek *f*; **chattel -** Mobiliarhypothek *f*; **closed -** eingelöste Hypothek; **collateral - bonds** Obligationen (für die vom Schuldner verpfändete Hypotheken als Sicherheit dienen); **common -** Verkehrshypothek *f*; **consolidated -** (US) Gesamthypothek *f* **construction -** Bauhypothek *f*; **contributory -** für mehrere Gläubiger bestellte Hypothek; **creation of a -** Hypothekenbestellung *f*; **direct reduction -** Hypothek mit direkter Tilgung; **equitable -** Billigkeitspfand *n*; **extinguish a -** eine Hypothek tilgen; **farm -** landwirtschaftliche Hypothek; **first -** erste Hypothek, erststellige Hypothek; **floating -** Gesamthypothek *f*; **foreclose a -** Zwangsvollstreckung aus einer Hypothek betreiben; **general -** Gesamthypothek *f*; **legal -** rechtsgültige Hypothek, gesetzliche Hypothek; **paid off -** abgelöste Hypothek; **puisne -** (GB) Nachgangshypothek *f*; **purchase money -** Restkaufgeldhypothek *f*; **raise a -** eine Hypothek aufnehmen; **real estate -** Hypothek *f*, hypothekarische Belastung, Hypothekenbrief *m*; **real estate - note** Hypothekenpfandbrief *m*, Hypothekenbrief *m*; **refunding -** Ablösungsschuldhypothek *f*; **register a -** eine Hypothek bestellen, eine Hypothek eintragen lassen; **repayment -** Tilgungshypothek *f*; **second -** Zweithypothek *f*; **senior -** Vorranghypothek *f*; **ship -** Schiffshypothek *f*; **statutory -** rechtsgültige Hypothek, gesetzliche Hypothek; **tacit -** stilliegende Hypothek; **trust -** Sicherungshypothek *f*; **underlying -** (US) Vorranghypothek *f*
mortgageable *adj* verpfändbar *adj*, hypothekenfähig *adj*, hypothekisierbar *adj*
mortgaged *adj* dinglich belastet, hypothekarisch belastet
mortgagee *n* Hypothekengläubiger *m*, Pfandgläubiger *m*, Hypothekenpfandgläubiger *m*
mortgager *n* Hypothekenschuldner *m*, Hypothekenpfandschuldner *m*
mortgages; burdened with - mit Hypotheken belastet
mortgagor *n* Hypothekenschuldner *m*, Hypothekenpfandschuldner *m*
most-favoured-nation clause Meistbegünstigungsklausel *f*
motors *n pl* Automobilaktien *f pl*
movable equipment leasing Mobilienleasing *n*
movable estate bewegliches Vermögen, Mobiliarvermögen *n*; **- goods** bewegliches Vermögen, Mobiliarvermögen *n*
movables *n pl* bewegliches Vermögen, Mobiliarvermögen *n*; **- and immovables** bewegliches und unbewegliches Vermögen
movement *n* Umsatz *m* (Bewegung auf einem Konto); **- of capital** Kapitalbewegung *f*; **bull -** Haussebewegung *f*
mover *n* (US) Möbelspediteur *m*
moving average gleitender Durchschnitt
MTN = medium-term note Schuldverschreibung mit mittlerer Laufzeit
mulct *n* Geldstrafe *f*, Buße *f*

multi function financial services Allfinanzdienstleistungen f pl
multi-currency clause Mehrwährungsklausel f
multi-currency credit line Kreditlinie für mehrere Währungen f
multilateral adj mehrseitig adj, multilateral adj
multinational bank multinationale Bank
multiple *certificate* Globalanteilschein m; **- *exchange rate*** gespaltener Wechselkurs; **- lien on property** Gesamtpfandrecht n, Gesamtgrundpfandrecht n; **- *office bank*** Filialbank f; **- *option financing facility (MOFF)*** Finanzierung mit Wahlrecht zwischen verschiedenen Währungen; **- *voting share*** Mehrstimmrechtsaktie f
multiple-branch banking Filialbanksystem n
multiplier bond Anleihe mit Wahlrecht zwischen Barzahlung und weiteren Anleihestücken
multiply v vervielfachen v, multiplizieren v
multi-point connection Mehrpunktverbindung f
multi-point drop Mehrpunktverbindung f
multi-programming n (EDP) Simultanarbeit f
multi-purpose field Mehrzweckfeld n
multi-source export finance Exportfinanzierung als Gesamtpacket aus verschiedenen Finanzierungsmöglichkeiten
multi-stage plan Stufenplan m

municipal adj städtisch adj, gemeindlich adj, kommunal adj; **- bank** Kommunalbank f; **- bond** (US) Kommunalschuldverschreibungen f pl, Stadtanleihe f, Kommunalanleihe f, Kommunalobligationen f pl; **- securities** Kommunalschuldverschreibungen f pl, Stadtanleihe f, Kommunalanleihe f, Kommunalobligationen f pl
municipals n pl Kommunalschuldverschreibungen f pl, Stadtanleihe f, Kommunalanleihe f, Kommunalobligationen f pl
muniment Eigentumsurkunde f
MUST = medium-term USD/SFR transaction Doppelwährungsanleihe auf US-Dollar und Schweizer Franken
mutilated adj beschädigt adj (Wertpapiere), verstümmelt adj (Telegramm)
mutilation n Verstümmelung f, Beschädigung f
mutual *fund* Investmentgesellschaft mit offenem Anlageportefeuille, (US) offener Fonds; **- *fund share*** (US) Investmentanteil m, Fondsanteil m; **- *insurance*** Versicherung auf Gegenseitigkeit; **- *loan association*** (US) genossenschaftliche Bausparkasse; **- *savings bank*** (US) Sparkasse f; **- *testament*** gegenseitiges Testament, Berliner Testament n; **- *will*** gegenseitiges Testament, Berliner Testament n
mystic will unverständliches Testament

N

naked *debenture* (GB) ungesicherte Obligation; *- guarantee* abstrakte Garantie f; *- option* ungedeckte Option; *- position* ungesicherte Position; *- warrant* ungedeckter Optionsschein

Napoleon Napoleon m (französische 20-Franken-Goldmünze)

narrow market enger Markt

NASD = National Association of Securities Dealer Dachorganisation der amerikanischen Aktienmakler

national bank (US) mit Genehmigung der Bundesregierung im Rahmen eines Nationalbankgesetzes gegründete Bank, Nationalbank f, Staatsbank f

National Bank Surveillance System Überwachungssystem der US-Bankenaufsichtsbehörde

national *banking system* (US) Nationalbankwesen n, vom Bundesstaat zugelassene Banken; *- currency* Landeswährung f; *- debt* Staatsschuld f

National Debt Office nationale Schuldenverwaltung Großbritanniens

national *debt register* Schuldbuch n; *- economy* Wirtschaftswissenschaft f, Nationalökonomie f, Volkswirtschaft n; *- issue* Inlandsmission f; *- product* Bruttosozialprodukt n

National Savings Bank Postsparkasse f; *- Union of Bank Employees* britischer Bankangestelltenverband

national wealth Volksvermögen n

nationalize v verstaatlichen v

natural capital Grundbesitz m

near banks bankähnliche Unternehmen; *- liquid asset* Quasigeld n

near-bank (US) bankähnliche Finanzgesellschaft (z.B. Bausparkassen)

near-bank banking Finanzdienstleistungen banknaher Unternehmen

near-limit order (near-order) Zirka-Auftrag m, Zirka-Limit n

need; *customer's -* Kundenbedürfnis n; *in case of -* im Bedarfsfall, Notadresse auf Wechseln

needy adj bedürftig adj, arm adj

negative *interest* Minuszins m; *- mortgage clause* negative Hypothekenklausel; *- pledge clause* Negativklausel m

negligence n Leichtfertigkeit f, Fahrlässigkeit f

negligent adj fahrlässig adj, leichtfertig adj

negotiability n Bankfähigkeit f, Börsenfähigkeit f, Marktfähigkeit f, Übertragbarkeit f, Indossierbarkeit f, Begebbarkeit f

negotiable adj begebbar adj, marktfähig adj, verkäuflich adj, übertragbar adj, handelbar adj; *- instruments* verkäufliche Wertpapiere; *- papers* begebbare Wertpapiere; *- securities* begebbare Wertpapiere

negotiate v verhandeln v, begeben v, handeln v, unterbringen v (Wechsel, Anleihen), zustandebringen v, negoziieren v

negotiation n Verhandlung f, Vertragsabschluß m, Negozierung f; *- of bills* Diskontierung von Wechseln

negotiating bank negoziierende Bank

negotiator n Unterhändler m, Vermittler m

nest-egg n Sparpfennig m, Notgroschen m

net n Netto-; *-* v netto-, abwerfen v, erbringen v; *- amount* Nettobetrag m, Reinbetrag m; *- asset value* Inventarwert m (eines Investmentfonds); *- assets* Reinvermögen n; *- avails* (US) Nettoerlös m, Gegenwert m; *- barter terms of trade* Nettoaustauschverhältnis n (Außenhandel); *- earnings* Nettoverdienst m; *- income* Nettoeinkommen n, Reinertrag m; *- interest* Nettozinsen m pl; *- interest return* Nettoverzinsung f; *- operating income (profit)* Betriebsüberschuß m; *- plant* feste Anlage abzüglich vorgenommener Abschreibungen; *- proceeds* Reingewinn m, Nettogewinn m; *- profit*

Reingewinn *m*, Nettogewinn *m*; **- profit on financial operations** Nettoertrag aus Finanzgesellschaften; **- property** feste Anlage abzüglich vorgenommener Abschreibungen; **- sale** Nettoumsatz *m*; **- value** Nettowert *m*; **- working capital** Nettobetriebskapital *n*; **- worth** Eigenkapital *n*, Eigenvermögen *n*; **- yield** Nettorendite *f*; Reinertrag *m*; **- of branch offices** Filialnetz *n*, Geschäftsstellennetz *n*; **appropriation of - profit** (GB) Verwendung des Reingewinns; **corporate - profit** Gesellschaftsreingewinn *m*

netting Netting *n*, Glattstellung von Verbindlichkeiten im Konzernverbund

network *n* Übertragungsnetz *n*; **- configuration** Netzaufbau *m*; **- lay-out** Netzaufbau *m*; **- of branch offices** Filialnetz *n*, Geschäftsstellennetz *n*

neutral banking transaction bilanzneutrales Bankgeschäft

new accounting period neue Rechnung; **- business department** (US) Abteilung einer Bank zur Entwicklung neuer Dienstleistungen; **- issue market** Neuemissionsmarkt *m* **- issue of shares** (for cash) Ausgabe neuer oder junger Aktien (gegen Barzahlung); **- shares** junge Aktien; **- start-ups** Existenzgründer *m*

New Year's bond Silvester-Anleihe *f*

New York Interbank Offered Rate = NIBOR New Yorker Interbanken-Angebotszinssatz

New York Stock Exchange = NYSE New Yorker Wertpapierbörse *f*

NF = abbreviation for »no funds« ungenügende Kontoguthaben, keine Deckung (Bankvermerk auf Schecks)

nickel *n* (US) Fünfcentstück *n*

nick-name *n* Börsenname *m* (von Effekten)

night depository (US) Nachtsafe *m*, Nachttresor *m*; **- safe** Nachtsafe *m*, Nachttresor *m*

nil growth Nullwachstum *n*

ninety days loan Dreimonatsgeld *n*

ninety-day deposits Dreimonatsgelder *n pl*

no dealings Kurs gestrichen *m* (Börse); **- expense** »ohne Kosten«; **- funds** keine Deckung; **- noting** Wechselprotest nicht möglich; **- value** ohne Wertangabe

no-claims bonus Schadensfreiheitsrabatt *m*

nominal *adj* nominell *adj*, Nenn- (in Zus.), Nominal- (in Zus.); **- account** Sachkonto *n*; **- amount** Nominalbetrag *m*; **- capital** Nennkapital *n*; **- consideration** (GB) formaler Gegenwert; **- par** Nennwert *m*, Nominalwert *m*, Pariwert *m*; **- partner** (GB) nicht aktiver Teilhaber; **- value** Nennwert *m*, Nominalwert *m*, Pariwert *m*

nominate *v* nominieren *v*, vorschlagen *v*, ernennen *v*

nomination *n* Berufung *f*

nominee *n* Kandidat *m*, Normierter; **- account** Mündelkonto *n*

non voting share stimmrechtslose Aktien

non-acceptance Akzeptverweigerung *f*, Nichtakzeptierung *f*, Annahmeverweigerung *f*, Nichtannahme *f*

non-accrual loan notleidender Kredit (US)

non-apportionable annuity Leibrente ohne Zahlung im Todesfall

non-assessable nicht nachschußpflichtig, abgabenfrei *adj*

non-assessable stocks nicht nachschußpflichtige Aktien

non-bank banking Finanzdienstleistungen von Nichtbanken

non-callable bond unkündbare Anleihe

non-cancellable unkündbar *adj*

non-cash item Unbarposten *m*

non-collectable nicht eintreibbar

non-commercial letter of credit Reisekreditbrief *m*

non-convertible nicht konvertierbar

non-credit business of banks neutrales Bankgeschäft

non-cumulative dividend nicht kumulative Dividende

non-deductible nicht absetzbar

non-delivery Nichtlieferung *f*

non-durable goods Konsumgüter *n pl*

non-exchange market außerbörslicher Markt

non-free share unfreie Aktie

non-interest-bearing zinsfrei, *adj* zinslos *adj*, unverzinslich *adj*

non-interest-bearing bond unverzinsliche Schuldverschreibung

non-legals Wertpapiere n pl (die nicht den rechtlichen Vorschriften entsprechen)
non-leverage company Investmentgesellschaft, die zum Kauf von Anlagen kein Fremdkapital einsetzt
non-liability clause Freizeichnungsklausel f, Angstklausel f
non-local transaction Distanzgeschäft n
non-marketable nicht börsenfähig, nicht marktfähig
non-member bank Bank außerhalb des Clearingsystems
non-member broker freier Makler, nicht zur offiziellen Börse zugelassener Makler
non-negotiable nicht übertragbar, nicht begebbar
non-negotiable bill Rektawechsel m
non-negotiable instrument Rektapapier n
non-par bank Bank außerhalb des Clearing-Systems
non-participating preferred stocks Vorzugsaktien ohne zusätzliche Gewinnbeteiligung (US)
non-payment Nichtbezahlung f, Nichtzahlung f
non-personnel cost Sachkosten plt
non-profit corporation gemeinnützige Gesellschaft
non-quoted Kurs gestrichen m (Börse)
non-recourse factoring echtes Faktoring
non-recourse financing Forfaitierung f
non-resident gebietsfremd adj
non-resident securities account Ausländerdepot n
non-statutory capital reserves freiwillige Rücklagen
non-taxable steuerfrei adj, nicht steuerpflichtig
non-transferable unübertragbar adj
non-value bill Gefälligkeitswechsel m
non-voting preference share Vorzugsaktie ohne Stimmrecht
non-warranty Haftungsausschluß m
no-par share nennwertlose Aktie, Aktie ohne Nennwert
no-par stock nennwertlose Aktie, Aktie ohne Nennwert
no-quotation Kurs gestrichen m (Börse)
no-recourse basis keine Rückgriffsmöglichkeit

normal condition Normalkondition f
Norway Krone Norwegische Krone f
nostro account Nostrokonto n
not easy marketable schwer handelbar; ~ **negotiable** nur zur Verrechnung; ~ **to order clause** Rektoklausel f
notarial adj notariell adj, vor einem Notar; ~ **act** Notariatsakt m; ~ **fees** Notariatsgebühren f pl; ~ **protest certificate** Protesturkunde f
notariate n Notariat n
notarize v notariell beglaubigen, in notarieller Form abschließen
notary n Notar m, Urkundsbeamter m; ~ **public** Notar m, Urkundsbeamter m
note n Mitteilung f, Bescheid m, Rechnung f, Banknote f, Wechsel m, Schuldschein m, Schuldverschreibung f, Obligation f; ~ **broker** (US) Diskontwechselhändler m; ~ **loan** Schuldscheindarlehen n; ~ **of blocking** Sperrvermerk m; ~ **of charges** Gebührenrechnung f; ~ **of disbursements** Auflagenrechnung f; ~ **of hand** Solawechsel m, Eigenwechsel m; ~ **of protest** Protesturkunde f; ~ **teller** (US) Angestellter zur Überwachung der Einlösung fälliger Wechsel; **acceleration** ~ Schuldscheinverpflichtung mit dem Recht vorzeitiger Rückzahlung; **bank** ~ Banknote f; **bond** ~ Zollbegleitschein m; **bought** ~ Schlußnote f, Schlußschein m; **broker's** ~ Schlußnote f, Schlußschein m; **cash** ~ (GB) Auszahlungsanweisung f, Kassenanweisung f; **cognovit** ~ schriftliche Schuldanerkenntnis f; **collateral** ~ Verpflichtungsschein über erfolgte Hinterlegung von Effekten zwecks Deckung eines Kredits; **commercial** ~ Handelswechsel m, Warenwechsel m; **confirmation** ~ Bestätigungsschreiben n; **consignment** ~ Frachtbrief m; **contract** ~ Schlußnote f, Schlußschein m; **cover** ~ (GB) vorläufige Deckungszusage f; **covering** ~ vorläufige Deckungszusage; **credit** ~ Gutschrift f, Gutschriftsanzeige f; **customer's** ~ Kundenwechsel m; **customs** ~ Zollvormerkschein m; **state** ~ Staatsschuldschein m; **trade** ~ Handelsdokument n

noted *bill* protestierter Wechsel; *- for protest* (bill of exchange) protestiert *adj* (Wechsel)

notes *in circulation* Banknotenumlauf *m*; *- payable* (US) fällige Wechsel, Wechselverbindlichkeit *f pl*, Wechselschulden *f pl*; *- receivable* (US) Debitoren aus Schuldscheinen, Wechseln und Akzepten; ***collateral trust*** *- * pfandrechtlich gesicherte Obligationen; ***foreign - and coin*** ausländische Banknoten und Münzen, Sorten

not-holder Schuldscheininhaber *m*

notice *n* Bekanntmachung *f*, Ankündigung *f*, Anzeige *f*, Veröffentlichung *f*; *- n* Kündigung *f*; *- deposits* Spareinlagen *f pl*; *- of delivery* (US) Zustellungsurkunde *f*, Empfangsbestätigung *f*; *- of dividend* Dividendenankündigung *f*; *- of drawing* Auslosungsanzeige *f*; *- of intention* (US) Antrag auf Erteilung einer Bankkonzession; *- of loss* Schadensanzeige *f*; *- of protest* (US) Protestbenachrichtigung *f*; *- of rights* Bezugsrechtsankündigung *f*; *- of withdrawal period* Kündigungssperrfrist *f*; ***bankruptcy*** *- * Konkurserklärung *f*, Konkursanmeldung *f*, Bankrotterklärung *f*; ***seven days'*** *- * wöchentliche Kündigung; ***term of*** *- * Kündigungsfrist *f*; ***written*** *- * schriftliche Kündigung

noticeable *adj* nennenswert *adj*, spürbar *adj*

notification *n* Bekanntmachung *f* (förmlich), Mitteilung *f*, Notifikation *f*, Benachrichtigung *f*; *- factoring* offenes Factoring; *- of credit* Akkreditivanzeige *f*; *- of dividend* Dividendenankündigung *f*

notify *n* informieren *v*, mitteilen *v*, unterrichten *v* (in Kenntnis setzen), benachrichtigen *v*; *- address* Notadresse *f*

noting of a bill Protestaufnahme *f*

not-issuing bank Notenbank *f*

not-issuing power Banknotenausgaberecht *n*, Notenprivileg *n*

not-issuing privilege Notenmonopol *n*

nsf = abbreviation for »not sufficient funds« ungenügende Kontoguthaben, keine Deckung (Bankvermerk auf Schecks)

Nugget Nugget *m* (auch australische Goldmünze; 1 Unze Feingold)

null and void null und nichtig

nullification *n* Annullierung *f*, Nichtigkeitserklärung *f*

nullify *v* annullieren *v*, aufheben *v*, widerrufen *v*, für nichtig erklären

number *of accounts* Kontenzahl *f*; *- of print positions* Schreibbreite *f* (eines Schnelldruckers); *- of transactions* Buchungspostenzahl *f*

numbered account Nummernkonto *n*; *- safekeeping account* Nummerndepot *n*; ***consecutively*** *- * fortlaufend numeriert

numbering principle Numerierungsprinzip *n*

numerical order Zahlenfolge *f*

numismatics Numismatik *f*, Münzkunde *f*, Sammeln von Münzen

nursery unit Kleinbetrieb *m*, kleine Fabrik

nursing an account (GB) ein faules Konto sanieren

Nylies = New York Life Insurance Companies New Yorker Lebensversicherungsgesellschaften

NYSE = New York Stock Exchange New Yorker Wertpapierbörse *f*

object

O

object *n* Gegenstand *m*

objection *n* Beanstandung *f*, Beschwerde *f*, Reklamation *f*; ~ *n* Einrede *f*, Rechtseinwand *m*, Einwand *m*; **technical** ~ formaler Einwand

obligation *n* Verpflichtung *f*, Schuldverhältnis *n*, Anleihe *f*, Schuldschein *m*, Schuldverschreibung *f*, Verbindlichkeit *f*; ~ **to provide additional security** Nachdeckungspflicht *f*; ~ **to provide extra funds** Nachschußpflicht *f*; **alternative** ~ Alternativverpflichtung *f*; **bond of** ~ Schuldverschreibung *f*, Schuldschein *m*

obligations; assume ~ Verbindlichkeiten eingehen; **partnership** ~ Verpflichtungen einer Gesellschaft, Gesellschaftsverpflichtungen

obligator *n* Schuldner *m*, Verpflichtete *f* u. *m*, Obligationsschuldner *m*

oblige *v* gefällig sein

obligee *n* Gläubiger *m*, Kreditor *m*, Forderungsberechtigter *m*

obliging *adj* entgegenkommend *adj*

obligor *n* Schuldner *m*, Verpflichtete *f* u. *m* Obligationsschuldner *m*

obsolete securities (US) aufgerufene und für ungültig erklärte Obligationen

occupation code Berufsgruppenschlüssel *m*

occupied *adj* beschäftigt *adj*

occupier Bewohner *m*; **beneficial** ~ Nießbrauchberechtigte *f* u. *m*

odd lot (US) Börsenabschluß *m* (dessen Mindestbetrag im allgemeinen unter 100 Stücken liegt), Restposten *m*, Kleinauftrag *m*

OECD = Organization for Economic Cooperation and Development Organisation für wirtschaftliche Zusammenarbeit *f*

off ermäßigt, mit Ermäßigung, unter, von, außer; ~ **securities** nicht notierte Wertpapiere (US)

off-balance-sheet business bilanzneutrales Bankgeschäft

off-board market (US) Freiverkehr *m*

offense; currency ~ Devisenvergehen *n*

offer *v* anbieten *v*; ~ *n* Offerte *f*, Gebot *n* Anerbieten *n*; ~ **for sale** Anleiheverkaufsangebot *n* (GB); ~ **for sale by tender** Ausschreibung einer Emission zu einem variablen Kurs; ~ **for subscription** Zeichnungsangebot *n*; ~ **price** Briefkurs *m*; **capital stock exchange** ~ Aktienumtauschangebot *n*; **credit** ~ Kreditangebot *n*

offerer *n* Anbieter *m*

offering price Ausgabekurs *m*, ~ **prospectus** Zeichnungsprospekt *m*; ~ **terms** Emissionsbedingungen *f pl*

offerings *n pl* (US) Angebot *n* (Börse), Material *n* (Börse)

office *n* Büro *n*, Geschäftszimmer *n*, Zweigniederlassung *f*; Stellung *f* (Amt), Position *f*; ~ **building** Geschäftshaus *n*; ~ **banking** Bankgeschäftsstelle *f*; ~ **branch** - Niederlassung *f*, Zweigstelle *f*, Filiale *f*, Nebenstelle *f*, Depositenkasse *f*, Geschäftsstelle *f*; **brokerage** ~ Maklerfirma *f*, Maklergeschäft; **business** ~ Geschäftslokal *n*, Geschäftsräume *m pl*; **district** ~ Bezirksagentur *f*; **term of** ~ Amtsdauer *f*

officer *n* Beamter *m*, Angestellter *m*; ~ **in charge** zuständiger Beamter

official *adj* dienstlich *adj*, amtlich *adj*, offiziell *adj*, Amt-, Dienst-; ~ **broker** amtlicher Makler *m*; ~ **cash market quotation** amtlicher Einheitskurs; ~ **check** Bankscheck *m* (US); ~ **certification** Beglaubigung *f*; ~ **discount rate** offizieller Diskontsatz *m*; ~ **exchange rate** amtlicher Wechselkurs; ~ **gold price** amtlicher Goldpreis; ~ **listing** (US) offizielle Zulassung zum Börsenhandel; ~ **price (rate)** amtlicher Kurs, Angebotssatz *m*; ~ **reserves** offene Reserven; **bank** ~ Bankangestellte *f* u. *m*, Bankbeamte *m*; **customs** ~ Zollbeamte *m*; **government** ~ Regierungsbeamte *m*

officially quoted amtlich notiert

offset v kompensieren v, ausgleichen v; - **n** Gegenforderung f (Aufrechnung), Ausgleich m, Aufrechnung f; - **account** Verrechnungskonto n; - **agreement** Verrechnungsabkommen n; - **transactions** Kompensationsgeschäfte n pl

offsetting Verrechnung f, Aufrechnung f

offshore banking Offshore-Bankgeschäfte n pl; - **financial center** Offshore-Finanzplatz m; - **fund** Investmenttrust in einem steuerbegünstigten Land, Exotenfonds m

off-shore banking Bankgeschäfte außerhalb nationaler Grenzen

off-the-exchange außerbörslich adj

oils Erdölaktien f pl

old age pension Altersrente f

OMF = Open-Market de France elektronische Optionsbörse von Frankreich (Sitz: Paris)

ombudsman n Schlichter bei Beschwerden von Bankkunden

omission n Unterlassung f, Versäumnis n; **errors and -s expected** Versäumnisse vorbehalten

omit a dividend eine Dividende ausfallen lassen

omnibus account Gemeinschaftskonto n; - **credit** Warenkredit m

omnium n (GB) Gesamtwert einer öffentlichen Anleihe

on demand (payable on demand) auf Sicht (zahlbar auf Sicht); - **margin** mit Kredit finanzierte Börsengeschäfte

on-board bill of lading Bordkonnossement n

oncosts Fixkosten

one financial services Allfinanzdienstleistungen f pl; - **man business** (GB) Einzelfirma f

one-stop banking Universalbank f, Finanzsupermarkt m

on-line adj on-line adj, direkt verfügbar, angeschlossen

on-line accounting system Direktbuchungssystem n

on-line debit system Sofortabbuchungssystem n

on-line information system Sofortauskunftssystem n

on-line posting Direktbuchung f

on-line posting program Direktbuchungsprogramm n

on-shore banking Bankgeschäfte innerhalb nationaler Grenzen

OPEC = Organization of Petroleum Exporting Countries Organisation Erdöl exportierender Länder f

open account Kontokorrentkonto n, laufendes Konto, Konto in laufender Rechnung, offenes Konto; - **account policy** Warenkreditversicherung f; - **a credit** ein Akkreditiv stellen; - **an account** ein Konto eröffnen; - **banking hall** offene Schalterhalle; - **check** Barscheck m, offener Scheck, ungekreuzter Scheck; - **credit** Kontokorrentkredit m, offener Kredit; - **fund** Investmentgesellschaft mit offenem Anlageportefeuille; - **market** freier Markt, offener Markt; - **Market de France = OMF** elektronische Optionsbörse in Frankreich (Sitz: Paris); - **market policy** n Offenmarktpolitik f; - **money market** freier Kapitalmarkt; - **order** Wertpapierkauf oder Verkaufsauftrag mit Kurslimit; - **outcry** Preisermittlung durch Zuruf oder Handzeichen (Börse); - **policy** offene Police; - **position** ungedecktes Engagement; - **rate** Geldsatz am offenen Markt; - **safekeeping account** offenes Depot; - **trust** Investmentgesellschaft, die laufend Zertifikate ausgibt und zurückkauft; **on the - market** freihändig

open-end bonds (US) Anleihe ohne Begrenzung des Gesamtbetrags

opening n Eröffnung f; - **balance** Eröffnungsbilanz f; - **balance sheet** Eröffnungsbilanz f; - **capital** Anfangskapital n; - **price** Anfangskurs m, Eröffnungskurs m

open-to-borrow arrangement Rahmenkreditvertrag m

operate v handeln v, handhaben v, verwalten v, betreiben v, bedienen v (Gerät)

operating account Kontokorrentkonto n; - **assets** Betriebsvermögen n; - **company** aktive

operation

Geschäfte betreibende Gesellschaft; **~ deficit** Betriebsverlust *m*; **~ expenses** (US) variable Geschäftsunkosten, Betriebsunkosten *pl*t, Verwaltungsaufwendungen *m pl*; **~ ratio** (US) Verhältnis der veränderlichen Geschäftsunkosten zur Roheinnahme; **~ result** Betriebsergebnis *n*; **~ surplus** Betriebsgewinn *m*

operation *n* Geschäft *n*, Unternehmen *n*, Transaktion *f*; **bear ~** Baisse-Spekulation *f*; **bearish ~** Baisse-Spekulation *f*; **bull ~** Hausse-Spekulation *f*; **cash ~** Bargeschäft *n*, Kassageschäft *n*; **cost of ~** Betriebskosten *plt*

operational accounting Betriebsbuchhaltung *f*

operations research betriebliche Unternehmensforschung; **banking ~** Bankgeschäfte *n pl*; **credit ~** Kreditgeschäfte *n pl*

operator *n* Bedienungskraft *f*; **~ n** (US) Börsenmakler *m*, Unternehmer *m*; **~ error** Bedienungsfehler *m*; **~ instructions** Bedienungsanleitung *f* (Operator-Anweisung); **currency ~** Währungsspekulant *m*

opinion book (GB) Auskunftsbuch über Kunden; **counsel's ~** Gutachten *n* (eines Rechtssachverständigen)

opportunity *n* Gelegenheit *f*, Chance *f*, Möglichkeit *f*; **market ~** Absatzmöglichkeit *f*

optical character recognition (OCR) optische Zeichenerkennung

option *n* Option *f* (Börse); **~ buyer** Optionskäufer *m*; **~ clause** Fakultativklausel *f*; **~ currency** Optionswährung *f*; **~ deal** Prämiengeschäft *n*; **~ dealing** Prämiengeschäft *n*; **~ fund** Optionsfonds *m*; **~ loan** Optionsanleihe *f*; **~ on new stock** Bezugsrecht auf neue Aktien; **~ price** Prämienkurs *m*, Optionspreis *m*; **~ put and call** (US) Prämiengeschäft *n*; **~ stock** Prämienwerte *f pl*; **~ taker** Optionserwerber *m*, Optionsnehmer *m*; **~ to purchase** Kaufoption *f*; **~ seller (writer)** Optionsverkäufer *m*; **abandonment of the ~ money** Prämienaufgabe *f*; **annuity ~** Rentenwahlrecht *n*; **buyer's ~** Kaufoption *f*; **call ~** Kaufoption *f*; **call an ~** ein Prämiengeschäft eingehen

optional bonds (US) kündbare Obligationen; **~ dealings** Prämiengeschäfte *f pl*, Optionshandel *m*

optionee *n* Optionsberechtigter *m*

optioner *n* Optionsgeber *m*

options exchange Optionsbörse *f*; **~ trading** Optionshandel *m*; **declaration of ~** Prämienerklärung *f*;

order *v* bestellen *v*; **~ n** Order *f*, Auftrag *m*, Anweisung *f*, Bestellung *f*, Kommission *f*; **~ bill of lading** Orderkonnossement *n*; **~ book** Auftragsbuch *n*, Auftragsbestand *m*; **~ check** Ordercheck *m*; **~ flow** Auftragseingang *m*; **~ for collection** Inkassoauftrag *m*; **~ instrument** Orderpapier *n*; **~ of magnitude** Größenordnung *f*; **~ of precedence** Rangordnung *f*; **~ of priority** Rangfolge *f*; **~ paper** Orderpapier *n*; **~ to pay** Zahlungsbefehl *m*; **armament ~** Rüstungsauftrag *m*; **ascending ~** aufsteigende Reihenfolge; **bank money ~** Bankanweisung *f*, Zahlungsanweisung *f*, Banküberweisung *f*; **banker's ~** (GB) Bankauftrag *m*; **blanket ~** Blankoauftrag *m*; **by ~ and for account of** im Auftrag und für Rechnung; **cable ~** Kabelauftrag *m*; **cash ~** Barzahlungsauftrag *m*, (GB) Sichtwechsel *m*; **check to ~** Ordercheck *m*; **conditional ~** bedingter Auftrag; **covering ~** Deckungsauftrag *m*; **credit ~** Kreditauftrag *m*; **cross ~** Kompensationsauftrag *m*, **customer's ~** Kundenauftrag *m*; **descending ~** absteigende Reihenfolge; **give an ~** einen Auftrag erteilen; **in ~ to** zwecks; **purchase ~** Kaufauftrag *m*, Bestellung *f*; **standing ~** Dauerauftrag *m*

orderly market geregelter Markt

orders not to pay Schecksperrung *f*

ordinaries *n pl* (GB) Stammaktien *f pl*

ordinary *adj* normal *adj*, gewöhnlich *adj*; **~ debts** Buchschulden *f pl*; **~ guarantee** einfache Bürgschaft *f*; **~ interest** Zinsen *m pl* (berechnet auf der Basis von 360 Tagen); **~ partnership** Offene Handelsgesellschaft *f*; **~ safekeeping account**

344

offenes Depot; **~ share** Stammaktie f; **~ stock** Stammaktie f
organic growth inneres Wachstum
organization Organisation f, Gesellschaft f, Verein m, Verband m, Gründung f; **~ chart** Organigramm n
organize v organisieren v, einrichten v, gestalten v
origin; certificate of ~ Ursprungszeugnis n, Herkunftsbescheinigung f
original n Original n, Urschrift f, Urtext m; **~ capital** Grundkapital n, Stammkapital n; **~ investment** Gründungseinlage f; **~ subscriber** Erstzeichner m; **~ syndicate** Übernahmesyndikate n; **~ value** Anschaffungswert m
originating house Konsortialführerin f (US)
orphan n Waise f
OTC = over the counter außerbörslicher Handel mit nicht notierten Wertpapieren
other assets sonstige Vermögensgegenstände; **~ charges** sonstiger Aufwand; **~ income** sonstige Erträge; **~ earnings reserves** andere Gewinnrücklagen; **~ expenses** sonstige betriebliche Aufwendungen; **~ income** sonstige betriebliche Erträge; **~ liabilities** sonstige Verpflichtungen, sonstige Verbindlichkeiten
out of town market Provinzbörse f
outbid v überbieten v, übersteigern v
outdoor staff Außendienstmitarbeiter m
outflow of capital Kapitalabfluß m
outgoing cash letters (US) versandte Fernschecks; **~ partner** ausscheidender Gesellschafter
outlay n Ausgabe f, Auslage f, Auszahlung f; **capital ~** Kapitalaufwand m
outlet n (market) Absatzmarkt m
outline n Entwurf m, Umriß m; ~ v umreißen v
outlook business Geschäftsaussichten f pl
output n Produktion f, Förderung f; **annual ~** Jahresproduktion f
outright buying (US) Kassakauf m; **~ forward transaction** Devisentermingeschäft n; **~ operations** Outright-Geschäfte n pl, einfache Devisentermingeschäfte

outside broker freier Makler, nicht zur offiziellen Börse zugelassener Makler; **~ exchange hours** außerbörslich adj; **~ financing** Fremdfinanzierung f; **~ market** Freiverkehr m; **~ securities** nicht an der Börse notierte Wertpapiere
outstanding adj ausstehend adj, unbezahlt adj, offenstehend adj, in Umlauf; **~ coupon** unbezahlter Kupon, ausstehender Kupon; **~ expenses** unbezahlte Ausgaben; **to be ~** ausstehen v
outvote v überstimmen v
outward freight Hinfracht f
over business Schaltergeschäft n, außerbörslicher Effektenhandel; **~ dealer** Freiverkehrshändler m; **~ market** Markt im Telefonverkehr und am Schalter, Freiverkehrsmarkt m; **~ quotation** Freiverkaufskurs m; **~ trading** Schalterverkehr m
overagio n (GB) Extraprämie f
overall adj global adj; **~ liquidity** Gesamtliquidität f
overbid v überbieten v, übersteigern v
overborrowed überschuldet
overbought adj überbezahlt adj
over-capitalize v überkapitalisieren v
overcertification n (US) Bestätigung eines Schecks für einen Betrag, der hoher als das Guthaben des Ausstellers ist
overcertify v (US) einen ungedeckten oder nicht voll gedeckten Scheck bestätigen
overcharge v zuviel belasten, überbelasten v; **~** n Mehrbelastung f, Zuschlag m, Aufschlag m
overcheck v überziehen v; **~** n Überziehungsscheck m
overcheque n (GB) über ein festgesetztes Kreditlimit hinausgezogener Scheck
overcredit v zuviel Kredit gewähren, überkreditieren v
overdebit v zuviel belasten, überbelasten v
over-depreciation n übermäßige Abschreibung
overdraft n Kontoüberziehung f, Kreditüberschreitung f; **~** Überziehungsbetrag m; **~ facility** Überziehungskredit m, Überziehungsrecht n; **~ facility in current account** Kontokorrentkredit m,

offener Kredit; *- list* Überziehungsliste f; *commission on -* Überziehungsprovision f; *technical -* technische Kontoüberziehung; *temporary -* kurzfristige Kontoüberziehung
overdraw v überziehen v; *- an account* ein Konto überziehen
overdrawing Überziehung f
overdrawn account überzogenes Konto
overdue adj überfällig adj, notleidend adj; *- bill* überfälliger Wechsel, notleidender Wechsel; *- check* überfälliger Scheck, verfallener Scheck; *- coupon* notleidender Kupon; *- payment* rückständige Zahlung; *amount -* überfälliger Betrag; *to be -* ausstehen v
overextended accounts (US) nicht genügend gedeckte Konten
overhead n Gemeinkosten plt, Generalkosten plt; *- charges* allgemeine Kosten; *- expenses* allgemeine Unkosten
overindebtedness Überschuldung f
over-insurance n Überversicherung f
overinvestment n übermäßige Investition
overlay n Doppelbelegung f (bei Großspeicherorganisation)
overnight loan (US) Darlehen (das am folgenden Tage zurückgezahlt werden muß); *- cash holdings* Abendkassenbestände m pl; *- money* (GB) Darlehen n (von Banken an Wechselmakler vom Nachmittag eines Tages bis zum folgenden Tag)
overpayment n Überbezahlung f
overprice v überbewerten v, überschätzen v; *- n* Überpreis m
overproduction n Überproduktion f
overrider commission Superprovision f
overruns Mehrkosten f pl

overseas trade Außenhandel m
oversell v über den Bestand verkaufen, leer verkaufen
oversubscribe v überzeichnen v; *- a loan* eine Anleihe überzeichnen
oversubscription n Überzeichnung f
over-the-counter (OTC) über den Bankschalter, außerbörslich adj (Handel mit nicht notierten Wertpapieren)
overtime n Überstunden f pl
overvaluation n Überbewertung f
overvalue v überbewerten v, überschätzen v
owe v schulden v, schuldig sein
own v besitzen v (als Eigentümer), Eigentümer sein; *- business for -* account Eigengeschäft n; *- financing* Selbstfinanzierung f, Eigenfinanzierung f; *- outright* voll und ganz besitzen
owner n Eigentümer m, Besitzer m; *absolute -* unbeschränkter Eigentümer; *beneficial -* Nutznießer m, materieller Eigentümer; *beneficiary -* Nutznießer m, materieller Eigentümer; *property -* Grundstückseigentümer m; *rightful -* rechtmäßiger Eigentümer
owners' capital Eigenkapital n, Eigenvermögen n
ownership n Eigentümereigenschaft f, Eigentumsrecht n, Eigentumsverhältnis n; *- certificate* Bescheinigung über das Eigentum (an einem bestimmten Wertpapier); *absolute -* unbeschränktes Eigentumsrecht; *assume -* Eigentum übernehmen; *beneficial -* materielles Eigentum, wirtschaftliches Eigentum, Nießbrauchrecht n; *change of -* Besitzwechsel m; Eigentumswechsel m; *collective -* Gemeinschaftseigentum n; *joint -* Miteigentum n; *state -* Staatseigentum n

P

package *deal* Kopplungsgeschäft n; *- merger* Fusion mehrerer Unternehmen; *- mortgage* Gesamthypothek f (mit Mobiliar)
packing *credit* Akkreditivvorschuß m; *- method* Verdichtungsmethode f
page reader Seitenleser m (EDV)
paid adj bezahlt adj; *- check* eingelöster Scheck
paid-in capital eingezahltes Kapital
paid-off ausbezahlt adj, ausgezahlt adj
paid-off creditor abgefundener Gläubiger
paid-off mortgage abgelöste Hypothek
paid-up capital eingezahltes Kapital
paid-up policy volleingezahlte Police
Panda = 100 Yuan Chinese gold coin Panda m (chinesische Goldmünze; 100 Yuan, mit 1 Unze Feingehalt)
panel n Ausschuß m, Gremium n; *consumer -* Verbrauchertestgruppe f
panic n Panik f (an der Börse); *- sales* Panikverkäufer f pl (Börse)
paper n Papier n, Wertpapier n, Wechsel m, Banknote f, Urkunde f, Brief m, Dokument n; *- basis* Papierwährung f, Papiervaluta f; *- burster* Papiertrennmaschine f; *- currency* Banknotenumlauf m, Papiergeld n, Banknoten f pl; *- cutter* Papierschneidemaschine f; *- decollator* Papiertrennmaschine f; *- money* Banknotenumlauf m, Papiergeld n, Banknoten f pl; *- profits* (US) Scheingewinne m pl, unrealisierte Gewinne; *- securities* Effekten plt, Papierwerte m pl; *- standard* Papierwährung f; *- surplus* Papiergewinne m pl; *- tape* Lochstreifen m; *bank -* bankfähiges Papier; *blank -* Blankopapier n; *business -* Warenwechsel m; *commercial -* kurzfristiger Schuldschein aus kommerziellen Transaktionen; *commodity -* (US) Dokumententratte f; *continuous - tape* Endlospapierstreifen m; *convertible - currency* konvertierbares Papiergeld; *corporation* *-* (US) begebbares Papier einer Aktiengesellschaft; *purchased -* per Kasse gekauftes Wertpapier; *stamped -* Stempelpapier n; *trade -* Handelsdokument n
paperless payments belegloser Zahlungsverkehr m
**papers; clearance -* Verzollungspapiere n pl; *commercial -* Handelspapiere n pl; *negotiable -* begebbare Wertpapiere; *second-class -* zweitklassige Wertpapiere
paperwork n Schreibarbeit f
par n pari; *- collection* Inkasso zu Pari; *- exchange rate* Wechselkurssatz m; *- list* (US) Verzeichnis von Banken, die auf sie gezogene Schecks spesenfrei einlösen; *- issue* Pariemission f, Emission zum Nennwert; *- of exchange* Wechselparität f; *- rate* Parikurs m; *- value* Nennwert m, Nominalwert m, Pariwert m; *- value stock* (US) Nennwertaktie f; *at -* zum Nennwert; *below -* unter dem Nennwert, unter Pari; *bill at -* Pariwechsel m
parallel financing Parallelfinanzierung f; *- market* Parallelmarkt m, freier Devisenmarkt; *- run* Parallellauf m; *- standard* Doppelwährung f; *- work* Simultanarbeit f
parameter card Steuerkarte f (Informationsverarbeitung)
par-bond Zinserlaß-Obligation f
parcel of shares Aktienpaket n
parcener n Miterbe m, Miteigentümer m (von ererbtem Grundbesitz)
pardon v verzeihen v
parent bank Stammbank f; *- company* Muttergesellschaft f, Dachgesellschaft f, Stammgesellschaft f
pari passu gleichberechtigt
participation certificate Genußschein m, Partizipationsschein m
Paris Interbank Offered Rate = PIBOR Pariser Interbanken-Angebotszinssatz
parity n Parikurs m, Parität f, Pariwert m, Umrechnungskurs m; *- clause*

Paritätsklausel f; **purchasing power** - Kaufkraftparität f

parked funds Zwischenanlagen f pl, geparkte Mittel n pl

part n Teil m, Tranche f (eines Kredits), Anteil m; **- owner** Miteigentümer m, Parteninhaber m, Miteigentümer eines Schiffs; **- ownership** Miteigentum n; **- payment** Teilzahlung f; **- with** (sich) trennen von, aufgeben v

partial acceptance Teilakzept n; **- amount** Teilbetrag m; **- bill of lading** Teilkonnossement n; **- endorsement** Teilindossament n

participant n Teilnehmer m, Teilhaber m

participate v teilhaben v, beteiligt sein

participating adj gewinnberechtigt adj; **- annuity** Rente mit Gewinnbeteiligung; **- bonds** (US) Obligationen mit Gewinnbeteiligung; **- certificate** Genußschein m; **- dividend** Vorzugsdividende f; **- fee** Anteil der Konsorten an der Führungsprovision; **- insurance** Versicherung mit Gewinnbeteiligung; **- loan** Konsortialkredit m; **- preference shares** (GB) Vorzugsaktien mit zusätzlicher Gewinnbeteiligung; **- preferred stocks** (US) Vorzugsaktien mit zusätzlicher Gewinnbeteiligung; **- stocks** Aktien mit Gewinnbeteiligung; **cumulative - preference shares** Vorzugsaktien mit besonderer Dividendenberechtigung

participation n Mitwirkung f, Teilnahme f, Gewinnbeteiligung f, Mitbeteiligung f, Beteiligung f; **- certificate** (US) Anteilschein m; **- loan** Konsortialkredit m; **business -** Geschäftsbeteiligung f

participator Gesellschafter m

particular adj besonders adj, einzeln adj, Sonder- (in Zus.), genau adj; **- partnership** Gelegenheitsgesellschaft f

particularity n Besonderheit f, Ausführlichkeit f, Eigenheit f

partition n Aufteilung f (Teilung)

partly adj teilweise adj, zum Teil; **- paid-up ordinary share** teileingezahlte Stammaktie

partner n Mitinhaber m, Mitbesitzer m, Teilhaber m, Partner m; Gesellschafter m, Beteiligter m; **acting -** geschäftsführender Gesellschafter, geschäftsführender Teilhaber; **associated -** unbeschränkt haftender Teilhaber; **bankrupt -** in Konkurs gegangener Teilhaber; **dormant -** Geldgeber m (in einer GmbH oder Kommanditgesellschaft), stiller Teilhaber, Kommanditist m; **limited -** Kommanditist m, beschränkt haftender Gesellschafter, beschränkt haftender Teilhaber; **managing -** geschäftsführender Gesellschafter, geschäftsführender Teilhaber; **nominal -** (GB) nicht aktiver Teilhaber; **responsible -** persönlich haftender Gesellschafter; **senior -** Hauptinhaber m; **silent -** (US) Geldgeber m (in einer GmbH oder Kommanditgesellschaft), stiller Teilhaber, Kommanditist m; **sleeping -** (GB) Geldgeber m (in einer GmbH oder Kommanditgesellschaft), stiller Teilhaber, Kommanditist m; **special -** Kommanditist m, beschränkt haftender Gesellschafter, beschränkt haftender Teilhaber

partners' interests Gesellschafteranteile f pl; **- investments** Kapitaleinlagen der Gesellschafter; **- meeting** Gesellschafterversammlung

partnership n Handelsgesellschaft f, Teilhaberschaft f, Personalgesellschaft f, Gesellschafterverhältnis n; **- agreement** Gesellschaftsvertrag m; **- assets** Gesellschaftsvermögen n (einer OHG); **- assurance** (GB) Teilhaberversicherung f; **- capital** Gesellschaftskapital n (einer OHG); **- creditor** Gesellschaftsgläubiger m; **- debt** Gesellschaftsschuld f; **- insurance** Teilhaberversicherung f; **- obligations** Verpflichtungen einer Gesellschaft, Gesellschaftsverpflichtungen f pl; **- property** Gesellschaftsvermögen n, Gesellschaftseigentum n; **assets of a -** Gesellschaftsvermögen n (einer OHG); **change a - to a corporation** eine Personalgesellschaft in eine juristische Person umwandeln; **commercial -** Handelsgesellschaft f; **dormant -** stille Gesellschaft; **general -** offene Handelsgesellschaft (OHG); **limited -** Kommanditgesellschaft f (KG)

part-paid stock teileingezahlte Aktien

party to a bill Wechselbeteiligte f u. m, Wechselverpflichtete f u. m; **~ to an estate** Miterbe m, Miterbin f; **contracting ~** Kontrahent m, vertragsschließender Teil, Vertragspartei f
pass v annehmen v, verabschieden v, genehmigen v
passbook n (US) Sparbuch n, Bankbuch n, Einlageheft n, Einlagenbuch n, Kontobuch n, Depositenbuch n; **~ account** Sparkonto n (US); **~ balance** Buchsaldo m (im Sparbuch eingetragener Saldo); **~ chute** Vorsteckeinrichtung f (für Sparbücher) **~ loan** durch ein Sparbuch abgesicherter Kredit
passenger clause Reisebestimmungen f pl
passing of a dividend Dividendenausfall m
passive bond unverzinsliche Schuldverschreibung; **~ debt** unverzinsliche Schuld
pass-through bank Durchleitungsbank f
pass-through loans Durchleitungskredite m pl
patent v patentieren v; **~ n** Patent n, Konzession f; **~ rights** Patentrechte n pl
patentability n Patentfähigkeit f
patentable adj patentierbar adj; patentfähig adj
patented adj patentiert adj, gesetzlich geschützt
patentee n Patentinhaber m
pathfinder prospectus vorläufiger Emissionsprospekt
patronage letter Patronatserklärung, garantieähnliche Erklärung
pattern n Muster n, Schema n, Struktur f; **~** v ausrichten nach, orientieren an
pawn v verpfänden v, versetzen v; **~ n** Pfand n, Faustpfand n, Pfandgegenstand m, Pfandsache f; **~ bank** Pfandbank f; **~ office** Pfandbank f
pawnbroker n Pfandleiher m
pawnbrokery n Pfandleihgeschäft n
pawnbroking n Pfandleihgeschäft n
pawned stock (GB) lombardierte Aktien, verpfändete Aktien
pawnee n Pfandnehmer m, Pfandinhaber m
pawning n Pfandbestellung f, Verpfändung f
pay v zahlen v, bezahlen v; **~ n** Bezahlung f, Gehalt n, Lohn m; **~ a call** eine Teilzahlung auf Aktien leisten; **~ back** zurückzahlen v, rückvergüten v, rückerstatten v, abdecken v, tilgen v, ersetzen v; **~ day** (GB) Zahltag m; **~ down** Anzahlung f
payable adj zahlbar adj, fällig adj, schuldig adj; **~ at sight** bei Sicht zahlbar; **~ bill** fälliger Wechsel m; **~ dividend** fällige Dividende f; **~ in advance** im voraus zahlbar, pränumerando; **~ in arrears** postnummerando; **~ on demand** bei Sicht zahlbar; **~ on presentation** zahlbar bei Vorlage; **~ to** lautend auf; **~ to bearer** zahlbar an Überbringer; **~ to order** zahlbar an Order; **accounts ~** Kreditoren m pl (aus Buchlieferantenschulden); **make ~** zahlbar stellen
payables n pl (US) Verbindlichkeiten f pl, Kreditoren m pl
payback period Kapitalrückflußdauer
pay-check Lohn-, Gehaltsscheck m
payee n Empfänger m (von Überweisungsgutschriften); **~ n** Zahlungsempfänger m, Begünstigter m; **~ of a bill** Remittent m, Wechselnehmer m; **~ of a cheque** Scheckbegünstigter m; **account of ~** für Rechnung des Remittenten (Kreuzung auf Schecks); **alternative ~** Alternativbegünstigter m
payee's bank Empfängerinstitut n, Empfängerbank f
payer n Zahler m, Bezogener m, Trassat m; **~ of a bill** Wechseleinnehmer m
paying agent Zahlstelle f, Einlösungsstelle f; **~ bank** auszahlende Bank; **~ department** Auszahlungskasse f, Kassenabteilung f; **~ habits** Zahlungsgewohnheiten f pl; **~ off** Auszahlung f, Abfindung f; **~ office** Zahlstelle f, Einlösungsstelle f; **~ slip** Einzahlungsbeleg m; **~ teller** (US) Kassierer für Auszahlungen; **~ teller's window** (US) Auszahlungskassenschalter m
paying-in book (GB) Einzahlungsbuch n
payment n Zahlung f, Einzahlung; **~ against documents** Zahlung gegen Dokumente; **~ bond** Zahlungsbürgschaft f; **~ by instal(l)ments** Ratenzahlung f; **~ countermanded** Scheck gesperrt; **~ default policy** Kreditversicherung f; **~ for**

honour Ehreneintritt *m*, Ehrenzahlung *f*; *- habits* Zahlungsgewohnheiten *f pl*; *- in full* volle Zahlung; *- media* Zahlungsmittel *n pl*; *- on account* Anzahlung *f*; Ratenzahlung *f*, Abschlagszahlung *f*, Abzahlung *f*, Teilzahlung *f*; *- order* Zahlungsanweisung *f*; *- received* erhaltene Zahlung; *- slip* Einzahlungsschein *m*; *- standstill* Zahlungsmoratorium *n*; *- stop* Schecksperre *f*; *- system* Zahlungssystem *n*; *- transactions* Zahlungsverkehr *m*; *action for -* Klage auf Zahlung; *additional -* Nachzahlung *f*; *amortization -* Amortisationszahlung *f*, Tilgungsleistung *f*; *anticipated -* Vorauszahlung *f*, vor Fälligkeit geleistete Zahlung; *anticipating -* Vorauszahlung *f*, vor Fälligkeit geleistete Zahlung; *application for -* Zahlungsaufforderung *f*; *apply for -* Zahlung beantragen, mahnen *v*; *arrears of -* Zahlungsrückstände *m pl*; *banker's -* Bankzahlung *f*, Bankanweisung *f*; *bonus -* Tantiemeauszahlung *f*; *cash -* Barzahlung *f*, sofortige Zahlung; *cash-down -* Barzahlung *f*, sofortige Zahlung; *compensation - * Abfindungszahlung *f*; *deferred -* gestundete Ratenzahlung; *delated against -* verspätete Zahlung *f*; *documents against -* Dokumente gegen Zahlung, Kasse gegen Dokumente; *in - of our account* zum Ausgleich unserer Rechnung; *lump sum -* Pauschalzahlung *f*; *overdue -* rückständige Zahlung *f*; *preferential -* Vorzugszahlung *f*; *redemption -* Amortisationszahlung *f*, Tilgungsleistung *f*; *terms of -* Zahlungsbedingungen *f pl*; *token -* Teilzahlung in Anerkennung einer Verpflichtung; *upon - of* gegen Zahlung von

payments; *appropriation of -* Zweckbestimmung von Zahlungen; *balance of -* Zahlungsbilanz *f*; *cash -* Kassenausgänge *m pl*; *clearance of -* Zahlungsausgleich *m*

pay off abbezahlen *v*, tilgen *v*, auszahlen *v*

pay out ausbezahlen *v*, ausgeben *v*

payout-ratio *n* ausgeschüttete Dividende in Prozenten des Kapitalertrags

payroll *n* Lohnliste *f*, Gehaltsliste *f*; *- account* Lohnkonto *n*, Gehaltskonto *n*; *- accounting* Lohnabrechnung *f*

payroller *n* Lohnempfänger *m*, Gehaltsempfänger *m*

peak Höchststand *m*; *- load* Spitzenbelastung *f*; *- price* Höchstpreis *m*

peculation *n* Unterschlagung *f*, Veruntreuung *f*

pecuniary *adj* pekuniär *adj*, geldlich *adj*, finanziell *adj*, Geld- (in Zus.); *- loss insurance* (US) Veruntreuungsversicherung *f*

peg *v* anbinden *v*, stützen *v*, unverändert halten; *- n* Festsatz *m*, Kursstützung *f*, Preisstützung *f*, Marktstützung *f*

pegged exchange künstlich gehaltener Devisenkurs; *- market* (US) in engem Rahmen gehaltener Markt

pegging purchase Stützungskauf *m*

penal interest Verzugszinsen *m pl*

penalty *n* Strafe *f*, Buße *f*, Geldstrafe *f*, Konventionalstrafe *f*

pence rates (GB) in Pennies notierte Devisenkurse

pending *adj* in der Schwebe befindlich, noch anhängig

penny (GB) Penny, (US) Centstück; *- bank* Sparkasse *f*; *- stocks* (US) spekulative Aktien (die unter 1 Dollar gehandelt werden)

pension *n* Pension *f*, Rente *f*; *- n* Pensionszuwendung *f*, Ruhegeld *n*; *- account* Pensionskonto *n*; *- fund* Pensionskasse *f*; *- off* pensionieren *v*; *- plan* Pensionsplan *m*, Altersversorgungsplan *m*; *- scheme* Betriebsrente *f*, betriebliche Altersversorgung; *bill in -* Depotwechsel *m*, Pensionswechsel *m*

pensioner *n* Rentner *m*, Pensionär *m*

PER = price/earnings ratio Kurs-Gewinn-Verhältnis *n* (KGV)

per *anum* im (pro) Jahr; *- capita* pro Kopf; *- cent* Prozent *n*

per-capita-income Pro-Kopf-Einkommen *n*

percentage *n* Prozentsatz *m*, Prozent *n*; *- of loan value* Beleihungswert *m*; *- of profits*

Gewinnbeteiligung f; **- of recovery** Konkursquote f

percentaged adj prozentual adj, in Prozenten ausgedrückt

percental adj prozentual adj

percentile n Hundertstel n

perforated tape Lochstreifen m

performance n (of a mutual fund) Leistung f (eines Investmentfonds), Wertentwicklung f (eines Investmentfonds); **- bond** Erfüllungsgarantie f; **- fund** auf hohen Wertzuwachs ausgerichteter Investmentfonds; **- warranty** Leistungsgarantie f, Erfüllungsgarantie f

period n Zeit f, Zeitraum m, Periode f, Dauer f, Laufzeit; **- bill** Nachsichtwechsel m; **- of limitation** Verjährungsfrist f; **- of notice** Kündigungsfrist f; **- of prescription** Verjährungsfrist f; **contractual -** Vertragsperiode f; **- credit** Laufzeit eines Kredits; **limited -** Frist f

permanent adj dauerhaft adj, ständig adj; **- assets** Anlagevermögen n; **- debt** konsolidierte Schuld f; **- holding** dauernde Beteiligung f

permission; customs - zollamtliche Erlaubnis

permit n Erlaubnis f, Genehmigung f, Zollfreischein m; **- v** genehmigen v, erlauben v, gestatten v

permitted band zulässige Bandbreite

perpetual annuity lebenslängliche Rente, Lebensrente f, Leibrente f; **- bond** Rentenanleihe f; **- debenture** Dauerschuldverschreibung f; **- floating rate note (bond)** zinsvariable Anleihe ohne Laufzeitbegrenzung; **- government loan** Rentenanleihe f; **- inventory** permanente Inventur

per-share asset value Inventarwert je Fondsanteil

persistent inflation schleichende Inflation

person; artificial - juristische Person; **juridical -** juristische Person; **legal -** juristische Person

personal account Privatkonto n; **- banking market** Privatkundengeschäft n; **- computer (PC)** Personal Computer m (PC); **- credit** Personalkredit m; **- estate** Besitz an beweglichem Vermögen; **- identification number** persönliche Kennummer f (Geldautomat); **- loan** (US) Personalkredit m; **- loan broker** (US) Geldmakler für die Vermittlung von Personalkrediten; **- loan company** (US) Abzahlungsfinanzierungsgesellschaft f; **- loan department** Personalkreditabteilung f; **- loan institutions** Privatkreditinstitute n pl; **- property** bewegliches Eigentum, Mobilien plt; **- property tax** Vermögenssteuer f; **- security** persönliche Bürgschaft, persönliche Sicherheit, nicht durch dingliches Vermögen abgesicherte Bürgschaft; **- wealth** Privatvermögen n

personality; legal - Rechtspersönlichkeit f

personnel department Personalabteilung f; **- division** Personalabteilung f; **skilled -** gelerntes Personal, ausgebildetes Personal

peseta Peseta f (Währung in Spanien)

petition; bankruptcy - Konkursantrag m; **creditor's -** Konkurseröffnungsantrag eines Gläubigers; **debtor's -** Konkurseröffnungsantrag eines Schuldners

petro dollars Petro-Dollars, Dollarerlöse der Erdöl exportierenden Länder

petty cash Portokasse f, kleine Kasse; **- expenses** geringe Aufwendungen

physical assets materielle Vermögenswerte, Sachanlagevermögen n

PIBOR = Paris Interbank Offered Rate Pariser Interbanken-Angebotszinssatz

pick out auswählen v

pick-up of time Zeitgewinn m

piece n Stück n; **- price** Stückpreis m

PIN = personal identification number persönliche Kennummer (PIN)

pit n (US) Maklerstand m, Börsenring m; **- trader** (US) für eigene Rechnung spekulierender Produktmakler

place in escrow zu getreuen Händen übergeben; **- of business** Geschäftssitz m; **- of delivery** Erfüllungsort m, Lieferort m; **- of jurisdiction** Gerichtsstand m; **- of payment** Zahlungsort m; **- of**

performance Erfüllungsort m; **banking ~** Bankplatz m

placement n Plazierung f, Unterbringung f, Stellenvermittlung f; **~ on commission** kommissionsweise Plazierung f

placing n Plazierung f; **~ of an issue** Plazierung einer Emission; **~ price** Emissionspreis m

plain bonds ungesicherte Obligationen

plan v planen v, vorsehen v, ausarbeiten v; **~ n** Plan m, Entwurf m, Aufstellung f, Projekt n; **bonus ~** Prämiensystem n; **pension ~** Pensionsplan m, Altersversorgungsplan m

planned economy Planwirtschaft f

planning n Planung f; **corporate ~** Unternehmensplanung f

plant n Fabrikanlage f, Maschinenanlage f, Werk n; **company ~** Werkanlage f; **gross ~** feste Anlagen f; **net ~** feste Anlage abzüglich vorgenommener Abschreibungen

plastic money Plastikgeld n

platinum Platin n

pledge v verpfänden v, versetzen v; **~ n** Pfand n, Faustpfand n, Pfandgegenstand m, Pfandsache f; **~ n** Pfandrecht n, Verpfändung f; **~ loan** Pfandanleihe f; **contract of ~** Verpfändungsvertrag m; **hold in ~** als Pfand unterhalten; **put in ~** verpfänden v, versetzen v; **redeem a ~** ein Pfand einlösen

pledged securities lombardierte Effekten; **~ collaterals** verpfändete Sicherheiten f pl

pledgee n Pfandnehmer m, Pfandinhaber m

pledger n (GB) Verpfänder m, Pfandschuldner m, Pfandgeber m

pledging n Pfandbestellung f, Verpfändung f; **~ of securities** Verpfändung von Wertpapieren

pledgor n (US) Verpfänder m, Pfandschuldner m, Pfandgeber m

plum n (US) Extradividende f, Gratisaktie f

plunge v stürzen v (Kurs, Preis), sinnlos spekulieren

plunger n wahnsinniger Spekulant

plural vote Mehrstimmenrecht n

pocket key Fachschlüssel m (beim Beleglesen)

point n Punkt m (bei der Notierung an der Börse); **~ of sale (POS)** Verkaufsstelle f

point-to-point connection Standverbindung f (EDV)

poison pills (US) Maßnahmen zur Abwehr von Firmenübernahmen, Übernahmeabwehr durch Wandlung von Anleihen in Aktien; **~ put** (US) Anleihe mit Tilgungsoption bei einer feindlichen Übernahme

policy n Politik f; **~ n** Versicherungsschein m, Police f; **~ holder** Versicherungsnehmer m, Versicherungsbeleihung f; **~ of insurance** Versicherungspolice f; **~ value** Versicherungswert m; **accounting ~** Bilanzpolitik f; **blank ~** Generalpolice f; **blanket ~** Generalpolice f; **cargo ~** Frachtpolice f; **credit ~** Kreditpolitik f; **currency ~** Währungspolitik f; **cyclical ~** Konjunkturpolitik f; **deflationary ~** Deflationspolitik f; **floating ~** gleitende Neuwertversicherung, Pauschalversicherung f; **marine insurance ~** Seeversicherungspolice f; **open ~** offene Police; **paid-up ~** volleingezahlte Police; **time ~** Versicherung für einen befristeten Zeitraum

poll; deed ~ einseitige Rechtserklärung

polling mode Abrufbetrieb m (EDV)

pool n Kartell n, Pool m, Ring m; **~ support** Stützungskäufe der Poolbeteiligten; **bull ~** Haussegruppe f

pooling n Zusammenschluß m, Poolbildung f; **~ agreement** Kartellvertrag m; **~ of interests** Organschaft f; Gewinn-und-Verlust-Abführungsvertrag m; **~ of profits** Gewinnteilung f; **~ of risk** Risikoverteilung f

poor adj bedürftig adj, arm adj

port bill of lading Hafenkonnossement n; **~ of lading** Ladehafen m

portfolio n Effektenportefeuille n, Wertpapierbesitz m, Wertpapierbestand m, Effektenbestand m; **~ n** Portefeuille n; **~ analysis** Portefeuilleanalyse f, Depotbewertung f; **~ evaluation** Depotbewertung f; **~ insurance** Depotabsicherung f; **~ management** Vermögensverwaltung f; **~ manager** Vermögensverwalter f; **~ of bills**

Wechselportefeuille n; **- value** Depotbewertung f; **bills in -** Wechselportefeuille n, Wechselbestand m
portion n Anteil m (Teil), Quote f
POS = point of sale Verkaufsstelle f
position n Position f, Bestand m, Lage f, Stellung f, Rang m, Stand f, Saldo m; -v positionieren v; **- sheet** Devisenposition f, Aufstellung der Devisenengagements; **competitive -** Wettbewerbssituation f; **open -** ungedecktes Engagement
positioning Positionierung f
possession n Besitz m; **proprietary -** Eigenbesitz m; **take - of** in Besitz nehmen
possessor n Besitzer m, Eigentümer m, Inhaber m
possessorship n Besitz m
possessory title Besitztitel m, Besitzurkunde f
post n Stand m (Börse), Buchhaltungsposten m; **- code** Postleitzahl f; **- entry** Nachverzollung f; **- into the ledger** in das Hauptbuch eintragen; **- up** tagfertig buchen
postage n Porto n, Portogebühr f, Portospesen plt; **- paid** Lieferung ohne Versandspesen
postal check (US) Postscheck m; **- cheque** (GB) Postscheck m; **- collecting order** (US) Postauftrag m; **- giro transfer** Postgiro n; **- giro service** Postscheckverkehr m; **- money order** Postanweisung f; **- order** (GB) Postanweisung f (für kleine Beträge); **- payment order** Zahlungsanweisung im Postscheckverkehr; **- receipt** Postempfangsschein m; **- savings account** Postsparkassenkonto n; **- savings bank** Postsparkasse f; **- savings deposit** Postsparkassenguthaben n, Postsparguthaben n
postdate v vordatieren v; **- a check** einen Scheck vordatieren
postdated adj vordatiert adj; **- check** vordatierter Scheck
postil n (US) Anmerkung bei einem Buchhaltungsposten

posting n Verbuchung f; **certificate of -** Postquittung f, Einlieferungsschein bei der Post
postings n pl Buchungen f pl
post-inscription Nachcodierung f
postpone v aufschieben v, verschieben v
post-qualification (MICR) Nachcodierung f
post-tax profit Gewinn nach Steuern
potential stocks nicht ausgegebene Aktien
pound sterling Pfund Sterling n
poundage pro Pfund berechnete Gebühr
power of attorney Vertretungsvollmacht f, Handlungsvollmacht f, Prozeßvollmacht f; **- to contract** Abschlußvollmacht f; **- to draw** Verfügungsberechtigung f; **blank - of attorney** Blankovollmacht f; **unlimited - of attorney** Generalvollmacht f
powers of the central bank Notenbankinstrumentarium n; **corporate -** Gesellschaftsbefugnisse f pl
practicable adj gangbar adj
practice v ausüben v; -n Usance f; **banking -** Bankpraxis f, Bankusancen f pl; **commercial -** Geschäftspraxis f
practices; brokerage - Maklerusancen f pl
practitioner; accounting - Bilanzexperte m
pre dealings Nebenbörsengeschäfte n pl; **clause of -** Vorverkaufsklausel f
preauthorized payment method Abbuchungsverfahren n
precarious loan unsicheres Darlehen
precedence; order of - Rangordnung f
precious metals Edelmetalle n pl
preclusion clause Ausschlußklausel f
pre-emption Vorkaufsrecht n
pre-emptive right Bezugsrecht n, Optionsrecht n
preference n Vorzug m, Begünstigung f, Präferenz f; **- bond** Vorzugsobligation f, Obligation mit Vorzugsrecht; **- shares** (GB) Vorzugsaktien f pl; **- stocks** (US) Vorzugsaktien f pl; **cumulative - stocks** kumulative Vorzugsaktien; **participating - shares** (GB) Vorzugsaktien mit zusätzlicher Gewinnbeteiligung
preferences n pl Vorzugsaktien f pl

preferential

preferential *adj* mit einem Vorzug ausgestattet; **~ creditor** (GB) Vorzugsgläubiger *m*, bevorrechtigter Gläubiger, bevorzugter Gläubiger; **~ debt** bevorrechtigte Schuld, bevorrechtigte Forderung; **~ payment** Vorzugszahlung *f*; **~ shares (stocks)** Vorzugsaktien *f pl*; **~ terms** Vorzugskonditionen *f pl*

preferred bond Vorzugsobligation *f*, Obligation mit Vorzugsrecht; **~ creditor** (US) Vorzugsgläubiger *m*, bevorrechtigter Gläubiger, bevorzugter Gläubiger; **~ debt** bevorrechtigte Schuld, bevorrechtigte Forderung; **~ dividend** Vorzugsdividende *f*; **~ ordinary share** Vorzugsstammaktie *f*; **~ stocks** (US) Vorzugsaktien *f pl*; **convertible ~ stock** Vorzugsaktie mit Umtauschrecht; **participating ~ stocks** (US) Vorzugsaktien mit zusätzlicher Gewinnbeteiligung; **redeemable ~ stocks** kündbare Vorzugsaktien; **second ~ stocks** (US) Vorzugsaktien zweiter Klasse

pre-financing Vorfinanzierung *f*
preliminary contract Vorvertrag *m*
pre-market price Kurs der Vorbörse
premises *n pl* Grundstücke mit allen Nebengebäuden, Einleitung zu einem Vertrag; **business ~** Geschäftslokal *n*, Geschäftsräume *m pl*
premium *n* Prämie *f*, Agio *n*, Aufgeld *n*, Report *m*, Bonus *m*, Zuschlag *m*, Aufschlag *m*, Reuegeld *n*, Rücktrittsprämie *f*; **~ bargain** Prämiengeschäft *n*; **~ bond** Prämienschein *m*, Prämienobligation *f*, Aufzinsungsanleihe *f*; **~ deal** Prämiengeschäft *n*; **~ loan** Policendarlehen *n*; **~ rate** Aufgeld *n*; **amount of ~** Prämienhöhe *f*; **bond ~** Obligationsagio *n*, Pfandbriefagio *n*; **buy at a ~** über pari kaufen; **risk ~** Risikoprämie *f*

prepaid *adj* vorausbezahlt *adj*, freigemacht *adj*, frankiert *adj*; **~ card (electronic purse)** Wertkarte *f*, Geldkarte *f*; **~ expenses** transitorische Aktiva, aktive Rechnungsabgrenzungsposten; **~ interest** im voraus vorgenommener Zinsabzug
prepay *v* vorausbezahlen *v*, freimachen *v*, frankieren *v*

prepayment *n* Vorauszahlung *f*, Vorkasse *f*
prescribe *v* vorschreiben *v*, verordnen *v*, verjähren *v*
prescribed; to become ~ verjähren *v*
prescription *n* Vorschrift *f*, Verordnung *f*; **period of ~** Verjährungsfrist *f*
prescriptive right Verjährungsrecht *n*, Gewohnheitsrecht *n*
present again wiedervorlegen *v*; **~ value** Barwert *m*
presentation *n* Vorlage *f*
presenter *n* Einreicher *m*
presentment for acceptance Vorlage zum Akzept, Vorlage zur Annahme, Akzeptbesorgung *f*; **~ for payment** Vorlage zur Zahlung; **~ of a bill** Wechselvorlage *f*, Wechselpräsentierung *f*
president *n* (US) geschäftsführender Direktor, Generaldirektor *m*; **~ n** Präsident *m*; **vice ~** Direktor *m*
presidential chair Präsidentenstuhl *m*
pre-sort *n* Grobsortierung *f* (beim Beleglesen)
press conference Pressekonferenz *f*
pressure *n* Druck *m*; **~ group** Interessengruppe *f*
pre-tax Gewinn vor Steuerabzug, vor Steuern
pre-tax profit Gewinn vor Steuern
prevailing *adj* vorherrschend *adj*, üblich *adj*
price *n* Notierung *f*, Notiz *f*, Börsentierung *f*, Börsennotiz *f*, Preisangabe *f*, Preisstellung *f*, Preis *m*; **~ advance** Kurssteigerung *f*; **~ after hours** Kurs der Nachbörse; **~ bid** Geldkurs *m*, (Börse); **~ cap** Kursobergrenze *f*; **~ caring** Kurspflege *f*; **~/cash flow ratio** Kurs-Cash-flow-Verhältnis *n*; **~ decline** Kursrückgang *m*; **~ difference** Kursdifferenz *f*; **~ differential** Preisunterschied *m*; **~ drawn by lot** Loskurs *m*; **~/earnings ratio (PER)** Kurs-Gewinn-Verhältnis *n* (KGV); **~ escalator clause** Preisgleitklausel *f*; **~ fixing** Preisfestsetzung *f*; **~ fluctuation** Kursschwankung *f*; **~ increase** Kursanstieg *m*; **~ index number** Kursindex *m*; **~ information system** Kurs-Informations-und-Service-System *n* (KISS); **~ jump** Kurssprung *m*; **~ limit**

354

Kurslimit n - **list** Kurszettel m, Preisliste f; - **margin** Kursspanne f; - **markdown** Kursabschlag m; - **movement** Kursbildung f, Kursbewegung f, Kursentwicklung f; - **offered** Briefkurs m; - **paid** Bezahltkurs m; - **range** Kursbildung f, Kursbewegung f, Kursentwicklung f; Preisspielraum m (innerhalb gewisser Grenzen); - **run-up** Kursanstieg m; - **slippage** Nachgeben der Kurse; - **support** Kursstützung f, Preisstützung f, Marktstützung f; **actual** - Marktpreis m; **asked** - Briefkurs m; **bargain** - Vorzugspreis m, Ausverkaufspreis m; **basic** - Grundpreis m; **bid** - Geldkurs m, gebotener Preis; **bond** - Obligationenkurs m, Rentenkurs m; **boom** - Haussekurs m; **ceiling** - Höchstpreis m; **closing** - Schlußkurs m; **competitive** - Konkurrenzpreis m, konkurrenzfähiger Preis; **contract** - Vertragspreis m; **controlled** - Stoppreis m, gebundener Preis; **cost** - Kostenpreis m, Wareneinstandspreis m; **curb market** - nachbörslicher Kurs, außerbörslicher Kurs; **current** - Tageskurs m, Tagessatz m, Marktpreis m; **cut-throat** - Wucherpreis m; **forward** - Terminkurs m; **offer** - Briefkurs m; **opening** - Anfangskurs m, Eröffnungskurs m; **put up** - Taxpreis m; **reasonable** - annehmbarer Preis, vernünftiger Preis; **share** - Aktienkurs m, Aktienpreis m, Aktiennotierung f; **sharp** - **advance** n plötzliche Kurssteigerung; **starting** - Anfangskurs m, Eröffnungskurs m; **stock** - **average** Börsenindex m; **top** - höchster Kurs

prices have decreased die Kurse liegen schwächer; - **have improved** die Kurse haben sich gebessert; **bargain basement** - Ausverkaufspreise m pl, Spottpreise m pl; **commodity** - Warenpreise m pl; **securities** - Effektenkurse m pl

pricing Preisbildung f, Preisgestaltung f; - **policy** Preispolitik f, Gebührenpolitik f; - **schedule** Gebührentabelle f

primary account data Stammdaten plt (für ein Konto); - **account number** Stammkontonummer f; - **dealer** (GB) Marktmacher m, Händler mit Staatspapieren, Primärhändler m; - **deposit** (US) Einlage (die nicht aus der Gutschrift eines eingeräumten Kredits entstanden ist); - **market** Markt für Neuemissionen, Primärmarkt m

prime acceptances Primadiskonten m pl; - **bill** erstklassiger Wechsel, prima Wechsel; - **cost** Selbstkosten plt, Gestehungskosten plt; - **rate** (US) Zinssatz der Banken für Kredite an erstklassige Adressen, Leitzinssatz m, Privatdiskontsatz m

principal n Kapital n (im Gegensatz zu »Zinsen«); - n Vollmachtgeber m, Auftraggeber m; - **and interest** Kapital und Zinsen; - **bill debtor** Hauptwechselschuldner m; - **debtor** Hauptschuldner m; - **mortgage** erstrangige Hypothek; - **repayment** Kapitalzurückzahlung f; - **shareholder** Hauptaktionär m

principle n Grundsatz m; - adj grundsätzlich adj; - **currency** - Golddeckungsprinzip n; - **of dual control** Vier-Augen-Prinzip n

principles; credit - Kreditgrundsätze m pl

print buffer Druckpuffer m; - **file** Druckdatei f; - **file on disc** Druckplatte f (Plattenspeicher, der Druckdaten enthält); - **line** Druckzeile f; - **tape** Druckband n

printer layout Listenbild n

printing format Druckbild n; - **rate** Druckgeschwindigkeit f; **bank note** - Banknotendruck m

printout n Protokoll n (Informationsverarbeitung)

prior adj früher adj, vorausgehend adj; - **lien** bevorrechtigtes Pfandrecht, bevorrechtigtes Zurückbehaltungsrecht; - **preferred stocks** erstrangige Vorzugsaktien; - **to maturity** vor Fälligkeit

priority n Priorität f, Vorrang m, Vorzug m, Dringlichkeit f, Dringlichkeitsstufe f; - **shares** Vorzugsaktien f pl

private adj privat adj, persönlich adj, nicht öffentlich; - **account** Privatkonto n; - **bank** Privatbank f, Privatbankhaus n; - **banker** Privatbankier m; - **company** (GB) etwa: Gesellschaft mit beschränkter Haftung (GmbH); - **discount rate** Privatdiskontsatz m; - **enterprise** Privatunternehmen n; - **income** Privateinkommen n; - **limited company** (GB) Gesellschaft mit beschränkter Haftung; - **means** Privatvermögen n; - **placement** nicht am Markt plazierte Anleihe, Privatplazierung f; - **property** Privatvermögen n, Privateigentum n; - **trust** Familienstiftung f; - **wire house** (US) Börsenmitglieder (die private Telegraphenlinien unterhalten)

privatization n Privatisierung f

privilege n (US) Prämiengeschäft n, Privileg n, Vorrecht n, Vorzugsrecht n, Sonderrecht n; - **broker** (US) Prämienmakler m

privileged adj privilegiert adj, bevorrechtigt adj, mit Sonderrechten ausgestattet; - **common stock** Vorzugsstammaktie; - **creditor** bevorrechtigte Gläubiger m; - **debt** bevorrechtigte Schuld, bevorrechtigte Forderung; - **stocks** Vorzugsaktien f pl

prize n Preis m (Gewinn), Belohnung f, Prämie f; - **bond** Prämienanleihe f, Losanleihe f

probate v ein Testament gerichtlich bestätigen lassen; - n gerichtliche Testamentsbestätigung und Erbscheinerteilung; - **court** Nachlaßgericht; - **duty** Erbschaftssteuer f; - **register** Testamentshinterlegungsstelle f

problem definition Aufgabenstellung f; - **lendings** ausfallgefährdete Ausleihungen

procedure n Prozedur f (EDV); - n Verfahren n; **court** - Gerichtsverfahren n

proceedings Verfahren n, Prozeß m; **bankruptcy** - Konkursverfahren n; **composition** - Vergleichsverfahren n

proceeds n pl Erlös m, Ertrag m, Gewinn m, Diskonterlös m, Einnahmen f pl; **application of** - Verwendung des Gegenwertes; **business** - Geschäftsertrag m, Betriebsertrag m; **cash** - Barerlös m; **credit the** - **to an account** Gegenwert einem Konto gutschreiben; **gross** - Rohertrag m, Bruttoertrag m; **net** - Reingewinn m, Nettogewinn m

processing n Bearbeitung f; - **phase** Arbeitsphase f; - **sequence** Arbeitsablauf m; - **time** Verarbeitungszeit f; **text** - Textverarbeitung f

procura Prokura f, Vertretungsvollmacht f

procuration n Prokura f; - **endorsement** Vollmachtsindossament n

procuratory n (US) Vollmacht f

procure v beschaffen v, erlangen v, besorgen v, beibringen v, einholen v

produce v fabrizieren v, herstellen v, bringen v, erzielen v; - **exchange** Warenbörse f, Produktenbörse f; - **loan** Warenkredit m

producer n Fabrikant m, Hersteller m, Industrieller m, Fabrikbesitzer m, Erzeuger m, Produzent m; **marginal** - Grenzbetrieb m

product n Produkt n, Erzeugnis n; - **management** Produktmanagement n, Produktentwicklung f

production n Produktion f, Herstellung f; - **loan** Produktionskredit m; **annual** - Jahresproduktion f; **settled** - gleichmäßige Produktion

productive adj produktiv adj, ertragsfähig adj, rentabel adj

productivity n Produktivität f, Ertragskraft f

profession n Beruf m (freier oder akademischer)

professional traders Berufshandel m; - **troubleshooter** (informal) Krisenmanager m

profit n Ertrag m, Gewinn m, Verdienst m; - **and loss account** Erfolgsrechnung f, (GB) Gewinn-und-Verlust-Rechnung f; Erträgnisaufstellung f, Ertragsrechnung f; - **and loss accounts** Aufwand-und-Ertrags-Konten n pl; - **balance** Guthabensaldo m; - **break-even point** Gewinnschwelle f; - **brought forward** Gewinnvortrag f; - **center** Profitzenter n, Geschäftsbereich mit Ertragsverantwortung; - **derived from capital** Kapitalgewinn m, Kapitaleinkommen n; - **expectation** Gewinnerwartung f; - **forecast** Gewinnprognose f; - **margin**

Gewinnspanne f; ~ **mark-up** Gewinnzuschlag m; ~ **participation certificates outstanding** Genußrechtskapital n; ~ **rise** Gewinnsteigerung f; ~ **sharing** Gewinnbeteiligung f; ~ **shrinkage** Gewinnschrumpfung f, Flaute f; ~ **taking** Gewinnmitnahme f, Gewinnrealisierung f; ~ **transfer agreement** Gewinnabführungsvertrag m; **actual** ~ echter Gewinn; **accumulate** ~ v Gewinn thesaurieren v; **approval of** ~ **and loss account** Genehmigung der Gewinn-und-Verlust-Rechnung; **book** ~ Buchgewinn m; **boom** ~ Konjunkturgewinn m; **business** ~ Geschäftsgewinn m; **clear** ~ Reingewinn m, Nettogewinn m; **commercial** ~ Geschäftsgewinn m; **consolidated** ~ **and loss statement** konsolidierte Gewinn-und-Verlust-Rechnung; **contingent** ~ noch nicht realisierter Gewinn; **corporate** ~ Gesellschaftsgewinn m; **gross** ~ Bruttogewinn m, Rohgewinn m; **leave a** ~ einen Gewinn abwerfen; **net** ~ Reingewinn m, Nettogewinn m; **pre-tax** ~ Gewinn vor Steuern; **pure** ~ Reingewinn m, Nettogewinn m; **trading** ~ Betriebsgewinn m, Geschäftsgewinn m

profitability n Rentabilität f

profitable adj lukrativ adj, gewinnbringend adj, rentabel adj, einträglich adj

profit-making gewinnbringend adj, rentabel adj

profits; calculation of ~ Gewinnberechnung f, Rentabilitätsberechnung f; **distributed** ~ ausgeschütteter Gewinn, verteilter Gewinn; **distribution of** ~ Gewinnverteilung f; **paper** ~ (US) Scheingewinne m pl, unrealisierte Gewinne; **pooling of** ~ Gewinnteilung f; **retained** ~ zurückbehaltene Gewinne, nicht ausgeschüttete Gewinne; **surplus** ~ (US) Gewinnüberschuß m, Überschuß m, Überfluß m, unverteilter Reingewinn; **taxable** ~ steuerpflichtige Gewinne; **unappropriated** ~ (US) unverteilter Reingewinn; **undivided** ~ unverteilter Reingewinn

profit-sharing bonds Obligationen mit Gewinnbeteiligung

proforma invoice Proformarechnung f

programmable adj programmierbar adj

programme v programmieren v; ~ n Programm n; ~ **error** Programmfehler m; ~ **package** Programmpaket n; ~ **subdivision** Programmaufteilung f; ~ (US: program) **trading** Programmhandel m

programmed check programmierte Kontrolle; ~ **instruction** programmierte Unterweisung

programmer n Programmierer m

programming n Programmierung f

progress n Verlauf m, Fortschritt m; ~ v fortschreiten v, vordringen v

progression n Progression f

progressive interest calculation progressive Zinsrechnung

prohibitive adj untragbar adj, unerschwinglich adj, vorbeugend adj

project n Plan m, Projekt f, Vorhaben f; ~ v planen v

project financing Projektfinanzierung f

prolong v prolongieren v, verlängern v, erneuern v

prolongation n Prolongation f, Verlängerung f

prominent adj bekannt adj, namhaft adj; ~ adj führend adj

promise of a credit Kreditzusage f

promising adj chancenreich adj

promissory note Schuldschein m, Solawechsel m, Eigenwechsel m

promote v befördern v, gründen v, werben v

promoter n Förderer m, Gründer m

promotion Förderung f, Werbung f; ~ **of exports** Exportförderung f; **cost of** ~ Gründungskosten plt

prompt adj sofort adj, prompt adj, pünktlich adj

proof of debt Nachweis einer Forderung

property n Eigentum n, Immobilien plt, Grundstück n, Vermögen n, Besitz m; ~ **account** Anlagekonto n, Immobilienkonto n, Sachkonto n; ~ **assets** feste Anlagen; ~ **bond fund** Immobilienfonds m; ~ **depreciation** Grundstücksabschreibung f; ~ **dividend** (US) Sachwertdividende f, Dividende in Form von Gratisaktien anderer Aktiengesellschaften; ~ **income**

Einkommen aus Grundbesitz; **- insurance** Sachversicherung f; **- investments** Anlagevermögen n; **- management** Vermögensverwaltung f; **- market** Grundstücksmarkt m; **- owner** Grundstückseigentümer m; **- reserve** Vermögensreserve f; **- risk** Risiko, dessen Höhe sich aus dem beim Kreditnehmer vorhandenen Eigentum ergibt; **- statement** Vermögensaufstellung f, Vermögenserklärung f; **- tax** (GB) Grund- und Gebäudesteuer, (US) Vermögenssteuer für bewegliches und unbewegliches Vermögen; **- value** Grundstückswert m, Vermögenswert m; **accession of -** Vermögenszuwachs m; **acquisition of -** Eigentumserwerb m; **administration of -** Vermögensverwaltung f; **adventitious -** Erbschaftsvermögen n; **alien -** Ausländervermögen n; **attachment of -** Vermögensbeschlagnahme f; **beneficial -** Nießbrauch an einem Vermögen; **blocking of -** Vermögenssperre f; **business -** Geschäftsgrundstück n, Betriebsgrundstück n; **capital -** Kapitalvermögen n; **contingent -** Reservekapital n; **conveyance of -** Eigentumsübertragung f; **damage to -** Sachschaden m, Vermögensschaden m; **declaration of -** Vermögenserklärung f; **deed of -** Vermögensübertragung f; **dotal -** Mitgift f, Aussteuer f; **gross -** feste Anlagen; **immovable -** Immobilien plt, unbewegliches Vermögen; **landed -** Immobilien plt, Grundbesitz m, Grund und Boden, Grundeigentum n, Grundstückseigentum n, Liegenschaften f pl; **net -** feste Anlage abzüglich vorgenommener Abschreibungen; **partnership -** Gesellschaftsvermögen n, Gesellschaftseigentum n; **personal -** bewegliches Eigentum, Mobilien plt; **private -** Privatvermögen n, Privateigentum n; **real -** Immobilien plt, Grundbesitz m, Grund und Boden, Grundeigentum n, Grundstückseigentum n, Liegenschaften f pl; **registration of a title to -** Eintragung eines Eigentumsrechts in das Grundbuch

proportion n Anteil m (Verhältnis), Teil m (Verhältnis), Verhältnisziffer f

proportional adj verhältnismäßig adj, proportional adj

proportionately adj verhältnismäßig adj, pro rata, nach Verhältnis, anteilmäßig adj

proposer Antragsteller m

proprietary n Besitzstand m; **- account** Kapitalkonto n; **- capital** Eigenkapital n, Eigenvermögen n; **- company** Holdinggesellschaft f, Dachgesellschaft f, Grundstücksgesellschaft f, kontrollierende Gesellschaft; **- equity** Barbetrag aus einem Grundbesitz; **- possession** Eigenbesitz m; **- right** Eigentumsrecht n

proprietor n Besitzer m, Eigentümer, Inhaber m; **- of a bank** Bankinhaber m, Bankherr m

proprietorship n Eigentumsrecht n, Eigenkapital n

prospect n zukünftiger Kunde, Aussicht f

prospective customer voraussichtlicher Kunde

prospector n Goldgräber m, Prospektor m, Spekulant m

prospects; business - Geschäftsaussichten f pl

prospectus n Zeichnungsprospekt m

prosperity n Wohlstand m; **business -** Geschäftskonjunkturauftrieb m, Hochkonjunktur f

protect v sicherstellen v, schützen v, sichern v

protecting; check - device (US) Scheckschutzvorrichtung f, Apparat zur Verhütung von Fälschungen

protection n Schutz m; **- of a bill** Wechseleinlösung f; **- of creditors** Gläubigerschutz m; **- of savers and depositors** Sparer-und-Anleger-Schutz m; **- of transmitted data** Übertragungssicherung f (EDV); **consumer -** Verbraucherschutz m; **tariff -** Zollschutz m

protectionism n Protektionismus m, Schutzsystem n

protest v protestieren v, Einspruch erheben; **- n** Protest m, Einspruch m, Reklamation f; **- charges** Protestkosten plt; **- for nonacceptance** Protest wegen Nichtannahme; **- for nonpayment**

Protest mangels Zahlung; *- of a bill of exchange* Wechselprotest m; *act of -* Protesterhebung f, Protesturkunde f; *bill -* Wechselprotest m; *bill of - * Protesturkunde f; *certificate of -* Protesturkunde f; *deed of -* Protesturkunde f; *enter - of a draft* einen Wechsel protestieren lassen; *notarial - certificate* Protesturkunde f; *note of -* Protesturkunde f; *notice of -* (US) Protestbenachrichtigung f; *raise a -* Protest erheben

protested bill protestierter Wechsel; *- check* protestierter Scheck

protesting of a bill Protestaufnahme f

provable debts nachweisbare Schulden

prove v beweisen v, nachweisen v, beglaubigen v; *- a claim in bankruptcy* Konkursforderung anmelden; *- a will* ein Testament gerichtlich bestätigen lassen; *- one's identity* (sich) legitimieren v

provide a bill with acceptance Wechsel mit Akzept versehen

provided adj (with) versehen adj (mit)

provident bank Sparkasse f, Sparbank f; *- fund* Fürsorgefonds m, Pensionsfonds m; *- reserve fund* Spezialreserve f, außerordentliche Reserve; *beneficiary of - fund* Bezugsberechtigter einer Versorgungsstiftung

provincial adj provinziell adj, regional adj, Provinz- (in Zus.)

provision n Rückstellung f, Rücklage f, Reserve f, Bestimmung f (Vertrag), Vorsorge f; *- against specific debts* Einzelwertberichtigung f; *- for taxes* Steuerrückstellungen f pl; *call -* Bestimmung f, nach der Obligationen jederzeit zurückgezahlt werden können; *check without -* ungedeckter Scheck

provisional adj vorläufig adj; *- bond* Zwischenschein für eine Obligation; *- certificate* Zwischenschein für eine Obligation oder Aktie

provisions (reserves) Rückstellungen für Kreditverluste; *- of a contract* Vertragsbestimmungen f pl; *legal -* Rechtsvorschriften f pl

proviso n Bedingung f (Vorbehalt); *- clause* Vorbehaltsklausel f

proxy n Bevollmächtigter m, Vollmacht f, Stellvertretung f (auf Grund einer Vollmacht); *- endorsement* Prokuraindossament n; *- holder* Vollmachtsbesitzer m; *- voting right* Auftragsstimmrecht n, Depotstimmrecht f; *by -* in Vertretung, in Vollmacht

prudential adj vorsichtig adj; *- committee* (US) Beirat m

public n Öffentlichkeit f (Allgemeinheit); *- adj* öffentlich adj, staatlich adj, Staats- (in Zus.); *- account* (GB) Staatskonto n; *- accountant* Bücherrevisor m, Wirtschaftsprüfer m, Buchprüfer m, Rechnungsprüfer m, Revisor m; *- authority* Behörde f; *- bonds* Staatsanleihe f, Staatspapiere f pl; *- business* Staatsbetrieb m; *- company* (GB) gemeinwirtschaftliches Unternehmen; *- credit* öffentliche Anleihe, öffentlicher Kredit; *- creditor* Staatsgläubiger m, öffentlicher Gläubiger; *- debt* Staatsschuld f, öffentliche Schuld; *- finance* staatliches Finanzwesen, öffentliches Finanzwesen; *- funds* Staatsgelder n pl, öffentliche Gelder; *- liability insurance* Haftpflichtversicherung f; *- limited company* Aktiengesellschaft f, Kapitalgesellschaft f; *- loan* öffentliche Anleihe, öffentlicher Kredit; *- money* Staatsgelder n pl, öffentliche Gelder; *- offering* Zeichnungsangebot n, Zeichnungsofferte f; *- placing* öffentliche Plazierung; *- registry* Grundbuchamt n; *- relations* (PR) Öffentlichkeitsarbeit f; *- sale* öffentliche Versteigerung; *- sector securities* Schuldtitel öffentlicher Stellen (Bilanzposition); *- utilities* Aktien oder Obligationen (von privaten Versorgungsbetrieben); *- works* öffentliche Arbeiten; *certified - accountant* (US) vereidigter Wirtschaftsprüfer

publicity n Publizität f, Werbewesen n; *- department* Werbeabteilung f

published reserves offene Reserven, offene Rücklagen

puisne mortgage (GB) Nachgangshypothek f

pull off abwickeln v, an Land ziehen; **- out** aussteigen v, zurücktreten v
pump v ankurbeln v, antreiben v
punch card Lochkarte f; **- card machine** Lochkartenmaschine f
punched tape Lochstreifen m
punctual adj pünktlich adj
Punt Irische Pfund n (Währung in Irland)
purchase n Kauf m, Ankauf m, Einkauf m, Anschaffung f, Erwerb m; **-** v kaufen v, erwerben v, ankaufen v; **- agreement** Emissions-und-Übernahme-Vertrag m; **- at auction** ersteigern v; **- at option** Prämienkauf m (Börse); **- commitment** Kauf- Abnahmeverpflichtung f; **- debts** v Forderungen abkaufen; **- for acceptance** Kauf gegen Akzept; **- money** Kaufpreis m, Kaufsumme f; **- money mortgage** Restkaufgeldhypothek f; **- of real property** Grundstückserwerb m; **- on account** Kauf auf Kredit; **- order** Kaufauftrag m, Bestellung f; **- syndicate (group)** Übernahmekonsortium n; **abatement of - money** Kaufpreisherabsetzung f, Kaufpreisminderung f; **bull -** (US) Haussekauf m; **cash -** Barkauf m; **certificate of -** Grunderwerbsbescheinigung f; **charge -** Kreditkauf m; **contract of -** Kaufvertrag m, Kaufbrief m; **covering -** Deckungskauf m; **pegging -** Stützungskauf m; **supporting -** Stützungskauf m
purchased paper per Kasse gekauftes Wertpapier
purchaser n Käufer m; **- in good faith** gutgläubiger Erwerber
purchases; assets - Anlagekäufe m pl; **speculative -** Meinungskäufe m pl

purchasing n Kauf m, Ankauf m, Einkauf m, Anschaffung f, Erwerb m; **- power** Kaufkraft f; **- power index** Kaufkraftindex m; **- power parity** Kaufkraftparität f; **consumer - power** Konsumentenkaufkraft f

pure gold Feingold n; **- interest** Nettozinsen m pl; **- profit** Reingewinn m, Nettogewinn m

push up hinauftreiben v, hochtreiben v

put v festsetzen v, festlegen v, legen v, setzen v; **-** n Verkaufsoption f, Rückprämie beim Börsenprämiengeschäft; **- and call** Stellagengeschäft n; **- and call broker** (US) Prämienmakler m; **- and call price** Stellagekurs m, Steilpreis m; **- bond** Anleihe mit Kündigungsschutzrecht des Gläubigers; **- capital into a business** Kapital in ein Geschäft stecken; **- into circulation** in Umlauf bringen; **- into utterance** in Umlauf setzen; **- of more** Nochgeschäft n (Börse); **- option** Rückprämie f (Börsenprämiengeschäft), Verkaufsoption f; **- out money** Geld ausleihen; **- to account** Rechnung stellen; **- up price** Taxpreis m; **- warrant** Verkaufsoptionsschein m

puts n pl Verkaufsoptionen f pl

puttable bond kündbare Anleihe; **- swap** kündbarer Swap

pyramiding n (US) Benutzung von noch nicht realisierten Spekulationsgewinnen zu neuen Spekulationen, Aufnahme von Geldern zur Bezahlung bereits bestehender Verpflichtungen

pyramid selling Schneeballvertriebssystem n

Q

qualification *n* Qualifikation *f*; **- procedure** Zulassungsverfahren *n*

qualified; - acceptance bedingtes Akzept, bedingte Annahme; **- audit certificate** eingeschränkter Bestätigungsvermerk; **- endorsement** bedingtes Indossament; **- for dividend** dividendenberechtigt; **- for tax relief** steuerbegünstigt; **- sale** Verkauf mit Eigentumsvorbehalt

qualifying date Stichtag *m*; **- period** Wartezeit *f*, Karenzzeit *f* (Versicherung); **- shares** Pflichtaktien *f pl*

quality *n* Qualität *f*, Güte *f*, Eigenschaft *f*; **- control** Qualitätskontrolle *f*

quantity *n* Quantum *n*, Quantität *f*, Masse *f*, Menge *f*; **- discount** Mengenrabatt *m*; **- theory of money** Quantitätstheorie *f*

quanto warrent Quanto-Optionsschein *m*

quarter *n* Viertel *n*, Quartal *n*, Vierteljahr *n*, 25-Cent-Stück *n*

quarterage *n* Quartalsbetrag *m*

quarterly *adj* vierteljährlich *adj*; **- dividend** Quartalsdividende *f*

quash *v* annullieren *v*, ungültig machen, aufheben *v*

quasi partner Scheingesellschafter *m*

quasi-negotiable instrument quasi begebbares Wertpapier, quasi übertragbares Wertpapier

quay *n* Lagerhaus *n*, Lagerplatz *m*, Dock *n*, Kai *m*

quayage *n* Dockgebühren *f pl*, Dockgeld *n*, Löschgeld *n*, Landungszoll *m*, Kaigeld *n*

queer money (US) Falschgeld *n*

query bill fauler Wechsel

quick assets leicht realisierbare Aktiva (liquides Umlaufvermögen); **- liabilities** kurzfristig zurückzahlbare Schulden; **- ratio** Verhältnis des Umlaufvermögens zu den laufenden Verbindlichkeiten

quintal *n*, Doppelzentner *m* (100 kg)

quitclaim *v* verzichten *v*, Verzicht leisten; **-** *n* Verzicht *m*, Verzichtleistung *f*

quittance *n* Quittung *f*, Schulderlaß *m*, Entlastung *f*

quorum *n* Beschlußfähigkeit *f*, beschlußfähige Mehrheit

quota *n* Quote *f*, Kontingent *n*, Rate *f* (Satz), Anteil *m*; **- fixing** Kontingentierung *f*; **subscription -** Zeichnungsbetrag *m*, Übernahmebetrag *m*

quotable *adj* notierbar *adj*

quota-free kontingentfrei

quota-system Kontingentierungssystem *n*

quotation *n* Notierung *f*, Notiz *f*, Börsennotierung *f*, Börsennotiz *f*, Preisangabe *f*, Preisstellung *f*, Preis *m*; **- board** Kursanzeigetafel *f*; **- fee** Börsenzulassungsgebühr *f*; **- list** Kursblatt *n*; **- on the stock exchange** Börsennotierung *f*; **- on spot exchange** Devisenkassanotierung *f*; **- ticker** (US) Börsenfernschreiber *m*, Börsentelegraph *m*; **asked -** Briefkurs *m*; **firm -** verbindliche Kursnotierung; **market -** Marktnotierung *f*, Börsennotierung *f*; **share -** Aktienkurs *m*, Aktienpreis *m*, Aktiennotierung *f*

quotations; bids and asked - Geld-und-Brief-Kurs *m*

quote *v* notieren *v*, Preise angeben; **-** *n* Notierung *f*, Kurs *m*

quote sheet *n* Kursblatt *n*

quoted *adj* börsennotiert *adj*, kotiert *adj* (Schweiz); **- company** börsennotiertes Unternehmen; **- equities** börsennotierte Aktien; **- value** Börsenkurs *m*, Kurswert *m*

R

racing inflation galoppierende Inflation
racket n (US) Geschäftemacherei f, Schiebung f; *- busting* (US) Aufdecken von Schiebungen; *currency -* Devisenschiebung f
racketeer n (US) Schieber m, Betrüger m
rack-rent n überhöhte Miete, Wuchermiete f, Jahresmiete f
radial transmission network sternförmiges Leitungsnetz
radio and TV advertising Radio-und-Fernseh-Werbung f
raffle n Auslosung f (von Wertpapieren), Verlosung f
rag money (US) entwertetes Papiergeld
ragged bonds (US) Obligationen mit abgetrennten, noch nicht fälligen Coupons
raider aggressiver Unternehmensaufkäufer m
Raiffeisen banks Raiffeisenbanken f pl (landwirtschaftliche Genossenschaftsbanken)
rail consignment note Eisenbahnfrachtbrief m
rail; *carriage by -* Eisenbahntransport m
railroad; *- bill of lading* Eisenbahnfrachtbetrieb m; *- freight rate* Gütertarif m; *- stocks* Eisenbahnwerte m pl
rails; *American -* (GB) amerikanische Eisenbahnwerte
railway bond Eisenbahnschuldverschreibung f; *- debenture* Eisenbahnobligation f; *- express agency* bahnamtlicher Spediteur, Bahnspedition f; *- loan* Eisenbahnanleihe f; *- rate* Gütertarif m; *- tariff* Bahntarif m
raise v erhöhen v, in die Höhe treiben, aufstocken v; *- n* Erhöhung f, Aufstockung f; *- a claim* Anspruch erheben, Anspruch geltend machen; *- a mortgage* eine Hypothek aufnehmen; *- a protest* Protest erheben; *- funds* Geldmittel auftreiben; *- money* Geld auftreiben

raised *bill* (US) durch Werterhöhung gefälschte Banknote; *- check* (US) durch Werterhöhung gefälschter Scheck
rake n (US) Provision f, Gewinnbeteiligung f
rally n (stock exchange) Erholung f (Börse)
rand Rand (Währung in Südafrika)
random *access* direkter Zugriff; *- selection process* Zufallsauswahlverfahren n
range n Bereich m, Umfang m (Reichweite); *- n* Kursschwankung f; *- for cable transfers* Satz für Kabelauszahlungen; *- of application* Anwendungsbereich m; *- of prices* Preislage f, Preisskala f; *- of products* Fertigungsprogramm n, Produktionsskala f; *- of services* Dienstleistungsangebot n; *- warrants* Bandbreiten-Optionsscheine; *- warrent* Kurskanal-Optionsschein, Hamster Optionsschein
rank n Rang m, Stellung f; *- v* Rang einnehmen, einordnen v
ranking Rangordnung f, Klassifizierung f, Rangfolge f; *- of creditors* Rangfolge der Gläubiger; *- of mortgage* Hypothekenrangordnung f
ratability n Steuerbarkeit f, Zollpflichtigkeit f, Umlagepflicht f, Steuerpflicht f
ratable adj anteilmäßig adj, im Verhältnis, umlagepflichtig adj, steuerpflichtig adj; *- value* Steuerwert m, Einheitswert m
rate n Gebühr f, Kurs m, Prämie f, Satz m, Tarif m, Umlage f; *- v* einschätzen v, bewerten v, bemessen v, besteuern v, beurteilen v, taxieren v; *- a coin* eine Münze schätzen; *- asked* Briefkurs m; *- basis* Frachtberechnungsgrundlage f; *- calculation* Kurswertberechnung f; *- ceiling* Zinsobergrenze f; *- development* Kursentwicklung f (Devisen); *- hedged* kursgesichert adj
rate-hedging Kurssicherung f, Zinssatzsicherung f
rate *increase* Gebührenerhöhung f, Prämienerhöhung f; *- of commission* Provisionssatz m; *- of compensation*

Kompensationskurs m; *- of consideration* Prämiensatz m; *- of conversion* Konversionssatz m; *- of customs* Zollsatz m, Steuersatz m; *- of depreciation* Abschreibungssatz m; *- of discount* Diskontsatz m; *- of duty* (GB) Steuerrate f, Zollsatz m; *- of exchange* Devisenkurs m, Umrechnungskurs m, Wechselkurs m, Umtauschkurs m; *- of increase* Steigerungsrate f; *- of interest* Zinssatz m, Zinsfuß m; *- of investment* Investitionsrate f; *- of issue* Emissionskurs m, Ausgabekurs m; *- of redemption* Rückzahlungskurs m, Einlösungskurs m; *- of return* Kapitalverzinsung f; *- of shares* Aktienkurs m, Aktienpreis m, Aktiennotierung f; *- of subscription* Zeichnungskurs m; *- of taxation* Steuersatz m; *- of the day* Tageskurs m, Tagessatz m, Marktpreis m; *- on deposit account* Zinsen für Spareinlagen; *- spread* Zinsspanne f; **backwardation** *-* Deportkurs m; **bank** *-* (of discount) Diskontsatz der Notenbank; **bill discount** *-* Wechseldiskontsatz m; **borrowing** *-* Kreditzinssatz m, Darlehenszinssatz m, Ausleihungssatz m; **buying** *-* Geldkurs m, Kaufkurs m; **cable transfer** *-* Kabelauszahlung f (Kurs), telegraphische Auszahlung (Kurs); **call** *-* Tagesgeldzinssatz m, Satz für Tagesgeld; **cash** *-* Scheckkurs m, Kassakurs m; **check** *-* Scheckkurs m; **church** *-* (GB) Kirchensteuer f; **clearing** *-* Verrechnungskurs m; **commercial** *- of exchange* (US) Devisenkurs m, Umrechnungskurs m, Wechselkurs m, Umtauschkurs m; **credit** *-* Habenzinssatz m; **cross** *-* Umtauschsatz m, Umtauschverhältnis n, Usance-Kurs m, Cross-Rate f; **deposit** *-* Habenzinssatz m; **foreign exchange** *-* Devisenkurs m, Umrechnungskurs m, Wechselkurs m, Umtauschkurs m; **telegraphic transfer** *-* Kabelauszahlung f (Kurs), telegraphische Auszahlung (Kurs)

rates n pl (GB) Kommunalsteuern f pl; *- and taxes* Gebühren und Abgaben; *change of -* Kursänderung f; **collecting** *-* Inkassotarif m; **continental** *-* (GB) Sorten- und Devisenkurse bei Banken des europäischen Kontinents; **currency** *-* (GB) in Pfund Sterling notierte Devisenkurse

ratification n Ratifizierung f, Genehmigung f, Bestätigung f

rating n Bewertung f, Einschätzung f, Taxierung f, Bemessung f, Schätzung f; **bond** *-* Schätzung des Nettowertes festverzinslicher Wertpapiere; **capital** *-* Kapitalbewertung f; **credit** *-* (US) Kreditwürdigkeitsprüfung f, Einschätzung der Kreditwürdigkeit

ratings n pl (US) Effektenbewertung f, TV-Einschaltquoten

ratio n Verhältnis n, Wertverhältnis n, Verhältniszahl f; *- analysis* Bilanzanalyse f; **capital** *-* Kapitalverhältnis n; **clearing** *-* Verrechnungsschlüssel m; **cover** *-* Deckungsverhältnis n; **market** *-* (US) Marktverhältnis n; **price-earnings** *- (PER)* Kurs-Gewinn-Verhältnis n, Verhältnis des Aktienkurses zum Reingewinn; **quick** *-* Verhältnis des Umlaufvermögens zu den laufenden Verbindlichkeiten

rationalization n Rationalisierung f

raw material Rohmaterial n, Rohstoff m

reaccount Rückrechnung f

reacquired capital stock Portefeuille eigener Aktien

reaction n Reaktion f, Rückgang m (Kurse), Rückschlag m (Börse), Rückwirkung f, Auswirkung f; *- of a stock* (US) Kursrückgang einer Aktie

readjustment of capital stock Kapitalberichtigung f

ready market aufnahmefähiger Markt; *- money* Bargeld n, bares Geld, flüssige Mittel; *buy for - money* gegen bar kaufen

real adj real adj, Real-, tatsächlich adj, echt adj, eigentlich adj, wirklich adj; *- assets* Immobilien plt, Grundbesitz m, Grund und Boden, Grundeigentum n, Grundstückseigentum n, Liegenschaften f pl; *- bill* (US) echter Wechsel; *- estate* Immobilien plt, Grundbesitz m, Grund und Boden, Grundeigentum n, Grundstückseigentum n,

real-time

Liegenschaften f pl; **- estate bonds** (US) Grundkreditpfandbriefe m pl, Grundstücksobligationen f pl; **- estate broker** (US) Grundstücksmakler m, Immobilienmakler m; **- estate business** Immobiliengeschäft n; **- estate dealer** Grundstücksmakler m, Immobilienmakler m; **- estate financing** Immobilienfinanzierung f; **- estate firm** Immobiliengesellschaft f; **- estate fund** Immobilienfonds m; **- estate investment** Immobilienanlage f, Grundbesitzanlage f; **- estate investment trust = REIT** (US) Immobilienfonds auf Aktien; **- estate loan** Hypothekarkredit m, Hypothekenkredit m, Grundstückskredit m; **- estate market** Immobilienmarkt m; **- estate mortgage** Hypothek f, hypothekarische Belastung, Hypothekenbrief m; **- estate mortgage note** Hypothekenpfandbrief m, Hypothekenbrief m; **- estate recording** (US) Grundbucheintragung f; **- estate register** (US) Grundbuch n, Kataster m; **- estate tax** Grundsteuer f; **- estate value** Grundstückswert m; **- interest** Realzins m; **- investment** Sachanlage f; **- property** Immobilien pl t, Grundbesitz m, Grund und Boden, Grundeigentum n, Grundstückseigentum n, Liegenschaften f pl; **- property tax** Grundsteuer f; **- security** Grundpfand n, dingliche Sicherheit; **- servitude** Grunddienstbarkeit f

real-time Echtzeit f

real value effektiver Wert, Sachwert m; **appreciation of - estate** Wertzuwachs eines Grundstücks; **credit on - estate** Realkredit m; **deed of - estate** Grundstücksvertrag m

realizable adj realisierbar adj, kapitalisierbar adj, verwertbar adj, verkäuflich adj, ausführbar adj; **- stock** börsengängige Wertpapiere, Börsenwerte m pl

realization n Realisierung f, Kapitalisierung f, Flüssigmachung f, Liquidierung f, Verkauf m, Versilberung f (bildlich); **- and liquidation account** Liquidationskonto n; **- (liquidation) of a security** Sicherheitsverwertung f

realize v realisieren v, flüssig machen, versilbern v, verkaufen v, veräußern v; **- shares** Aktien veräußern

re-allot v reparieren v

realtor n (US) Grundstücksmakler m, Immobilienmakler m

realty n Immobilien pl t, Grundbesitz m, Grund und Boden, Grundeigentum n, Grundstückseigentum n, Liegenschaften f pl; **- transfer tax** Grunderwerbsteuer f

reappraisal n Neubewertung f, Neuschätzung f

reappraise v neubewerten v

reasonable price annehmbarer Preis, vernünftiger Preis

reasonableness check Plausibilitätsprüfung f

reassess v neu bewerten (Kreditrisiken)

reassign v zurückübertragen v, wieder übertragen

re-assignment n Rückübertragung f, Wiederabtretung f

reassurance (re-assurance) n Rückversicherung f

reassure (re-assure) v rückversichern v, beruhigen v

rebatable steuerlich absetzbar

rebate n Rabatt m, Preisnachlaß m, Rückvergütung f

rebated acceptance (US) vor Fälligkeit bezahltes Akzept

rebound v sich erholen, wieder anziehen (Börse) v; **- in prices** Börsenumschwung m

recall for redemption Aufforderung zur Rückzahlung; **- from circulation** aus dem Verkehr ziehen

recapitalization n Rekapitalisierung f, Umwandlung von Krediten in Eigenkapital, Neufinanzierung f, Neukapitalisierung f; **- of business** Sanierung f

recapitalize v neufinanzieren v, nochmals kapitalisieren, sanieren v

receding quotations nachgebende Kurse f pl (Börse)

receipt v quittieren v, Quittung ausstellen; **- n** Empfangsbescheinigung f, Quittung f; **- for shipment bill of lading**

Empfangskonnossement n, Übernahmekonnossement n; **- in full** Gesamtquittung f, Gesamtabrechnung f; **acknowledge -** den Empfang bestätigen; **acknowledgement of -** Empfangsbestätigung f; **bank -** Bankquittung f; **banker's -** Depotschein m; **binding -** Deckungszusage f; **carriage -** Ladeschein m (Landtransport); **cash -** Kassenquittung f; **certificate of -** Übernahmeschein m, Verladeschein m; **custody -** Depotquittung f, Depotschein m; **customhouse -** Zollquittung f; **customs -** Zollschein m; **deposit -** Depotquittung f, Depotschein m; **make out a -** quittieren v, Quittung ausstellen; **statutory -** gesetzlich vorgeschriebene Quittung; **withdrawal -** Quittung über Kontoabhebung

receipted bill of exchange quittierter Wechsel

receipts n pl Einnahmen f pl; **bill of - and expenditures** Einnahmen-und-Ausgaben-Rechnung; **book of - and expenditures** Einnahmen-und-Ausgaben-Buch; **cash -** Bareinnahmen f pl

receivable; accounts - Außenstände m pl, ausstehende Forderungen, Debitoren m pl, Buchforderungen f pl; **bill -** einzulösender Wechsel; **bills -** Kundenwechsel m pl (Bilanz), Wechselforderungen f pl; **trade notes -** Kundenwechsel m pl (Bilanz), Wechselforderungen f pl

receivables n pl (US) Außenstände m pl, ausstehende Forderungen, Debitoren m pl, Buchforderungen f pl; **- discounting** Diskontierung von Buchforderungen; **contingent -** ungewisse Forderungen, bedingte Forderungen; **current -** Umlaufvermögen n, flüssige Aktiva, flüssige Mittel

receive v empfangen v, entgegennehmen v, einnehmen v

received for shipment bill of lading - Bordkonnossement n

receiver v Empfänger m, Konkursverwalter m, Zwangsverwalter m, Liquidator m, Vermögensverwalter m, Treuhänder m, Masseverwalter m; **bank -** Bankkassierer m

receivership n (US) Konkursverwaltung f, Zwangsverwaltung f, Konkursantrag stellen

receiving note Ladeschein m; **- teller** Kassierer für Einzahlungen, Scheckkontrolleur m (US)

reception pocket Ablagefach n

recession n Konjunkturrückgang m, Rückschlag m; **business -** Rezession f, Geschäftskonjunkturrückgang m; **material -** beträchtlicher Rückgang, wesentlicher Rückgang

recipient n Empfänger m (Bedachter)

reciprocal adj reziprok adj, gegenseitig adj, beiderseitig adj; **- contract** gegenseitiger Vertrag; **- credit** Gegenkredit m

reciprocate v sich revanchieren, mitziehen v, (sich) Gegendienste erweisen

reckless adj fahrlässig adj, leichtfertig adj

recklessness n Leichtfertigkeit f, Fahrlässigkeit f

reckoning n Rechnen n, Rechnung f, Zählung f

reclaimable tax rückerstattungsfähige Steuer

reclamation proceedings (US) Aussonderungsverfahren n

recognizance n Schuldschein m, Schuldanerkenntnis f, Sicherheitsleistung für eine Anerkennung

recognizor n Schuldscheinaussteller m

recoin v umprägen v, wiederprägen v

recoinage n Umprägung f

recommendation; customer - Kundenempfehlung f

recommendatory letter Einführungsschreiben n

reconcile v abstimmen v, in Übereinstimmung bringen

reconciliation n (of accounts) Abstimmung f (von Konten); **- of bank accounts** Kontenabstimmung f (Bank); **- of statement** (GB) Kontoauszug m (in dem sämtliche noch nicht verbuchten Posten berücksichtigt sind); **- statement** Richtigkeitsbestätigung f

Reconstruction Finance Corporation (US) Kreditanstalt für Wiederaufbau f

reconstruction n Wiederaufbau m; **~ accounts** Sanierungsbilanz f

reconveyance n Rückübertragung f, Rückübertragung f (von Grundbesitz)

record v registrieren v, eintragen v, protokollieren v, aufzeichnen v; ~ n Protokoll n (Gerichts-), Niederschrift f, Bericht m, Urkunde f, Dokument n, Zeugnis n, Register n, Eintrag m, Aufzeichnung f; **~ date** Stichtag m; **~ insertion** Neubelegung f (von Lücken auf Großspeicherdaten); **~ of stock holder** Aktionärsregister n; **cash ~** Kassenbeleg m; **cost ~** Kostenbeleg m, Spesenzettel m; **variable ~ length** variable Satzlänge (EDV)

Record Office (US) Grundbuchamt n

recording Eintragung f, Beurkundung f, Registrierung f; **~ fee** Eintragungsgebühr f

records n pl Archiv n; **bank ~** Bankbelege m pl; **bookkeeping ~** Buchungsunterlagen f pl; **business ~** Geschäftsbücher n pl

recount v nachzählen v, durchzählen v

recourse n Regreß m, Rückgriff m; **~ against third parties** Rückgriff gegen Dritte; **~ claim** Rückgriffsforderung f; **~ debtor** Rückgriffsschuldner m; **~ factoring** unechter Forderungsverkauf (Factoring); **~ for want of acceptance** Regreßmangel, Annahme f; **~ leasing** unechtes Leasing; **liable to ~** regreßpflichtig adj; **without ~** ohne Obligo

recover v wiedererlangen v, aussondern v (Konkurs), einziehen v, Regreß nehmen, zurückerhalten

recoverable adj eintreibbar adj, erstattungsfähig adj, aussonderungsfähig adj, einziehbar adj, eintreibbar adj, beitreibbar adj; **~ debt** beitreibbare Forderung

recovery n Aufschwung m, Wiederbelebung f, Einzug m, Eintreibung f, Geschäftsbelebung f, Erholung f, Festigung der Börse; **~ charges** Einziehungsspesen plt, Einziehungskosten plt; **~ claims on public authorities** Ausgleichsforderungen gegen die öffentliche Hand (Bilanzposten); **~ of debts** Einziehung von Forderungen; **business ~** Konjunkturbelebung f, Wirtschaftsbelebung f; **to be past ~** unwiederbringlich verloren sein

re-credited adj wiedergutgebracht adj, wiedergutgeschrieben adj

rectify v korrigieren v, berichtigen v, verbessern v, abändern v

rectifying entry Berichtigungsbuchung f

recycling n Recycling n, Rückschleusung von Geldern, Wiederverwertung f, Rückgewinnung von Rohstoffen f

red clause credit Akkreditivbevorschussung f; **~ chips** chinesische (ohne Staatserlaubnis) in Hongkong notierte Aktien; **~ numbers** Zinszahlen f pl; **to be in the ~** (US) Verluste haben

redeem v tilgen v, ablösen v, rückzahlen v, ausgleichen v, einlösen v, wiedergutmachen v; **~ a pledge** ein Pfand einlösen

redeemable adj einkassierbar adj, einlösbar adj, eintreibbar adj, einziehbar adj; **~ adj** tilgbar adj, amortisierbar adj, zurückzahlbar adj, ablösbar adj, auflösbar adj, kündbar adj; **~ bonds** kündbare Obligationen; **~ loan** Tilgungsdarlehen n; **~ mortgage** Tilgungshypothek f; **~ preference share** rückzahlbare Vorzugsaktie; **~ preferred stock** kündbare Vorzugsaktien; **~ stock** zurückzahlbare Werte

redeemableness n Amortisierbarkeit f, Tilgbarkeit f, Ablösbarkeit f

redeemed adj amortisiert adj, getilgt adj

redefinition n Neubelegung f (COBOL)

redemand v zurückfordern v, kündigen v (Kapital)

redemption n Amortisation f, Tilgung f, Rückzahlung f, Ablösung f, Rückkauf m (von Aktien); **~ agreement** Tilgungsabkommen n; **~ bond** Amortisationsanleihe f; **~ bonds** Ablösungsanleihe f; **~ capital** Ablösungsbetrag m; **~ check** (US) Verrechnungsscheck für Ausgleichsbeträge; **~ date** Tilgungszeitpunkt m; **~ discount** Rückkaufsdisagio n; **~ fund** Tilgungsfonds m; **~ loan** Tilgungsanleihe f; **~ mortgage** Amortisationshypothek f; **~ notice** Anleihekündigung f; **~ payment** Amortisationszahlung f, Tilgungsleistung f; **~ plan** Schuldentilgungsplan m; **~ price** Rücknahmepreis m; **~ rate** Tilgungskurs m; **~ reserve** Tilgungsrücklage f; **~ service** Tilgungsdienst m; **~ table** Tilgungsplan m; **~ value** Rückzahlungswert m, Rückkaufswert m; **amount of ~** Ablösungssumme f; **bond** ~ Obligationstilgung f; **call for ~** Kündigung f (einer Anleihe); **capital ~** Tilgung von Vorzugsaktien; **certificate of ~** Tilgungsbescheinigung f; **debt ~** Schuldentilgung f; **rate of ~** Rückzahlungskurs m, Einlösungskurs m

redeposit v wiedereinzahlen v

rediscount n (US) Diskont m, Rediskont m; ~ v rediskontieren v; **~ credit** (US) Diskontkredit m, Rediskontkredit m; **~ rate** (US) Diskontsatz m, Rediskontsatz m

rediscountable paper Rediskontpapiere f pl; **~ (eligible) bill of exchange at the Bundesbank** bundesbankfähiger Wechsel

redistribute v umverteilen v, neu verteilen

redistribution of wealth Vermögensumverteilung f

redraft; account of ~ Rückwechselkonto n

reduce v reduzieren v, ermäßigen v, verbilligen v, im Preis herabsetzen

reduced capital herabgesetztes Kapital

reduction n Abschreibung f, ~ n Herabsetzung f, Ermäßigung f, Verbilligung f, Abschlag m, Berichtigung f, Abnahme f, Abzug m, Preisermäßigung f, Steuererlaß m, Zollerlaß m; **~ in the discount rate** Diskontermäßigung f; **~ of capital stock** (US) Kapitalherabsetzung f, Kapitalzusammenlegung f; **~ of dividends** Dividendenkürzung f; **~ of share capital** (GB) Kapitalherabsetzung f, Kapitalzusammenlegung f; **cost ~** Kostensenkung f

redundancy n Arbeitslosigkeit f, Entlassung f

re-exchange n Rückrechnung f (Auslandswechsel)

re-export Wiederausfuhr f

referee n Schiedsrichter m, Schlichter m, Sachverständiger m; **~ in bankruptcy** Konkursrichter m; **~ in case of need** Notadressat

reference n Referenz f, Bezug m, Zeichen n; **~ number** Geschäftszeichen n; **bank ~** Bankauskunft f; **banker's ~** Bankauskunft f; **business ~** geschäftliche Empfehlung, geschäftliche Referenz

refinance v refinanzieren v

refinancing n Refinanzierung f; **~ swap** Refinanzierungs-Swap

refine v veredeln v

reflation Reflation f, Ankurbelung der Wirtschaft

reform budgetary Haushaltsreform f; **currency ~** Währungsreform f

refund v zurückzahlen v, zurückerstatten v, rückvergüten v; **~ n** Zurückzahlung f, Rückerstattung f, Rückvergütung f; **tax ~** Steuerrückerstattung f

refunding n Rückerstattung f, Rückzahlung f; **~ bonds** Ablösungsschuldverschreibungen f pl; **~ mortgage** Ablösungsschuldhypothek f

refundment n Rückerstattung f, Rückzahlung f

refusal n Ablehnung f, Absage f, Abweisung f, Weigerung f; **~ of acceptance** Nichtannahme f; **~ to pay** Zahlungsverweigerung f

refuse v ablehnen v, abschlagen v, verweigern v

refused Annahme verweigert; **~ acceptance** Annahmeverweigerung f

regional adj provinziell adj, regional adj, Provinz- (in Zus.); **~ bank** Regionalbank f, Landesbank f

register v registrieren v, eintragen v, protokollieren v, aufzeichnen v; **~ n** Register n, Verzeichnis n, Kontobuch n, Protokoll n, Grundbuch n; **~ a mortgage** eine Hypothek bestellen, eine Hypothek eintragen lassen; **~ of charges** Register für Grundstücksbelastungen; **~ of companies** (GB) Handelsregister n; **~ of mortgages** Hypothekenregister n; **~ of securities** Effektendepot n, Wertpapierdepot n; **~ of shares** Aktienbuch n; **~ office** Registratur f, Annahmestelle f, (GB) Standesamt n, Handelsregisteramt n; **acceptance ~** Obligobuch n; **bill ~** Wechseleingangsbuch n, Wechselregister n, Wechsellogierbuch n; **bond ~**

registered

Obligationenbuch n; **cash** ~ Registrierkasse f; **check** ~ Scheckliste f; **customers'** ~ Kundenliste f; **discount** ~ Wechselkopierbuch n, Wechsellogierbuch n, Wechselbuch n, Wechselobligo n (Buch), Wechselverfallbuch n; **draft** ~ Wechselverzeichnis n

registered adj eingetragen adj, registriert adj, auf den Namen lautend; **~ bonds** Namensschuldverschreibungen f pl; **~ capital** (GB) eingetragenes Kapital; **~ certificate** Namenspapier n; **~ charge** Grundschuld f; **~ check** (US) Bankscheck m; **~ company** eingetragene Handelsgesellschaft; **~ coupon bonds** Namenspapiere mit Zinsschein; **~ debenture** Namensobligation f; **~ lien charge** Pfandrecht an einer beweglichen Sache; **~ mail** Einschreibesendung f; **~ securities** Namenspapiere n pl, Rektapapiere n pl, nicht registrierte Wertpapiere; **~ share** (GB) Namensaktie f; **~ share with restricted transferability** vinkulierte Namensaktie; **~ stock** (US) Namensaktie f; **~ transferability** Vinkulierung f

registrable adj registrierungsfähig adj, eintragungsfähig adj

registrar n Registrator m, Registerführer m, Standesbeamter m; **~ of deeds** (US) Grundbuchbeamter m; **~ of mortgages** Grundbuchbeamter m

registration Anmeldung f, Eintragung f, amtliche Registrierung; **~ of a company** (GB) Handelsregistereintragung einer Gesellschaft; **~ of a title to property** Eintragung eines Eigentumsrechts in das Grundbuch; **~ of charges** Eintragung von Belastungen; **~ of deeds** Eintragung von Urkunden; **~ of mortgage** Hypothekeneintragung f; **~ of stock** Eintragung im Aktionärsregister; **decree of ~** Anerkenntnisurteil n

Registry of Deeds (US) Grundbuchamt n

regular checking account Kontokorrentkonto n (US); **~ collateral** (US) Sicherheit durch Hinterlegung guter Effekten; **~ customer** Stammkunde m; **~ lot** (US) Einheit, in der Abschlüsse an einer Börse getätigt werden; **~ income** festes Einkommen

regulation n Verordnung f, Verfügung f, Regelung f, Ausführungsbestimmung f, Durchführungsbestimmung f; **~ account** Ausgleichskonto n

regulations n pl Satzungen f pl; **currency ~** Devisenbestimmungen f pl

rehabilitate v rehabilitieren v, normalisieren v, wiedereinsetzen v

rehabilitation n Rehabilitierung f, Normalisierung f, Wiedereinsetzung f

rehypothecate v weiter verpfänden, bombardieren v, wiederverpfänden v

reimbursable adj rückzahlbar adj

reimburse v erstatten v, rückvergüten v, rückzahlen v, rückerstatten v

reimbursement n Erstattung f, Rückvergütung f, Rembours m; **~ credit** Sichtakkreditiv n; **~ recourse** Remboursrückgriff m

reimport v wiedereinführen v

reimportation n Wiedereinfuhr f, Rückeinfuhr f

reinstallment value insurance Neuwertversicherung f

reinstate v wiedereinsetzen v, ersetzen v, Ersatz leisten

reinstatement n Wiedereinsetzung f, Ersatzleistung f

reinsurance n Rückversicherung f

reinsure v rückversichern v

reinsurer n Rückversicherer m

reinvest v reinvestieren v, neu anlegen, wiederanlegen v

reinvestment n Wiederanlage f, Neuanlage f, Reinvestment n; **~ discount** Wiederanlagerabatt m

reissuable adj wieder begebbar, wieder ausgebbar; **~ notes** wieder ausgebbare Banknoten

reissue v wieder begeben, neu auflegen; ~ n Wiederausgabe f, Neuemission f; **~ of a bill of exchange** Wiederausgabe eines Wechsels

reissued adj neu aufgelegt

REIT = real estate investment trust (US) Immobilienfonds auf Aktien

reject v aussondern v (Qualitätskontrolle), zurückweisen v, ablehnen v

related company Konzerngesellschaft f
relation; *contractual* - Vertragsverhältnis n
relations; *business* - Geschäftsverbindung f, Geschäftsbeziehungen f pl
relationship banking Hausbankverbindung f
release v freistellen v, befreien v, entlasten v, entbinden v, verzichten v, aufgeben v; - n Freigabe f, Entlastung f, Erlaß m, Übertragung f, Quittung f; *- from debts* Schuldenerlaß m; *- funds* Guthaben freigeben; *- of a blocked account* Kontofreigabe f; *- of credits* Freiwerden von Krediten; *- of mortgage* Hypothekenlöschung f
re-lease v wiedervermieten v
reliability n Zuverlässigkeit f
reliable adj vertrauenswürdig adj, zuverlässig adj, kreditwürdig adj
relief n Hilfe f, Unterstützung f, Nachlaß m (Steuer), Ermäßigung f (Steuer); *- fund* Unterstützungsfonds m, Hilfsfonds m, Unterstützungskasse f; *tax -* Steuerermäßigung f
relinquish v aufgeben v, verlassen v, abtreten v, verzichten v
relocation of industry Industrieverlagerung f
remainder n Restbetrag m, Restbestand m, Saldo m; *- estate* Anwartschaftsgut n
remainderman n Nacherbe m
remaining adj unverkauft adj; *- amount* Restbetrag m, Restbestand m, Saldo m
remargin v (US) nachschießen v
remargining n (US) Nachschußzahlung f
reminder n Mahnung f, Mahnbrief m, Erinnerungsschreiben n; *- entry* Erinnerungsposten m
remission n Erlaß m (Schuld, Strafe); *- of taxes* Steuerzurückzahlung f
remit v remittieren v, überweisen v, senden v, abtreten v, Deckung anschaffen
remittance n Überweisung f, Rimesse f, Wertsendung f, Geldsendung f; *- account* Überweisungskonto n; *- fee* Überweisungsgebühr f; *- form* Überweisungsformular n; *- in cash* Barsendung f; *- order* Überweisungsauftrag m; *- slip* Überweisungsträger m; *bank post -* Postüberweisung im Auftrag der Bank; *cash -* Barüberweisung f; *specie -* Geldsendung f; *to make a -* in bar übersenden

remittances; *book of* - Überweisungsbuch n
remittee n Überweisungsempfänger m
remitter n Übersender m, Geldsender m
remitting bank überweisende Bank
remonetize v wieder in Kurs setzen
remote data processing Datenfernverarbeitung f; *- entry* Fernbuchung f; *- processing* Fernverarbeitung f
removal *contractor* (GB) Möbelspediteur m; *- from the stock exchange list* Streichung der amtlichen Notierung; *- of business* Geschäftsverlegung f
remove v entfernen v, ausziehen v, entlassen v, beiseite bringen
remunerate v vergüten v, bezahlen v
remunerated gegen Vergütung
remuneration n Vergütung f, Lohn m, Entgelt n, Belohnung f, Honorar n; *- of the supervisory board* Aufsichtsratsvergütung f
remunerative adj lukrativ adj, gewinnbringend adj, rentabel adj, einträglich adj
render *a profit* Gewinn abwerfen; *- an account* Rechnung vorlegen, Rechnung legen
rendering of account Rechnungslegung f
renegotiate v neu verhandeln, neu festlegen
renew v prolongieren v, verlängern v, erneuern v
renewable adj prolongationsfähig adj, verlängerungsfähig adj, erneuerungsfähig adj
renewal n Erneuerung f, Prolongation f; *- bill* Prolongationswechsel m; *- coupon* Talon m, Erneuerungsschein m, Allonge f; *- of credit* Kreditprolongation f
renounce v verzichten v, Verzicht leisten
renouncement n Verzicht m, Verzichtleistung f
renowned adj bekannt adj, namhaft adj

rent v mieten v, pachten v, vermieten v, verpachten v; ~ n Miete f (Wohnungsmiete), Pacht f (Zahlung); **~ account** Mietkonto n; **~ charge** Grunddienstbarkeit f, Erbzins m; **~ collection** Mieteinzug m; **~ collector** Mieteinzieher m; **~ income** Mieteinkommen n, Pachteinkommen n; **~ money** Mietgeld n, Pachtgeld n; **~ payer** Mieter m, Pächter m; **~ receipts** Mieteinnahmen f pl, Pachteinnahmen f pl; **~ return** Mietertrag m; **dead ~** (GB) Minimalpacht f, Bergregalabgabe f
rentable adj vermietbar adj, verpachtbar adj zu vermieten, zu verpachten
rental n Mietzins m, Pachtzins m; **~ value** Pachtwert m
rentals n pl Mietsätze m pl, Pachtsätze m pl
rented adj vermietet adj, verpachtet adj
renter n Mieter m, Pächter m
rentier n Rentner m
rentless adj zinslos adj, ertraglos adj
rents n pl Einkünfte plt; **accrued ~** Mietrückstände m pl; **collection of ~** Mietinkasso n
reopen business Geschäft wiedereröffnen, Geschäft wiederaufnehmen
reorder n Nachbestellung f
reorganization n (US) Gläubigervergleich m; **~ n** Reorganisation f, Umorganisation f; **~ n** Reorganisation f, Sanierung f; **~ n** Reorganisationsablauf m (bei Großspeicherdateien); **~ account** Sanierungskonto n; **~ bond** US Gewinnschuldverschreibung f (in Zusammenhang mit einer Reorganisation); **~ of the stock exchange** Börsenreform f
reorganize v umorganisieren, sanieren v
reparation n Entschädigung f, Ersatz m, Wiedergutmachung f
repartition n Verteilung f, Zuteilung f, Gewinnverteilung f
repatriate v repatriieren v, zurückführen v
repatriated bonds repatriierte Anleihen
repatriation n Repatriierung f; Rückführung f; **~ of capital** Kapitalrückführung f; **~ of prosit** Gewinnabführung f

repay v zurückzahlen v, rückvergüten v, rückerstatten v, abdecken v, tilgen v, ersetzen v
repayable adj rückzahlbar adj
repayment n Rückzahlung f, Tilgung f; **~ date** Rückzahlungstermin m (eines Kredits); **~ on due date** fristgemäße Rückzahlung; **~ plan** Tilgungsplan m; **~ rate** Tilgungsrate f
repeal v außerkraftsetzen v, aufheben v, für ungültig erklären
repeat option business Nachgeschäft n; **~ orders** (Börsen-) Folgeaufträge m pl
replace v ersetzen v
replacement n Anlageerneuerung f, Ersatz m; **~ costs** Wiederbeschaffungskosten plt; **~ investment** Ersatzinvestition f; **~ value** Wiederbeschaffungswert m
replenish v auffüllen v, aufstocken v
replenishment loan Auffüllkredit m
replevisor n Kläger der gegen unberechtigte Pfändung klagt
report v ausweisen, bilanzieren v; **~ n** Bericht m; **~ of balances** Saldenliste f; **agency** ~ (US) Kreditauskunfteibericht m; **annual** ~ Jahresbericht m, jährlicher Geschäftsbericht m; **audit** ~ Buchprüfungsbericht m, Revisionsbericht m; **bank** ~ Bankausweis m; **bullish** ~ Haussenachricht f; **business** ~ Geschäftsbericht m; **corporate** ~ Geschäftsbericht m, Gesellschaftsbericht m; **corporation** ~ Geschäftsbericht m, Gesellschaftsbericht m; **credit** ~ Kreditauskunft f; **credit bureau** ~ Kreditauskunft f
reported loss ausgewiesener Verlust; **~ profit** ausgewiesener Gewinn
reporting period Berichtszeitraum m, Bilanzierungszeitraum m, Bilanzjahr n; **~ requirement** Ausweispflicht f
representative money (US) Papiergeld n; **~ stocks** Standardwerte m pl
re-price v neu bewerten, Preis neu festsetzen v
repricing clause Preisänderungsklausel f
repurchase Rückkauf m, Rückerwerb m, Rücknahme f; **~ v** zurückkaufen v, zurückerwerben v; **~ agreement**

residual

Pensionsgeschäft n; **- price** Rücknahmepreis m
reputation n Ansehen n; **business -** geschäftliches Ansehen
request v beantragen v; - n Ersuchen n; - n Initiative f (z. B. vom Datenendplatz aus)
requirement n Anforderung f, Bedürfnis n; **credit -** (US) Kreditbedürfnis n
requirements; capital - Kapitalbedarf m; **financial -** Kapitalbedarf m
re-rating Neubewertung f, Neufestsetzung f
resale n Wiederverkauf m, Weiterverkauf m
reschedulding of loans Umschuldung von Krediten
reschedule v umschulden v
rescind v aufheben v, rückgängig machen
rescindable adj annullierbar adj, aufhebbar adj
rescission n Aufhebung f, Rückgängigmachung f; **- bonds** Schuldverschreibung zur Ablösung ungültig ausgegebener Garantien
rescue v sanieren, auffangen v, retten v; - n Rettung f, Hilfe f; **- operation** Rettungsaktion f, Sanierung f
research department Forschungsabteilung f; **advertising -** Werbeforschung f; **business -** Konjunkturforschung f
resell v wiederverkaufen v, weiterverkaufen v
reseller n Wiederverkäufer m
reselling n Wiederverkauf m
reservation n Reservierung f, Vorbehalt m; Einschränkung f
reserve v reservieren v, zurückstellen v, vorbehalten v; - n Reserve f, Rücklage f, Rückstellung f, Vorrat m; **- account** Reservekonto n, Rückstellungskonto n; **- bank credit** Darlehen der Landeszentralbank; **- currency** Reservewährung f; **- for amortization** Rückstellung für Anlageerneuerung; **- for bad debts** Rückstellung für zweifelhafte Forderungen, Rückstellung für dubiose Forderungen, Debitorenreserve f; **- for contingent liabilities** Rückstellung für zweifelhafte Schuldner; **- for debt**

redemption Rückstellung für Schuldentilgung; **- for depreciation** Abschreibungsreserve f, Abschreibungsfonds m, Abschreibungsrücklage f; **- for renewals and replacement** Erneuerungsrücklage f; **- funds** Reservefonds m pl; **- item** Rückstellungsposten m; **- liability** Nachschußpflicht f; **- requirements** Mindestreservevorschriften f pl; **- amortization** Rückstellung für Amortisationen; **bad debt -** Rückstellungen für uneinbringliche Forderungen; **bank -** Bankreserve f; **banking -** Bankreserve f; **bonus -** Prämienreserve f, Dividendenreserve f; **bullion -** Goldreserve f, Gold- und Silberbestand; **cash -** Kassenreserve f, Barreserve f; **claim -** Schadenreserve f, Prozeßrückstellung f; **contingency -** Sicherheitsrücklage f, Delkredererückstellung f, Rückstellung für unvorhergesehene Ausgaben; **contingent -** Sicherheitsrücklage f, Delkredererückstellung f, Rückstellung für unvorhergesehene Ausgaben; **legal -** gesetzlich vorgeschriebene Reserve; **minimum -** Mindestreserve f; **monetary -** Währungsreserve f; **second -** Reserve zweiten Ranges; **special -** Sonderrückstellung f; **surplus -** (US) zweckgebundene Rücklage, Gewinnrückstellung f; **under usual -** unter üblichem Vorbehalt
reserved interest zweifelhafte Zinszahlung; **- interest account** (GB) Konto für Zinsen
reserves n pl Rückstellungen f pl, Rücklagen f pl; **- for contingencies** Rückstellungen für noch nicht erkennbare Risiken; **accumulation of -** Reservebildung f; **hidden -** stille Reserven; **inner -** stille Reserven; **liquid -** flüssige Mittel, flüssige Reserven; **official -** offene Reserven; **statutory -** nach der Satzung vorgeschriebene Rückstellungen
reserving due payment Eingang vorbehalten
residence n Wohnsitz m, Geschäftsdomizil n
resident n Inländer m, Gebietsansässiger m, Deviseninländer m
residual claim Restforderung f; **- costs** Restbuchwert m; **- purchase price**

371

residuary

financing Kaufpreisrestfinanzierung f; **- value** Restbuchwert m
residuary estate Restnachlaß m, Nachlaß nach Zahlung aller Verbindlichkeiten; **- legacy** Restvermächtnis n, Vermächtnis nach Abzug der Nachlaßverbindlichkeiten; **- legatee** Nachvermächtnisnehmer m
residue n Restbetrag m, Rest m, Nachlaßrest m
resolution n Beschluß m, Resolution f, Entschließung f, Beschlußfassung f
resources n pl Hilfsmittel n pl, Geldmittel n pl, Vermögenswerte m pl; **bank -** Aktiva einer Bank; **cash -** Kassenmittel n pl; **credit -** Kreditquellen f pl; **liquid -** flüssige Mittel, flüssige Reserven
respite n Aufschub m, Bedenkzeit f, Zahlungsaufschub m; **- n** Stundung f; **- money** Prolongationsgebühr f; **- of payment** Zahlungsaufschub m, Moratorium n; **accord a - in payment** eine Zahlung stunden; **days of -** Respekttage m pl, Verzugstage m pl, Fristtage m pl
respondentia n Hypothekenkredit auf die Schiffsladung; **- bond** Bodmereibrief auf Schiff und Ladung
response n Rückmeldung f; **- time** Antwortzeit f
responsibility n Verantwortlichkeit f, Zuständigkeit f, Haftung f, Zahlungsfähigkeit f, Solidität f
responsible adj verantwortlich adj, kompetent adj, zuständig adj, haftpflichtig adj, zahlungsfähig adj, solid adj, solvent adj; **- age** geschäftsfähiges Alter; **- partner** persönlich haftender Gesellschafter
rest capital (GB) Reservefonds m, Reservekapital n
restart program Wiederanlaufprogramm n; **- routine** Wiederanlaufroutine f (EDV)
restitution n Restitution f, Wiedererstattung f, Rückgabe f, Wiedergutmachung f
restraint of competition Wettbewerbsbeschränkung f
restrict v beschränken v, einschränken v
restricted adj beschränkt adj, limitiert adj, begrenzt adj; **- cash** Termineinlage f

restriction n Begrenzung f; **- n** Beschränkung f, Einschränkung f; **- of credit** Kreditverknappung f; **- of exports** Ausfuhrbeschränkungen f pl; **- of investment** Investitionsbeschränkungen f pl; **- of trade** Handelsbeschränkung f, Konkurrenzbeschränkung f; **credit -** Krediteinschränkung f, Kreditrestriktion f
restrictions; currency - Devisenbeschränkungen f pl; **foreign exchange -** Devisenbeschränkungen f pl
restrictive endorsement beschränktes Giro, Rektaindossament n
result n Resultat n, Ergebnis n, Erfolg m; **- fee** Erfolgshonorar n; **operating -** Betriebsergebnis n
resume payments Zahlungen wiederaufnehmen
retail n Einzelhandel m; **- banking** Privatkundengeschäft n, Massengeschäft n; **- book credit** Kundenkredit m, Konsumentenkredit m; **- credit** (US) Kundenkredit m, Konsumentenkredit m; **- customer** Privatkunde m (Bank); **- firm** Einzelhandelsfirma f; **- instalment financing** Teilzahlungsfinanzierung f; **- price** Detailpreis m; **- price index** Einzelhandelspreisindex m; **- trade** Einzelhandel m
retailer n Einzelhändler m, Detaillist m
retailing n Einzelhandel m, Einzelverkauf m
retain v zurückbehalten v, einbehalten v
retained earnings zurückbehaltene Gewinne, nicht ausgeschüttete Gewinne; **- correspondence** adj banklagernd adj; **- income** zurückbehaltenes Einkommen, Gewinnrücklage f; **- profits** zurückbehaltene Gewinne, nicht ausgeschüttete Gewinne
retainer n Honorarvorschuß m
retaining fee Gebührenvorschuß m, Vorschuß m (Anwaltsgebühren); **- lien** Zurückbehaltungsrecht n
retarded protest verspäteter Protest
retention n Selbstbehalt m, Einbehaltung f, Zurückbehaltung f; **- money** einbehaltene Garantiesumme; **- of title** Eigentumsvorbehalt m

retire v in den Ruhestand treten, in Pension gehen, ausscheiden v, zurücktreten v, tilgen v, ausbuchen v, aus dem Verkehr ziehen, ausstreichen v; **- a bill** einen Wechsel einlösen, einen Wechsel honorieren; **- a debt** eine Schuld einlösen, eine Schuld bezahlen; **- a loan** Anleihestücke zurückkaufen; **- from business** Geschäft aufgeben

retirement n Ausbuchung f, Einziehung f, Abgang m, Rücktritt m (vom Amt), Austritt m, Pensionierung f, Ruhestand m; **- benefits** Pensionszuwendung f, Ruhegeld n; **- of a bill** vorzeitige Einlösung eines Wechsels; **- of credits** Tilgung von Krediten f; **- of stock** Kapitaleinziehung f; **- pension** Pensionszuwendung f, Ruhegeld n; **- plan** Pensionsplan m, Altersversorgungsplan m; **- rate** Rückzahlungskurs m

retractible bond Anleihe mit möglicher Laufzeitverkürzung

retraining n Umschulung f

retreat n Rückzug m, allgemeiner Kursrückgang

retrenchment n Kürzung f, Abbau m, Einschränkung f

retroactive adj rückwirkend adj

retrocede v wiederabtreten v, zurückübertragen v

retrograde adj rückläufig adj (Börse)

return v zurückzahlen v, zurückerstatten v, einbringen v, abwerfen v (Gewinn), umsetzen v, zurückkommen v, zurückkehren v, zurücksenden v; **-** n Ertrag m, Rendite f, Gewinn m, Rückzahlung f, Umsatz m, Rückgabe f, Antwort f, Bankausweis m; **- account** Rückrechnung f; **- debit voucher** Rückbelastungsaufgabe f; **- draft** Rückwechsel m; **- of a bill to drawer** Wechselrückgabe f; **- on capital employed** Kapitalrentabilität f; **- on sales** Gewinnspanne f; **- remittance** Rücküberweisung f; **- to fixed parities** Rückkehr zu festen Wechselkursen; **annual -** (GB) Jahresbericht m, jährlicher Geschäftsbericht; **monthly -** (GB) Monatsausweis m; **rate of -** Kapitalverzinsung f; **rent -** Mietertrag m; **tax -** Steuererklärung f

returned adj zurückgesandt adj; **- bill** Rückwechsel m; **- check** Rückscheck m

returner n Remittent m

returns n pl Gewinn m, Einkünfte plt, Rücksendungen f pl, Einkünfte aus Kapitalvermögen; **- account** Retourenkonto n; **- credit voucher** Retouren-Gutschrift f

revalorization of a currency Aufwertung einer Währung; **- rate** Aufwertungssatz m

revalorize v aufwerten, neu bewerten v

revaluation n Aufwertung f (einer Währung); **-** n (of property) Neubewertung f (von Vermögen)

revalue v aufwerten v

revalued currency aufgewertete Währung

revenue n Einkommen n, Ertrag m, Einkünfte f pl; **- account** Gewinn-und-Verlust-Konto; **- bonds** (US) Kommunalanleihen (deren Rückzahlung und Zinsen auf dem Einkommen bestimmter Projekte basieren); **- department** Steuerverwaltung f, Fiskus m; **- expenditure** (US) Kapitalaufwand (zwecks Ersatz von verbrauchten Werten); **- reserves** (GB) Kapitalreserve f, Reservekapital n; **- sources** Einnahmequellen f pl; **special -** Sondereinnahme f; **tax -** Steuereinkommen n

reversal n Umschwung m, Umkehr f, Rückschlag m, Umbuchung f, Stornierung f (Rückbuchung), Gegenbuchung f; **- entry** Stornoumsatz m; **- voucher** Stornobeleg m

reverse adj umgekehrt adj, entgegengesetzt adj; **-** v zurückbuchen v, stornieren v (Buchung), ungültig erklären; **-** n Rückseite f; **- bidding** Gegenübernahmeangebot n; **- dual currency bond** Doppelwährungsanleihe mit variablem Wechselkurs für die Rückzahlung; **- floater** (FRN) umgekehrt variabel verzinsliches Wertpapier; **- split** Aktienzusammenlegung f; **- stock check** Anweisung zur Zahlung auf dem ausländischen Markt gekaufter Aktien; **- yield curve** inverse Zinsstruktur

reverser n Hypothekenschuldner m

reversionary adj anwartschaftlich adj; **- interest** Anwartschaftsrecht n

reversioner n Anwartschaftsberechtigter m

review n Übersicht f (Bericht), Überprüfung f, Durchsicht f; **financial -** Finanzprüfung f
revision service Änderungsdienst m
revitalize v sanieren v
revocable credit widerruflicher Kredit; **- documentary credit** widerrufliches Dokumentenakkreditiv; **- letter of credit** widerrufliches Akkreditiv; **- stock order** widerrufbarer Börsenauftrag
revocation n Widerruf m, Annullierung f, Heimfall m, Zurücknahme f
revoke v widerrufen v, rückgängig machen, zurücknehmen v
revoking n Zurückziehung f
revolving adj revolvierend adj; **- account** revolvierendes Konto; **- assets** Umlaufvermögen n, flüssige Aktiva, flüssige Mittel; **- credit** revolvierender Kredit, sich automatisch erneuernder Kredit; **- documentary credit** revolvierendes Akkreditiv n; **- letter of credit** automatisch sich erneuerndes Akkreditiv; **- payments** wiederkehrende Zahlungen; **- underwriting facility (RUF)** kurzfristiger Schuldtitel auf revolvierender Basis
reward v belohnen v; **-** n Belohnung f, Vergütung f, Honorar n
riches n pl Vermögen n, Reichtum m
rider n Anhang m, Zusatzklausel f, Wechselallonge f
rig n Börsenmanöver n; **- the market** ein Börsenmanöver durchführen, eine Kurssteigerung an der Börse herbeiführen
rigged bid Scheinangebot n
rigging; market - Kurstreiberei f, Börsenmanöver n
right n Recht n, Berechtigung f, Anspruch m, Anrecht n, Aktienbezugsrecht n; **- of action** Klagerecht n, einklagbarer Anspruch m; **- of admission** Zulassungsanspruch m; **- of calling** Abnahmerecht n (beim Prämiengeschäft); **- of coinage** Münzhoheit f; **- of conversion** Wandlungsrecht n; **- of first refusal** Vorkaufsrecht n; **- of inheritance** Erbberechtigung f, Erbschaftsanspruch m; **- of lien** Pfandrecht n; **- of preemption** Option f, Vorkaufsrecht n; **- of**

recourse Rückgriffsrecht n; **- of recovery** Schadenersatzanspruch m; **- of renewal** Prolongationsrecht n; **- of retention** Zurückbehaltungsrecht n; **- of separation** Aussonderungsrecht n (Konkurs); **- of set-off** Aufrechnungsanspruch m; **- of succession** (GB) Erbfolgerecht n; **- of usufruct** Nießbrauch m, Nutznießung f; **- to issue bank notes** Banknotenprivileg n, Notenprivileg n; **- to notice** Kündigungsrecht n; **- to subscribe** Bezugsrecht n, Optionsrecht n; **- to succeed** Erbberechtigung f, Erbschaftsanspruch m; **assignment of a -** Rechtsübertragung f; **beneficial -** Nießbrauch m, Nutznießung f; **bonus -** Gratisrecht n; **contingent -** Anwartschaftsrecht n; **customary -** Gewohnheitsrecht n; **prescriptive -** Verjährungsrecht n, Gewohnheitsrecht n; **proprietary -** Eigentumsrecht n; **subscription -** Bezugsrecht n, Optionsrecht n; **voting -** Stimmrecht n

rightful claimant Forderungsberechtigte f u. m; **- owner** rechtmäßiger Eigentümer
rights: acquired - wohlerworbene Rechte; **chartered -** verbriefte Rechte; **contractual -** Vertragsrechte n pl; **ex -** ohne Bezugsrecht; **patent -** Patentrechte n pl; **vested -** wohlerworbene Rechte
rigid adj unelastisch adj; **- trust** Trust mit beschränkter Kapitalanlage
ring n Börsenring m (Schweizer Börse)
rise v steigen v, ansteigen v, sich erhöhen; **-** n Steigerung f (Börse), Steigen n, Anstieg m, Erhöhung f, Zunahme f; **buy for the -** auf Hausse spekulieren, im Hinblick auf eine Hausse kaufen
rising n Steigerung f (Börse), Steigen n; **-** adj kursanziehend adj, steigend adj; **- market** anziehende Kurse
risk v wagen v, riskieren v; **-** n Risiko n; **- arbitrage** Risikoarbitrage f; **- assurance** Risikoversicherung f; **- capital** Risikokapital n, Spekulationskapital n; **- free** risikolos; **- management** Risikomanagement n; **- premium** Risikoprämie f; **- rating** Risikobewertung f; **- return** risikoneutraler Ertrag; **- spread** Risiko-

verteilung f; **- taking** Risikoübernahme f; **- underwriting** Versicherung von Risiken; **-/yield (return) profile** Risiko-Rendite-Profil n; **amount of -** Risikobetrag m; **credit -** Kreditrisiko n; **distribution of -** Risikoverteilung f; **pooling of -** Risikoverteilung f

risky adj gewagt adj, riskant adj

rival bank Konkurrenzbank f

robbery insurance Raubüberfallversicherung f; **credit -** Kreditbetrug m

rock bottom Niedrigpreis m, Schleuderpreis m

rocket v haussieren, in die Höhe steigen v

rolling capital Betriebskapital n, Umlaufkapital n, Betriebsmittel n pl

roll-over credit Rollover-Kredit, Kredit mit Zinsbindung an den Interbanksatz

Romalpa clause Eigentumsvorbehaltsklausel des Lieferanten

room; board - Börsensaal m, Sitzungssaal des Direktoriums

rough balance Rohbilanz f; **- draft of contract** Vertragsentwurf m (erster, konzeptartiger); **- sort** Grobsortierung f (beim Beleglesen)

round-tripping Aufnahme und Verleihung von Fremdmittel, Kauf und unverzüglicher Verkauf von Wertpapieren; **- lot** Mindestbetrag m, (Obligation)

rounding-off buying Arrondierungskäufe m pl

route items (US) Wechsel m pl, Schecks m pl (die durch Boten eingezogen werden müssen)

routing symbol Bankleitzahl f

royalty n Royalty f, Tantieme f (Autoren-), Lizenzgebühr f, Regal n

rubber check (US) Scheck ohne (volle) Deckung; ungedeckter Scheck

rubbers n pl Gummiaktien f pl (Gummiverarbeitende Industrie)

RUF = revolving underwriting facilities Wertpapiere des Euromarktes mit kurzer Laufzeit (Euronotes)

ruin n Ruin m, Zusammenbruch m

rule n Vorschrift f, Usance f; **- book** Satzung f

rules of the stock exchange Börsenordnung f, Usancen der Börse; **bankruptcy -** Konkursbestimmungen f pl; **credit -** Kreditrichtlinien f pl

ruling price Marktpreis m

run v laufen v (z. B. von Wechseln), gelten v, sich belaufen auf, bedienen v; **-** n Ansturm von Kunden auf die Banken, Run m, Andrang m; **- a cheque** Ausstellen von Schecks durch Computer; **-** n Maschinendurchlauf m; **- into heavy selling** schlechten Absatz finden, sich schwer verkaufen lassen; **- into money** kostspielig sein; **- on stocks** große Nachfrage nach Aktien; **- to** betragen v, (sich) belaufen auf

runaway inflation galoppierende Inflation f

running adj laufend adj, regelmäßig adj, nacheinander adj; **-** n Führung f, Kontoführung f, Laufzeit f; **- account** Kontokorrentkonto n, laufendes Konto, Konto in laufender Rechnung, offenes Konto; **- broker** Wechselmakler m; **- interest** Stückzinsen f pl; **- yield** (GB) laufende Verzinsung, Umlaufrendite f

run-up in shares Aktienhausse f

rural credit landwirtschaftlicher Kredit

rush v übereilen v, (US) Kurse in die Höhe treiben; **-** n Eile f; **-** n äußerst lebhafte Nachfrage

S

safe n Safe m Tresor m, Geldschrank m; ~ **adj** sicher adj; ~ **box** Schrankfach n Bankfach n, Schließfach n; Stahlfach n; ~ **custodies** (GB) Depotgeschäft n; ~ **custody** (GB) Wertpapierdepot n; ~ **custody account** (GB) Depot n (bei Bank), Depotkonto n; ~ **custody department** (GB) Depotabteilung f; ~ **custody deposit** Effektenkonto n, Wertpapierdepot n; ~ **custody fee** Depotgebühr f; ~ **deposit box** Schrankfach n, Bankfach n, Schließfach n; ~ **deposit box insurance** Depotversicherung f; ~ **deposit department** Tresorabteilung f; ~ **deposit fee** Safemiete f, Schrankfachgebühr f, Schließfachgebühr f; ~ **investment** sichere Anlage

safeguard v sicherstellen v, schützen v, sichern v; ~ n Schutz m; ~ **interest** Interesse wahren

safeguarding of credits Kreditsicherstellung f; ~ **of the currency** Währungssicherung f

safekeeper n Verwahrer m

safekeeping n (US) sichere Verwahrung; ~ **account** Depotverwahrung f; ~ **account analysis** Depotanalyse f; ~ **address** Lagerstelle f (im Depotgeschäft); ~ **fee** Depotgebühr f

safety n Sicherheit f; ~ **measures** Sicherungsmaßnahmen f pl; ~ **precautions** Sicherungsvorkehrungen f pl

sag n Sinken n Abflauen n, Abschwächung f

sagging market abgeschwächter Markt

sal(e)able adj marktfähig adj, börsenfähig adj, absatzfähig adj; ~ **value** Verkaufswert m

salaried adj festes Gehalt beziehen, fest angestellt

salary n, Lohn m, Gehalt n, Bezüge m pl; ~ **account** Gehaltskonto n; ~ **payment by bank giro credit** bargeldlose Gehaltszahlung f; **advance of** ~ Gehaltsvorschuß m; **anticipate** ~ Vorschuß nehmen

sale n Verkauf m Absatz m; Vertrieb m; ~ **and leaseback** Verkauf und Rückmiete (Leasingverfahren); ~ **and repurchase agreement** Pensionsgeschäft n; ~ **by tender** Verkauf einer Anleihe im Ausschreibungsverfahren (Tenderverfahren); ~ **of an option** Stillhaltergeschäft n; ~ **on commission** Kommissionsverkauf m kommissionsweiser Verkauf; **bargain** ~ Ausverkauf m (Verkauf zu herabgesetzten Preisen); **bill of** ~ Kaufvertrag m, Kaufbrief m; **cash** ~ Barverkauf m; **charge** ~ Kreditverkauf m; **clearance** ~ Ausverkauf m (Räumungsverkauf); **clearing** ~ Ausverkauf m (Räumungsverkauf); **conditions of** ~ Verkaufsbedingungen f pl; **contract of** ~ Kaufvertrag m; Kaufbrief m; **credit** ~ Kreditverkauf m; **deed of** ~ Kaufvertrag m; Kaufbrief m

sales n pl (US) Umsatz m, Umschlag m; ~ **analysis** Verkaufsanalyse f; ~ **check** Rechnung f (US); ~ **company** Vertriebsgesellschaft f; ~ **financing** Absatzfinanzierung f; ~ **literature** Prospektmaterial n; ~ **note** Schlußnote f, Schlußschein m ~ **promotion** Absatzförderung f, Verkaufsförderung f; ~ **price** Verkaufspreis m; ~ **revenue** Umsatzerlöse f pl; ~ **tax** Umsatzsteuer f (US); **gross** ~ Bruttoumsatz m; **share** ~ Aktienverkäufe pl

salesman n (US) Verkäufer m (Beruf), Kaufmann m, Effektenhändler m

salvage n Bergung f; ~ **money** Bergelohn m

sample n Muster n, Probe f, Auswahl f; ~ **test** Stichprobe f

samurai bond Yen-Auslandsanleihe f

satellite loan office kleine Bankzweigstelle

satisfaction of mortgage Hypothekenlöschung

save v sparen v, ersparen v, Ersparnisse machen

save-as-you-earn staatliche Sparförderung (US)

saver n Sparer m

saving n Sparen n, Ersparnis f, Sparvorgang m; **cost ~** Kostenersparnis f

savings n pl Ersparnisse f pl, erspartes Geld, Spareinlagen f pl, Spargelder n pl; **~ account** Sparkonto n, Spareinlage f, Sparguthaben n; **~ activity** Sparverkehr m; **~ and loan association = S&L** (US) Bausparkasse f; Sparkasse f, Sparbank f; **~ association** (US) Sparverein m, Sparkasse f, Sparbank f; **~ bank** Sparkasse f, Sparbank f; **~ banking** Sparkassenwesen n; **~ bond** Sparbrief m; **~ bonds** Obligationen mit kleiner Stückelung; **~ book** Sparkassenbuch n, Sparbuch n; **~ capital** Sparkapital n; **~ certificate** (GB) Postsparschein m; **~ department** Sparabteilung f; **~ deposit** Spareinlage f; **~ depositor** Spareinleger m; **~ passbook** Sparkassenbuch n, Sparbuch n; **~ plan** Sparplan m, Sparvertrag m; **~ securities** mündelsichere Anlagepapiere n, mündelsichere Wertpapiere, mündelsichere Papiere; **accumulation of ~** Spareinlagenbildung f; **business ~** geschäftliche Einsparungen, betriebliche Einsparungen; **cooperative ~ organization** Kreditgenossenschaft f; **credit with a ~ bank** Sparkassenguthaben n; **industrial ~** Betriebssparen n, Werkssparen n

scale of commission (GB) Courtagetarif m

scaling down Zuteilung (Repartierung) von Wertpapieren

scalp v (US) schnell Gewinn mit kleinem Nutzen realisieren, auf schnellen Gewinn spekulieren

scalper n (US) spekulativer Händler, Spekulant m

scalping n (US) Mitnahme kleinster Spekulationsgewinne

scare n Panik f (an der Börse); **~ buying** Angstkäufe m pl; **~ up money** Geld auftreiben

scattered investments gestreute Anlagen; **~ rises** einzelne Kursgewinne

schedule n Aufstellung f, Anhang m, Werbeplan m, Inventar n, Reiseplan m; **~ of commission charges** Gebührenordnung f, Courtagetarif m; **~ of property** Vermögensaufstellung f

scheme n Plan m, Entwurf m, Aufstellung f, Projekt n; **pension ~** Betriebsrente f, betriebliche Altersversorgung

scheme of arrangement Vergleichsvorschlag m

schilling Schilling (Österreichische Währung)

school; business ~ Handelsschule f

scope n Bereich m, Umfang m (Reichweite); **~ of business** Geschäftsrahmen m, Geschäftsbereich m

score an advance einen Kursgewinn verzeichnen

scramble n (GB) heftige Nachfrage (nach Aktien)

scrap n Schrott m; **~ value** Restbuchwert m

scrip n Berechtigungsschein m, Interimsschein m; **~ bonus** Gratisaktie f; **~ certificate** (US) Anteilschein einer Aktie, (GB) Interimsschein m; **~ issue** Kapitalberichtigungsaktien f pl Gratisaktien f pl

scrutineer n Stimmenzähler m

SDR = special drawing rights Sonderziehungsrechte n pl

sea insurance Seeschadenstransportversicherung f, Seeversicherung f; **~ carriage by ~** Seetransport m

seal v versiegeln v, verschließen v, plombieren v; **~** n Siegel n, Plombe f

sealed adj versiegelt adj, verschlossen adj, plombiert adj; **~ deposit** verschlossenes Depot; **~ safekeeping account** geschlossenes Depot

search n Grundbucheinsicht f, das Grundbuch einsehen; **~ v** suchen v

seasonal loan Saisonkredit m, (US) Erntekredit m; **~ tendency** Saisontendenz f; **subject to ~ influences** saisonabhängig adj

seasoned securities n Favoriten m pl, gut renommierte Wertpapiere; **~ issue** Emission mit existierendem Sekundärmarkt

seat n (on the stock exchange) Börsensitz m

SEC = Securities and Exchange Commission Börsenaufsichtsbehörde in den USA

second distress Anschlußpfändung f; **~ buy** Kaufoption f (US)

Second Vice President (US) Chefprokurist m, stellvertretender Direktor

secondary adj sekundär adj, zweitrangig adj, untergeordnet adj; **~ deposit** Einlage (auf dem laufenden Konto durch Belastung auf dem Kreditsonderkonto); **~ credit** Gegenakkreditiv n; **~ liabilities** Eventualverbindlichkeiten f pl; **~ loan** nachrangige Anleihe; **~ market** Markt zweiter Ordnung, Sekundärmarkt m; **~ offering** Zweitplazierung; **~ stocks** Nebenwerte m pl

second-class papers zweitklassige Wertpapiere

second-hand adj gebraucht adj, aus zweiter Hand

second lien nachrangiges Pfandrecht; **~ mortgage** nachrangige Hypothek, zweitstellige Hypothek; **~ of exchange** Sekundärwechsel m, zweite Wechselausfertigung; **~ preferred stock** (US) Vorzugsaktien zweiter Klasse; **~ reserve** Reserve zweiten Ranges

secrecy; bank ~ Bankgeheimnis n

secret adj geheim adj, Geheim-; **~ reserves** stille Rücklagen; **business ~** Geschäftsgeheimnis n, Betriebsgeheimnis n

secretariat n Sekretariat n

secretary n Sekretär m, Verwaltungsdirektor m, Schriftführer m, Syndikus m

section n Gruppe f, Abteilung f, Abschnitt m, Bereich m

sector n Sektor m

secure v sicherstellen v, schützen v, sichern v; **~ interests** Beteiligungen erwerben; **~ profits** Gewinne erzielen

secured adj gesichert adj, sichergestellt adj, bevorrechtigt adj (Konkursrecht); **~ advance** gedecktes Darlehen; **~ bond** hypothekarisch gesicherte Obligation, hypothekarisch gesicherte Schuldverschreibung; **~ credit** gesicherter Kredit, abgesicherter Kredit; **~ creditor** gesicherter Gläubiger; **~ debt** bevorrechtigte Schuld, bevorrechtigte Forderung; **~ loan** gesicherter Kredit, abgesicherter Kredit

securities n pl Effekten pl/t, Wertpapiere n pl; **~ account** Wertpapierkonto n; **~ accounts department** Depotbuchhaltung f; **~ administration** Wertpapierverwaltung f; **~ analysis** Wertpapieranalyse f; **~ blotter** (US) Effektenstrazze f; **~ broker** Effektenmakler m; **~ clearing bank** Effektengirobank f, Kassenverein m; **~ collateral loan** Lombardkredit m, Lombarddarlehen n, abgesicherter Kredit; **~ custody** Depotverwahrung f; **~ dealer** Effektenhändler m, Börsenhändler m; **~ department** Effektenabteilung f; **~ description** Wertpapierbezeichnung f; **~ exchange** Börse f, Effektenbörse f, Wertpapierbörse f; **~ holdings** Effektenbestand m, Wertpapierbesitz m; **~ information system** Wertpapierinformationssystem n; **~ investment trust** Wertpapierfonds m; **~ issue** Wertpapieremission f; **~ listing by categories** Wertpapiergattungsaufnahme f; **~ market** Effektenbörse f, Effektenmarkt m, Wertpapiermarkt m; **~ number** Valorennummer f, Wertpapierkennummer f, Ordnungsnummer eines Wertpapiers; **~ on offer** Angebot n (Börse), Material n (Börse); **~ pool** Sicherheitspool m; **~ portfolio** Effektenportefeuille n, Wertpapierbestand m; **~ prices** Effektenkurse m pl; **~ repurchase (repo) agreement** Wertpapierpensionsgeschäft n; **~ safekeeping account** Wertpapierdepot n; **~ safekeeping account bookkeeping** Depotbuchhaltung f; **~ safekeeping account charges** Depotgebühren f pl; **~ tax** Wertpapiersteuer f; **~ trading department** Börsenabteilung f; **~ trading settlement** Effektenabrechnung f; **active ~** Wertpapiere n pl (die täglich an der Börse gehandelt werden); **admission of ~** Zulassung von Effekten zum Börsenhandel; **advance money on ~** Effekten beleihen; **advances against ~** Effektenbeleihung f, Effektenlombard m, Effektenlombardkredit m; **advances on ~** Effektenbeleihung f, Effektenlombard m, Effektenlombardkredit m; **armament ~** Rüstungswerte m pl; **as-**

sented ~ im Sammeldepot hinterlegte Wertpapiere; **balance of** ~ Wertpapierbilanz f; **bearer** ~ Inhaberpapiere n pl, Inhabereffekten plt; **business in** ~ Effektengeschäft n; **carry** ~ Wertpapiere besitzen; **collateral** ~ beliehene, lombardierte Wertpapiere; **convertible** ~ wandelbare Wertpapiere; **credit on** ~ Lombardkredit m, Lombarddarlehen n, abgesicherter Kredit; **fixed income** ~ festverzinsliche Wertpapiere; **fixed interest bearing** ~ festverzinsliche Wertpapiere; **foreign** ~ Auslandswertpapiere n pl, Auslandswerte m pl; **gilt-edged** ~ mündelsichere Anlagepapiere, mündelsichere Wertpapiere, mündelsichere Papiere; **government** ~ Staatspapiere n pl; **industrial** ~ Industriepapiere n pl, Industriewerte m pl; **international** ~ international gehandelte Effekten, international gehandelte Wertpapiere; **lend money on** ~ Effekten beleihen; **lodge** ~ Effekten hinterlegen; **marketable** ~ börsengängige Wertpapiere, Börsenwerte m pl; **mining** ~ Wertpapiere von Bergwerksunternehmen; **municipal** ~ Kommunalschuldverschreibungen f pl, Stadtanleihe f, Kommunalanleihe f, Kommunalobligationen f pl; **negotiable** ~ begebbare Wertpapiere; **obsolete** ~ (US) aufgerufene und für ungültig erklärte Obligationen; **outside** ~ nicht an der Börse notierte Wertpapiere; **paper** ~ Effekten plt, Papierwerte m pl; **pledged** ~ bombardierte Effekten; **registered** ~ Namenspapiere n pl; **savings** ~ mündelsichere Anlagepapiere, mündelsichere Wertpapiere, mündelsichere Papiere; **seasoned** ~ Favoriten m pl, gut renommierte Wertpapiere; **senior** ~ bevorrechtigte Wertpapiere; **stock exchange** ~ börsengängige Wertpapiere, Börsenwerte m pl; **transferable** ~ übertragbare Wertpapiere; **unassented** ~ (US) nicht abgestempelte Effekten; **war** ~ Rüstungswerte m pl

Securities and Exchange Commission = SEC Börsenaufsichtsbehörde in den USA

securitised loan verbriefter Kredit

securitization Securitisierung f, Verbriefungstendenz f, wertpapiermäßige Unterlegung von Kreditforderungen

securitize v als Wertpapier gestalten

security n Sicherheit f, Garantie f, Bürgschaft f, Kaution f, Pfand n, Wertpapier n; ~ **account** (US) Effektendepot n, Wertpapierdepot n; ~ **analysis** Wertpapieranalyse f; ~ **bond** Bürgschaftsschein m, Bürgschaftsurkunde f; ~ **clearing** Effektengiroverkehr m; ~ **code** Sicherungsschlüssel m (EDV); ~ **dealer** Effektenhändler m, Börsenhändler m; ~ **deposit** Sicherstellungsdepot n; ~ **identifikation number** Wertpapierkennnummer; ~ **market** Effektenbörse f, Effektenmarkt m, Wertpapiermarkt m; ~ **measures** Sicherungsmaßnahmen f pl; ~ **note** Effektenkauf- bzw. Verkaufsabrechnung f; ~ **numbering system** Valorenregister n; ~ **precautions** Sicherungsvorkehrungen f pl; ~ **prices** Effektenkurse m pl; ~ **trading** Wertpapierhandel m; **abandonment of** ~ Verzicht auf Sicherheit; **ample** ~ genügende Sicherheit; **bill of** ~ Garantie f, Sicherheitswechsel m; **collateral** ~ zusätzliche Sicherheit; **continuing** ~ Kreditbürgschaft f, Dauergarantie f; **dead** ~ wertlose Sicherheit; **personal** ~ persönliche Bürgschaft, persönliche Sicherheit, nicht durch dingliches Vermögen abgesicherte Bürgschaft; **provide ~ for** sicherstellen v, schützen v, sichern v; **real** ~ Grundpfand n, dingliche Sicherheit; **speculative** ~ Spekulationspapier n

seed money Startkapital n

seesaw market Schaukelbörse f

segment of the market Marktsegment n, Marktabschnitt m

segregate v absondern v, aussondern v, trennen v, getrennt verwahren

segregated account (US) Sonderkonto n

segregation n (US) Streifbanddepotverwahrung f

seignorage n Münzgebühr f, Münzgewinn m

seizable adj pfändbar adj, beschlagnahmefähig adj, einziehbar adj

seize v beschlagnahmen v, einziehen v, pfänden v, in Besitz nehmen, mit Beschlag belegen

seizin n Besitz m, Besitzergreifung f

seizure n Beschlagnahme f, Einziehung f, Pfändung f; **~ for security** Sicherheitspfändung f, Sicherheitsbeschlagnahme f

select v auswählen v

selection n Auswahl f; **~** n Selektion f

self-checking account number selbstprüfende Kontonummer

self-employed adj freiberuflich adj, selbständig adj

self-financing n Selbstfinanzierung f, Eigenfinanzierung f

self-insurer n Selbstversicherer m

self-liquidation credit Kredit (der aus dem Erlös des mit ihm finanzierten Geschäfts abgedeckt wird)

self-service bank Selbstbedienungsbank f

self-supporting adj finanziell unabhängig

self tender (US) Tenderofferte einer Gesellschaft zum Aufkauf der eigenen Aktien

sell v verkaufen v, absetzen v, abgeben v, veräußern v; **~ a bear** auf Baisse spekulieren, fixen v; **~ at a disadvantage** mit Verlust verkaufen; **~ at auction** versteigern v; **~ by auction** versteigern v; **~ forward** auf Termin verkaufen; **~ on credit** auf Kredit verkaufen; **~ short** leer verkaufen, fixen v; **~ out stocks** Wertpapiere abstoßen (Panikverkäufe); **buy and ~** handeln v (Handel treiben)

seller n Verkäufer m, Veräußerer m; **~ of an option** Stillhalter m; **bear ~** Baissespekulant m, Baissier m, Fixer m

seller's market Verkäufermarkt m; **~ option** Verkäuferoption f; **~ rate** Briefkurs m

sellers over (GB) mehr Angebot als Nachfrage

selling brokerage Verkaufsprovision f; **~ commission** Vertriebsprovision f; **~ for a fall** Verkauf auf Baisse m; **~ foreign currency** Devisenverkauf m; **~ group** Bankenkonsortium für den Verkauf von Obligationen; **~ order** Verkaufsauftrag m; **~ out** Zwangsverkauf m; **~ rate** Briefkurs m; **~ short**
Leerverkauf m; **heavy - pressure** massiver Abgabedruck (Börse)

semi account halbjährlicher Kontoauszug

semi-annual adj halbjährlich adj

semi-fixed fund Investmentfonds mit begrenzt auswechselbarem Portefeuille

semi-monopolistic adj monopolähnlich adj

send up hinauftreiben v, hochtreiben v

sender n Adressant m, Absender m

senior adj älter adj, vorrangig adj, übergeordnet adj; **~ bond** Vorzugsobligation f, Obligation mit Vorzugsrecht; **~ director** Seniorchef m; **~ mortgage** Vorranghypothek f; **~ partner** Hauptinhaber m; **~ securities** bevorrechtigte Wertpapiere; **~ shares** (GB) Stammaktien f pl; **~ stocks** (US) Vorzugsaktien f pl

Senior Vice President Direktor m

sensitive market leicht reagierende Börse, empfindlich reagierende Börse

sentimental value Liebhaberwert m

separate v aussondern v, trennen v; **~** adj gesondert adj, getrennt adj; **~ custody of securities** Einzelverwahrung f (E. von Wertpapieren); **~ estate** Vorbehaltsgut n, Sondervermögen n, eingebrachtes Gut

separation of estates Gütertrennung f

SEQA = Stock Exchange Automated Quotation System elektronische System der Börsennotierung und des Börsenhandels an der Londoner Börse

sequence; ascending ~ aufsteigende Reihenfolge; **descending ~** absteigende Reihenfolge

sequester v sequestrieren v, beschlagnahmen v

sequestered account beschlagnahmtes Konto, Konto unter Zwangsverwaltung

sequestrable adj beschlagnahmefähig adj

sequestrator n Zwangsverwalter m, Sequester m, Verwalter m

serial bond Serienanleihe f

serve v Dienst leisten, dienen v, bedienen v

service n Dienstleistung f, Kundendienst m, Service m, Zustellung f; **~ apportionments** Pensionszuschüsse m pl; **~ charge** Konto-Bearbeitungsgebühr f, Bearbeitungsgebühr f, Dienstleistungsgebühr f; **~ credit** Überziehungskredit m (US); **~ department** Kunden-

dienstabteilung f; **consular** - Konsulatsdienst m; **coupon** - Kuponeinlösung f; **- of securities** Verwaltung von Wertpapieren
servicing a loan Bedienung einer Anleihe
serving Zustellung f
servitude Grunddienstbarkeit f
session n Sitzung f, Versammlung f, Tagung f; **trading** - Börsenzeit f, Börsensitzung f
set v festlegen v, festsetzen v, bestimmen v; - n Satz m, Dokumentensatz m; **- apart** aussondern v; **- of exchange** ein Satzwechsel; **- of forms** Formularsatz m; **- off** Gegenforderung f (Aufrechnung), Ausgleich m, Aufrechnung f, in Gegenrechnung stellen; **full - of documents** n voller Satz Dokumente
setback n Rückschlag m
settle v regeln v, begleichen v, abmachen v, liquidieren v, aussetzen v (Rente), abfinden v, ein Geschäft gründen, bezahlen v (Rechnung); **- a claim** Anspruch befriedigen; **- an account** ein Konto ausgleichen
settled adj abgerechnet adj, abgeschlossen adj, ausgeglichen adj, erledigt adj, bezahlt adj (Rechnung); **- income** festes Einkommen; **- production** gleichmäßige Produktion
settlement n Begleichung f, Abmachung f, Erledigung f, Abrechnung f, Liquidation f, Vergleich m (außergerichtlich), Geschäftsgründung f, Abschluß m, Saldierung f, Skontierung f; **- account** Liquidationskonto n; **- (settling) date** Liquidationstag, Abwicklungsstag m; **- out of court** außergerichtliches Vergleichsverfahren; **- of a debt** Bezahlung einer Schuld; **- of property** Eigentumsübertragung f; **- risk** Abwicklungsrisiko, Erfüllungsrisiko n; **account of** - Abschlußrechnung f, Schlußabrechnung f; **bill in full** - Ausgleichswechsel m; **claim** - Schadenregulierung f; **deed of** - Abfindungsvertrag m; **fortnightly** - Halbmonatsabrechnung f; **marriage** - Ehevertrag m; **mid-year** - Halbjahresrechnung f, Halbjahresabschluß m

settling day Schlußabrechnungstag m, Liquidationstag m, Abrechnungstag m
settlor n Treugeber m, Testator m, Begründer m, Stifter m
set-up v eröffnen v, gründen v, einsetzen v
seven days' notice wöchentliche Kündigung
several estate Sondervermögen n
shading n geringfügiger Kursrückgang
shady adj fragwürdig adj, zweifelhaft adj
shake v erschüttern v
shakeout (shake out) n Glattstellung von Wertpapierenpositionen, Personalabbau m, Gesundschrumpfen n, Werte abstoßen
shaking out (US) Börsenmanöver n
sham dividend Scheindividende f, fiktive Dividende
share v teilen v, verteilen v, teilnehmen v; - n Aktie f, Teil m, Kapitalanteil m, Gewinnanteil m, Anteil m; - n (in a business) Geschäftsanteil m; **- account** Kapitalkonto n; **- block** Aktienpaket n; **- bonus** Gewinnprämie f; **- capital** Gesellschaftskapital n (einer AG), Aktienkapital n; **- certificate** Aktienzertifikat m, Aktienanteilschein m, Aktienschein m; **- (stock) certificate** Aktienmantel m; **- certificate (of an investment company)** Anteilschein m (eines Investmentfonds); **- consolidation** Aktenzusammenlegung f; **- deal** Unternehmensübernahme durch Kauf der Anteile; **- denomination** Aktienstückelung f; **- dividend** Aktiendividende f; **- index** Aktienindex m; **- issue** Aktienausgabe f; **- ledger** (GB) Aktienbuch n; **- list** Aktienkurszettel m, Aktienkursliste f; **- listed on the stock exchange** börsengängige Aktie; **- loan** Effektenbeleihung f, Effektenlombard m, Effektenlombardkredit m; **- market** Aktienmarkt m; **- movements** Kursbewegungen f pl; **- of a mining company** Aktie einer Bergwerksgesellschaft, Kux f; **- of no par value** nennwertlose Aktie, Aktie ohne Nennwert; **- of profits** Tantieme f; **- premium** Aktienagio, Emissionsagio n; **- price** Aktienkurs m, Aktienpreis m, Aktiennotierung f; **- (stock)**

381

portfolio Aktiendepot n; **~ pusher** betrügerischer Aktienverkäufer; ***~ quotation*** Aktienkurs m, Aktienpreis m, Aktiennotierung f; **~ rating** Bewertung einer Aktie f; **~ register** Aktienbuch n; **~ sales** Aktienverkäufe m pl; **~ split** Aktiensplit m, Aktienaufteilung f; **~ trading** Aktienhandel m; **~ (stock) underwriting group** Aktienübernahmekonsortium n; **~ warrant** Aktienzertifikat n, Aktienanteilschein m, Aktienschein m; **~ warrant to bearer** Inhaberaktienzertifikat n; **bank ~** Bankaktie f; **bearer ~** Inhaberaktie f; **bonus ~** (GB) Gratisaktie f, Kapitalberichtigungsaktie f; **capital ~** Kapitalanteil m; **common ~** Stammaktie f; **fully paid ~** voll eingezahlte Aktie; **non-free ~** unfreie Aktie; **no-par ~** nennwertlose Aktie, Aktie ohne Nennwert; **ordinary ~** Stammaktie f; **registered ~** (GB) Namensaktie f; **stock ~** Kapitalanteil m; **voting ~** stimmberechtigte Aktie

shareholder n Aktionär m, Aktieninhaber m, Anteilseigner m, Gesellschafter m; **~ value** Wertzuwachs für Aktionäre; **bank ~** Bankaktionär m; **major ~** Großaktionär m; **principal ~** Hauptaktionär m

shareholders; annual meeting of ~ (GB) ordentliche Hauptversammlung der Aktionäre

shareholders' equity Eigenkapital n (Bilanz); **~ ledger** Aktionärsbuch n, Aktionärsverzeichnis n; **~ meeting** Hauptversammlung f, Generalversammlung f, Aktionärsversammlung f; **~ register** (GB) Aktionärsverzeichnis n

shareholdings n pl Aktienbesitz m, Aktienbestand m; **~ n pl** Beteiligungen f pl

sharepushing n Börsenmanöver m

sharer n Mitinhaber m, Teilhaber m

shares in a cooperative society Genossenschaftsanteile m pl; **~ of no-par value** Quotenaktien f pl; **allocate ~ to all applicants** Aktien voll zuteilen; **allocation of ~** Aktienzuteilung f; **announce ~** Aktien auflegen; **assignation of ~** Aktenübertragung f, Aktienumschreibung f; **block of ~** Aktienpaket n; **consolidation of ~** Zusammenlegung des Aktienkapitals; **deferred ~** Nachbezugsaktien f (können erst nach Befriedigung der vorgehenden Aktien Dividende beanspruchen); **displaced ~** nicht notierte Aktien; **industrial ~** Industriepapiere n pl, Industriewerte m pl; **management ~** Vorstandsaktien f pl; **parcel of ~** Aktienpaket n; **preference ~** (GB) Vorzugsaktien f pl; **rate of ~** Aktienkurs m, Aktienpreis m, Aktiennotierung f; **senior ~** (GB) Stammaktien f pl; **shipping ~** Schiffahrtsaktien f pl, Schiffswerte m pl; **take up ~** Aktien zeichnen, Aktien beziehen; **transfer of ~** (GB) Aktienübertragung f, Aktienumschreibung f; **transmission of ~** Depotumbuchung f; **unallotted ~** nicht zugeteilte Aktien; **unissued ~** nicht ausgegebene Aktien; **unlisted ~** an der Börse nicht eingeführte Aktien

sharing n Beteiligung f; **profit ~** Gewinnbeteiligung f

shark repellants Übernahmeabwehr durch gesellschaftsvertragliche Regelungen f

sharp drop Baisse f; **~ price advance** n plötzliche Kurssteigerung; **~ rise** Hausse f

sheared n (US) geprellter Börsenspekulant

sheet n Kursblatt n, Bogen m; **contract ~** Abrechnung des Börsenmaklers; **coupon ~** Kuponbogen m, Zinsscheinbogen m

shell company Firmenmantel m

sheriff's sale Zwangsversteigerung f

shifting of capital Kapitalumschichtung f

ship broker Schiffsmakler m, Frachtenmakler m; **~ mortgage** Schiffshypothek f; **cargo ~** Frachtschiff n

shipment Verschiffung f, Verladung f, Fracht f; **certificate of ~** Ladeschein m, Verschiffungsbescheinigung f, Versandschein m

shipowner n Reeder m, Schiffseigentümer m

shipper n Verschiffer m, Ablader m, Versender m, Verfrachter m, Spediteur m; **country ~** Inlandsspediteur m

shipper's draft Tratte des Verladers; **~ papers** Verladepapiere n pl

shipping n Verladung f, Versendung f, Spedition f, Verschiffung f; **~ code** Versandartschlüssel m; **~ documents**

Verladedokumente n pl, Verschiffungspapiere n pl; ~ **exchange** Frachtenbörse f; ~ **issues** Schiffahrtsaktien f pl, Schiffswerte m pl; ~ **papers** Verladepapiere f pl; ~ **shares** Schiffahrtsaktien f pl, Schiffswerte m pl; **stale** ~ **documents** nicht rechtzeitig eingereichte Verschiffungspapiere

ship's protest Havarieerklärung f; ~ **register** Schiffsregister n

shipyard n Werft f

shogun bond japanische Auslandsanleihe (nicht in Yen)

shop buying Wertpapierkäufe des Berufshandels; ~ **in shop** (US) Bankgeschäfte im Warenhaus (u.ä. Einrichtungen); ~ **selling** Wertpapierverkäufe des Berufshandels

shopkeeper n Ladenbesitzer m

short adj kurz adj, knapp adj, beschränkt verfügbar sein, Aktien leerverkaufen; ~ n (Leer-) Verkäufer m, Kurzläufer m, Baisse-Spekulant m, Baissier m, Fixer m; ~ **amount** Minderbetrag m; ~ **bill** Inkassowechsel m; ~ **bond (maturity)** Kurzläufer m; ~ **call** verkaufte Kaufoption; ~ **certificate** Sparbrief mit kurzer Laufzeit; ~ **credit** (loan) kurzfristiger Kredit, Überbrückungskredit m; ~ **dated** kurzfristig adj; ~ **futures position** Futuresverkaufsposition f; ~ **hedge** Verkaufshedge n, Terminverkauf m; ~ **in cash** Kassendefizit n, Kassenfehlbetrag m; ~ **market** Baisse-Markt; ~ **position** Baissier-Engagement m, Leerverkaufsposition f; ~ **sale** Leerverkauf m, Verkauf ohne Deckung; ~ **selling** Leerverkäufe auf Baisse; ~ **side** Baisse-Partei f; ~ **stock sale** Leerverkauf von Aktien

short-sighted loan kurzfristiger Kredit, kurzfristiges Darlehen, kurzfristige Anleihe

shortage of cash Kassendefizit n, Kassenfehlbetrag m; **capital** ~ Kapitalknappheit f

shortened adj abgekürzt adj, gekürzt adj, gerafft adj

shorts Papiere mit kurzen Laufzeiten n pl (bis zu 5 Jahren)

short-term adj kurzfristig adj

short-term bill kurzfristiger Wechsel, Wechsel auf kurzfristige Sicht

short-term credit kurzfristiger Kredit, kurzfristiges Darlehen, kurzfristige Anleihe

short-term deposits Einlagen mit kurzer Kündigungsfrist

short-term financing Zwischenfinanzierung f, kurzfristige Finanzierung

short-term liabilities kurzfristige Verbindlichkeiten f pl

short-term loan kurzfristiger Kredit, kurzfristiges Darlehen, kurzfristige Anleihe

short-term notes kurzfristige Wechsel

show a balance of einen Saldo von Aufweisen; ~ **a profit** einen Gewinn aufweisen, einen Nutzen abwerfen

shrinkage in value Wertminderung f

shut for dividend Dividendenschluß m

SIBOR = Singapore Interbank Offered Rate Singapurer Interbanken-Angebotszinssatz

sick market (US) uneinheitlicher Markt, lustloser Markt

side n Partei f, Seite f; **credit** ~ Habenseite f; **debit** ~ Debitseite f

sideline market Nebenmarkt m (Börse)

sight a bill einen Wechsel zum Akzept vorlegen, einen Wechsel mit Sichtvermerk versehen; ~ **bill** Sichtwechsel m; ~ **deposit** Sichteinlage f; ~ **documentary credit** Sichtakkreditiv n; ~ **draft** Sichttratte f; ~ **exchange** Sichtwechselkurs m; ~ **items** Sichtpapiere n pl; ~ **letter of credit** Sichtakkreditiv n; ~ **rate** Sichtkurs m; **at** ~ bei Sicht; **bill at** ~ Sichtwechsel m; **bill of** ~ Zollerlaubnisschein m; **draft at** ~ Sichttratte f

sign v zeichnen v (Unterschrift leisten), unterzeichnen v, unterschreiben v; **authority to** ~ Zeichnungsberechtigung f, Unterschriftsvollmacht f

signatory power Unterschriftsvollmacht f (bei Staatsverträgen)

signature n Unterschrift f, Unterzeichnung f, Namenszug m; ~ **book** Unterschriftenverzeichnis n; ~ **card** Unterschriftskarte f; ~ **verification** Unterschriftsprüfung f; **authorized** ~ berechtigte Unterschrift; **blank** ~ Blankounterschrift f; **certification of** ~ Unter-

schriftsbeglaubigung f; **confirmation of ~** Unterschriftsbeglaubigung f
signing n Unterzeichnung f (Vorgang)
silent partner (US) Geldgeber m (in einer GmbH oder Kommanditgesellschaft), stiller Teilhaber, Kommandist m
silver bar Silberbarren m; **~ coin** Silbermünze f; **~ standard** Silberwährung f
simple debenture ungesicherte Schuldverschreibung; **~ debt** nicht bevorrechtigte Konkursforderung; **~ guarantee** einfache Bürgschaft; **~ interest** Kapitalzinsen m pl
simulate v vortäuschen v, simulieren v, fingieren v
Singapore Interbank Offered Rate = SIBOR Singapurer Interbanken-Angebotszinssatz
single adj einzeln adj; **~ bill** Solawechsel m, Eigenwechsel m; **~ option** einfache Option; **~ premium** Einmalprämie f (Lebensversicherung)
single-copy form Einzelformular n
single-currency interest rate swap währungsgleicher Zinsswap m
single-digit sort Vereinzelungslauf m (beim Beleglesen)
single-name paper Schuldschein m
sink v tilgen v, amortisieren v, fallen v, heruntergehen v
sinking n Tilgung f, Amortisation f; **~ fund** Amortisationsfonds m, Ablösungsfonds m; Tilgungsrücklage f; **~ loan** Tilgungsanleihe f; **~ round table** Tilgungsplan m; **~ spell** kurzfristiger Kursrückgang m; **bond ~ fund** Amortisationsfonds für Obligationen
sinking-fund bond Tilgungsanleihe f
sister company Schwestergesellschaft f
sit v eine Sitzung abhalten, tagen v
site n Grundstück n, Bauplatz m, Lage eines Grundstücks
situation credit kreditpolitische Situation
six-month's Libor Sechsmonats-Libor m
sixes n pl sechsprozentige Papiere
size n Umfang m
skilled personnel erfahrenes Personal, ausgebildetes Personal
skyrocketing n (US) raketenartiges Steigen der Kurse

slack adj flau adj, matt adj, lustlos adj, geschäftslos adj, still adj; **~ demand** spärliche Nachfrage
slacken v nachlassen v
slaughter v mit Verlust verkaufen, verschleudern v, unter Preis verkaufen; **~** n (US) Verschleuderung f
sleeping partner (GB) Geldgeber m (in einer GmbH oder Kommanditgesellschaft), stiller Teilhaber, Kommandist m
slice in the market Marktanteil m
slide sharply v stark nachgeben (Börse); **~ in equities** Rückgang der Aktienkurse
slight improvement of share prices leichtes Anziehen der Effektenkurse; **~ rally** leichte Kurserhöhung
slip n Beleg m, Schein m; **deposit ~** Depotquittung f, Depotschein m
slowdown Abschwung m, Verlansgsammung f, Verringerung f
slump n plötzlicher Kurssturz, Verlangsamung f, Verringerung f, Baisse f
small and medium-sized enterprises (SME) kleine und mittlere Unternehmen (KMU), mittelständische Unternehmen; **~ bonds** Obligationen mit kleiner Stückelung; **~ business loan** gewerblicher Kleinkredit; **~ caps** kleine und mittlere Unternehmen; **~ change** Kleingeld n; **~ company** Kleinunternehmen n; **~ loan** Kleinkredit m, Teilzahlungskredit m; **~ trade** Handwerk m
small-saver certificate Sparbrief m
smart card elektronische Kreditkarte, integrierte Zahlkarte f
Snake of the European Currency Europäische Währungsschlange f
sneak attack (US) heimlicher Aufkauf eines größeren Aktienpakets
soaring prices haussierende Kurse
social disbursements Sozialaufwendungen f pl; **~ insurance** Sozialversicherung f; **~ insurance benefits** Sozialversicherungsleistung f pl; **~ report** Sozialbilanz f; **~ security** Sozialversicherung f; **~ security expenses** soziale Abgaben

socialization *n* Sozialisierung *f*, Überführung in Gemeineigentum

socialize *v* sozialisieren *v*, vergesellschaften *v*

society *n* Gesellschaft *f*, Verein *m*; *- benefit* Versicherungsverein auf Gegenseitigkeit, Unterstützungsverein *m*; *building -* (GB) Bausparkasse *f*; *cashless -* bargeldlose Gesellschaft; *credit -* Kreditgesellschaft *f*

soft *adj* weich *adj*, nachgiebig *adj* (Börse); *- currency* weiche Währung

softening Kursrückgang *m*, Kursabschwächung *f*

softer schwacher *adj* (Kurse)

sola *bill* Solawechsel *m*, Eigenwechsel *m*; *- of exchange* Solawechsel *m*, Eigenwechsel *m*

sole *adj* alleinig *adj*, ausschließlich *adj*; *- bill of exchange* Solawechsel *m*, Eigenwechsel *m*; *- proprietorship* (US) Einzelfirma *f*

solicitor *n* (GB) Jurist *m*, Rechtsanwalt *m*, Anwalt *m*; *- n* Rechtsvertreter *m*, Rechtsbeistand *m*

solvency *n* Solvenz *f*, Zahlungsfähigkeit *f*, Liquidität *f*, Flüssigkeit *f*; *- factor* Solvenzkoeffizient *m* *credit -* Bonität *f*; *declaration of -* Liquidationsmeldung bei Gesellschaftsauflösung

solvent *adj* solvent *adj*, zahlungsfähig *adj*, liquide *adj*, kreditwürdig *adj*, kreditfähig *adj*; *- debtor* zahlungsfähiger Schuldner

sort *v* sortieren *v*; *- n* Sortierlauf *m*; *- bills away in the bill case* Wechsel in das Wechselportefeuille einsortieren; *- criterion* Sortierkriterium *n*; *- generator* Sortiergenerator *m*; *- key* Sortierkriterium *n*; *- method* Sortierverfahren *n*; *- out* aussondern *v*; *- pattern* Sortiermodell *n* (beim Beleglesen); *- philosophy* Sortiergesichtspunkt *m*; *- run* Sortierlauf *m*; *final - pass* Ausgangssortierung *f* (beim Beleglesen)

sorting *code* Bankleitzahl *f*; *- method* Sortierverfahren *n*

sound *adj* solide *adj*, gesund *adj*, kreditwürdig *adj*, kreditfähig *adj*; *- value* Verkehrswert *m* (Versicherung)

soundness *n* Bonität *f*

source of error Fehlerquelle *f*; *- program* Primärprogramm *n*

sovereign debt (GB) Schuldtitel staatlicher Kreditnehmer

Sovereign British gold coin Sovereign *m* (englische Goldmünze; 20-Schilling-Goldstück)

sovereignty; monetary - Währungshoheit *f*

S & P = Standard and Poors US-Unternehmen für Bonitätsbewertungen von Wertpapieren und Kreditverpflichtungen

spaced payment Ratenzahlung *f*

spare *adj* übrig *adj*, überschüssig *adj*; *- v* erübrigen *v*; *- capital* flüssiges Kapital, flüssige Mittel; *- cash* übriges Geld; *- money* Notgroschen *m*, verfügbares Geld

special *adj* speziell *adj*, besonders *adj*, Sonder-, außerordentlich *adj*; *- account* Sonderkonto *n*, Separatkonto *n*; *- allowance* Sonderwertberichtigung *f*; *- capital* Kommanditkapital *n*; *- crossing* (of a check) besondere Kreuzung (eines Schecks); *- delivery* Eilsendung *f*, Expreßbrief *m*; *- deposit* (US) Sonderdepot *n*, Werte außer Bargeld bei einer Bank zur Aufbewahrung; *- dividend* Bonus *m*, Extradividende, Sonderdividende *f*, Superdividende *f*, außerordentliche Dividende *f*; *- drawing rights* (SDR's) Sonderziehungsrechte *n pl* (IMF); *- endorsement* Vollgiro *n*, volles Wechselgiro, ausgefülltes Giro; *- field* Sachgebiet *n*; *- fund* Spezialfonds *m*; *- indorsement* Vollgiro *n*, volles Wechselgiro, ausgefülltes Giro; *- interest account* (US) Sparkonto *n*, Spareinlage *f*, Sparguthaben *n*; *- interest department* (US) Sparkassenabteilung *f*; *- items with partial reserve character* Sonderposten mit Rücklageanteil (Bilanzposten); *- lien* Zurückbehaltungsrecht *n* (an einem bestimmten Gegenstand); *- partner* Kommanditist *m*, beschränkt haftender Gesellschafter, beschränkt haftender Teilhaber; *- quota* Sonderkontingent *n*; *- reserve* Sonderrückstellung *f*; *- revenue*

specialized bank

Sondereinnahme f; **- stocks** (US) Spezialwerte m pl, Sonderwerte m pl; **- trust** (US) Pflegschaft mit besonderen Pflichten
specialized bank Spezialbank f
specie n Metallgeld n, Münzsorte f; **- account** Sortenkonto n; **- payment** Zahlung in Hartgeld f; **- point** Goldpunkt m; **- remittance** Geldsendung f
specific deposit Sonderdepot n; **- guaranty** (US) Garantievertrag m; **- lien** Zurückbehaltungsrecht n (an einem bestimmten Gegenstand)
specify v einzeln aufführen, spezifizieren v, nach Posten gliedern
specimen signature Unterschriftsprobe f
speculate v spekulieren v (an der Börse), gewagte Geschäfte machen; **- for a rise** auf Hausse spekulieren, im Hinblick auf eine Hausse kaufen; **- on a fall** auf Baisse spekulieren, fixen v
speculation n Spekulation f, gewagtes Geschäft; **- in futures** Terminspekulation f; **- in stocks** Aktienspekulation f; **bear -** Baissespekulation f; **bull -** Haussespekulation f
speculative adj spekulativ adj; **- gain** Spekulationsgewinn m; **- purchases** Meinungskäufe m pl; **- security** Spekulationspapier n; **- stock** Spekulationsaktie f; **- transaction** Spekulationsgeschäft n; **- venture** riskantes Unternehmen
speculator n Spekulant m; **- for a rise** Haussespekulant m, Haussier m
spend v ausgeben v, aufwenden v, verausgaben v, verbrauchen v
spending; deficit - Ankurbelung der Volkswirtschaft durch staatliche Ausgaben
spendthrift trust Unterhaltsfonds m
spent bill of lading erloschener Frachtbrief
sphere n Bereich m (Wirkungskreis), Sphäre f; **- of business** Geschäftsrahmen m, Geschäftsbereich m
spillover selling Ausschlußkäufe f pl (Börse)
spinoff v eine Tochtergesellschaft ausgliedern
spin-off Konzernentflechtung f
split splitten, aufteilen, aufspalten v; **- n** Split m, Aktienteilung f, Einkommensteilung f; **- of shares** Aktiensplit m,

Aktienaufteilung f; **- order** (US) Börsenauftrag m (der in zwei oder mehreren Abschnitten zu verschiedenen Kursen ausgeführt wird); **- quotation** Kursnotierung in Bruchteilen; **- rate of exchange** gespaltener Wechselkurs; **- stocks** gesplittene Aktien
splitting n Spaltung f, Teilung f; **- n** Split m, Aktienteilung f, Einkommensteilung f
split-up Aktiensplit m
sponsor n Sponsor m, Schirmherr m, Förderer m, Bürge m (für Einwanderer)
sponsoring (sponsorship) Sponsoring n, finanzielle Förderung
spot adj sofort lieferbar adj, sofort zahlbar adj; **- n** Sofortpreis m, Werbespot m; **- cash** sofort lieferbar, sofort zahlbar; **- deal** Kassageschäft n; **- delivery** Kassalieferung f; **- exchange** Kassadevisen f pl; **- exchange market** Devisenkassamarkt m; **- market** Kassamarkt m; **- payment** sofortige Zahlung f; **- price** Kassakurs m (Effektenbörse); **- purchase of currencies** Devisenverkauf m; **- rate** Lokopreis m (Warenbörse), Kassakurs m (Devisenmarkt); **- transaction** Kassageschäft n
spread n Konsortialprovision f, Marge f, Differenz f (zwischen Preisen, Kursen), Stellagegeschäft n, Spanne f; **- of interest rates** Zinsspanne f
spreading operations (GB) Geschäfte in verschiedenen Effekten
spurious adj falsch adj, unecht adj
spurt n plötzliche Kurssteigerung, Kurssprung m
squander v verschleudern v
square v glattstellen v
squaring; book - Glattstellen von Positionen
squeeze n Zwang zu Deckungskäufen, Liquiditätsmangel m; **credit -** Kreditknappheit f
stability n Stabilität f, Beständigkeit f
stabilization (stabilisation) n Stabilisierung f, Festigung f; **- fund** Währungsausgleichsfonds m; **- loan** Aufwertungsanleihe f; **currency -** Währungsstabilisierung f

stabilize (stabilise) v stabilisieren v, festigen v
stabilizing factors of the market Kursstützungsfaktoren m pl
stable currency stabile Währung
stacker n Ablagefach n
staff n Belegschaft f, Personal n; **- expenses** Personalaufwand m; **- guarantee fund** (GB) Bankgarantiefonds m; **- member** Mitarbeiter m; **- pension fund** Angestelltenpensionskasse f; **- register** (GB) Personalkonto n; **permanent -** Stammpersonal n
stag n (GB) Konzertzeichner m; **- the market** den Markt durch Konzertzeichnungen beeinflussen
stagflation Stagflation f, Inflation bei stagnierender Wirtschaftslage
stagger v staffeln v
staggered prices gestaffelte Preise
stagging Konzertzeichnung f, Majorisierung f
stagnancy n Stagnation f, Stockung f, Flaute f, Lustlosigkeit f
stagnant adj stagnierend adj, stockend adj, flau adj, lustlos adj
stagnate v stagnieren v, stocken v, flau sein, lustlos sein, darniederliegen v
stagnation n Stagnation f, Stockung f, Flaute f, Lustlosigkeit f
stale adj flau adj, verfallen adj, abgelaufen adj; **- bear** geschlagener Baissier; **- bull** geschlagener Haussier; **- check** (US) verjährter Scheck; **- market** flauer Markt, flaue Börse; **- shipping documents** nicht rechtzeitig eingereichte Verschiffungspapiere
stamp v stempeln v, frankieren v, freimachen v, prägen v; **- n** Stempel m, Briefmarke f, Postwertzeichen n, Stempelmarke f; **- book** Portokassenbuch n, Portobuch n; **- duty** Stempelgebühr f, Stempelsteuer f, Stempelabgabe f; **- duty on securities** Effektenstempelsteuer f; **- note** (GB) Zollfreigabeschein m; **- tax** (US) Stempelgebühr f, Stempelsteuer f, Stempelabgabe f; **adhesive -** Stempelmarke f; **bank -** Bankindossament n; **bill -** Wechselsteuermarke f, Wechselstempelmarke f; **check -** Scheckstempel m; **contract -** Vertragsstempel m, Schlußscheinstempel m; **postage -** Briefmarke f

stamped adj abgestempelt adj, freigemacht adj, frankiert adj; **- paper** Stempelpapier n
stamping n Abstempelung f, Verstempeln n, Versteuerung f
stand guarantee for haften für; **- surety** Bürgschaft leisten
standard n Standard m, Grad m, Feingehalt n, Münzfuß m; **- currency** Einheitswährung f; **- form** Normvordruck m; **- gold** Feingold m; **- interest** normaler Zinssatz; **- of living** Lebensstandard m; **- of rate** Wertmaßstab m, Wertmesser m; **- wage** Tariflohn m; **cost -** Kalkulationsnorm f; **double -** Doppelwährung f; **monetary -** Münzfuß m, Währungsstandard m, Währungseinheit f; **paper -** Papierwährung f; **parallel -** Doppelwährung f
Standard and Poors = S&P US-Unternehmen für Bonitätsbewertungen von Wertpapieren und Kreditverpflichtungen
standardization n Standardisierung f, Vereinheitlichung f, Normierung f
standardized loan normierter Kredit
standards; audit - Revisionsrichtlinien f pl; **credit -** Kreditrichtlinien f pl
standby credit Kreditzusage f, Beistandskredit m; **- agreement** Emissionsübernahmegeschäft mit Plazierungsrisikoübernahme
standing n Rang m, Ansehen n, Ruf m, Bonität f, Stellung f; **- credit** laufender Kredit; **- order** Dauerauftrag m; **credit -** Kreditwürdigkeit f, Kreditfähigkeit f
starting price Anfangskurs m, Eröffnungskurs m
start-up dividend Anlaufdividende f
start-up financing Neugründungsfinanzierung f
state v festsetzen v, festlegen v, bestimmen v, angeben v; **- n** Staat m, Bundesstaat m, Status m (Rang), wöchentlicher Bankausweis, Stellung f; **- bank** (US)

stated value

Staatsbank f, von einem Einzelstaat zugelassene Bank; **~ bank examiner** (US) staatlicher Bankenkommissar; **~ banking department** (US) staatliche Bankenaufsicht; **~ bonds** (US) Obligationen der amerikanischen Bundesstaaten; **~ borrowing** Staatsschuldenaufnahme f; **~ budget** Staatshaushalt m; **~ creditor** Staatsgläubiger m; **~ controlled** staatlich gelenkt; **~ debt** Staatsschuld f; **~ funds** Staatsgelder n pl; **~ loans** Staatskredite m pl, staatliche Kreditmittel; **~ note** Staatsschuldschein m; **~ of credit** Kreditsituation f; **~ of economy** Konjunkturlage f; **~ of the market** Konjunkturlage f, Marktlage f; **~ tax** Staatssteuer f

stated value Nominalwert m

state-guaranteed loan staatlich garantierte Anleihe

statement n Kontoauszug m Aufstellung f, Bilanz f, Erklärung f, Status m, Vermögensstand m; **~ analysis** Bilanzanalyse f; **~ department** (US) Kontoauszugsabteilung f; **~ heading** Bilanzschema n; **~ of account** Abrechnung f, Kontoauszug m Rechnungsauszug m; **~ of affairs** Status m (Übersicht über die Vermögenslage), Vermögensaufstellung f; **~ of assets and liabilities** (US) Bilanz f, Bilanzaufstellung f, Bilanzbogen m; **~ of condition** (US) Tagesbilanz f, Tagesbericht m, Bilanzaufstellung f; **~ of securities deposited** Depotaufstellung f; **~ of sources and applications of funds** (US) Liquiditätsstatus m; **accounting ~** Rechnungsaufstellung f; **accounts receivable ~** Debitorenaufstellung f; **annual ~** Jahresausweis m; **bank ~** Bankauszug m; **bank reconciliation ~** Kontoabrechnung f; **closing ~** Abschlußbericht m, Kontoabschluß m; **company ~** Gesellschaftsbilanz f, Firmenbilanz f; **corporate ~** Gesellschaftsbilanz f, Firmenbilanz f; **income ~** (US) Erfolgsrechnung f, Gewinn- und-Verlust-Rechnung, Ertragsaufstellung f, Ertragsrechnung f; **monthly ~** Monatsausweis m; **surplus ~** Gewinnübersicht f, Erfolgsbilanz f

Statements of Standard Accounting Practice (SSAP) Bilanzrichtlinien f pl (in den USA)

state-owned company Staatsbetrieb m, Staatsunternehmen n

stater; average ~ Dispacheur m, Havarievertreter m, Havarieagent m

state-trading country Staatshandelsland n

statistical evaluation statistische Auswertung

statistics Statistiken f pl, statistische Unterlagen

status inquiry Anfrage wegen einer Kreditauskunft; **~ report** Kreditauskunft f; **consular ~** Konsularstatus m; **legal ~** Rechtslage f, Personenstand m

statute n Gesetz n, Vorschrift f, Satzung f; **~ book** Gesetzessammlung f; **~ law** Gesetzesrecht n; **~ of limitations** Verjährungsbestimmungen f pl; **bankruptcy ~** Konkursordnung f

statute-barred adj (GB) erloschen adj, verjährt adj

statute-barred; to become ~ verjähren v

statutory adj statutengemäß adj, satzungsmäßig adj, gesetzlich adj; **~ books** gesetzlich vorgeschriebene Bücher; **~ company** Körperschaft des öffentlichen Rechts; **~ corporation** Körperschaft des öffentlichen Rechts; **~ declaration** eidesstattliche Erklärung, Affidavit n; **~ interest** gesetzlicher Zinssatz; **~ mortgage** rechtsgültige Hypothek, gesetzliche Hypothek; **~ receipt** gesetzlich vorgeschriebene Quittung; **~ reserve** Mindestreserve f; **~ reserves** nach der Satzung vorgeschriebene Reserven

steadiness of prices Kursstabilität f, Preisstabilität f

steady adj stabil adj, beständig adj; **~** v sich behaupten, sich befestigen (Kurse) v; **~ market** feste Börse, fester Markt; **~ prices** feste Kurse, feste Preise

steels Stahlaktien f pl

step-up bond Anleihe mit während der Laufzeit zunehmender Verzinsung f

step-up swap Stufenswap m, Kombination aus endfälligem und Termin-Swap

sterling n englisches Pfund; ~ *adj* echt *adj*, unverfälscht *adj*; ~ *area* Sterlingblock m, Sterlinggebiet n; ~ *block* Sterlingblock m, Sterlinggebiet n; ~ *bonds* Sterlingobligationen f pl; ~ *gold* echtes Gold; ~ *loan* Pfundanleihe f

sticky *assets* schwer verwertbare Aktiva; ~ *prices* unbewegliche Kurse

stiff *adj* fest *adj*, hart *adj*, versteift *adj*; ~ *market* feste Börse; ~ *price* hoher Preis

stiffen v fester werden, (sich) versteifen v

stiffening of prices Anziehen der Preise

stimulate v anregen v, beleben v, stimulieren v, intensivieren v, ankurbeln v

stimulus to savings Sparanreiz m

stipulate v festsetzen v (vereinbaren), ausbedingen v, ausmachen v, vereinbaren v

stipulated *adj* festgesetzt *adj*, ausgemacht *adj*

stipulation n Festsetzung f, Bedingung f, Abmachung f, Vereinbarung f; ~ *of payment* Zahlungsvereinbarung f

stipulator n Kontrahent m, vertragsschließender Teil, Vertragspartei f

stitched *adj* broschiert *adj*

stock Aktie f, Wertpapier f, (GB) festverzinsliches Wertpapier, Kapital n, Warenbestand m, Vorratsvermögen n, Lagerbestand m; ~ *account* Kapitalkonto n; ~ *adventure* (GB) Effektenspekulation f; ~ *basket* Aktienkorb m; ~ *broking (stock market transactions)* Börsengeschäfte n pl; ~ *call option* Aktienkaufoption f; ~ *capital* Gesellschaftskapital n (einer AG), Aktienkapital n; ~ *certificate* Aktienzertifikat n, Aktienanteilschein m, Aktienschein m; ~ *clerk* Lagerverwalter m, Lagerhalter m; ~ *company* Aktiengesellschaft f; ~ *corporation* (US) Aktiengesellschaft f; ~ *deposit* Wertpapierdepot n; ~ *dividend* (US) Dividende in Form von Gratisaktien; ~ *exchange* n Börse f, Effektenbörse f, Wertpapierbörse f

Stock Exchange Automated Quotation System = SEAQ elektronisches System der Börsennotierung und des Börsenhandels an der Londoner Börse

stock *exchange commission* Effektenprovision f; ~ *exchange customs* Börsenusancen f pl, Börsenbrauch m; ~ *exchange dealings* Börsengeschäfte n pl; ~ *exchange list* Börsenzettel m, Kurszettel m, Kursblatt n, Börsenkurszettel m; ~ *exchange manoeuvre* Börsenmanöver n; ~ *exchange operator* Börsianer m; ~ *exchange order* Börsenorder f, Börsenauftrag m; ~ *exchange quotation* Börsenkurs m, Börsennotiz f; ~ *exchange regulations* Börsenordnung f, Usancen der Börse; ~ *exchange securities* börsengängige Wertpapiere, Börsenwerte m pl; ~ *exchange settlement* Börsenabrechnung f; ~ *exchange transactions* Börsengeschäfte n pl; ~ *exchange turnover* Börsenumsätze m pl; ~ *futures and options trading* Aktienterminhandel m; ~ *index futures* Aktienindex Future m; ~ *in hand* Inventar n, Warenbestand m, Vorrat m, Bestand m; ~ *insurance company* Versicherungsaktiengesellschaft f; ~ *issue* Aktienemission f; ~ *ledger* Aktionärsverzeichnis n; ~ *list* (US) Aktienkurszettel m, Aktienkursliste f; ~ *loan* Effektenbeleihung f, Effektenlombard m, Effektenlombardkredit m; ~ *market* Börse f, Effektenbörse f, Wertpapierbörse f, Effektenmarkt m, Wertpapiermarkt m; ~ *office* Effektenabteilung f, Börsenabteilung f; ~ *option* Aktienoption f, Bezugsrecht auf neue Aktien; ~ *picking* Aktienauswahl unter Renditeaspekt; ~ *power* (US) Effektenverkaufsvollmacht f; ~ *price average* Börsenindex m; ~ *purchase (purchase of shares)* Aktienkauf m; ~ *share* Kapitalanteil m; *(share) purchase option* Optionsrechte auf Aktien; ~ *split* Aktiensplit m; ~ *tender offer* Aktienübernahmeangebot n; ~ *trade* Aktiengeschäft n; ~ *transfer* Aktienübertragung f, Aktienumschreibung f; ~ *transfer tax* (US) Börsenumsatzsteuer f; ~ *transfer warrant* (GB) Aktienzertifikat n, Aktienanteilschein m, Aktienschein m; ~ *trust certificate* Aktienzertifikat n, Aktienanteilschein m, Aktienschein m; ~ *value* *stockbroker*

Kurswert m; **~ warrant** Aktienbezugsrecht n, Aktienoptionsschein m, Aktienzertifikat m, Aktienanteilschein m, Aktienschein m; **~ watering** Verwässerung von Aktienkapital (Grundkapital); **~ yield** Aktienrendite f; **active ~** gängige Aktie; **amendment of ~ laws** Aktienrechtsreform f; **amount of ~** Kapitalanteil m; **assignment of ~** Aktienübertragung f, Aktienumschreibung f; **authorized ~** (US) genehmigtes Kapital; **baby ~** (US) neu ausgegebene Aktie; **bank ~** Bankaktien f pl; **bearer ~** Inhaberaktie f; **blue chip ~** Standardwerte m pl, Spitzenwerte m pl, erstklassige Wertpapiere; **bonus ~** (US) Gratisaktie f, Kapitalberichtigungsaktie f; **capital ~** (US) Grundkapital n, Stammkapital n; **certificate of ~** (US) Aktienzertifikat n, Aktienanteilschein m, Aktienschein m; **civil ~** Schuldverschreibungen der öffentlichen Hand; **closing ~** Schlußbestand m; **committee of the ~ exchange** Börsenvorstand m; **common ~** (US) Stammaktie f; **consolidated ~** (GB) konsolidierte Papiere; **convertible loan ~** Wandelanleihe f; **cooperative ~** Genossenschaftskapital n; **dead ~** unverkäufliche Waren; **deal on the ~ exchange** Börsencoup m; **debenture ~** (US) Vorzugsaktie f, hypothekarisch gesicherte Obligation, (GB) Obligation (die man in Teilbeträgen überweisen kann); **deferred ~** Aktienkapital mit hinausgeschobener Zinszahlung; **eighth ~** (US) in kleiner als üblichen Posten (1/8 über oder unter regulärem Kurs gehandelte Aktien); **foreign ~** Auslandswertpapiere n pl, Auslandswerte m pl; **inscribed ~** (GB) Namensaktie f; **issued ~** (US) effektiv ausgegebenes Aktienkapital, effektiv ausgegebenes Kapital; **loan ~** festverzinsliche Anleihe; **monetary ~** (US) gesamter Geldbestand; **nopar ~** nennwertlose Aktie, Aktie ohne Nennwert; **ordinary ~** Stammaktie f; **par value ~** (US) Nennwertaktie f; **participating ~** Aktien mit Gewinnbeteiligung; **pawned ~** (GB) bombardierte Aktien, verpfändete Aktien; **potential ~** nicht ausgegebene Aktien; **realizable ~** börsengängige Wertpapiere, Börsenwerte m pl; **redeemable ~** zurückzahlbare Werte; **registered ~** (US) Namensaktie f; **senior ~** (US) Vorzugsaktien f pl; **speculative ~** Spekulationsaktie f; **transfer of ~** (US) Aktienübertragung f, Aktienumschreibung f; **treasury ~** eigene Aktien; **unified ~** (GB) konsolidierte Anleihe; **unissued ~** nicht ausgegebene Aktien; **unsubscribed ~** nicht gezeichnete Aktien; **voting ~** Stimmrechtsaktien f pl; **widow and orphan ~** (US) mündelsichere Anlagepapiere, mündelsichere Wertpapiere, mündelsichere Papiere

stockbroker n Effektenmakler m

stockbrokerage n Courtage f, Maklergebühr f

stockbroking n Effektenhandel m, Börsenhandel m, Aktienhandel m; **~ transaction** Börsenkommissionsgeschäft n

stock-financing loan Vorratskredit m

stockholder n Aktionär m, Aktieninhaber m, Anteilseigner m, Gesellschafter m; **~ group** Aktionärsgruppe f; **~ of record** eingetragener Aktionär m

stockholders meeting Hauptversammlung f, Generalversammlung f, Aktionärsversammlung f; **~ tax** Kuponsteuer f, Kapitalertragsteuer f; **annual meeting of ~** (US) ordentliche Hauptversammlung der Aktionäre

stockholders' equity (US) Eigenkapital n (Bilanz); **~ ledger** Aktionärsbuch n, Aktionärsverzeichnis n; **~ liability** Einzahlungsverpflichtung des Aktionärs

stockholding n Aktienbesitz m, Aktienbestand m

stockjobber n Börsenhändler m, Zwischenmakler m, Effektenhändler m, Fondshändler m

stockmaster Stockmaster m, elektronische Erfassung von Wertpapierinformationen

stockowner n Effektenbesitzer m, Aktienbesitzer m

stock out nicht mehr am Lager

stockpile v horten v

stocks n pl Aktien f pl, Effekten plt, Wertpapiere n pl, Obligationen f pl, Schuldverschreibungen f pl; **~ and bonds department** Börsenabteilung f; **absorb**

~ Wertpapiere aufnehmen; **barometer** ~ (US) Standardwerte *m pl*; **building** ~ (US) Bauaktien *f pl*; **classified** ~ in verschiedenen Serien ausgegebene Schuldverschreibungen; **corporation** ~ (GB) Kommunalschuldverschreibungen *f pl*, Stadtanleihe *f*, Kommunalanleihe *f*, Kommunalobligationen *f pl*; **county** ~ (GB) Papiere der verschiedenen englischen Grafschaften; **cumulative** ~ (US) kumulative Aktien; **curb** ~ (US) im Freiverkehr gehandelte Wertpapiere; **dealer in** ~ (US) Effektenhändler *m*, Börsenhändler *m*; **defensive** ~ Aktien mit einer gleichmäßigen Gewinnerzielung; **deferred** ~ (US) nicht bevorrechtigte Aktien (in bezug auf Dividendenzahlungen); **glamour** ~ Wachstumsaktie mit stark spekulativem Einschlag; **guaranteed** ~ Aktien mit garantierter Dividendenzahlung; **industrial** ~ Industriepapiere *n pl*, Industriewerte *m pl*; **international** ~ (US) international gehandelte Effekten, international gehandelte Papiere, international gehandelte Wertpapiere; **non-assessable** ~ nicht nachschußpflichtige Aktien; **preference** ~ (US) Vorzugsaktien *f pl*; **preferred** ~ (US) Vorzugsaktien *f pl*; **representative** ~ Standardwerte *m pl*; **special** ~ (US) Spezialwerte *m pl*, Sonderwerte *m pl*

stocktaking *n* Bestandsaufnahme *f*; Inventur *f*

stop order Auftrag, Aktien billigst zu kaufen; ~ **payment** Zahlungen einstellen; ~ **payment of a check** einen Scheck sperren; ~ **payment order** Schecksperre *f*, Sperre *f* (eines Schecks)

stop-loss order Wertpapierverkaufauftrag eines Kunden (sobald ein gewisser Kurs unterschritten ist), Stopp-Loss-Auftrag, Verlustbegrenzungsauftrag *m*

stoppage *n* Zahlungsstopp *m*, Gehaltsabzug *m*, Einstellung *f* (Beendigung); ~ **of credit** Kreditsperre *f*; ~ **of payment** Zahlungssperre *f*

stopped check gesperrter Scheck *m*

stopping of a check Schecksperre *f*; ~ **list** Oppositionsliste, Sperrliste *f*

storage Lagerung *f*, Lagerkosten *f pl*; ~ **agency bill** Vorratsstellenwechsel *m*; ~ **bin** Ablagefach *n*; ~ **capacity** Speicherkapazität *f* (EDV)

store *n* Laden *m*, Geschäft *n*, Lager *n*; ~ **card** Kunden(kredit)karte *f*, Servicekarte *f*; ~ **keeper** Lagerverwalter *m*, Lagerhalter *m*; ~ **owner** (US) Ladenbesitzer *m*; **bill of** ~ (US) Wiedereinfuhrgenehmigung *f*, Wiedereinfuhrschein *m*

storehouse *n* Lagerhaus *n*, Magazin *n*, Lager *n*

stores Kaufhauswerte *m pl*

straddle *n* (US) Stellagegeschäft *n*, kombiniertes Optionsgeschäft, Kauf-und-Verkaufs-Optionsschein mit dem gleichen Basiswert

straight bill of lading (US) Namenskonnossement *n*; ~ **bonds** (straights) Festzinssatzanleihen *f pl*, Festsatzbonds *m*; ~ **letter of credit** bestätigtes unwiderrufliches Akkreditiv; ~ **loan** nicht handelbare Anleihe; ~ **note** Straight-Anleihe, Anleihe ohne Wandel- oder Optionsklausel; ~ **promissory note** (US) ungesicherter Schuldschein

straighten accounts Rechnungen bezahlen, Rechnungen in Ordnung bringen

straight-line depreciation lineare Abschreibung

strain on liquidity Liquiditätsanspannung *f*; **credit** ~ Kreditanspannung *f*

strap Stellagegeschäft mit Kaufoption

straw bid Scheinangebot *n*

street loan (US) kurzfristiges Darlehen an Börsenmakler unter Beleihung von börsengängigen Effekten; ~ **price** Freiverkehrskurs *m*

strengthen *v* sich festigen *v* (Börse)

strengthening of prices Kursbefestigung *f*

stress of money Geldanspannung *f*

strike a dividend eine Dividende ausschütten; ~ **coins** münzen *v*, prägen *v*; ~ **the balance** den Saldo ziehen

striking (exercise) price Basissatz *m*

stringency *n* Strenge *f*, Knappheit *f*; **credit** ~ Kreditknappheit *f*

stringent *adj* streng *adj*, gedrückt *adj*, knapp *adj*

strip Mantel und Zinskupon einer Anleihe trennen

stripped bond Anleihe, bei der Mantel und Zinsscheine getrennt sind; strap Kombination: 2 Kauf- (Call) und 1 Verkaufsoption (Put); strip Kombination: 1 Kauf- (Call) und 2 Verkaufsoptionen (Put)

stripped bonds vom Mantel und Bogen getrennte Anleihe

stripper *n* Unternehmensausschlachter *m*

stripping *v* ein Unternehmen ausschlachten

strips = stripped US-Treasury zero bonds Nullkuponanleihen *f pl*, Anleihe des US-Schatzamtes nach Trennung der Kupons vom Mantel

strips market getrennter Markt für Mäntel und Kupons

strong box Stahlkassette *f*; *- market* feste Börse; *- room* Panzergewölbe *n*, Tresor *m*, Stahlkammer *f*

struck balance Zwischenbilanz *f*

structure *n* Struktur *f*, Aufbau *m*, Gefüge *f*; *- v* gestalten *v*, strukturieren *v*; *cost - * Kostengefüge *n*

struggle; *business* - Konkurrenzkampf *m*

stub *n* (US) Kontrollblatt *n*, Scheckabschnitt *m*

student employee Praktikant *m*

stumer *n* (GB) ungedeckter Scheck, gefälschter Scheck, falsche Banknote

style; *business* - Firmierung *f*

suable *adj* klagbar *adj*, prozeßfähig *adj*

sub-account *n* Unterkonto *n*

sub-branch Zweigstelle *f* (einer Bank), Depositenkasse *f*

subcharter *v* unterverfrachten *v*

subcompany Tochtergesellschaft *f* (US)

subcontractor Subunternehmer *m*

subfund Subfonds *m* (Teil- oder Unterfonds eines Umbrellafonds)

subject *n* Sachgebiet *n*; *- to call* täglich kündbar; *to collection* Eingang vorbehalten; *- to commission* kommissionspflichtig *adj*; *- to notice* kündbar *adj*; *- to rent* zinspflichtig *adj*; *- to taxation* steuerpflichtig *adj*

sublease *v* untervermieten *v*, unterverpachten *v*; *- n* Untervermietung *f*, Untermiete *f*, Unterpacht *f*

sublessor *n* Untervermieter *m*

sublet *v* untervermieten *v*, unterverpachten *v*

sub-manager Unterdirektor *m*

sub-office Zweigstelle *f* (einer Bank), Depositenkasse *f*

subordinated *liabilities* nachrangige Verbindlichkeiten; *- loan* nachrangige Anleihe; *- mortgage* nachrangige Hypothek

subordination Rangrücktritt *m*

sub-participation Unterbeteiligung *f*

sub-partner (GB) persönlich nicht haftender Gesellschafter

subreption *n* Erbschleichung *f*

subscribe *v* zeichnen *v* (z. B. Anleihen), subskribieren *v*

subscribed *allotment* Repartierung, Zuteilung bei einer überzeichneten Emission; ***capital*** gezeichnetes Kapital; *- capital stock* ausstehende Einlagen auf das Grundkapital

subscriber *n* Zeichner *m* (z. B. einer Anleihe)

subscription *n* Zeichnung *f* (z. B. einer Anleihe), Subskription *f*, Abonnement *n*, Mitgliedsbeitrag *m*; *- blank* (US) Zeichnungsformular *n*, Zeichnungsschein *m*; *- certificate* Bezugsschein *m*; *- form* Zeichnungsformular *n*, Zeichnungsschein *m*; *- in excess* Überzeichnung *f*; *- ledger* Aktienzeichnungsbuch *n*; *- list* Zeichnungsliste *f*, Zeichnungsbogen *m*, Zeichnungsschein *m*; *- money* Zeichnungsbetrag *m*; *- period* Zeichnungsfrist *f*; *- quota* Zeichnungsbetrag *m*, Übernahmebetrag *m*; *- right* Bezugsrecht *n*, Optionsrecht *n*; *rate of -* Zeichnungskurs *m*; *- right valuation* Bezugsrechtsbewertung *f*; *subsequent - * Nachzeichnung von Aktien

subsequent *adj* nachfolgend *adj*, folgend *adj*; *- bankruptcy* Ausschlußkonkurs *m*; *- endorsement* Nachindossament *n*; *- entry* Nachtragsbuchung *f*; *- machine processing* maschinelle Weiterverarbeitung; *- processing* Folgearbeit *f* (z. B. im Anschluß an Verbuchungsprogramme); *- subscription* Nachzeichnung von Aktien

subsidiary *n* Konzerngesellschaft *f*, Tochtergesellschaft *f*; *- account number*

Unterkontonummer f; **- accounting department** Nebenbuchhaltung f; **- coin** Scheidemünze f; **- company** Konzerngesellschaft f, Tochtergesellschaft f

subsidization n Subventionierung f

subsidize v subventionieren v, unterstützen v, durch Staatsgelder stützen; **- exports** die Ausfuhr fördern

subsidized adj subventioniert adj, durch Staatszuschüsse unterstützt

subsidy n Subvention f, staatliche Unterstützung f, staatlicher Zuschuß f; **- for interest** Zinszuschuß f

substitute v ersetzen v; **-** n Stellvertreter m, Vertreter m; **- document** Ersatzbeleg m

substitution n Vertretung f (Ersatz), Stellvertretung f; **- of debt** Schuldübernahme f, Schuldauswechselung f, Novation f

sub-subsidiary Enkelgesellschaft f

subtract v subtrahieren v, abziehen v (Math.)

subtraction n Subtraktion f

sub-underwriter Unterkonsorte m

subvention n Subvention f, staatliche Unterstützung f, staatlicher Zuschuß

subventioned adj subventioniert adj, durch Staatszuschüsse unterstützt

subventionize v subventionieren v

succeed; right to - Erbberechtigung f, Erbschaftsanspruch m

succession n Nachfolge f, Erbfolge f

successor n Rechtsnachfolger m, Erbe

sue v verklagen v, klagen v, Klage erheben

sufferance; bill of - Erlaubnis zollfreier Warenausfuhr von Hafen zu Hafen

suit n Zivilprozeß m, Klageerhebung f, Klage f

suitor n Kläger m

sum n Summe f, Geldbetrag m; **- insured** Versicherungssumme f; **- up** zusammenrechnen v, addieren v, aufrechnen v

summary n Auszug m (kurze Übersicht); **- advice** Sammelavis m; **- bill enforcement procedure** Wechselstrenge f; **- of assets and liabilities** Bilanzauszug m, verkürzte Bilanz

sums; allow for - paid in advance Anzahlungen verrechnen

sundries n pl Verschiedenes n, Diverses n, diverse Unkosten; **- account** Konto »Verschiedenes«, Konto für Diverses, Konto pro Diverse

sundry creditors account (GB) »diverse Kreditoren« (Kontobezeichnung)

sunrise industries innovative Unternehmen

sunset industries veraltete Unternehmen

super new account (US) verzinsliches Geldmarktkonto für öffentliche Stellen

superdividend n Bonus m, Extradividende f, Sonderdividende f, Superdividende f, außerordentliche Dividende

superintendend of banks Bankkommissar m, Bankinspektor m

supervise v beaufsichtigen v

supervision n Kontrolle f (Überwachung)

supervisory board Aufsichtsrat m, Direktorium n

supplement n Anlage f, Beilage f; **-** n Supplement n, Ergänzung f, Nachtrag m

supplementary benefit Sozialhilfe f; **- claim** Nachforderung f; **- entry** Nachtragsbuchung f

supplier n Lieferant m

supplier's bill Lieferantenwechsel m

supplies n pl Vorräte m pl, Lagerbestände m pl, Warenbestände m pl

supply v liefern v, bereitstellen v, versorgen mit; **-** n Angebot n, Versorgung f, Vorrat m, Lieferung f; **- and demand** Angebot und Nachfrage; **- of capital** Kapitalbereitstellung f; **- service** (GB) Ergänzungskredit m; **currency -** Zahlungsmittelversorgung f; **the floating -** tägliches Angebot

support v unterstützen v; **-** n Unterstützung f, Stützungsangebot n, Stützungskäufe m pl, Marktpflege f, Kurspflege f, Besicherung f; **- fee** Avalprovision f (US); **banking -** Bankenstützungsaktion f, Bankenintervention f; **pool -** Stützungskäufe der Poolbeteiligten; **- program** Förderprogramm n

supported price gestützter Kurs

supporting purchase Stützungskauf m

support-measures Stützungsmaßnahmen f pl

surety n Bürge m, Garant m, Gewährsmann m; ~ n Garantie f, Bürgschaft f; **- acceptance** Avalkredit m; **- business** Kautionsversicherungsgeschäft n; **- company** (US) Kautionsversicherungsgesellschaft f; **- credit** Avalkredit m; **bankrupt** ~ in Konkurs gegangener Bürge; **bill** ~ Wechselbürge m; **bond with** ~ Schuldverschreibung mit zusätzlicher Bürgschaft; **joint** ~ Mitbürge m, Gesamtbürgschaft f; **stand** ~ Bürgschaft leisten

suretyship n Garantie f, Bürgschaft f; **contract of** ~ Bürgschaftsvertrag m

surge Anstieg m, Auftrieb m; **- in equities** Aktienhausse f

surplus Gewinn m, Überschuß m, Rücklagen f pl; **- account** (US) Gewinnüberschußkonto n; **- accumulation** Gewinnansammlung f; **- analysis** Gewinnanalyse f; **- brought forward** (US) Gewinnvortrag m; **- dividend** Bonus m, Extradividende f, Sonderdividende f, Superdividende f, außerordentliche Dividende, Zusatzdividende f; **- earnings** (US) Gewinnüberschuß m, Überschuß m, Überfluß m, unverteilter Reingewinn; **- profits** (US) Gewinnüberschuß m, Überschuß m, Überfluß m, unverteilter Reingewinn; **- reserve** (US) zweckgebundene Rücklage, Gewinnrückstellung f; **- statement** Gewinnübersicht f, Erfolgsbilanz f; **accumulated** ~ Gewinnvortrag m; **appropriation of** ~ Reservebildung f; **availability** ~ nicht zweckgebundener Gewinn; **book** ~ buchmäßiger Überschuß; **capital** ~ Kapitalreserven f pl, Kapitalüberschuß m; **company's** ~ Gesellschaftsgewinn m; **consolidated** ~ (GB) Konzernüberschuß m; **credit** ~ Aktivüberschuß m; **earned** ~ Betriebsgewinn m; **paper** ~ Papiergewinne m pl

surrender n Aufgabe f, Verzicht m, Übergabe f, Aushändigung f; **- for exchange** zwecks Umtausch übergeben; **- value** Rückkaufswert m (einer Versicherungspolice); **cash - value** Rückkaufswert m (einer Versicherungspolice)

surtax n Ergänzungssteuer f; ~ n Steuerzuschlag m

survey n Geschäftsbewertung f, Grundstücksbewertung f, Gutachten n, Übersicht f; **commercial** ~ Markanalyse f; **habit** ~ Untersuchung über Verbrauchergewohnheiten

surveyor Gutachter m, Sachverständiger m

surviving debts Restschulden f pl

sushi bond Euroanleihe japanischer Emittenten in fremder Währung (nicht in Yen)

suspend v unterbrechen v, einstellen v, abbestellen v, aufhören v

suspended account transitorisches Konto, vorläufiges Konto

suspense account transitorisches Konto, vorläufiges Konto, Durchlaufkonto n, Conto pro Diversa n (CpD); **- interest account** (GB) Konto für Zinsen, deren Eingang zweifelhaft ist; **- items** vorläufige Posten, Übergangsposten m pl, Schwebeposten m pl; **- liabilities** transitorische Passiva

suspension n einstweilige Aufhebung, vorübergehende Einstellung, Aufschub m; **- of aquotation** Kursaussetzung f; **- of specie payments** Aufhebung der Einlösungspflicht von Banknoten

sustained rally anhaltende Kurserholung

swap v tauschen v (Swapgeschäft durchführen); ~ n Swapgeschäft n, Tauschgeschäft n (Börse), Tausch m, Austausch m, Umtausch m; **- offer** Umtauschangebot n; **- operations** Swapgeschäfte n pl; **- rate** Swapsatz m

swaption Swaption f, Option auf einen Swap

sweating coins Gewinnung von Gold- und Silberstaub aus Münzen durch Gewichtsverringerung

sweetener zusätzlicher Anreiz

SWIFT = Society for Worldwide Interbank Financial Telecommunication internationales Kommunikationssystem für den Zahlungsverkehr

swing n (US) Swing m, Schwankungsbreite f, Konjunkturperiode f

swingline facility Kreditlinie zur Überbrückung von Zeitgrenzen oder der Kreditart

Swiss Bankers Association Schweizer Bankiervereinigung f; *- Franc* Schweizer Franken m; *- National Bank* Schweizer National Bank f

switch v switchen v, Switchgeschäft machen; *- n* Switchgeschäft n

sworn *broker* vereidigter Makler; *- declaration* eidesstattliche Erklärung, Affidavit n

syndic n Syndikus m, Rechtsberater m, Bevollmächtigter m

syndicate n Syndikat n, Konsortium n, Interessengemeinschaft f; *- business* Konsortialgeschäft n; *- credit* Konsortialkredit m; *- loan* (US) Konsortialkredit m; *- manager* führende Bank eines Konsortiums; *- member* Konsortialmitglied n; *- offering* Konsortialangebot n; *- operation* Konsortialgeschäft n; *- participation* Konsortialbeteiligung f; *- share* Konsortialanteil m; *banking -* Bankenkonsortium n; *business -* Wirtschaftsvereinigung f; *original -* Übernahmesyndikat n; *underlying -* (US) Übernahmekonsortium n; *underwriting -* Emissionskonsortium n

syndicated loan Konsortialkredit m

synergy Synergieeffekt m

system configuration Anlagenkonfiguration f; *- loading* Auslastung f (eines Systems); *- of crawling pegs* System der Wechselkursanpassung in kleinen Schritten, System gleitender Bandbreiten; *- of fixed (floating)* (exchange rates) System fester (gleitender) Wechselkurse; *- utilization* Auslastung f (eines Systems); *monetary -* Geldsystem n, Währungssystem n

systematic *chart of accounts* Kontenrahmen m; *- schedule of accounts* Kontenrahmen m

systems failure Systemausfall m

T

table n Tabelle f; **- format** Tabellenform f; **- look-up time** Tabellensuchzeit f; **- search time** Tabellensuchzeit f
tabular bookkeeping amerikanische Buchführungsmethode
tacit mortgage n Sicherungshypothek f, Zwangshypothek f
tacking of mortgages Hypothekenvereinigung f, Zusammenfassung von Hypotheken
take v nehmen v, einnehmen v, unternehmen v, durchführen v; **- n** Gewinn m, Einnahmen plt; **- as a set-off** in Gegenrechnung stellen; **- effect** wirksam werden; **- inventory** v eine Inventur durchführen; **- on discount** diskontieren v; **- over** übernehmen v; **- possession of** in Besitz nehmen; **- up a bill** einen Wechsel einlösen, einen Wechsel honorieren; **- up shares** Aktien zeichnen, Aktien beziehen; **final -** Restrisikoposition einer Finanzierung (Spezialfinanzierung)
take-home pay Nettoverdienst m
takeover Unternehmensübernahme f; **- bid** Übernahmeangebot n; **- candidate** Übernahmekandidat m; **- defence** Übernahmeabwehr f; **- financing** Übernahmefinanzierung f
take-over bid Übernahmeangebot n
taker n Abnehmer m (Börse), Käufer m (Börse); **- n** (US) Vermächtnisnehmer m; **- for a call** Verkäufer einer Rückprämie (Verkaufsoption); **- for a put** Käufer einer Rückprämie (Kaufoption); **- of an option** Prämiennehmer m, Stillhalter m, Optionsgeber m
taking for the call Verkauf einer Rückprämie; **- for the put** Kauf einer Rückprämie; **- out of a mortgage** Hypothekenaufnahme f; **- over** Übernahme f; **- over a company** Übernahme einer Gesellschaft; **- up a loan** Kreditaufnahme f
takings Einnahmen f pl, Erlöse f pl

tally n Kontrolliste f; **- v** übereinstimmen v (Konten); **- n** Kontobuch n, Übereinstimmen von Konten
talon n Talon m, Erneuerungsschein m, Allonge f
tampering with a balance sheet Bilanzfrisur f
tangible fixed assets Sachanlagen f pl; **- assets** Sachanlagevermögen n, körperliche Wirtschaftsgüter
tap v eine Anleihe machen, leihen v; **- bill** Schatzwechsel m; **- issue** Regierungsanleihe f (GB); **- rate** Schatzwechselsatz m
tape card Lochstreifenkarte f; **- machine** Börsenfernschreiber m, Börsentelegraph m; **- organization** Bandorganisation f
tare; customs - Zollgewicht n
target n Ziel n; **- price** Richtpreis m; **- range** Zielkorridor m
targeted issue Emission für bestimmte Anleger(gruppe)
tariff n Zoll m, Tarif m, Gebührenverzeichnis n, Preisliste f; **- barrier** Zollschranke f; **- of charge** Gebührentabelle; **- protection** Zollschutz m; **- union** Zollunion f; **- wall** Zollschranke f; **customs -** Zolltarif m
tax v besteuern v, belasten v, veranlagen v, mit Steuern belegen; **- n** Steuer f, Abgabe f, Gebühr f, Taxe f; **- assessment note** Steuerbescheid m; **- assessment notice** Steuerbescheid m; **- at source** Quellensteuer f; **- balance sheet** Steuerbilanz f; **- bill** (GB) Steuerbescheid m; **- card** Steuerkarte f; **- credit** Steuergutschrift f; **- evasion** Steuerhinterziehung f; **- heaven corporation** Briefkastenfirma f; **- hike** Steuererhöhung f; **- liabilities** Steuerschulden f pl; **- loss company** Steuerabschreibungsgesellschaft f; **- office** (US) Finanzamt n, Steueramt n; **- on exports** Exportsteuer f; **- on imports** Importsteuer f; **- on increment value** Wertzuwachssteuer f; **- on real estate**

Grundstücksteuer f; *- payer* Steuerzahler m, Besteuerter m; *- position* Steuerklasse f; *- privilege* Steuervorteil m; *- rate* Steuertarif m; *- rebate* Steuernachlaß m; *- refund* Steuerrückerstattung f; *- relief* Steuervergünstigung f; *- remission* Steuererlaß m; *- reserves* Steuerrücklagen f pl; *- return* Steuererklärung f; *- revenue* Steuereinkommen n; *- scale* Steuertarif m; *- sheet* Steuererklärung f; *- shelters* steuerbegünstigte Wertpapiere; *- table* Steuertabelle f; *amusement -* Vergnügungssteuer f; *betterment -* Wertzuwachssteuer f; *beverage -* Getränkesteuer f; *capital -* Kapitalvermögenssteuer f; *capital gains -* Kapitalgewinnsteuer f, Kapitalzuwachssteuer f; *capital transaction -* Kapitalverkehrssteuer f; *capital yield -* Kapitalertragsteuer f; *corporation -* Körperschaftsteuer f; *income -* Einkommensteuer f, Lohnsteuer f; *property -* (US) Vermögenssteuer für bewegliches und unbewegliches Vermögen; *real estate -* Grundsteuer f; *securities -* Wertpapiersteuer f; *stamp -* (US) Stempelgebühr f, Stempelsteuer f, Stempelabgabe f; *turnover -* Umsatzsteuer f; *withholding -* Quellensteuer f

Tax; *Interest Equalization -* amerikanische Zinsausgleichssteuer auf Käufe ausländischer Wertpapiere

taxable adj besteuerbar adj, steuerbar adj, steuerpflichtig adj, gebührenpflichtig adj; *- income* steuerpflichtiges Einkommen; *- profits* steuerpflichtige Gewinne *- value* steuerpflichtiger Wert, steuerbarer Wert, Steuerwert m

taxableness n Besteuerbarkeit f

tax-anticipation note Steuergutschein m

taxation n Besteuerung f, Steuerveranlagung f, Steuerwesen n; *burden of -* Steuerlast f; *direct -* direkte Besteuerung; *double -* Doppelbesteuerung f; *rate of -* Steuersatz m; *subject to -* steuerpflichtig adj

taxational adj Steuern betreffend

tax-deductible steuerlich absetzbar adj

tax-deductibles steuerlich abzugsfähige Beträge

taxed adj besteuert adj

taxes Steuern f pl; *- payable* Steuerverbindlichkeiten f pl; *- reserved* Steuerrückstellungen f pl; *bill of -* Steuerbescheid m; *deferred -* Steuervorauszahlungen f pl; *provision for -* Steuerrückstellungen f pl

tax-exempt amount Steuerfreibetrag m

tax-exemption Steuerfreiheit f, Steuerbefreiung f

tax-favo(u)red loan steuerbegünstigte Anleihe

tax-free adj steuerfrei adj, nicht steuerpflichtig

taxing authority Steuerbehörde f; *- power* Steuerhoheit f

taxpayer n Steuerzahler m

tax-sheltered steuerbegünstigt adj

technical analysis technische Analyse; *- objection* formaler Einwand; *- overdraft* technische Kontoüberziehung; *- reaction* technische Reaktion

technology stocks Technologiewerte m pl

tel quel rate (GB) Nettokurs m, Telquelkurs m

telebanking Telebanking n, elektronische Abwicklung von Bankgeschäften

telegraphic acceptance Drahtakzept n; *- address* Drahtwort n, Drahtanschrift f; *- code* Telegrammschlüssel m; *- key* Telegrammschlüssel m; *- money order* telegrafische Geldüberweisung; *- transfer* telegrafische Überweisung

teleprinter n Fernschreiber m; *by -* fernschriftlich

teleprocessing n Datenfernverarbeitung f; *- n* Fernverarbeitung f

teletypewriter n Fernschreiber m

telex n Fernschreiben n; *by -* fernschriftlich

teller n (US) Kassierer m; *- machine* Schalterbuchungsmaschine f; *- posting machine* Schalterbuchungsmaschine f; *- receipting machine* Schalterquittungsmaschine f; *- stamp* (US) Kassenstempel m; *bank -* Bankkassierer m; *coupon -* Kuponkassierer m

teller's department (US) Kasse f (Abteilung); **~ proof** Kassenabschluß m, Kassenrevision f; **~ window** Auszahlungsschalter m

temporary adj vorläufig adj; **~ annuity** Zeitrente f; **~ credit** Zwischenkredit m; Überbrückungskredit m; **~ overdraft** kurzfristige Kontoüberziehung; **~ storage** Zwischenspeichern n (EDV)

tenancy n Pachtverhältnis n, Mietverhältnis n, Pachtdauer f; **~ agreement** Mietvertrag m, Pachtvertrag m

tenant n Mieter m, Pächter m

tenantable adj mietbar adj, pachtbar adj, bewohnbar adj

tendencies of the market Börsenentwicklung f

tendency n Tendenz f, Entwicklung f; **bearish ~** Baissetendenz f; **bullish ~** Haussetendenz f

tender v anbieten v, ausschreiben v, vorlegen v, bieten v, einreichen v; **~ n** Tenderverfahren n, Ausschreibung von Wertpapieremissionen, Angebot n, Kostenvoranschlag m, Offerte f, Kostenanschlag m; **~ for treasury bills** Zeichnungsangebot für Schatzwechsel; **~ guarantee** Bietungsgarantie f; **~ of documents** Vorlage von Dokumenten; **~ offer** Übernahmeangebot n; **~ period** Einreichungsfrist f; **~ price** Angebotspreis m; **~ procedure** Tenderverfahren n; **accept the ~** Zuschlag erteilen; **fixed-rate ~** Mengentender m

tenders; invite ~ zur Abgabe von Zeichnungsangeboten auffordern

tenor of a bill Laufzeit eines Wechsels; **~ of a deed** Wortlaut einer Urkunde

tenure n Ausstellung f, Amtszeit f

term n Bezeichnung f, Ausdruck m; **~ n** Laufzeit f, Termin m, Frist f, Verfallzeit f; **~ account** Festgeldkonto n; **~ bill** Nachsichtwechsel m; **~ credit** Akzeptakkreditiv n; **~ deposits** Festgelder n pl, Termineinlagen f pl; **~ loan** befristetes Darlehen; **~ money** Festgelder n pl; **~ of a loan** Laufzeit einer Anleihe, Dauer einer Anleihe; **~ of notice** Kündigungsfrist f; **~ of office** Amtsdauer f; **~ sheet** (Basis)Konditionen einer Finanzierung (Spezialfinanzierung); **at fixed ~** terminiert adj; **balance sheet ~** bilanztechnischer Ausdruck; **expiry of a ~** Fristablauf m, Termin m; **fixed ~** fester Termin

terminable contract kündbarer Vertrag

terminal bond Bahnleihe f (US); **~ bonus** Schlußdividende f; **~ market** Terminmarkt m, Warenterminbörse f

terminate v beendigen v, zum Abschluß bringen

termination Beendigung f, Auflösung f, Kündigung f

terms n pl (of a loan) Ausstattung f (einer Anleihe); **~ n pl** Bedingungen f pl, Bestimmungen f pl; **~ of a loan** Anleihebedingungen f pl; **~ of delivery** Lieferungsbedingungen f pl, Lieferbedingungen f pl; **~ of interest** Zinskonditionen f pl; **~ of payment** Zahlungsbedingungen f pl; **contract ~** Vertragsbedingungen f pl; **credit ~** Kreditbedingungen f pl, Kreditkonditionen f pl

test data Testdaten plt (EDV); **~ mode** Testbetrieb m (EDV); **~ number** Stichzahl f, Kontrollnummer f; **~ operation** Testbetrieb m (EDV); **~ program** Testprogramm n

testable adj testierfähig adj

testacy n Testierfähigkeit f

testament n Testament n, letztwillige Verfügung, letzter Wille; **mutual ~** gegenseitiges Testament, Berliner Testament

testamentary adj letztwillig adj, testamentarisch adj; **~ capacity** Testierfähigkeit f; **~ trustee** Testamentsvollstrecker m

testate; die ~ unter Hinterlassung eines Testaments sterben

testation n testamentarische Verfügung, letztwillige Verfügung

testator n Erblasser m, Testator m

testatrix n Erblasserin f

text key Textschlüssel m

The Single European Act Einheitliche Europäische Akte f

theft insurance Diebstahlversicherung f

theory of money Geldtheorie f; **commodity ~ of money** Geldwerttheorie f

thin market schwacher Markt, enger Markt
third *market* Börsen-Drittmarkt *m*;
~ ***market stock*** (US) Freiverkehrswerte *m pl*
Third World *n* Dritte Welt *f*
third-party liability insurance Haftpflichtversicherung *f*
third-party property Fremdbesitz *m*
three *months bill* Dreimonatswechsel *m*; ~ ***months draft*** Dreimonatswechsel *m*
threefold dreifach
threshold price Schwellenpreis *m*
thrift *n* Sparsamkeit *f*; ~ ***account*** (US) Sparkonto *n*, Spareinlage *f*, Sparguthaben *n*; ~ ***box*** (US) Sparbüchse *f*; ~ ***department*** (US) Sparabteilung *f*; ~ ***deposit*** Spargelder *n pl*
through bill of lading Transitkonnossement *m*, Durchkonnossement *n*
tick Tick *m* (0,01%), Mindestkursschwankung *f*, (informal) Pump *m*; ~ ***off (items)*** anhaken *v*, abhaken *v* (von Posten)
ticker *n* (US) Börsenfernschreiber *m*, Börsentelegraph *m*, Ticker *m*; ~ ***abbreviations*** (US) Börsenabkürzungen *f pl*; ~ ***firm*** Börsenmakler *m*; ~ ***service*** (US) Börsenfernschreibdienst *m*, Tickerdienst *m*; ~ ***symbol*** Aktiensymbol *n*; ~ ***tape*** Papierband *n* (auf dem die Börsenkurse verzeichnet werden)
ticket *n* Zettel *m*, Beleg *m*, Einzahlungsbeleg *m*; ***broker's*** ~ Börsenabrechnung *f*; ***call*** ~ Zahlungsaufforderungsschein *m*; ***charge*** ~ Belastungsanweisung *f*; ***debit*** ~ Belastungsanweisung *f*
tickler; maturity ~ (US) Verfallbuch *n*
tie *v* anbinden *v*, koppeln *v*; ~ ***to gold*** Goldbindung *f*; ~ ***to the European Currency Unit (ECU)*** an die Europäische Währungseinheit anbinden
tied loan zweckgebundenes Darlehn
tied-up claims eingefrorene Forderungen
tight *adj* angespannt *adj* (Börse); ~ ***credit policy*** restriktive Kreditpolitik; **to be** ~ in Geldverlegenheit sein, knapp bei Kasse sein
tightness of money Geldknappheit *f*

till *n* Geldkasse *f*, Ladenkasse *f*; ~ ***book*** Kassenbuch *n*; ~ ***cancelled*** bis auf Widerruf; ~ ***money*** Kassenbestand *m*, Kassenreserve *f*
time account Festgeldkonto *n*; ~ ***advantage*** Zeitvorteil *m*; ~ ***bargain*** Termingeschäft *n*; ~ ***bill*** Zeitwechsel *m*; ~ ***certificate of deposit*** Zeitwechsel *m*; ~ ***deposit*** befristete Einlage, Termineinlage *f*, Festgeld *n*; ~ ***deposit account*** Festgeldkonto *n*, Termingeldkonto *n*; ~ ***draft*** Zeitwechsel *m*; ~ ***loan*** befristetes Darlehen; ~ ***payment*** Ratenzahlung *f*; ~ ***policy*** Versicherung (für einen befristeten Zeitraum); ~ ***purchase*** Termingeschäft *n*, Terminkauf *m*; ~ ***required*** Zeitbedarf *m*; ~ ***requirement*** Zeitbedarf *m*; ***buy on*** ~ auf Kredit kaufen
times over überzeichnet *adj*
time-sharing *n* Timesharing, zeitlich begrenzte Nutzungsrechte, Gemeinschaftsbetrieb *m*
timing *n* Erfassen des richtigen Zeitpunkts; ~ ***factor*** Zeitfaktor *m*
tip Börsentip *m*, Ratschlag *m*, vertrauliche Information
tippee *n* Dritter *f u. m* (die/der Börsengeschäfte durch Insiderinformationen tätigt)
title *n* Anrecht *n*, Eigentumsrecht *n*, Rechtsanspruch *m*, Rechtstitel *m*; ~ ***Überschrift*** *f*; ~ ***deed*** Erwerbsurkunde *f*, Eigentumsurkunde *f*, Besitzurkunde *f*; ~ ***holder*** Eigentümer *m*; ***bad*** ~ mangelhafter Rechtstitel; ***change of*** ~ Besitzwechsel *m*, Eigentumswechsel *m*; ***claim a*** ~ Eigentum beanspruchen; ***conveyance of*** ~ Rechtsübertragung *f*; ***defect of*** ~ Rechtsmangel *m*, Mangel im Recht *m*; ***document of*** ~ urkundlicher Rechtstitel; ***possessory*** ~ Besitztitel *m*, Besitzurkunde *f*; ***unmarketable*** ~ unverkäufliches Wertpapier

to the order of Orderklausel *f*, zahlbar an
today's balance Tagesbilanz *f*; ~ ***rate*** Tageskurs *m*, Tagessatz *m*, Marktpreis *m*; ~ ***tentative balance*** Tagesrohbilanz *f*

token

token *n* Zeichen *n*, Symbol *n*; *- coin* Wertmarke *f*; *- money* Wertmarke *f*; *- payment* Teilzahlung in Anerkennung einer Verpflichtung

tolerance *n* (US) Sperrgeld *n*, Zollabgabe *f*, Zollgebühr *f*

toll *n* Zoll *m*, Abgabe *f*, Gebühr *f*, Hafengebühr *f*

tollable *adj* zollpflichtig *adj*

tombstone (informal) Emissionsanzeige *f*

tone *of the market* Börsenklima *n*; *cheerful -* freundliche Stimmung (Börse)

tools and implements Werkzeuge und Geräte

top *level* Höchststand *m*; *- market* überhöhte Aktienkurse; *- price* höchster Kurs

top-heavy *adj* überbewertet *adj*

tort *n* Delikt *n*, Gesetzesverstoß *m*

total *n* Gesamtsumme *f*, Summe *f* (Gesamt-), Betrag *m* (Gesamt-); *- adj* gesamt *adj*, ganz *adj*, völlig *adj*, absolut *adj*; *- amount* Gesamtbetrag *m*; *- assets* Summe der Aktiva; *- commitment* Gesamtengagement *n*; *- costs* Gesamtkosten *pl*; *- expenses* Summe der Aufwendungen; *- income* Summe der Erträge; *- liabilities* Summe der Passiva; *- life* Gesamtdauer *f*; *- receipts* Gesamteinnahmen *f pl*; *- value* Gesamtwert *m*; *- balance sheet -* Bilanzsumme *f* (Bilanzvolumen)

town *bill* (US) Platzwechsel *m*; *- check* Platzscheck *m*

tracer *n* Inkassobericht *m*, Laufzettel *m*

track record Erfolgsbilanz *f*, Erfolgs- und Leistungsbilanz

trade *v* Handel treiben, handeln *v*, tauschen *v*; *- n* Handel *m*, Geschäft *n*, Gewerbe *n*, Handwerk *n*, Branche *f*, Fach *n*, Beruf *m* (praktischer); *- acceptance* Handelsakzept *n*, Kundenakzept *n*, Warenakzept *n*; *- agreement* Handelsabkommen *n*, Handelsvertrag *m*; *- allowance* Warenskonto *n*, Großhandelsrabatt *m*, Rabatt für Wiederverkäufer; *- and commerce* Handel und Gewerbe; *- and industry* Handel und Industrie; *- balance* Handelsbilanz *f*; *- bill* Handelswechsel *m*, Warenwechsel *m*; *- center n* Markt *m*, Handelszentrum *n*; *- credit* Warenkredit *m*, Handelskredit *m*; *- creditor* Gläubiger aus Kontokorrentgeschäften; *- debtors* Warenforschungen *f pl*; *- debts* Warenverbindlichkeiten *f pl*; *- deficit (gap)* Außenhandelsdefizit *n*; *- financing* Handelsfinanzierung *f*; *- margin* Handelsspanne *f*, Kalkulationsaufschlag *m*; *- name* Firmenname *m*, Firmenbezeichnung *f*, Handelsbezeichnung *f*; *- note* Handelsdokument *n*; *- notes receivable* Kundenwechsel *m pl* (Bilanz), Wechselforderungen *f pl*; *- paper* Handelsdokument *n*; *- surplus* Außenhandelsüberschuß *m*; *- union* Gewerkschaft *f*; *- union bank* Arbeiterbank *f*, Gewerkschaftsbank *f*; *active - balance* aktive Handelsbilanz; *balance of -* Handelsbilanz *f*; *banking -* Bankwesen *n*, Bankgeschäft *n*, Bankbetrieb *m*, Kreditgewerbe *n*, Bankgewerbe *n*; *court of -* Kammer für Handelssachen; *cross -* Börsenkompensationsgeschäft *n*; *domestic -* Binnenhandel *m*; *illegal -* Schmuggel *m*, Schleichhandel *m*; *wholesale - n* Großhandel *m*, Großhandelsverkauf *m*, Massenverkauf *m*

Trade; *Board of -* (US) Handelskammer *f*, (GB) Handelsministerium *n*, Wirtschaftsministerium *n*

traded options börsengehandelte Optionen

trademark *n* Warenzeichen *m*, Handelszeichen *n*, Fabrikzeichen *n*

trader *n* Händler *m*, Makler *m*, Kaufmann *m*

traders *n pl* Handelsstand *m*, der Handel

tradesman *n* Händler *m*, Makler *m*, Kaufmann *m*

trading *n* Handel *m*, Handelsverkehr *m*; *- account* Betriebskonto *n*, Verkaufskonto *n*; *- capital* Betriebskapital *n*, Umlaufkapital *n*, Betriebsmittel *n pl*; *- company* Handelsgesellschaft, Erwerbsgesellschaft *f*; *- corporation* Handelsgesellschaft *f*, Erwerbsgesellschaft *f*; *- enterprise* Handelsunternehmen *n*; *- floor* Börsensaal *m*, Parkett *n* (Börse); *- for cash* Kassageschäfte *f pl*; *- hours* Börsenstunden *f pl*, Börsensitzung *f*; *- in calls* Vorprämiengeschäfte *n pl*; *- in*

futures Terminhandel m; **- in options** Optionshandel m; **- limit** Kurslimit n (Börse); **- loss** Betriebsverlust m; **- partner** Handelspartner m; **- price** Abschlußkurs m; **- profit** Betriebsgewinn m, Geschäftsgewinn m; **- session** Börsensitzung f; **- unit** Handelseinheit f; **- year** Geschäftsjahr n; **bond -** Anleihehandel m, Obligationenhandel m, Pfandbriefhandel m; **forward -** Terminhandel m; **option -** Optionshandel m

trailer n (EDP) Beisatz m (EDV)

trainee n Volontär m, Praktikant m, Informand m, Kursteilnehmer m, Auszubildender m, Lehrling m

training n Ausbildung f, Schulung f; **academic -** akademische Ausbildung; **course of -** Ausbildungskurs m

tranche Abschnitt m, Tranche f, Quote f; **credit -** Kredittranche f (IMF)

transact v abwickeln v, durchführen v

transaction n Transaktion f, Abschluß m, Vergleich m, Geschäftsabschluß m, Geschäftsvorfall m, Geschäft n; **- for cash** Kassageschäft f; **- input** Umsatzeingabe f; **- loan** kurzfristiger Kredit m (US); **- list** Umsatzliste f; **- statistics** Umsatzstatistik f; **- tape** Umsatzband n; **banking -** Bankgeschäfte n pl; **bear -** Baissegeschäft n; **bill -** Wechselgeschäfte n pl; **blank -** Blankogeschäft n; **bona fide -** gutgläubiger Erwerb m; **bull -** Haussegeschäft n; **business -** Geschäftsabschluß m; **cash -** Bargeschäft n, Kassageschäft n; **check and bill -** (GB) Scheck-und-Wechsel-Verkehr; **commercial -** Handelsgeschäft n; **speculative -** Spekulationsgeschäft n; **underlying -** Grundgeschäft n

transfer v transferieren v, übertragen v (Recht, Vermögen), überweisen v, übergeben v, umbuchen v, zedieren v, versetzen v (Personal); **-** n Transfer m, Übertragung f, Überweisung f, Umbuchung f, Abtretung f, Zession f, Übergabe f, Versetzung f (Personal); **- account** Kontokorrentkonto n, Girokonto n; **- agent** Transferstelle f; **- bank** Girobank f; **- by means of indorsement** Übertragung durch Giro; **- check** Überweisungsscheck m; **- deed** Zessionsurkunde f; **- department** Überweisungsabteilung f; **- fee** Transfergebühr f, Umschreibgebühr f, Überweisungsspesen plt; **- of property** Eigentumsübertragung f; **- of shares** (GB) Aktienübertragung f, Aktienumschreibung f; **- of stock** (US) Aktienübertragung f, Aktienumschreibung f; **- of title to land** Grundstücksübertragung f, Grundstücksumschreibung f; **- order** (GB) Übertragungsanweisung f, Überweisungsauftrag m; **- price** (GB) Tageskurs m; **- risk** Transferrisiko n; **- slip** Überweisungsformular n; **- stamp duty** (GB) Börsenumsatzsteuer f; **- tax** Börsenumsatzsteuer f; **- voucher** Überweisungsformular n; **as t of -** Abtretungserklärung f; **bank -** Banküberweisung f; **blank -** Blankogiro n; **book -** Umbuchung f; **capital -** Kapitaltransferierung f; **certificate of -** Übertragunsbescheinigung f; **stock -** Aktienübertragung f, Aktienumschreibung f

transferable adj übertragbar adj; **- documentary credit,** übertragbares Akkreditiv; **- loan facility** Kreditteilbetrag m; **- securities** übertragbare Wertpapiere

transferee n Zessionar m, Forderungsübernehmer m

transference n Übertragung f, Umschreibung f

transferor n Zedent m, Abtretender m

transire n Zollbegleitschein m, Zolldurchlaßschein m

transit n Zwischenhandel m, Durchfuhr f, Transit m, Durchgangsverkehr m; **- account** Übergangskonto n; **- bill** Durchfuhrschein m, Transitschein m; **- duty** Durchfuhrzoll m Transitzoll m; **- trade** Transithandel m; **item in -** Durchgangsposten m

translation Übersetzung f; Wechselkursumrechnung f, Konvertierung f; **- gains** Wechselkursgewinne f pl (Bilanz)

translator n Übersetzer m

transmission charges Überweisungsgebühren f pl; **- difficulties** Übertragungsschwierigkeiten f pl; **- error** Übertragungsfehler m; **- of shares** Depotumbuchung f

transmit v überweisen v

transport n Beförderung f Transport m; **- charges** Frachtkosten f pl; **means of -** Beförderungsmittel n

transportable adj transportierbar adj, beförderungsfähig adj

transportation n Beförderung f, Transport m; **- difficulties** Transportschwierigkeiten f pl; **- stocks** Aktien von Verkehrsunternehmen

transshipment n Umladung f; **- bill of lading** Umladekonnossement n

travel agent Reisebüro n; **- funds** Reisegeld n, Reisedevisen f pl

travel(l)er commercial Handlungsreisende f u. m

traveler's check Reisescheck m Travellerscheck m; **- cheque** (GB) Reisescheck m Travellerscheck m; **- letter of credit** (US) Reisekreditbrief m

travel(l)ing salesman Handlungsreisende f u. m

treasure n Schatz m

treasurer n Finanzdirektor m, Finanzverwalter m, Leiter der Finanzabteilung, Schatzmeister m

Treasuries Schuldtitel des US-Schatzamtes

treasury bill Schatzwechsel m

Treasury Board (GB) Finanzministerium n

treasury bond Schatzanleihe f

treasury certificates US-Schatzscheine m pl

Treasury Department (US) Finanzministerium n

treasury management Liquiditätssteuerung f (und Finanzplanung); **- notes** US-Schatzanweisungen f pl; **- obligations** Schuldtitel des US-Schatzamtes; **- stocks** britische Staatstitel

treat v behandeln

treaty n (Staats-) Vertrag m; **commercial -** Handelsabkommen n, Handelsvertrag m

trend n Trend m, Verlauf m, Tendenz f, Entwicklung f; **- indicator** Stimmungsbarometer n; **- of affairs** Geschäftsgang m; **- consumption -** Verbrauchsrichtung f, Konsumtrend m; **cyclical -** Konjunkturtendenz f

trial Gerichtsverhandlung f, Prozeß m, Verhandlung f, Probe f; **- balance** Probebilanz f, provisorische Bilanz

triangular exchange Devisenarbitrage in drei verschiedenen Währungen

trillion n (US) Billion f (1.000.000.000.000)

triple adj dreifach

triplicate n dritte Ausfertigung; **in -** in dreifacher Ausfertigung

true adj echt, unverfälscht, authentisch

truncate v verkürzen

truncation n (Ver-)Kürzung f, beleglose Scheckeinzugsverfahren; **- fee** Scheckinkassogebühr f

trust n Trust m, (Unternehmensorganisation) Konzern m, Kartell m; **- account** Treuhandkonto n; **- agreement** Treuhandvertrag m Sicherungsübereignung f; **- area** Wertpapierbereich m; **- bank** Bank f (für Anlageberatung und Vermögensverwaltung); **- bond** Schuldverschreibung f (über eine bevorrechtigte Forderung); **- company** Treuhandgesellschaft f, Treuhandbank f; **- debenture** Schuldverschreibung f (über eine bevorrechtigte Forderung); **- deed** Treuhandvertrag m, Sicherungsübereignung f; **- department** Vermögensverwaltung f, (Bankabteilung), Treuhandabteilung f; **- estate** Treuhandvermögen n, Treuhandgut n, Stiftungsvermögen n, Mündelgelder n pl; **- fund** Treuhandvermögen n, Treuhandgut n, Stiftungsvermögen n, Mündelgelder n pl; **- instrument** Treuhandvertrag m, Sicherungsübereignung f; **- investment officer** Vermögensverwalter m; **- letter** Treuhandschein m; **- money** Mündelgeld n; **- mortgage** Sicherungshypothek f; **- property** Treugut n; **- stock** mündelsichere Wertpapiere m; **- transaction** fiduziarisches Rechtsgeschäft; **buy on -** auf Kredit kaufen; **flexible -** Investmenttrust m (dessen Verwaltung bei Vornahme von Kapitalanlagen Bewegungsfreiheit hat); **irrevocable ~ fund** unwiderruflicher Treuhandfonds; **living ~** (US) lebenslängliche Treuhandverwaltung; **management ~** Kapitalanlagegesellschaft f (mit Anlageverwaltung); **open-end ~** Investmentgesellschaft f (die laufend Zertifikate ausgibt und zurückkauft); **special ~** (US) Pflegschaft f (mit besonderen Pflichten); **unit ~** (GB) Investmentgesellschaft f (mit offenem Anlageportefeuille)

trustee n Vermögensverwalter m, Treuhänder m, Bevollmächtigter m, Verwalter m, Pfleger m; **~ in bankruptcy** Konkursverwalter m; **~ investments** (GB) mündelsichere Kapitalanlage; **~ investment status**, Mündelsicherheit f; **~ of an estate** Nachlaßverwalter m; **~ securities** mündelsichere Anlage f; **~ under a deed of arrangement** Vergleichsverwalter m (GB); **custodian ~** Vermögensverwalter m, Treuhänder m, Bevollmächtigter m, Verwalter m, Pfleger m

trusteeship n Treuhandverwaltung f; **~ in bankruptcy** Konkursverwaltung f

trustor Treugeber m

trustworthy adj vertrauenswürdig adj, zuverlässig adj, kreditwürdig adj

tun n Tonne f, Fuder n auch: »ton« tun: Faß, ton: Tonne (Gewichtseinheit)

turn n (US) vollständig durchgeführte Börsentransaktion; **~ down** ablehnen v, abschlagen v, verweigern v; **~ in the market** Umschwung am Markt; **~ over** umsetzen v; **for a ~** (US) kurzfristig angelegt (Effekten)

turn around Trendwende f, Umscherung f, Sanierung f, Kauf und Verkauf am selben Tag, Zäsur f

turnaround n Trendwende f, Umscherung f, Sanierung f, Kauf und Verkauf am selben Tag, Zäsur f; **~ situation** (US) Verbesserung der Lage innerhalb einer Gesellschaft oder Branche

turnover n Umsatz m, Umschlag m; **~ of goods** Warenumschlag m; **~ tax** Umsatzsteuer f; **account ~** Kontoumsatz m; **annual ~** Jahresumsatz m; **capital ~** Kapitalumsatz m; **cash ~** Kassenumsatz m

twenty per cent rule (US) 20-Prozent-Regel f (d. h., von einem Kredit sind im allgemeinen 20 Prozent als unverzinsliche Sichteinlagen zu unterhalten)

24-hour banking 24-Stunden-Bankservice m

twin shares Zwillingsaktien f pl

two-part offering Anleiheemission in zwei Tranchen

two-part tariff gespaltener Tarif

two-point arbitrage Mehrfacharbitrage f

two-tier market zweigeteilter Markt

two-tier tender (US) zweiteilige Tenderofferte

two-tranche issue zweiteilige Emission

two-way market Kauf-und-Verkaufs-Geschäft n

two-way price Geld-und-Brief-Kurs m, doppelte Kursnotierung

tycoon Industriemagnat m, wichtiger Geschäftsmann m

tying agreement Ausschließlichkeitsklausel f

type of account Kontenart f; **~ of securities deposit** Depotverwahrungsart f; **~ of payment** Zahlungsart f

typewrite v tippen v, auf der Schreibmaschine schreiben

U

ultimate balance letzte Bilanz
ultimo *n* letzter Tag des Monats
umbrella fund Umbrellafonds, Fonds aus mehreren Teil- oder Subfonds; **- organisation** Dachorganisation *f*
unable to contract geschäftsunfähig *adj*
unacceptable paper nicht rediskontfähiges Papier
unaccepted bill nicht akzeptierter Wechsel
unaccounted nicht bilanziert *adj*
unadjusted liabilities schwebende Verbindlichkeiten
unalienable property unverkäuflicher Grundbesitz
unallocated reserves freie Rücklagen
unallotted shares nicht zugeteilte Aktien
unappropriated *earned surplus* (US) unverteilter Reingewinn; **- *funds*** nicht verteilte Mittel; **- *income*** nicht vorkalkulierter Ertragsüberschuß; **- *profits*** (US) unverteilter Reingewinn
unassented securities (US) nicht abgestempelte Effekten
unassignable *adj* nicht zuteilbar; **- *shares*** nicht übertragbare Aktie
unaudited accounts nicht testierten Abschluß
unauthorized nicht berechtigt, unberechtigt *adj*
unavailed credit nicht in Anspruch genommener Kredit
unbalanced *adj* nicht saldiert, unausgeglichen
unbankable *adj* nicht bankfähig, nicht diskontfähig
unbanked *adj* ohne Bankverbindung, nicht eingelöst, nicht bei einer Bank hinterlegt
unbilled *adj* nicht in Rechnung gestellt
unbusinesslike *adj* nicht geschäftsmäßig, unkaufmännisch
uncalled bond ungekündigte Anleihe
uncalled capital nicht eingezahltes Kapital
uncashed *adj* nicht eingelöst
uncertain *adj* zweifelhaft, unsicher
uncertified *adj* unbeglaubigt, nicht beglaubigt

unchanged unverändert, behauptet (Börsenkurs)
unchecked ungeprüft *adv*
unclaimed dividend nicht beanspruchte Dividende
unclean bill of lading fehlerhaftes Konnossement
uncoined *adj* ungemünzt, ungeprägt
uncollectable *adj* nicht einziehbar, nicht Einkassierbar
unconditional *adj* vorbehaltlos; **- *acceptance*** uneingeschränktes Akzept; **- *commitment*** unbedingte Verpflichtung
unconfirmed letter of credit nicht bestätigtes Akkreditiv
uncovered *adj* nicht gedeckt, ohne Deckung, ungedeckt; **- *call/put option*** ungedeckte Kauf-und-Verkaufs-Option; **- *check*** ungedeckter Scheck; **- *loan*** Blankokredit *m*
uncredited *adj* ohne Kredit, nicht gutgeschrieben
uncrossed check Barscheck *m*, offener Scheck, nicht gekreuzter Scheck
undated bond Schuldverschreibung ohne Fälligkeitstermine
undeclared unverzollt *adj*
under *bond* unter Zollverschluß; **- *usual reserves*** Eingang vorbehalten
underbid *v* unterbieten
underbidder *n* Mitbieter *m*
undercapitalization *n* Unterkapitalisierung *f*
undercapitalize *v* unterkapitalisieren
undercharge zu wenig berechnen
undercut *v* unterbieten *v*
underemployed unterbeschäftigt, nicht ausgelastet
underestimate *v* unterbewerten, unter dem Wert einschätzen, zu niedrig bewerten
underestimation *n* Unterbewertung *f*
underfreighter *n* Unterverfrachter *m*, Weiterverfrachter *m*
underinsurance Unterversicherung *f*

underlease n Untermietvertrag m, Unterpachtvertrag m

underlying bonds (US) durch Vorranghypothek gesicherte Obligationen; **~ mortgage** (US) Vorranghypothek f; **~ stock** Basisaktie f, Basiswert m; **~ syndicate** (US) Übernahmekonsortium n; **~ transaction** Grundgeschäft n

underrated share zu niedrig bewertete Aktie

undersell unter Wert verkaufen, auf Baisse spekulieren; **~ the market** eine erwartete Baisse am Markt im voraus berücksichtigen

underselling Verkauf unter Wert, Baissespekulation

understaffed; to be ~ Personalmangel haben

undersubscribed bond nicht in voller Höhe gezeichnete Anleihe

undertake v übernehmen, sich verpflichten, unternehmen, vornehmen

undertaking n Unternehmen n, Betrieb m, Engagement n, Sicherheitsleistung f, Verpflichtung f; **~ of guarantee** Garantieübernahme f

undervaluation n Unterbewertung f

undervalue v unterbewerten v, unter dem Wert einschätzen, zu niedrig bewerten

underweight adj untergewichtig, nicht ausgeglichen

underwrite v zeichnen; **~ a stock issue** eine Aktienemission zeichnen

underwriter n Anleihegarant m, Emissionsbank f; Emissionsfirma f; **bonding ~** Übernahmekonsortium für Obligationen (Pfandbriefe)

underwriters Konsortium m; Plazierungskonsortium n; **fire ~** Feuerversicherungsgesellschaft f; **marine insurance ~** Seeversicherungsgesellschaft f

underwriting n Emissionsübernahmegeschäft n, Effektengarantie f, Übernahme von Versicherungen; **~ agreement** Konsortialvertrag m; **~ business** Emissionsgeschäft n; **~ commission** Provision aus Konsortialbeteiligungen, Konsortialprovision f; **~ conditions** Zeichnungsbedingungen f pl; **~ house** Emissionsfirma f; **~ office** Versicherungsunternehmer n; **~ share** Konsortialanteil m; **~ syndicate** Emissionskonsortium n; **firm ~** Festübernahme f

undeveloped country Entwicklungsland n

undisclosed assignment stille Abtretung; **~ reserves** stille Reserven

undiscountable nicht diskontierbar

undistributed profit nicht ausgeschütteter Gewinn

undivided profits unverteilter Reingewinn

undrawn overdraft facility nicht in Anspruch genommene Kreditlinie

unearned income Kapitalertrag m

uneconomical adj unwirtschaftlich adj

unemployed adj arbeitslos

unemployment n Arbeitslosigkeit f; **mass ~** Massenarbeitslosigkeit f

unencumbered adj unbelastet, schuldenfrei, hypothekenfrei

unendorsed adj ohne Giro, nicht giriert, ungiriert adj, nicht indossiert

unexpired bills noch nicht fällige Wechsel

unfair competition unlauterer Wettbewerb

unfilled orders Auftragsbestand m

unfreeze funds Guthaben freigeben

unfunded debt schwebende Schuld, unfundierte Schuld

ungeared adj ohne Fremdkapital

unhedged currency exposure ungesicherte Währungsposition

unified bonds Ablösungsschuldverschreibungen f pl; **~ mortgage bonds** Einheitshypothek f, durch Gesamthypothek gesicherte Schuldverschreibungen; **~ stock** (GB) konsolidierte Anleihe

Uniform Customs and Practice for Documentary Credits (UCP) Einheitliche Richtlinien für Dokumentenakkreditive (ERA)

unincorporated adj nicht eingetragen; **~ bank** Privatbank f (US); **~ company** Personengesellschaft f (US)

unincumbered adj unbelastet adj, schuldenfrei adj, hypothekenfrei adj

unindorsed adj ohne Giro, nicht giriert, ungiriert adj, nicht indossiert

uninsurable adj nicht versicherungsfähig

uninsured adj unversichert adj

union n Gewerkschaft f, Verband m, Vereinigung f; **credit ~** Kreditverein m, Kreditgenossenschaft f, Volksbank f; **customs ~** Zollunion f; **monetary ~** Währungsunion f; **tariff ~** Zollunion f; **trade ~** Gewerkschaft f

unissued *capital* nicht ausgegebene Aktien; **~ debentures** noch nicht ausgegebene Schuldverschreibungen; **~ shares** nicht ausgegebene Aktien; **~ stock** nicht ausgegebene Aktien

unit n Einheit f, Stück n; **~ of account** Verrechnungseinheit f, Rechnungseinheit f; **~ of currency** Währungseinheit f; **~ price** Stückpreis m, Anteilkurs m; **~ pricing** Festsetzung eines Stückpreises (Einheitskurs); **~ teller** Kassierer für Ein- und Auszahlungen; **~ trust** (GB) Investmentgesellschaft mit offenem Anlageportefeuille; **cost ~** Kosteneinheit f; **currency ~** Zahlungsmitteleinheit f; **monetary ~** Geldeinheit f, Münzeinheit f, Währungseinheit f

universal financing Allfinanz f

unlimited adj unlimitiert adj, nicht limitiert, nicht eingeschränkt; **~ company** Offene Handelsgesellschaft f; **~ partner** unbeschränkt haftender Gesellschafter; **~ partnership** (US) Offene Handelsgesellschaft

unlisted adj (US) nicht notiert, unnotiert adj; **~ securities** Freiverkehrswerte m pl; **~ shares** an der Börse nicht eingeführte Aktien

unmarketable securities nicht börsengängige Wertpapiere; **~ title** unverkäufliches Wertpapier

unmortgaged adj unbelastet adj, schuldenfrei adj, hypothekenfrei adj

unnegotiable adj nicht begebbar

unofficial *broker* Freiverkehrsmakler m; **~ market** (GB) Freiverkehrsbörse f, Freibörse f, Freiverkehrsmarkt m, Nachbörse f

unowned adj herrenlos adj

unpaid adj unbezahlt adj, nicht bezahlt, rückständig adj, nicht freigemacht, unfrankiert adj; **~ check** nicht eingelöster Scheck

unpledged adj unverpfändet adj

unprofitable adj unrentabel adj

unqualified audit certificate uneingeschränkter Bestätigungsvermerk

unquoted shares (stocks) nicht notierte Aktien

unredeemed *loan* noch nicht getilgte Anleihe; **~ pledge** nicht eingelöstes Pfand

unseasoned issue Emission ohne existierenden Sekundärmarkt

unsecured *credit* Blankokredit m, Blankovorschuß m; **~ creditor** ungesicherter Gläubiger; **~ loan** unbesichertes Darlehen, unbesicherte Anleihe; **~ personal loan** ungedeckter Personalkredit

unsettled adj in der Schwebe befindlich, noch anhängig

unsubscribed stock nicht gezeichnete Aktien

until *cancelled* bis auf Widerruf; **~ recalled** bis auf Widerruf

untransferable adj nicht übertragbar

upbringing n Erziehung f

update v aktualisieren; **~** n Aktualisierung f

updating service Änderungsdienst m

upon entry nach Eingang

upset price m Vorbehaltspreis m

upside potential Kursspielraum nach oben

upsurge in stock prices Aktienhausse f

upvaluation n (of a currency) Aufwertung f (einer Währung)

upward trend Aufwärtstrend m

usage n Usance f; **banking ~** Bankusance f

usages; business ~ Handelsbräuche m pl, Usancen f pl

usance n Frist f, Wechselfrist f, Wechsellaufzeit f; **~** n Usance f

usance credit Remboursakkreditiv n

use; credit in ~ in Anspruch genommener Kredit; **make ~ of** Gebrauch machen von

used adj gebraucht, aus zweiter Hand

user n Benutzer m, Anwender m; **~ value** Gebrauchswert m

user-friendly adj benutzerfreundlich

usufruct n Nießbrauch m, Nutznießung f

usufructuary n Nießbraucher m

usurer n Wucherer m

usurious adj wucherisch

usury *n* Wucher *m*; ***bill*** - Wechselwucher *m*
utilities *n pl* Versorgungswerte *m pl*, Versorgungsbetriebe *m pl*
utility *program* Dienstprogramm *n*; ***marginal*** - Grenznutzen *m*

utilization *n* Verwendung *f*, Nutzung *f*, Benutzung *f*, Auslastung *f* (eines Systems); ***capacity*** - Kapazitätsausnutzung *f*
utterance; *put into* - in Umlauf setzen
uttering false notes Falschgeld verbreiten

V

vacancy n freie Stelle, Vakanz f
vacation club account Feriensparkonto n (ein Sparkonto, das angelegt wird, um die Kosten für einen Urlaub aufzubringen)
valid adj gültig adj; **~ contract** rechtsgültiger Vertrag; **~ for one day** börsengültig für einen Tag
validate v gültig machen, legalisieren, für rechtgültig erklären; **~ contract** rechtsgültiger Vertrag
validation n Gültigkeitserklärung f
validity n Gültigkeit f, Rechtswirksamkeit f, Validität f
valorization n Aufwertung f (eines Marktpreises)
valorize v aufwerten
valuables n pl Wertgegenstände m pl, Wertsachen f pl; **consignment of ~** Wertsendung f
valuation n Wertansatz m, Bewertung f, Wert m, Schätzung f, Schätzwert m; **~ clause** Wertklausel f; **~ date** Bewertungsstichtag f; **~ items** Wertberichtigungen f pl; **~ reserve** Rückstellung für Wertberichtigungen; **assets ~** Anlagebewertung f; **bond ~** Wertberechnung einer Obligation; **capital ~** Kapitalbewertung f
value v schätzen, valutieren, bewerten; **~ n** Wert m; **~ assessed** Steuerwert m; **~ date** Wert m (Datum), Valuta f (Datum), Wertstellung f, Wertstellungszeitpunkt m; **~ for collection** Wert zum Einzug, Wert zum Inkasso; **~ given clause** Valutaklausel f; **~ insured** Versicherungswert m; **~ of money** Geldwert m, Kaufkraft f; **~ safeguarding clause** Wertsicherungsklausel f; **absorption ~** berichtigter Wert; **accounting ~** Buchwert m; **actual ~** effektiver Wert; **annuity ~** Rentenbarwert m, Rentenrückkaufswert m; **appraised ~** Schätzwert m, Taxwert m; **appreciation ~** Wertsteigerung f; **approximate ~** Annäherungswert m; **assets ~** Aktivwert m; **balance ~** Bilanzwert m; **basic ~** Einheitswert m (eines Grundstücks); **book ~** Buchwert m; **bullion ~** Gold- oder Silberwert einer Münze; **clear ~** Nettowert m **collateral ~** Beleihungswert m, Lombardwert m; **commercial ~** Handelswert m, Marktwert m; **commodity ~** Warenwert m, Sachwert m; **cost ~** Anschaffungswert m, Erwerbswert m; **currency ~** Währungswert m; **current ~** Marktwert m; **declaration of ~** Wertangabe f; **loan ~** Beleihungswert m, Lombardwert m; **market ~** Marktwert m; **quoted ~** Börsenkurs m, Kurswert m; **real ~** effektiver Wert, Sachwert m; **real estate ~** Grundstückswert m; **sentimental ~** Liebhaberwert m; **sound ~** Verkehrswert m (Versicherung); **stated ~** Nominalwert m; **surrender ~** Rückkaufswert m (einer Versicherungspolice); **taxable ~** steuerpflichtiger Wert, steuerbarer Wert, Steuerwert m
value-added tax Mehrwertsteuer f
valuer n (GB) Schätzer m, Taxator m
valueless securities wertlose Wertpapiere, Nonvaleurs m pl
variable adj veränderlich, variabel, schwankend; **~ interest loan** Kredit mit variabler Verzinsung; **~ portion** variabler Teil (bei Bestandssätzen); **~ price quotation** fortlaufende Notierung; **~ rate** variabler Kurs; **~ record length** variable Satzlänge (EDV); **~ yield bond** Schuldverschreibung mit variablem Ertrag
variation n Veränderung f, Schwankung f, Wechsel m, Abweichung f
variations in market price Kursschwankungen f pl
variety n Auswahl f
vault n Panzergewölbe n, Tresor m, Stahlkammer f; **~ cash** (US) Barreserve f; **bank ~** Banktresor m; **safety ~** Tresorraum m
velvet n (US) ein leicht erzielter Börsengewinn
vendee n Käufer m
vendor n Verkäufer m, Veräußerer m

vendue Auktion f; **~ master** Auktionär m
venture n Vorhaben n, Unterfangen n, Risiko n, Wagnis n; ~ v riskieren, wagen; **~ capital** Beteiligungskapital n; Risikokapital n, Spekulationskapital n, Venture Capital, Wagniskapital n; **speculative ~** riskantes Unternehmen
venture capitalist Wagniskapitalgeber m; **~ (capital) fund** Wagnisfinanzierungsfonds
Venture Consort EU-Aktionsprogramm zur Finanzierung neuer Technologien von KMU
venue n (of court) Gerichtsstand m
verification n Überprüfung f
verify v nachprüfen, bestätigen, kontrollieren
vertical merger vertikale Fusion
vest v übertragen (Vermögen), verleihen (Vollmacht)
vested persönliches Interesse; **~ rights** wohlerworbene Rechte
vesting n Übertragung f, Verleihung f
vet v (über)prüfen
vice president Direktor m
victory loan (GB) Kriegsanleihe f
video data terminal Datensichtgerät n; **~ display** Datensichtgerät n
view n Ansicht f, Meinung f
violation; contract ~ Vertragsverletzung f
vis major höhere Gewalt
visibiles Export- bzw. Importvolumen n
voiceless adj nicht stimmberechtigt
void adj nichtig adj, ungültig adj, unwirksam adj
voidable contract anfechtbarer Vertrag
volatile adj schwankend

volatility n Volatilität f, Kursschwankungsausmaß n (z. B. bei einer Aktie), Kursschwankungsbreite f
volume n Volumen n, Menge f, Umfang m; **~ of business** Geschäftsvolumen n, Umsatz m; **~ of money** Geldmenge f
voluntary adj freiwillig; **~ bankruptcy** Konkursverfahren auf Antrag des Schuldners; **~ reserves** freiwillige Reserven; **~ savings** freie Ersparnisse; **~ settlement** außergerichtlicher Vergleich
vostro account Vostrokonto n
vote v abstimmen v (Wahl), beschließen v, wählen v (durch Abstimmung); **~ n** Abstimmung f (Wahl), Beschluß m, Votum n; **~ plural** Mehrstimmenrecht n
voting Abgabe f, Stimmabgabe f; **~ power** Stimmrecht n; **~ right** Stimmrecht n; **~ stock** Stimmrechtsaktien f pl
voting shares stimmberechtigte Aktien; **~ shareholder** stimmberechtigter Aktionär
vouch v bezeugen, bürgen
voucher n Beleg m, Auszahlungsbeleg m, Buchungsbeleg m, Gutschein m, Quittung f; **~ check** (US) Verrechnungsscheck m; **booking ~** Buchungsbeleg m, Buchhaltungsbeleg m; **cash ~** Kassenbeleg m; **debit ~** Lastschriftenbeleg m, Sollbeleg m
vouching n vorbereitende Buchungsmaßnahmen
voyage policy Reiseversicherung f
Vreneli (Swiss 20 Francs gold coin) Vreneli n (Schweizer 20-Franken-Goldmünze)

W

wage n Lohn m, Arbeitsentgelt n; **- dividend** Gratifikation f, Bonus m; **- earner** Lohnempfänger m; **- group** Tarifgruppe f; **- rates** Lohntarife m pl; **standard -** Tariflohn m
wage-cost inflation Lohnkosteninflation f
wager policy Wettpolice f
wages n pl Lohn m, Arbeitsentgelt n; **- and salaries** Löhne und Gehälter; **- bill** Lohn- und Gehaltsaufwendungen f pl; **- check** Lohnscheck m; **- settlement** Tarifvertrag m; **advance on -** Lohnvorschuß m
wages-prices-spiral Lohn-Preis-Spirale f
wait-and-see attitude abwartende Haltung (= Attentismus) am Kapitalmarkt
waiter n (GB) Börsendiener m
waive v verzichten auf; **- a claim** auf einen Rechtsanspruch verzichten
waiver n Verzicht m, Aufgabe f, Verzichterklärung f; **- clause** Verzichtsklausel f; **- of interest** Zinsverzicht m
walk-out Warnstreik m
walks bill Platzwechsel m
Wall Street Wall Street f (New Yorker Effektenbörse)
wallpaper Emission bei Aktienumtausch
want; for - of payment mangels Zahlung
wantage n Defizit n, Fehlbetrag m
wanted Geld n, Geldkurs m
war loan Kriegsanleihe f; **- risk clause** Kriegsrisikoklausel f; **- securities** Rüstungswerte m pl
ward n Mündel m
warehouse n Lagerhaus n, Magazin n, Lager n; **- certificate** (US) Lagerschein m; **- receipt** Lagerschein für sicherungsübereignete Waren; **- space** Lagerraum m; **- warrant** Lagerschein m, Orderlagerschein m, Lagerpfandschein m; **customs -** Zollager n
warehouseman n Lagerverwalter m, Lagerhalter m
warehousemen's lien Lagerhalterpfandrecht n

warehousing charges Lagergeld n
warrant v garantieren, Bürgschaft leisten, Gewähr leisten, bürgen; **- n** Vollmacht f, Befugnis f, Lagerschein m, Warenschein m, Schatzanweisung f, Bürgschaftsvertrag m, Zollbegleitschein m, Optionsschein m; **- into negotiable government securities = WINGS** Optionsschein zum Bezug von US-Schatzanleihen; **- issue** Optionsanleihe f; **- market** Optionsscheinmarkt m; **- of attorney** Mandat n, Vollmacht für einen Rechtsanwalt; **- offering price** Ausgabekurs des Optionsscheins; **dividend -** Dividendenschein m, Gewinnanteilschein m; **stock transfer -** (GB) Aktienzertifikat n, Aktienanteilschein m, Aktienschein m
warrantee n Garantieempfänger m, Sicherheitsnehmer m, Sicherheitsempfänger m, Bürgschaftsempfänger m, Warrantee m
warrantor n Sicherheitsgeber m, Bürge m, Garant m
warrants n pl Sicherheiten f pl
warranty n Garantie f, Gewährleistung f; **- deed** (US) Grundstücksübertragungsurkunde f; **clause of -** Garantieklausel f
wash sale (GB) Scheinkauf und -verkauf von Wertpapieren
washing n (US) Börsenscheingeschäfte n pl
waste v verschwenden; **- book** Kassenkladde f
wasting assets abnutzbare Wirtschaftsgüter, kurzlebige Wirtschaftsgüter
watered capital verwässertes Aktienkapital; **- stock** (US) verwässertes Aktienkapital
watering of stock Kapitalverwässerung f
waterway; inland - Binnenschiffahrtsweg m
waybill n Frachtbrief m, Beförderungsschein m, Warengeleitschein m; **blanket -** Kollektivfrachtbrief m
weak market schwacher Markt; **- currency** Weichwährung f

weaken v nachgeben v, abschwächen v (Börsenkurs)

wealth n Reichtum m; *- tax* Vermögenssteuer f

wear; *allowance for - and tear* Absetzung für Abnutzung

weight n Gewicht n, Bedeutung f, Wichtigkeit f; *- of taxation* Steuerlast f; *bill of -* Gewichtsschein m, Wiegenote f; *customs -* Zollgewicht n

welfare fund Wohlfahrtsfonds m

well-known adj bekannt adj, namhaft adj

wharf n Lagerhaus n, Lagerplatz m, Dock n, Kai m

wharfage n Dockgebühren f pl, Dockgeld n, Löschgeld n, Landungszoll m, Kaigeld n

wheelage n Rollgeld n

when issued (WI) Handel per Erscheinen

white *elephant* (US) unrentables Geschäft; *- knight* (US) Übernahmeabwehr durch Beteiligung von Fusionspartnern; *- paper* erstklassiges Handelspapier

White paper Weißbuch n

white-collar crime Wirtschaftsverbrechen n

white-collar union Angestelltengewerkschaft f

whizz kid (informal) Senkrechtstarter in der Finanzwelt

whole-life insurance Lebensversicherung auf den Todesfall

wholesale n Großhandel m; *- bank* Universalbank f; *- banking* Großkundengeschäft n (Bank); *- dealer* Grossist m, Großhändler m; *- financing* Großhandelsfinanzierung f; *- market* Firmenkundenmarkt m (Bank); *- trade* n Großhandel m, Großhandelsverkauf m, Massenverkauf m

wholesaler n Grossist m, Großhändler m

wide quotation variabler Kurs m

widely spread share holdings Streubesitz m

widow and orphan stock (US) mündelsichere Anlagepapiere, mündelsichere Wertpapiere, mündelsichere Papiere

wild cat company (US) Schwindelfirma f; *- cat securities* sehr spekulative und häufig gänzlich wertlose Effekten; *- satter* wilder Spekulant

will n Testament n, letztwillige Verfügung, letzter Wille; *ability to make a -* Testierfähigkeit f; *clause of a -* Testamentsbestimmung f; *dispute a -* ein Testament anfechten; *double -* gegenseitiges Testament, Berliner Testament; *draw up a -* ein Testament errichten; *mutual -* gegenseitiges Testament, Berliner Testament; *mystic -* unverständliches Testament; *prove a -* ein Testament gerichtlich bestätigen lassen

win v gewinnen v, erwerben v, verdienen v

wind bill (GB) Gefälligkeitswechsel m, Kellerwechsel m, Reitwechsel m; *- up* v liquidieren v, abwickeln v, auflösen v

windfall n unerwarteter Gewinn; *- profit tax* Sondergewinnsteuer f, Spekulationssteuer f (US)

winding-up by creditors Liquidationsvergleich m (GB)

winding-up compulsory Zwangsliquidation f

windmills n pl (GB) Gefälligkeitswechsel m, Kellerwechsel m, Reitwechsel m

window *closing time* Schalterschluß m; *- traffic* Schalterverkehr m

window-dressing Bilanzbildverbesserung f, Bilanzfrisur f

WINGS = warrant into negotiable government securities Optionsschein zum Bezug von US-Schatzanleihen

wipe off abschreiben (Schuld oder Forderung)

wire fate Ersuchen um telegrafische Nachricht über das Schicksal eines Schecks oder Wechsels; *- transfer* elektronischer Zahlungsverkehr

with profits mit Gewinnbeteiligung

withdraw v zurückziehen v, abheben v, entnehmen v, entziehen v; *- from circulation* außer Umlauf setzen

withdrawal n Entnahme f, Rücktritt m (von einer Vereinbarung), Widerruf m, Entwertung f, Abhebung f; *- of funds* Geldabhebung f; *- of a loan* Kreditkündigung f; *- receipt*

Quittung über Kontoabhebung; **bank -** Bankabhebung f
withhold v zurückbehalten, einbehalten
withholding tax Quellensteuer f, Verrechnungsteuer f
without *recourse* ohne Rückgriff; *- our liability* ohne Obligo; *- protest* ohne Protest; *- using cash* bargeldlos
witness v als Zeuge unterschreiben, bezeugen v, zeugen v
woll exchange Baumwollbörse f
wording n Wortlaut m
work n Arbeit f, Handlung f; *- out* ausarbeiten v; *- phase* Arbeitsphase f; *- segment* Arbeitsgang m (Stufe, Abschnitt)
workable adj gangbar adj
worker n Arbeiter m, Berufstätiger m
workforce n Belegschaft f, Arbeiterschaft f
working *account* umsatzreiches Konto; *- capital* Betriebskapital n, Umlaufkapital n, Betriebsmittel n pl; *- capital loan* Betriebsmittelkredit m; *- capital ratio* (US) Verhältnis der flüssigen Aktiven zu den laufenden Verbindlichkeiten; *- credit* Betriebskredit m; *- expenses* Betriebskosten plt; *- fee* Provision f (z.B. für eine neue Finanzierungsstruktur); *net - capital* Nettobetriebskapital n
workload n Arbeitsbelastung f
works n Werk n, Fabrik f, Unternehmen n

work-sharing Arbeitsteilung f
workstation n Arbeitsplatz m
World Bank = International Bank for Reconstruction and Development (IBRD) Weltbank f
world *of commerce* Handelswelt f
world-wide adj weltweit, global
worth n Wert m; **net -** (US) Eigenkapital n
worthless adj wertlos
wraparound mortgage Zusatzhypothek f
wreck n Schiffbruch m, Wrack n, Konkursfirma f, Ruin m
write a call Verkauf einer Kaufoption; *- off* v abschreiben (Schuld oder Forderung); *- options* Optionen verkaufen
write-downs of and adjustments to claims and certain securities Abschreibungen und Wertberichtigungen auf Forderungen und bestimmte Wertpapiere
write-off n Abschreibung f (Schuld oder Forderung)
write-offs n pl (US) nicht einziehbare Werte
writer n Stillhalter m; *- of a check* Scheckaussteller m; *- of an option* Optionsverkäufer m, Stillhalter m
writing back Stornierung f
written notice schriftliche Kündigung
written-down value Buchwert m, Restbuchwert m, Nettobuchwert m

x = ex ohne, außer, nach Abzug von (Bezeichnung im internationalen Finanzverkehr)
x-inefficiency (GB) Ineffizienz f, Unwirtschaftlichkeit f, Leistungsunfähigkeit f
Xmas = Christmas Weihnachten n
Xmas Club (US) Sparkonto für Weihnachtseinkäufe

Y

yankee bond Yankee-Anleihe f (in den USA emittierte US-Dollar Anleihe eines nicht-US-Schuldners)

year book n Jahrbuch n; **boom ~** Konjunkturjahr n; **business ~** Geschäftsjahr n; **financial ~** (GB) Geschäftsjahr n, Finanzjahr n, Wirtschaftsjahr n, Rechnungsjahr n, Betriebsjahr n, Steuerjahr n; **trading ~** Geschäftsjahr n

year-end n Jahresultimo m

year-end settlement Jahresultimoabschluß m

yearling bond Schuldverschreibung (mit 12monatiger Laufzeit)

yearly account Jahreskonto n; **~ accounts** Jahresabschluß m; **~ statement of deposited securities** Depotjahresauszug m

Yellow Book (GB) Zulassungsvorschriften zum geregelten Freiverkehr

Yen Yen m (japanische Währungseinheit)

yield v einbringen, Ertrag abwerfen, Zinsen bringen; **~** n Ertrag m, Rendite f, Verzinsung f, Zinsertrag m; **~ capacity** Ertragskraft f; **~ forecasting** Ertragsvorschau f; **~ interest** Zinsen bringen; **~ of a bond** Anleiherendite f; **~ on capital** Kapitalertrag m; **~ on savings** Spareinlagenverzinsung f; **~ prospect** Ertragschance f; **~ spread** Renditespanne f; **~ table** Renditetabelle f; **~ tax** Kapitalertragsteuer f; **~ to maturity** interner Zinsfuß eines festverzinslichen Wertpapiers; **capital ~** Kapitalertrag m; **current ~** laufender Ertrag, laufender Gewinn, laufende Rendite; **dividend ~** Dividendenertrag m; **earnings ~** Gewinnrendite (d. h. Prozentsatz des Aktienkurswertes, der auf diese Aktie bei restloser Auszahlung entfallen würde); **effective ~** Effektivverzinsung f

yield-curve note umgekehrter Floater m

yielding interest eine Rente abwerfend, verzinslich

Yuan Yuan m (chinesische Währungseinheit)

Z

ZEBRAS = **zero coupon eurosterling** gestrippte englische Pfund-(Sterling)-Staatsanleihe

zero *coupon bond* abgezinste Anleihe, Nullprobe f; *- coupon eurosterling =* **ZEBRAS** gestrippte englische Pfund-(Sterling)-Staatsanleihe; *- growth* Nullwachstum f

zero-cost cap Zinsbegrenzungsvereinbarung nach oben und unten

zero-interest loan zinsloses Darlehen

zero-rated mehrwertsteuerfrei

zero-rating Mehrwertsteuerbefreiung f

zip code Postleitzahl f

zloty Zloty m (Währung in Polen)

zone n Zone f, Gebiet n; *- rates* Zonentarif m; *free trade -* Freihandelszone f

zoom v in die Höhe schnellen

zooming *costs* sprunghaft steigende Kosten; *- equities* Aktienhausse f

Antworten auf alle Fragen des Bankgeschäftes.

Das Standardwerk für alle Praktiker des Bank-, Geld- und Kreditwesens.

**Hans E. Büschgen,
Das kleine
Bank-Lexikon,**
2. aktualisierte
Auflage 1997,
1.504 Seiten,
Fadenheftung,
Pappband, DM 98,-
ISBN: 3-87881-108-X

Die grundlegend überarbeitete Neuauflage des Standardwerks „Das kleine Bank-Lexikon" erfaßt auf 1.500 Seiten mit mehr als 17.000 Stichwörtern alle klassischen Inhalte des Bank-, Geld- und Kreditwesens sowie der Bankgeschäftspolitik. Die umfangreichen Aktualisierungen machen den hohen Grad neuer Entwicklungen seit Erscheinen der ersten Auflage gerade im deutschen und internationalen Bank- und Finanzwesen deutlich.

Verlag Wirtschaft
und Finanzen
Postfach 101102 • 40002 Düsseldorf

BESTELLKARTE

Hiermit bestelle(n) ich (wir) zur sofortigen Lieferung gegen Rechnung (zzgl. Versandkosten):

___ Expl. Art.-Nr. 78 100 31: Hans E. Büschgen,
Das kleine Bank-Lexikon
2. aktualisierte Auflage 1997. 1.504 Seiten, gebunden, DM 98,–.

___ Expl. Art.-Nr. 78 100 36: Feldbausch/Feldbausch,
Bank-Wörterbuch, Deutsch-Englisch/Englisch-Deutsch
4. erweiterte Auflage 1997. Ca. 430 Seiten, gebunden, DM 52,–.

Expl. Art.-Nr. 78 100 26: U. Rettberg/D. Zwätz,
___ **Das kleine Terminhandels-Lexikon**
4. aktualisierte Auflage 1995. 404 Seiten, gebunden, DM 32,–.

Expl. Art.-Nr. 78 100 28: Klaus-Dieter Schroth,
___ **Das kleine Lexikon des Wirtschaftsrechts**
1. Auflage 1995. 712 Seiten, gebunden, DM 58,–.

Expl. Art.-Nr. 78 100 29: Geml/Geisbüsch/Lauer,
___ **Das kleine Marketing-Lexikon**
1. Auflage 1995. 452 Seiten, gebunden, DM 58,–.

Expl. Art.-Nr. 78 100 33: Harz/Hub/Schlarb,
___ **Sanierungs-Management. Unternehmen aus der Krise führen**
1. Auflage 1996. 214 Seiten, gebunden, DM 98,–.

Fax-Bestellung an: (02 11) 8 87 17 70.

Bitte unbedingt auch die Vorderseite dieser Karte ausfüllen.

Verlagsgruppe
Handelsblatt GmbH
Vertriebs-Service
Postfach 10 27 17

40018 Düsseldorf

Name

Vorname

Firma

Straße

PLZ/Ort

Datum   Unterschrift

Verlag Wirtschaft und Finanzen ∎ Ein Unternehmen der Verlagsgruppe Handelsblatt